SOMETHING ABOUT THE AUTHOR®

Something about
the Author *was named
an* **"Outstanding
Reference Source,"**
*the highest honor given
by the American
Library Association
Reference and Adult
Services Division.*

ISSN 0276-816X

something
About the
Author®

**Facts and Pictures about Authors
and Illustrators of Books for Young People**

volume 146

GALE®

THOMSON

GALE

Detroit • New York • San Diego • San Francisco • Cleveland • New Haven, Conn. • Waterville, Maine • London • Munich

Something About the Author, Volume 146

Project Editor
Jenai A. Mynatt

Editorial
Katy Balcer, Shavon Burden, Sara Constantakis, Natalie Fulkerson, Michelle Kazensky, Julie Keppen, Joshua Kondek, Mary Ruby, Lemma Shomali, Susan Strickland, Maikue Vang, Tracey Watson

Research
Tracie Richardson

Permissions
Lori Hines, Jacqueline Key, Mari Masalin-Cooper, Shalice Shah-Caldwell

Imaging and Multimedia
Lezlie Light, Michael Logusz, Denay Wilding

Composition and Electronic Capture
Kathy Sauer

Manufacturing
Lori Kessler

LIBRARY OF CONGRESS CATALOG CARD NUMBER 62-52046

ISBN 0-7876-6992-X
ISSN 0276-816X

Printed in the United States of America
10 9 8 7 6 5 4 3 2 1

Contents

Authors in Forthcoming Volumes

Below are some of the authors and illustrators that will be featured in upcoming volumes of *SATA*. These include new entries on the swiftly rising stars of the field, as well as completely revised and updated entries (indicated with *) on some of the most notable and best-loved creators of books for children.

Bill Amend ▮ Amend is most widely known for his comic strip *Fox-trot,* created in 1988. With over 1,000 newspapers subscribing to his comic strip, Amend joins an elite group of cartoonists breaking the four-figure circulation mark. The Fox family antics have received a warm reception from the public since their inception, and continue to delight readers of all ages.

Wayne Anderson ▮ Award-winning British illustrator Anderson has provided the artwork for more than forty children's books, including such modern classics as *Ratsmagic, A Mouse's Tale, Thumbelina, Dragon, Invasion of the Giant Bugs, The Leprechaun Companion, Year of the Dragon, Gnomes and Gardens,* and *The Tin Forest.* Anderson has illustrated his own titles as well as those by writers such as Nigel Suckling, Helen Ward, Ben Butterworth, W. J. Corbett, Joan Aiken, and A. J. Wood.

Dianne Bates ▮ Prolific Australian writer Bates is the author of more than eighty-five books for children and young adults. Although Bates approaches tragedy and difficult issues in her writing, many of her books focus on happier subjects. *The Funnies: Cartoons and Comics* discusses comic strips and cartoons and shows kids how to draw them. Bates shares her life with her husband, writer Bill Condon, and the two have collaborated on several books.

Barbara Elleman ▮ A noted authority in the field of children's literature, Elleman has served on advisory committees, award juries, and editorial boards. Her expertise in the field and her familiarity with some of the best in children's literature has led Elleman to author several books of her own, among them *Tomi dePaola: His Art and His Stories* and *Virginia Lee Burton: A Life in Art.* Elleman has received many awards for her efforts including the Hope S. Dean Award, from the Foundation for Children's Literature.

*Will Hillenbrand ▮ Hillenbrand is an award-winning author/illustrator whose works include almost forty picture books for young readers. In addition to his own self-illustrated titles such as *Down by the Station, Fiddle-I-Fee,* and *Here We Go Round the Mulberry Bush,* he has also illustrated the works of prominent

children's writers and re-tellers, including Eric A. Kimmel, Phyllis Root, Judy Sierra, and David A. Adler.

*Naomi Shihab Nye ▮ Nye is a prolific, critically acclaimed poet who has turned her hand to children's books that in one way or another deal with the idea of connections-connections as simple as the everyday lives of people around the world, or of ancestry played out in daily tasks. Her works for children include poetry, picture books such as *Sitti's Secrets,* and novels, such as the highly praised *Habibi.*

*Alice Provensen ▮ Over the course of more than thirty years, Provensen and her husband Martin created the artwork for a score of their own and other authors' picture books, earning high regard for their realistic and charming illustrations. After Martin's death, Provensen launched a successful solo career, producing several more self-illustrated titles, including award winners such as *Punch in New York, Count on Me, The Master Swordsman and the Magic Doorway,* and 2003's *A Day in the Life of Murphy.*

*Kate Spohn ▮ Combining simple texts with illustrations that range from colored-pencil drawings to pastels to impressionistic oils, Spohn has created several well-received books for children. In addition to picture books such as *Christmas at Anna's, The Mermaid's Lullaby,* and *Snow Play,* Spohn has also written and illustrated books for beginning readers. She has received high praise from a number of high profile book reviewers, including Library Journal and Kirkus Reviews.

*Ellen Stoll Walsh ▮ Children's author and illustrator Walsh is the creator of over a dozen picture books focused on helping young readers learn important skills, such as counting, mixing colors, and overcoming fears. In 2001, Walsh began a series about a pair of detective mice, Dot & Jabber, which served to introduce children to simple science concepts. *Dot & Jabber and the Big Bug Mystery* received the 2004 National Outdoor Children's Book Award.

Dirk Zimmer ▮ German-born children's book illustrator Zimmer has created the artwork for over thirty titles authored by some of the most prominent names in children's literature. Books that Zimmer has complemented with his incredible touch include *The Moonbow of Mr. B. Bones, Seven Spiders Spinning, One Eye, Two Eyes, Three Eyes: A Hutzul Tale* and *King of Magic, Man of Glass: A German Folktale.*

Introduction

Something about the Author (*SATA*) is an ongoing reference series that examines the lives and works of authors and illustrators of books for children. *SATA* includes not only well-known writers and artists but also less prominent individuals whose works are just coming to be recognized. This series is often the only readily available information source on emerging authors and illustrators. You'll find *SATA* informative and entertaining, whether you are a student, a librarian, an English teacher, a parent, or simply an adult who enjoys children's literature.

What's Inside *SATA*

SATA provides detailed information about authors and illustrators who span the full time range of children's literature, from early figures like John Newbery and L. Frank Baum to contemporary figures like Judy Blume and Richard Peck. Authors in the series represent primarily English-speaking countries, particularly the United States, Canada, and the United Kingdom. Also included, however, are authors from around the world whose works are available in English translation. The writings represented in *SATA* include those created intentionally for children and young adults as well as those written for a general audience and known to interest younger readers. These writings cover the entire spectrum of children's literature, including picture books, humor, folk and fairy tales, animal stories, mystery and adventure, science fiction and fantasy, historical fiction, poetry and nonsense verse, drama, biography, and nonfiction. Obituaries are also included in *SATA* and are intended not only as death notices but also as concise overviews of people's lives and work. Additionally, each edition features newly revised and updated entries for a selection of *SATA* listees who remain of interest to today's readers and who have been active enough to require extensive revisions of their earlier biographies.

Autobiography Feature

Beginning with Volume 103, *SATA* features two or more specially commissioned autobiographical essays in each volume. These unique essays, averaging about ten thousand words in length and illustrated with an abundance of personal photos, present an entertaining and informative first-person perspective on the lives and careers of prominent authors and illustrators profiled in *SATA*.

Two Convenient Indexes

In response to suggestions from librarians, *SATA* indexes no longer appear in every volume but are included in alternate (odd-numbered) volumes of the series, beginning with Volume 57.

SATA continues to include two indexes that cumulate with each alternate volume: the Illustrations Index, arranged by the name of the illustrator, gives the number of the volume and page where the illustrator's work appears in the current volume as well as all preceding volumes in the series; the Author Index gives the number of the volume in which a person's biographical sketch, autobiographical essay, or obituary appears in the current volume as well as all preceding volumes in the series.

These indexes also include references to authors and illustrators who appear in *Gale's Yesterday's Authors of Books for Children, Children's Literature Review,* and *Something about the Author Autobiography Series.*

Easy-to-Use Entry Format

Whether you're already familiar with the *SATA* series or just getting acquainted, you will want to be aware of the kind of information that an entry provides. In every *SATA* entry the editors attempt to give as complete a picture of the person's life and work as possible. A typical entry in *SATA* includes the following clearly labeled information sections:

PERSONAL: date and place of birth and death, parents' names and occupations, name of spouse, date of marriage, names of children, educational institutions attended, degrees received, religious and political affiliations, hobbies and other interests.

ADDRESSES: complete home, office, electronic mail, and agent addresses, whenever available.

CAREER: name of employer, position, and dates for each career post; art exhibitions; military service; memberships and offices held in professional and civic organizations.

MEMBER: professional, civic, and other association memberships and any official posts held.

AWARDS, HONORS: literary and professional awards received.

WRITINGS: title-by-title chronological bibliography of books written and/or illustrated, listed by genre when known; lists of other notable publications, such as plays, screenplays, and periodical contributions.

ADAPTATIONS: a list of films, television programs, plays, CD-ROMs, recordings, and other media presentations that have been adapted from the author's work.

WORK IN PROGRESS: description of projects in progress.

SIDELIGHTS: a biographical portrait of the author or illustrator's development, either directly from the biographee—and often written specifically for the *SATA* entry—or gathered from diaries, letters, interviews, or other published sources.

BIOGRAPHICAL AND CRITICAL SOURCES: cites sources quoted in "Sidelights" along with references for further reading.

EXTENSIVE ILLUSTRATIONS: photographs, movie stills, book illustrations, and other interesting visual materials supplement the text.

How a *SATA* Entry Is Compiled

A *SATA* entry progresses through a series of steps. If the biographee is living, the *SATA* editors try to secure information directly from him or her through a questionnaire. From the information that the biographee supplies, the editors prepare an entry, filling in any essential missing details with research and/or telephone interviews. If possible, the author or illustrator is sent a copy of the entry to check for accuracy and completeness.

If the biographee is deceased or cannot be reached by questionnaire, the *SATA* editors examine a wide variety of published sources to gather information for an entry. Biographical and bibliographic sources are consulted, as are book reviews, feature articles, published interviews, and material sometimes obtained from the biographee's family, publishers, agent, or other associates.

Entries that have not been verified by the biographees or their representatives are marked with an asterisk (*).

Contact the Editor

We encourage our readers to examine the entire *SATA* series. Please write and tell us if we can make *SATA* even more helpful to you. Give your comments and suggestions to the editor:

Editor
Something about the Author
The Gale Group
27500 Drake Rd.
Farmington Hills MI 48331-3535

Toll-free: 800-877-GALE
Fax: 248-699-8054

Something about the Author Product Advisory Board

The editors of *Something about the Author* are dedicated to maintaining a high standard of excellence by publishing comprehensive, accurate, and highly readable entries on a wide array of writers for children and young adults. In addition to the quality of the content, the editors take pride in the graphic design of the series, which is intended to be orderly yet inviting, allowing readers to utilize the pages of *SATA* easily and with efficiency. Despite the longevity of the *SATA* print series, and the success of its format, we are mindful that the vitality of a literary reference product is dependent on its ability to serve its users over time. As literature, and attitudes about literature, constantly evolve, so do the reference needs of students, teachers, scholars, journalists, researchers, and book club members. To be certain that we continue to keep pace with the expectations of our customers, the editors of *SATA* listen carefully to their comments regarding the value, utility, and quality of the series. Librarians, who have firsthand knowledge of the needs of library users, are a valuable resource for us. The *Something about the Author* Product Advisory Board, made up of school, public, and academic librarians, is a forum to promote focused feedback about *SATA* on a regular basis. The nine-member advisory board includes the following individuals, whom the editors wish to thank for sharing their expertise:

Eva M. Davis
Youth Department Manager,
Ann Arbor District Library,
Ann Arbor, Michigan

Joan B. Eisenberg
Lower School Librarian,
Milton Academy,
Milton, Massachusetts

Francisca Goldsmith
Teen Services Librarian,
Berkeley Public Library,
Berkeley, California

Susan Dove Lempke
Children's Services Supervisor,
Niles Public Library District,
Niles, Illinois

Robyn Lupa
Head of Children's Services,
Jefferson County Public Library,
Lakewood, Colorado

Victor L. Schill
Assistant Branch Librarian/Children's Librarian,
Harris County Public Library/Fairbanks Branch,
Houston, Texas

Caryn Sipos
Community Librarian,
Three Creeks Community Library,
Vancouver, Washington

Steven Weiner
Director,
Maynard Public Library,
Maynard, Massachusetts

Acknowledgments

Grateful acknowledgment is made to the following publishers, authors, and artists whose works appear in this volume.

ANDERSON, M.T. ▌ Anderson, M. T. From a cover of his *Feed.* Candlewick Press, 2002. Reproduced by permission of the publisher Candlewick Press, Inc., Cambridge, MA.

ASHBY, GIL ▌ Ashby, Gil, illustrator. From a cover of *Dear Mother, Dear Daughter: Poems for Young People,* by Jane Yolen and Heidi Stemple. Boyds Mills Press, 2001. Illustrations copyright © 2001 by Boyds Mills Press. All rights reserved. Reproduced by permission. /Ashby, Gil. Self-Portrait, pencil on paper. © Gil Ashby. Reproduced by permission.

BAKER, ALAN ▌ Baker, Alan, illustrator. From an illustration in *The Odyssey,* retold by Robin Lister. Kingfisher, 1987. Copyright © 1987 Kingfisher Publications Plc. Reproduced by permission of the publisher, all rights reserved. /Baker, Alan, illustrator. From an illustration in his *Gray Rabbit's Odd One Out.* Kingfisher, 1995. Illustration © 1995 by Alan Baker. Reproduced by permission of Kingfisher Publications Plc. All rights reserved. Reproduced by permission. /Baker, Alan, photograph. Reproduced by permission Alan Baker.

BEATY, MARY ▌ Beaty, Mary, photograph. Reproduced by permission.

BLOOM, BARBARA LEE ▌ Chinese and French officials signing a treaty in 1858, photograph. © Bettmann/Corbis. Reproduced by permission.

BRAGER, BRUCE L ▌ Eichmann, Adolf, in a glass booth during his 1961 trial for being a Nazi collaborator during World War II, photograph. © Bettmann/Corbis. Reproduced by permission.

BURGESS, MELVIN ▌ Fiedler, Joseph Daniel, illustrator. From a jacket of *The Baby and Fly Pie,* by Melvin Burgess. Simon & Schuster Books for Young Readers, 1996. Reproduced by permission of the illustrator. /Foster, Jon, illustrator. From a jacket of *Bloodtide,* by Melvin Burgess. Tom Doherty, 2001. Reproduced by permission. /Burgess, Melvin, photograph. Reproduced by permission.

BURLEIGH, ROBERT ▌ Colon, Raul, illustrator. An illustration from *Pandora,* by Robert Burleigh. Harcourt, Inc., 2002. Illustrations copyright © 2002 by Raul Colon. All rights reserved. Reproduced by permission Harcourt. /Los, Marek, illustrator. An illustration from *Lookin' for Bird in the Big City,* by Robert Burleigh. Harcourt, 2001. Illustrations copyright © 2001 by Marek Los. All rights reserved. Reproduced by permission of Harcourt. /Wimmer, Mike, illustrator. An illustration from *Flight: The Journey of Charles Lindbergh,* by Robert Burleigh. Illustrations copyright © 1991 by Mike Wimmer. Used by permission of Philomel Books, a Division of Penguin Young Readers Group, A Member of Penguin Group (USA) Inc., 345 Hudson Street, New York, NY 10014. All rights reserved

CASILLA, ROBERT ▌ Casilla, Robert, photograph. Reproduced by permission.

CHORON, SANDRA ▌ Schulder, Lili, illustrator. From a cover of *The Book of Lists for Teens,* by Sandra and Harry Choron. Houghton Mifflin Company, 2002. Cover illustration © Lili Schulder. Reproduced by permission of Houghton Mifflin Company. /Choron, Sandra, photograph by Harry Choron. Reproduced by permission.

CHWAST, SEYMOUR ▌ Chwast, Seymour, illustrator. From an illustration in his *Harry I Need You.* Houghton Mifflin, 2002. Reproduced by permission of Houghton Mifflin Company. /Chwast, Seymour, illustrator. From an illustration in his *Traffic Jam.* Houghton Mifflin Company, 1999. Illustrations copyright © 1999 Seymour Chwast. All rights reserved. Reproduced by permission of Houghton Mifflin Company. /Chwast, Seymour, photograph. Reproduced by permission of Seymour Chwast.

CROSS, TOM ▌ Cross, Tom, photograph. Reproduced by permission

DAVOL, MARGUERITE W ▌ Roth, Robert , illustrator. From an illustration in *Why Butterflies Go By on Silent Wings,* by Marguerite W. Davol. Orchard Books, 2001. Illustrations copyright © 2001 by Robert Roth. All rights reserved. Reproduced by permission. /Smith, Cat Bowman, illustrator. From a jacket of *The Loudest, Fastest, Best Drummer in Kansas,* by Marguerite W. Davol. Orchard Books, an imprint of Scholastic Inc., 2000. Illustration copyright © 2000 by Cat Bowman Smith. Reprinted by permission. /Heo, Yumi, illustrator. From an illustration in *The Snake's Tales,* by Marguerite W. Davol. Orchard Books, 2002. Illustrations copyright © 2002 by Yumi Heo. All rights reserved. Reproduced by permission. /Davol, Marguerite W, photograph. Reproduced by permission.

DOUGHERTY, TERRI L ▌ From a photograph in *Mark McGwire,* by Terri Dougherty. ABDO Publishing Company, 1999. Reproduced by permission of AP/Wide World Photos.

DRAPER, SHARON M ▌ All photographs reproduced by permission of the author.

EMBERLEY, BARBARA ▌ Emberley, Ed, illustrator. From an illustration in *Drummer Hoff,* adapted by Barbara Emberley. Aladdin, 1987. Copyright © 1967 by Edward R. Emberley and Barbara Emberley. Reprinted with the permission of Simon & Schuster Books for Young Readers, an imprint of Simon & Schuster Children's Publishing Division. /Emberley, Barbara and Ed Emberley, photograph. Reproduced by permission by Barbara Emberley.

EMBERLEY, ED ▌ Emberley, Ed, illustrator. From an illustration in his *Go Away, Big Green Monster.* Little Brown, 1992. Copyright © 1993 by Ed Emberley. Reproduced by permission of Little, Brown and Company, (Inc.). /Emberley, Ed, illustrator. From an illustration in his *The Wing on a Flea: A Book about Shapes.* Little, Brown

ENGLART, MINDI ▌ Casolino, Peter, photographer. From a photograph in *How Do I Become An...? Architect,* by Mindi Englart. Blackbirch Press, 2002. © Peter Casolino. Reproduced by permission of Gale Group.

FARISH, TERRY ▌ Root, Barry, illustrator. From an illustration in *The Cat Who Liked Potato Soup,* by Terry Farish. Candlewick Press, 2003. Illustration copyright © 2003 by Barry Root. Reproduced by permission of the publisher Candlewick Press, Inc., Cambridge, MA.

FEARRINGTON, ANN ▌ Fearrington, Ann, illustrator. From an illustration in her *Christmas Lights.* Houghton Mifflin, 1996. Reproduced by permission of Houghton Mifflin Company. /Laroche, Giles, illustrator. From an illustration in *Who Sees the Lighthouse?* by Ann Fearrington. G. P. Putnam, 2002. Illustrations copyright © 2002 by Giles Laroche. Reproduced by permission of G.P. Putnam's Sons, a Division of Penguin Young Readers Group, A Member of Penguin Group (USA) Inc., 345 Hudson Street, New York, NY 10014. All rights reserved. /Fearrington, Ann photograph. Reproduced by permission of Ann Fearrington.

FRAUSTINO, LISA ▌ All photographs reproduced by permission of the author.

GAIMAN, NEIL ▌ Potter, J.K., photographer. From a cover of *Smoke and Mirrors: Short Fictions and Illusions,* by Neil Gaiman. Perennial, 2001. Reproduced by permission HarperCollins Publishers. /Russell, P. Craig. From an illustration in *The Sandman # 50,* by Neil Gaiman. DC Comics, 1993. © 1993 DC Comics. All Rights Reserved. Used with Permission. /Gaiman, Neil, photograph by Kelli Bickman. © Kelli Bickman. Reproduced by permission.

GARRISON, MARY ▌ Garrison, Mary. Photograph reproduced by permission of the author..

GLUBOK, SHIRLEY ▌ Glubok, Shirley, walking down New York City street, photograph by Jeff Mermelstein. Reproduced by permission. /All photographs reproduced by permission of the author.

HEELAN, JAMEE RIGGIO ▌ Heelan, Jamee Riggio. Photograph reproduced by permission of the author.

HELQUIST, BRETT. ▌ Helquist, Brett, illustrator. From an illustration in *A Series of Unfortunate Events: The Bad Beginning,* by Lemony Snicket. HarperCollins, 1999. Illustration copyright © 1999 by Brett Helquist. Reproduced by permission of HarperCollins Publishers. /Helquist, Brett, illustrator. From an illustration in *A Series of Unfortunate Events: The Miserable Mill,* by Lemony Snicket. HarperCollins, 2000. Illustrations copyright © 2000 by Brett Helquist. Reproduced by permission of HarperCollins Publishers, Inc.

HEO, YUMI ▌ Heo, Yumi, illustrator. From an illustration in *Pirican Pic and Pirican Mor,* by Hugh Lupton. Barefoot Books, 2003. Illustrations copyright © 2003 by Yumi Heo. Reproduced by permission. /Heo, Yumi, illustrator. From an illustration in *Sometimes I'm Bombaloo,* by Rachel Vail. Scholastic Press, a division of Scholastic Inc., 2002. Illustrations copyright © 2002 by Yumi Heo. Reproduced by permission..

ICHIKAWA, SATOMI ▌ Ichikawa, Satomi, illustrator. From an illustration in her *My Pig Amarillo.* Philomel Books, 2002. Reproduced by permission of Philomel Books, a division of Penguin Putnam Inc. /Ichikawa, Satomi, illustrator. From an illustration in *Tanya and the Magic Wardrobe,* by Patricia Lee Gauch. Puffin Books, 1997. Illustrations copyright © Satomi Ichikawa, 1997. Reproduced by permission of Puffin Books, a division of Penguin Put-

nam Inc. /Ichikawa, Satomi, illustrator. From an illustration in her *The First Bear in Africa.* Philomel Books, 2001. Reproduced by permission of Philomel Books, a division of Penguin Putnam Inc. /Ichikawa, Satomi, photograph by Marianne Veron. Reproduced by permission of Satomi Ichikawa.

JAMES, J. ALISON ▌ Duroussy, Nathalie, illustrator. From an illustration in *Stormy Night,* by Hubert Flattinger. Translated by J. Alison James. North-South Books, Inc., 2002. Copyright © 2002 by Nord-Süd Verlag AG, Gossau, Zurich, Switzerland. Used by permission of North-South Books, Inc., New York. /Heyne, Ulrike, illustrator. From an illustration in *Midnight Rider,* by Krista Ruepp. Translated by J. Alison James. North-South Books, Inc., 1996. Copyright © 1996 by Nord-Süd Verlag AG, Gossau, Zurich, Switzerland. Used by permission of North-South Books, Inc., New York. /Pfister, Marcus. From an illustration in his *The Rainbow Fish.* Translated by J. Alison James. North-South Books, 1992. Copyright © 1992 by Nord-Süd Verlag AG, Gossau Zurich, Switzerland. Used by permission of North-South Books, Inc., New York. /Tharlet, Eve, illustrator. From an illustration in *Hugs and Kisses,* by Christophe Loupy. Translated by J. Alison James. North-South Books, Inc., 2001. Copyright © 2001 by Nord-Süd Verlag AG, Gossau, Zurich, Switzerland. Used by permission of North-South Books, Inc., New York.

JOHNSON, DONALD B. ▌ Johnson, Donald B., photograph by Medora Hebert. Reproduced by permission.

KJELLE, MARYLOU MORANO ▌ Kjelle, Marylou Morano. From a photograph in her *Helping Hands: A City and a Nation Lend Their Support At Ground Zero.* Chelsea House Publishers, 2002. Reproduced by permission of AP/Wide World Photos.

KOTZWINKLE, WILLIAM. ▌ Colman, Audrey, illustrator. From an illustration in *Walter the Farting Dog,* by William Kotzwinkle and Glenn Murray. Frog, Ltd., 2001. Illustration copyright © 2001 Audrey Colman. Reprinted by permission of the publisher. /Servello, Joe, illustrator. From an illustration in *Hearts of Wood and Other Timeless Tales,* by William Kotzwinkle. David R. Godine, 1986. Illustrations copyright © 1986 by Joe Servello. Reproduced by permission. /Kotzwinkle, William, photograph. © Jerry Bauer. Reproduced by permission.

LANDSTROM, LENA AND OLOF ▌ Landstrom, Lena, illustrator. From an illustration in her *The Little Hippos' Adventure.* Translated by Joan Sandin. R & S Books, 2002. Reproduced by permission of Lena Landstrom. /Landstrom Olof and Lena, illustrators. From an illustration in their *Boo and Baa Get Wet.* R & S Books, 2000. Reproduced by permission of Lena Landstrom. /Landstrom, Olof, illustration. From a illustration in *Boris's Glasses,* by Peter Cohen. Translated by Joan Sandin. R & S Books, 2003. Pictures copyright © 2002 by Olof Landstrom. Reproduced by permission of Lena Landstrom. /Landstrom, Lena, photograph by Olof Landstrom. Reproduced by permission.

LEE, DOM ▌ Lee, Dom and Keunhee, illustrators. From an illustration in *Journey Home,* by Lawrence McKay, Jr. Lee & Low Books, Inc., 1998. Illustrations copyright © 1998 by Dom and Keunhee Lee. Reproduced by permission of Lee & Low Books, Inc. /Lee, Dom, illustrator. From an illustration in *Baseball Saved Us,* by Ken Mochizuki. Lee & Low Books Inc., 1995. Illustrations copyright © 1993 by Dom Lee. Reproduced by permission of Lee & Low Books Inc. /Lee, Dom, photograph. Reproduced by permission.

LEUCK, LAURA ▌ McMullen, Nigel, illustrator. From an illustration in *Goodnight, Baby Monster,* by Laura Leuck. HarperCollins Publishers, 2002. Illustrations copyright © 2002 by Nigel McMullen. All rights reserved. Reproduced by permission of HarperCollins Publishers. /Parkins, David, illustrator. From an illustration in *Jeepers Creepers: A Monstrous ABC,* by Laura Leuck. Chronicle, 2003. Illustrations © 2003 by David Parkins. All rights reserved. Reproduced by permission.

MARSDEN, JOHN ▮ Goodman, Vivienne, illustrator. From a jacket of *Darkness Be My Friend*, by John Marsden. Houghton Mifflin Company, 1999. Jacket art © 1999 by Vivienne Goodman. Reproduced by permission of Houghton Mifflin Company. /Goodman, Vivienne, illustrator. From a jacket of *The Night is for Hunting*, by John Marsden. Houghton·Mifflin Company, 2001. Reproduced by permission of Houghton Mifflin Company. /Hillenbrand, Will, photographer. From a jacket of *Tomorrow, When the War Began*, by John Marsden. Houghton Mifflin Company, 1995. Jacket art © 1995 by Will Hillenbrand. Reproduced by permission. /Marsden, John, 1994, photograph by David Furphy. Reproduced by permission.

MAYFIELD, SUE ▮ Brak, Syd, illustrator. From a cover of *A Time To Be Born*, by Sue Mayfield. Scholastic, 1995. Illustration copyright © Syd Brak. All rights reserved. Reproduced by permission of Scholastic Ltd.

MCCLINTOCK, BARBARA ▮ McClintock, Barbara, illustrator. From an illustration in her *The Gingerbread Man*. Retold by Jim Aylesworth. Scholastic Press, a division of Scholastic Inc. Illustration copyright © 1998 by Barbara McClintock. Reproduced by permission. /McClintock, Barbara, with a boy, photograph by Lawrence DiFiori. Reproduced by permission of Barbara McClintock.

MCDANIEL, LURLENE ▮ Hefferman, Phil, illustrator. From a cover of *Time to Let Go*, by Lurlene McDaniel. Bantam Books, 1990. Reproduced by permission of Dell Publishing, a division of Random House, Inc. /Vojnar, Kamil, illustrator. From a cover of *Angels Watching Over Me*, by Lurlene McDaniel. Laurel-Leaf Books, 2003. Cover art copyright © 1996 by Kamil Vojnar. Reproduced by permission of Dell Publishing, a division of Random House, Inc. /McDaniel, Lurlene, photograph by Robert Copeland. Reproduced by permission Copeland Photography.

MCDONNELL, FLORA ▮ McDonnell, Flora, illustrator. From an illustration in *ABC*, by Flora McDonnell. Candlewick Press, 1997. Copyright © 1997 by Flora McDonnell. Reproduced by permission of the publisher Candlewick Press, Inc., Cambridge, MA, on behalf of Walker Books Ltd., London. /McDonnell, Flora, illustrator. From an illustration in her *Splash*, by Flora McDonnell. Candlewick, 1999. Copyright © 1999 by Flora McDonnell. Reproduced by permission of the publisher Candlewick Press, Inc., Cambridge, MA, on behalf of Walker Books Ltd., London.

MEAD, ALICE ▮ Hale, Christy, illustrator. From an illustration in *Billy and Emma*, by Alice Mead. Farrar, Straus & Giroux, 2000. Illustration copyright © 2000 by Christy Hale. Reproduced by permission of Farrar, Straus & Giroux, LLC. /From a jacket of *Junebug In Trouble*, by Alice Mead. Farrar Straus Giroux, 2002. Copyright © 2003 by Alice Mead. Reproduced by permission of Farrar Straus Giroux, a division of Farrar, Straus and Giroux, LLC.

MENENDEZ, SHIRLEY ▮ Menendez, Shirley, photograph. Reproduced by permission.

MOCHIZUKI, KEN ▮ Tauss, Marc, photographer. From a jacket of *Beacon Hill Boys*, by Ken Mochizuki. Scholastic Press, a division of Scholastic Inc., 2002. Illustration copyright © 2002 by Scholastic Inc. Reprinted by permission. /Lee, Dom, illustrator. From an illustration in *Heroes*, by Ken Mochizuki. Lee & Low Books Inc., 1997. Illustrations copyright © Dom Lee. Reproduced by permission of Lee & Low Books, Inc. /Lee, Dom, illustrator. From an illustration in *Passage to Freedom: The Sugihara Story*, by Ken Mochizuki. Lee & Low Books, 1997. Illustrations copyright © 1997 by Dom Lee. Reproduced by permission of Lee & Low Books, Inc.

MONTGOMERY, HUGH ▮ Poullis, Nick, illustrator. From an illustration in *The Voyage of the Arctic Tern*, by Hugh Montgomery. Can-

dlewick Press, 2000. Illustrations Copyright © 2002 by Nick Poullis. Reproduced by permission of the publisher Candlewick Press, Inc., Cambridge, MA, on behalf of Walker Books Ltd., London.

NEWMAN, MARJORIE ▮ Bowman, Peter, illustrator. From an illustration in *Is That What Friends Do?*, by Marjorie Newman. Red Fox, 2001. Illustrations copyright © Peter Bowman 1998. Used by permission of The Random House Group Limited. /Bowman, Peter, illustrator. From an illustration in *The King and the Cuddly*, by Marjorie Newman. Hutchinson, 2001. Used by permission of The Random House Group Limited.

NOONAN, DIANA ▮ Blobel, Colin, photographer. From a photograph in *The Emperor Penguin*, by Diana Noonan. Chelsea Clubhouse, 2002. Reproduced by permission of Colin Blobel/ANTphoto.com.au. /Six, A. & J. , photographers. From a photograph in *The Butterfly*, by Diana Noonan. Chelsea House, 2002. © Pascal Goetgheluck. Reproduced by permission of Auscape International.

PEARCE, JACQUELINE ▮ Pearce, Jacqueline, photograph. Reproduced by permission.

PETERSON, SHELLEY ▮ Handley, Christina, photographer. From a cover of *Abby Malone*, by Shelley Peterson. *The Porcupine's Quill*, 1999. Reproduced by permission. /Leck, Karl photographer. From a cover of *Dancer*, by Shelley Peterson. Porcupine's Quill, 1996. Reproduced by permission. /Peterson, Shelley, photograph by Anna Bratt. Reproduced by permission.

READ, NICHOLAS ▮ Read, Nicholas, photograph. Reproduced by permission.

ROWE, JOHN A. ▮ Rowe, John, photograph. Reproduced by permission.

SEINFELD, JERRY ▮ Bennett, James, illustrator. From an illustration in *Halloween*, by Jerry Seinfeld. Little, Brown and Company, 2002. Copyright © 2002 Columbus 81 Productions, Inc. and Byron Preiss Visual Publications, Inc.. Reproduced by permission of Little, Brown and Company, (Inc.). /Seinfeld, Jerry, New York City, 1998, photograph by Richard Drew. AP/Wide World Photos. Reproduced by permission.

SHAW, JANET ▮ Farnsworth, Bill, illustrator. From *Changes for Kaya: A Story of Courage*, by Janet Shaw. American Girl, 2002. Reproduced by permission. /Farnsworth, Bill, illustrator. From *Kaya's Escape: A Survival Story*, by Janet Shaw. American Girl, 2002. Reproduced by permission. /Farnsworth, Bill, illustrator. From *Kaya's Hero: A Story of Giving*, by Janet Shaw. American Girl, 2002. Reproduced by permission.

SHULMAN, DEE ▮ Porter, Sue. From an illustration in *Cuddly Board Book: Our New Baby*, by Dee Shulman. Scholastic Inc., 2000. Illustration copyright © 2000 by Sue Porter. Reprinted by permission of Scholastic Inc. /Porter, Sue, illustrator. From an illustration in *Cuddly Board Book: Birthday Bunny*, by Dee Shulman. Scholastic, 2000. Illustrations copyright © 2000 by Sue Porter. Reproduced by permission of Scholastic Inc.

SMALLS-HECTOR, IRENE. ▮ Geter, Tyrone, illustrator. From an illustration in *Irene and the Big Fine Nickel*, by Irene Smalls. Illustrations copyright © 1991 by Tyrone Geter. Reproduced by permission of Little, Brown and Company, (Inc.). /Hays, Michael, illustrator. From an illustration in *Kevin and His Dad*, by Irene Smalls. Illustrations copyright © 1999 by Michael Hays. By permission of Little, Brown and Company, (Inc.).

something about the author

ANDERSON, M. T(obin) 1968-

Personal

Born November 4, 1968, in Cambridge, MA; son of Will (an engineer) and Juliana (an Episcopal priest) Anderson. *Education:* Attended Harvard University, 1987; Cambridge University, B.A., 1991; Syracuse University, M.F.A., 1998.

Addresses

Office—Union Institute & University, Vermont College, 36 College St., Montpelier, VT 05602.

Career

Writer. Candlewick Press, Cambridge, MA, editorial assistant, 1993-96; *Boston Review,* intern; WCUW-Radio, disc jockey; Union Institute & University, Vermont College, Montpelier, VT, instructor in M.F.A. program in writing for children, 2000—.

Awards, Honors

Boston Globe/Horn Book Nonfiction Honor, 2002, for *Handel: Who Knew What He Liked;* National Book Award finalist, National Book Foundation, 2002, Best Book for Young Adults selection, American Library Association, *Boston Globe/Horn Book* Honor Book for Fiction, and *Los Angeles Times* Book Award, all 2003, all for *Feed.*

Writings

Thirsty, Candlewick Press (Cambridge, MA), 1998.
Burger Wuss, Candlewick Press (Cambridge, MA), 1999.
Handel: Who Knew What He Liked, illustrated by Kevin Hawkes, Candlewick Press (Cambridge, MA), 2001.
Feed, Candlewick Press (Cambridge, MA), 2002.
Strange Mr. Satie, Viking Penguin (New York, NY), 2003.
The Game of Sunken Places, Scholastic (New York, NY), 2004.
Just Me, All Alone, at the End of the World, Candlewick Press (Cambridge, MA), in press.

Contributor of articles and reviews to periodicals, including *Improper Bostonian, BBC Music, Pulse!,* and *Cobblestones.* Contributor of short story to *Open Your Eyes: Extraordinary Experiences in Far Away Places,* edited by Jill Davis, Viking (New York, NY), 2003.

Work in Progress

A gothic novel for adults about the textile industry in nineteenth-century New England.

Sidelights

Author M. T. Anderson is noted for his young adult novels that challenge readers to look at the world in new ways. "Writing is a kind of weakness, I think," he once told *SATA.* "We write because we can't decipher things the first time around. As a reader, I like best those books in which the author, mulling things over for him or herself, enables readers to see a world anew." Anderson's novels, such as *Thirsty,* about a teenage vampire, *Burger Wuss,* about revenge in a fast-food restaurant, or *Feed,* about rebellion against futuristic media control of the world, use wit and satire to jab at contemporary society. "We are so used to the bizarre images, cabals, rituals, and rites that constitute our lives that they seem natural, even invisible, to us," Anderson once told *SATA.* "I admire books that facilitate renewed awareness of the way we live, and this is what I'm attempting in my own work: renewed awareness both for myself and, I hope, for my readers. That's my goal, in any case."

Anderson's debut novel, *Thirsty,* set in a small town in Massachusetts, features a high school freshman named Chris who realizes that he is on the verge of growing into a vampire—despite his town's very elaborate and ritualistic attempts to fight the dreaded monsters, which seem to reap a steady New England harvest. "Chris's turbulent transformation . . . is paralleled by and inextricable from the changes of adolescence: insatiable appetite, sleepless nights, and a deep sense of insecurity and isolation," noted *Horn Book* reviewer Lauren Adams, who added: "The unusual blend of camp horror and realistic adolescent turmoil and the suspenseful plot affirm a new talent worth watching." A *Kirkus Reviews* critic also praised *Thirsty,* calling it a "startling, savagely funny debut," and *School Librarian*'s Julie Blaisdale found the work "at once creepy and yet extremely funny." In *Publishers Weekly,* a reviewer concluded that *Thirsty* is a "vampire novel a bloody cut above the usual fare" despite some flaws in the plot.

The young adult novels *Burger Wuss* and *Feed* take place in a setting that is both disturbing and familiar. In the former, the teenage narrator, Anthony, is set upon getting revenge on another teen who has "stolen" his girlfriend. The other teen, Turner, is a hot-shot worker at the local burger joint, and by getting a job at the fast-food restaurant, Anthony plots his revenge. According to a *Publishers Weekly* critic, "Anderson's witty tale of a lovelorn boy and his corporate antagonists is both a tasty read and a stinging satire." Also focusing on the novel's abundant "black humor and satire," *Booklist*'s Jean Franklin cited "a marvelous parody of a television commercial" for particular praise, and *Horn Book* reviewer Peter D. Sieruta likewise commented on Anderson's "eye for the dark and demented aspects of everyday life," which through Anthony's narration "serves up a lot of laughs."

With *Feed,* Anderson goes one step further, taking readers into a more distant and frightening future in which the media controls the world and everyone is linked into this system with an electronic feed inserted in the brain. Titus, like other typical teenagers, is connected to the educational system, entertainment, merchandise, and friends through this feed. With this constant information stream, there is little need to speak, read, or write. While vacationing on the moon with a group of friends, Titus

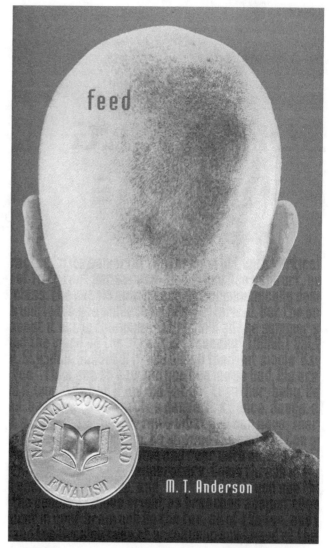

Titus lives in a world where a "feed" controls all aspects of his life. From the novel **Feed,** *written by M. T. Anderson.*

meets Violet, who has been home-schooled and is somewhat of a Luddite in that she eschews technology. When hackers temporarily disconnect the vacationers' feeds and Titus wakes up in the hospital, he experiences silence for the first time. Violet tries to recruit him to resist the feed and all that it implies, but he is unable to reject his previous lifestyle.

Reviewers saw much to like in *Feed,* particularly Anderson's wit and imagination. Among the work's enthusiasts are a *Kirkus Reviews* contributor, who called it "satire at its finest," and a *Publishers Weekly* critic, who described Titus as a "believably flawed hero" and the work a "thought-provoking and scathing indictment." According to Elizabeth Devereaux, writing in the *New York Times Book Review, Feed* is "subversive, vigorously conceived, [and] painfully situated at the juncture where funny crosses into tragic." Although, as Sharon Rawlins of *School Library Journal* remarked, "Violet and her father are the only truly sympathetic characters," the work as a whole, she asserted, is a "gripping, intriguing, and unique cautionary novel." Several reviewers noted Anderson's use of language, particularly his tone and creation of original language. "Anderson's hand is light throughout; his evocation of the death of language is as hilarious as it is frightening," wrote *Horn Book*'s Lauren Adams. "Inventive details help evoke a world that is chillingly plausible," she continued. "Like those in a funhouse mirror, the reflections the novel shows us may be ugly and distorted, but they are undeniably ourselves." Winner of the *Los Angeles Times* Book Award, *Feed* was a finalist in the competition for the National Book Award, as well as a *Boston Globe/Horn Book* Honor Book and an American Library Association Best Book for Young Adults selection.

Anderson has expressed his interest in music as a reviewer for *BBC Music* and through two picture-book biographies of composers, eighteenth-century German-English composer George Frideric Handel and twentieth-century French composer Erik Satie. *Handel: Who Knew What He Liked* illustrates much about the life of Handel through anecdotes told in a "saucy style, [with] impeccable pacing, and a richness of content," in the words of Wendy Lukehart of *School Library Journal*. One such anecdote is how the young Handel, whose parents did not want him to become a musician, smuggled a clavichord into the attic of his parents' house. Others give background on the composition of such works as the *Music for the Royal Fireworks*, which bombed upon its first performance, his failure as an opera composer, and the creation of the *Messiah* oratorio, which earned the composer lasting fame. Several reviewers commented on the appropriateness of Anderson's language and tone, including a *Publishers Weekly* contributor, who dubbed the work "wittily irreverent." Using "plain words and short sentences," Anderson tells about Handel's life "with warmth and color, humor and humanity," applauded *Booklist* reviewer Carolyn Phelan, and in *Horn Book*, Mary M. Burns, who deemed *Handel* "worthy of a standing ovation," praised Anderson's balanced tone and "lively text, sufficiently detailed but not overburdened with minutiae."

In *Strange Mr. Satie*, Anderson continues his foray into the lives of famous men in music, using his "offbeat," but compelling, storytelling skills, claimed *Booklist* contributor GraceAnne A. DeCandido. An unusual man, French composer Erik Satie is perhaps not as well known as Handel, but he is noted for his influence on modern music as well as for his interesting lifestyle, once throwing his girlfriend out of a window, never bathing with soap, and displaying a general disdain for rules, be they of music or society. Again, critics found Anderson's narrative style well suited for a biographical work. Writing in *Horn Book*, Lolly Robinson claimed, "Anderson's words flow naturally and hypnotize the reader with oceanic rhythms." Similarly, DeCandido remarked that the author's "text has a fine rhythm, and it doesn't shirk at the strangeness" of the composer's life.

Pointing out that the author's text closely mirrors Satie's own circular musical style, *School Library Journal*'s Jody McCoy found *Strange Mr. Satie* "a splendid alliance of topic, text, and illustration, produc[ing] a hauntingly compelling biography."

Biographical and Critical Sources

PERIODICALS

Booklist, November 15, 1999, Jean Franklin, review of *Burger Wuss,* p. 613; December 15, 2001, Carolyn Phelan, review of *Handel: Who Knew What He Liked,* p. 727; October 15, 2002, Frances Bradburn, review of *Feed,* pp. 400-401; January 1, 2003, review of *Feed,* p. 795; November 1, 2003, GraceAnne A. DeCandido, review of *Strange Mr. Satie,* p. 512.
Book Report, September-October, 1997, Charlotte Decker, review of *Thirsty,* p. 30.
General Music Today, winter, 2002, Richard Ammon, review of *Handel,* p. 31.
Horn Book, May-June, 1997, Lauren Adams, review of *Thirsty,* p. 313; November, 1999, Peter D. Sieruta, review of *Burger Wuss,* p. 732; November-December, 2001, Mary M. Burns, review of *Handel,* pp. 767-768; September-October, 2002, Lauren Adams, review of *Feed,* pp. 564-566; September-October, 2003, Lolly Robinson, review of *Strange Mr. Satie,* p. 624.
Kirkus Reviews, January 1, 1997, review of *Thirsty,* p. 56; September 15, 2001, review of *Handel,* p. 1352; September 1, 2002, review of *Feed,* p. 1301.
New York Times Book Review, November 17, 2002, Elizabeth Devereaux, review of *Feed,* p. 47; December 8, 2002, review of *Feed,* p. 74.
Publishers Weekly, January 27, 1997, review of *Thirsty,* p. 108; August 2, 1999, review of *Burger Wuss,* p. 86; October 15, 2001, review of *Handel,* p. 72; July 22, 2002, review of *Feed,* p. 181; September 1, 2003, review of *Strange Mr. Satie,* p. 89.
School Librarian, fall, 1998, Julie Blaisdale, review of *Thirsty,* p. 155.
School Library Journal, March, 1997, Joel Shoemaker, review of *Thirsty,* p. 184; December, 2001, Wendy Lukehart, review of *Handel,* p. 117; September, 2002, Sharon Rawlins, review of *Feed,* p. 219; October, 2003, Jody McCoy, review of *Strange Mr. Satie,* p. 143.

*　　　*　　　*

ASHBY, Gil 1958-

Personal

Born February 13, 1958; son of Madison and Inez Ashby; married; wife's name Maura; children: Madison. *Ethnicity:* "African American." *Education:* School of Visual Arts, B.F.A., M.F.A. *Hobbies and other interests:* Jazz music, classical music, theater, dance, drama.

Gil Ashby

National Foundation for Advancement in the Arts award, 1994; Kids' Pick of the Lists selection, American Booksellers Association, 2001, and Best Children's Books of the Year selection, Bank Street College of Education, both for *Dear Mother, Dear Daughter: Poems for Young People;* Certificate of Merit, Society of Illustrators, 2002; Certificate of Design Excellence, Print's Regional Design Annual, 2002, Honorable Mention, Scarab Club's Advertising Annual Exhibition, 2002.

Writings

ILLUSTRATOR

Eloise Greenfield, *Rosa Parks,* HarperCollins (New York, NY), 1996.

Dennis Brown and Pamela A. Toussaint, *Mama's Little Baby: The Black Woman's Guide to Pregnancy, Childbirth, and Baby's First Year,* Dutton (New York, NY), 1997.

Evangeline Nicholas, *Summer Sands,* Wright Group (Bothell, WA), 1997.

Jane Yolen and Heidi E. Y. Stemple, *Dear Mother, Dear Daughter: Poems for Young People,* Boyds Mills Press (Honesdale, PA), 2001.

Addresses

Office—College for Creative Studies, 201 E. Kirby, Detroit, MI 48202-4034. *E-mail*—gashby@ccscad.edu.

Career

School of Visual Arts, New York, NY, instructor; Kutz Town University, Kutz Town, PA, instructor; College of Creative Studies, Detroit, MI, associate professor and chair of illustration department, 1999—. Freelance illustrator, whose clients include NBC News, Bell Atlantic, *Black Enterprise,* Clairol, Cold Chillin Records, D.C. Comics, *Essence,* Johnson Publications, *New York Times Book Review,* Backer Spielvogel, Arista Records, Time & Life, Time Warner, Inc., Chelsea House Publications, Agency for Interracial Books, Marvel Comics, McGraw-Hill, Franklin Watts, Harcourt Brace, Houghton Mifflin, Home Box Office, SONY Music Entertainment, and the Jackie Robinson Foundation. *Exhibitions:* Work has appeared in solo exhibitions at the School of Visual Arts, New York, NY, 1991, and in Savannah, GA, 1996, and in group exhibitions in Detroit, New York, San Francisco, and Seoul, South Korea.

Member

Society of Illustrators.

Awards, Honors

Appreciation Award, mayor of New York, in recognition of the exhibition "Lady Legends of Jazz," 1988;

Book cover illustration from Dear Mother, Dear Daughter: Poems for Young People, *written by Jane Yolen and Heidi E. Y. Stemple and illustrated by Gil Ashby.*

Work in Progress

Akila's Adventure, about "the adventures of a little girl who gets to meet her idol when she takes a chance to go beyond her boundaries."

Sidelights

In addition to creating and showing artworks at exhibits throughout the country, Gil Ashby works not only as an art professor but also illustrates books and offers his services to numerous commercial clients. He has brought his talent to bear on several books for children, including a joint effort by the mother-daughter writing team of Jane Yolen and Heidi E. Y. Stemple, *Dear Mother, Dear Daughter: Poems for Young People.* The topics of these poems presented from opposite generational viewpoints include typical subjects of interest to adolescent girls: school, appearance, dating, self-assurance, and allowances. Each set of poems covers a full-page spread and is illustrated with a pencil sketch by Ashby, whose artwork features girls of different backgrounds. Sometimes Ashby also created doodles similar to those that might appear in a teenage girl's notebook, remarked *School Library Journal* critic Susan Scheps.

Biographical and Critical Sources

PERIODICALS

Childhood Education, September 15, 2001, Jeanie Burnett, review of *Dear Mother, Dear Daughter: Poems for Young People,* p. 394.
Publishers Weekly, January 15, 2001, "Rhyme Time," review of *Dear Mother, Dear Daughter,* p. 78.
Reading Teacher, March, 2002, Nancy J. Johnson and Cyndi Giorgis, "Children's Books Relationships."
School Library Journal, May, 2001, Susan Scheps, review of *Dear Mother, Dear Daughter,* p. 174.

ONLINE

College of Creative Studies, http://www.ccscad.edu/ (May 22, 2003).

B

BAKER, Alan 1951

Personal
Born November 14, 1951, in London, England; son of Bernard Victor (a welder) and Barbara Joan (a tracer; maiden name, Weir) Baker; divorced. *Education:* Attended Croydon Technical College, 1969-71, Hull University, 1971-72, and Croydon Art College, 1972-73; Brighton Art College, B.A. (honours), 1976. *Politics:* Green. *Religion:* Agnostic. *Hobbies and other interests:* Music, waking.

Addresses
Home and office—St. Michaels, Telscombe Village, near Lewes, East Sussex BN7 3HZ, England. *E-mail*—info@alanbakeronline.com.

Career
Author and freelance illustrator of children's books. Part-time teacher of illustration at Northbrook College.

Awards, Honors
Whitbread Award and Carnegie Medal commendation, both 1978, both for *The Battle of Bubble and Squeak,* written by Ann Philippa Pearce; Silver Award, Campaign Press Awards, 1990; Gold Award, Creative Circle Awards, 1990; Children's Choice selection, International Reading Association/Children's Book Council, 1996, for *Gray Rabbit's Odd One Out;* several of Baker's works have been selected for annual "Best Books" commendations.-

Writings

FOR CHILDREN; SELF-ILLUSTRATED

Benjamin and the Box, Deutsch (London, England), Lippincott (Philadelphia, PA), 1977.

Alan Baker

Benjamin Bounces Back, Deutsch (London, England), Lippincott (Philadelphia, PA), 1978.
Benjamin's Dreadful Dream, Deutsch (London, England), Lippincott (Philadelphia, PA), 1980.
Benjamin's Book, Deutsch (London, England), Lothrop (New York, NY), 1982.
A Fairyland Alphabet, Deutsch (London, England), 1984.
Benjamin's Portrait, Deutsch (London, England), Lothrop (New York, NY), 1986.
One Naughty Boy, Deutsch (London, England), 1989.
Goodnight William, Deutsch (London, England), 1990.
Benjamin's Balloon, Deutsch (London, England), Lothrop (New York, NY), 1990.
Two Tiny Mice, Kingfisher (London, England), 1990, Dial (New York, NY), 1991.
Jason's Dragon, BBC Publications (London, England), 1992.
Where's Mouse?, Kingfisher (London, England, and New York, NY), 1992.

Black and White Rabbit's ABC (also see below), Kingfisher (London, England, and New York, NY), 1994.

Brown Rabbit's Shape Book (also see below), Kingfisher (London, England, and New York, NY), 1994.

Gray Rabbit's 1, 2, 3 (also see below), Kingfisher (London, England, and New York, NY), 1994.

White Rabbit's Colour Book, Kingfisher (London, England), 1994, published as *White Rabbit's Color Book* (also see below), Kingfisher (New York, NY), 1994.

Brown Rabbit's Day, Kingfisher (London, England, and New York, NY), 1995.

Gray Rabbit's Odd One Out, Kingfisher (London, England, and New York, NY), 1995.

Little Rabbit's First Word Book, Kingfisher (London, England, and New York, NY), 1996.

Mouse's Christmas, Copper Beach Books (Brookfield, CT), 1996.

I Thought I Heard: A Book of Nighttime Noises, Aladdin (London, England), Copper Beach Books (Brookfield, CT), 1996.

Little Rabbit's Play and Learn Book (contains *White Rabbit's Color Book, Gray Rabbit's 1, 2, 3, Black and White Rabbit's ABC,* and *Brown Rabbit's Shape Book*), Kingfisher (New York, NY), 1997.

Mouse's Halloween, Copper Beach Books (Brookfield, CT), 1997.

Little Rabbit's Snack Time, Kingfisher (London, England, and New York, NY), 1998.

Little Rabbit's Bedtime, Kingfisher (London, England, and New York, NY), 1998.

Little Rabbit's Tell the Time Book, Kingfisher (London, England), published as *Little Rabbit's First Time Book,* Kingfisher (New York, NY), 1999.

Little Rabbit's Picture Word Book, Kingfisher (London, England), 1999.

Look Who Lives in the Ocean, Macdonald (Hove, England), 1998, Bedrick (New York, NY), 1999.

Look Who Lives in the Rain Forest, Macdonald (Hove, England), 1998, Bedrick (New York, NY), 1999.

Look Who Lives in the Arctic, Macdonald (Hove, England), Bedrick (New York, NY), 1999.

Look Who Lives in the Desert, Macdonald (Hove, England), Bedrick (New York, NY), 1999.

Little Rabbit's First Farm Book, Kingfisher (London, England, and New York, NY), 2001.

ILLUSTRATOR

Ann Philippa Pearce, *The Battle of Bubble and Squeak,* Deutsch (London, England), 1978.

Eleanor Bourne, *Heritage of Flowers,* Hutchinson (London, England), 1980.

Deirdre Headon, *Mythical Beasts,* Hutchinson (London, England), 1981.

Rudyard Kipling, *The Butterfly That Stamped,* Macmillan (London, England), Bedrick (New York, NY), 1982.

Kate Petty, *Snakes,* F. Watts (London, England, and New York, NY), 1984.

Kate Petty, *Dinosaurs,* F. Watts (London, England, and New York, NY), 1984.

Kate Petty, *Frogs and Toads,* F. Watts (London, England, and New York, NY), 1985.

Kate Petty, *Spiders,* F. Watts (London, England, and New York, NY), 1985.

Michael Rosen, *Hairy Tales and Nursery Crimes,* Deutsch (London, England), 1985.

Gene Kemp, *Mr. Magus Is Waiting for You,* Faber (London, England), 1986.

Robin Lister, reteller, *The Odyssey,* Kingfisher (London, England), 1987, Doubleday (New York, NY), 1988.

Robin Lister, reteller, *The Story of King Arthur,* Kingfisher (London, England), 1988.

Verna Wilkins, *Mike and Lottie,* Tamarind (London, England), 1988, Child's Play (New York, NY), 1993.

Judith Nicholls, *Wordspells,* Faber (London, England), 1988.

Judith Nicholls, *What on Earth?: Poems with a Conservation Theme,* Faber (London, England), 1989.

Jill Bailey, *Gorilla Rescue,* Steck-Vaughn (Austin, TX), 1990.

Jill Bailey, *Mission Rhino,* Steck-Vaughn (Austin, TX), 1990.

Jill Bailey, *Project Panda,* Steck-Vaughn (Austin, TX), 1990.

Jill Bailey, *Save the Tiger,* Steck-Vaughn (Austin, TX), 1990.

Michael Rosen, *Mini Beasties,* Firefly (London, England), 1991, Carolrhoda (Minneapolis, MN), 1992.

Kate Petty, *Stop, Look and Listen, Mr. Toad!,* Hodder & Stoughton (London, England), Barron's (New York, NY), 1991.

Kate Petty, *Mr. Toad to the Rescue,* Barron's (Hauppauge, NY), 1992.

Joni Mitchell, *Both Sides Now,* Scholastic (New York, NY), 1992.

Kate Petty, *Mr. Toad's Narrow Escapes,* Barron's (Hauppauge, NY), 1992.

Gloria Patrick, *A Bug in a Jug and Other Funny Rhymes,* D.C. Heath (Lexington, MA), 1993.

Jill Bennett, *Sorry for the Slug,* Heinemann (London, England), 1994.

Dan Abnett, *Treasure Hunt in the Creepy Mansion,* Salamander (London, England), 1995.

Dan Abnett, *Treasure Hunt in the Lost City,* Salamander (London, England), 1996.

Judy Allen, *Hedgehog in the Garden,* Leopard, 1996.

Fit-a-Shape: Animals; Colors; Opposites; Shapes; Bugs; Patterns; Cloths; Numbers, Running Press (Philadelphia, PA), 1996.

Anita Ganeri, reteller, *Dragons and Monsters,* Macdonald (Hove, England), 1996.

Kate Petty, *Little Rabbit's First Number Book,* Kingfisher (New York, NY), 1998.

Louis De Bernieres, *Red Dog,* Secker and Warburg (London, England), Pantheon (New York, NY), 2001.

David Stewart, *Seasons,* F. Watts (London, England, and New York, NY), 2002.

Dawn Allette, *Caribbean Animals,* Tamarind (London, England), 2004.

Contributor of illustrations to *Creatures Great and Small,* written by Michael Gabb, Lerner (Minneapolis, MN), 1980.

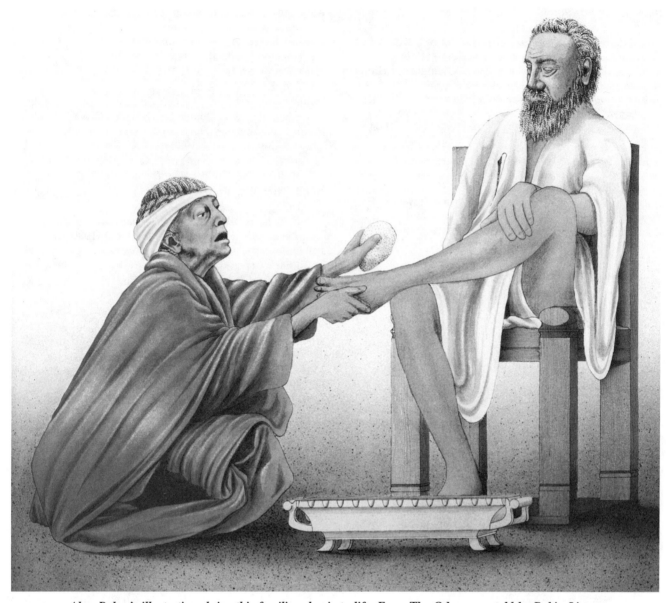

Alan Baker's illustrations bring this familiar classic to life. From **The Odyssey,** *retold by Robin Lister.*

Adaptations

Benjamin and the Box was featured on the Canadian Broadcasting Corporation (CBC-TV) series *The Friendly Giant,* in March and April of 1980, and on British and Norwegian television.

Work in Progress

Three children's books.

Sidelights

Alan Baker is an English author/illustrator who is best known for his "Rabbits" series of picture books for preschoolers. Baker favors pen-and-ink drawings that depict animals in meticulous detail. At the same time, critics note that his mice, hamsters, and rabbits appeal to youngsters because they have young and beguiling expressions themselves. This is particularly the case in

the "Rabbits" series, where bunnies of different hues introduce concepts such as the alphabet, color, shape, and telling time. Another popular Baker work is the "Look Who Lives In" series, in which readers discover interesting animals and plants from various ecosystems. Some commentators contend that Baker's simple texts are merely a vehicle for his extravagant illustrations. But, though the visual element often takes precedence in Baker's work, "I like to think of the writing as adding a further dimension to the illustrations," Baker once commented. "The words hold the story line when the idea cannot be illustrated."

In *Benjamin and the Box,* Baker introduces preschoolers to a hapless, nearsighted, persistent little hamster named Benjamin, a character based on a pet from Baker's childhood. In this first book, Benjamin comes upon a box, which he persistently tries to open, using tools, magic spells, and even dynamite. "It was love at first meeting," a reviewer for *Publishers Weekly* declared of *Benjamin and the Box*. In *Benjamin Bounces Back*, the nearsighted Benjamin fails to read the "NO ENTRY" sign on a door, and reluctantly embarks on a series of wild adventures after he pushes through the forbidden entrance. *Benjamin's Dreadful Dream* similarly finds the accident-prone hamster inadvertently touching off a pile of fireworks that blasts him into outer space, when all he really wanted was a midnight snack. "The tenuous story is clearly an excuse for the sparkling illustrations," observed a reviewer for *Junior Bookshelf*, but a *Publishers Weekly* critic maintained that "charmed readers won't forget this larky escapade."

The same brightly colored, realistically detailed illustrations characterize the other stories about Benjamin, including *Benjamin's Book*, in which the hamster accidentally puts a paw print on a clean sheet of paper. In his increasingly frantic attempts to repair the damage, the page gets ever messier, until Benjamin replaces the sheet altogether, but accidentally marks it with another paw print as he leaves. "This is visually appealing, has a quiet humor, and tells a story that's just right in length, scope, and familiarity for the preschool child," noted Zena Sutherland in the *Bulletin of the Center for Children's Books*. *Benjamin's Portrait* finds the determined hamster attempting a self-portrait after going to a portrait gallery. "Preschoolers will identify with Benjamin's eagerness to try things for himself, as well as his encounters with unexpected troubles," remarked Susan Nemeth McCarthy in *School Library Journal*. Benjamin flies off under the power of a purple balloon in *Benjamin's Balloon*, which *Growing Point*'s Margery Fisher called a "gentle and congenial comedy."

Baker's other recurring animal characters include a number of rabbits featured in some highly regarded concept books that teach very young children about shapes, colors, letters, and numbers. Invariably, critics found that Baker's concept books give a fresh twist to familiar themes. *Black and White Rabbit's ABC* starts with an apple, as many alphabet books do, but then is transformed as a black and white rabbit enters the picture and attempts to paint the apple, beginning the reader on "a wry and often very messy journey from A to Z," according to a *Publishers Weekly* reviewer. *Brown Rabbit's Shape Book* features balloons of different shapes, and *White Rabbit's Color Book* is "perhaps the best book of the bunch," according to Ilene Cooper in *Booklist*. In *White Rabbit's Color Book*, originally published as *White Rabbit's Colour Book*, a white rabbit falls into a series of paint cans, demonstrating how primary colors mix to become other colors. Throughout each of these concept books, a *Publishers Weekly* critic noted, "sweet-natured humor infuses the clear, precise artwork."

Baker's subsequent "Rabbit" titles are also distinguished by a gently humorous text and striking illustrations combined with a unique slant on a learning concept. In *Brown Rabbit's Day*, a simple story offers the opportunity for color and object identification, counting, and telling time. In *Gray Rabbit's Odd One Out*, preschoolers help Gray Rabbit find his favorite book while learning to sort objects according to a variety of schemes. *Little Rabbit's First Farm Book* takes Rabbit to a farm, where he participates in the chores and meets the resident animals. A *Publishers Weekly* reviewer felt that the title "is perfect for preschoolers."

Baker introduces his readers to animals common to the English forest through which his little heroes travel in *Two Tiny Mice*, another self-illustrated picture book. A *Kirkus Reviews* critic singled out Baker's "expansive, delicately detailed illustrations" for special mention in a review of this work. Introducing animals also forms the basis for Baker's story *Where's Mouse?*, in which Mother Mouse questions one forest animal after another in her search for Baby Mouse. *Where's Mouse?* has accordion-fold pages whose holes give the illusion of three-dimensionality to the illustrations, which *School Library Journal* contributor Christine A. Moesch praised as "delicate and cleverly laid out." Baker employs a similar format in *Mouse's Christmas*, in which Mouse's friends plan a surprise party for him on Christmas Eve.

The "Look Who Lives In" series introduces early readers to the plants and animals in some of the world's more extreme ecosystems. The books offer teasers in which each page shows an animal and hints at the animal on the next page, too. In a *Science Books and Film* review of *Look Who Lives in the Rain Forest*, Michele H. Lee declared that "young children will enjoy guessing the animals' identities" in this "delightful book." A *Kirkus Reviews* critic likewise found *Look Who Lives in the Rain Forest* to be "a good introduction to a habitat" often studied by young students.

Baker's illustrations are acclaimed for their fine detail and for the humor they add to the author's simple tales. According to reviewers, Baker perfected this combination in his popular "Benjamin" series; "Even when one sees only [Benjamin's] feet encased in a snowball, the comic character of the furry creature is unmistakable," remarked Lori A. Janick in *School Library Journal*. Although some critics have found Baker's plots meager, especially when compared to his arresting artwork, reviewers of such concept books as *Gray Rabbit's 1,2,3* and *White Rabbit's Color Book* felt that Baker's plots were suitable for holding the attention of his preschool audience. *School Library Journal* contributor Marsha McGrath avowed that Baker's books are "instructional titles that are lots of fun for prereaders."

Biographical and Critical Sources

PERIODICALS

Booklist, July, 1994, Ilene Cooper, review of *Black and White Rabbit's ABC, Brown Rabbit's Shape Book*, and

Clean, innovative artwork helps early learners grasp concepts in Gray Rabbit's Odd One Out. *(Written and illustrated by Baker.)*

White Rabbit's Color Book, p. 1952; December 1, 1999, Kathy Broderick, review of *Little Rabbit's First Time Book,* p. 708; November 15, 2001, Ilene Cooper, review of *Little Rabbit's First Farm Book,* p. 580.

Bulletin of the Center for Children's Books, July, 1983, Zena Sutherland, review of *Benjamin's Book,* p. 202.

Growing Point, January, 1978, Margery Fisher, review of *Benjamin and the Box,* p. 3251; November, 1982, Margery Fisher, review of *Benjamin's Book,* p. 3990; March, 1991, Margery Fisher, review of *Benjamin's Balloon,* p. 5486.

Junior Bookshelf, June, 1978, review of *Benjamin and the Box,* p. 133; April, 1979, review of *Benjamin Bounces Back,* p. 91; October, 1980, review of *Benjamin's Dreadful Dream,* p. 232.

Kirkus Reviews, June 15, 1980, review of *Benjamin's Dreadful Dream,* p. 773; May 1, 1991, review of *Two Tiny Mice,* p. 611; December 1, 1992, review of *Where's Mouse,* p. 1500; June 15, 1999, review of *Look Who Lives in the Rain Forest,* p. 960.

Publishers Weekly, February 27, 1978, review of *Benjamin's Box;* December 11, 1978, review of *Benjamin Bounces Back,* p. 70; review of *Benjamin's Dreadful Dream,* p. 340; November 23, 1992, review of *Where's Mouse,* p. 61; March 7, 1994, review of *Gray Rabbit's 1, 2, 3, Black and White Rabbit's ABC, Brown Rabbit's Shape Book,* and *White Rabbit's Color Book,* p. 68; September 30, 1996, review of *Mouse's Christmas,* p. 90; November 12, 2001, review of *Little Rabbit's First Farm Book,* p. 61.

School Library Journal, May, 1987, Susan Nemeth McCarthy, review of *Benjamin's Portrait,* p. 81; December, 1990, Lori A. Janick, review of *Benjamin's Balloon,* p. 70; February, 1993, Christine A. Moesch, review of *Where's Mouse,* p. 68; Marsha McGrath, March, 1996, review of *Brown Rabbit's Day* and *Gray Rabbit's Odd One Out,* p. 166; February, 2002, Carolyn Janssen, review of *Little Rabbit's First Farm Book,* p. 96.

Science Books and Film, September, 1999, Michele H. Lee, review of *Look Who Lives in the Rain Forest,* p. 220.

*   *   *

BEATY, Mary (T.) 1947-

Personal

Born April 5, 1947, in Minneapolis, MN; daughter of George A. and Dorothy (a teacher; maiden name, Snouffer) Hannon; married Richard Beaty, December 21, 1969; children: Taran, Maev. *Ethnicity:* "Danish-American heritage." *Education:* University of Iowa, B.Ed.; University of Toronto, M.L.S. *Politics:* "Progressive." *Religion:* "Humanist." *Hobbies and other interests:* Activities related to human rights, social justice, intellectual freedom, and ethics education.

Addresses

Home—576 Henry St., Apt. 3, Brooklyn, NY 11231. *E-mail*—elibrarian@earthlink.net; beaty@sprint.ca.

Career

Toronto Public Library, Toronto, Ontario, Canada, children's librarian, 1975-80; Kingston-Frontenac Public Library, Kingston, Ontario, Canada, coordinator of children's and youth services, 1980-99; New York Cares, New York, NY, coordinator of Community Resource Center, 2001—. United Nations, moderator of Council of Ethics Based Organizations, 2001—; United Nations, member of Working Group on the Rights of the Child of the Congress of NGOs.

Member

American Library Association, American Coalition for the International Criminal Court, National Writers Union, American Humanist Association (United Nations representative, 2000—), Humanist Society of Metropolitan New York.

Awards, Honors

Children's Service Award of Merit, Ontario Library Association, 1996.

Writings

(With Maureen Garvie) *George Johnson's War* (young adult novel), Groundwood Books (Toronto, Ontario, Canada), 2002.

Contributor to library journals, magazines, and newspapers.

Mary Beaty

Work in Progress

A publication project dealing with ethics and non-profit organizations.

Sidelights

Mary Beaty told *SATA:* "George Johnson's story emerged on a series of rural car trips through the Mohawk Valley and Loyalist country in southern Ontario. My coauthor, Canadian Maureen Garvie, and I, a transplanted Minnesotan living in Kingston, Ontario, had spent two years tuning our librarians' DNA to unearthing information about Mohawk matron Molly Brant, as we approached the bicentennial of her death in 1996. My little nineteenth-century cottage in Kingston was built on Molly's land grant, a gift from a grateful British government for her aid during the War for American Independence. We followed this trail backwards, on the path of many historians in both New York and Canada, trying to find the heartbeat behind this mysterious and dynamic woman, who impressed so many people but left little physical trace.

"Molly's bicentenary was celebrated with appropriate ceremonies and participation from the Native community, the church, and local dignitaries. A statue was commissioned, speeches and plaques presented. We wrote a newspaper piece and continued to sift legend, politics, history, and family records, trying to extract a picture of the extreme changes and contrasts Molly and her children encountered as the American Revolution changed the destiny of so many lives.

"Our novel started from Molly's point of view, but we gradually switched to her daughter Peggy, and then, somehow George's voice emerged. We knew George had owned a house just down the hill from where Molly, her grandchildren, and their good friend Reverend John Stuart were buried. We knew George had claimed Molly's property after her death but was denied that legacy when he could not produce a legal marriage certificate for his parents. He left the city to become a schoolmaster near the Six Nations settlement on the Grand River, and the Johnson-Brant legacy faded. George, the only surviving son, who bridged the Native, white, British, and new Canadian world, and who was constantly surrounded by all those sisters and mothers and clan mothers, seemed both a real character and a cipher. On our backwoods car trips, we began to simply try to tell the story through George's eyes. Then I moved to New York City, and we continued our long-distance research in two countries and wrote our book by e-mail.

"The clues were so few in either country that often all we had was a glimpse from afar: prehistoric Indian pottery and French crystal fragments from Molly's privy, a copy of the Mohawk prayer book, a fragile store ledger with the mark of Little Abraham, a soldier's record of the Valley raid. Images were absent; there were paintings of Sir William Johnson and more paintings of George's uncle Joseph Brant, scattered and copied from Philadelphia to Cooperstown (and eventually reproduced as a ubiquitous decal on an old Victrola record player). But except for a heartbreakingly copy-of-a-copy of a posthumous painting of Peter and a poor picture of his aunt Anne, we can only guess that George resembled his uncle.

"We have had, instead, to walk the hills of the Mohawk, and the banks of the St. Lawrence, and the trails of our imaginations. We hope that we did not do ill to the memories of these real people. We have obviously created our own version of time and circumstance. But we trust that some of it is based on the wisps of the lives we have glimpsed in the corners of experience.

"We also hope that the story of one child, and one family, caught in a war not of their making, but one in which they showed great courage and resilience, will help inform the lives of other children and families facing events in our own times, and in times to come."

Biographical and Critical Sources

PERIODICALS

Resource Links, October, 2002, Brenda Dillon, review of *George Johnson's War,* p. 34.

*   *   *

BEELER, Janet
See SHAW, Janet

BLOOM, Barbara Lee 1943-

Personal

Born April 11, 1943, in Long Beach, CA; daughter of Verdon Bradley and Shirley Andrews; married Thomas K. Bloom (a university professor); children: Heidi, Heather. *Ethnicity:* "Mixed." *Education:* University of California—Los Angeles, B.A.; California State University—Long Beach, M.A.; University of Vermont, Ed.D. *Hobbies and other interests:* Running, biking, hiking, skiing, reading.

Addresses

Home—41 Henderson Terrace, Burlington, VT 05401. *E-mail*—bloom@champlain.edu.

Career

Writer, historian, and educator. Champlain College, assistant professor, 1980-90, professor of history, 1990—. Vermont Governor's Institute faculty, summers, 1982-1985; Vermont Council on the Humanities and Social Sciences Scholar, 1985-1995; Universidad Regiomontana, Monterrey, Mexico, visiting professor, 1997. Worked on curriculum development for the Center for World Education.

Member

Vermont Sierra Club, National Council of the Social Sciences, Society of Children's Book Writers and Illustrators.

Awards, Honors

University Scholars Fellowship, Rotary International, 1997.

Writings

Exploring Historical Fiction, Scholastic (New York, NY), 1992.
The Chinese Americans, Lucent Books (San Diego, CA), 2002.
The Mexican Americans, Lucent Books (San Diego, CA), 2004.

Work in Progress

Research on American women suffragists and on cultures and peoples of the world.

Sidelights

Writer and historian Barbara Lee Bloom relies on the techniques of both fiction and nonfiction to examine historical subjects. Bloom, a professor of history at

In 1858, treaties were signed to allow commerce between France and China. From **The Chinese Americans,** *written by Barbara Lee Bloom.*

Champlain College in Vermont, is the author of factually accurate but fictionalized accounts of history in books such as *Exploring Historical Fiction.* Her story "Ain't I a Woman?" concerns Sojourner Truth, a former slave who became an evangelist, speaker, abolitionist, and women's rights crusader in the United States during the middle 1800s.

In her two nonfiction books, *The Chinese Americans* and *The Mexican Americans,* Bloom describes in detail the reasons and results of Chinese and Mexican immigration to the United States. The books explore why the immigrants left their home countries, the types of work they undertook in the United States, the problems and prejudices they encountered, and their struggles and victories in making a new life in a new, sometimes dramatically unfamiliar, country. Diane S. Marton, writing in *School Library Journal,* remarked favorably upon the "clear, lively" writing in *The Chinese Americans,* noting that Bloom offers "many first-person accounts" as well as additional detail "in numerous sidebars and boxes."

The book pays special attention to Chinese immigrants in Hawaii, with a separate chapter on their lives in this U.S. island state. Marton called *The Chinese Americans* an "in-depth" book as well as a "solid choice for reports." Similarly, Bloom's *The Mexican Americans* offers a detailed account of the reasons behind Mexican immigration to the United States, as well as the cultural, economic, and social effects on immigrants and their families.

"I wrote my first book when I was ten years old," Bloom told *SATA.* "It wasn't published, but instead it was hidden in a secret compartment in my best friend's closet. We coauthored this book about Elizabeth's adventures in a private girls' school in Massachusetts. We had done our research by pretending to be parents of Elizabeth and writing letters to various private institutions and asking about their schools. To a young girl growing up in Long Beach, California, attending an Eastern girls' school sounded far away and far more exciting than my public school in a beach community.

"Since then, I have continued to love to do research and to learn about far-away places. I have traveled a great deal in Europe and Latin America and even spent the spring of 1997 in Monterrey, Mexico. As a historian, I am now careful about getting the facts and writing as accurately as possible about what I've discovered. My writings include historical fiction, biography, and historical nonfiction. For my biographical story about Sojourner Truth, 'Ain't I a Woman?,' I was paid in Australian pounds when the school system of New South Wales included it in one of their textbooks. That same story was put on the Internet for Colorado legislatures to read. As a historian, I know the importance of telling the story as accurately as possible, but as a professor of history, I know the importance of finding the interesting details of the past to interest my students.

"Currently, I teach courses in American and world history," Bloom told *SATA*. "I am the director of the international exchange program at my college. In the past I have developed, with others, multicultural curriculum for grades five through twelve."

Biographical and Critical Sources

PERIODICALS

School Library Journal, July, 2002, Diane S. Marton, review of *The Chinese Americans,* p. 129.

*   *   *

BRAGER, Bruce L. 1949-

Personal

Born 1949, in Chester, PA. *Education:* George Washington University, B.A. *Hobbies and other interests:* Photography.

Addresses

Home—1020 North Quincy St., Apt. 807, Arlington, VA 22201. *E-mail*—bbrager@juno.com.

Career

Writer, editor, and researcher.

Writings

The Trial of Adolf Eichmann: The Holocaust on Trial ("Famous Trials" series), Lucent Books (San Diego, CA), 1999.
The Texas 36th Division: A History, Eakin Press (Austin, TX), 2002.
Petersburg, Chelsea House (Philadelphia, PA), 2003.
The Monitor vs. the Merrimack ("Great Battles" series), Chelsea House (Philadelphia, PA), 2003.

The Iron Curtain: The Cold War in Europe ("Arbitrary Borders" series), Chelsea House (Philadelphia, PA), 2003.

Author of more than eighty published magazine and journal articles and letters to the editor.

Work in Progress

Stonewall Jackson: You Can Be Whatever You Resolve to Be; Context, Causes, and Connections: Decision Making, Unintended Consequences, and the Real American Way of War.

Sidelights

Bruce L. Brager's works focus on issues in military history, government, and defense. His books cover a variety of time periods and historical events, including the U.S. Civil War, World War I and II, and the Holocaust. He has also written about modern political and technical topics, such as the energy industry, the U.S. defense industry, foreign and domestic government, and political science.

In *The Texas 36th Division: A History,* Brager explores the formation and history of this noted military unit. The 36th Division was formed in 1917, shortly after the United States became involved in World War I. Brager's detailed history covers the division's early years, World War I service, status as a Texas National Guard unit between the wars, and the division's combat service in Italy and France during World War II.

Brager takes up volatile post-World War II issues in *The Trial of Adolf Eichmann: The Holocaust on Trial.* Eichmann was a senior Nazi official responsible for, among other things, the development of the railway system that carried Jews and others to the concentration camps. Eichmann had eluded capture after World War II, but in the late 1950s, reports began to surface that he had been seen in Argentina. Brager's book provides an in-depth account of the search, Eichmann's eventual capture, his return to Israel in 1961, and his subsequent trial for war crimes. Prior to Eichmann's capture, many Holocaust survivors had been unwilling to talk about their horrifying experiences. The capture and trial of a pivotal figure in the Nazi Reich finally allowed some survivors in Israel and throughout the world to open up and discuss their traumas. As *School Library Journal* critic David N. Pauli observed, the trial itself served to "showcase the horror of the Nazi regime and to document the Holocaust." Writing in *Booklist,* Randy Meyer called Brager's book "a fine supplement to the Holocaust curriculum."

In addition to his books and articles, Brager has researched and written scripts and served as editor for an interactive CD-ROM on the American Civil War. He wrote and edited multimedia training materials on issues in the hydrocarbon industry, including production, industrial design, management, and safety; researched low-intensity warfare for U.S. Army contingency plan-

Adolf Eichmann, a Nazi criminal, had to be kept behind bulletproof glass while in the courtroom. From The Trial of Adolf Eichmann: The Holocaust on Trial, *written by Bruce L. Brager.*

ning studies; and prepared technical manuals and guides on energy production, urban development, and recycling. He also created, edited, and published a newspaper on southern Africa. Brager told *SATA* his work habits are characterized by "persistence, sometimes past reason."

Brager is also an avid photographer. "I sometimes think I prefer photography to writing," Brager told *SATA*. "But I realize this is because with photography I just get the fun part, no revisions, no retyping, etc., etc."

Biographical and Critical Sources

PERIODICALS

Booklist, May 1, 1999, Randy Meyer, review of *The Trial of Adolf Eichmann: The Holocaust on Trial,* p. 1584.
Military History of the West, fall, 2002, Adrian R. Lewis, review of *The Texas 36th Division: A History.*

Multicultural Review, September, 1999, review of *The Trial of Adolf Eichmann.*
School Library Journal, August, 1999, David N. Pauli, review of *The Trial of Adolf Eichmann,* p. 166.
Southwestern Historical Quarterly, July, 2003, John Atkins, review of *The Texas 36th Division.*

*   *   *

BURGESS, Melvin 1954-

Personal

Born April 25, 1954, in Twickenham, Surrey, England; son of Christopher (an educational writer) and Helen Burgess; married Avis von Herder (marriage ended); married Judith Liggett; children: Oliver von Herder, Pearl, Sam. *Politics:* "Left."

Addresses

Home—Manchester, England. *Agent*—c/o Author Mail,

Melvin Burgess

Andersen, 20 Vauxhall Bridge Rd., London SW1V 2SA, England. *E-mail*—melvin.burgess@ntlworld.com.

Career

Writer.

Member

Society of Authors.

Awards, Honors

Carnegie Medal runner-up, British Library Association, 1991, for *The Cry of the Wolf*, and 1993, for *An Angel for May;* Carnegie Medal, British Library Association, and *Guardian* Award for Children's Fiction, both 1997, both for *Junk;* Lancashire Children's Book Award, for *Bloodtide.*

Writings

The Cry of the Wolf, Andersen (London, England), Tambourine Books (New York, NY), 1990.
Burning Issy, Andersen (London, England), 1992, Simon & Schuster (New York, NY), 1994.
An Angel for May, Andersen (London, England), 1992, Simon & Schuster (New York, NY), 1995.

The Baby and Fly Pie, Andersen (London, England), 1993, Simon & Schuster (New York, NY), 1996.
Loving April, Andersen (London, England), 1995.
Junk, Andersen (London, England), 1996, published as *Smack,* Holt (New York, NY), 1998.
Tiger, Tiger, Andersen (London, England), 1996.
Earth Giant, Andersen (London, England), Putnam (New York, NY), 1997.
Kite, Andersen (London, England), 1997, Farrar, Straus & Giroux (New York, NY), 2000.
The Copper Treasure, illustrated by Richard Williams, A & C Black (London, England), 1998, Holt (New York, NY), 2000.
Bloodtide, Andersen (London, England), 1999, Tor (New York, NY), 2001.
Old Bag, illustrated by Trevor Parkin, Barrington Stoke (Edinburgh, Scotland), 1999.
The Birdman, illustrated by Ruth Brown, Andersen (London, England), 2000.
Billy Elliot: A Novel (novelization of the screenplay by Lee Hall), Chicken House (London, England), Scholastic (New York, NY), 2001.
The Ghost behind the Wall, Andersen (London, England), 2001, Holt (New York, NY), 2003.
Lady: My Life as a Bitch, Andersen (London, England), 2001, Holt (New York, NY), 2002.
Robbers on the Road ("Tudor Flashbacks" series), A & C Black (London, England), 2002.
Highwayman ("Tudor Flashbacks" series), A & C Black (London, England), 2002.
Doing It, Andersen (London, England), 2003, Holt (New York, NY), 2004.

Adaptations

Junk was adapted into a play of the same name by John Retallack and published by Methuen Drama (London, England), 1999; *An Angel for May* was adapted into a motion picture, directed by Harley Cokeliss, with a screenplay by Peter Milligan, 2003.

Work in Progress

City of Light, a sequel to *Bloodtide.*

Sidelights

Melvin Burgess is the author of several novels for middle-graders and teenage readers that combine fantasy with down-to-earth stories of young protagonists attempting to cope with various problems. Beginning his career as a young adult author in 1990 with *The Cry of the Wolf*, British-born Burgess has produced a series of titles that showcase his creative and unique views on the experience of adolescence. Burgess is quoted in *Authors and Artists for Young Adults* as saying: "My books are about anything that interests me, but they nearly all have this in common: they are life seen from the underside, not (usually) from on top."

Taking place in Surrey, England, *The Cry of the Wolf* features a young boy who inadvertently threatens the wolf population near his home. Ten-year-old Ben tells a stranger identified only as "the Hunter" about a wolf pack that lives in the forest nearby; the Hunter, on a mission to gain notoriety for killing the last of the wolves surviving in the wild in England, arms himself with a crossbow and hunts them down. "This is indeed a powerful first novel, and sinister too," noted a reviewer in *Junior Bookshelf.* Calling the novel "a dramatic and horrifying tale of the tragedy of extinction," Susan Oliver added in *School Library Journal* that *The Cry of the Wolf* is "an ecological thriller that will draw nature lovers and horror fans alike."

Tiger, Tiger recalls Burgess's first novel in its focus on the plight of animals. The story revolves around a Chinese businessman's attempts to use several hundred square miles in Yorkshire as a safari park featuring Siberian tigers, rare animals that are said to have magical properties. When one of the great cats—a female called Lila—escapes and encounters several children living in a nearby village, a merger between cat and human on both physical and intellectual levels is the result. "The adroit combination of fact and fantasy is expertly managed with no concession to the tenderhearted," explained a *Junior Bookshelf* critic, who also noted the story's use of the folklore of werewolves and human-to-animal shape shifting. Linda Newbery praised the work in *School Librarian,* declaring that *Tiger, Tiger* "ends with a poignant reflection on the status of wild animals in the modern world."

An Angel for May, first published in England in 1992, finds Tam, a twelve-year-old upset over his parents' recent divorce, spending a great deal of time roaming through the moors and the charred ruins of a farmhouse near his country home. On one of his rambles, Tam by chance encounters an unusual bag lady named Rosey who draws him fifty years into the past—the World War II era—where he meets a young retarded child named May. May helps the boy to put his own family situation into perspective and he, in turn, becomes an important, caring presence in her life. Calling the novel "a sad, strange little story," a *Junior Bookshelf* reviewer stated that Burgess's book "hits the right note throughout" and is written "with a restraint which is all the more moving for its quietness." Merri Monks, in a *Booklist* assessment, lauded Burgess's tale as "a story of courage, moral development, friendship, and love."

In *Burning Issy,* published originally in England in 1992, Burgess draws readers into the seventeenth century, depicting the life of a young, orphaned woman who befriends both white and black witches. She is eventually accused of witchcraft in this era of superstition when witch hunters and the church persecuted herbal healers and others with supposed "magical" powers. As the story unfolds, Issy, who was badly burned as a small child, realizes that her recurrent nightmares of fire are actually recollections of being almost burned alongside her mother, a convicted witch who was burned at the stake. When she herself is imprisoned, Issy is determined to escape, whatever the cost.

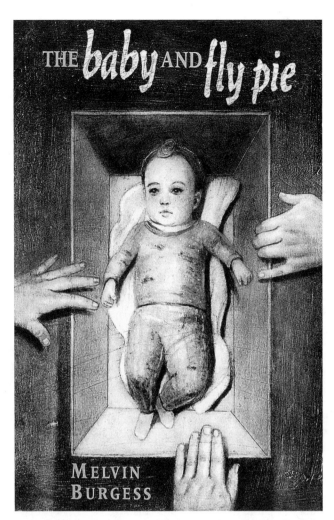

Orphans find a kidnapped baby in a dump in **The Baby and Fly Pie,** *by Melvin Burgess. (Illustrated by Joseph Daniel Fiedler.)*

Helen Turner, in a review in *Voice of Youth Advocates,* called the book "a riveting exploration into some dark corners of history." *Burning Issy* was also hailed by *Horn Book* contributor Nancy Vasilakis as "a compelling story with a thoughtful message on the destructive force of superstition."

From the distant past, Burgess moves ahead to the not-so-distant future in his novel *The Baby and Fly Pie.* The book's unusual title comes from the two main characters: Fly Pie, an orphaned teen surviving on the London streets as one of the scavenging "Rubbish Kids," and the infant daughter of a wealthy family whom Fly Pie and his friend Sham intercept during a kidnapping attempt gone awry. When the kidnapper dies of his wounds, the teens find themselves surrogate parents and must decide whether to return infant Sylvie to her distraught parents or hold out for ransom. While some reviewers felt the novel was too bleak to interest teens, the book received high marks from several critics. A *Junior Bookshelf* commentator noted that the novel's "topical theme and its sympathetic treatment, its social message and its refusal to compromise with the harsh reality of shanty town economy make it strong meat for early teenagers." *Booklist* contributor Anne O'Malley maintained: "The stunning characterizations, fascinating scenario, well-plotted, virtually nonstop action, and mounting suspense pull the reader right in from start to tragic end."

Winner of the 1997 Carnegie Medal and the *Guardian* Children's Fiction Award, *Junk,* published in the United States as *Smack,* follows the story of two fourteen-year-old runaways, Tar and Gemma. Fleeing disturbing home environments, the pair find their place among the squatters in Bristol and embark on a delinquent lifestyle that eventually includes shoplifting, prostitution, and heroin addiction. Critics praised Burgess for offering without condescension an accurate depiction of teen drug abuse. Writing in *Observer,* reviewer Neil Spencer noted the "absence of adult finger-wagging" in the book. He went on to praise Burgess for leaving the book's ending open, but with "a sense of hope rather than despair" for the characters. Calling the novel "complex, multifoliate, and tremendously powerful," a contributor to *Books for Keeps* applauded the author's ability to capture the "addicts' self-deluding psychobabble," saying "the chill authenticity of their ramblings is frightening."

Burgess also received critical praise for his 1999 effort *Bloodtide,* which won the Lancashire Children's Book Award. Based on the thirteenth-century Icelandic Volsunga Saga, the story is set many years later in a post-apocalyptic London where two warring human clans live among a breed of half-men. With character names and a story line taken from the Volsunga Saga, the story revolves around the power struggle between the Conors and the Volsons to see who will rule London. In the midst of the story, which is narrated by multiple characters, the leaders of the two clans hope to unite through a marriage between the head of the Connor clan and a fourteen-year-old girl named Signy. However, the Connors use the marriage as a trap and end up slaughtering the entire Volson clan. Only Signy and her twin brother survive the massacre, and the story follows them in their search for vengeance against the Conors. Amid the ensuing battle between the two clans, the Norse gods Odin and Loki play significant roles, just as they do in the Volsunga Saga.

While praising the book, several literary critics warned readers of the tale's darker elements. According to a contributor for *Publishers Weekly,* the book "does not stint on graphic portrayals of violence." Sally Estes of *Booklist* called the work "a grim, disturbing dystopia." Despite such forewarning, Julia Eccleshare, who reviewed the book for *Guardian,* felt its "moments of tenderness offset the brutality." Estes felt it was a tale that "readers . . . won't forget."

Burgess continued his work for young adults into the new century, publishing *Lady: My Life as a Bitch* in 2001. With this title, the author attracted the same kind of controversy that he did with *Junk.* Including scenes

In Burgess's dystopian novel **Bloodtide,** *two families battle over what is left of London. (Jacket art by Jon Foster.)*

of teenage sex, *Lady* is about seventeen-year-old, angst-ridden Sandra Fancy, who is transformed into a dog after an encounter with a tramp. Far from perplexed by her metamorphosis, Sandra actually enjoys her new life because it allows her to pursue hedonistic pleasures without worrying about how human society will perceive her actions. "I just decided to get off on anything I could find to get off on," Sandra says in the book. "And it was just great. I was so much happier." In a 2001 interview with a contributor for *Bookseller,* Burgess attempted to answer his critics, who accused him of endorsing amoral behavior. "People tend to write books for young adults and children that say, you can go anywhere and explore anything, so long as you come home at the end. So it was a real pleasure to write a book where the female character left home at the end—and for all the wrong reasons," Burgess said in the interview. In another 2001 interview, this time with *Guardian,* Burgess said he tackled the issues of "lust, desire and sexual irresponsibility" in the book. Despite the book's controversial subject matter, several literary critics lauded the effort, including a contributor for *Bookseller,* who called it "a vivid account, both realistic, and fantastical, of a teenager's experiences, and one in which the morality is not reducible to a cautionary lesson." *Daily Telegraph* critic Rachel Cusk felt the work was a "funny, punchy, well-written, original book."

Burgess's 2003 novel, *Doing It,* also became the subject of much debate in England, even before the book appeared in print. Written to a mature young adult audience, *Doing It* revolves around the experiences of three seventeen-year-old boys and their relationships with women. As much of the work features frank discussions of sex, some reviewers in the British press found the dialogue inappropriate for teenagers, including children's laureate Anne Fine who, calling *Doing It* "filth, whichever way you look at it" in an article for *Guardian,* disparaged the work for being a "grubby book, which demeans both young women and young men." However, as Burgess himself has remarked, other reviewers found the title addressing a genre largely ignored in literature for teens, adolescent male romance. As he wrote on his Web site, "I wrote *Doing It* because I do believe that we have let young men down very badly in terms of the kind of books written for them. . . . This is changing these days, and *Doing It* is my go at trying to bring young, male sexual culture into writing." Considering his characters "nice boys" who are simply interested in sex and what it involves physically as well as emotionally, Burgess defended his work to *Evening Standard* critic Catherine Shoard by claiming that the criticism surrounding this work "confirmed my feeling that *Doing It* was a good thing to do. Lads of that age get terribly neglected because of these so-called moral guardians." As he observed on his Web site, "Boy/girl books are always for girls, and this is certainly not because the boys aren't interested. What is it about young male sexuality that is so unacceptable that no one writes about it? . . . *Doing It* is an attempt on my part to chronicle a side of that culture, sexually, emotionally, psychologically, and of course, humorously as well."

As an author who writes novels he feels will appeal to teenagers despite the opinions of reviewers, Burgess has earned several prestigious awards for his sometimes controversial work. Having his first book published while in his mid-thirties, the author finds his experiences outside the world of literature only enhance his writings. As he once commented: "I wanted to write ever since I was fourteen, and never went into adult education as I felt I'd get more from doing other things. I think to write well you need to have lived at least three different lives and been at least three different people."

Biographical and Critical Sources

BOOKS

Authors and Artists for Young Adults, Volume 28, Gale (Detroit, MI), 1999.

Beacham's Guide to Literature for Young Adults, Volume 12, Gale (Detroit, MI), 2001.
Burgess, Melvin, *Lady: My Life as a Bitch,* Andersen (London, England), 2001, Holt (New York, NY), 2002.

PERIODICALS

Booklist, October 15, 1992, p. 428; May 1, 1995, pp. 1571-1572; May 15, 1996, p. 1586; April 15, 1998, p. 1435; April 1, 1999, p. 1383; March 15, 2000, p. 1371; October 15, 2001, Sally Estes, review of *Bloodtide,* p. 387; June 1, 2002, Anne O'Malley, review of *Lady: My Life as a Bitch,* p. 1716; April 15, 2003, Anne O'Malley, review of *The Ghost behind the Wall,* p. 1470.
Bookseller, June 1, 2000, p. 1890; August 3, 2001, p. 32; August 24, 2001, p. 24.
Books for Keeps, May, 1997, review of *Junk,* p. 27.
Bulletin of the Center for Children's Books, July, 1995, pp. 378-379; May, 1996, pp. 294-295.
Daily Telegraph, December 1, 2001, Rachel Cusk, review of *Lady,* p. 4.
Evening Standard, April 25, 2003, Catherine Shoard, "The Truth about Teenagers."
Guardian, October 12, 1999, p. 2; November 30, 1999, p. 4; June 2, 2001, p. 10; March 29, 2003, Anne Fine, "Filth, whichever way you look at it."
Horn Book, March-April, 1995, Nancy Vasilakis, review of *Burning Issy,* p. 193.
Junior Bookshelf, February, 1991, pp. 29-30; June, 1992, pp. 117-118; February, 1993, pp. 26-27; April, 1994, p. 64; August, 1995, pp. 142-143; August, 1996, pp. 146, 153-154.
Kirkus Reviews, October 15, 1992, p. 1307; October 1, 1997, p. 1529.
Library Journal, November 15, 2001, p. 101.
Observer, March 30, 1997, Neil Spencer, review of *Junk,* p. 17.
Publishers Weekly, February 16, 1998, p. 123; April 3, 2000, p. 82; September 24, 2001, p. 73; November 26, 2001, pp. 62-63; March 4, 2002, review of *Lady: My Life as a Bitch,* p. 81; July 1, 2002, Emily Jenkins, "The British Invasion: PW Speaks to Five Authors Who Have Crossed the Atlantic and Found American Readers," p. 26; April 14, 2003, review of *The Ghost behind the Wall,* p. 70.
School Librarian, November, 1992, pp. 156-157; May, 1993, p. 59; August, 1996, p. 117.
School Library Journal, September, 1992, p. 250; December, 1994, p. 106; June, 1995, p. 108; April, 2000, p. 129; July, 2000, p. 100; July, 2002, Miranda Doyle, review of *Lady: My Life as a Bitch,* p. 114; July, 2003, Beth L. Meister, review of *The Ghost behind the Wall,* p. 124.
Voice of Youth Advocates, April, 1995, pp. 19-20; August, 1996, p. 154.

ONLINE

Melvin Burgess Home Page, http://web.onetel.net.uk/~melvinburgess/ (January 1, 2004).*

BURLEIGH, Robert 1936-

Personal

Born January 4, 1936, in Chicago, IL; married; children: three. *Education:* Attended DePauw University, 1953-57; University of Chicago, 1958-62.

Addresses

Home—415 W. North Ave., Chicago, IL 60610. *E-mail*—roburleigh@aol.com.

Career

Author and artist. Worked for Society of Visual Education as a writer and artist.

Awards, Honors

Orbis Pictus Award, National Council of Teachers of English, 1992, for *Flight: The Journey of Charles Lindbergh.*

Writings

FOR CHILDREN

A Man Named Thoreau (picture book biography), illustrated by Lloyd Bloom, Atheneum (New York, NY), 1985.

Flight: The Journey of Charles Lindbergh (picture book biography), illustrated by Mike Wimmer, Philomel (New York, NY), 1991.

Who Said That? Famous Americans Speak (picture book biography), illustrated by David Catrow, Holt (New York, NY), 1997.

Hoops (picture book), illustrated by Stephen T. Johnson, Silver Whistle (San Diego, CA), 1997.

Home Run: The Story of Babe Ruth (picture book biography), illustrated by Mike Wimmer, Silver Whistle (San Diego, CA), 1998.

Black Whiteness: Admiral Byrd Alone in the Antarctic (picture book biography), illustrated by Walter Lyon Krudop, Atheneum (New York, NY), 1998.

It's Funny Where Ben's Train Takes Him, illustrated by Joanna Yardley, Orchard (New York, NY), 1999.

Hercules, illustrated by Raul Colon, Silver Whistle (San Diego, CA), 1999.

Edna, illustrated by Joanna Yardley, Orchard (New York, NY), 2000.

Messenger, Messenger, illustrated by Barry Root, Atheneum (New York, NY), 2000.

Lookin' for Bird in the Big City, illustrated by Marek Los, Harcourt (San Diego, CA), 2001.

I Love Going through This Book, illustrated by Dan Yaccarino, HarperCollins (New York, NY), 2001.

Goal (picture book), illustrated by Stephen T. Johnson, Harcourt (San Diego, CA), 2001.

Chocolate: Riches from the Rainforest, Abrams (New York, NY), 2002.

Pandora, illustrated by Raul Colon, Harcourt (San Diego, CA), 2002.

The Secret of the Great Houdini, illustrated by Leonid Gore, Simon & Schuster (New York, NY), 2002.

Into the Air: The Story of the Wright Brothers' First Flight (picture book biography), illustrated by Bill Wylie, Silver Whistle (San Diego, CA), 2002.

Into the Woods: John James Audubon Lives His Dream, illustrated by Wendell Minor, Atheneum (New York, NY), 2003.

(Editor) *Earth from Above for Young Readers,* photographs by Yann Arthus Bertrand, illustrated by David Giraudon, Abrams (New York, NY), 2003.

(Editor) *Volcanoes: Journey to the Crater's Edge,* photographs by Philippe Bourseiller, illustrated by David Giraudon, Abrams (New York, NY), 2003.

(Editor) *The Sea: Exploring Life on an Ocean Planet,* photographs by Philip Plisson, illustrated by Emmanuel Cerisier, Abrams (New York, NY), 2003.

Amelia Earhart: Free in the Skies, illustrated by Bill Wylie, Silver Whistle (San Diego, CA), 2003.

Langston's Train Ride, illustrated by Leonard Jenkins, Orchard (New York, NY), 2004.

Martin Luther King, Jr.: Until Justice Runs Down Like Water, illustrated by Bill Wylie, Silver Whistle (San Diego, CA), 2004.

American Moments: Scenes from American History, illustrated by Bruce Strachan, Holt (New York, NY), 2004.

Seurat and La Grande Jatte: Connecting the Dots, Abrams (New York, NY), 2004.

(With Tiki and Ronde Barber) *By My Brother's Side,* Simon & Schuster (New York, NY), 2004.

OTHER

(With Mary Jane Gray) *Basic Writing Skills,* Society for Visual Education (Chicago, IL), 1976.

The Triumph of Mittens: Poems, Boardwell-Kloner (Chicago, IL), 1980.

Colonial America, illustrated by James Seward, Doubleday (Garden City, NY), 1992.

Also writer and producer of over one hundred filmstrips and cassettes on educational subjects.

Sidelights

A writer of informational books of biography and history as well as a poet, Robert Burleigh is noted for introducing difficult historical topics to young readers in an accessible and effective manner. Characteristically using a picture book format, the author presents facts about his subjects—most often notable Americans such as Henry David Thoreau, Charles Lindbergh, Babe Ruth, Harry Houdini, and Admiral Richard Perry—in simple language and present-tense narration. Burleigh favors clipped, staccato texts in both his prose and his poetry, a style credited with expressing the ideas, drama, and importance of each of his topics in an evocative fashion. Reviewers also note the successful marriage of the author's texts with the illustrations of such artists as Lloyd Bloom, Mike Wimmer, and Stephen T. Johnson.

Nineteenth-century writer and philosopher Henry David Thoreau is the subject of Burleigh's first biography, *A Man Named Thoreau*. Considered a balanced overview of Thoreau's life and influence, the book addresses its subject's time at Walden Pond, his love for nature, his literary works, and his civil disobedience, among other topics. Burleigh presents Thoreau and his ideas by combining biographical facts with quotes from the philosopher's popular work *Walden*. Writing in *School Library Journal*, Ruth Semrau called *A Man Named Thoreau* a book that "unfolds new pleasures on every page" and deemed it an "exquisitely simple introduction to a difficult subject." David E. White observed in *Horn Book* that the quotations "interspersed throughout the text . . . are beneficial in capturing the essence of this noted figure." A reviewer for the *Bulletin of the Center for Children's Books* declared that to "have simplified concepts so much without distortion is a gift to the younger reader or listener."

In his picture book *Flight: The Journey of Charles Lindbergh,* Burleigh describes Lindbergh's famous non-stop flight from New York to Paris in 1927. Basing his text on Lindbergh's memoir *The Spirit of St. Louis,* Burleigh focuses on the pilot's journey at the age of twenty-five. Once again, the author is credited with successfully conveying a sophisticated concept, in this case the difficulty of, in the words of *New York Times Book Review* contributor Signe Wilkinson, "staying awake, alert and in charge of a plane and one' life for two days and a very long, lonely night before sleep" to an audience "too young to appreciate what pulling an all-nighter feels like." *Horn Book* reviewer Ann A. Flowers remarked that the text conveys Lindbergh's bravery, the drain on him personally, and the primitive state of his plane in "completely convincing detail" and noted that Burleigh's use of the present tense "keeps the reader in suspense from the moment the plane takes off until [its arrival in] Paris." Flowers concluded that the book is a "pioneer example of the 'right stuff,' splendidly and excitingly presented." Burleigh's use of sentence fragments and single-sentence paragraphs "conveys the excitement of Lindbergh's historic flight," noted a critic in *Kirkus Reviews,* who called *Flight* a book "that brings new life to one of the stories of the century." Burleigh received the Orbis Pictus Award in 1992 for this work.

Shifting to sports, Burleigh wrote a picture book biography of baseball's most widely known hero in *Home Run: The Story of Babe Ruth,* as well as two picture books of poetry, *Hoops* and *Goal,* that describe basket-

A pilot made history in 1927 when he crossed the Atlantic solo in a plane named **The Spirit of St. Louis,** *from Flight: The Journey of Charles Lindbergh. (Written by Robert Burleigh. Illustrated by Mike Wimmer.)*

ball and soccer in verses that simulate the action of the players and the excitement of the game. Filled with tactile imagery, *Hoops* and *Goal* outline the way the game feels to its players. "An ode to the game for older children, veteran players, and NBA fans," declared a *Publishers Weekly* reviewer of *Hoops,* "this book will give language to teenagers' experience both on and off the court." A *Kirkus Reviews* critic noted that *Goal* uses soccer as a frame "to demonstrate the power of teamwork to achieve success." The critic concluded that the book is "a real winner."

In his picture book *Black Whiteness: Admiral Byrd Alone in the Antarctic,* Burleigh retells the explorer's incredible six-month stay alone in the Antarctic. Based on Byrd's daily journal, *Black Whiteness* includes detailed descriptions of Byrd's enduring hardships—sub-zero temperatures, continuous darkness with limited lighting equipment, and loneliness. "Burleigh's spare prose eloquently captures the spartan surroundings in which Byrd conducted daily meteorological studies," observed a critic in *Kirkus Reviews,* who concluded that the explorer's story is "severe, often depressing, and always riveting." A similar adventurous hero can be found in *Into the Woods: John James Audubon Lives His Dream.* Burleigh uses rhyming couplets to communicate Audubon's decision to give up business in order to wander through the wilderness, painting and drawing the sights he sees during his adventures. A *Publishers Weekly* reviewer wrote of *Into the Woods* that Audubon's "philosophy wafts through the volume like a summer breeze." A *Kirkus Reviews* critic called the book a "tribute" to Audubon and a "feast for bird lovers."

Musician Miles Davis travels to New York to find a jazz partner, in Lookin' for Bird in the Big City, *written by Burleigh. (Illustrated by Marek Los.)*

Burleigh is as comfortable writing about big cities as he is about wilderness explorers. *Messenger, Messenger* follows a bike messenger through his busy day, from waking up in his book-filled apartment to making deliveries throughout the city. At the book's end, the tired worker returns to his flat to be warmly greeted by his cat. Writing in *Booklist,* Gillian Engberg felt that the picture book "beautifully captures the energizing pulse of urban life and satisfying work." In *Lookin' for Bird in the Big City,* a teenaged Miles Davis, trumpet in hand, makes music in the city streets as he goes in search of his hero, Charlie Parker. Once again, Burleigh employs poetic language and rhythms to convey the flavor of jazz music and the enthusiasm Davis feels for it. "Words and art harmonize in this creatively imagined account," observed a *Publishers Weekly* reviewer. *School Library Journal* contributor Mary Elam concluded that the work offers "a lovely and lyrical look at this all-American art form."

Ancient Greece abounds with mythical tales about super-human exploits and misadventures. Burleigh has

brought two of these to younger readers with his *Hercules* and *Pandora.* In *Hercules,* the hero tests his mettle against supernatural challenges, culminating in his descent to the underworld to battle the three-headed dog, Cerberus. *Booklist*'s Ilene Cooper liked the fact that *Hercules* uses "language that draws on the strength of its subject yet speaks in the lilt of poetry." In her *Booklist* review, Stephanie Zvirin felt that *Hercules* would inspire young readers to search for other ancient myths about Hercules and other Greek gods, calling the book a "beautiful retelling." *Pandora* puts a human face to the curious woman who, according to Greek myth, unleashed all the world's ills by opening a container. In his version of the story, Burleigh uses verse to illuminate how Pandora's curiosity becomes an obsession, despite her understanding of the danger she faces opening the jar. In a *School Library Journal* review of the work, Patricia Lothrop-Green praised "the graceful drama that unfolds" in the story, concluding: "This Pandora is tempting." Gillian Engberg of *Booklist* found *Pandora* to be "another fine retelling of a Greek myth."

Retelling of the Greek myth Pandora, *in which a woman becomes obsessed with her need to know what is contained in a forbidden jar.* (Written by Burleigh. Illustrated by Raul Colon.)

Burleigh offers middle grade readers a detailed look at a favorite confection in *Chocolate: Riches from the Rainforest.* The illustrated book covers many aspects of chocolate, from its history as a food of the Maya and Aztecs to its journey from cacao pod to candy bar. The author writes about the slave labor once used in the cacao and sugar industries, and about how Milton Hershey revolutionized the sale of milk chocolate from his factory in Pennsylvania. In a *School Library Journal* review, Augusta R. Malvagno praised the "delightful" book for its "kaleidoscope of fascinating information," while a contributor to *Kirkus Reviews* concluded that the title is "a well-conceived and executed work on a subject of great interest."

Some critics have particularly praised Burleigh's *The Secret of the Great Houdini.* Burleigh explores Houdini's escape from a trunk hurled into deep water from the point of view of a youngster named Sam and

his Uncle Ezra, who have joined a crowd to watch the feat. While Sam and Uncle Ezra anxiously await Houdini's escape, Uncle Ezra tells Sam about Houdini's childhood and hardscrabble youth. Sam can hardly concentrate on what his uncle is saying, so terrified is he of the possibility that Houdini will drown. "Burleigh achieves immediacy by writing his poetic text in the present tense," observed Marianne Saccardi in *School Library Journal.* "Houdini is a fascinating figure for all ages," maintained a *Kirkus Reviews* critic. "This snapshot of one incredible feat . . . may spur further exploration, and inspiration." In her *Booklist* review, Gillian Engberg declared that the work "captures the mystique of its famous subject."

Burleigh lives and works in Chicago. In addition to his writing, he enjoys making presentations to schools on the subjects he writes about and the uses of poetry in literature. He has also served as the writer and producer of a variety of educational filmstrips and cassettes and has worked as a writer and artist for the Society of Visual Education.

Biographical and Critical Sources

PERIODICALS

Booklist, February 1, 1999, Stephanie Zvirin, review of *It's Funny Where Ben's Train Takes Him,* p. 979; August, 1999, Ilene Cooper, review of *Hercules,* p. 2050; March 15, 2000, Carolyn Phelan, review of *Edna,* p. 1377; May 15, 2000, Gillian Engberg, review of *Messenger, Messenger,* p. 1742, and Stephanie Zvirin, review of *Hercules,* p. 1758; February 15, 2001, Bill Ott, review of *Lookin' for Bird in the Big City,* p. 1152; June 1, 2001, Marta Segal, review of *I Love Going through This Book,* p. 1888; June 1, 2002, Gillian Engberg, review of *Pandora,* p. 1711; July, 2002, Gillian Engberg, review of *The Secret of the Great Houdini,* p. 1854; January 1, 2003, Julie Cummins, review of *Into the Woods: John James Audubon Lives His Dream,* p. 874.

Bulletin of the Center for Children's Books, December, 1985, review of *A Man Named Thoreau,* p. 63.

Horn Book, March, 1986, David E. White, review of *A Man Named Thoreau,* pp. 215-216; November, 1991, Ann A. Flowers, review of *Flight: The Journey of Charles Lindbergh,* p. 752.

Kirkus Reviews, August 15, 1991, review of *Flight,* p. 1086; December 1, 1997, review of *Black Whiteness: Admiral Byrd Alone in the Antarctic,* p. 1773; February 1, 2001, review of *Goal,* p. 180; March 1, 2002, review of *Chocolate: Riches from the Rainforest,* p. 330; May 1, 2002, review of *Pandora,* p. 650; June 15, 2002, review of *The Secret of the Great Houdini,* p. 876; January 1, 2003, review of *Into the Woods,* p. 58.

New York Times Book Review, January 26, 1992, Signe Wilkinson, review of *Flight,* p. 21.

Publishers Weekly, October 6, 1997, review of *Hoops,* p. 83; August 9, 1999, review of *Hercules,* p. 352; May 14, 2001, review of *Lookin' for Bird in the Big City,* p. 82; June 19, 2000, review of *Messenger, Messenger,* p. 54; June 4, 2001, review of *I Love Going through This Book,* p. 79; April 1, 2002, review of *Pandora,* p. 83; June 3, 2002, review of *The Secret of the Great Houdini,* p. 88; December 2, 2002, review of *Into the Woods,* p. 52.

School Library Journal, January, 1986, Ruth Semrau, review of *A Man Named Thoreau,* p. 64; October, 1999, Nina Lindsay, review of *Hercules,* p. 135; April, 2000, Kate McClelland, review of *Edna,* p. 92; April, 2001, Lee Bock, review of *Goal,* p. 129; June, 2001, Marianne Saccardi, review of *I Love Going through This Book,* p. 104, and Mary Elam, review of *Lookin' for Bird in the Big City,* p. 104; April, 2002, Augusta R. Malvagno, review of *Chocolate,* p. 129; May, 2002, Patricia Lothrop-Green, review of *Pandora,* p. 134; July, 2002, Marianne Saccardi, review of *The Secret of the Great Houdini,* p. 85; September, 2002, Dona Ratterree, review of *Into the Air,* p. 241; January, 2003, Laurie von Mehren, review of *Earth from Above for Young Readers,* p. 150; February, 2003, Robyn Walker, review of *Into the Woods,* p. 128.

Teacher Librarian, June, 2000, Jessica Higgs, review of *Hercules,* p. 54.*

C

CASILLA, Robert 1959-

Personal
Born April 16, 1959, in Jersey City, NJ; son of Miriam (Castro) Casilla; married Carmen Torres (a real estate adjuster), May 1, 1982; children: Robert, Jr., Emily. *Ethnicity:* "Puerto Rican heritage." *Education:* School of Visual Arts, B.F.A., 1982. *Religion:* Protestant Christian. *Hobbies and other interests:* Museums, fine art, baseball, movies.

Addresses
Home and office—101 Southside Ave., 3B, Hastings-on-Hudson, NY 10706. *E-mail*—robertcasilla@aol.com.

Career
Freelance illustrator, 1983—.

Member
Society of Illustrators, Society of Children's Book Writers and Illustrators.

Awards, Honors
Washington Irving Children's Book Choice Award for Illustration, 1996, Notable Book selection, American Library Association, *Reading Rainbow* selection, and Pick of the List selection, American Booksellers Association, all for *The Little Painter of Sabana Grande.*

Robert Casilla

ILLUSTRATOR:
David A. Adler, *Martin Luther King, Jr.: Free at Last,* Holiday House (New York, NY), 1986.

Elizabeth Howard, *The Train to Lulu's,* Bradbury Press (New York, NY), 1988.

Myra Cohn Livingston, *Poems for Fathers,* Holiday House (New York, NY), 1989.

David A. Adler, *Jackie Robinson: He Was the First,* Holiday House (New York, NY), 1989.

David A. Adler, *A Picture Book of Martin Luther King, Jr.,* Holiday House (New York, NY), 1989.

Eileen Roe, *Con mi hermano/With My Brother,* Bradbury Press (New York, NY), 1991.

David A. Adler, *A Picture Book of Eleanor Roosevelt,* Holiday House (New York, NY), 1991.

David A. Adler, *A Picture Book of John F. Kennedy,* Holiday House (New York, NY), 1991.

David A. Adler, *A Picture Book of Simón Bolívar,* Holiday House (New York, NY), 1992.

David A. Adler, *A Picture Book of Jesse Owens,* Holiday House (New York, NY), 1992.

Patricia Murkin, *The Little Painter of Sabana Grande,* Bradbury Press (New York, NY), 1993.

David A. Adler, *A Picture Book of Rosa Parks,* Holiday House (New York, NY), 1993.

Gary Soto, *The Pool Party,* Delacorte Press (New York, NY), 1993.

David A. Adler, *A Picture Book of Jackie Robinson,* Holiday House (New York, NY), 1994.

Jonelle Toriseva, *Rodeo Day,* Bradbury Press (New York, NY), 1994.

Gary Soto, *Boys at Work,* Delacorte Press (New York, NY), 1995.

Jane Q. Saxton, reteller, *The Good Samaritan,* Time-Life for Children (Alexandria, VA), 1996.

Natasha Wing, *Jalapeño Bagels,* Atheneum (New York, NY), 1996.

David A. Adler, *A Picture Book of Thurgood Marshall,* Holiday House (New York, NY), 1997.

Jo Harper, *The Legend of Mexicatl,* published simultaneously in Spanish as *La leyenda de Mexicatl,* Turtle Books (New York, NY), 1998.

John Micklos, Jr., *Daddy Poems,* Boyds Mills Press (Honesdale, PA), 2000.

L. King Pérez, *First Day in Grapes,* Lee and Low (New York, NY), 2002.

Carolyn Marsden, *Mama Had to Work on Christmas,* Viking (New York, NY), 2003.

Contributor of illustrations to the *New York Times, Reader's Digest* and *Highlights for Children.* Several titles illustrated by Casilla have been translated into Spanish.

Work in Progress

Illustrations for *The Drama on Blanca's Wall* and *Midnight Forest,* both forthcoming from Boyds Mills Press.

Sidelights

Robert Casilla is an illustrator of children's books who is known for the warmth and detail he brings to his work. Using watercolors, line drawings, and pastels, Casilla creates realistic renderings that critics consider especially appropriate for the many picture-book biographies he has illustrated for author David A. Adler. Raised by parents born in Puerto Rico, the illustrator brings to his work a multicultural perspective that has enhanced books such as *The Pool Party* and *Boys at Work,* both by noted author Gary Soto, as well as Jo Harper's *The Legend of Mexicatl,* which tells the story of a boy chosen by the Great Spirit to lead his people out of the desert and into the region now known as Mexico. Using watercolors in earthy shades of gold, rust, and brown, Casilla's illustrations for *The Legend of Mexicatl,* published simultaneously in Spanish as *La leyenda de Mexicatl,* "complement the text perfectly," according to *School Library Journal* reviewer Monica Scheliga Carnesi, "infusing the story with both realism and magic."

Casilla has collaborated with Adler on illustrated biographies of a number of men and women who have excelled at their field and made important contributions to society as well. Athlete Jackie Robinson joins civil rights advocates Rosa Parks and Dr. Martin Luther King, Jr., as well as U.S. Supreme Court Justice Thurgood Marshall and first lady Eleanor Roosevelt, in a series of books a *Publishers Weekly* contributor praised as "a highly effective . . . way to introduce the life and legacy of important Americans" to pre-readers. In each book, Casilla creates full-page watercolor paintings representing significant events from the subject's life, giving special attention to portraits and period details. Praising *A Picture Book of Thurgood Marshall* in *School Library Journal,* Margaret Bush noted that the author and illustrator work together to "offer a succinct, visually handsome presentation of the youth and the career highlights of the history-making Marshall." The life of the Alabama-born woman who sparked the civil rights movement of the twentieth century is depicted in 1993's *A Picture Book of Rosa Parks.* Casilla uses "dramatic color" in illustrations that reveal the historic backdrop to Parks' life—from Ku Klux Klan rallies lit by flaming torches to inspiring speeches by Dr. King—and include intimate portraits of Parks that "capture the ordinary person who made a difference," in the words of *Booklist* contributor Hazel Rochman.

Poems reflecting the special relationship between children and their fathers are the center of *Daddy Poems,* edited by John Micklos, Jr. In creating the illustrations for this 2000 poetry collection, Casilla used his own two children as models. The illustrator depicts children as they "dance, snuggle, and rest across the warmly illustrated pages," remarked Jeanie Burnett in her *Childhood Education* review. Praising the collection of twenty poems as a wonderful way to reinforce the many different relationships children may have with a father, *School Library Journal* reviewer Nina Lindsay commended in particular Casilla's "realistic paintings of families of diverse backgrounds."

The life of a migrant farmworker family is the focus of L. King Pérez's 2002 book *First Day in Grapes.* The story follows Chico as he begins third grade in a new school where he knows no one and where he will only stay until the grape harvest is complete and his family moves on to the next job. While an initially unhappy Chico prepares to be hounded by schoolyard bullies and given homework he is unable to complete, he finds he has a skill with math due to his work in the fields and comes home from his first day confident and excited about the year to come. Casilla's colored pencil and watercolor illustrations "excel in conveying Chico's emotions through facial expressions," noted a *Kirkus Reviews* critic, while in *School Library Journal,* Rosalyn Pierini complimented the illustrator's work for adding "warmth and color to this portrait of life in rural California."

In addition to illustrating children's books, Casilla also works with clients as a professional artist, and has created art for magazines and even designed a postage stamp. He lives and works in Hastings-on-Hudson, New York, with his wife, Carmen, and his children Emily and Robert, Jr. When not working in his studio, Casilla enjoys spending time with young people and sharing what he does for a living; he visits schools and explains to students how the book illustration process works, from reading the manuscript and meeting with the author through "thumbnail" sketches, finished drawings, and final watercolor paintings.

Casilla once commented: "When I illustrate biographies, I try to learn as much as possible about the person I am illustrating so when I am working on the art, I feel I know the person intimately. I find great rewards and satisfaction in illustrating for children. I hope to be able to help kids learn and grow and enjoy reading."

Biographical and Critical Sources

PERIODICALS

Booklist, March 1, 1993, Julie Corsaro, review of *The Little Painter of Sabana Grande,* p. 1237; October 15, 1993, Hazel Rochman, review of *A Picture Book of Rosa Parks,* p. 444; June 1, 1996, Stephanie Zvirin, review of *Jalapeño Bagels,* p. 1737; November 15, 1997, Carolyn Phelan, review of *A Picture Book of Thurgood Marshall,* p. 552; November 15, 1998, Isabel Schon, review of *La leyenda de Mexicatl,* p. 599; November 15, 2002, Linda Perkins, review of *First Day in Grapes,* p. 612.
Childhood Education, winter, 2000, Jeanie Burnett, review of *Daddy Poems,* p. 107.
Kirkus Reviews, October 1, 2002, review of *First Day in Grapes,* p. 1477.
Knight Ridder/Tribune News Service, June 15, 2000, Linda DuVal, review of *Daddy Poems.*
Publishers Weekly, November 24, 1989, review of *A Picture Book of Martin Luther King, Jr.,* p. 71; February 15, 1993, review of *The Little Painter of Sabana Grande,* p. 237; September 22, 2003, review of *Mama Had to Work on Christmas,* p. 72.
School Library Journal, May, 1988, Jeanette Lambert, review of *The Train to Lulu's,* p. 84; November, 1994, Charlene Strickland, review of *Rodeo Day,* p. 92; December, 1994, Tom S. Hurburt, review of *A Picture Book of Jackie Robinson,* p. 94; July, 1996, Beth Tegart, review of *Jalapeño Bagels,* p. 75; January, 1998, Margaret Bush, review of *A Picture Book of Thurgood Marshall,* p. 96; May, 1998, Monica Scheliga Carnesi, review of *La leyenda de Mexicatl,* p. 161; October, 2002, Nina Lindsay, review of *Daddy Poems,* and Rosalyn Pierini, review of *First Day in Grapes,* p. 125.

ONLINE

Author-Illustrator Source, http://author-illustr-source.com/ (June 11, 2003), "Robert Casilla, Illustrator."

Sandra Choron

Portfolios.com, http://www.portfolios.com/ (December 26, 2003), "Robert Casilla Illustration."
Robert Casilla Home Page, http://www.robertcasilla.com/ (June 11, 2003).
ZAKS Illustrator Source, http://www.illustrators.net/ (December 26, 2003), "Robert Casilla."

OTHER

"Robert Casilla" (publicity pamphlet), Holiday House, c. 1992.

*   *   *

CHORON, Sandra (Zena Samelson) 1950-

Personal

Born March 10, 1950, in New York, NY; daughter of Kalman (a tailor) and Fay (a tailor; maiden name: Rabinowitz) Samelson; married Harry Choron (a graphic designer), 1972; children: Casey. *Education:* Lehman College (Bronx, NY), B.A., 1971. *Religion:* Jewish.

Addresses

Home—4 Myrtle St., Haworth, NJ 07641. *E-mail*—schoron@aol.com.

Career

Writer, editor, literary agent, designer, and book packager. March Tenth, Inc., Haworth, NJ, founder and president, 1981—. Worked as an editor at Hawthorn Books and Dell Publishing. Founding editor, *Rock & Rap Confidential* newsletter. Instructor, Lehman College, 1998.

Member

American Book Producers Association (member of board of directors, 1983-84), American Society of Journalists and Authors.

Writings

(Adapter from the screenplay by John Hughes) *National Lampoon's Class Reunion,* Dell Publishing (New York, NY), 1982.

(With Edward Malca) *Everybody's Investment Book: How to Invest Up to 5,000 Dollars Even If You Don't Have It,* Bantam (New York, NY), 1984.

(With Dave Marsh and Debbie Geller) *Rocktopicon: Unlikely Questions and Their Surprising Answers,* Contemporary Books (Chicago, IL), 1984.

The Big Book of Kids' Lists, illustrated by John Lane, World Almanac Publications (New York, NY), 1985.

(Compiler, with Bob Oskam) *Elvis!: The Last Word: The 328 Best (and Worst) Things Anyone Ever Said about "The King,"* Carol Publishing Group (Secaucus, NJ), 1991.

(With husband, Harry Choron) *The Book of Lists for Kids,* Houghton Mifflin (New York, NY), 1995, revised edition published as *The All-New Book of Lists for Kids,* Houghton Mifflin (New York, NY), 2002.

(With husband, Harry Choron) *The Book of Lists for Teens,* Houghton Mifflin (New York, NY), 2002.

(With Sasha Carr) *The Caregiver's Essential Handbook: More than 1200 Tips to Help You Care For and Comfort the Seniors in Your Life,* McGraw Hill (New York, NY), 2003.

The Book of College Lists, Houghton Mifflin (New York, NY), 2004.

Sidelights

Sandra Choron's career is deeply intertwined with multiple aspects of books and publishing. A writer, literary agent, editor, book packager, and designer, Choron has written several works of her own and helped many high-profile clients publish their own books. She founded a literary agency called March Tenth, Inc., in 1981, and has represented more than 100 authors in a variety of subject areas, including reference, fiction, humor, and health. The agency has packaged more than 200 titles for both commercial publishers and individual clients. In addition, March Tenth, Inc., has created DVD and record packages for a number of prominent recording artists, including Bruce Springsteen, Shania Twain,

Mark Knopfler, and Sting. Choron has also taught a college-level class in book production at Lehman College in New York City.

With her husband, Harry, Choron wrote *The Big Book of Kids' Lists* and *The Book of Lists for Teens.* The books provide trivia, history, lifestyle suggestions, and other focused lists covering topics of interest to young people and teenagers. In *The Big Book of Kids' Lists,* readers can find more than three hundred lists of statistics and facts covering problems and issues sometimes faced in childhood and adolescence, including such topics as ten things to do if you are afraid of the dark, six ways kids can help to change the world, and five ways to stop a nosebleed. The book also includes information on bike safety, lists of books banned from public schools, kids' legal rights, and information on how kids can fight censorship. There are also lists of topics intended for fun, including how to tell what is in a box of chocolates, listings of the twenty-five best U.S. amusement parks, seven ways to ward off Dracula, films featuring monster vegetables, and ten little-known things about Superman. The material is "clearly written and often of merit," wrote Eva Elisabeth Von Ancken in *School Library Journal.* Kristiana Gregory, writing in *Los Angeles Times,* commented that "Readers ages seven to seventeen can gorge on trivia here and not feel flabby, for this isn't just junk trivia. Most of the facts here are worth digesting."

Similarly, *The Book of Lists for Teens* offers a "captivating collection of tips, advice, opinions, and more, both silly and serious," intended for teenagers and young adults, wrote Paula Rohrlick in *Kliatt.* The lists are grouped in chapters covering overall topics such as school, relationships, entertainment, facts, the world at large, and personal issues. There are lists of suggestions for solving problems that many teenagers face, such as nine ways to defeat bullies, twenty organizations that work with the problems of young people, twenty-eight ideas to fight prejudice, and eleven ways to share bad news with parents. Lighter topics include twelve steps to forming a band, twenty popular songs of the 1990s, and ten notable hip-hop albums. "Filled with trivia, facts, and fun, this book inspires, informs, and entertains," wrote Elaine Baran Black in *School Library Journal.*

"No one in my family was surprised that books became my passion in life; 'book' was the first word I ever uttered, and as a child, I had no better friends than the many volumes I was encouraged to take out of the library each week," Choron told *SATA.* "As an adult, I have been lucky enough to be able to submerge myself in every aspect of the book world: I'm an agent, a writer, a book designer, and a lover of information. Working on *The Book of Lists for Kids* and *The Book of Lists for Teens,* I was able to combine so many of the skills I had acquired in my publishing career, including research and consulting, plus it gave me a chance to organize the hundreds of ideas I had for these books. I

There's a list to manage just about everything in the Book of Lists for Teens, *written by Sandra and Harry Choron. (Cover illustration by Lili Schulder.)*

think list-making can be a valuable tool for young readers (and older ones, too!) in that the process gives us a chance to catalog our thoughts, define subjects, and keep track of a world that's changing faster than ever."

Biographical and Critical Sources

PERIODICALS

Kliatt, Paula Rohrlick, review of *The Book of Lists for Teens,* p. 40.

Los Angeles Times, July 7, 1985, Kristiana Gregory, review of *The Big Book of Kids' Lists,* p. B6.

Publishers Weekly, March 22, 1985, review of *The Big Book of Kids' Lists,* p. 57; June 3, 2002, review of *The All-New Book of Lists for Kids,* p. 90.

School Library Journal, February, 1986, Eva Elisabeth Von Ancken, review of *The Big Book of Kids' Lists,* p. 82; January, 2003, Elaine Baran Black, review of *The Book of Lists for Teens,* p. 152.*

CHWAST, Seymour 1931-

Personal

Born August 18, 1931, in New York, NY; son of Aaron Louis (a file clerk and waiter) and Esther (Newman) Chwast; married Jacqueline Weiner (an artist), 1952 (divorced, 1971); married Paula Scher (a designer), 1973 (divorced, 1979, re-married, 1989); married Barbara Wool, 1980 (divorced, 1982); children: (with Weiner) Eve, Pamela. *Education:* Cooper Union Art School, diploma, 1957.

Addresses

Home—Grammercy Park, Manhattan, NY. *Office*—Pushpin Group, Inc., 55 East 9th Street, New York, NY 10003.

Career

Graphic artist, designer, and illustrator, 1956—; *New York Times,* New York, NY, junior designer; worked variously for *Esquire, House and Garden,* and *Glamour;* Push Pin Studios, New York, NY, founding partner, originator, and director of studio publication, *Push Pin Graphic,* 1954-80, studio director, 1975-82; Pushpin, Lubalin, Peckolick, Inc., New York, NY, partner, 1982-86; Pushpin Group, president and director, 1982—. Cooper Union Art School, New York, NY, instructor of design and illustration, 1975-81; Parsons School of Design, visiting lecturer. American Institute of Graphic Arts, vice-president and member of board of directors; New York Art Directors Guild, member of board of directors. *Exhibitions:* Work has been featured at Musee Des Arts Decoratif, the Louvre, Paris, France, 1971, 1973; "A Century of American Illustration," Brooklyn Museum, 1973; American Institute of Graphic Arts; Art Directors Club of New York; Society of Illustrators; Type Directors Club of New York; Art Directors Club of Chicago; Lincoln Center for the Performing Arts; California State University; and Galerie Delpire, Paris, France. One-man shows include: Cooper Union, New York, NY, 1986; Jack Gallery, New York, NY, 1987; Lustrare Gallery, New York, NY, 1991; Bradley Gallery, Milwaukee, WI, 1992; GGG Gallery, Tokyo, Japan, 1992, Recruit Gallery, Osaka, Japan, 1992; Michael Kisslinger Gallery, New York, NY, 1994; Kunstschalter Gallery, New York, NY, 1994; School of Visual Arts Master Series, 1997; and Warsaw Poster Museum, 2000. Works are held in the Museum of Modern Art (New York, NY), the Cooper-Hewitt Museum, the Brooklyn Museum, the Whitney Museum of American Art, and the Smithsonian Institute.

Member

Alliance Graphique Internationale, Art Directors Club, American Institute of Graphic Arts.

Awards, Honors

Best Illustrated Book of the Year, *New York Times,* 1969, for *Sara's Granny and the Groodle,* and 1970, for *Finding a Poem;* American Institute of Graphic Arts'

Seymour Chwast

Fifty Books selections, 1969, for *Still Another Alphabet book,* 1972, for *Still Another Children's Book* and *The Pancake King,* and 1973, for *The House That Jack Built;* Children's Book Showcase selection, 1972, for *Rimes de la Mere Oie: Mother Goose Rendered into French;* St. Gavden's Medal, Cooper Union; Hall of Fame, New York Art Directors Club, 1984; Gold Medal, American Institute of Graphic Arts, 1985; Parents' Choice Picture Book Award, 1988, and Jewish Book Council Award for Illustration, 1989, both for *Just Enough Is Plenty: A Hanukkah Tale;* Parents' Choice Picture Book Award, 1991, for *The Alphabet Parade;* Cooper Union Citation for Excellence; honorary Ph.D., Parsons School of Design, 1992; Master Series Award, School of Visual Arts, 1997.

Writings

CHILDREN'S BOOKS; SELF-ILLUSTRATED

(With Martin Stephen Moskof) *Still Another Alphabet Book,* McGraw (New York, NY), 1969.
(With Martin Stephen Moskof) *Still Another Number Book,* McGraw (New York, NY), 1971.
Mother Goooose, Random House (New York, NY), 1972.
(With Martin Stephen Moskof) *Still Another Children's Book,* McGraw (New York, NY), 1972.
Limerickricks, Random House (New York, NY), 1973.
Bushy Bride: Norwegian Fairy Tale, Creative Education (Mankato, MN), 1983.

Tall City, Wide Country: A Book to Read Forward and Backward, Viking (New York, NY), 1983.
The Alphabet Parade, Harcourt (New York, NY), 1991.
Paper Pets: Make Your Own Three Dogs, Two Cats, One Parrot, One Rabbit, One Monkey, Abrams (New York, NY), 1993.
The Twelve Circus Rings, Harcourt (New York, NY), 1993.
Mr. Merlin and the Turtle, Greenwillow (New York, NY), 1996.
Traffic Jam, Houghton (Boston, MA), 1999.
Harry, I Need You!, Houghton (Boston, MA), 2002.

CHILDREN'S BOOKS; ILLUSTRATOR

Joan Gill, *Sara's Granny and the Groodle,* Doubleday (Garden City, NY), 1969.
Eve Merriam, *Finding a Poem,* Atheneum (New York, NY), 1970.
Phyllis La Farge, *The Pancake King,* Delacorte (New York, NY), 1971.
(With Milton Glaser and Barry Zaid) Ormande deKay Jr., translator, *Rimes de la Mere Oie: Mother Goose Rendered into French,* Little, Brown (Boston, MA), 1971.
The House That Jack Built, Random House (New York, NY), 1973.
Steven Kroll, *Sleepy Ida and Other Nonsense Poems,* Pantheon (New York, NY), 1977.
Dan Weaver, adapter, *The Little Theater Presents "A Christmas Carol": A Play in Three Acts Adapted from the Story by Charles Dickens,* Viking (New York, NY), 1986.
Harriet Ziefert, *Keeping Daddy Awake on the Way Home from the Beach,* Harper (New York, NY), 1986.
Harriet Ziefert, *My Sister Says Nothing Ever Happens When We Go Sailing,* Harper (New York, NY), 1986.
Barbara Diamond Goldin, *Just Enough Is Plenty: A Hanukkah Tale,* Viking (New York, NY), 1988.
Harriet Ziefert, *Harry's Bath,* Bantam (New York, NY), 1990.
Deborah Johnston, *Mathew Michael's Beastly Day,* Harcourt (New York, NY), 1992.
Judith Martin, *Out of the Bag: The Paper Bag Players Book of Plays,* Hyperion (New York, NY), 1997.
Gloria Nagy, *The Wizard Who Wanted to Be Santa,* Sheer Bliss Communications (Newport, RI), 2000.
Harriet Ziefert, *Moonride,* Houghton (Boston, MA), 2000.
Harriet Ziefert, *Ode to Humpty Dumpty,* Houghton (Boston, MA), 2001.
Jerry Spinelli, *My Daddy and Me,* Knopf (New York, NY), 2003.
Had Gadya = One Little Goat: A Passover Song, Roaring Brook Press (Brookfield, CT), 2004.

OTHER

(Designer) *The Illustrated Cat: A Poster Book,* compiled by Jean-Claude Suares and edited by William E. Maloney, Harmony Books (New York, NY), 1976.
(Designer) Emily Blair Chewning, *The Illustrated Flower,* Harmony Books (New York, NY), 1977.

(Editor, with Jean-Claude Suares) *The Literary Cat,* Windhover Books (New York, NY), 1977.

(Editor and compiler, with Steven Heller) *The Art of New York,* Abrams (New York, NY), 1983.

(Illustrator) Erica Heller and Vicki Levites, *300 Ways to Say No to a Man,* Simon & Schuster (New York, NY), 1983.

(With D. J. R. Bruckner and Steven Heller) *Art against War: 400 Years of Protest in Art,* Abbeville Press (New York, NY), 1984.

(Self-illustrated) *The Left-Handed Designer,* edited by Steven Heller, Abrams (New York, NY), 1985.

(Self-illustrated) *Happy Birthday Bach,* Doubleday (Garden City, NY), 1985.

(Illustrator, with Alkan Cober and Guy Billout) *Everybody's Business: A Fund of Retrievable Ideas for Humanizing Life in the Office,* edited by Malcolm Clark and William Houseman, Herman Miller Research Corporation (Zeeland, MI), 1985.

(With Donald Barthelme) *Sam's Bar,* Doubleday (Garden City, NY), 1987.

(Compiler and editor, with Barbara Cohen and Steven Heller) *New York Observed: Artists and Writers Look at the City, 1650 to the Present,* Abrams (New York, NY), 1987.

(Illustrator) Steven Heller, *Design Career: A Handbook for Illustrators and Graphic Designers,* Van Nostrand Reinhold (New York, NY), 1987.

(Illustrator) *Visions of Peace,* edited by Vito Perrone, North Dakota Quarterly Press (Grand Forks, ND), 1988.

(With Steven Heller) *Graphic Style: From Victorian to Post-Modern,* Abrams (New York, NY), 1988.

(With Barbara Cohen and Steven Heller) *Trylon and Perisphere: The 1939 New York World's Fair,* Abrams (New York, NY), 1989.

(Editor, with Steven Heller) *Sourcebook of Visual Ideas,* Van Nostrand Reinhold (New York, NY), 1989.

(With Vicki Gold Levi and Steven Heller) *You Must Have Been a Beautiful Baby: Baby Pictures of the Stars,* Hyperion (New York, NY), 1992.

(Self-illustrated) *Bra Fashions by Stephanie,* Warner Books (New York, NY), 1994.

(With Steven Heller) *Jackets Required: An Illustrated History of the American Book Jacket 1920-1950,* Chronicle Books (San Francisco, CA), 1995.

(With James Fraser and Steven Heller) *Japanese Modern: Graphic Design between the Wars,* Chronicle Books (San Francisco, CA), 1996.

(Illustrator) D. K. Holland, *Illustration America: Twenty-five Outstanding Portfolios,* Rockport Publishers (Gloucester, MA), 1996.

(With Steven Heller) *Graphic Style: From Victorian to Digital,* Abrams (New York, NY), 2000.

Author of *The Book of Battles,* privately published, 1957; designer of *Connoisseur Book of the Cigar,* 1967. Also creator of illustrations, posters, typographic designs, and animated commercials for print and television advertising, book jackets, record albums, packages, brochures and magazines, and art for theatrical productions.

Adaptations

The Twelve Circus Rings was adapted as a CD-ROM in 1996.

Sidelights

Seymour Chwast is considered one of the most influential commercial artists of the twentieth century in the United States. Some of his works are held in major U.S. museums, and he is known worldwide for his innovations in graphic design. Since the mid-1950s, he has expressed his political perspective in cartoons rendered in pen and ink, on posters designed with woodcuts, and, more recently, in steel sculptures. As Chwast explained to Steven Heller in *Innovators of American Illustration,* he is a "nonconformist" who recognizes that "art has to establish its own order and authority while attacking the existing one." Chwast added: "Therefore I try to use my assignments as platforms for whatever I have to say."

Chwast's contribution has not been limited, however, to adult audiences. He is the author or illustrator of over twenty books for children, many of which feature his unmistakable cartoon style. A *Publishers Weekly* reviewer noted that his "distinctive, poster-styled art" suits children's books very well, as "his subjects are simply and boldly delineated; his palette is vivid and cheery." According to Steven Heller on the *American Institute of Graphic Arts (AIGA)* Web site, "It would be difficult to imagine contemporary American and European graphic design and illustration without the presence of Seymour Chwast. . . . For over thirty years he has continued to ride above the twists and turns of fashion; today his art is even more energized and varied than when it originally altered a generation's perceptions."

Chwast was born in the Bronx, New York. He lived some of his childhood years on Coney Island, where he spent a great deal of time drawing. During his Depression-era youth, he attended art classes sponsored by the Works Progress Administration (WPA). When he entered Lincoln High School in New York City, his talent for art was apparent, and he was encouraged by his art teacher, Leon Friend. Heller observed: "It was at Lincoln that Chwast learned to appreciate type, graphic images, and the possibilities of commercial art. Friend believed that there was no greater glory for an artist than to have his work printed, and demanded that his students enter all competitions open to them. Chwast entered many. At sixteen, his first illustration was published in a reader's column in *Seventeen* magazine."

Chwast later attended Cooper Union Art School, where he studied printmaking, woodcut techniques, and typography. Upon graduating from that institution, Chwast teamed up with other Cooper Union-trained artists to publish *The Push Pin Almanack.* Chwast, Milton Glaser, and Edward Sorel formed the Push Pin Studios in 1954.

A kitten is rescued in **Traffic Jam,** *written and illustrated by Seymour Chwast.*

The Push Pin Group, in some organizational form or another, challenged traditional, sentimental illustration and graphic design for decades, earning its members admiration and respect. They also renewed styles popular in years past. Chwast explained to Heller in *Innovators of American Illustration,* "I found that around 1950 designers had come to the end of a period of evolving style. We came to that point because extensive publishing allowed us to observe and digest everything that had been done before. We started borrowing from the past, and that seemed to progress chronologically." Some of the styles that Chwast and his partners have worked in include Victoriana, art nouveau, and art deco.

In addition to his work with the Push Pin Group, Chwast has taken on a number of other projects over the years. He told Heller in *Innovators of American Illustration,* "I'm always working on half a dozen things simultaneously. While I'm working on drawings, I might be conceptualizing and designing with other members of my studio." On the *AIGA* Web site, Heller wrote: "Chwast's approach—regardless of media—was always humorous and aggressive without being crass. His virtuosity has always been demonstrated in his ability to master both elegance and pop."

Chwast created his first children's books with Martin Stephen Moskof in the late 1960s. Their first collaboration, the 1969 work *Still Another Alphabet Book,* was praised by critics for its originality, colorful pictures with hidden words, and gaiety. The illustrations in the volume, according to Zena Sutherland of the *Bulletin of the Center for Children's Books,* are "a graphic triumph over tedium." A *Publishers Weekly* critic wrote that the book was "to be looked at with the greatest happiness." Similarly, *Still Another Number Book,* published in 1971, was described as "absolutely glorious" by a *Publishers Weekly* commentator. Zena Sutherland, in a *Bulletin of the Center for Children's Books* appraisal, called it an "imaginative introduction to numbers."

In the early 1980s, Chwast created *Tall City, Wide Country: A Book to Read Forward and Backward.* This book has what Ann A. Flowers described in *Horn Book* as an "ingenious format." Double-page, horizontal illustrations present country life, and vertical illustrations (which require the reader to turn the book ninety degrees) capture city life. "Chwast's bright, wobbly cartoons are still droll," wrote a *Kirkus Reviews* critic. *The Alphabet Parade,* published in 1991, showcases marchers and floats representing every letter of the alphabet

Harry imagines what surprise his mother has in store for him in **Harry, I Need You!** *(Written and illustrated by Chwast.)*

in sequence. The people watching the parade also contribute to the fun. The book was lauded as "cheerfully inventive" by a *Kirkus Reviews* critic. Joanne Oppenheim, writing in the *New York Times Book Review,* similarly praised the book as "truly playful."

Chwast's 1993 picture book, *The Twelve Circus Rings,* gives the familiar verses of "The Twelve Days of Christmas" a new twist. On double-page, light-blue colored spreads, circus clowns and monkeys, jugglers and elephants, and horseback riders present themselves in a variety of permutations. A *Publishers Weekly* critic applauded the "cumulative counting book," particularly its "glossy, simply outlined figures" that help children identify mathematical patterns. Writing in *Booklist,* Deborah Abbott praised the overall work as "an entertaining package."

After more than a half century as a designer and illustrator, Chwast continues to please adults and children alike with his graphic style. *Mr. Merlin and the Turtle,* a 1996 book, was written and illustrated by Chwast in pen, ink, and color film. The result, in the words of a *Publishers Weekly* critic, is a "clever lift-the-flap volume." The story concerns Mr. Merlin, who becomes bored with his pet turtle and decides to turn him into a bird. Mr. Merlin finds fault with the bird, however, and soon changes it into a monkey. The transformations continue through a camel and elephant before Mr. Merlin realizes that his old turtle was not so bad after all. Readers participate in the story by using various flaps to transform the turtle into the different animals. A *Kirkus Reviews* contributor commented favorably on the story's illustrations, stating that, like comic strips, they remain "perfectly balanced between telling a story and telling a joke."

Traffic Jam turns one of daily life's annoyances into a comic celebration. When a mother cat seeks to take her errant kitten across a busy intersection, a traffic snarl

develops and, as the pages unfold to a lengthy panel, gets worse and worse. Chwast livens the scene by presenting the various drivers' and passengers' thoughts in bubbles above their heads. Eventually the cats find their way home safely, and the traffic slowly begins to flow again. A *Publishers Weekly* critic felt that the book "may well give kids something to think about the next time they are stuck in traffic."

An imaginative youngster indulges in flights of fancy in *Harry, I Need You!* Harry's mother wakes him one morning by calling, "Harry, I need you!" As he rises from bed, Harry tries to imagine why his mother would summon him so urgently. He concocts scenarios, one more worrisome than the next, as he makes his way to the kitchen. All is well in the end—Harry's cat has had kittens. In her *School Library Journal* review, Marlene Gawron felt that the illustrations "seem intentionally awkward" but are nonetheless "innovative." Gawron concluded that "the story is timeless."

In addition to illustrating his own work, Chwast has provided pictures for both adult and children's books written by others. He has collaborated with Harriet Ziefert on several children's titles, including *Moonride,* a story of a youngster's fanciful ride across the sky on the back of the moon. *School Library Journal* contributor Corinne Camarata described Chwast's illustrations for that book as "soft, endearing ink-and-colored-pencil drawings." In *My Daddy and Me,* by Jerry Spinelli, a puppy anxiously awaits his father's return from work and then plays with Dad exuberantly upon his arrival. A *Publishers Weekly* critic wrote of the work: "The warmth emanating from parent and child is comfortingly universal." *Ode to Humpty Dumpty,* also by Ziefert, takes up the story of Humpty Dumpty after the egg's great fall, showing how the citizens of the kingdom seek to comfort their grieving ruler. A *Publishers Weekly* commentator maintained that Chwast's drawings "ably deliver some comical images of monuments to Humpty's memory."

On the *AIGA* Web site, Heller concluded: "A famous illustrator once said . . . 'Illustration is a young man's game.' If that is true then Chwast has discovered a fountain of youth. . . . He has more sparks of inspiration and longer fires of brilliance than most younger colleagues. No one can argue with his influence on illustration or his breakthroughs in design. His palette and design forms were new wave when most new wavers were still finger painting. . . . His art for commerce and his creative art are as fresh and uncompromised as when he first put pen to paper." Chwast lives and works in New York City.

Biographical and Critical Sources

BOOKS

Contemporary Designers, 3rd edition, St. James (Detroit, MI), 1997.
Heller, Steven, editor, *Innovators of American Illustration,* Van Nostrand Reinhold (New York, NY), 1986.
Siegel, RitaSue, *American Graphic Designers,* McGraw-Hill (New York, NY), 1984.

PERIODICALS

Arithmetic Teacher, May, 1994, David J. Whitin, review of *The Twelve Circus Rings,* p. 562.
Booklist, March 15, 1993, Deborah Abbott, review of *The Twelve Circus Rings,* p. 1352.
Bulletin of the Center for Children's Books, July, 1970, Zena Sutherland, review of *Still Another Alphabet Book,* p. 173-174; September, 1971, Zena Sutherland, review of *Still Another Number Book,* p. 2.
Horn Book, August, 1983, Ann A. Flowers, review of *Tall City, Wide Country: A Book to Read Forward and Backward,* p. 429.
Kirkus Reviews, June 1, 1983, review of *Tall City, Wide Country,* p. 617; August 15, 1991, review of *The Alphabet Parade,* p. 1096; June 15, 1996, review of *Mr. Merlin and the Turtle,* p. 896.
New York Times Book Review, November 10, 1991, Joanne Oppenheim, "Books to Play With," p. 32; March 9, 2003, Sean Kelly, review of *Harry, I Need You!,* p. 24.
Publishers Weekly, August 25, 1969, review of *Still Another Alphabet Book,* p. 284; July 15, 1971, review of *Still Another Number Book,* p. 50; September 6, 1991, review of *The Alphabet Parade,* p. 102; March 1, 1993, review of *The Twelve Circus Rings,* p. 56; June 24, 1996, review of *Mr. Merlin and the Turtle,* p. 60; October 18, 1999, review of *Traffic Jam,* p. 81; March 26, 2001, review of *Ode to Humpty Dumpty,* p. 93; September 16, 2002, review of *Harry, I Need You!,* p. 68; February 17, 2003, review of *My Daddy and Me,* p. 73.
School Library Journal, December, 2000, Corinne Camarata, review of *Moonride,* p. 128; May, 2001, Shara Alpern, review of *Ode to Humpty Dumpty,* p. 139; September, 2002, Marlene Gawron, review of *Harry, I Need You!,* p. 182.

ONLINE

American Institute of Graphic Arts, http://www.aiga.org/ (June 12, 2003), Steven Heller, "Seymour Chwast."*

* * *

CROSS, Tom 1954-

Personal

Born February 8, 1954, in Johnson City, NY; son of Gerald W. and Elsie J. Cross; married Patti (an artist and designer), 1990; children: Amber. *Ethnicity:* "Caucasian." *Education:* Attended Broome Community College and Ohio State University; University of Florida, B.S.

Addresses

Home and office—P.O. Box 774, Osprey, FL 34229. *E-mail*—info@tomcross-artist.com.

Career

Artist, illustrator, designer, computer consultant, zoologist, and writer. Designer and illustrator for clients such as Franklin Mint, Lean'n Tree Cards, Ceaco Puzzles, Lenox China, Lovelace Family Gifts, Sarasota Bay National Estuary Program, Iron Crown Enterprises, Pelican Press, Binghamton Press, and U.S. National Park Service. Contributing author and editor to the Cousteau Society. Sarasota County Manatee Protection Committee, natural resources chair; Sarasota County Midnight Pass Blue Ribbon Panel. *Exhibitions:* Works exhibited at a number of national and international galleries and shows, including Germanton Gallery, Germanton, NC, 1996-2002; Sarasota Visual Arts Center, Sarasota, FL, 1998-2000; Golden Lynx Gallery, Mendon, NY, 1999; Nihon Gallery, Nagoya, Japan, 1999; Selby Gallery, Ringling School of Art and Design, 2000; Phillippi Estate, Sarasota, FL, 2001; and ARTEVENTI, Italy, France, and Switzerland, 2002-2005.

Awards, Honors

Environmental Hero Top Twenty, *Sarasota* magazine.

Writings

(Creator and illustrator) Constance Barkley Lewis, *Fairy Garden: Fairies of the Four Seasons,* Andrews McMeel Publishing (Kansas City, MO), 1998.
(Illustrator) Marcia Zina Mager, *Believing in Faeries: A Manual for Grown-Ups,* C. W. Daniel (Essex, England), 1999.
The Way of Wizards, Andrews McMeel Publishing (Kansas City, MO), 2001.

Tom Cross

Contributor to numerous periodicals, including *Renaissance, Inform Art, Art Club Times, Art Business News, Computer Artist, Sarasota Herald Tribune, Starlog, Dragon,* and *BookPage.* Contributor to books, including *Aquaculture: The Ecological Issues,* Blackwell Publishers (Malden, MA) 2003. Contributor of art and illustrations to publishers such as Lionheart Books Ltd., Harper & Row Junior Books, and Classical Kids Publishing. Limited edition prints and artwork published by Mill Pond Press, Applejack/National Wildlife Editions, and Tom Cross, Inc.

Work in Progress

The Everyday Tree; Trapped Magic; How a Wizard Spells.

Sidelights

Illustrator and writer Tom Cross combines traditional art techniques with modern computer image technology to create his lush illustrations of wizards, nature, and fairies. "My paintings are ancient in content and look, but I use both traditional tools and tools of the future to implement them," Cross said in a profile on his Web site *The Wondrous Worlds of Tom Cross.* Using a computer to visualize, manipulate, and experiment with the image releases Cross from the physical restrictions of illustration—such as cleaning brushes and finding the right materials—and "frees up the creative process to

be more responsive to the ideas and inspiration when it begins to really flow," he continued.

Cross often begins his illustrations with a traditional hand-drawn sketch that is scanned in or captured from video and turned into an electronic computer file. Using Photoshop and a Wacom drawing tablet, Cross then works on the image digitally, adding, changing, resizing, and "drawing" with pixels rather than ink or paint. "Much time and care is spent in pushing pixels as one would paint traditionally at this stage to build up the color, detail, and overall finished look of the work," Cross explained. Using computer image technology, "I can almost move, resize, re-configure, and experiment as fast and furious as the ideas and possibilities pop into my head," Cross commented on his Web site.

A major benefit of using the computer is that each drawing variation or new experiment can be saved as a separate illustration; there is no need to start over from the beginning if some new addition to the picture does not work or if Cross is not happy with the way the illustration is coming together. Using electronic files, Cross can always pick up at any point where he left off and try something different, all the while leaving the basic illustration intact and ready to be worked on again. "You can experiment, make mistakes, let the happy accidents and discoveries occur," Cross remarked on his Web site. "The paint is never dry. No mistake is forever!"

Cross checks each drawing from a photo-quality printout, then sends to image to a giclée printer. Giclée (pronounced ZHEE-clay, and derived from the French word for "squirt") is a special type of printing process where microscopic dots of archival-quality inks are sprayed at high speed onto fine art paper, canvas, or other material. The process creates extremely high-quality prints that are so good, they are often hard to tell from originals. Using giclée, "The artist gets the best possible reproduction of his or her work, [and] the collector [gets] an exquisite print," Cross explained. Once the giclée print is prepared, Cross will often add to the print with acrylics, colored pencils, pastels, or other art materials. The final result, he observed, is "a very unique, not reproducible original work. A bit backwards I guess in that the original often comes last!"

In *Fairy Garden: Fairies of the Four Seasons,* Cross and collaborator Constance Barkley Lewis present a look at the mystical worlds where fantasy and nature meet. The book contains almost fifty images of fairies for each season, accompanied by Lewis's poetry. Similarly, in *The Way of Wizards,* Cross creates an entire world populated by crafty mages and wise wizards. The book is "gorgeously illustrated" and "physically beautiful," wrote a reviewer in *Globe and Mail.* The book contains more than 200 illustrations depicting "the fantastical world of wizards," wrote Gregory Harris in an interview with Cross on the *BookPage* Web site. "At times," Harris observed, "the book resembles a tome from a wizard's library."

Cross's artwork displays a deep respect for nature and other living creatures on Earth, an attitude that is reinforced by his education in zoology and background as a coastal ecologist. As a scientist and specialist in barrier island and beach ecology, Cross has worked with organizations such as the Cousteau Society, the Conservation Program, and the National Estuary Program. Whether writing, teaching, or illustrating ecological subjects, Cross uses a combination of folklore and scientific fact to present his message. "I try to explain nature and ecological principles in a lighthearted way," Cross commented in a biography on his Web site. "Seeing how our predecessors viewed the world around them—through their stories, their art, and their superstitions—often softens the blow and makes learning about our world much more enjoyable."

"It's so easy with our busy pace of life and technology out there—faxes, phones, modems—to forget the medium that we are all swimming through together," Cross continued. "And that is nature." While Cross may not consider himself a wizard, he recognizes that under-standing and explaining nature often requires a little bit of magic. "If you think about it, every culture has wizards, whatever they call them," he remarked in the *BookPage* interview. "It's usually been the guy or the woman who was most in tune with nature."

Biographical and Critical Sources

PERIODICALS

Globe and Mail, December 1, 2001, review of *The Way of Wizards*, p. D23.

ONLINE

BookPage, http://www.bookpage.com/ (June 17, 2003), Gregory Harris, interview with Tom Cross.
Wondrous Worlds of Tom Cross, http://www.tomcross-artist.com/ (September 3, 2003).*

D

DAVOL, Marguerite W. 1928-

Personal

Born July 2, 1928, in East Peoria, IL; daughter of Eugene P. Welcher (a real estate broker) and Vera Ruth Peteit (maiden name, Huber); married Stephen H. Davol (a psychology professor), March 19, 1950 (deceased, July 8, 1982); married Robert L. Greenberg (an engineer), September 12, 1992; children: Susan M. Carlson, Jonathan Davol, Sarah R. Davol-Kelley. *Education:* University of Colorado, B.A., 1951; graduate work at Kansas State University, 1953-54, and University of Rochester, 1955-56. *Politics:* Democrat. *Hobbies and other interests:* Music, children's theater.

Addresses

Home—124 College St., #19, South Hadley, MA 01075-0578; New Hampshire. *E-mail*—davol@ttlc.net.

Career

Rocky Ford Junior High School, Rocky Ford, CO, teacher, 1952-53; various part-time town and school library jobs, 1953-64; Gorse Child Study Center, Mount Holyoke College, South Hadley, MA, preschool teacher, 1964-92. Active in local Parent-Teacher Associations and Know Your Town. Leader of school workshops on creative writing and storytelling. Speaker at numerous storytelling, reading, and children's literature conferences.

Member

Society of Children's Book Writers and Illustrators (national and New England chapters), League for the Advancement of New England Storytelling, National Storytelling Association.

Awards, Honors

Honor Book citation, *Storytelling World,* Pick of the Lists citation, American Booksellers Association, Notable Book citation, American Library Association, Notable Children's Trade Books in the Field of Social Studies citation, National Council for the Social Studies/

Marguerite W. Davol

Children's Book Council, Parents' Choice Honor Book, and Golden Kite Award, Society of Children's Book Writers and Illustrators, all 1998, all for *The Paper Dragon;* Dr. Toy's Best Children's Products citation and Best Socially Responsible Products citation, both 2001, both for *Why Butterflies Go By on Silent Wings.*

Writings

The Heart of the Wood, illustrated by Sheila Hamanaka, Simon & Schuster (New York, NY), 1992. Black,

White, Just Right!, illustrated by Irene Trivas, A. Whitman (Morton Grove, IL), 1993.

Papa Alonzo Leatherby: A Collection of Tall Tales from the Best Storyteller in Carroll County, illustrated by Rebecca Leer, Simon & Schuster (New York, NY), 1995.

How Snake Got His Hiss, illustrated by Mercedes McDonald, Orchard (New York, NY), 1996.

Batwings and the Curtain of Night, illustrated by Mary GrandPré, Orchard (New York, NY), 1997.

The Paper Dragon, illustrated by Robert Sabuda, Atheneum (New York, NY), 1997.

The Loudest, Fastest, Best Drummer in Kansas, illustrated by Cat Bowman Smith, Orchard (New York, NY), 2000.

Why Butterflies Go By on Silent Wings, illustrated by Robert Roth, Orchard (New York, NY), 2001.

The Snake's Tales, illustrated by Yumi Heo, Orchard (New York, NY), 2002.

Contributor of short story "Flesh and Blood" to *Werewolves,* Harper (New York, NY), 1988. *The Paper Dragon* was included in the "McGraw Hill Reading" text book for fifth grade.

Sidelights

A former preschool teacher, Marguerite W. Davol has put her experience to work in a selection of picture books that are firmly rooted in the tradition of fable and folktale. Although her stories are original, they are considered to have a timeless quality because they seek to explain such elemental questions as how the world began and why butterflies are so brightly colored and so silent. Davol is also at home with the tall tale. Her award-winning 1997 title *The Paper Dragon* illuminates the resourceful mind of an ordinary man challenged by a fire-breathing dragon, while *Papa Alonzo Leatherby: A Collection of Tall Tales from the Best Storyteller in Carroll County* is a collection of improbable pioneer stories. To quote a *Publishers Weekly* reviewer, the author's "narrative images are palpable enough to conjure up a new world in readers's minds."

Davol's cumulative tale *The Heart of the Wood* follows a sycamore tree from the forest, where it is felled by a woodcutter, to the sawmill, then to a craftsman's table, where the lumber is made into a fiddle, and finally, into a musician's hands, where the fiddle makes joyous music. "Davol sheds some gentle light on the interconnected worlds of art and nature in her first picture book," wrote a *Publishers Weekly* critic. *Bulletin of the Center for Children's Books* contributor Betsy Hearne found the book's success in its "merging of a subject—singing and dancing—with a style that sings and dances." Critics also commended Sheila Hamanaka's illustrations, which Lisa Dennis described as "rich and vivid" in a *School Library Journal* review.

In *Black, White, Just Right!,* Davol gives voice to the child of a mixed-race marriage who cheerfully expresses her parents' differences and proudly declares herself, "Just right!" Hazel Rochman, writing in *Booklist,* lauded the book for highlighting the individuality of the family members, as each cultivates tastes and pursues interests that are not limited by stereotype or convention. Dad, who is white, dances to rap, while Mom, who is black, prefers ballet. A *Publishers Weekly* critic expressed concern that the book failed to address any of the problems a child in this situation might face outside the family, but added, "The book's upbeat tone is welcoming and refreshing."

Both *How Snake Got His Hiss* and *Batwings and the Curtain of Night* are *pourquoi* tales, about snakes and bats respectively. Snake begins as a round creature who must puff himself up and roll from place to place. This proves so disruptive to the other animals that eventually Elephant steps on him, flattening him and leaving him with a perpetual hiss. Writing in *Booklist,* Janice M. Del Negro commended the story for its "dynamic forward momentum and a satisfying, cumulative plot line." A *Publishers Weekly* reviewer suggested that the wealth of silly sounds and misadventures "will have preschoolers rolling—and eventually slithering—around on the floor." In *Batwings and the Curtain of Night,* the Mother of All Things shakes her skirts, and all living things roll out of them to live on the Earth. It is the bats who become fascinated with the "curtain of night" and tear holes in it with their claws. According to *Booklist* contributor Susan Dove Lempke, in this read-aloud, "the story and illustrations almost dance off the page."

The author enjoys creating fanciful stories featuring human beings, too. Papa Alonzo Leatherby, in the book of the same title, goes out on the coldest night of the year and tells stories. When his words freeze, his wife puts them in jars to save. One by one the stories are taken out, thawed, and retold, each sillier and more outrageous than the last. "Readers who love nonsense and absurdity will find these entertaining," a *Kirkus Reviews* critic stated. Another tall tale unfolds in *The Loudest, Fastest, Best Drummer in Kansas.* Feisty Maggie of Serena, Kansas, is a born drummer who dismantles her crib in search of a way to beat out rhythms. At age six, she gets her first real drum—and promptly raises a ruckus through town. Only after Maggie has foiled a plague of wasps and a deadly tornado is her talent welcomed by the other townspeople. A *Publishers Weekly* reviewer liked Maggie's "true spitfire nature" and noted that Davol "finds a happy beat with this boisterous story." In *Booklist,* Todd Morning observed that the "goofy and implausible humor" gives the tale "a certain retro appeal."

One of Davol's best known works is *The Paper Dragon.* She teamed with illustrator Robert Sabuda to create the story of Mi Fei, a Chinese artist who is called upon to save his village from a ferocious, fire-breathing dragon. Mi Fei, scrolls and paints in hand, accepts three challenges from the dragon and through quick thinking solves all three. The book abounds in gate-fold illustrations that communicate the dragon's massive size and strength—as opposed to Mi Fei's diminutive stature. A winner of multiple awards and citations, *The Paper Dragon* was warmly reviewed by most critics. *Horn Book* correspondent Hanna B. Zeiger deemed it "a strong tale with plenty of action for the story-hour

Maggie shakes up the town with her drumming in **The Loudest, Fastest, Best Drummer in Kansas,** *by Marguerite W. Davol.* (Illustrated by Cat Bowman Smith.)

audience." In her *Booklist* review, Susan Dove Lempke noted that the book is "so cleverly crafted it sounds as if it has been told for centuries." A *Publishers Weekly* critic concluded: "Both artists have come together to celebrate their gifts in this ode to the simplest of all: love."

Why Butterflies Go By on Silent Wings explains how the colorful insects acquired their looks and nature. In the beginning of time, butterflies were drab and noisy, complaining and bickering amongst themselves. When a thunderstorm knocks them into the mud, the butterflies emerge with a new respect for nature, as well as with more colorful wings. *School Library Journal* critic Joy Fleishhacker felt that the story "is well written and the language is evocative." She added: "There is a lot to think about here."

People and animals interact in *The Snake's Tales*, an adaptation of a traditional Seneca story. In a time before stories, a family works hard to make a living. When Father and Mother send the children out to gather fruit, a wily snake strikes a bargain. In return for the fruit, the snake will tell the children some stories. Never having heard of stories, the children agree. Only when the bargain includes apples does Father discover what has been happening to the fruit as he sees the lumpy snake in the forest. All is well when the children share the tales the snake has told them. A *Publishers Weekly* reviewer found *The Snake's Tale* a "pleasing, original story" with "folktale rhythm and simple imagery." *Booklist*'s Connie Fletcher called the picture book "imaginative." Fletcher added that the narrative "cleverly contemplates the genesis of storytelling—an activity close to the hearts of us all."

"I've had a long apprenticeship—over twenty-five years—in learning to write children's books," Davol once told *SATA*. "And I am still learning!

"As a preschool teacher in a college laboratory school with excellent library facilities, I was able to choose

A mystical snake charms two children with his stories, in Davol's Snake's Tales, *illustrated by Yumi Heo.*

Davol spins a tale about noise in **Why Butterflies Go by on Silent Wings.** *(Illustrated by Rob Roth.)*

from an extensive collection of books, books which we read every day. I soon learned from experience those which appealed, those which failed to capture the interest and imagination of young children. I learned which books were too old or too young, too long or too dull, and those with unappealing illustrations. And why were some books literally worn out from children's choosing to look at them over and over and others not given a second glance? I worked at sharpening my critical sense of what a child's book should be.

"Throughout all my years of teaching, I often could not find just the right story or poem or song to fit whatever themes or ideas I wished to explore with the children. I began to write my own stories, songs, and poems, often with input from the children themselves. Searching for just the right word, the appropriate metaphor, was a challenge and a struggle. No less difficult was learning to hear with an inner ear the rhythm and texture and sound of my words. I learned from my successes and failures. (A wiggling four year old announcing loudly, 'I'm tired!' is a most honest critic!)"

Biographical and Critical Sources

BOOKS

Davol, Marguerite W., *Black, White, Just Right!*, A. Whitman (Morton Grove, IL), 1993.

PERIODICALS

Booklist, November 1, 1993, Hazel Rochman, review of *Black, White, Just Right!*, p. 528; April 15, 1996, Janice M. Del Negro, review of *How Snake Got His Hiss,* p. 1445; April 15, 1997, Susan Dove Lempke, review of *Batwings and the Curtain of Night,* p. 1434; October 15, 1997, Susan Dove Lempke, review of *The Paper Dragon,* p. 402; March 15, 2000, Todd Morning, review of *The Loudest, Fastest, Best Drummer in Kansas,* p. 1386; January 1, 2003, Connie Fletcher, review of *The Snake's Tales,* p. 904.

Bulletin of the Center for Children's Books, February, 1993, Betsy Hearne, review of *The Heart of the Wood,* p. 173.

Horn Book, January-February, 1998, Hanna B. Zeiger, review of *The Paper Dragon,* p. 63.

Kirkus Reviews, October 15, 1995, review of *Papa Alonzo Leatherby: A Collection of Tall Tales from the Best Storyteller in Carroll County,* p. 1489.

Publishers Weekly, August 10, 1992, review of *The Heart of the Wood,* p. 69; October 25, 1993, review of *Black, White, Just Right!,* p. 62; January 29, 1996, review of *How Snake Got His Hiss,* p. 100; March 3, 1997, review of *Batwings and the Curtain of Night,* p. 75; September 29, 1997, review of *The Paper Dragon,* p. 88; March 6, 2000, review of *The Loudest, Fastest, Best Drummer in Kansas,* p. 110; July 22, 2002, review of *The Snake's Tales,* p. 177.

School Library Journal, October, 1992, Lisa Dennis, review of *The Heart of the Wood,* p. 86; May, 2000, Ginny Gustin, review of *The Loudest, Fastest, Best Drummer in Kansas,* p. 139; August, 2001, Joy Fleishhacker, review of *Why Butterflies Go By on Silent Wings,* p. 144; September, 2002, Susan Pine, review of *The Snake's Tales,* p. 183.

ONLINE

Marguerite Davol, Author, http://www.author-illustr-source.com/margueritedavol.htm/ (June 18, 2003), information about the author and her books.

Marguerite W. Davol Home Page, http://www.margueritewdavol.com/ (January 4, 2004).

*　　　*　　　*

DICKINSON, Mary-Anne
See RODDA, Emily

*　　　*　　　*

DOUGHERTY, Terri (L.) 1964-
(Terri Sievert)

Personal

Born October, 1964, in Appleton, WI; daughter of Veryle (a tire store owner) and Virgie (a homemaker and bookkeeper; maiden name, Hartwig) Sievert; married Denis Dougherty (a sports copy editor), September 10, 1988; children: Kyle, Rachel, Emily. *Ethnicity:* "Caucasian." *Education:* University of Wisconsin—Oshkosh, B.S. (journalism and English), 1987. *Religion:* Lutheran. *Hobbies and other interests:* Reading, jogging, playing soccer, cross-country skiing, "playing games with my children, volunteering at my children's school," teaching Sunday school.

Addresses

Home—Appleton, WI. *Agent*—c/o Author Mail, Lucent Books, 10911 Technology Pl., San Diego, CA 92127. *E-mail*—writetd@att.net.

Career

Writer. *Oshkosh Northwestern* (newspaper), Oshkosh, WI, reporter and editor, 1987-1991; freelance writer, 1992—. University of Wisconsin—Oshkosh, teaching adjunct, 1991 and 1999-2000; Thrivent Financial for Lutherans, in corporate communications, 1996-1997.

Writings

"JAM SESSION" SERIES; EDITED BY HUSBAND, DENIS DOUGHERTY

Barry Sanders, ABDO Publishing Company (Edina, MN), 1998.

Brett Favre, ABDO Publishing Company (Edina, MN), 1999.

Kevin Garnett, ABDO Publishing Company (Edina, MN), 1999.

Lisa Leslie, ABDO Publishing Company (Edina, MN), 1999.

Tara Lipinski, ABDO Publishing Company (Edina, MN), 1999.

Mark McGwire, ABDO Publishing Company (Edina, MN), 1999.

Sammy Sosa, ABDO Publishing Company (Edina, MN), 1999.

Tiger Woods, ABDO Publishing Company (Edina, MN), 1999.

Terrell Davis, ABDO Publishing Company (Edina, MN), 1999.

Jeff Gordon, ABDO Publishing Company (Edina, MN), 1999.

Kobe Bryant, ABDO Publishing Company (Edina, MN), 2000.

Derek Jeter, ABDO Publishing Company (Edina, MN), 2000.

Kurt Warner, ABDO Publishing Company (Edina, MN), 2000.

Mia Hamm, ABDO Publishing Company (Edina, MN), 2000.

Ken Griffey, Jr., ABDO Publishing Company (Edina, MN), 2001.

Shaquille O'Neal, ABDO Publishing Company (Edina, MN), 2001.

Barry Bonds, ABDO Publishing Company (Edina, MN), 2002.

Ichiro Suzuki, ABDO Publishing Company (Edina, MN), 2004.

Tony Hawk, ABDO Publishing Company (Edina, MN), 2004.

"PEOPLE IN THE NEWS" SERIES

Brad Pitt, Lucent Books (San Diego, CA), 2002.
Prince William, Lucent Books (San Diego, CA), 2002.
Julia Roberts, Lucent Books (San Diego, CA), 2003.
Tim Allen, Lucent Books (San Diego, CA), 2003.
Elijah Wood, Lucent Books (San Diego, CA), 2004.

UNDER NAME TERRI SIEVERT

The World's Fastest Superbikes, Capstone Press (Mankato, MN), 2002.
The World's Fastest Trains, Capstone Press (Mankato, MN), 2002.
U.S. Airforce at War, Capstone Press (Mankato, MN), MN, 2002.
U.S. Army at War, Capstone Press (Mankato, MN), 2002.
Illinois, Capstone Press (Mankato, MN), 2003.
Texas, Capstone Press (Mankato, MN), 2003.
Motocross Racing, Capstone Press (Mankato, MN), 2004.
Dirt Bike History, Edge Books (Mankato, MN), 2004.
Loch Ness Monster, Edge Books (Mankato, MN), in press.
UFOs, Edge Books (Mankato, MN), in press.

OTHER

Sam Walton, Blackbirch Press (San Diego, CA), 2004.
Argentina, Lucent Books (San Diego, CA), 2004.

Contributor of "Family Fun," a weekly column that offers family activity ideas, to the *Post-Crescent* (Appleton, WI). Contributor to numerous magazines and newspapers.

Work in Progress

French and the Fox: The Cannon Battle over Wisconsin's Fur Trade; Syria, for Lucent Books (San Diego, CA).

Sidelights

Terri Dougherty has combined the two major interests in her life, family and writing, into a successful career as an author of children's books. Dougherty told *SATA,* "I have wanted to be a writer ever since my first book, 'The Farm Mystery,' was published (stapled together) by my third-grade teacher. My desire to write was nurtured by my love of reading, from 'Nancy Drew' books to *Harriet the Spy.*" After earning her degree in journalism and English from the University of Wisconsin—Oshkosh, she began work as a reporter, a background that "greatly helped my career as a freelance writer, teaching me how to write concisely and quickly as well as providing research and interview skills." Specializing in nonfiction accounts of interesting people, she has written biographical sketches about contemporary athletes and people in the news.

The "Jam Session" series offers slim volumes about individual athletes that give brief personal histories and highlight professional achievements. In her *Horn Book Guide* review of eight books in the "Jam Session" series, Carrie Harasimowicz described the books as "an enthusiastic introduction for new fans." Although reviewers noted that the volumes are short, *School Library Journal* critic Tom S. Hurlburt, reviewing *Mark McGwire* and *Sammy Sosa,* commented that "these highly visual titles are serviceable introductions for young and reluctant readers."

Dougherty does not confine her efforts to sports alone. Other books of interest cover businessmen, actors, actresses, and the U.S. Army and Airforce. Dougherty told *SATA*, "My favorite part of my job is learning something new every day. I hope I am passing this love of learning on to my children and all those who read my books."

Biographical and Critical Sources

PERIODICALS

Horn Book Guide, January-June, 1999, Carrie Harasimowicz, review of "Jam Session" series, p. 365; January-June, 2001, Carrie Harasimowicz, review of "Jam Session" series, p. 396.
School Library Journal, August, 1999, Tom S. Hurlburt, review of *Mark McGwire* and *Sammy Sosa,* pp. 145-146, and Barb Lawler, review of *Lisa Leslie* and *Tara Lipinski,* p. 145; August, 2003, Kathleen Simonetta, review of *Iowa,* p. 147.

*   *   *

DRAPER, Sharon M(ills) 1950-

Personal

Born 1950, in Cleveland, OH; daughter of Victor D. (a hotel manager) and Catherine (a gardener) Mills; married Larry E. Draper (an educator); children: Wendy, Damon, Crystal, Cory. *Ethnicity:* "African American." *Education:* Pepperdine University, B.A., 1971; Miami

In **Mark McGwire,** *author Terri Dougherty gets up close and personal with the baseball legend.*

University (Oxford, OH), M.A. *Hobbies and other interests:* Reading; "I won't read junk; there's no time to waste on poorly written books."

Addresses

Office—P.O. Box 36551, Cincinnati, OH 45236.

Career

Public speaker, poet, and author. Walnut Hills High School, Cincinnati, OH, English teacher and head of department, 1972—; Mayerson Academy, associate; Duncanson artist-in-residence at Taft Museum.

Member

International Reading Association, American Federation of Teachers, National Board for Professional Teaching Standards (member of board of directors, 1995—), National Council of Teachers of English, Ohio Council of Teachers of English Language Arts, Conference on English Leadership, Delta Kappa Gamma, Phi Delta Kappa, Women's City Club.

Awards, Honors

First prize, *Ebony* Literary Contest, 1991, for short story "One Small Torch"; Coretta Scott King Genesis Award, American Library Association (ALA), Best

Book for Young Adults, ALA, Best Books, Children's Book Council (CBC)/Bank Street College, Books for the Teen Age, New York Public Library, and Notable Trade Book in the Field of Social Studies, National Council for the Social Studies, all 1995, for *Tears of a Tiger,* and all 1998, for *Forged by Fire;* named Outstanding High School English Language Arts Educator, Ohio Council of Teachers of English Language Arts, 1995; Midwest regional winner, National Council of Negro Women Excellence in Teaching Award, 1996; Ohio Governor's Educational Leadership Award, 1996; National Teacher of the Year, 1997; ALA Best Book designation, International Reading Association (IRA) Notable Book designation, and Books for the Teen Age designee, New York Public Library, all 2000, all for *Romiette and Julio;* IRA Children's Choice, 2001, and IRA Young-Adult Choice, 2003, both for *Darkness before Dawn;* CBC Notable Social Studies Trade Book, and ALA among ALA Top Ten Sports Books, both 2003, both for *Double Dutch;* Milken Family Foundation National Educator Award; YWCA Career Woman of Achievement; Dean's Award, Howard University School of Education; Pepperdine University Distinguished Alumnus Award; Marva Collins Education Excellence Award; named Ohio State Department of Education Pioneer in Education. Honorary degrees include D.H.L, College of Mount Saint Joseph, and D.H., Cincinnati State University.

Writings

FOR YOUNG ADULTS

Tears of a Tiger, Simon and Schuster (New York, NY), 1994.
Forged by Fire, Simon and Schuster (New York, NY), 1997.
Romiette and Julio, Simon and Schuster (New York, NY), 1999.
Jazzimagination, Scholastic (New York, NY), 1999.
Darkness before Dawn, Simon and Schuster (New York, NY), 2001.
Double Dutch, Simon and Schuster, 2002.
The Battle of Jericho, Simon and Schuster, 2003.

FOR CHILDREN

Ziggy and the Black Dinosaurs, Just Us Books (East Orange, NJ), 1994.
Lost in the Tunnel of Time, Just Us Books, (East Orange, NJ), 1996.
Shadows of Caesar's Creek, Just Us Books (East Orange, NJ), 1997.

FOR ADULTS

Teaching from the Heart: Reflections, Encouragement, and Inspiration, Heinemann (Portsmouth, NH), 2000.

Not Quite Burned out but Crispy around the Edges: Inspiration, Laughter, and Encouragement for Teachers, Heinemann (Portsmouth, NH), 2001.

Also author of *Let the Circle Be Unbroken* (children's poetry), and *Buttered Bones* (poetry for adults). Contributor of poems and short stories to literary magazines; contributor of essay "The Touch of a Teacher" to *What Governors Need to Know about Education,* Center for Policy Research of the National Governor's Association.

Adaptations

Draper's books have been recorded on audiocassette, Recorded Books.com.

Sidelights

Sharon M. Draper is a teacher and writer with a philosophy that guides her in how she teaches and what she writes. That philosophy is evident in remarks she made about being honored as the 1997 National Teacher of the Year: "It is a wonderful honor, but also an awesome responsibility—to be the spokesperson and advocate for education in America. I was ready for this challenge, however, because I had been preparing for this work my entire life." Reading, teaching, and writing are all connected for Draper, who wanted to be a teacher since childhood. As she once told an interviewer, "I was an avid reader. I read every single book in the elementary school library, all of them. I did not plan to be a writer until much, much later. I tell students all the time that in order to be a good writer it is necessary first to be a good reader. You need some information in your head. Reading is input. Writing is output. You can't write without input."

Born to Victor and Catherine Mills in Cleveland, Ohio, Draper was the eldest of three children raised in a close-knit neighborhood. Her father worked as a hotel manager and her mother as an administrator at the *Cleveland Plain Dealer.* Theirs was a family where education was a given. The question was not "would you attend college, it was where and to study what," Draper explained in her interview. Draper entered Cleveland Public Schools in the 1950s from a home where she had grown up surrounded by books. Her mother read stories, poems, fairytales, and nursery rhymes to Draper and her siblings from the time they were very young. She recalls a teacher who once "gave me O's for outstanding, saying an A wasn't good enough." A fifth grade teacher gave Draper and her fellow students poetry by Langston Hughes and Robert Frost. They read and loved Shakespeare. "We didn't know we weren't supposed to be able to do that in fifth grade. She gave it to us and we loved it," Draper said. "It was part of making me the teacher I am today."

Draper attended Pepperdine University as a National Merit Scholar, majoring in English. Upon graduation in 1971, she returned to Ohio where she married and assumed a teaching position in Cincinnati Public Schools where she still works. Her experience teaching public school since 1972 has given her some definite ideas on the reading habits of teens. "I know what kids like—what they will read, and what they won't. Although I have nothing against Charles Dickens, many teenagers would rather gag than read him. Dickens wrote for his contemporaries—young people of a hundred and fifty years ago. American students might need to know about the world of London in the 1860s, but they would much rather read about their own world first. Not only will they read about recognizable experiences with pleasure, but they will also be encouraged to write as well."

According to an essayist in the *St. James Guide to Young Adult Writers,* "Draper's works address the problems African Americans face in a predominantly white society, specifically stereotyping of black males. They also examine the dynamics of African American families and communities. Her . . . fiction is energetic and intense, as characters become self aware and attain emotional growth. She often creates mystery plots as a means for characters to be introspective and explore their identities. She sets her books in Cincinnati where she lives and teaches, suggesting a familiarity with her characters and community that enhances their realism."

In 1994 Draper began her "Ziggy" series, writing for a young audience about African-American history and folklore. Ziggy and his friends, who call themselves the Black Dinosaurs, begin their adventures in the first book, *Ziggy and the Black Dinosaurs,* In the second book, *Lost in the Tunnel of Time,* Ziggy and friends, on a field trip to the Ohio River, learn about the Underground Railroad and the tunnels the slaves used to escape the South. In the third volume, *Shadows of Caesar's Creek,* Draper makes connections between African Americans and Native Americans.

In 1994 Draper published the young-adult novel *Tears of a Tiger,* a story about Andy Jackson, a black youth who struggles to make sense of the death of his best friend, Robert, in an automobile accident in which Andy was the driver. Andy must live with his friend's last words: "Oh God, please don't let me die like this! Andy!" The two teenagers had been drinking beer with their friends Tyrone and B. J. in celebration of a victory by their high school basketball team. Tyrone and B. J. are able to move past the awful pain caused by the accident: Tyrone finds support from his girlfriend Rhonda, B. J. through religion. Andy, however, is racked with guilt, grief, and pain that does not subside with time.

According to critics, *Tears of a Tiger* shows the difficulties in healing a damaged teenager. Draper also places in her narrative characters who represent institutional attitudes confronting the young black male: In one episode, teachers discuss how Andy's grief cannot be all that serious since he is black. Andy also internalizes ideas about himself that prevent him from realizing his full capabilities; for example, he thinks he cannot be

successful academically because he is a basketball player. Merri Monks, writing in *Booklist,* observed that "Andy's perceptions of the racism directed toward young black males—by teachers, guidance counselors, and clerks in shopping malls—will be recognized by African American YAs."

Critics of *Tears of a Tiger* found that Draper effectively uses dialog to advance the story. Kathy Fritts, writing in the *School Library Journal,* pointed out that "the characters' voices are strong, vivid, and ring true. This moving novel will leave a deep impression." Furthermore, Draper's use of news stories, journal entries, homework assignments, and letters give the novel an immediacy that adds to its power. Although some critics faulted Draper for a tendency to be preachy, most commented similarly to Monks, who remarked that the work's "characters and their experiences will captivate teen readers." In *Publishers Weekly,* a reviewer concluded that "the combination of raw energy and intense emotions should stimulate readers." Dorothy M. Broderick, critiquing the work in *Voice of Youth Advocates,* wrote: "Suffice to say, not only is Draper an author to watch for, but that this is as compelling a novel as any published in the last two decades." Roger Sutton, writing in the *Bulletin of the Center for Children's Books,* stated that "rather than a tidy summary of suicide symptoms and 'ways to help,' readers instead get a grave portrait of unceasing despair and a larger picture of how young African-American men like Andy get lost in a system that will not trust or reach out to them." *Tears of a Tiger* received several honors, including the Coretta Scott King Genesis Award.

Forged by Fire, the 1997 sequel to *Tears of a Tiger,* has a similar socially relevant focus. Child sexual abuse and drug addiction replace suicide and racism, yet both books reach a tragic finality. Draper wrote *Forged by Fire*'s first chapter as a short story, "One Small Torch," published in *Ebony.* The novel went on to win Draper her second Coretta Scott King Award.

Gerald Nickelby—a minor character in *Tears of a Tiger*—at age three was burned in a fire when left alone by his mother, Monique. After his hospital stay, Gerald goes to live with his Aunt Queen, a loving and supportive woman. Six years later, Monique reenters Gerald's life after Aunt Queen dies. Monique has married Jordan Sparks, the father of Angel, Gerald's new half-sister. Gerald learns that Sparks has sexually abused Angel and through the testimony of the children, Sparks is sent to prison. When Sparks returns six years later, Monique, who indulges too much in drugs, lets him return to family life where he once again attempts to sexually harm Angel.

Tom S. Hurlburt, reviewing *Forged by Fire* in *School Library Journal,* assessed the book's impact this way: "There's no all's-well ending, but readers will have hope for Gerald and Angel, who have survived a number of gut-wrenching ordeals by relying on their constant love and caring for one another." Candace Smith, writing in *Booklist,* concluded that "Draper faces some big issues (abuse, death, drugs) and provides concrete options and a positive African American role model in Gerald."

In *Darkness before Dawn* Draper tells the story of high schooler Keisha Montgomery, who has just lost her ex-boyfriend to suicide and now must deal with an overly-aggressive track coach. Debbie Carton in *Booklist* believed that "the graduation scene, in which class president Keisha gives the closing speech, is moving and triumphant, showing Draper and her vibrant characters at their best." While Angela J. Reynolds in *School Library Journal* found that "readers may be overwhelmed by the soap-opera feel of this issue-laden world," Odette Cornwall, writing in the *Journal of Adolescent and Adult Literacy,* concluded that "not only did Draper make Keisha real, but she also wove many prominent social issues faced by young adults today into the story line."

Double Dutch concerns a group of eighth graders with serious problems. Delia cannot read and does not want anyone to find out; her friend Randy fears that his father has deserted the family; and the violent Tolliver twins scare their new classmates. "Draper adeptly paints a convincing portrayal of how young people think, act, feel, and interact with one another," Connie Tyrrell Burns commented in *School Library Journal.* A critic for *Kirkus Reviews* found that "Delia and her friends are delightful, and the reader is rooting for them all the way."

Draper once commented: "I feel very blessed that I have had so much success in such a short time. I hope that my books can continue to make a difference in the lives of young people." In a statement posted on her Web site, Draper proclaimed: "I approach the world with the eyes of an artist, the ears of a musician, and the soul of a writer. I see rainbows where others see only rain, and possibilities when others see only problems."

Biographical and Critical Sources

BOOKS

Contemporary Black Biography, Gale (Detroit, MI), Volume 16, 1998.

St. James Guide to Young Adult Writers, 2nd edition, St. James Press (Detroit, MI), 1999.

PERIODICALS

American Libraries, June, 1995, "Two New Awards," p. 487.

American Visions, December-January, 1995, p. 39.

Booklist, November 1, 1994, p. 492; April 1, 1995, p. 1416; March 15, 1996, p. 1278; February 15, 1997, pp. 1016-1017; January 1, 2001, review of *Darkness before Dawn,* p. 939.

Bulletin of the Center for Children's Books, January, 1995, p. 164; June, 1997, p. 355.

Children's Book Review Service, February, 1997, p. 82.

Children's Bookwatch, February, 1995, p. 3.

Christian Science Monitor, May 5, 1997, David Holmstrom, "America's Top Teacher Gives Tough Assignments—And Plenty of Support," p. 12.

Ebony, December, 1990, pp. C18-19.

Emergency Librarian, September, 1996, p. 24.

English Journal, January, 1996, p. 87.

Journal of Adolescent and Adult Literacy, April, 2002, Arina Zonnenberg, review of *Romiette and Julio,* p. 660, and Odette Cornwall, review of *Darkness before Dawn,* p. 661.

Kirkus Reviews, December 1, 1996, p. 1735; June 1, 2002, review of *Double Dutch,* p. 804.

Ohioana, 2002, Virginia Schaefer Horvath, review *Darkness before Dawn.*

Publishers Weekly, October 31, 1994, p. 64; January 15, 1996, p. 463; March 25, 1996, p. 85; December 16, 1996, p. 61; June 17, 2002, review of *Double Dutch,* p. 66.

School Library Journal, February, 1995, p. 112; March, 1995, p. 202; August, 1996, p. 142; March, 1997, p. 184; September, 1999, Jane Halsall, review of *Romiette and Julio,* p. 222; February, 2001, Angela J. Reynolds, review of *Darkness before Dawn,* p. 117; June, 2002, Connie Tyrrell Burns, review of *Double Dutch,* p. 137.

Social Education, April, 1995, p. 215.

USA Today, April 17, 1997, "An 'A' for Creativity: Variety Is on Teacher of the Year's Lesson Plan," p. D4.

Voice of Youth Advocates, February, 1995, p. 338; June, 1997, p. 108; December, 1999, Deborah L. Dubois, review of *Romiette and Julio.*

ONLINE

Ohio Department of Education Web site, http://schoolimprovement.ode.ohio.gov/ (June 5, 1998), "Sharon Draper.".

Sharon Draper Web site, http://sharondraper.com/ (November 4, 2003).

Autobiography Feature

Sharon M(ills) Draper

Earliest Memories

I guess I always knew I was going to be a teacher, but I had no idea that I'd become a writer as well. Sometimes you choose your path; sometimes the path is chosen for you. Of course I couldn't know any of that when I was an infant, but the paths were being drawn for me even before I was born. After eating a ham and egg sandwich on the way to the hospital, and for some reason that's my favorite kind of sandwich still, my mother gave birth to me on a hot sunny day in August. My father's birthday was the twelfth of August, and I was supposed to be born on his birthday, but I waited almost two weeks until the twenty-first to make my arrival into the world. Children born in August are supposedly sunny and cheerful, and I certainly filled that bill. I loved the warmth of the sunshine on me—it made me feel warm and loved. Which I was. Fiercely. Since I was the first-born child, my mother treated me like a princess. She sang to me constantly—my earliest memories are filled with song. She had a beautiful, operatic voice—she sang first soprano and should have been a

Sharon M. Draper

star with the Metropolitan opera, but she gave up any chances for a career in singing because she fell in love with my dad, got married, and had me. I remember her voice as she hung up clothes outside to dry, as she fixed dinner, as she worked in the huge flower garden she grew in the front of our house. She filled our house with laughter, music, and song. And books. Lots of books. My mother read to me even before I could walk or talk. One of my earliest memories is the sound of my mother's voice, reading to me. Her voice, melodic and beautiful, drew images for me in my mind as she read of cats and queens and pretty maids all in a row. I remember the "lullaby lady from hush-a-bye street" who lulled me to slumber at the end of the day. Somehow that lady from the poem and my mother became intertwined in my mind as I began to carve memories from dreams.

She'd hold me tight and tell me stories. She'd read bright, colorful picture books to me, and even though I didn't know what those squiggles on the page were, I knew the pictures were glorious, and the sound of my mother's voice made the stories magic. She read tall tales and fables and wonderful stories. She read nursery rhymes and poetry. The early rhythms of those rhymes became the background for words I wouldn't write for many years to come. The itsy, bitsy spider climbed into my mind and memory. The power of "Fee-Fi-Fo-Fum" thrummed in my head, even though I was unaware that I loved the power and repetition in those words. It was the cadence of my mother's voice and the rhythm of the repetitions that first fostered my love of books and the magic of words.

By the time I was three, I knew hundreds of poems and stories and nursery rhymes, never quite sure where the reality ended and the magic began. My early years were filled with impossible notions that made sense only in the mind of a child. Of course a mouse could run up a clock and a cow could jump over a moon. I'd

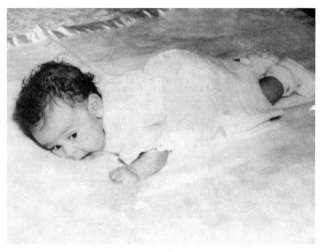

The author at two months old

never had porridge, and still have never tasted any, but that never stopped me from loving the rhythms of "pease porridge hot, pease porridge cold."

One of the earliest poems I remember begins with "I think that I shall never see/A poem lovely as a tree." It talks of leafy arms and golden boughs. A word picture formed in my head, and even now, when I look at the glory and majesty of a full grown tree silhouetted against the sky, I am awed. By the time I could walk, my mother introduced me to the library. She and I would walk to our neighborhood library once a week, where the chairs were just the right size, and the books were placed low to the floor, just at the right level for little people like me. Library visits were a special trip—it was hard to sleep the night before. I reveled in the magnificent array of books from which I could choose, especially brand new books, still crisp and un-soiled by little hands. The pages, stiff like brand new soldiers, turned slowly, almost squeaking on the binding as they opened to page after page of unimagined pleasures. I loved the crackle of the plastic coverings, the smell of the ink on the page, the feel of the thick, golden pages on my fingers, the bold words that cavorted on the pages, making nonsense, much sense, and magic. I loved Dr. Seuss and how he played with words and characters. Gentle Horton, who heard a Who, and hatched an egg. Bartholomew and his five hundred hats. Thidwick, the big-hearted Moose. The magic of McElligot's Pool.

I remember the ducks crossing a busy street in *Make Way for Ducklings*. I'd never been to Boston, and for that matter, had never seen a real duck, but that didn't make the story any less compelling. I remember the kindly face of the policeman who helped the ducks cross the street and the triumphant face of Mrs. Duck as she herded her family where it needed to go. That book led me to McCloskey's *Blueberries for Sal.* I'd certainly never encountered a bear, and I know I'd never picked blueberries, but the books became my passage-way into a world so much larger and more exciting than the small house we lived in.

I delighted in the antics of Tigger and Winnie the Pooh, not the animated, television version that children now associate with those characters, but the words and pictures which came alive as I read the books. I knew I'd recognize the Hundred Acre Woods should I ever pass by, and Christopher Robin would be a delightful playmate, I was sure, even if he did wear those short pants all the time. I remember thinking that Christopher Robin's mother had very little fashion sense!

I marched in a line with Madeline, but I wondered about the whereabouts of the mothers of all those little girls, and enjoyed the adventures of Curious George, and was lulled to sleep by the soothing words of *Good-night, Moon*.

By the time I started school, I was a fluent reader. I don't remember ever learning to read—it just happened gradually as I progressed from listening to the stories my mother read, to reading them with her, to finally reading them by myself. I breezed through kindergarten, even though the teacher frowned on children being "too advanced" and knowing "too much" before getting to her classroom. She felt that parents just didn't have the knowledge to teach a child to read, and surely I had learned something incorrectly. But since she had her hands full teaching the rest of the class how to read the "right" way, I had plenty of time to look at books and read on my own. By first and second grade, we were deeply immersed in the "Dick and Jane" books. These were the required readers that our school, and most schools in the country, used at this time. The stories surrounded a white, upper-class family that consisted of Mom, Dad, Dick, Jane, Baby Sally, and Jip the dog. They lived in a lovely house, drove a nice blue car, and nothing bad ever happened to them. "See Jane run. Run, run, Jane. Jane can hop." These were the kind of sentences found in the early books. It never occurred to me that this family did not represent my own, or those of most of the children in my class. I thrilled in their adventures, and each year, the text would become more difficult, and the adventures of Dick and Jane would get more complicated, but still, nothing worse than a rain storm ever happened. I read them, absorbed them, and even identified with the characters and adventures presented to me. It was all I had.

Actually, there was one character who was not pale and perfect. His name was Little Black Sambo, and even though I admired his resourcefulness against the tigers, he embarrassed me and made me feel inferior. Somehow, as he ate his pancakes triumphantly at the end with his mother Mumbo and his father Jumbo, little Sambo was somehow something to be laughed at, rather than admired. I rejected him and moved on to other books. I continued my weekly trips to the library, always excited about the possibilities that awaited me. I loved big books, books with chapters and plot twists, and learned to appreciate books without pictures. As I got older, and was able to go to the library by myself, I discovered Beverly Cleary. Beezus and Ramona, Henry Huggins and Ribsy—all characters I could accept, laugh

Sharon (far right) at age six, with sister Vicky and brother Jeffrey

with, and understand. Even though their world was still very uniracial, everything wasn't perfect in their world. They didn't have much money, and they had real, albeit humorous, difficulties. I'll never forget Henry Huggins trying to get that dog home in a box on the city bus!

Every summer our library sponsored a summer reading book club. The names of children who read books each week of summer vacation were put on a chart, and a small sticker was placed next to each name as a book was read. Most children read one book a week, some read two. I, however, considered this a challenge and read as many books as I could. Ten books was a slow week for me. They ran out of room for stickers next to my name and had to put stickers all on the margin and the edges of the poster board the librarians used to make the summer display. I think the highest number of books I read in a summer was 175. The next year they left extra space next to my name. I filled it up.

I discovered horses around the fourth grade after reading *Black Beauty,* and went on to devour every book Marguerite Henry ever wrote. My dream was to get to Chincoteague Island and buy my own pony. It never happened, of course.

I read all of the "Little House" books by Laura Ingalls Wilder, and then all of the books by Louisa May Alcott. Spiced up with fanciful tales of Danny Dunn and his homework machine, a brilliant invention as far as I was concerned, I proceeded to steal from the rich and feed the poor with Robin Hood, run away from home and get lost with Pinocchio and Tom Sawyer, and long for home with Heidi. I read all of Kipling, all the Baum stories about the Wizard of Oz, and delighted in Peter Pan's Neverland, where children were rulers and could fly!

I love the smell of a library, and whenever I enter I breathe deeply of that almost intoxicating library odor. It's sort of like dust and ink and magic all mixed together. The library of my childhood had wooden floors, which gleamed first thing in the morning with

fresh wax, and creaked when you tiptoed across it to find a book on the shelf. The shelves, also made of wood, held row upon row of possibilities, all brightly jacketed and waiting to be opened and discovered.

The smell of a good book, when it is opened, is powerful. The plastic jacket creaks a little, bending to accommodate the opening of the treasure it holds. The pages are slightly yellowed, sometimes a little thick, but that makes them easy to turn. Each page I turn is like a gulp—rich and delicious. The print, clear and bright, calls out to me to read.

By the time I got to the sixth grade, I had read most of the books in our small school library and most of those on the children's side of the public library. The librarians knew me by name and often let me take home ten or twelve books at a time. I read them all voraciously and took them back to be exchanged for more. One librarian in particular, Mrs. Pratt, a bespeckled woman of great girth, guided my reading, encouraged me to read wider and deeper, and even offered me new books to take home to review for the rest of the children who visited the library.

I was frustrated, however, because I had nowhere to grow. One had to be fourteen to get an adult card and I was only eleven and a half. Mrs. Pratt recognized my dilemma, and one day I walked in and she announced with great anticipation in her voice, "I have a surprise for you!"

"A new book has come in?" I asked.

"Better than that!"

"The sequel to *Caddie Woodlawn?*"

"No." She grinned like a schoolgirl, then handed me a green library card.

Now, library cards for children were yellow. Adult cards were white. I had never seen a green one. I looked at her quizzically. "What's this?" I asked.

"It's a special-permission card," she told me. "With this card, you may check out books from the adult side of the library. The green card means someone will check to make sure you don't check out books that are too grown-up for you, but as of today, the rest of the library belongs to you!" I think I saw tears in her eyes. I jumped with excitement, gave her a hug, and ran with joyful anticipation to the great adventure of reading the rest of the books in the library. I am still there. I was more a reader than a writer for most of my life. In third grade, I wrote a poem called "Clouds." I think some of the lines were, "the clouds can sometimes be so funny/ sometimes they look just like a bunny." It really wasn't a very good poem, but my teacher loved it, and it was placed in the front hall, on display for the whole school to see. I remember not being proud of it, but being a little ashamed because it was not my best work. I've always been very critical of things I write, and always wanting it to be better. Even now, when people tell me how good they think something is that I have written, I secretly wish I had changed a couple of things, improved a couple of things, and made it better.

In junior high I kept a journal of really horrible writing. It was all about teen problems and the fear of the unknown. I wrote to express some of the normal teenaged confusion I felt. It was full of passion, but not much power.

High School and College

High school and college went by in a blur. I know when you are in school, the days seem endless, and freshmen look bleakly to their senior year, because it seems as if it will never arrive. But it does, and all too quickly. I had happy, pleasant high school years. I was in the top classes, I made good grades, and I had friends. I was not the most popular girl in the school, but I had a circle of friends that I could talk to and trust. My high school was made up of an interesting mixture of races and ethnicities. African American families were just moving into the white neighborhoods, but the high school kids, regardless of their race, seemed to get along pretty well. In addition, our school had a large population of students from Slovakian heritage. Many of them had last names that were difficult for us to pronounce. Many of their parents did not speak English, being first generation immigrants, but the kids learned the language and the culture quickly, and melted into our school society with the rest of us.

As I look back at my high school yearbook, we look old, even then. Perhaps it was the hairstyles; perhaps we just wanted to look old and serious for those yearbook photos. But we looked a lot older than we felt. We had the same insecurities and fears that teenagers face today. What will happen after graduation? Will we go to college? Will we get married? What about the military? At that time, the draft was in force, and all young men who did not go to college were immediately drafted into the armed forces. Many of them were sent to Vietnam, and many of them died there. When I visit the Vietnam War Memorial in Washington, D.C., I can trace the names of boys who sat next to me in French or Biology—boys who went to war and never came home.

I was sixth in a graduating class of 602. I missed being valedictorian of the class because I've never been very good in gym, and my gym grades kept my academic average down. Most years I got straight A's and a C in gym. It bothered me, but there was nothing I could do about it. I don't remember why the valedictorian did not give the graduation speech, and why I was asked to do it instead, but that was my first major public presentation. The topic was "A Time for Us." I took the title from a song from *West Side Story,* my favorite movie at the time. I talked about how our generation would change the world. I think all graduation speeches are basically the same, but I really meant what I said.

I had the choice of lots of colleges—I was a National Merit Scholar, and I probably could have gone to any school I wanted to. But I chose Pepperdine Univer-

The author at seventeen

sity, a small, Christian college in Los Angeles, California. I picked it because it was associated with my church, and far away from home. I loved my parents, and my brother and sister, but I wanted to test my independence, and try to make it on my own. I also wanted to test my relationship with my boyfriend, who I had dated through most of high school. Actually, I'd known him all my life—there was never time when he wasn't a part of what I did. It was time to see if this was the real thing, or just a pleasant habit.

I remember the day I left for college. It was to be my first plane ride, and I'd be going alone. Now, it seems, young people have their parents pack up a U-Haul to take the microwave, the TV, furniture—plus all their clothes and earthly belongings, to their first adventure in college. I had a small trunk, a couple of suitcases, and high hopes. That's it. I remember that after the plane took off, I cried.

A family friend met me at the airport, and took me to the campus, where I was delighted to find palm trees lining the walkways, and a small, cozy campus. I encountered my first real example of racism on that first day. I found my room, chose which bed I wanted, started to unpack, and waited eagerly for my roommate to appear. She did. Tall, blond, and very surprised to see me, she wondered if perhaps I had the wrong room. I told her no, and continued to unpack. She and her parents huddled and whispered together, gesturing and pointing at me, not sure what to do.

She finally said to me, "Perhaps you'll be happier with another roommate."

"No," I told her, pretending I didn't know what she meant, "I'm sure you and I will get along just fine."

Her mother joined in the conversation. "We think you'd be happier in another room, dear."

Now, I've been taught to respect my elders, but I knew where this lady was coming from. So I took a deep breath and told her, "But I was here first. If she wants to move, that's fine with me."

They seemed to think I should be the one to leave, but I had already plotted out the corner bed next to the window, and I had no intention of leaving. "It will be better all around if you just pack up and move out now, dear," her mother insisted.

I wanted to cry. My breathing felt tight and my insides felt like they were burning. But I sat on the bed, which I had made up with my pretty orange bedspread, and refused to budge. They hurried out of the room to find an administrator to make me leave the room to which I had been assigned.

They returned with an administrator of dorms, who, instead of doing what was clearly the right thing, took me aside and suggested I give in just this once, and she'd find me a real nice room with other "colored" students, where I'd be much happier. I did cry then. But I refused to budge. I insisted that if she was unhappy with me, she should find another room. The dorm lady whispered to the parents, promised the girl a nicer room than freshmen were supposed to have, and left me alone in my little victory. Two days later, I got two roommates—one was white and one was black, and the three of us still remain close friends today.

I like the fact that I went to a small college. I gradually met most of the students on campus, and I felt like I was in a small family. I knew the teachers, and where they lived—I'd even been to their homes occasionally. They knew me, my strengths, and abilities. It felt good to be accepted. And although racism did show its ugly head occasionally, basically, I breezed through college with success and a smile.

One teacher from college I remember particularly was my freshman English teacher. He was from Tennessee, and talked with such a strong southern twang I could hardly understand him. I just knew he had to be the least intelligent man I'd ever met. How could he ever teach me, the English scholar, anything at all about literature? But I was quickly humbled by his quick wit, his discerning analysis of my writing, and his ability to spot "bull" when I shoved it out in a paper.

One day he gave us a pop quiz on several poems he had assigned us to read the night before. For some reason, I had not read them at all, none of them. He asked us some general questions about the poetry, and then to analyze the structure and essence of a couple in particular. I didn't know what to do. My heart started to pound—I couldn't get an F on this! Then I remembered a line from the poem, "Ars Poetica" by Archibald MacLeish—"a poem should not mean, but be." I think MacLeish was saying that sometimes we over-analyze poetry, and that sometimes we just enjoy the poem for what it is—something lovely. That's what I wrote for my quiz answer. I turned it in and hurried out of class, swearing never to skip another reading assignment.

The next day, when he returned the papers, he had written, "Good use of just plain bull, Sharon. I'll let you slide this time, but next time, I'll expect you to be prepared!" He turned out to be the best teacher I had there—I learned much from him.

I didn't do much writing in college. I think I got a poem published in our literary magazine, but, like that bunny poem from third grade, I wasn't particularly pleased or proud of it. What I did in college, although I didn't know it then, was to learn to write by reading. Since I was an English major, I had to read all the classics—Keats, Byron, Shakespeare, Dickens, Twain, Whitman and hundreds of others. I read wonderful writers who could take a word and make it dance upon the page, and I read horribly boring writers who were so caught up in esoteric nonsense that the book was ponderous and very unsatisfying. I didn't know it at the time, but reading all those writers gave me the basic ingredients that would simmer for many years before I'd be ready to write words of my own. My focus was on becoming a teacher—the very best one that I could be. I had no desire to be a writer. I just loved to read good writing.

Shortly before I graduated from Pepperdine, I was offered a job to teach there in the English department. It was a great honor, but I felt I wasn't ready. I was 21 years old and not much older than the students I might be teaching. Besides, I wanted to teach high school and middle school. Those students, I felt, would be a lot more fun.

At our graduation ceremony, once again I was asked to give the commencement speech. This time my theme focused on vision and maturity and passion for beliefs. It was probably just a more mature version of my high school speech, but I got lots of compliments, and my parents were very proud.

Early Years of Teaching

I finished college in January, moved back to Ohio, and got married that June—to the young man I had run away from. We have not been apart since. We both got teaching jobs in the same school system—he at the high school, teaching biology, and me at the junior high, teaching English—two first-year teachers struggling with new jobs, a new marriage, and new responsibilities.

Sharon on her wedding day

I remember working really hard to teach ALL my students, not just the good kids—the superstars. There was this one young man whose name was Bo who had difficulty with reading and writing and anything having to do with the English curriculum. But he tried. I worked with him at lunch time, and I'd give him alternate assignments on which he could feel some success. But I found out that was not the correct "policy" of the school district.

The department head approached me one day and asked me, "So how does a student like Bo make a B in your class? He's failing everything else."

I smiled, sure I was about to be complimented. "I've been working with Bo, and I've given him extra help and special assignments so he can feel some success."

"You mean you varied from the adopted text?" He looked at me as if I had just robbed a bank.

"Well, yes, I did. Bo has never had any success in school, and he has shown so much improvement lately!" I was very proud of Bo's achievements.

"You are never to vary from the adopted text again!" he told me sternly.

"But Bo, and many other students like him, will fail if I just use that book!" I pleaded.

"Bo and students like him are meant to fail," he told me harshly. "You're wasting your time on giving him extra help. It won't make any difference. And if you continue to vary from the prescribed assignments in the adopted text, you're in danger of losing your job!" He slammed the door and left.

I was stunned. This wasn't why I went into teaching. I continued to help Bo, but he knew what the expectations were. Bo DID fail that year, and he dropped out a couple of years after that. That department head retired that summer, and was replaced by a woman who was warm and not so narrow-minded. But it was too late for Bo.

I learned to teach by teaching. There is no book that tells you what to do if a students barks just to cause trouble, or if he vomits in front of the class, or if a child's parent dies. There is no book that tells how to get the magic flow of teaching and learning, of chaos and control. It is learned by practice, by making mistakes, and by getting better at it because you love what you do. I loved books, and reading, and writing, so it was easy for me to transfer that love to my students. I remember what is was like to be twelve or fourteen, so I tried to make class interesting, and exciting. I used to hate boring classes, so I tried very hard for my classes never to be like that. We'd act out plays, or write poetry to music, or create stories out of newspaper articles. Always something new and exciting and different. Of course, not every day is exciting, but the passion was always there—the passion for learning and reading, and teaching kids how to appreciate books.

How the Writing Started

In January of 1977, I watched, fascinated, along with the rest of America, the televised version of Alex Haley's monumental book called *Roots*. Over 130 million people tuned in to watch the story of a slave called Kunta Kinte and how this young man, snatched from his native land and transported in the hold of a slave ship to this country, became the ancestor of a strong family of African Americans, the family of Alex Haley.

I was teaching at a junior high school at the time, and I remember that all the discussions, whether in the teacher's lounge or in the classroom, surrounded that powerful story. The situation was tense and polarized. The black students felt angry and confrontational, while the white students, who the day before had been their friends, felt guilty and defensive. Class discussions brought out previously unspoken feelings and deeply hidden biases and hurts. Even though the dramatization sought to end each story with a message of hope, it was impossible to escape the realities of slavery, degradation, and human depravity. The film, and the book on which it was based, detailed the horrors of the hold of the slave ship, the shame of the auction block, the pain and confusion of families split apart, and the realities of forced labor under terrible conditions. But it also showed the unquenchable will to live, the determination to survive and overcome, and the power of the human spirit. The dramatization of that book changed the lives of all us who witnessed it.

Alex Haley became a household name. His family history, and how he had been able to trace his roots back to Africa, a feat rarely accomplished by any Black American up to that point, became our own. He awakened an interest in genealogy, particularly among African Americans, and, finally, a way to reflect on the hideous past of slavery with something close to pride. He helped to transpose everyone's view of history. I admired him for his skill, his ability to write and draw a picture with words, as well as his humanity and humility.

Alex Haley was raised on a farm in Henning, Tennessee. There, he sat on the wide front porch of the family home, listening to stories from his maternal grandmother, Cynthia Palmer, who traced the family genealogy to Haley's great-great-great-great-grandfather, who was an African, called "Kin-tay" and brought by slave ship to America. Years later, Haley embarked on an odyssey that took eleven years and is now part of literature history. On the basis of family tradition and his own research, Haley traveled to the village of Juffure, to trace his own ancestors. He met with the village *griot,* oral historian, who could name Haley's own ancestor Kunta Kinte.

The resulting book, *Roots,* was published in 1976 to much critical acclaim. The book sold in one year more than a million copies, one of which belonged to me.

I cherished that book and all it meant, and kept it on a special place in my bookcase. I used excerpts from the book, and later, from the videotapes when they were released, in my classroom. We discussed issues of fairness and racism and bigotry and redemption. We connected the ideas in the book with history lessons as well as with American literature of that period. We read poetry of Paul Dunbar, Claude McKay, and Walt Whitman, as well as Maya Angelou. We read the life of Lincoln, and the life of Frederick Douglass. My students devoured the concepts, accepted the challenges, and absorbed the underlying lessons that were offered through this integrated study. It was multicultural, cross-curricular teaching and learning at its best, and I didn't even know it. I just knew they were thriving and enjoying the learning process with no pain and much gain. Alex Haley helped me to do that.

By 1990, I was teaching ninth grade at a junior-senior high school, still focusing on cross-curricular lessons which touched on important concepts and issues. A student once asked me, "Don't you know you're an English teacher? Why you keep givin' us all this history and stuff?"

I just smiled and told him that a piece of literature made no sense unless you could understand its historical context. "You gotta know where the author is coming from," I explained. He looked at me doubtfully, but he truly enjoyed our choral reading of Robert Hayden's poem "Middle Passage" as we began our unit of American literature and history and culture that year, which was always climaxed by excerpts from the videotapes of *Roots.*

A large part of any English classroom is, of course, writing assignments, and I did my best to give mean-

The author in her early years of teaching

ingful assignments, and even opportunities for students to have their work published in various venues, like the library journal, or poetry contests. One day, a student named Jared came to me and handed me a crumpled piece of paper that had been ripped from a magazine. On it was an application for a short story contest. He said to me in that deep, almost gravel-sounding voice of challenge that only ninth-graders can have, "Here! You think you so bad—why don't YOU write something!"

I looked at him, grinned, and said, "Well, Jared, maybe I'll just do that!" I tossed it in my bag, along with cut slips, red pens, dozens of paperclips, six books, and three hundred ungraded papers, and forgot about it.

On the way home, I stopped by the grocery store to pick up fixings for dinner, thinking only of whether or not spaghetti sauce was on sale this week. I was pushing my cart down an aisle, when a woman came toward me from the other direction. In her cart was a chubby, almost cherubic-looking three-year-old, standing amidst the food items his mother had selected. He was grinning and reaching for her. Just as I passed them, instead of reaching for her son, I heard her say to him, "If you don't sit your stinkin', useless butt back down in that shopping cart, I swear I'll bust your greasy face in!"

Shocked, I looked at her sharply, but I said nothing. The child sat down heavily, his smile gone. She rushed past me and headed to the checkout lane. I found the spaghetti sauce and pasta I was looking for, but I was no longer hungry. I couldn't get the face of that child out of my mind. What kind of life must he have at home? If she treats him like this in public, what might she do in private?

When I got to the parking lot of the grocery store, I searched for the child and his mother, but they had vanished. Thinking back, perhaps I should have said something to her. Perhaps I should have followed her out and copied down the license plates of her car. To tell whom? The police? Social services? And tell them what? That she yelled at her child? That's not against the law.

I got home, fixed dinner, but I was distracted and impatient with my family. I could not stop thinking about that child. I sat down at my computer, and before I was consciously aware of it, I started writing. In two hours it was finished—only three typed pages—a powerful little short story that took that little boy home and saw his life through the eyes of my imagination.

I pulled out the application that Jared had given me, filled out the entry form, put the whole thing in an envelope and sealed it. I grabbed my coat, drove to the post office, and mailed it before I could think about it or change my mind. I was driven purely by emotion, not reason.

The next day I sheepishly told Jared that I had written something for the contest, and we continued with class. Eventually, I forgot about it.

Four months later, I was at home, sitting on my bed grading papers, which is a dangerous idea because sleep jumps up and grabs you in the middle of a paragraph! The phone rang, and a deep, cultured voice said, "May I speak to Sharon Draper, please?"

"Speaking."

"I'm from *Ebony* magazine, and I'm in charge of the short story contest. We had thousands of entries, you know."

"I'm glad I didn't have to grade them," I chuckled. "How did I do?"

"I'm pleased to announce that your story, 'One Small Torch,' came in first place!"

"You're kidding! What does that mean?"

"It means your story will be published and very shortly we will be sending you a check for *five thousand dollars*!"

I gasped and screeched and I think I jumped on the bed, stepping all over graded and ungraded essays on Shakespeare.

When the story was printed, it was as if I had won the Pulitzer Prize. Reporters from the local newspaper asked to interview me. I got my picture, in full color, on the front page of the Tempo section, with a wonderful article on the story and its power and simplicity. I was a little overwhelmed. People started asking me for autographs.

"My autograph?" I asked. "I don't know how to sign an autograph! I sign detention slips!"

I got letters from people from all over the country, people who had read the story and were touched by it. I was amazed. But the most amazing and most treasured letter came in early 1991. On his own letterhead paper, written in his own handwriting, was a letter from someone I would never in a million years expect to hear from. It said, "Dear Mrs. Draper, I read your story and I think it is wonderful. You are a skilled writer and have much to offer. Keep up the good work." It was signed ALEX HALEY.

I trembled as I read it. I could not believe that the person I so admired, a writer I so respected, would take the time from his busy schedule to offer words of encouragement to me. He called me a writer! It was the first time that I even entertained the notion of being a "writer." I knew I was a teacher. I knew I was pretty good at editing student writing, but it never occurred to me that I, too, could be a writer.

I took the letter to school and showed my students and colleagues, where everyone was properly awed. Jared, the student who had started the whole process, had moved to another state, and I was never able to track him down and thank him, but the rest of my students and I celebrated with pizza and pop and, knowing me, probably a little poetry.

But the story doesn't end there. Just a year after he sent me that letter, Alex Haley died on February 10, 1992, and I was truly saddened. Not only was a great and generous man gone forever, but a voice in the darkness was forever silenced.

I continued to teach, using Alex Haley's words, his spirit, his ability to inspire in my lesson planning, and in my life as well. I decided I wanted to try to write a book, and was unbelievably successful with my first attempt, *Tears of a Tiger*.

Since I've been an English teacher for almost thirty years, I know what kids like, what they will read, and what they won't. Although I have nothing against Charles Dickens, most teenagers would rather gag than read him. Dickens wrote for his contemporaries—young people of a hundred and fifty years ago. That's one of the reasons he was so popular—he wrote for his contemporaries! American kids of course need to know about the world of London in the 1860s, but they would much rather read about their own world first. Not only will they read about recognizable experiences with pleasure, but they will also be encouraged to write as well. I started my writing career for those young people.

Tears of a Tiger was written in study hall, on weekends, before and after school and during summer vacation. It is written for high school students—on their level, in their style, about their world. It's written for all teenagers. The characters are just ordinary kids trying to get through high school. The book does not deal with drugs or gangs or sex. It does, however, deal with parents, girlfriends, and homework. It also discusses the problems of drinking and driving, racism and teen suicide. I sent it to twenty-five publishing companies and got twenty-four rejection notices. The very last letter was a letter of acceptance from Simon and Schuster.

While I was waiting for that one to finish the publication process—it takes about a year and a half—I wrote another book for younger students. It is called *Ziggy and the Black Dinosaurs,* and is written for children ages six to twelve. This one was accepted on the very first try. *Ziggy* is funny and a mystery, dealing with club houses and buried treasure and even includes a strong lesson on history that young readers learn without even knowing it. The response has been so wonderful that it has been made into a series. In the second book, Ziggy and his friends find an old, abandoned tunnel of the Underground Railroad and get lost in it. It's called *Lost in the Tunnel of Time.* The third book in this series is called *Shadows of Caesar's Creek,* and deals with the cultural connections of Native Americans, again through humor, excitement, and solid literary development. Kids can read this series and learn as well as enjoy the tale. Teachers can use these to teach.

Although it was not planned that way, both *Tears of a Tiger* and *Ziggy and the Black Dinosaurs* hit the bookstores on the very same day! The response was tremendous and overwhelming. Parents have asked "Where have you been?" Kids are clamoring for the sequels. Schools are starting to adopt them in their curriculums. I don't think I have ever had a young person read *Tears of a Tiger* that did not like it. Actually, many of the teenagers who read it tell me they have never read a whole book before in their life, but they read that one in one night.

Tears of a Tiger received wonderful reviews, several national awards, and was awarded the Coretta Scott King Genesis Award, as well as being selected as an ALA Best Books for Young Adults for 1995. Amazing for a first book. Two years later I wrote the sequel, called *Forged by Fire,* which is a powerful piece for young people on child abuse and survival It won the 1997 Coretta Scott King Award, as the best book published the year before for young people by an African-American author. It also won several other awards, but it is close to my heart because Chapter One of *Forged by Fire* is "One Small Torch," the story that won first prize in that short story contest! At the award ceremony, I took special pains to mention Alex Haley and how much influence he had had on my life.

Twenty-three years after the showing of *Roots* on television, nine years after I received the letter from Alex Haley, and three years after the publication of *Forged by Fire*, I sat in the back seat of a car, heading down the sunny roads of Tennessee, toward the little town of Clinton, toward Alex Haley's farm, the place he built when he became successful as a writer. I was giddy with excitement. Of course, the farm now belonged to the Children's Defense Fund, but many of the original buildings remained, and I knew that Alex Haley's spirit walked those lanes and breathed peacefully in the air of the library that had been built there.

The purpose of my visit there was to speak to a group of young people who had read *Forged by Fire* during their stay there and who wanted to hear from the author. These young people were special—not the top of their class or the children usually picked for special events like this one. These kids were difficult, troubled, needy in mind and spirit, and on the edge—just about ready to fall off, drop out, give up. But they were brought there to build up their spirits, to repair their damaged self-esteem, to offer them hope and possibilities. The only attention that these tenth graders had ever received in school was negative attention. In just a few days, like wilted daisies that just needed a little water and attention, I saw them blossom, bloom, and grow, as they received the nurturing attention of the staff. They were given encouragement for once in their lives; they were given goals and responsibilities. It was amazing to see the changes in them as they received something that we assume all young people are given, but unfortunately, too many of them grow to maturity without—positive reinforcement and love.

On the last day, they marched in proudly for the graduation ceremonies. They sang, they hugged, they wept. I spoke to them about dreams and rainbows and golden possibilities, which can be found in spite of the harsh realities of many of their lives. I told them of Alex Haley and how he had influenced my life and how, even long after his death, he touched and inspired all of us. And I charged them with heading out into the future with heads held high.

They cheered and we proceeded to that wide, welcoming porch, exactly like the one where long ago, Alex's grandmother told him those stories about the captured slave, and I signed copies of my books which had been inspired by his spirit. It was humbling and awesome.

I was almost finished and a young man approached me. He was long and gangly and had eyes that had seen pain in spite of the grin on his face. His name was Kyrus.

"You got any more of them *Tears of a Tiger* books?"

"I'm sorry, they're all gone," I replied with regret. I had brought a few books with me, and not realizing how powerful a good book can be in the hands of a child who needs it, I had not brought enough. I had just given away the last one.

"I ain't never read no book before—not all the way through. But your book was good. I couldn't put it down. My moms couldn't believe it—cause I was readin'. I read *Forged by Fire* in one night."

"I'll be glad to sign *Forged by Fire* for you, but we've run out of *Tears of a Tiger.* I'm really sorry."

"Oh, that's OK. Just write down the title. I don't hardly ever go to the library, but I'm gonna go to the library as soon as I get home and see if I can find it. I just gotta read that book!"

Now I had one copy left of *Tears of a Tiger.* It was the copy I used when I gave presentations and it was battered and torn and dirty, with markings all through it. It was in the bottom of my purse. I dug down and pulled it out slowly.

"This is my own copy, and it's a little beat up, but if you want it, you can have it."

"For real? Oh, I can?"

"I said it's yours," I said gently. I wrote, "For my friend Kyrus—may all your dreams come true," on the front page and signed my name. He was almost dancing with excitement. I was near tears.

"I'm gonna read this on the plane," he said. "I bet I'll have it finished before I get home. Wait till I show my moms! Thank you so much!"

I handed him the book and he bounded off the porch in two steps, crowing to his friends in exultation that he'd received the very last copy of *Tears of a Tiger.* He clutched the book to him like it was the Holy Grail. Maybe, in a sense, it was. I could feel the presence of Alex Haley smiling broadly.

National Teacher of the Year

People often ask, "So how do you get to be the Teacher of the Year anyhow?" A few years ago, I would not have been able to answer that question. I never had any great plans to grow up and be the National Teacher of the Year. I remember once seeing a glimpse of a teacher in the Rose Garden of the White House and wondering vaguely to myself, "How did she get to do that?" I bet I could do that, but I didn't have the foggiest notion how. I remember also reading about a National Teacher of the Year flying in Air Force One with the president. Wow. That's the kind of thing that happens to other people in other states. No one we know ever does wonderful things like that. Until now.

It all started very simply. It was May of 1997. The principal of my school handed me an application, about twenty pages in length, that said on the front cover, "Ohio Teacher of the Year—1997. He said, "Why don't you try this?" I shrugged and said, "OK, why not?" I had no notion of where that short conversation might lead. I had no grand plan. I filled out the application, which was thoughtful, required broad thinking, and good writing style.

Since then, I have found out that many states do the application process quite differently. In South Carolina, for example, a local winner is chosen from every single school in every single city. The winner of the city teacher of the year is announced at a breakfast and

celebrated at a formal dinner with gowns and tuxedos. Then that teacher's application goes to the country level, where the process is repeated, then finally to the state level. All this is a wonderful idea and should be emulated. It gives a glorious opportunity for dozens of teachers to be recognized, celebrated, praised and lauded as they should be. They are given plaques, or certificates or golden apples, and they go back to their classrooms refreshed, renewed, and rededicated.

But in Cincinnati, we simply fill out the application, and someone in the central office picks a candidate to go to the state competition. In 1997, they picked me. I think there were about six candidates. I got a phone call in June, telling me my application would be sent to the state. I was pleased, but I still had no sense of the big picture at that point. Shortly after school started in September, I got another phone call. I had been selected as one of the four finalists for Ohio Teacher of the Year!

On October 24, I was in the middle of sixth bell, teaching Chaucer to my seniors. The door to my classroom opened. In walked the principal, the assistant principal, several secretaries, the hall monitors, every teacher with a free bell, the superintendent of Cincinnati schools, the head of the school board, John Goff, the State Superintendent of Education, half a dozen reporters snapping photos and others with bright lights and video cameras, and my husband Larry and six of his students! Needless to say, I was at a loss for words. John Goff said, "Let me be the first to congratulate you as the 1997 Ohio Teacher of the Year!" My class went wild. The kids cheered. I grabbed my face in a gesture of surprise, and lifted my arms as if to say, "Wow!" That picture, in full color, appeared on the front page of the *Cincinnati Enquirer* the next day, covering almost the whole top half of the front page. I drove down the street, just marveling at my picture in those little newspaper stands, over and over and over!

Everyone was so supportive and so genuinely glad for me. From the lady at the cleaners, to the man at the drugstore, to the tellers at my local bank, who all stopped what they were doing when I walked in the door, to clap and cheer, everyone felt proud to share my success. I was a part of the community and I had made them all stand tall with pride. I was overwhelmed and humbled.

Being named Ohio Teacher of the Year was plenty for me. I still had no great dreams of heading for the National competition. The Ohio Teacher of the Year is a position of great responsibility, as are each of the State Teacher positions. I would travel all over the state of Ohio, speaking to teachers and educational organizations, but would still continue teaching. It promised to be an exciting year. But the application of each State Teacher of the Year is passed on to the national office, for consideration to be National Teacher of the Year.

I was certainly no greater than any of those fine teachers, any one of whom could have been chosen. One evening in January the phone rang. It was Jon

Quam, the director of the National Teacher of the Year program. He said, "I'm calling to tell you that you have been selected as one of four finalists for the 1997 National Teacher of the Year, and to ask you if you would like to accept this opportunity." Now this was the first moment where I started to get giddy, to look to the future, to imagine the possibilities. I grinned at the phone, told him, "Yes, of course, I'd be honored," and other sorts of correct phrases, and hung the phone up and screamed with delight.

From that time until March when the four finalists would meet the National Teacher of the Year committee, I studied, read *Education Week,* met with people in the educational field here in town that I respected and admired, such as our Superintendent of Education, Mike Brandt, and read as much as I could about all aspects of education. For now I was not only seeking to speak for the teachers in Ohio, but for all of the three million teachers in this country. I needed to be familiar with all aspects of the educational spectrum. I wanted to be knowledgeable, secure, confident. I had to prepare a ten-minute presentation for the committee, which is made up of fourteen members of the educational community, representing the major educational organizations, such the American Federation of Teachers, the National Education Association, the National School Boards Association, etc.

I flew to Washington, D.C., the first week of March. For three days the four of us who were finalists were put through the paces—interviews, press conferences, dinners, videotaping, a presentation, questions about education. It was thrilling, stimulating, exhausting, and probably the best educational process I had ever experienced. They sent us home then with a promise to call us in a week or so. I came home feeling confident, but not overly so. There is just no telling what reasons committees use to make decisions behind closed doors.

We had been told that if we were NOT selected as the National Teacher of the Year, we would receive a phone call from Jon Quam, the director of the program. If we WERE selected, we would receive a call from our State Superintendent of Education. In Ohio, that was John Goff. Either way, I would get a call from someone named John. All my family knew it. When the call came, I wasn't home. My daughter Crystal, who was fifteen, answered the phone.

When I got home, I asked, "Were there any calls?'

"Yes," she replied sweetly.

"Well," I asked, "who called?"

"Oh," she said innocently, "somebody named John called."

"John who?" I asked.

"I don't know," she replied, grinning with delight. "I forgot to ask."

Now she knew full well which John had called, but she really enjoyed making me sweat. Ten minutes later John Goff called and said, with real pleasure in his voice, "Sharon, once again, it is my pleasure to congratulate you. Let me be the first to say congratulations to the 1997 National Teacher of the Year!"

I didn't scream this time. I whispered. "Really?" I asked. My face was about to burst from the giant grin on my face.

"Yes, really," he replied. "We are all so proud of you. And by the way, you can't tell anybody!"

Now how was I going to keep such a wonderful thing a secret? My students, my friends, my parents? The White House placed an embargo on the news, which could not be officially announced until April, when the President of the United States greets the new National Teacher of the Year in the Rose Garden. I told my family, and my parents of course, and my principal and superintendent, but the news stayed under wraps until just a couple of days before we left for Washington.

It was a glorious journey, because every step was an unplanned adventure, a new height to climb to and reach. I never planned to reach the summit of that mountain, but the view was spectacular. I knew I had so much to offer the teachers of this country, and others who didn't know or understand the educational world as well. I was proud and ready to begin the next climb, which promised to be a full mountain range, with paths untouched and for which no map was written. But I was ready.

So many confused ideas—where does the rhetoric end and the true feelings begin? I say to people that I'm proud and humbled and surprised that I was selected as National Teacher of the Year, and I am, but in my heart of hearts, I knew I was ready. Through most of the process, I felt confident and relaxed and qualified. One statement that I made to the committee was very true, and I guess I said it with real passion because I really believed it. I have been preparing for this job since I was born, and I didn't even know it.

From my mother reading to me, and encouraging me through school, to all those days in classes, through college, I always liked school, loved learning, loved the mental challenge of sucking the information in and assimilating it, storing it, and being able to retrieve it, and then share it—effectively, and with style.

When I got up to give that speech, wearing a bright orange suit that I was sure would resonate on television, I felt no fear. I took a deep breath, looked at all those cameras, and began to speak. Even though I had the speech written, I gave it from memory. Proud, humbled, excited, and confident, I began.

White House Speech—April 18, 1997

Thank you, Mr. President. Mr. Secretary. Honored guests.

I am so very *proud* to be a *teacher!*

I am proud of all of the students whose lives have intersected with mine. And because of that moment in time together, all of us are better. For each of them taught me as well and to them I say, I love you all.

I am proud of my colleagues—three million of us—striving to make a difference in the lives of the children.

This apple, which shines with proud intensity for all teachers, represents

—the knowledge of the past,

—the responsibility of the present,

—and the hope of the future.

As we build this wonderful bridge to the twenty-first century, let us remember that we will need teachers to instruct us how to build it, teachers to guide us across its intricate paths, and teachers who stand ready in the twenty-first century to take us to new paths and bridges as yet undreamed.

And who will walk that path? The children. Imagine a child—any child, every child—hopeful, enthusiastic, curious. In that child sleeps the vision and the wisdom of tomorrow. The touch of a teacher will make the difference.

More on Writing

After being National Teacher of the Year, it's hard to go back to the world of classrooms and bells, homework and faculty meetings. I had had the opportunity to travel to almost every state, to dozens of cities, and hundreds of schools. I'd been to Russia. I had seen excellent teachers all over this country, and schools that did a wonderful job of educating young people. I'd been exposed to different kinds of teaching—innovative methods of reaching students. I had been in airports in strange cities at six in the morning, as well as at midnight. I'd experienced the glories of a hotel like the Ritz-Carlton, and the Spartan cleanliness of a Motel 6. How was I to return to my classroom? It wasn't that I felt that I was too "big" or famous to return; it's just that my world had expanded. I had been instrumental in helping teachers all over the country feel good about themselves, about how influential they are in the lives of the students they teach. My classroom stage had expanded.

So when I returned to Cincinnati after that glorious year, I wasn't sure what to do. The new National Teacher of the Year had taken my place, and, like Cinderella, I had to give up my coach and magic slippers to return to the real world. I decided to take a position in our professional development academy. It gave me an opportunity to work with teachers, and gave me a little more freedom than I would have had back in my classroom. I missed having students around, but I got to visit schools as part of my job, and that helped. But more than anything, I wanted to write. I had more books that had been published by this time—*Romiette and Julio,* and two more Ziggy books. My dream was to retire from teaching so I could dedicate myself to writing full time.

Two years later, I was able to do just that. I officially retired from teaching, and headed home to be a writer. What a glorious opportunity—to be able to get up each morning and sit down at my computer and write all my thoughts and dreams and ideas! Of course, reality is never quite like the dream, because I found that even though I didn't have to go to work, so many other things gobbled my time that I had to squeeze my writing in. I was asked to come and speak at schools and conferences. Since I was no longer teaching, I was free to do that. It was a little like the National Teacher of the Year experience, only on a less powerful channel.

I never really stopped teaching—I just changed my area of expertise. Writing and teaching are mixed up together and can't be separated. I started writing as a result of my teaching, and now, my writing has become a teaching tool. I starting writing for students, for the kids I knew who didn't like to read, who weren't inspired by books or literature. Now the books are used in schools all over the country, and teachers use them as learning tools for their classes. When I speak to students at schools, all I really do is an extended version of what I've always done, which is teach. I instruct, I inspire, I entertain—I love it! I know that working with young people in schools has helped my writing because I've been able to talk to students from all over the country, not just one classroom. In essence, thousands of classrooms are now mine and we get to share with each other through the books.

I like visiting schools because that gave me the opportunity to talk to young people—to see how they thought and even see what the latest fashion trends were. I couldn't write about kids wearing jeans with belts, for example, when it was clear that everyone wore their jeans down low on their behinds, held up with nothing but hips and hope.

After the success of *Tears of a Tiger, Forged by Fire,* and *Romiette and Julio,* I wasn't sure what to write next. But I started getting letters from young people—hundreds of them. They wanted to know what happened to Angel and Gerald, two of the characters from the first two books. They wanted to know if Rhonda and Tyrone, two young lovers mentioned in both novels, ever broke up. They believed in them as if the characters were real people.

When I was visiting a school, a young lady came up to me and said, "I need Keisha's home phone number!"

I told her quietly, "Keisha's not real. I made her up."

Not at all influenced by that, she continued, "Oh I know you changed her name to protect her privacy, but that girl got some issues, and I think I can help her. I gotta talk to her right away!"

Because of the huge amount of interest in the kids from Hazelwood High, I wrote the third book in what is now a trilogy. It's called *Darkness before Dawn,* and it takes all the characters from *Tears of a Tiger* and *Forged by Fire* and brings the story to a conclusion. I'm still getting letters, however, to write more about these kids. Perhaps one day I will, but right now, I'm working on new projects and new novels.

I still get dozens of e-mails a week. Many students tell me, "I never liked to read" or "I've never read a whole book before" but "I read your book in one night and I couldn't wait to read the others." They like the reality and the honesty of the stories and locations and characters.

Sometimes I get letters from young people or their teachers who want to know why I write about such powerful subjects—like abuse or suicide. I think that difficult or controversial subjects should be handled with skill and delicacy. It is possible to describe a horrible situation, such as child abuse, without using graphic details. Such subjects dealt with in this manner can then be discussed intelligently because it is the ideas and thoughts we want young readers to share, not the experience itself. We are all attracted to tragedy. That's why soap operas and sad movies are so popular. I think there's something within each of us that wants to look at tragedy from the outside so that we don't have to experience it personally. The other difficult issues or social problems I deal with are very real in the lives of many readers. We don't live in a world of sugarplum fairies and happily ever after. Perhaps reading about the difficulties of others will act like armor and protect my readers from the personal tragedies in their own lives.

Many of the letters I receive from students are very touching. Sometimes they tell me that reading one of the books changed their lives. I had a student tell me she called the child abuse hotline that is printed in the back of *Forged by Fire.*

She said, "I read your book. I called that number. You saved my life." I still get chill bumps when I think of that. Another student wrote that he was depressed and was thinking of taking his life, but after reading *Tears of a Tiger,* he decided to live. I counseled him to talk to someone he trusted, and he wrote me back that he had. Another student said she was reading *Tears of a Tiger* in class and that weekend some of her friends were drinking at a party. She thought about BJ in the book (who doesn't drink), so she called her mother to come and pick her up. Her friends were killed that night in an automobile accident. It's an awesome responsibility to have so much response to what I've written. That's why I try so hard to make every single book ring true and honest and why I try to be available to my readers. I try to answer every single e-mail and every single letter that I receive.

Some of the letters are funny, however. Often students write, "I have to do a report on you. Tell me everything you know about yourself. My report is due tomorrow, so please reply quickly."

The Writing Process

A typical writing day starts early in the morning—maybe around five or six. I must have absolute silence—no music, no telephone, not even a fan can be blowing. Then I find my "zone" and enter it. It's a magic flow of thoughts and words. Sometimes the thoughts come faster than I can type them. It's exciting, exhilarating, and wonderful. And it is truly a blessing. The characters come and they create themselves. They become like real people to me—living, breathing young people who share the same fears and frustrations that all teenagers experience.

I start with an idea, or a problem or a conflict, or even a situation that might be pertinent to the lives of young people, then the characters grow from that point. I try to make strong characters that change and develop and learn from their mistakes. I try to make characters so real that young people believe they are real people, and many do.

I'll write all day—maybe until eight or nine at night, when my fingers are so tired I can't write any longer. But I start again the next morning. I try to block off at least two weeks at a time to write, but I can't always do that.

I can write about a chapter a day if I have no interruptions, but usually there are interruptions—the dog has to go out, I have to go the post office, etc. When I come back to it, I revise it or expand it and change it, each time making it better and stronger. When I finish the whole book, usually in two to three months, I go back and edit it. I fix, change, and rearrange. Then I do it again. Then one more time. That may take several more months. Then I send it in to my editor who fixes and changes it even more. It may go through three or four or even five edits with her. Then, it goes through a final edit with the copy editor. That may take another six to eight months. Writing is easy. Editing is very tedious and painful. When a book is finally done, it may have taken more than a year to get it just right, and even then, I'm never really satisfied with it. I still wish I had perfected it just a little more

I try not to work on more than one project at a time, but during my breaks from a current project, I might do some research for something else, because that's next in line.

Writing for me is a very fluid process—I sit down a wait for the words to come. They usually do—in buckets and waves. It's amazing. I look upon it as a blessing because the words come so easily. The plot is born from the idea, then is crafted by the characters and how they respond to what happens to them. It's a thrilling, exciting process.

When people ask me how to become a writer, I tell them first of all that I understand their desire—that need to express themselves through writing. A real writer is thirsty for it, wants to write more than anything else in the world. I tell them, "If you find yourself scribbling on notebook paper, or daydreaming about storylines, or jotting down lines of poetry at the mall, you ARE a writer! A writer is not something you become. A writer is something that you are." That gives them validation and power to continue.

There is no secret to becoming a writer. The best way to become a writer is to write. I tell them to get one of those blank journals, and just keep on writing until it is filled. Then write some more and fill another one. You don't have to show it to anyone—just write whenever the need arises. It's like an athlete. Much practice is done alone. At game time, the athlete shines. Game time for a writing athlete is a paper due for school, or a short story, or a poem.

Then I try to show them the importance of reading. I tell them to read the classics—Faulkner, Tennyson, Shakespeare, Dickens—all of them. I tell them to read poetry as well because the rhythms are essential to good writing—Keats, Dunbar, Hughes, Whitman—all of them. Good writers are powerful motivators. I even tell them to read bad writers as well. How is one to know a good book if one has never read a bad book? Then they must write, write, write. Practice, revise, make it perfect, then do it again. Many times young writers are too anxious to get published, and not willing to do the necessary reading and studying to become really proficient at the art and skill of writing. An Olympic athlete starts by running laps with no audience at all. A true champion knows the power of practice.

New Projects

At the time of this writing, *The Battle of Jericho* has just been released. It deals with problems of peer pressure and dangerous choices in a high school. The main character is a tenth grader named Jericho who is asked to join a club at his school called The Warriors of Distinction. This club has secret initiation rites and all kinds of terrible secrets that lead to an unbelievable conclusion. It's a powerful book, and I'm really excited about it. I think it is the best thing I've ever written. If we are supposed to learn from our experiences, then I should have learned quite a bit about the writing process, about what makes a novel work. I tried to incorporate everything I've ever learned from my editor about how to make a story have the punch and power and needs to grab the attention of my readers. I've included memorable characters, strong descriptive scenes, and a plot that deals with real issues that young people face every day. Here's a brief excerpt:

Madison continued, "We ask for, no—we demand—your dedication, your absolute obedience, your very life, if necessary. In return, we pledge

to share with you our secrets, our connections, and our power. Any problems with that? If so, there's the door."

No one moved. Jericho wondered if anyone else felt as uncomfortable as he did. He wondered what Madison meant.

Eddie spoke next. "Since there seems to be full acceptance, we will continue with what we call The Bonding of the Brotherhood."

"The Bonding of the Brotherhood," Madison explained, "requires not only secrecy and obedience, but also responsibility, loyalty, and honor. Your first responsibility is to your pledge brothers. Look around you. The fifteen young men that you see here will depend on YOU for their success as well as their safety, and you will depend on each of them. You must provide ANYTHING your brother needs. Each pledge holds the responsibility for the other."

"Agreed?" Eddie Mahoney asked once more to the almost-trembling pledges.

"Agreed," they replied. Jericho shivered in the darkness with them, sitting together on the floor on that warehouse.

"In addition, you must agree to do ANYTHING you are asked to do," Madison said, an odd smile on his face.

"Agreed?" Eddie Mahoney demanded.

"Agreed," they replied quietly.

"I will lie if I must!" Eddie barked.

"I will lie if I must!"

"I will steal if it is necessary to help my brother!" Eddie continued. He looked almost demonic, it seemed to Jericho, in the dim light of the candles. He seemed to be enjoying himself as he chanted.

"I will steal if it is necessary to help my brother!" Jericho did not like the sound of this, but he didn't know how to get out of it. He whispered the words. His stomach was starting to hurt.

Madison turned the page of the book and continued to read. "As a pledge, you must also understand the concept of loyalty. Each of you must think of yourself as one link in a chain that has no beginning and no end. Therefore, all of you must succeed in every pledge activity, or none of you do. The group must work together to help the individual."

"Repeat after me," Eddie demanded. "All of us or none of us!"

"All of us or none of us!" the group of pledges replied.

Then Rick Sharp moved to the center of the circle. "These are the basic guidelines for the Bonding of the Brotherhood. Please repeat after me," he asked the pledges.

"Number One. A Warrior of Distinction is not afraid to lower himself for his brother."

"A Warrior of Distinction is not afraid to lower himself for his brother," they repeated. Jericho wondered what "lowering himself" actually meant.

"Number Two. A Warrior of Distinction does not show fear," Rick intoned.

"A Warrior of Distinction does not show fear." Jericho said the words with the rest of them, but he was feeling pretty fearful right now. He figured maybe this whole process was designed to intimidate and scare them. It was working.

"Number Three. A Warrior of Distinction is bonded to his brothers."

"A Warrior of Distinction is bonded to his brothers," the rest of the pledges repeated.

Jericho glanced over at Joshua, who looked intense and serious. He and Josh had been almost as close as brothers since they were born. Their birthdays were only a month apart and when they were younger, his parents and Josh's parents had apartments in the same building. Josh's dad had been working on his law degree, while Jericho's dad went through his training for the police academy. The two families shared everything back then—food, trips, babysitting. The two cousins had spent hours in the hallway of that apartment building, racing Hot Wheels cars down the long, polished hallways. Jericho wondered how he could ever be 'bonded' as close to the boys in this room as he already was to Joshua. He turned his attention back to the ceremony.

"Number Four. A Warrior of Distinction NEVER breaks the code of silence," Rick continued.

Receiving the National Teacher of the Year Award from President Bill Clinton, 1997

"A Warrior of Distinction never breaks the code of silence." Jericho wanted to think about that one, but the rest of the group repeated it without hesitation, so he joined with the others and said the words as well.

"Number Five. A Warrior of Distinction celebrates obedience," Rick said clearly.

"A Warrior of Distinction celebrates obedience," the pledges replied obediently.

Madison said to them, "Stand, young warriors. The road ahead will be difficult, but the rewards are great." Jericho, surprised at this sudden, secret confirmation of their membership, stood with the rest of the new pledges and stretched with pride. He hoped they would never be called upon to actually live up to all the words they had just said.

Students often ask me how I knew I wanted to write. I tell them it's because I must. I love it. Writing makes me happy. I wish the same for everyone.

E

ELLSWORTH, Mary Ellen (Tressel) 1940-

Personal
Born August 13, 1940, in Chicago, IL; daughter of Harry S. (a certified public accountant, actuary, and lawyer) and Marguerite (King) Tressel; married Michael H. Ellsworth, September 15, 1962; children: Robert H., M. Patrick, Mary Elizabeth, Kathleen. *Education:* Smith College, B.A., 1962; Columbia University, M.A., 1963, Ph.D., 1981. *Hobbies and other interests:* Gardening; sports like hiking, swimming, and cross-country skiing; animals; old houses; antiques.

Addresses
Home—P.O. Box 145, Eastford, CT 06242. *Office*—English Department, Connecticut College, Box 5225, 270 Mohegan Ave., New London, CT 06320.

Career
Rye Country Day School, Rye, NY, teacher of English and mathematics, 1963-65; Grace Church School, New York, NY, teacher of English and mathematics, 1960s; Queensborough Community College, lecturer in English, 1960s; Queens College, Queens, NY, lecturer in English, 1960s; Tunxis Community College, Farmington, CT, lecturer in English, 1970s; Quinebaug Valley Community College, Danielson, CT, lecturer in English, 1981-82, 1991-95; Eastern Connecticut State University, Willimantic, CT, lecturer in English, 1982-87, 1990, 1996-97, assistant professor of English, 1987-89; Three Rivers Community College, Norwich, CT, lecturer in English, 1992-93, 1995-97; St. Joseph College, West Hartford, CT, lecturer, 1992; Harford College for Women and University of Hartford, Hartford, CT, lecturer in English, 1995-96; Connecticut College, New London, CT, visiting assistant professor of English, 1997-98, 2001, 2002—.

Member
Association for the Study of Connecticut History, New England Historical Association; Stowe Society.

Awards, Honors
Connecticut Humanities Council Grant recipient, 1989-92; Yale visiting faculty fellow, 1994-95.

Writings
Gertrude Chandler Warner and the Boxcar Children, illustrated by Marie DeJohn, A. Whitman Co. (Morton Grove, IL), 1997.

A History of the Connecticut Academy of Arts and Sciences, 1799-1999, Connecticut Academy of Arts and Sciences (New Haven, CT), 1999.

Work in Progress
A children's story of friendship; a biography of a twentieth-century woman author; an edition of a twentieth-century poet's memoirs.

Sidelights
Mary Ellen Ellsworth told *SATA:* "I was asked by a colleague to give a presentation on a local author as part of the 300th anniversary celebration for Windam County in Connecticut, where I live. I soon found that the area author who seemed to have the greatest readership was Gertrude Chandler Warner, who had written nineteen volumes of the 'Boxcar Children' mystery series for children. Even though I don't think it was quite what the university expected, I gave my paper on Warner, and it seemed to be thoroughly enjoyed by all the colloquium participants. One participant, the president of Putnam's Aspinock Historical Society, asked me to give a talk on Warner at his group's spring meeting the following year. That meeting was a lot of fun; local residents and former Warner students came, bringing anecdotes and mementos, and we videotaped the evening. Then I put my Warner materials away as I went on with my teaching and other writing projects. Many months later, on a cold fall afternoon, I received a call from a college administrator in Florida, whom I did not know. She said that she had grown up in Putnam and had

Miss Warner as her teacher. Her mother had sent her the videotape of the Putnam evening for her birthday. Coincidentally, at a recent booksellers' meeting, a representative of the Albert Whitman Company, Warner's publisher, had mentioned to her that they were looking for someone to write Warner's biography. She was sure I was the one to do it! So I prepared a manuscript and gave it a trial-run on the second-graders in our local elementary school.

"I had Warner's own books to work with, and articles about her and her publications in the two local papers. I worked hard at trying to track down any other individuals who might have known Warner in the classroom or through her church or Red Cross work. Individuals at the Putnam Public Library and the Aspinock Historical Society were very helpful. We found photographs to go along with the time period. I visited the house where Warner had grown up and made the 'Sunday afternoon drive' to the Warner family farm. Eventually, as I talked to more individuals, I tracked down the names of surviving family members in Rhode Island and arranged a visit with them. We shared a wonderful day, and I was able to review some of the early childhood manuscripts I had not seen before. I also found that Albert Whitman and Company had selected another Connecticut person to do the drawings of the book. We arranged a Saturday together and spent the afternoon walking in Warner's Putnam footsteps. Marie DeJohn was able to verify the authenticity of her drawings. I think she did a wonderful job! I also continued to dig—to try to find more details about Warner family life. I confirmed even more thoroughly what a wonderful, spirited group the Warners were!

"Overall, this has been a labor of love. Our four children are all avid readers, and they all read the 'Boxcar Children' mysteries. So some of the Warner books are around the house (I keep all books!). The research took time and ferreting, but so many people shared an obvious enthusiasm that it was an enjoyable and positive experience.

"I wrote for children because they were and are Warner's primary readers. Warner clearly was an exemplary person and affected positively the lives of those around her here in the Putnam area. But her greatest impact was and is in what she did for young readers everywhere. By creating intelligent, independent children as her central characters—two girls and two boys—and setting them off on adventures written in a way that unsophisticated readers could fully enjoy—she added to the richness of the imaginative experiences of millions of young people worldwide. Now through my book, I hope these readers will have the opportunity to know this woman, who had a clear vision and purpose, but who, in many ways, had a most ordinary life in a most ordinary setting. A publicly reserved, dignified, rather quiet woman, living in small-town America without advanced education, great wealth, or the best of health, went her way and left an important legacy for all children.

"Children's writing, in some ways, presents the biggest challenge if it is well done. Ideas must be presented clearly, simply, and directly—in a well-organized fashion—without talking down or being simple-minded. Warner did that, and that is what I have tried to do in my biography about her.

"A note of interest: in February, 2003, the people of Putnam, Connecticut, purchased a boxcar similar to the one Warner wrote about. The boxcar was placed near the center of town and will be opened to house the Gertrude Chandler Warner Museum.

"I have been involved in public education all of my adult life, trying to do whatever I could to make it as effective as possible. Part of this stems from my own passion for ideas in general and for literature and writing in particular, and part, I know, from wanting the best for my own four children as they were growing up. One way to try to impact things in my local area—a rural region of northeastern Connecticut—was to be on the school board. So I got elected to the local school board and served for eighteen years. I also served on our community college's advisory councils for eight years, and as a member of the board of trustees of our local high school for many more years. These are all volunteer activities."

Biographical and Critical Sources

PERIODICALS

Booklist, August 1, 1997, review of *Gertrude Chandler Warner and the Boxcar Children.*
Horn Book Guide, September, 2000, review of *Gertrude Chandler Warner and the Boxcar Children.*
Kirkus Reviews, April 15, 1997, review of *Gertrude Chandler Warner and the Boxcar Children.*
Publishers Weekly, July 8, 2002, review of *Gertrude Chandler Warner and the Boxcar Children.*
School Library Journal, July, 1997, review of *Gertrude Chandler Warner and the Boxcar Children.*

ONLINE

Yale University Web Site, http://www.yale.edu/caas/ (June 19, 2003), publisher's summary of *The History of the Connecticut Academy of Arts and Sciences, 1799-1999.*

*   *   *

EMBERLEY, Barbara A(nne) 1932-

Personal

Born December 12, 1932, in Chicago, IL; maiden name, Collins; married Edward Randolph Emberley (a writer, artist, and designer), 1955; children: Rebecca Anne, Michael Edward. *Education:* Massachusetts School of Art, B.F.A. *Hobbies and other interests:* Sailing.

Ed and Barbara A. Emberley

Addresses

Home and office—6 Water St., Ipswich, MA 01938; 6 Sanctuary Rd., North Conway, NH 03860-5918.

Career

Author, reteller, and illustrator of children's books; also worked as a librarian at Brown University, Providence, RI. Founder, with husband Ed Emberley, of Bird in the Bush Press.

Awards, Honors

One Wide River to Cross, illustrated by Ed Emberley, received an Art Books for Children citation, Brooklyn Public Library, 1966, and was named a Caldecott Honor Book, American Library Association (ALA), 1967; *Drummer Hoff,* illustrated by Ed Emberley, won the Caldecott Medal, ALA, and the Lewis Carroll Shelf Award, both 1968.

Writings

ILLUSTRATED BY HUSBAND, ED EMBERLEY

Night's Nice, Doubleday (Garden City, NY), 1963.

(Reteller) *The Story of Paul Bunyan,* Prentice-Hall (Englewood Cliffs, NJ), 1963, Simon and Schuster (New York, NY), 1994.

(Reteller) *One Wide River to Cross,* Prentice-Hall (Englewood Cliffs, NJ), 1966, Little, Brown (Boston, MA), 1992.

(Reteller) *Drummer Hoff,* Prentice-Hall (Englewood Cliffs, NJ), 1967, published as a board book, Simon and Schuster (New York, NY), 1987.

Simon's Song, Prentice-Hall (Englewood Cliffs, NJ), 1969.

ILLUSTRATOR; WITH HUSBAND, ED EMBERLEY

Seymour Simon, *The BASIC Book,* HarperCollins (New York, NY), 1985.

Seymour Simon, *Bits and Bytes: A Computer Dictionary for Beginners,* HarperCollins (New York, NY), 1985.

Seymour Simon, *How to Talk to Your Computer,* Crowell (New York, NY), 1985.

Seymour Simon, *Meet the Computer,* HarperCollins (New York, NY), 1985.

Franklyn M. Branley, *Flash, Crash, Rumble, and Roll,* HarperCollins (New York, NY), 1985.

Seymour Simon, *Turtle Talk: A Beginner's Book of LOGO,* HarperCollins (New York, NY), 1986.

Franklyn M. Branley, *The Moon Seems to Change,* HarperCollins (New York, NY), 1987.

From Drummer Hoff, *adapted by Barbara A. Emberley and illustrated by Ed Emberley.*

Adaptations

Drummer Hoff was adapted for film by Gene Deitch and released by Weston Woods, 1969; it was released as both a sound filmstrip and, later, a video. *The Story of Paul Bunyan* was released as a filmstrip by Educational Enrichment Materials, 1969.

Sidelights

For sidelights, see sketch on husband, Ed Emberley.

Biographical and Critical Sources

BOOKS

Emberley, Ed, *Ed Emberley's Drawing Book of Animals,* Little, Brown (Boston, MA), 1970.

Emberley, Ed, *Go Away, Big Green Monster!,* Little, Brown (Boston, MA), 1992.

Hopkins, Lee Bennett, *Books Are by People: Interviews with 104 Authors and Illustrators of Books for Young People,* Citation Press (New York, NY), 1969.

Hopkins, Lee Bennett, *Pauses: Autobiographical Reflections of 101 Creators of Children's Books,* HarperCollins (New York, NY), 1995.

PERIODICALS

Booklist, October, 1998, Kathleen Squires, review of *Three: An Emberley Family Sketchbook,* p. 96.

Boston Globe, October 19, 1997, Liz Rosenberg, "The New Flexibility of the Board Book," p. P5.

Chicago Sunday Tribune Magazine of Books, May 14, 1961, Joan Beck, review of *The Wing on a Flea: A Book about Shapes,* section 2, p. 2.

Christian Science Monitor, May 7, 1970, Pamela Marsh, review of *Ed Emberley's Drawing Book of Animals,* p. B1.

Horn Book, February, 1964, Virginia Haviland, review of *The Story of Paul Bunyan,* p. 48; August, 1968, Barbara Emberley, "Ed Emberley," pp. 403-406; August, 1968, Ed Emberley, "Caldecott Award Acceptance," pp. 399-402; August, 1978, Ethel L. Heins, review of *Ed Emberley's ABC,* pp. 386-387; March, 1995, review of *The Story of Paul Bunyan,* p. 222.

Instructor, May, 1995, Judy Freeman, review of *Go Away, Big Green Monster!,* p. 78.

Kirkus Reviews, July 15, 1966, review of *One Wide River to Cross,* p. 683; March 15, 2003, review of *Thanks, Mom!*

Library Journal, December 15, 1967, Della Thomas, review of *Drummer Hoff,* p. 602.

New York Times Book Review, May 14, 1961, review of *The Wing on a Flea: A Book about Shapes,* p. 35; January 26, 1964, Barbara Wersba, review of *The Story of Paul Bunyan,* p. 26; October 16, 1966, Barbara Novak O'Doherty, review of *One Wide River to Cross,* p. 38; November 5, 1967, Eve Merriam, review of *Drummer Hoff,* p. 71; March 1, 1970, George A. Woods, review of *Ed Emberley's Drawing Book of Animals,* p. 34; July 2, 1978, Selma G. Lanes, review of *Ed Emberley's ABC,* p. 11.

Pittsburgh Post-Gazette Magazine, March 21, 2000, Karen MacPherson, "Artful Books Open Up World of Art to the Young."

Portsmouth Herald, September 30, 2003, Jeanne McCartin, "A Story-Book Existence."

Publishers Weekly, December 26, 1966, review of *One Wide River to Cross,* p. 99; July 25, 1980, "Ed Emberley," pp. 78-79; March 29, 1993, review of *Go Away, Big Green Monster!,* p. 54; March 24, 2003, review of *Thanks, Mom!,* p. 74.

School Library Journal, October, 1963, Eileen Lampert, review of *Night's Nice,* p. 190; March, 1968, Jean Reynolds, "Ed Emberley," pp. 113-114; September, 1978, Gemma DeVinney, review of *Ed Emberley's ABC,* p. 107.

Time, December 21, 1970, Timothy Foote, review of *Ed Emberley's Drawing Book of Animals,* p. 68.

ONLINE

Bulletin of the Center of Children's Books, http://alexia.lis.uiuc.edu/ (August 1, 2002), Jeannette Hulick, "True Blue: Ed Emberley."*

*   *   *

EMBERLEY, Ed(ward Randolph) 1931-

Personal

Born October 19, 1931, in Malden, MA; son of Wallace Akin (a carpenter and house painter) and Evelyn (a clerk in a clothing store; maiden name, Farrell) Emberley; married Barbara A. Collins (an author and illustrator), 1955; children: Rebecca Anne, Michael Edward. *Education:* Massachusetts School of Art, B.F.A.; also studied at the Rhode Island School of Art (now Rhode Island School of Design). *Religion:* Protestant. *Hobbies and other interests:* Sailing.

Addresses

Home and office—6 Water St., Ipswich, MA 01938; 6 Sanctuary Rd., North Conway, NH 03860-5918.

Career

Author and illustrator of children's books; illustrator of textbooks and for periodicals; designer. Also worked as a cartoonist and paste-up artist for a direct-mail advertising firm, Boston, MA. Founder, with wife, Barbara, of Bird in the Bush Press. Designer of children's merchandise for Boston Marathon, 2003. *Military service:* U.S. Army, two years.

Awards, Honors

Notable Book citation, American Library Association (ALA), 1961, for *The Wing on a Flea: A Book about Shapes;* award for best-illustrated book, *New York Times,* 1961, for *The Wing on a Flea,* and 1965, for *Punch and Judy: A Play for Puppets;* Junior Literary Guild selection, 1962, for *The Parade Book,* and 1966, for *Rosebud;* Art Books for Children citation, Brooklyn Public Library, 1966, and Caldecott Honor Book, ALA, 1967, both for *One Wide River to Cross;* New Jersey Authors Award for science, New Jersey Institute of Technology, 1968, for *Ladybug, Ladybug, Fly Away Home;* Caldecott Medal, ALA, and Lewis Carroll Shelf Award, both 1968, both for *Drummer Hoff;* Chandler Book Talk Reward of Merit, 1968; Black-Eyed Susan Book Award (Maryland), 1994-95, for *Go Away, Big Green Monster!*

Writings

SELF-ILLUSTRATED

The Wing on a Flea: A Book about Shapes, Little, Brown (Boston, MA), 1961, revised edition. 2001.

The Parade Book, Little, Brown (Boston, MA), 1962.

Cock a Doodle Doo: A Book of Sounds, Little, Brown (Boston, MA), 1964.

Punch and Judy: A Play for Puppets, Little, Brown (Boston, MA), 1965.

Rosebud, Little, Brown (Boston, MA), 1966.

Green Says Go, Little, Brown (Boston, MA), 1968.

Klippity Klop, Little, Brown (Boston, MA), 1974.

The Wizard of Op, Little, Brown (Boston, MA), 1975.

A Birthday Wish, Little, Brown (Boston, MA), 1977.

Ed Emberley's ABC, Little, Brown (Boston, MA), 1978.

Ed Emberley's Amazing Look-Through Book, Little, Brown (Boston, MA), 1979.

Ed Emberley's Crazy Mixed-up Face Game, Little, Brown (Boston, MA), 1981.

Six Nature Adventures (contains "The Butterfly," "The Dandelion," "The Chameleon," "The Chicken," "The Frog," and "The Hare"), Little, Brown (Boston, MA), 1982.

Go Away, Big Green Monster!, Little, Brown (Boston, MA), 1992.

Ed Emberley's Three Science Flip Books, Little, Brown (Boston, MA), 1994.

(With Anne Miranda) *Glad Monster, Sad Monster: A Book about Feelings,* Little, Brown (Boston, MA), 1997.

(With Rebecca and Michael Emberley) *Three: An Emberley Family Sketchbook,* Little, Brown (Boston, MA), 1998.

Ed Emberley's Rainbow, Little, Brown (Boston, MA), 2000.

Thanks, Mom!, Little, Brown (Boston, MA), 2003.

ILLUSTRATOR; WRITTEN BY WIFE, BARBARA EMBERLEY

Night's Nice, Doubleday (Garden City, NY), 1963.

(Reteller) *The Story of Paul Bunyan,* Prentice-Hall (Englewood Cliffs, NJ), 1963, Simon and Schuster (New York, NY), 1994.

(Reteller) *One Wide River to Cross,* Prentice-Hall (Englewood Cliffs, NJ), 1966, Little, Brown (Boston, MA), 1992.

(Reteller) *Drummer Hoff,* Prentice-Hall (Englewood Cliffs, NJ), 1967, published as a board book, Simon and Schuster (New York, NY), 1987.

Simon's Song, Prentice-Hall (Englewood Cliffs, NJ), 1969.

ILLUSTRATOR; WITH WIFE, BARBARA EMBERLEY

Seymour Simon, *The BASIC Book,* HarperCollins (New York, NY), 1985.

Seymour Simon, *Bits and Bytes: A Computer Dictionary for Beginners,* HarperCollins (New York, NY), 1985.

Seymour Simon, *How to Talk to Your Computer,* Crowell (New York, NY), 1985.

Seymour Simon, *Meet the Computer,* HarperCollins (New York, NY), 1985.

Franklyn M. Branley, *Flash, Crash, Rumble, and Roll,* HarperCollins (New York, NY), 1985.

Seymour Simon, *Turtle Talk: A Beginner's Book of LOGO,* HarperCollins (New York, NY), 1986.

Franklyn M. Branley, *The Moon Seems to Change,* HarperCollins (New York, NY), 1987.

SELF-ILLUSTRATED; "ED EMBERLEY'S DRAWING BOOK" SERIES

Ed Emberley's Drawing Book of Animals, Little, Brown (Boston, MA), 1970.

Ed Emberley's Drawing Book: Make a World, Little, Brown (Boston, MA), 1972.

Ed Emberley's Drawing Book of Faces, Little, Brown (Boston, MA), 1975.

Ed Emberley's Great Thumbprint Drawing Book, Little, Brown (Boston, MA), 1977.

Ed Emberley's Big Green Drawing Book, Little, Brown (Boston, MA), 1979.

Ed Emberley's Big Orange Drawing Book, Little, Brown (Boston, MA), 1980.

Ed Emberley's Halloween Drawing Book, Little, Brown (Boston, MA), 1980.

Ed Emberley's Big Purple Drawing Book, Little, Brown (Boston, MA), 1981.

Picture Pie: A Circle Drawing Book, Little, Brown (Boston, MA), 1984.

Ed Emberley's Big Red Drawing Book, Little, Brown (Boston, MA), 1987.

Ed Emberley's Christmas Drawing Book, Little, Brown (Boston, MA), 1987.

Ed Emberley's Drawing Box, Little, Brown (Boston, MA), 1988.

Ed Emberley's Second Drawing Box, Little, Brown (Boston, MA), 1990.

Ed Emberley's Thumbprint Drawing Box, Little, Brown (Boston, MA), 1992.

Mosaic: A Step-by-Step Cut and Paste Drawing Book, Little, Brown (Boston, MA), 1995.

Ed Emberley's Picture Pie Two: A Drawing Book and Stencil, Little, Brown (Boston, MA), 1996.

Ed Emberley's Fingerprint Drawing Book, Little, Brown (Boston, MA), 2000.

Ed Emberley's Drawing Book of Weirdos, Little, Brown (Boston, MA), 2002.

Ed Emberley's Drawing Book of Trucks and Trains, Little, Brown (Boston, MA), 2002.

Ed Emberley's Complete Funprint Drawing Book, Little, Brown (Boston, MA), 2002.

SELF-ILLUSTRATED; "ED EMBERLEY'S LITTLE DRAWING BOOK" SERIES

The Ed Emberley Little Drawing Book of Birds, Little, Brown (Boston, MA), 1973.

The Ed Emberley Little Drawing Book of Farms, Little, Brown (Boston, MA), 1973.

The Ed Emberley Little Drawing Book of Trains, Little, Brown (Boston, MA), 1973.

The Ed Emberley Little Drawing Book of Weirdos, Little, Brown (Boston, MA), 1973.

Ed Emberley's Little Drawing Book of Horses, Little, Brown (Boston, MA), 1990.

Ed Emberley's Little Drawing Book of Fish, Little, Brown (Boston, MA), 1990.

Ed Emberley's Little Drawing Book of Trucks, Little, Brown (Boston, MA), 1990.

Ed Emberley's Little Drawing Book of More Weirdos, Little, Brown (Boston, MA), 1990.

Ed Emberley's Little Drawing Book of Sea Creatures, Little, Brown (Boston, MA), 1990.

BOARD BOOKS; "FIRST WORDS" SERIES

Home, Little, Brown (Boston, MA), 1987.

Sounds, Little, Brown (Boston, MA), 1987.

Animals, Little, Brown (Boston, MA), 1987.

Cars, Boats, and Planes, Little, Brown (Boston, MA), 1987.

ILLUSTRATOR

Ruth Bonn Penn, *Mommies Are for Loving,* Putnam (New York, NY), 1962.

Franklyn M. Branley, *The Big Dipper,* Crowell (New York, NY), 1962.

Mary Kay Phelan, *The White House,* Holt (New York, NY), 1962.

Roma Gans, *Birds Eat and Eat and Eat,* Crowell (New York, NY), 1963.

Leslie Waller, *American Inventions,* Holt (New York, NY), 1963.

Richard Schackburg and others, *Yankee Doodle,* Prentice-Hall (New York, NY), 1965.

Letta Schatz, *Rhinoceros? Preposterous!,* Steck-Vaughn (Austin, TX), 1965.

Dorothy Les-Tina, *Flag Day,* Crowell (New York, NY), 1965.

Paul Showers, *Columbus Day,* Crowell (New York, NY), 1965.

M. C. Farquhar, *Colonial Life in America,* Holt (New York, NY), 1965.

Augusta Goldin, *The Bottom of the Sea,* Crowell (New York, NY), 1966.

Aguusta Goldin, *Straight Hair, Curly Hair,* Crowell (New York, NY), 1966.

Leslie Waller, *The American West,* Holt (New York, NY), 1966.

Judy Hawes, *Ladybug, Ladybug, Fly Away Home,* Crowell, 1967.

Heywood Broun, *The Fifty-first Dragon,* Prentice-Hall (Englewood Cliffs, NJ), 1968.

Leslie Waller, *Clothing,* Holt (New York, NY), 1969.

Mindel and Harry Sitomer, *What Is Symmetry?,* Crowell (New York, NY), 1970.

Ian Serraillier, *Suppose You Met a Witch,* Little, Brown (Boston, MA), 1973.

John G. Keller, *Krispin's Fair,* Little, Brown (Boston, MA), 1976.

Franklyn M. Branley, *Space City,* Harper (New York, NY), 1991.

OTHER

Emberley also has contributed to *Kid-Friendly Web Guide,* by Laura Leininger and others, Monday Morning Books, Inc. (Palo Alto, CA), 1997; *Kid-Friendly Computer Book,* by Elnora Chambers and others, Monday Morning Books, Inc. (Palo Alto, CA), 1997; and *Kid-Friendly Start-Ups: Activity Cards for Writing-Geography-Math,* by Elnora Chambers and others, Monday Morning Books, Inc. (Palo Alto, CA), 1998. *The Story of Paul Bunyan* was issued in Braille. *Growing Up Well—Squiggles, Dots, and Lines: A Kid's Video Guide to Drawing and Creating Featuring Illustrator Ed Emberley* was released by Inspired Corporation, 2002. A collection of Ed Emberley's manuscripts and art is included in the de Grummond Children's Literature Collection, University of Southern Mississippi, and the Cooperative Children's Book Center (Madison, WI).

Adaptations

Drummer Hoff was adapted for film by Gene Deitch and released by Weston Woods, 1969; it was released as both a sound filmstrip and, later, a video. *The Story of* *Paul Bunyan* was released as a filmstrip by Educational Enrichment Materials, 1969. *Ed Emberley's Three Science Flip Books* was featured on the television program *Reading Rainbow,* PBS Kids.

Sidelights

In a career that spans more than forty years, the husband-and-wife team of Ed and Barbara Emberley have become well respected for creating picture books that are noted for their rhythmic texts and vivid art. The pair has taken on the roles of author (Barbara) and artist (Ed) for their collaborations on original works and have acted together to illustrate science books for children by writers Seymour Simon and Franklyn M. Branley. The Emberleys are perhaps best known as the creators of *Drummer Hoff,* a retelling of an old folk song about the build-up to and aftermath of the firing of a cannon by a group of soldiers; *The Story of Paul Bunyan,* a recounting of the legends about the tall-tale hero; and *One Wide River to Cross,* an adaptation of an African-American spiritual about Noah's Ark. Several of the team's works are considered classic examples of juvenile literature and have won prestigious awards; for example, *Drummer Hoff* won the Randolph Caldecott Medal for its illustrations and the Lewis Carroll Shelf Award for its text and pictures, and *One Wide River to Cross* was named a Caldecott Honor Book. The Emberleys have not produced a book that is credited to both of them since 1969. However, Barbara has taken a behind-the-scenes role in helping to produce the works that are written and illustrated by her husband. These titles, which are published under Ed's name, chiefly are activity, concept, picture, and board books. Ed, who has developed a reputation as one of the most prolific and popular authors in the field, has received special attention for his "Drawing Books" series. These best-selling books present step-by-step instructions for creating a variety of subjects, both realistic and fantastic, by using simple geometric shapes. The volumes are credited with introducing young artists to artistic techniques in a particularly understandable and enjoyable manner. Ed also is commended as the creator of *Go Away, Big Green Monster!,* a toy book that uses cutout pictures in a cumulative effect to create and then disembody a scary monster; the book, which is praised for helping children to surmount their fears, often is considered a contemporary classic. Emberley also illustrates books by other authors, and his art has graced works by such writers as Paul Showers, Ian Serraillier, Letta Schatz, and Heywood Broun. In addition, Ed and Barbara's children, Rebecca and Michael Emberley, have worked with their parents on some of their books and have followed in their footsteps to become popular, award-winning author/artists.

As a literary stylist, Barbara employs crisp yet relaxed prose for her texts, which characteristically are drawn from folk songs, folktales, and nursery rhymes. As an illustrator, Ed uses mediums such as pencil, pen and ink, woodcuts, and computer graphics to create his

From Go Away, Big Green Monster! *written and illustrated by Ed Emberley.*

pictures. Emberley often is acknowledged for his originality and skill as both an artist and a designer. His knowledge of production and printing techniques—he and Barbara operate a private printing press and letterpress, Bird in the Bush Press, and publish limited editions of children's books—and strong graphic sensibility are credited with informing the works that he has illustrated. Ed, who tries to vary his technique with every book, characteristically creates energetic, expressive pictures in bold colors, though he also employs more subdued tones. The artist is considered particularly influential, particularly on the children who have learned to appreciate art through his instructional drawing books. Emberley sometimes has been faulted for including difficult elements in his drawing series, for teaching children to copy rather than to draw, and for continuing to produce these works after exhausting his formula; in addition, the quality of his illustrations generally is considered better than that of his texts. However, Emberley is noted as an artist of talent, inventiveness, and expertise and as an author who understands children and what appeals to them. Writing in *Bulletin of the Center for Children's Books,* Jeannette Hulick commented, "Kids definitely have their own ideas about the kind of books they think are fun and satisfying. Emberley's books are a good example of how sometimes it is perfectly O.K. to give kids what they want." Writing in *School Library Journal,* Jean Reynolds stated, "An Ed Emberley picture book leaves one with

a strange feeling of predestination. It is as if to say, 'Why, of course, it had to be done that way because no other way could be right.'" Reynolds concluded, "The deceptive simplicity of the finished book makes the exact basis for its lively appeal difficult to describe. The key seems to lie in that integration of technique, art work, and text that consistently marks an Ed Emberley picture book."

Born in Malden, Massachusetts, Ed Emberley grew up in the nearby town of Cambridge, which also is home to Harvard University; he washed dishes at Harvard for a year to earn money for art school. Emberley's maternal grandfather was a coal miner in Nova Scotia and his paternal grandfather was a sailor in Newfoundland. In his twenties, Emberley's father, Wallace Akin Emberley, left Newfoundland for America and settled in Massachusetts. He and his wife, Evelyn, encouraged Ed, who has said that he always knew that he would become an illustrator, in his early artistic endeavors. In an interview with his wife, Barbara, in *Horn Book,* Emberley stated that this encouragement came "mostly, by lack of discouragement and by having pencils and paper in the house at all times for us to use if we wanted to." Emberley, who liked to read as well as to draw, first began to write stories in kindergarten. Most of his personal library was composed of funny books and old *Life* magazines, although he also liked Beatrix Potter's *The Tale of Peter Rabbit,* Helen Bannerman's *The Story of Little Black Sambo,* and the "Oz" books by L. Frank Baum. As a boy, Emberley looked in vain for a book that would show him how to draw animals. He rectified that situation in 1970 with the publication of the first volume of his art-instruction series, *Ed Emberley's Drawing Book of Animals.* Emberley's dedication read, "For the boy I was, the book I could not find."

Encouraged by his parents and high-school teachers, Emberley went to the Massachusetts School of Art in Boston. Considered one of the best students at the school, he studied painting, illustration, and design as well as printing and production techniques. While at college, Emberley met Barbara Anne Collins, a fellow student who was studying fashion design. Born in Chicago, Illinois, Barbara grew up in Lexington, Massachusetts. After Ed and Barbara received their respective bachelor of fine arts degrees, they married in 1955. Then the Korean War began, and Ed entered the U.S. Army, where he completed a two-year assignment. While in the army, Ed worked as a sign painter and was assigned to a parade division on Governor's Island in New York City. His experience marching in parades later inspired Ed to write and illustrate *The Parade Book,* a nonfiction title for children that was published in 1962. It describes the sights and sounds of parades and features examples from Macy's Thanksgiving Parade in Manhattan, Mardi Gras in New Orleans, and the Tournament of Roses Parade in Pasadena, California, among others. After leaving the army, Ed continued his studies at the Rhode Island School of Art (now the Rhode Island School of Design) in Providence, Rhode

The Wing on a Flea: A Book about Shapes *helps young readers see the geometric shapes in everyday things. (Written and illustrated by Ed Emberley.)*

Island, where he studied illustration. During this time, Barbara worked as a librarian at Brown University in Providence. After Ed's course of study was completed, the couple moved to Boston, where Ed spent two years working as a paste-up artist and cartoonist for a direct-mail company.

Around the time that their children were born (Rebecca in 1958 and Michael in 1960), the Emberleys agreed that Ed should become a freelance illustrator. He then wrote his first book, *The Wing on a Flea: A Book about Shapes,* which was published in 1961. Described by Lee Bennett Hopkins in *Books Are by People: Interviews with 104 Authors and Illustrators of Books for Young People* as "an imaginative commentary on simple forms such as the triangle of a flea's wing or the beak of a bird," *The Wing on a Flea* uses upbeat rhymes and vigorous drawings in green and blue to demonstrate how to identify circles, rectangles, and triangles in everyday things. Writing in the *New York Times Book Review,* a critic concluded, "Only a real square would deny that here is a wonderful, lively way to learn." In 2001, Ed produced a newly illustrated version of *The Wing on a Flea* that includes full color art; printed on black paper, the book showcases pictures in bright primary colors and shiny accents in gold leaf.

Barbara Emberley's first work, *Night's Nice,* was published in 1963. This picture book soothes young readers and listeners by telling them that night is good for many things, such as sleeping, wishing on a star, and seeing city lights. Ed's illustrations portray the feeling of night by darkening oranges, reds, yellows, and greens while using other, brighter colors. Writing in *School Library Journal,* Eileen Lampert said, "Really effective illustrations illuminate this book." Lampert concluded that *Night's Nice* may lead readers to "consider the myriad beauties of his world at night." Also in 1962, Ed started to experiment with woodcuts. He sent out a mailer to various publishers of children's books showing a print of Paul Bunyan and Pinocchio along with a note stating that he would like to illustrate the stories of these characters. The publisher Prentice-Hall agreed; in 1963, they published *The Story of Paul Bunyan,* which includes Barbara's text and Ed's illustrations. This collection of anecdotes about the massive lumberjack and his companion Babe the Blue Ox is written in "easy, yarn-spinning prose," according to Barbara Wersba of the *New York Times Book Review,* and is illustrated in bold, detailed woodcuts in brown, blue, green, and white. Noting that the "robust and joyful" pictures "serve the story well," Wersba commented that the "comic exaggerations of the tall tale are beautifully rendered." Virginia Haviland of *Horn Book* called *The Story of Paul Bunyan* a "striking graphic arts achievement." Reviewing the reissued edition in another issue of the same magazine, a critic added that "the straightforward text is a fine introduction" to the tale of the legendary lumberjack.

In 1966, the Emberleys published *One Wide River to Cross,* an adaptation of the African-American spiritual that also serves as a counting book. Barbara describes the gathering of the animals on board the ark, first one by one, then two by two, and leading up to ten by ten; after this, the rains begin. Ed illustrates the book in woodcuts that feature silhouetted figures and pages of varying colors. He includes the animals associated with the ark as well as some figures from folklore, such as the unicorn and the griffin. Writing in the *New York Times Book Review,* Barbara Novak O'Doherty stated that *One Wide River to Cross* is "striking evidence that old themes, properly handled, are inexhaustible wells of inspiration." Alluding to the three books about Noah that had come out that year, a reviewer in *Publishers Weekly* claimed that the Emberleys' version "might well be the one that would have pleased him most of all." A critic in *Kirkus Reviews* suggested, "Buy it in twos, be prepared to have to reread it in tens." *One Wide River to Cross* was the sole runner-up for the Caldecott Medal in 1967.

The Emberleys produced their Caldecott Medal-winning book *Drummer Hoff* in 1967. The rhyming, alliterative text of this work is a retelling of the traditional poem "John Ball Shot Them All," which is about the making of a rifle. Barbara turned this verse into a cumulative rhyme about a group of happy soldiers who build a cannon that makes a loud explosion when their drummer fires it off. Ed's pictures—dynamic, stylized woodcuts that create the effect of thirteen colors through overprinting of red, yellow, and blue—give an antiwar subtext to the story. Both the soldiers and the cannon appear to have been destroyed by the blast; the last picture shows birds, ladybugs, and flowers—used as decorations in the previous pages—taking over the remains of the cannon. Emberley, who based his illustrations on the concept that a woodcut does not have to look like a woodcut, uses his woodcuts as if they were drawings, dropping colors into the open spaces left around the lines. By combining basic colors to create other tones, he was able to produce thirteen varied shades. Reviewers have praised the artist for both the originality of his idea and the success of its execution, and they have commended the reteller for the jaunty flavor of her text. Writing in the *New York Times Book Review,* Eve Merriam called *Drummer Hoff* "a perfect wedding of text and pictures. . . . You don't have to be married to produce this wry, well-bred humor, but in the Emberleys' case, it doesn't hurt." Della Thomas of *Library Journal* stated, "An old folk rhyme is the perfect vehicle for this talented author-artist team." Thomas continued by calling *Drummer Hoff* "one of the liveliest picture books of the year." In 1987, *Drummer Hoff* was issued as a board

book to mark its thirty-year anniversary. Liz Rosenberg of the *Boston Globe* commented that the book "continues strong in its board-book incarnation, as full of ferocity and wit as ever. . . . Barbara Emberley's adaptation is a galloping tour de force, and Ed Emberley's pictures a wild combination of the antique and the psychedelic."

In 1970, Ed Emberley produced the first of his "Drawing Book" series, *Ed Emberley's Drawing Book of Animals.* In this work, the artist demonstrates how to draw over fifty animals, from ants to whales, by using geometric shapes, letters, numbers, dots, curlicues, and other symbols. Emberley provides aspiring artists with clear verbal instructions and humorous visual examples. Writing in *Time,* Timothy Foote called *Ed Emberley's Drawing Book of Animals* "that all but unheard-of success, a 'how-to-draw' book that really works." Pamela Marsh of the *Christian Science Monitor* predicted that the book "can turn anyone over eight into an instant artist" and noted that "it makes an encouraging book for those, adults included, who imagine they can't draw for toffee." Writing in the *New York Times Book Review,* George A. Woods said that, after finishing Emberley's book, "I've got a pad full of impressive doodles and drawings and my kids think that I'm a genius!" Since the publication of his first drawing book, Emberley has added more than twenty-five titles to his series. These works, which are divided into "Drawing Books" and "Little Drawing Books," use a format similar to that in *Ed Emberely's Drawing Book of Animals* to center on colors, holidays, faces, birds, animals, motorized vehicles, supernatural characters, and other things that interest children. Emberley also includes works that use fingerprints and thumbprints as their jumping-off points. Throughout his series, the artist gives directions for drawing a wide variety of people, creatures, animals, and objects that reflect both the natural world and that of the imagination. Although these works have been called gimmicky, they generally are considered clever, appealing introductions to art instruction.

Among Emberley's most acclaimed works is *Ed Emberley's ABC,* a title published in 1978. In this book, the artist represents each letter of the alphabet in a double-page spread that contains four panels of pictures that show an animal constructing the individual letter (for example, an ant forms the letter "A" by skywriting in an airplane). Through hand-lettered text and vibrant illustrations, readers are encouraged to find numerous examples of objects that begin with the designated letter. Writing in the *New York Times Book Review,* Selma G. Lanes called it "an eye-dazzler" and "an alphabet not to be missed." Ethel L. Heins of *Horn Book* called *Ed Emberley's ABC* a "substantial and original piece of work. . . . [T]he pages show great ingenuity of conception and design, the color work is strikingly beautiful and subtle, and the whole book . . . constitutes a handsome, unified production." Gemma DeVinney of

School Library Journal predicted that *Ed Emberley's ABC* "will be snatched up by children eager to peruse its colorful, fun-loving, action-filled pages."

Ed Emberley is the creator of several interactive activity books that engage youngsters by having them do such things as hold pages to the light, turn them sideways, and lift flaps. One of his most popular titles in this genre is *Go Away, Big Green Monster!,* a book published in 1992. In this work, Emberley uses stiff, die-cut pages with peep holes to let children construct and deconstruct the title character. The book starts with a black page and two round yellow eyes that peer from the darkness. Each pages adds a new element, such as a long blue nose, a red mouth, sharp white teeth, and a big green face. Finally, the culmination produces the visage of a frightening monster; however, the text reads, "You Don't Scare Me! So Go Away." Each subsequent page then subtracts each of the scary pieces until the last page is black. The final text reads, "And Don't Come Back! Until I Say So." Writing in *Instructor,* Judy Freeman called *Go Away, Big Green Monster!* "a cleverly designed gem that all ages will adore." A reviewer in *Publishers Weekly* noted that Emberley "makes wonderful use of innovative production techniques in this ingenious offering."

Barbara and Ed Emberley consistently have involved their children Rebecca and Michael in their artistic lives. For example, both children helped their mother to make overlays with drawing instructions for their father's books. In an interview with Jeanne McCartin in the *Portsmouth Herald,* Rebecca said, "My father just wanted to hand down every thing he knew to me and my brother. He sure did that. . . . We spent a lot of time together as a family. Creating things was just life. It certainly was not an event. It was just what we did." Rebecca also called her mother a major influence. Barbara taught her daughter how to sew and to design clothing, and Ed taught her to work in silver, copper, and numerous paint mediums. When Rebecca was twelve and Michael ten, they each received sailing dinghy kits from their father. "We sailed [the boats] for years," Rebecca told McCartin. When Rebecca was in high school, her father started training her, taking her into his studio for three house each day during summer vacations. Rebecca recalled to McCartin, "Everything my father learned in college, I learned in high school. He also educated some of my boyfriends those summers. They came around long after they broke up with me." Rebecca and Michael now are both successful author/ illustrators of books for children. In 1998, they teamed up with their father to produce *Three: An Emberley Family Sketchbook.* A collection of narratives, drawings, and activities by each artist, the book includes fairy tales, stories, poems, recipes, and autobiographical information. Thematically, the concept of "three" appears throughout; artistically, the book reflects each illustrator's personal style. Ed uses computer-generated art, Rebecca uses woodcuts and paper collages, and Michael uses watercolors and bold ink-and-crayon art.

Booklist critic Kathleen Squires commented, "The Emberley family delivers a triple dose of fun. . . . Children will be intrigued by this big book of fun." Writing in the *Pittsburgh Post-Gazette Magazine,* Karen MacPherson called *Three: An Emberley Family Sketchbook* "a book that rings with energy" before concluding, "What's best about this book is its message that there are many different ways to be an artist."

Ed Emberley has also received favorable critical attention for his picture book *Thanks, Mom!,* a title published in 2003. The book features Kiko, a little mouse in a circus act. While performing in the center ring, Kiko spies a hunk of cheese and grabs it. He then is chased by a cat, a dog, a tiger, and an elephant—all animals of increasing size—who get their moment in the spotlight. Sailing through the air, Kiko's mother, Koko, frightens the elephant and frees Kiko, who thanks his mom politely and is welcomed warmly in return. At the end of the story, both mother and son enjoy the cheese. Emberley illustrates *Thanks, Mom!* with neon-hued geometric shapes, including stars, stripes, and polka dots, and colorful yellow highlights. A reviewer in *Publishers Weekly* noted, "At once buoyant and understated, Emberley's story. . . slyly delivers lessons in punctuation, pecking order, and manners." Calling *Thanks, Mom!* "a visual lollapalooza," a critic in *Kirkus Reviews* found the work "a classic turning of the tables [that] gives readers both an eyeful and a first taste of allegory."

In his Caldecott Medal acceptance speech, which was reprinted in *Horn Book,* Ed Emberley said, "There is more to illustrating a picture book than knowing how to draw pictures. To an illustrator the picture on the drawing board is merely a means to an end. The end is the printed picture. An illustration could be defined as a picture that can be printed. A good picture is a bad illustration if it cannot be printed well. And, of course, a bad picture is a bad picture no matter how well suited it is to the printing process. I work in many different techniques when preparing illustrations—woodcuts, pencil, pen and ink. But as varied as they are in appearance they have one thing in common—the illustrations are meant to be printed. Although I am primarily an artist and not a printing expert, the necessity to be both dreamer and realist is what fascinates me most about picture-book making." In assessing his career in the field of children's literature, Emberley told Lee Bennett Hopkins in *Pauses: Autobiographical Reflections of 101 Creators of Children's Books,* "Working in the field of children's books is challenging. It is a wonderful field to be involved in. It is one wide river to cross after another, and you never quite feel that you have reached the other side." In an interview in *Publishers Weekly,* Emberley stated, "I love books, even the *feel* of books, not to mention what's inside. And I don't consider myself an illustrator or an author or an instructor. I like to think I am a creator of books. If lightning should strike tomorrow and I could no longer write or draw, I would still find a way of making books my career."

Biographical and Critical Sources

BOOKS

Emberley, Ed, *Ed Emberley's Drawing Book of Animals,* Little, Brown (Boston, MA), 1970.

Emberley, Ed, *Go Away, Big Green Monster!,* Little, Brown (Boston, MA), 1992.

Hopkins, Lee Bennett, *Books Are by People: Interviews with 104 Authors and Illustrators of Books for Young People,* Citation Press (New York, NY), 1969.

Hopkins, Lee Bennett, *Pauses: Autobiographical Reflections of 101 Creators of Children's Books,* HarperCollins (New York, NY), 1995.

PERIODICALS

Booklist, October, 1998, Kathleen Squires, review of *Three: An Emberley Family Sketchbook,* p. 96.

Boston Globe, October 19, 1997, Liz Rosenberg, "The New Flexibility of the Board Book," p. P5.

Chicago Sunday Tribune Magazine of Books, May 14, 1961, Joan Beck, review of *The Wing on a Flea: A Book about Shapes,* section 2, p. 2.

Christian Science Monitor, May 7, 1970, Pamela Marsh, review of *Ed Emberley's Drawing Book of Animals,* p. B1.

Horn Book, February, 1964, Virginia Haviland, review of *The Story of Paul Bunyan,* p. 48; August, 1968, Barbara Emberley, "Ed Emberley," pp. 403-406; August, 1968, Ed Emberley, "Caldecott Award Acceptance," pp. 399-402; August, 1978, Ethel L. Heins, review of *Ed Emberley's ABC,* pp. 386-387; March, 1995, review of *The Story of Paul Bunyan,* p. 222.

Instructor, May, 1995, Judy Freeman, review of *Go Away, Big Green Monster!,* p. 78.

Kirkus Reviews, July 15, 1966, review of *One Wide River to Cross,* p. 683; March 15, 2003, review of *Thanks, Mom!*

Library Journal, December 15, 1967, Della Thomas, review of *Drummer Hoff,* p. 602.

New York Times Book Review, May 14, 1961, review of *The Wing on a Flea: A Book about Shapes,* p. 35; January 26, 1964, Barbara Wersba, review of *The Story of Paul Bunyan,* p. 26; October 16, 1966, Barbara Novak O'Doherty, review of *One Wide River to Cross,* p. 38; November 5, 1967, Eve Merriam, review of *Drummer Hoff,* p. 71; March 1, 1970, George A. Woods, review of *Ed Emberley's Drawing Book of Animals,* p. 34; July 2, 1978, Selma G. Lanes, review of *Ed Emberley's ABC,* p. 11.

Pittsburgh Post-Gazette Magazine, March 21, 2000, Karen MacPherson, "Artful Books Open Up World of Art to the Young."

Portsmouth Herald, September 30, 2003, Jeanne McCartin, "A Story-Book Existence."

Publishers Weekly, December 26, 1966, review of *One Wide River to Cross,* p. 99; July 25, 1980, "Ed Emberley," pp. 78-79; March 29, 1993, review of *Go Away, Big Green Monster!,* p. 54; March 24, 2003, review of *Thanks, Mom!,* p. 74.

School Library Journal, October, 1963, Eileen Lampert, review of *Night's Nice,* p. 190; March, 1968, Jean Reynolds, "Ed Emberley," pp. 113-114; September, 1978, Gemma DeVinney, review of *Ed Emberley's ABC,* p. 107.

Time, December 21, 1970, Timothy Foote, review of *Ed Emberley's Drawing Book of Animals,* p. 68.

ONLINE

Bulletin of the Center of Children's Books, http://alexia.lis. uiuc.edu/ (August 1, 2002), Jeannette Hulick, "True Blue: Ed Emberley."*

*   *   *

ENGLART, Mindi Rose 1965-

Personal

Born October 10, 1965, in Newark, NJ; daughter of Alan (a business owner) and Carol (a registered nurse) Englart; married Kiva Sutton (a humor writer, illustrator, and cartoonist). *Education:* Attended Fairleigh Dickinson University, 1983-85; University of Hartford, B.F. A., 1988; Wesleyan University, M.A., 2004. *Politics:* Democratic. *Religion:* Jewish. *Hobbies and other interests:* Learning, reading, traveling, camping, conversing.

Addresses

Office—East Rock Coaching & Consulting, LLC, 145 Cottage St., B1, New Haven, CT 06511. *E-mail*—m. Englart@comcast.net.

Career

Freelance writer and editor, 1990—; founder of East Rock Coaching & Consulting, LLC, New Haven, CT, 2001—; high school creative writing and journalism teacher, New Haven, CT, 2002—. Yoga teacher for chronically ill and the elderly, New Haven, CT, 1993—. Poetry judge for California Chapparal Poets; program coordinator for City Wide Open Studios (New Haven, CT). College essay advisor; writing coach; mentor for local young artists. Publisher of *Etcetera Journal,* Volumes 1-6, Etcetera Press (New Haven, CT), 1996-98. Coordinating Council for Children in Crisis, board member.

Member

Network Inc. of New Haven.

Awards, Honors

Fellowship, Yale Teachers Institute, Yale University, 2003; scholarship, Haystack Mountain School of Crafts.

Writings

"MADE IN THE USA" SERIES

Music CDs, Blackbirch Press (Woodbridge, CT), 2000.
Newspapers, Blackbirch Press (Woodbridge, CT), 2000.

In How Do I Become an ...? Architect, *readers learn what skills are needed to be successful in this field.* (Written by Mindi Rose Englart. Book photograph by Peter Casolino.)

Bikes, Blackbirch Press (Woodbridge, CT), 2002.
Helicopters, Blackbirch Press (Woodbridge, CT), 2002.
Pens, Blackbirch Press (Woodbridge, CT), 2002.

"HOW DO I BECOME A ?" SERIES

Architect, Blackbirch Press (Woodbridge, CT), 2002.
Chef, Blackbirch Press (Woodbridge, CT), 2002.
EMS Worker, Blackbirch Press (Woodbridge, CT), 2002.
Firefighter, Blackbirch Press (Woodbridge, CT), 2002.
Police Officer, Blackbirch Press (Woodbridge, CT), 2002.
TV Reporter, Blackbirch Press (Woodbridge, CT), 2003.
Veterinarian, Blackbirch Press (Woodbridge, CT), 2003.

OTHER

Also author of *2002 Success Calendar,* East Rock Coaching & Consulting, LLC (New Haven, CT), 2002. Author of *Rap as a Modern Poetic Form,* Yale University Press, 2003. Creative work has been published in *Poet's Park, Dirigible, Spirit Journal, Sun, New Haven Arts,* and *Etcetera Journal.* Editor of *Etcetera Journal,* Volumes 1-6, Etcetera Press (New Haven, CT), 1996-98.

Work in Progress

Stretch, a novel about a young woman's search for self, spirituality, and purpose while living in a yoga ashram for four years; ghostwriting an autobiography of Melvin H. Wearing, New Haven's retired police chief; research on building communities; research on the stories of elderly people.

Sidelights

Mindi Rose Englart's work focuses on providing creative and educational information for children. Her major contributions have been to two series of books published by Blackbirch Press: "Made in the USA" and "How Do I Become a . . .?" These slim volumes present factual and pictorial information geared to piquing the interest of youngsters and answering basic questions about everyday products and careers. Englart's interest in creative writing led her to develop a small press literary journal, *Etcetra,* which showcased the works of both established and emerging writers and artists. She also devotes considerable effort to encouraging young artists and writers in her community.

Geared towards grades three through six, Englart's "How Do I Become a . . .?" books "focus mostly on the schooling and training necessary to enter each field," observed Melinda Piehler in her review of *Architect* and *Chef* for *School Library Journal.* Piehler also found "both books . . . sound selections where needed." *Music CDs* and *Newspapers,* both from the "Made in the USA" series, "clearly explain and illustrate" the way the featured product is manufactured, commented Frieda F. Bostian in her *Horn Book Guide* review.

Biographical and Critical Sources

PERIODICALS

Booklist, May 15, 2003, Gillian Engberg, review of *Helicopters,* p. 1658.

Horn Book Guide, July-December, 2001, Frieda F. Bostian, review of *Music CDs* and *Newspapers,* p. 154.

School Library Journal, March, 2002, Linda Beck, review of *Music CDs,* p. 246; September, 2002, Sandra Welzenbach, review of *Bikes,* p. 211; March, 2003, Melinda Piehler, review of *Architect* and *Chef,* p. 216.

F

FARISH, Terry 1947-

Personal
Born June 8, 1947, in Waterbury, CT; daughter of Clifford and Eleanor (Bronson) Dickerson; married Stephen Farish (a U.S. Air Force officer), 1970; children: Elizabeth. *Education:* Texas Woman's University, B.S., 1969; California State University—Fullerton, M.L.S., 1976; Antioch University, M.A. (literature and creative writing), 1985. *Politics:* Democrat.

Addresses
Home—192 New Castle Ave., Portsmouth, NH 03801. *Agent*—Marilyn Marlow, Curtis Brown Ltd., 10 Astor Pl., New York, NY 10003. *E-mail*—spring@terryfarish.com.

Career
Ralston Public Library, Ralston, NE, director, 1976-82; Leominster Public Library, Leominster, MA, head of children's services, 1986-90; Cambodian Mutual Assistance Association, Lowell, MA, director of Young Parent Program, 1990-91; Rivier College, Nashua, NH, writing instructor, beginning 1993; Salt Institute for Documentary Studies, Portland, ME, instructor in nonfiction writing. Lecturer, workshop presenter, and literacy volunteer; involved in New Hampshire Theater Project, Arts Alliance of Northern New Hampshire, and Casey Family Services. Worked for American Red Cross in Cu Chi, Vietnam, 1969-70.

Member
Society of Children's Book Writers and Illustrators, National Writers Union, American Library Association.

Awards, Honors
New Hampshire individual artist fellow.

Writings
Why I'm Already Blue (young adult novel), Greenwillow (New York, NY), 1989.

Shelter for a Seabird (young adult novel), Greenwillow (New York, NY), 1990.
Flower Shadows (adult novel), Morrow (New York, NY), 1992.
If the Tiger (adult novel), Steerforth Press (South Royalton, VT), 1995.
Talking in Animal (young adult novel), Greenwillow (New York, NY), 1996.
A House in Earnest (adult novel), Steerforth Press (South Royalton, VT), 2000.
The Cat Who Liked Potato Soup (children's picture book), illustrated by Barry Root, Candlewick Press (Cambridge, MA), 2003.

Work in Progress
Braids, and More True Stories about Sudanese Teenagers, a nonfiction book about a group of teens living in Portland, Maine.

Sidelights
In her novels for both adults and teen readers, Terry Farish focuses on issues such as divorce, teen pregnancy, illness, and loss. Drawing from the people and places she has encountered, the author uses these elements to help create her characters and settings. Her work in Vietnam for the American Red Cross after she graduated from college brought her face to face with the realities of war, and her more recent work with immigrant teens from Africa and Asia have allowed her to see typical adolescent concerns from a broader-than-usual perspective.

Working for many years as a children's librarian, Farish began her writing career penning fiction for young adults. Her first novel, *Why I'm Already Blue,* examines the complex feelings of an adolescent girl whose parents are on the verge of divorce. Feeling as if the burden of family stability lies on her shoulders, twelve-year-old Lucy Purcell begins to retreat into herself after her older sister, Jane, leaves for nursing school. She also distances herself from her closest childhood friend,

Gus, who has muscular dystrophy. When Lucy's sister brings a baby from the hospital to the family cottage, Lucy reunites with Gus and begins to assume some responsibilities for the child's care. Thanksgiving dinner finally presents Lucy and her family with the opportunity to resolve differences, make plans, and adjust to new relationships in a novel that a *Publishers Weekly* reviewer described as "about the collision of emotions rather than a simple coming-of-age tale." *School Library Journal* contributor Bonnie L. Raasch noted the novel's serious tone, while a *Kirkus Reviews* critic called the story "atmospheric" and "moody," and maintained that Farish's "airy, elusive writing subtly conveys the full weight of each character's concerns."

With 1990's *Shelter for a Seabird,* Farish addresses a range of issues, including teen pregnancy, loss of community, and the desire for acknowledgment and understanding. Returning to her Shelter Island home after giving up her baby for adoption, sixteen-year-old Andrea is frustrated to find that her parents act as if nothing out of the ordinary has happened. For Andrea, her whole life and outlook has changed as a result of her summer fling and the consequential experiences of pregnancy and birth, and she soon realizes that this change has set her apart from her friends at school as well. Then Andrea meets Swede, an AWOL soldier who listens without judgment as Andrea talks about her life. Together, Andrea and Swede help each other deal with the erosion of stability in their lives and confront their problems responsibly in preparation for building a solid and mature relationship, in a novel a *Kirkus Reviews* contributor praised for its "ruggedly believable characters" and "pockets of tellingly placed details."

In *Talking in Animal,* pre-teen Siobhan realizes that her dog Tree, which has been a part of her family as long as she can remember, is quietly suffering great pain as he nears the end of his life. As if that imminent loss is not enough, her favorite person, wildlife rehabilitator Maddy Todd, is getting married, which means Maddy will not be able to spend as much time with Siobhan as she was once able. In frustration, she petulantly decides to make life miserable for Lester Grace, the girl who will soon be Maddy's stepdaughter. Ultimately, however, Siobhan comes to terms with her jealousy over Maddy's future and also summons the courage to take Tree to the vet to be euthanized. Calling Farish's protagonist "a really great kid" who makes the transition from her idealized world to reality "naturally and easily and believably," *Voice of Youth Advocates* critic Helen Turner dubbed the novel "a quiet, funny story," while in *Horn Book,* Jennifer Brabander noted that the author "writes with humor and precision about Siobhan's growing awareness of the many forms friendship can take."

Taking a break from more serious fare, Farish experimented with the picture-book genre in 2003's *The Cat Who Liked Potato Soup.* Illustrated by Barry Root, the book focuses on the close relationship between a curmudgeonly old man and a unique cat. Living together

in their rural Texas home, the pair have things down to a routine, and despite the occasional cross word, they get along just fine. Instead of catching birds, the cat prefers to eat potato soup, which the old man enjoys sharing. And rather than exhibiting a usual cat's aversion to water, this cat likes nothing more than to sit in the bow of the old man's fishing dingy, feeling the spray in her face as they row to a likely fishing spot each morning. The two seem inseparable until one day when the cat exhibits normal cat behavior and disappears for several days in retaliation for a slight change in their daily routine. Noting that Farish "demonstrates herself an exciting new talent" as a picture-book author, *Bulletin of the Center for Children's Books* contributor Deborah Stevenson praised *The Cat Who Liked Potato Soup* as a "casually told yet tender tale about the prickly friendship between an old man and his cat." In *Kirkus Reviews,* a contributor had special praise for the restrained illustrations by Barry Root, noting that Farish's "evocative language" is enhanced by "the rich array of subtle verbal and visual nuances" created by the author-illustrator collaboration.

In addition to her picture book and her novels for teen readers, Farish has also penned several fictional works for adults, among them *Flower Shadows, If the Tiger,* and *A House in Earnest.* Based on the author's own experiences in Vietnam as a war relief worker, *Flower Shadows* describes the horrors faced by female Red Cross volunteers during the Vietnam War. The main character's "breathless innocence makes this story a particularly heartbreaking and memorable one," declared a *Kirkus Reviews* critic.

Also set against the backdrop of the war in Southeast Asia, Farish's *If the Tiger* describes the impact of war on two young, motherless women—one Cambodian, one American—whose fathers fought on opposite sides during the Cambodian conflict. Chanty Sun is the only member of her family to have survived the war. Now living in the United States with her Cambodian-born husband, Kob, and her infant son, Chanty realizes that Kob's abusive, controlling behavior is not love. Meanwhile, college student Laurel Sullivan is trying to come to terms with her dictatorial Air Force colonel father and her mixed feelings toward a hippie mother who abandoned her. The paths of the two women cross in a Massachusetts mill town, sparking a chain of events that include a tragic death, a trip to a Buddhist temple to chase away spirits from the past, and an emotional reconciliation in a novel that *New York Times Book Review* writer Laura van Wormer described as "fresh and lyrical." In *Publishers Weekly,* a reviewer praised *If the Tiger* as "quiet, sensuous, and intensely moving," remarking in particular on Farish's skill in weaving Eastern spirituality and the emotional vestiges of war into a "universal human story."

Published in 2000, the novel *A House in Earnest* also involves the emotional aftermath of war, this time through the lives of young married couple Cristy and

A temperamental cat and an old man are an unlikely pair in Terry Farish's book, **The Cat Who Liked Potato Soup.** *(Illustrations by Barry Root.)*

Deborah Mahan. Through what a *Publishers Weekly* contributor described as a "languidly poetic story" covering the couple's twenty-five-year on-again, off-again relationship, Cristy remains haunted by violent memories of Vietnamese mine fields, while Deborah remains stuck in the hippie counterculture, where drugs, idealized fantasies of a better world, and a host of mundane worries fuel her disillusionment. While *Booklist* reviewer Michele Leber described Farish's protagonists as "alternately strikingly sensuous and exasperatingly introspective," Jim Dwyer wrote in his *Library Journal* review that through her writing skills, the novelist succeeds in portraying Cristy and Deborah as "multifaceted individuals with compelling stories."

Biographical and Critical Sources

PERIODICALS

Belles Lettres, fall, 1992, Bettina Berch, review of *Flower Shadows,* pp. 55-56.
Booklist, October 1, 1989, p. 347; November 15, 1990, p. 654; January 1, 1992, Cynthia Ogorek, review of *Flower Shadows,* p. 810; September 1, 1995, Joanne Wilkinson, review of *If the Tiger,* p. 38; May 1, 2000, Michele Leber, review of *A House in Earnest,* p. 1651.
Book Report, January-February, 1990, Rose M. Kent, review of *Why I'm Already Blue,* p. 46; March-April, 1991, Betty Jones, review of *Shelter for a Seabird,* p.

42; November-December, 1996, Holly Wadsworth, review of *Talking in Animal,* p. 39; May 1, 2000, Michele Leber, review of *A House in Earnest,* p. 1651; April 15, 2003, Carolyn Phelan, review of *The Cat Who Liked Potato Soup,* p. 1477.

Bulletin of the Center for Children's Books, June, 2003, Deborah Stevenson, review of *The Cat Who Liked Potato Soup.*

Choice, October, 1995, N. Tischler, review of *If the Tiger,* p. 291.

Horn Book, January-February, 1997, Jennifer Brabander, review of *Talking in Animal* p. 55.

Kirkus Reviews, November 1, 1989, review of *Why I'm Already Blue,* p. 1591; September 15, 1990, review of *Shelter for a Seabird;* October 15, 1991, review of *Flower Shadows,* pp. 1303-1304; June 15, 1996, review of *Talking in Animal,* p. 897; May 1, 2003, review of *The Cat Who Liked Potato Soup,* p. 676.

Library Journal, May 1, 1992, p. 144; April 15, 2000, Jim Dwyer, review of *A House in Earnest,* p. 122.

New York Times Book Review, January 14, 1996, Laura van Wormer, review of *If the Tiger,* p. 19; October 15, 2000, James Polk, review of *A House in Earnest,* p. 23.

Publishers Weekly, July 14, 1989, review of *Why I'm Already Blue,* p. 80; September 14, 1990, review of *Shelter for a Seabird,* p. 128; October 18, 1991, review of *Flower Shadow,* p. 54; May 8, 1995, review of *If the Tiger,* p. 289; October 7, 1996, review of *Talking in Animal,* p. 76; March 6, 2000, review of *A House in Earnest,* p. 80; May 5, 2003, review of *The Cat Who Liked Potato Soup,* p. 221.

School Library Journal, October, 1989, Bonnie L. Raasch, review of *Why I'm Already Blue,* p. 117; November, 1990, Judie Porter, review of *Shelter for a Seabird,* p. 138; November, 1996, Wendy D. Caldiero, review of *Talking in Animal,* p. 104; July, 2003, Steven Englefried, review of *The Cat Who Liked Potato Soup,* p. 95.

Times (London, England), April 14, 1990.

Times Educational Supplement, June 1, 1990, Mary Cadogan, review of *Why I'm Already Blue,* p. B8.

Voice of Youth Advocates, April, 1989, p. 29; October, 1989, p. 212; April, 1997, Helen Turner, review of *Talking in Animal,* p. 28.

Washington Post Book World, October 8, 1995, Hart Williams, review of *If the Tiger,* p. 8.

Women's Review of Books, July, 1995, Jeanne Schinto, review of *If the Tiger,* p. 31.

ONLINE

Terry Farish Home Page, http://www.terryfarish.com/ (January 3, 2004).*

*   *   *

FEARRINGTON, Ann (Peyton) 1945-

Personal

Born August 25, 1945, in Winston-Salem, NC; daughter of James Cornelius Pass (a physician) and Florence (a

Ann Fearrington

homemaker; maiden name: McCanless) Fearrington; married Hege Hill Russ, September 7, 1967 (deceased); married Vance Edwin Cox, Jr. (in sales), June 17, 1985; children: Charles Jonathan Cox, James Pass Fearrington Russ, Joseph Peyton Fearrington Russ. *Ethnicity:* "Caucasian." *Education:* Attended Randolph-Macon Woman's College; University of North Carolina—Chapel Hill, B.A. (English and secondary education); North Carolina State University, M.A. (botany and horticulture). *Religion:* Methodist. *Hobbies and other interests:* Reading, painting, watching TV (especially football, baseball, and basketball), Web surfing, movies, button collecting, lap swimming.

Addresses

Home and office—820 Lake Boone Trail, Raleigh, NC 27607. *Agent*—George Nicholson, Sterling Lord Literistic, 65 Bleecker St., New York, NY 10012. *E-mail*—annf@studioann.com.

Career

Writer, artist, and educator. Writer-in-residence, Raleigh-Wake County (NC) Schools, 1997-2000. Has worked as a middle school teacher of language arts, drama, and Latin; a designer of gardens; and a school library volunteer. *Exhibitions:* North Carolina Museum of Art, one-artist show of paintings from *Christmas Lights,* 1996.

Member

Society of Children's Book Writers and Illustrators, International Reading Association, Beatrix Potter Society, Wake County Reading Association.

Awards, Honors

Winner, national Clairol essay contest, 1991; Pick of the Lists selection, American Booksellers Association, for *Christmas Lights;* Newspaper Association of America Literacy Award, Southern Newspaper Publishers Association Literacy Award, and James B. Hunt Literacy Award, North Carolina Reading Association, all for *The Little Green Book: Eighteen Keys to Your Child's Reading Success.*

Writings

(And illustrator) *Christmas Lights,* Houghton Mifflin (Boston, MA), 1996.

The Little Green Book: Eighteen Keys to Your Child's Reading Success, Raleigh News & Observer (Raleigh, NC), 1998.

Teacher and Librarian Guide for The Little Green Book: Eighteen Keys to Your Child's Reading Success, Raleigh News & Observer (Raleigh, NC), 1999.

Who Sees the Lighthouse?, illustrated by Giles Laroche, Putnam (New York, NY), 2002.

Contributor of poems to literary magazines. *The Little Green Book* has been published in Spanish as *Pequeño Libro Verde,* Raleigh News & Observer (Raleigh, NC), 2000.

Sidelights

Ann Fearrington found the inspiration for her children's holiday book, *Christmas Lights,* in a family tradition she thought was restricted to her geographic area in Winston-Salem, North Carolina, but which was actually a nationwide ritual. While growing up, Fearrington and "her family would jump in the car and cruise the displays of Christmas lights neighbors had fashioned," wrote Megan Garvey in *News & Observer* (Raleigh, NC). "She thought it was a Winston-Salem thing. When she moved to Raleigh and the folks did the same, she thought it was a North Carolina thing. In Louisiana, a decade ago, she changed her mind." Fearrington realized that the fascination with Christmas lights, and the sense of holiday and celebration surrounding them, was something found in communities around the country.

Her insight sparked the idea for *Christmas Lights,* written and illustrated by Fearrington. In the book, a mother, father, and their pajama-wearing children climb into their station wagon one Christmas Eve to take a trip through the neighborhood, admiring the lights and holiday displays. On this dark, cold night, the family sees lights adorning factories, office buildings, balconies,

A family looks forward to celebrating Christmas traditions, in **Christmas Lights,** *written and illustrated by Ann Fearrington.*

trees, spires, and houses. Alliterative prose and descriptive language combine with Fearrington's pastel drawings as the family realizes that the lights they like best of all are the ones on their own Christmas tree in their own home. Kathy Broderick, writing in *Booklist,* remarked that the artwork is "well composed" and "capture[s] the thrill" of the holiday lights. A *Publishers Weekly* reviewer remarked that Fearrington's account "is bound to inspire many a Christmas Eve drive."

Fearrington worked on the text of *Christmas Lights* for a year and on the nine illustrations for another year, Garvey wrote. Without high expectations, she submitted the package to one of her favorite children's book publishers, fully expecting rejection. "But the rejection never came," Garvey wrote. Four days after submitting it, "I got a call from Houghton Mifflin," accepting the book, Garvey quoted Fearrington as saying. "I just about fainted."

A former middle school teacher with a B.A. in English and secondary education and an M.A. in botany and horticulture, Fearrington is a strong advocate of literacy and is also the author of *The Little Green Book: Eighteen Keys to Your Child's Reading Success.* In addition, she wrote and illustrated the *Teacher and Librarian Guide for The Little Green Book: Eighteen Keys to Your Child's Reading Success,* a guidebook for educators. She is also the creator of *StudioAnn.com,* an online resource for children, parents, librarians, and teachers.

The author's 2002 work, *Who Sees the Lighthouse?,* follows a counting book format as a variety of friendly people and animals are illuminated by a lighthouse's beacon, beginning with one sailor, then two pilots, three seagulls, and more. Even pirates and aliens are able to see the lighthouse in Fearrington's book. She also includes a collection of facts on lighthouses, their history, and their locations throughout the United States. A *Publishers Weekly* reviewer called the book "A handsome salute to a seafaring institution—and proof that even grownups take comfort in nightlights."

Biographical and Critical Sources

PERIODICALS

Booklist, September 1, 1996, Kathy Broderick, review of *Christmas Lights,* p. 136; November 15, 2002, Ilene Cooper, review of *Who Sees the Lighthouse?,* p. 609.

Kirkus Reviews, October 15, 1996, review of *Christmas Lights,* p. 1531; June 15, 2002, review of *Who Sees the Lighthouse?,* p. 879.

News & Observer (Raleigh, NC), December 5, 1996, Megan Garvey, "Point of Light: Ann Fearrington's bright idea turned a childhood tradition into a Christmas story for children."

Publishers Weekly, September 30, 1996, review of *Christmas Lights,* p. 89; June 17, 2002, review of *Who Sees the Lighthouse?,* p. 63.

School Library Journal, October, 1996, Jane Marino, review of *Christmas Lights,* p. 35; October, 2002, Laurie von Mehren, review of *Who Sees the Lighthouse?,* p. 105.

Summit Echoes, fall, 1996, "Childhood Memories Illuminate *Christmas Lights.*"

ONLINE

StudioAnn.com: Ann Fearrington Home Page, http://www.studioann.com/ (September 3, 2003).

*   *   *

FRAUSTINO, Lisa Rowe 1961-

Personal

Born May 26, 1961, in Dover-Foxcroft, ME; daughter of Franklin (a foreman) and Carole Linda (a postal clerk; maiden name, Reardon) Rowe; married Daniel V. Fraustino (an English professor), October 30, 1982 (divorced, 1999); children: Daisy, Dan, Olivia. *Education:* University of Maine at Orono, B.A. (with honors), 1984; University of Scranton, M.A., 1988; Binghamton University (formerly State University of New York), Ph.D., 1993. *Politics:* "Independent-minded Democrat."

Addresses

Office—Department of English, Eastern Connecticut State University, 83 Windham St., Willimantic, CT 06226. *E-mail*—FraustinoL@easternct.edu.

The lighthouse is seen by many different creatures. From Who Sees the Lighthouse?, *written by Fearrington. (Illustrated by Giles Laroche.)*

Career

National Education Corporation, Scranton, PA, editor, 1985-86; University of Scranton, Scranton, PA, instructor, 1987-90, 1994; Dick Jones Communications, Dalton, PA, associate editor, 1989-91; Institute of Children's Literature, Redding Ridge, CT, instructor, 1989-94; Wyoming Seminary Preparatory School, Forty Fort, PA, English teacher, 1995-2002; Eastern Connecticut State University, Willimantic, CT, assistant professor of literature, 2002—. Visiting professor, Hollins College, Roanoke, VA, 1995, and Western Maryland College Graduate Program in Education, Westminster, MD, 1999. Speaker and workshop presenter; symposium organizer and facilitator.

Member

Society of Children's Book Writers and Illustrators, Modern Language Association of America, Children's Literature Association, Rutgers University Council for Children's Literature.

Awards, Honors

PEN Syndicated Fiction Award, 1991, for "Christian Charity"; *Highlights for Children* fiction contest winner, 1992, for "Back to the River"; "best books for young adults" citation, American Library Association, and "best book for the teen age" citation, New York Public Library, both 1995, both for *Ash: A Novel;* "quick pick for reluctant readers" citation, American Library Association, and "best book for the teen age" citation, New York Public Library, both 1998, both for *Dirty Laundry: Stories about Family Secrets;* notable book citation, American Library Association, Oppenheim Toy Portfolio Gold Award, Center for Children's Books Blue Ribbon Book, notable book citation, National Council for Teachers of English, Children's Choice Award, International Reading Association, Carolyn Field Award Honor Book, Kansas Reading Association picture book award, and Parent Guide to Children's Media winner, all 2001, all for *The Hickory Chair.*

Writings

Grass and Sky, Orchard Books (New York, NY), 1994.
Ash: A Novel, Orchard Books (New York, NY), 1995.
(Editor and contributor) *Dirty Laundry: Stories about Family Secrets,* Viking (New York, NY), 1998.
The Hickory Chair (picture book), illustrated by Benny Andrews, Scholastic (New York, NY), 2001.
(Editor and contributor) *Soul Searching: Thirteen Stories about Faith and Belief,* Simon & Schuster (New York, NY), 2002.
(Editor) *Shonto Begay* (autobiography), Scholastic (New York, NY), 2004.
(Editor) *Surfing the Crimson Wave,* Simon & Schuster (New York, NY), 2004.
The Devil's Book ("Dear America" series), Scholastic (New York, NY), 2004.

Contributor of stories and essays to anthologies, including *Pegasus,* Kendall/Hunt, 1993; *Tana and the Artist Lady,* Highlights, 1995; Tricia Gardella, editor, *Writers in the Kitchen,* Boyds Mills Press, 1998; Jennifer Armstrong, editor, *Shattered: Stories about War,* Knopf (New York, NY), 2002; and *Sunscripts: Writing from the Florida Suncoast Writers Conference,* University of South Florida Press, 2002. Author of screenplays: *The Olden Days,* 1988, and *Empty Words.* Contributor of short stories to *Wee Wisdom, Pennywhistle Press, With, Clubhouse, Pegasus Anthology,* and *Highlights for Children;* contributor of articles to periodicals, including *Best Sellers, Babytalk, Children's Writer,* and *Once Upon a Time.* Contributor of nonfiction articles to periodicals, including *Children's Literature Association Newsletter, Children's Writer, Byline,* and *Young Authors Magazine.* Copy editor, *The Legal Studies Forum,* 1985-87.

Work in Progress

Editor and contributor to the anthology *Don't Cramp My Style: Stories about That Time of the Month.*

Sidelights

"The only thing I hope to achieve in my books is the best storytelling I can possibly wring out of myself," Lisa Rowe Fraustino told *SATA.* "I dream that my best will be enough to carry a young reader through my book and straight to the library for another by someone else.

"My desk holds piles of manuscripts in various stages of completion. I write many, many drafts of each story. Rather than work straight through on one project until it's publishable, I'll set aside draft three of one story to work on draft six of another or perhaps finish the first draft of something new. When I have a new idea that keeps me awake at night, I'll get up and write it down.

"If I start listing the authors who have influenced me and my work, I will definitely leave important people out because I read so much and try to be someone on whom nothing is lost. But perhaps I've learned the most from studying the works of Katherine Paterson. Also, in no particular order, I love Natalie Babbitt, J. M. Barrie, Beverly Cleary, A. A. Milne, E. L. Konigsburg, Sid Fleischman, Robert Cormier, Paul Zindel, and J. D. Salinger. My view of these and many other contemporary writers and their work is jealous and admiring."

Fraustino's fiction for young adults looks at families caught in difficult, bewildering situations. In *Grass and Sky,* young Timmi learns to accept her grandfather's imperfections and to understand why he has been long absent from the family. Wes, the narrator of *Ash: A Novel,* watches his beloved older brother fall victim to paranoid schizophrenia. In both novels, young protagonists must face the devastating consequences of mental illnesses not only for the sick individual but also for the family dynamics as a whole. Needless to say, Fraustino's books—and her short stories as well—demonstrate an awareness of sensitive issues that are rarely discussed outside the stricken families themselves.

In her *Booklist* review of *Grass and Sky,* Hazel Rochman noted that Fraustino creates situations and characters "drawn with restraint and painful comedy." This same dark humor is evident in *Ash,* as Wes tries to leaven his anxieties in the face of his brother's mental and physical disintegration. *Horn Book* contributor Maeve Visser Knoth described *Ash* as a "forceful, disturbing story about mental illness and the impact it has on a family." A *Publishers Weekly* reviewer likewise found the book "memorable" for its ". . . heartfelt observations of a family's shared pain."

Fraustino's picture book, *The Hickory Chair,* is told from the point of view of a boy who is blind. He enjoys a special relationship with his grandmother—formed through the senses of smell, taste, hearing, and feeling—and is especially bereaved when she passes away. The family discovers that Grandmother has left behind little notes to her loved ones, hidden here and there throughout her house. Although the boy finds notes left for others, he never discovers the note his grandmother wrote to him—until he is a grandfather himself, sitting in the hickory rocking chair that belonged to her. A winner of numerous awards, *The Hickory Chair* received warm reviews from some critics who liked its evocation of sightlessness and its theme of family love. A *Publishers Weekly* reviewer commented that Fraustino's "uncommonly visual prose . . . effectively conveys the lasting bond across generations." In *School Library Journal,* Susan Hepler called *The Hickory Chair* "a finely crafted story of handed-down family treasures . . . and loving connections across the generations."

Fraustino also writes short stories for young adults, and she has edited theme volumes of stories, including *Dirty Laundry: Stories about Family Secrets* and *Soul Searching: Thirteen Stories about Faith and Belief.* As its title implies, *Dirty Laundry* presents a series of stories— some comic, some tragic—about skeletons in the family closet. In Fraustino's contribution to the work, "FRESH PAINt," a girl learns about her ancestor by visiting a patient in a mental hospital. Another story features a teen narrator who discovers that he has an uncle who is undergoing a gender change. *Soul Searching* introduces stories from a variety of religious traditions about young people who seek a relationship with a higher power. According to Elizabeth M. Reardon in *School Library Journal,* the collection is "especially appropriate . . . for church-related discussion groups or ethics and morality classes."

Fraustino once told *SATA:* "My advice to aspiring writers is to read every book you can; books hold the best writing lessons. Live the fullest life you can; experiences hold the best writing details—provided that you notice details. And write every minute you can; you have to write hundreds of pages, and learn from hundreds of mistakes, before you can be in control of your craft. It takes years of study and practice to write well, but don't be discouraged. Consider the time an enjoyable apprenticeship."

Biographical and Critical Sources

PERIODICALS

Booklist, March 15, 1994, Hazel Rochman, review of *Grass and Sky,* p. 1347; April 1, 1995, Stephanie Zvirin, review of *Ash: A Novel,* p. 1387; May 15, 1998, Hazel Rochman, review of *Dirty Laundry: Stories about Family Secrets,* p. 1617; October 1, 2002, Ilene Cooper, review of *Soul Searching: Thirteen Stories about Faith and Belief,* p. 340.

Horn Book, July-August, 1995, Maeve Visser Knoth, review of *Ash,* p. 457.

Kirkus Reviews, April 15, 1994.

Publishers Weekly, February 28, 1994, review of *Grass and Sky,* p. 88; April 10, 1995, review of *Ash,* p. 63; June 8, 1998, review of *Dirty Laundry,* p. 61; February 19, 2001, review of *The Hickory Chair,* p. 90; November 25, 2002, review of *Soul Searching,* p. 64.

School Library Journal, February, 2001, Susan Hepler, review of *The Hickory Chair,* p. 99; December, 2002, Elizabeth M. Reardon, review of *Soul Searching,* p. 137.

Autobiography Feature

Lisa Rowe Fraustino

I, then Lisa Anne Rowe, wrote my first story on the toilet when I was four years old. With a crayon in hand—I think it might have been orange—I looped my words across the white plastic seat cover. I'll never forget how wonderful it felt. And I will never forget the response of my mother when I asked her to read what I had written. She informed me that my masterpiece was nothing but scribbles and got out the cleanser. My heart nearly broke, but I didn't give up on writing.

I made an important realization that day: Writing is a secret code. To write, I would have to learn how to form the combinations of letters that formed the words that formed the sentences that formed the stories I wanted to tell. Before I could write what others could read, I would have to go to school and learn the secret code. But before I could go to school, many other events happened that made me into a writer of children's literature.

When I was a mere fifteen months old, something happened that ruined my life as I knew it, and paved the way for many story conflicts to come: the birth of Angela Lynn Rowe, my sister. I was born in Dover-Foxcroft, Maine, on May 26, 1961, the eldest daughter of an eldest daughter who was herself the eldest daughter of her generation. It was a very special position to be in, making me the center of the family universe. With the birth of my sister, all of that doting attention that had been focused entirely on me—the only child, the only grandchild, the only niece—now had to be divided in two.

Math would never be my best subject. At that tender age, I didn't understand the concept of division. What was in reality the same amount of love and attention, shared, seemed to me a total loss. Of course, I have no conscious memory of those feelings, but the pictures tell the story, as do the relatives. Allegedly, I begged my parents to take Angie back to the hospital. The camera caught me hiding her baby bottle behind the couch.

In later years, once my own memories started staying put and piling up, I recall feeling intense jealousy over the attention paid my sister. Sibling rivalry, so normal, so universal, seemed like my own private torture. I wrote about my jealousy in the introduction to the first collection of young adult short stories that I edited, *Dirty Laundry: Stories about Family Secrets* (Viking 1998).

Lisa Rowe Fraustino

My conscious fascination with family secrets began the year paper-clip necklaces were the rage. You'd string regular paper clips into a chain, then cover each clip with colorful contact paper. My year-younger sister, the pretty one, therefore the popular one, managed to find a benefactor in the cool group and got herself a chain early in the craze. I, however, did not have the proper connections, and my parents refused to waste their meager resources on paper clips and contact paper. Without a string of paper clips around my neck, I was marked as an outcast for all to see.

Not only did I have green eyes, I had the green-eyed monster. And yet, I am so glad that Angie came along and ruined my life. For along with the stories of

The author on her mother's lap (right) and her sister Angie on her father's lap, 1963

hidden bottles, my family tells how I took Angie everywhere I went and would say, "I love my Sissa." Even though her presence meant I got less attention from the adults, I now had complete attention from her. I had a playmate close in age who would go wherever I went—a portable friend. That was no small matter. We moved four times before I started school, and after that we moved twice more. Of course, moving to different school districts made it difficult to fit in, but at least I had Angie to share the experience. We also shared a room until I went to college. We shared clothes, we shared birthday parties, we shared just about everything.

As if a pretty and popular sister weren't difficult enough on my fragile young ego, in 1965 my parents went and ruined what was left of it by having another child. This time it was worse. It was a brother. Boys, as I would come to learn, got a special kind of attention from the day they were born—not just at home but everywhere. Girls had to take care of them! Thus was born another theme for my future writing: the battle of the sexes. And now that I was four years old, I was old enough to remember exactly how Roger Loring Rowe changed the household: how he pushed out my mother's shirt, how she went away to have him, how she came back with a little red bundle that screamed for her attention constantly and tired her out so she had less and less time for me. Mama was especially protective of this new baby because he was born six weeks premature.

Today, as a mother of three myself, I empathize with my mother and am rather in awe of how she managed to take care of three small children, out in the woods without much money. However, at the time I felt very sorry for myself. Here I was with nothing to do except yearn for the attention my mother was giving my bawling little brother. I had to find ways to soothe my feelings of abandonment and neediness. Through

use of my imagination, I began the lifelong task of learning to be alone without being lonely, to entertain myself without being bored, and most importantly to adjust to change. These abilities have served me well as a writer.

We three Rowe kids were fortunate to be brought up in a very old-fashioned place and time. We had no phone back then, much less a computer with Internet access. When we did get a phone, upon moving from Charleston to Dexter when I was going into the third grade, it was a party phone. That meant several different homes shared the same line. The phone would ring a different number of times with a different combination of long and short rings for each household so everyone would know who was getting a call. Our form of caller ID was to pick up the phone to see if anyone was on it.

There were no CD players, and we didn't have a stereo, though many people did. We had a simple record player that spun black grooved disks recorded by the Supremes, the Beatles, and other groups that my uncle liked. He gave us some of his records when he moved up to the latest in modern musical technology, the 8-track tape deck.

I remember getting our first television set. It was black and white. It received the three network channels fairly clearly, plus PBS in the days before *Sesame Street*. Each day when it was time for Captain Kangaroo to come on, Angie, Roger, and I eagerly gathered in front of the screen—but not too close, because our mother warned us that it would give us cancer. Mr. Green Jeans brought Mr. Rabbit carrots from his garden, and ping-pong balls hailed down on Mr. Moose. Why weren't there any women around Captain Kangaroo's place? My favorite part of the show was story time, when a character would read a book while the camera showed the pictures. We were also addicted to the daily half hour of Warner Brothers cartoons with Bugs Bunny, Porky Pig, and my favorite, Yosemite Sam. Saturday

Lisa (right) with sister Angie and brother Roger

mornings all the stations ran cartoons, and we fought over which to watch. My top choices were Rocky and Bullwinkle, the Jetsons, the Flintstones, and Wonder Woman. By the time she came along, we had color TV.

The nearest cinema was an hour's drive away in the city of Bangor, and VCRs or DVDs hadn't been invented yet, so the only movies I saw growing up were on the television. On Sunday evenings we watched *The Wonderful World of Disney*. The first time I got to see a film at the cinema was in the fourth grade, when I was invited to go with a friend on her birthday. We saw a Disney classic that didn't show on TV, *Snow White*. I was amazed at the big screen, in full color, with sound that filled my ears.

From the television also came the voice of Walter Cronkite on the evening news. Mostly I thought the news was very boring, except for the parts that were scary. I didn't like hearing about the riots, the protests, and especially the body counts from the war in Vietnam. Perhaps hearing those news reports on television at such an impressionable age formed the basis of my adult aversion to war. It certainly sparked the theme of "Things Happen," which appeared in *Shattered,* a fiction anthology edited by Jennifer Armstrong (Knopf 2002). The protagonist of the story hides a draft dodger in her family's place of business, a junk yard inspired by a sprawling one I used to drive by in Pennsylvania.

I would be in college before I ever used a computer, and that was only in a computer programming class. My papers were typed on a manual typewriter I bought in the days before electronic models came out. This was not the same children's typewriter I received at age nine as a Christmas present from my parents, who saw me writing all the time: letters to pen pals and distant relatives, poems, stories, plays. Loving to draw, especially houses, trees, and flowers, I sometimes illustrated my writing and still have an interest in drawing. When I was working on my novel *Ash,* I took a drawing class that inspired me to make funny cartoon drawings for the book. Someday I hope to take more classes and pursue art as a hobby.

My first "published" work was a play I wrote for my fourth-grade class to perform. The princesses saved the princes from the dragon (I, the budding feminist, played a princess). To this day I enjoy turning stereotypes on their heads. Perhaps I wrote the play on that first little plastic typewriter, or perhaps I was given the typewriter because I had written the play—I don't remember. What I do remember was the rapid demise of my beloved Christmas gift when a neighbor boy who shopped in the husky section sat upon it. It's tempting to give his name because it's funny, but I will keep it to myself to protect the guilty.

During my childhood, Pac Man hadn't been invented yet, to say nothing of Mario and Luigi or Everquest. Without cable television, the World Wide Web, or video games to occupy our time, we kids spent our early years playing. Often the whole family played

Lisa with a typewriter she got for Christmas, 1970

sports and games with us, even the Grammies and Grampies. We weren't shuffled around from one activity to the next the way I drove my own three children straight from dance class to music lessons to sporting events during the 1980s and 90s. In the 1960s and 70s, our parents thought there was plenty of time to get serious about organized hobbies in junior high and high school. Until that time we played right in our own neighborhood with kids who rode bikes from a mile around.

Kickball, keepaway football, toss. Freeze tag, Mother May I, and Red Rover. Hide-and-seek. The girls made the boys play house and the boys made the girls play war. We built villages with Tonkas, populated by Barbies and GI Joes. Alone or in pairs we jumped rope, threw jacks, shot marbles, played hopscotch, and dug to China. We had Hula Hoop contests. (I'm still pretty good at that.) We turned cartwheels and backflips and rolled down grassy hills. When we got tired of the jungle gym or swing set, we climbed to the tops of trees. We made go-carts out of scrap lumber and training wheels off our old bikes, and rode them down the middle of the country roads. Once I fell off mine while it was speeding downhill and wound up with a huge tar burn on my outer thigh that left a scar to prove it. My brother landed in a stream.

Summers were spent at the lake swimming, boating, catching frogs, picking wild berries. In the winter we made snow families, snow angels, snow forts, and snow tunnels in the high banks left by the plows. We went ice skating and snowmobiling. On days when weather kept us inside we put puzzles together, drew pictures, colored in coloring books, and played cards or board games. We made up plays to perform. Mama taught Angie and me to cook, knit, and sew; Daddy taught all three of us to use a hammer. I read voraciously while my sister and brother complained of boredom.

Now when I look back at my childhood, I am amazed at the freedom we were given. The adults provided us with plenty of guidance, but they saw no need to control our every move. The environment of trust extended to the community at large. My parents left the front door unlocked when they went to work. They left the keys in the car overnight, too. Once my mother's cousin came in when we were gone and gutted some fish, leaving a stinky mess that made my parents discuss the possibility of locking up, but nothing was ever stolen. We were taught to keep our distance from strangers and never to get into a vehicle with someone we didn't know, and with these warnings we felt safe to explore the woods and fields of the neighborhood.

In the writing of my young adult novel *Ash,* I incorporated a number of my own childhood escapades as part of narrator Wes Libby's experiences growing up. For instance, when I was about five years old I learned from my father's cousins that it was exhilaratingly fun to ride sleds or even just slide on our butts down the steep barn roof and land in the snow below. It was also great fun to stand at the edge of the roof and turn a somersault in the air, landing on our backs in soft new snow. Sometimes we'd land feet first and our boots would come off. We'd dig around until we found them. My parents discovered that we were performing these snowy escapades after I lost my boots and couldn't find them. We were forbidden to slide off the roof thereafter, not only to protect life and limb but also to avoid having to spend the money for more boots.

The novel takes the form of a secret diary written by Wes to his older brother, Ash. Wes likes to draw funny pictures of the situations he describes. Here's the drawing of Wes stuck in the snow, waiting for Ash to rescue him before their parents get home:

Now that I've passed the age of forty, it makes a lot more sense to me that my parents worried about such silly things as broken legs and necks. As a kid I felt strong and invincible. The pleasure of sliding down the roof was irresistible. I continued to sneak roof slides and somersaults for many years after the buried boots incident. I just made sure I didn't get caught again!

And so I had written for all of my life—from toilet seat scribbles to letters to poems, plays, and stories, too few of them written on the typewriter sat upon by the neighbor boy. Okay, I can't resist. His name was Jo-Jo Tibbetts. Still, when it came time to go to college, I didn't think I had it in me to become what I wanted most to be: a writer of children's books. I didn't think I knew enough. In my mind, "real" writers were not only older and wiser than I but also had something important to write about. I knew I could learn the skills of narration, description, plotting, character development, and the like, but what good was technique if I didn't have great stories in me?

*

The author's drawing of Little Wes Beethoven, a character from her Ash: A Novel

What could a girl of eighteen who grew up in the boonies possibly have to say? I despaired of ever being able to create a character like those who had held my own young imagination in firm grip: Pippi Longstocking, Queenie Peavy, Henry Huggins, Ramona Quimby, Mr. Popper and his penguins, Christopher Robin and Pooh, Fern and Wilbur and Charlotte and Templeton. How could I possibly come up with plot after plot for my own equivalent of Nancy Drew? I had only left my home state twice: once on a weekend trip to Quebec so I could babysit my cousins while my aunt and uncle went out in the evening, and once on a day trip to Boston to see the Red Sox play at Fenway Park. Sure, I had a way with words—my teachers said so—but I had no ideas of interest to anyone else. Or so I thought.

Now, looking back on the stories and books that I have written over the past twenty years, I can't help but laugh and shake my head at my silly college-bound self. How wrong I was! The most important part of what I needed to know to become a writer, I knew when I wrote that first story on the toilet seat at age four. No, I hadn't yet cracked the secret code of text at that point. However, before I learned about book learning, I nevertheless had an instinctive understanding of what made a good story that would interest an audience. I'm not saying I was a born writer; nobody's that. We're raised. We're raised first by the storytellers around us, including real people as well as Rocky and Bullwinkle. The stories we read continue the upbringing.

My parents, my grandparents, my aunts and uncles—all of them told stories, wonderful stories that we children begged to hear again and again. My mother's father, Dana Reardon, often sang stories, too, my favorite being "Froggy Went A-Courting." He also told colorful tall tales about family members that I believed were only slightly exaggerated truth until I got to college and studied folklore. Turns out we weren't related to Paul Bunyan after all! The storytelling grandfather in my first book, *Grass and Sky,* was a lot like Grampy Reardon.

An oft-repeated story by my father's mother, Grammy Dot Rowe, became the basis of my first children's story ever accepted for publication in a magazine, "Billy's Surprise" (*Pennywhistle Press,* September 1988). Before she married, Grammy Rowe spent a year as a teacher in a one-room schoolhouse. She had a student who hated to sit still and do his schoolwork, and she struggled to keep him focused until one day she brought in a surprise that caught his attention. She lived on a farm and had noticed some frog's eggs in the cow pond, so she brought the eggs to school in a jar to use as a science lesson. The little boy who hated school loved the frog's eggs. He gave her his full attention every day until the eggs hatched and it was time to release the tadpoles back to the pond. She allowed him the privilege of emptying the jar. To Grammy's surprise, the boy came back to school the next day with a cow in tow to give her as a present to thank her! With such entertaining material, my story practically wrote itself.

Some members of my family joke, "Watch out what you do or say around Lisa or you will wind up in a book." They're only partly right. It's true that real life often provides inspiration for me. Then again, in my fiction I never use any family story exactly how it happened, and I take care to give my fictional characters their own unique personalities.

My picture book text *The Hickory Chair* has two real-life inspirations. In the story, a blind boy named Louis has a very special relationship with his grandmother. Upon her death, the family goes on a scavenger hunt to find the notes she has hidden in her favorite things indicating who gets what keepsake. Louis, using his other senses, has a gift for finding the notes and teaches the others his keen "blind sight." Blind sight is a way of seeing without eyes, a form of insight combining the senses with common sense and emotional truth. I got the idea for this concept from knowing my daughter Olivia's godfather, Dr. Louis D. Mitchell.

Louis Mitchell became blind as an adolescent from retinitis pigmentosa; however, that didn't stop him from doing anything he wanted to do. He earned a Ph.D. in English literature, specializing in the difficult area of eighteenth century poetry. He composed music, cooked gourmet meals, collected artwork and teapots, and answered letters to Santa at Christmas time, sending children the gifts they requested. Coming from mixed ancestry—black, Native American, Cuban, Spanish, and others—he served on the board of the NAACP. However, it is only a wonderful twist of fate that a black artist was chosen to illustrate the book, since the publisher, Arthur Levine, didn't know about the real-life

Dr. Louis D. Mitchell, godfather of the author's daughter Olivia and the inspiration for **The Hickory Chair**

Louis until after he had decided on the brilliant Benny Andrews. Louis spoke several languages, traveled the world, and lived in Madrid during breaks between college semesters. In fact, he forged such close relationships wherever he went that friends came from all over the world for his funeral. He had five godchildren.

When I moved to Pennsylvania as a newlywed in 1982, my husband's colleague Louis Mitchell was a full professor in the English Department at the University of Scranton. His other senses were so acute that, according to student myth, he could hear a senior fall asleep in the back row. I myself overheard students swear that Dr. Mitchell was only pretending to be blind. At one party, Louis lifted his head in an alert manner and said, "Pat Lawhon is here." I looked up across the crowded room, and sure enough, there was Pat. "How did you know she was here, Louis?" I asked. "I can smell the bleach," he said. Pat Lawhon had thirteen children. Apparently she always smelled of bleach, though only Louis noticed it. Bleach became a refrain in *The Hickory Chair* (Arthur Levine/Scholastic 2001). Narrated by Louis, the book begins:

> Sundays when I was small, that Gran of mine was good at hiding. The first time I played hide-and-seek with her and the older grandchildren, she disguised me as the pillow on the bed that Gramps had carved long ago for my father. Nobody found me.

When I was the seeker, I could almost always sniff everyone out, even Gran the time she stood inside her robe behind the bathroom door. She had a good alive smell—lilacs, with a whiff of bleach.

My father, who so often played with us kids, was actually the one who in real life had hidden me as a pillow. The other inspiration for *The Hickory Chair* was my mother's mother, Barbara Reardon. She has always made each family member feel special by being the favorite. Of course, I am the favorite oldest grandchild. In the book, Louis is the favorite youngest grandchild. Our whole family already knows that Grammy Reardon has placed labels on the backs of many keepsake items to make sure they go to the right people when she dies. In the story, though, I made Gran more mischievous. The family doesn't know about the notes until they read Gran's will.

Because I was the eldest of my generation in a family with a tradition of marrying young, I had the rare good fortune of knowing some of my great-grandparents. In fact, between the years of eight and twelve or so, I made a hobby of going around to visit my parents' grandparents and talking to them, soaking up their stories. I knew Grammy and Grampy Edes as well as Grammy Williams on my father's side, and Grampy Ladd on my mother's side. My mother's grandmother Ladd was alive too, but I never was allowed to meet her because she was in the hospital. She had cancer.

As a child I'd beg to go along when my mother or grandmother went to see Grammy Ladd. No, they always said; children weren't allowed to visit in the hospital. I didn't think that was fair, of course, but rules were rules, so I didn't dwell on it. I figured when she got out of the hospital I'd meet her then, but that was not to be. She died when I was young, and I was not allowed to attend the funeral. Oh, how I complained about that! How unjust, to have had a great-grandmother all my life and never even get a chance to see her face, much less hear any of her stories. Even though I had never known her, I felt a terrible sense of mourning at her loss. In fact, I drew on that emotion when writing about the death of Gran in *The Hickory Chair.*

Only as a young adult would I discover that, though my great-grandmother Ladd did indeed die of cancer, the hospital where she lived was the Bangor Mental Health Institute. She had suffered a nervous breakdown when my grandmother was a child and had remained in the mental hospital for the rest of her life. The youngest in the family were always sheltered from this information. In fact, as I grew older, I discovered that was only one of many family secrets.

The theme of family secrets has always intrigued me—for where there's a secret, there's always a story—and so it became the topic of the first young adult fiction anthology that I edited, *Dirty Laundry: Stories about Family Secrets.* And for my own contribution to

Top to bottom: Lisa's grandmother, mother, Lisa, and daughter, 1989

that collection, a story called "FRESH PAINt," I drew on the experience of discovering the truth about my great-grandmother. I say "drew on" because, like most of my fiction, the story is a work of imagination that merely springboards from autobiographical experience without depicting it as it really happened. My character Susie MacReavy volunteers at a mental hospital, something I did when I was in college. She discovers connections between a patient and a family secret. Because I knew how it felt to learn about mental illness in the family, and because I had spent time soaking up the sensory experiences on a ward of mentally ill elderly patients, I could create a story with vivid, true-to-life details. However, Susie is not my clone, and the events of her plot did not really happen to me.

Even though she hasn't shown up in print yet, the greatest influence on me from the great-grandparent generation was Grammy Dot Rowe's mother, Grace Williams. Grammy Williams was very old and frail during my tender years and lived on the family farm with my father's Aunt Mary. We visited the farm often, and I would beeline for Grammy's room off the kitchen on the first floor. She sat there in a rocker picking the knots out of balls of string because "Waste not, want not." She spoke in the deep, gravelly voice of the very old, with the slow drawl of a classic Maine accent. "What's your name?" would always be the first question followed by, "Who are your mother and father?" It didn't hurt my feelings that she didn't remember who I was; I understood that old age had stolen her memory for all things recent.

Grammy Williams hadn't lost a single memory from years past, however. She'd been a schoolteacher in her glory days, and she was a teacher till her dying day. "Can you name the days of the week?" was the first of the academic questions that inevitably followed once she got the child's identity out of the way. I soon learned to rattle off all seven. Next came: "Do you know the months of the year?" From her I learned the traditional ditty,

> 30 days in September,
> April, June, and November
> And the rest have 31
> All except a leap year
> When February has 29
> Instead of 28

After that, things got tough. "Can you name the fifty states?" I never got beyond twenty or thirty states while Grammy Williams was alive, nor did I ever master the toughest question of all: "Can you name the presidents in order?" She could rattle them all off, all the states and all the presidents up until Harry Truman. She couldn't name Kennedy or Johnson, though. The current events I absorbed from Walter Cronkite were about the only things I knew that Grammy Williams didn't, besides what we'd just had for supper.

Once we got through the schoolhouse drill, it was then time for stories. Unlike the rest of the storytellers in my father's family, Grammy Williams was a scholar and got her material from books. It was she who first introduced me to the pleasures of children's literature. She would gather the young ones around her on her bed and read Astrid Lindgren's *Pippi Longstocking*. She pronounced the two I's in Pippi the same, and dropped the g at the end, so it was Pippih Longstockin'. Oh, how I yearned to be like Pippi! I was transported to Villa Villekulla!

*

Clearly, I needed school so I could crack the secret code and read like Grammy Williams. I would stand at the door each morning with my nose pressed against the glass, watching with bitter envy as the big yellow school bus went by without me on it. Aunt Mary's children, who were just a few years older than I, often complained about the drudgery of reading, writing, and 'rithmetic. To me, complaining about school made about as much sense as complaining about going to the heaven we learned about every week in Sunday school.

There was no kindergarten in Charleston, Maine, in 1967, so I had to wait until first grade to get to book heaven. Once in school, I discovered a treasure I never knew existed. Not only did the teacher show us how to read books, but she had whole shelves full of them that we could borrow. We could take her books home and read them to our little sisters and brothers. And even though my sister and brother had ruined my life by being born, I loved reading to them as much as I loved being read to by Grammy Williams.

If Grammy Williams infected me with the reading bug, then Grammy Reardon kept it alive. When I was in the second grade, Grammy Reardon enrolled my sister in a monthly mail-order book club. Of course, I with the green eyes was very jealous that the books came in my sister's name and not mine. Why, I was the one who loved reading them, not her! In fact, I was the one who read the book club books to her and our little brother, Roger. I vividly remember *Harry the Dirty Dog, Danny and the Dinosaur,* and a book about a boy named Gregory (which I thought for years was pronounced Gray-gory because that was how Grammy Williams said it). Only later, looking back, did I understand and forgive my Grammy Reardon's logic for buying the books for Angie. She hoped to foster in my sister the love of reading for which I needed no encouragement.

In later years, Grammy Reardon would come back from one of her summer vacations with copies of *Charlotte's Web* and *The Witch of Blackbird Pond,* which would join the list of my favorite children's novels. When we visited her, she would sneak me a quarter or two that I could use to buy a book from the school book club circular. That was how I got my own copy of *Queenie Peavy,* which I read so many times that it fell apart.

Of course, I always wanted to read whatever novel Grammy was reading, and I didn't understand why she would say, "When you are old enough." Eventually she did let me have at the box of paperback novels she kept under the bed at "camp" (Maine talk for a summer cottage). I discovered that the formerly forbidden novels contained the sorts of things adults don't want to admit that their kids already know about—sex, violence, and most importantly, swear words. These books, the bestsellers of their time by such authors as Danielle Steel, Stephen King, and V.C. Andrews, were irresistible and kept me up many a night reading under the covers with a flashlight.

At four, I wasn't yet a writer because I couldn't write. However, I was a storyteller. And that's where writing begins. The second step to becoming a writer is to become a reader. Grammy Williams and Grammy Reardon set me on that path, my first teachers encouraged me along it, and then something huge happened to change my life forever. My mother went to work, and we kids went to a babysitter during school vacations. This babysitter had eight children herself and lived in town. One day we went to a place on a hill, and to my awe, I walked into a concrete building filled with shelves, and the shelves were filled with books we could borrow for a whole week. At the age of eight, I had discovered the library. Before long I was bringing home books by the armload, typically reading one a day during the school year and as many as three a day during the summer. By the time I got out of high school, I had read out three different libraries. And that's what I tell people who ask why I write primarily for children instead of adults.

My parents delight in telling how I loved school. "Lisa was the first one in and the last one out," Daddy says, when he's not saying. "Lisa walked into the school at age six and didn't come out until she was eighteen." Of course, in the early years learning itself was the major appeal. I simply couldn't get enough of books and the ideas within them. In the fifth grade I got an award for the highest average in science, which I have always loved. I liked math, too—at least before it turned into algebra—and have fond memories of my father setting up problems for me to practice. History I liked for the story part, but the dates gave me trouble on tests. I voraciously read biographies, especially biographies of queens. Mary, Queen of Scots, was my favorite historical figure. One of my early magazine publications was a biography of the great fiction writer Katherine Anne Porter. I have also written a historical novel about the Salem witch trials for Scholastic's "Dear America" series, and I hope to do more historical writing in the future.

Once I reached junior high, the extracurricular and social activities began to compete with academics for my interest. I still loved learning, but I often watched the clock as the day wore on, wishing the afternoon would go faster so I could get to whatever activity I was doing after school. The scrapbook I kept in junior high and high school grew thick with photos, newspaper clippings, and certificates. I acted in several plays and took part in the annual school-wide speaking contest, which I won during both my sophomore and junior years. In the band I played first chair flute; I sang and played flute in the jazz band that performed at the boys' basketball games; and I sang alto in the school chorus, also participating in the Maine All-State Chorus junior and senior years. And there were always sports: field hockey in the fall, basketball in the winter, softball in the spring.

In high school I did everything I possibly could simply because it was exhilarating fun. Little did I know that my multiple interests and talents would later serve me as a writer, in multiple ways. Obviously, knowing about sports, music, and drama provides me a broad range of possibilities for characters and plots. The protagonist of my first novel, Timmi Lafler, is a star pitcher on her baseball team who has to miss the big tournament to visit her estranged grandfather. Susie MacReavy

in "FRESH PAINt" first visits the mental hospital when she has to perform a story for a school project. She, like Ash, sings.

All of my athletic and artistic experiences did more than give me material, however. Perhaps even more importantly, they instilled me with the discipline necessary to learn the craft of writing. Just as it takes years of practicing foul shots to get those two points consistently in games, it takes many hours of practice to make writing techniques appear effortless. I couldn't pick up my flute that first time I tried it in the third grade and play "Flight of the Bumblebee," nor could I sit down at the typewriter and dash off a publishable novel on the first try. Furthermore, my musical training gave me a good ear for rhythm, which is an essential part of graceful writing even in prose, but especially in poetry. Some day I hope to write a book of poetry that children will enjoy.

*

Upon graduation from high school, I had to decide on a college major that would put me on a career track. Obviously, my favorite subject had been English. Not only did I love reading and writing, I loved diagramming sentences. In an old notebook I still have Mrs. Brown's eighth grade grammar rules written out in careful penmanship. "If the subject acts, then the noun that follows the verb is its direct object." And no autobiography of me would be complete without Miss Edna May Littlefield, who once divided our senior English class into two sections. "Those who want to learn, sit on this side. Those who don't, sit on that side," she said. To our surprise, she gave independent study work to us on the want-to-learn side and spent the rest of the term forcing language skills into the foolish heads of the lazy kids on the other side of the room. Miss Littlefield assigned reading, writing, and speaking every week and taught us more than many students learn in college today. She was the best teacher I ever had in twenty-four years of school.

But I'd have to make a living after college. What could I do with an English major?

Teach? Yes, I'd enjoyed helping grade school teachers correct spelling tests—I was always a strong speller and won the Piscataquis County spelling bee in the eighth grade. Yes, I enjoyed tutoring classmates who needed extra help in reading. And yes—I cringe to admit—I'd even fantasized about writing and grading my own tests. So I gave teaching serious thought. However, there was a major recession going on at the time, with upwards of 10 percent unemployment, and the job market for English teachers was horrendous.

Act? Did I have the talent? Maybe. I didn't have the right appearance to become star material, though—and probably not enough passion to survive as a starving artist.

Write? No doubt, I had a way with words. And passion! But remember: I didn't think I had anything to say. But I was great at reports and assignments. Ta-da! Reporters had assignments! I would major in journalism and hope, hope, hope I could land a job for a newspaper.

My first semester at Saint Michael's College in Winooski, Vermont—where, by the way, I got a marvelous work study job at the library—I took a required course for journalism majors. The professor sat in front of the room with his legs stretched out, smoking cigarettes the whole time as he rambled on about personal things that didn't have much to do with the material we'd been assigned to read. He put impossibly picky questions on his tests instead of important material. Many years of college later, I realized that the guy was simply a lousy teacher. However, at the time I held the mistaken viewpoint that college instructors must all be top experts teaching exactly what we were supposed to know, or they wouldn't be there. If that professor represented the life of a journalist, I wanted no part of it!

At the same time, I was taking the required freshman composition class and having a very different experience. My professor, Dr. John Reiss, taught us through example. We read and discussed great essays by the likes of George Orwell and Joan Didion, then tried to mimic them in our own writing. In those days before photocopying became commonplace, handouts were run off on ditto machines with purple ink, and I still remember that delicious ink-on-paper smell as Dr. Reiss would distribute student examples for discussion. He always chose good examples to dicuss, never negative ones, and he chose mine several times, giving my confidence a much-needed boost.

I kept the work completed in that class. In my early years of trying to become a professional writer, I would often feel discouraged by rejection. To keep myself from quitting altogether I would go back and read what Dr. Reiss wrote on one of my papers: "You impress me as being the best writer I have taught in 11 years of Freshman English and one of the best writers I have taught at any level." Aspiring writers need to hear that sort of thing. When working with students who have a passion for writing, I always remember what Dr. Reiss's words meant to me and try to encourage those with talent.

Knowing that I came from Maine, the home of E. B. White, one of my favorite children's book writers as well as author of our class text—and also knowing that I would like to write for children some day—Dr. Reiss encouraged me to send a letter to Mr. White asking if I might visit him. It seemed a bold move to me! But I trusted Dr. Reiss, and so I sent the letter. To my delight, I did receive a reply. For years I kept it in my yellowed copy of *The Elements of Style,* the little handbook by Strunk and White himself that we had memorized in Dr. Reiss's class. When I went to reproduce the letter for this autobiography, to my dismay, it was gone. The letter was typed on a manual typewriter with crooked keys and faded ribbon. Mr. White thanked me for my interest, and said that he received many letters like mine, and had become too old to spend his energy with such visits. But he wished me well.

By my primitive logic, Dr. Reiss was an English professor, and that meant English professors were the best, and that meant English was the best major for me. I switched majors after that first semester, and at the end of that year was one of the rare freshmen to be elected an English Honors Scholar.

After one year at St. Mike's, I transferred to the University of Maine at Orono, closer to home. There, teachers again identified me as a good writer, and I was chosen to train as a peer tutor in the writing lab. I worked there and also tutored in the Upward Bound program for underprivileged students. To make ends meet, I took other jobs as well, working at T.J. Maxx one year, and another year at The Bear's Den, the campus pub and eatery. During the school year I always worked twenty-five to thirty hours per week to pay my tuition and living expenses. Summers I worked full time.

Fun and lucrative jobs were scarce during the recession of the early 80s, especially for young people just entering the work force. I wound up living with my parents and working at nearby factories for minimum wages. Factory work made me all the more intent on having a profession that used my brains instead of my brawn. Finally, the summer before my senior year, a college friend told me his mother, a hotel manager, was looking for someone with my abilities to take on a new position and recommended me for the job. The remote lodge was located on an island in Fish River Lake—which is closer to Canada than it is to another U.S. state. To get there, we had to drive several hours north of the university, then drive another hour along a winding dirt road made just for logging trucks, park the car, and get into a boat.

Sky Lodge Island was named after its central building, a huge octagonal lodge made of logs, which housed the kitchen, dining room, and living room around the largest stone fireplace I've ever seen. Fires could be built on three sides of it. Guests stayed in smaller log cabins scattered along the shoreline. Cabins for the staff had the less scenic locations in the center of the Island, along with storage sheds and gardens. We had no electricity except when our manager deemed it necessary to fire up the gas-operated generator to run the washer, dryer, or vacuum cleaner. The Island was supplied with large tankfuls of propane fuel delivered over the frozen ice in winter, and so we had refrigerators, stoves, and lights. Unlike my family's camp on Lake Manhannock, the Island did have the luxury of running water (both hot and cold), showers, and flush toilets.

The Island had only three employees that summer. Along with my best friend from high school and college, Wendy Moynihan (the class valedictorian, incidentally—she got me through Algebra II and Physics), I

The author (left) with Susan Campbell Bartoletti at their first Society of Children's Book Writers and Illustrator's conference in Malibu, CA, 1989

was responsible for all of the cooking, cleaning, gardening, painting, patching, publicity, business correspondence—whatever needed to be done. Our manager, the son of the new owner, did the hardier labor of carpentry, splitting wood, maintaining equipment, and the like. The previous owners had gone out of business and left the Island vacant for several years, so that summer we had very few guests. Our work consisted mostly of bringing the place back to life. Every night I fell into bed exhausted from the hard work.

We didn't work every waking minute, though. I played flute, I knit sweaters, I read *War and Peace* and many other musty-smelling books on the shelves in the lodge and the cabins, including all of Jane Austin's books. My favorite was *Emma.* We waded out into the lake for a better view of the most incredible double rainbow I've ever seen. Wendy taught me to make homemade bread, kneading it by hand. Several times a week we got in the boat and visited neighbors or had them over to eat and play cards—neighbors being the family who lived a mile away on the shoreline. We put together jigsaw puzzles. It was one of the most rewarding experiences of my life, and that setting provided the inspiration for my first children's novel, *Grass and Sky.*

I began writing that novel soon after graduating from college. During my senior year at the University of Maine, I married a professor named Daniel Fraustino and moved with him to his new job at the University of Scranton. After the birth of our first child, Daisy, in 1983, I got my first electronic typewriter and began writing what was at that time titled *Adventures at Fish Lake,* rocking Daisy in her umbrella stroller with my foot as I typed. In my typical pattern of twisting real-life experience around in fiction, the book was about a family who had a camp on the shoreline and sometimes visited the Island.

Soon I began the Master's program in English at "da U." Over the next few years, I had two more chil-

dren: Dan in 1984 and Olivia in 1986. How I adored having small children to share my beloved books! We wore out *Caps for Sale, Where the Wild Things Are, The Cat in the Hat, Danny and the Dinosaur,* and *The Story of Ferdinand the Bull.* For a time I worked as a project editor at a correspondence school located in Scranton, but after my third child was born I worked freelance out of my home office, shifting over from editing textbooks to writing them.

Somehow during those years in the midst of mothering, working, and schooling, I managed to write several major revisions of that first novel about Fish Lake, each time making a huge leap in my literary craft. That novel taught me to write. When I visit schools or teach writing workshops to graduate students, I show them several first pages to illustrate the evolution of a creative writer. Each revision sample in just a few sentences shows a major leap in a different story element: first point of view, then characterization, then voice, then plotting, and finally bringing it all together smoothly.

In between revisions of the book that became *Grass and Sky,* and of course between teaching classes and meeting my educational text writing contracts, I wrote other stories, articles, and books. For many years, I sent work out only sporadically, and always received rejections back—by the dozens. The first time I ever sent out a story hoping it would be published, I was still a college senior. I had written a class assignment, been told it was good, and thought I'd try sending it to *Cricket,* known as the highest quality literary magazine for children. I received a standard rejection slip and was so embarrassed that I hid the envelope behind a book on my shelf and didn't write again for months, until I pulled out my file of papers from Dr. Reiss's class and twisted up my courage to try again.

*

My on-again, off-again writing and submission pattern came to an end on New Year's Day, 1987, when I made a resolution that I would put my all into learning everything I could about the profession, writing regularly, and keeping my work in circulation. If by the end of that year I hadn't received an acceptance, I would know I didn't have what it took to be a writer, and I would turn my attention to one of my many other interests, like upholstering furniture. Everyone needs slipcovers.

That year, I read, read, read—but no longer like the child reader who used to lose herself in the story world. Now I read like a writer and a scholar, studying the themes and analyzing the techniques used to get them across. For my master's I specialized in children's literature and delved into my reading list with obsessive gusto. In *Bridge to Terabithia* Katherine Paterson taught me to use active style and narration that mimics the honest viewpoint of the child. In *Tuck Everlasting* Natalie Babbitt taught me to use figurative language that grows directly out of the story itself. In *The Whipping Boy* Sid Fleischman taught me to say a lot in a few words, often humorously. Many other books taught me many other things, as well. And I wrote, wrote, wrote, trying to incorporate all that I had observed.

During that breakthrough year, my first three acceptances came within four days of each other. In addition to "Billy's Surprise," I published an article in *Baby Talk* called "Shopping for an Obstetrician" (July 1987) and a story in *Wee Wisdom* called "The Jaffe News" about a child who creates a family newspaper to keep relatives informed about each other's lives (December 1987). It would be a year before I had anything else accepted, but that was okay. Now I didn't need Dr. Reiss to tell me I was a writer. I had clips from magazines with my name on them. Now I was a professional.

At my first writer's conference, held by *Highlights for Children* magazine in Chautauqua, New York, I made my first professional connections and learned about the Society of Children's Book Writers and Illustrators. Immediately I joined the SCBWI and, in fact, founded a chapter in Northeastern Pennsylvania, serving as its first Regional Advisor for ten years. Through organizing an SCBWI event I met the editor who would later accept my first book, Harold Underdown. In fact, I have met most of my editors as well as my current agent at writer's conferences. At the Bread Loaf conference in Vermont I worked with Nancy Willard, who taught me how to invest emotion in objects and recommended that I send work to her editor.

Upon finishing my master's degree, I began teaching part time at the University of Scranton and found I loved helping college students learn to write. During that time I also began attending conferences on the teaching of writing, and at one of those events in 1987 I met the woman who was to become my closest friend, Susan Campbell Bartoletti. Sue was an eighth grade English teacher in a nearby town who had published some educational texts and also wanted to write children's books. She had a great sense of humor, which has always attracted me to people. It wasn't long before we had started a writer's critique group.

With another group member who joined us a couple of years later, Laura Lee Wren, Sue and I originated the annual SCBWI Pocono Mountains Retreat for writers, illustrators, agents, and editors of children's books. Over the ten years we organized the conference, we learned from some of the greatest writers and editors in the business. Patricia Lee Gauch went back and forth with me on several drafts of *The Hickory Chair,* Richard Peck hooked me up with an agent, and I am indebted to a long list of others who helped me in various ways, but I have a word limit.

Throughout those years I wrote and taught happily, but I missed being a student myself. In 1990 Sue suggested we take a graduate course at the State University

of New York at Binghamton. Studying the British romantic period greatly enriched our writing, and so I decided to go for my doctorate full time. At SUNY-Binghamton, I took a number of fabulous classes with great teachers, and I worked on my dissertation over a period of three years with Liz Rosenberg as my director. Liz, the author of one of my all-time favorite picture books, *Monster Mama,* taught me a great deal about making my characters real. With her gentle guidance, I pinpointed what had been a major weakness in my plotting: avoidance of conflict. Just as I didn't like to fight in real life, I didn't like to put my characters into emotionally difficult situations. Finally, I was able to revise the plot of *Grass and Sky* successfully. It was finally accepted for publication and arrived on my doorstep in 1994, exactly ten years after I started writing the first draft!

While that book was in production, I was busy at work finishing up the sixth draft of my creative dissertation, a young adult novel. On the very afternoon that I defended *Ash: A Novel* in front of the English Department and became Dr. Lisa, I received a call from my editor, Harold Underdown. He had received the manuscript that morning and couldn't put it down. He wanted to publish it. That was a really great day!

In 1994 I attended my first conference in another organization that has been pivotal in my career, the Children's Literature Association, a group composed primarily of college professors. Wow, hundreds of smart and funny children's book addicts from all over the world, all in one room! Never had I felt so at home in a new group of people. I became an active member, serving on committees and even organizing the annual con-

The author's children: Daisy (standing), Olivia (kneeling), and Dan, performing a skit scripted by a student in the Graduate Program in Children's Literature at Hollins University, 1995

vention myself in 2002. In the airport on the way home from that first ChLA conference in Missouri, I was invited to join the visiting faculty of the Graduate Program in Children's Literature at Hollins University in Roanoke, Virginia. Every other summer I return to work with talented critics and writers. Alexandria LaFaye, Hillary Homzie, and Betty Hicks are some former students of mine who have gone on to publish books. Just as I have benefited from the mentorship of experienced teachers and writers, I feel deep satisfaction in helping others along the journey of writing children's books and getting them published.

The same pleasure fuels my interest in editing fiction anthologies. After the success of *Dirty Laundry,* I went on to propose a second anthology, *Soul Searching: Thirteen Stories of Faith and Belief* (Simon and Schuster 2002). The piece I wrote for *Soul Searching,* "The Tin Man" is about a teenage girl waiting for a heart transplant, and I got the idea from my own father's six-month hospital wait for a heart transplant.

Unlike other anthologies, for which I simply ask all sorts of authors whose work I like, this one required me to find authors from specific cultural backgrounds and/or experiences. I also wanted to distinguish this anthology from others on similar themes by finding authors whose voices have not been as often heard—people who weren't necessarily the obvious choices to represent their religions. Some of the authors I already knew about, some were previously unpublished authors I discovered in my travels as a teacher, and others I located by searching the Internet for authentic voices from world religions. Though the stories were all finished before the terrorist attacks of September 11, 2001, I had to write the introduction the following week. It was difficult.

> The main reason that I don't know what I should write in this introduction is that I don't know what is going to happen in the name of religion between now and next year, when this anthology comes out. I don't even know what is going to happen between today and tomorrow. But one thing I know I can say, because this truth won't change no matter what happens, war or no war: in times of peace as well as times of stress, we all need stories such as those found in these pages. Not only are they soul searching, they're soul food.

My third anthology is called *Don't Cramp My Style: Stories about That Time of the Month,* and it's the first

Signing books at Young Authors Day, Wyoming, 2001

of my books to be pitched to me by an editor, the visionary Alyssa Eisner. It includes stories about menstruation from various historical and cultural perspectives, from a Lenni-Lenape girl's first experience in the Woman's House to a modern day adolescent boy's heroic quest to buy tampons for his girlfriend. My contribution to the book, "Sleeping Beauty," has almost no inspiration in real-life experience—at least not my own. I got the idea from a newspaper account of a college freshman who died in a dorm bathroom after giving birth, and nobody had even known she was pregnant. The girl does have to complete a writing prompt that I have given to my students, though.

My three children, Daisy, Dan, and Olivia, have provided me with ample inspirations for future stories I'll tell, once they're adult enough not to be embarrassed. Meanwhile, I have plenty of ideas from the fifth graders whom I taught at Wyoming Seminary for the seven years after graduate school. In 1999 I was divorced, and in 2002 I moved to a new job as Assistant Professor of English at Eastern Connecticut State University. I get up at 5:00 a.m. to write for a couple of hours before the shower because, as investment advisors say, if you want to succeed, pay yourself first. In my spare time I like to hang out with my kids and other loved ones, cook, eat what I cook, sing in the chorus, exercise, garden, sew, travel, watch movies, and decorate my home. Hmmmm, I think that toilet seat could use a little color . . .

G

GAIMAN, Neil (Richard) 1960-

Personal
Born November 10, 1960, in Portchester, England; son of David Bernard (a company director) and Sheila (a pharmacist; maiden name, Goldman) Gaiman; married Mary Therese McGrath, March 14, 1985; children: Michael Richard, Holly Miranda, Madeleine Rose Elvira. *Politics:* "Wooly." *Religion:* Jewish. *Hobbies and other interests:* "Finding more bookshelf space."

Addresses
Home—Near Minneapolis, Minnesota; western Wisconsin; England. *Agent*—Merilee Heifetz, Writer's House, 21 West 26th St., New York, NY 10010.

Career
Freelance journalist, 1983-87; full-time writer, 1987—.

Member
Comic Book Legal Defense Fund (board of directors), International Museum of Cartoon Art (advisory board), Science Fiction Foundation (committee member), Society of Strip Illustrators (chair, 1988-90), British Fantasy Society.

Neil Gaiman

Awards, Honors
Mekon Award, Society of Strip Illustrators, and Eagle Award for best graphic novel, both 1988, both for *Violent Cases;* Eagle Award for best writer of American comics, 1990; Harvey Award for best writer, 1990 and 1991; Will Eisner Comic Industry Award for best writer of the year and best graphic album (reprint), 1991; World Fantasy Award for best short story, 1991, for "A Midsummer Night's Dream;" Will Eisner Comics Industry Award for best writer of the year, 1992; Harvey Award for best continuing series, 1992; Will Eisner Comics Industry Award for best writer of the year and best graphic album (new), 1993; Gem Award, Diamond Distributors, for expanding the marketplace for comic books, 1993; Will Eisner Comics Industry Award for best writer of the year, 1994; Guild Award, International Horror Critics, and World Fantasy Award nomination, both 1994, both for *Angels and Visitations: A Miscellany* and short story "Troll Bridge;" GLAAD Award for best comic of the year, 1996, for *Death: The Time of Your Life;* Eagle Award for best comic, 1996; Lucca Best Writer Prize, 1997; *Newsweek* list of best children's books, 1997, for *The Day I Swapped My Dad for Two Goldfish;* Defender of Liberty Award, Comic Book Legal Defense Fund, 1997; MacMillan Silver Pen Award, 1999, for *Smoke and Mirrors: Short Fictions and Illusions;* Hugo Award nomination, 1999, for *Sandman: The Dream Hunters;* Mythopoeic Award for best

novel for adults, 1999, for *Stardust: Being a Romance Within the Realms of Faerie;* Nebula Award nomination, 1999, for screenplay for the film *Princess Mononoke;* Hugo Award for best science fiction/fantasy novel, Bram Stoker Award for best novel, Horror Writers Association, and BSFA Award nomination, all 2002, all for *American Gods;* British Science Fiction Association Award for best short fiction, Elizabeth Burr/Worzalla Award, Bram Stoker Award, Horror Writers Association, Hugo Award nomination, and Prix Tam Tam Award, all 2003, all for *Coraline.* Gaiman has received international awards from Austria, Brazil, Canada, Finland, France, Germany, Italy, and Spain. His script *Signal to Noise* received a SONY Radio Award.

Writings

FOR CHILDREN

The Day I Swapped My Dad for Two Goldfish (picture book), illustrated by Dave McKean, Borealis/White Wolf (Clarkson, GA), 1997, HarperCollins (New York, NY), 2004.

Coraline (fantasy), illustrated by Dave McKean, Bloomsbury (London, England), HarperCollins (New York, NY), 2002.

The Wolves in the Walls (picture book), illustrated by Dave McKean, HarperCollins (New York, NY), 2003.

GRAPHIC NOVELS AND COMIC BOOKS

Violent Cases, illustrated by Dave McKean, Titan (London, England), 1987, Tundra (Northampton, MA), 1991, Dark Horse Comics (Milwaukie, OR), 2003.

Black Orchid (originally published in magazine form in 1989), illustrated by Dave McKean, Titan (London, England), D.C. Comics (New York, NY), 1991.

Miracleman, Book 4: The Golden Age, illustrated by Mark Buckingham, Eclipse (London, England, and Forestville, CA), 1992.

Signal to Noise, illustrated by Dave McKean, Gollancz (London, England), Dark Horse Comics (Milwaukie, OR), 1992.

The Books of Magic (originally published in magazine form, four volumes), illustrated by John Bolton and others, D.C. Comics (New York, NY), 1993.

The Tragical Comedy, or Comical Tragedy, of Mr. Punch, illustrated by Dave McKean, VG Graphics (London, England), 1994, Vertigo/D.C. Comics (New York, NY), 1995, also published as *Mr. Punch.*

(Author of text, with Alice Cooper) *The Compleat Alice Cooper: Incorporating the Three Acts of Alice Cooper's The Last Temptation,* illustrated by Michael Zulli, Marvel Comics (New York, NY), 1995, published as *The Last Temptation,* Dark Horse Comics (Milwaukie, OR), 2000.

Angela, illustrated by Greg Capullo and Mark Pennington, Image (Anaheim, CA), 1995, published as *Spawn: Angela's Hunt,* Image (Anaheim, CA), 2000.

Stardust: Being a Romance within the Realms of Faerie, illustrated by Charles Vess, Titan (London, England), D.C. Comics (New York, NY), 1997-98, text published as *Stardust,* Spike (New York, NY), 1999.

(Author of text, with Matt Wagner) *Neil Gaiman's Midnight Days,* Vertigo (London, England), D.C. Comics (New York, NY), 1999.

Green Lantern/Superman: Legend of the Green Flame, D.C. Comics (New York, NY), 2000.

Harlequin Valentine, illustrated by John Bolton, Titan (London, England), Dark Horse Comics (Milwaukie, OR), 2001.

Murder Mysteries (based on play of the same title, also see below), illustrated by P. Craig Russel, Dark Horse Comics (Milwaukie, OR), 2002.

"SANDMAN" SERIES

Sandman: The Doll's House (originally published in magazine form), illustrated by Mike Dringenberg and Malcolm Jones III, D.C. Comics (New York, NY), 1990.

Sandman: Preludes and Nocturnes (originally published as *Sandman,* volumes 1-8), illustrated by Sam Keith, Mike Dringenberg, and Malcolm Jones III, Titan (London, England), D.C. Comics (New York, NY), 1991.

Sandman: Dream Country (originally published as *Sandman,* volumes 17-20; contains "A Midsummer's Night's Dream"), illustrated by Kelley Jones, Charles Vess, Colleen Doran, and Malcolm Jones III, D.C. Comics (New York, NY), 1991.

Sandman: Season of Mists (originally published as *Sandman,* volumes 21-28), illustrated by Kelley Jones, Malcolm Jones III, Mike Dringenberg, and others, Titan (London, England), D.C. Comics (New York, NY), 1992.

Sandman: A Game of You (originally published as *Sandman,* volumes 32-37), illustrated by Shawn McManus and others, Titan (London, England), D.C. Comics (New York, NY), 1993.

Sandman: Fables and Reflections (originally published as *Sandman,* volumes 29-31, 38-40, 50), illustrated by Bryan Talbot, Titan (London, England), D.C. Comics (New York, NY), 1994.

Death: The High Cost of Living (originally published in magazine form, three volumes), illustrated by Dave McKean, Mark Buckingham, and others, Titan (London, England), D.C. Comics (New York, NY), 1994.

Sandman: Brief Lives (originally published as *Sandman,* volumes 41-49), illustrated by Jill Thompson, Dick Giordano, and Vince Locke, Titan (London, England), D.C. Comics (New York, NY), 1994.

Sandman: World's End (originally published as *Sandman,* volumes 51-56), illustrated by Dave McKean, Mark Buckingham, Dick Giordano, and others, Titan (London, England), D.C. Comics (New York, NY), 1994.

(Author of text, with Matt Wagner) *Sandman: Midnight Theatre,* illustrated by Teddy Kristiansen, D.C. Comics (New York, NY), 1995.

(Editor, with Edward E. Kramer) *The Sandman: Book of Dreams,* Voyager (London, England), HarperPrism (New York, NY), 1996.

Sandman: The Kindly Ones (originally published as *Sandman*, volumes 57-69), illustrated by Marc Hempel, Richard Case, and others, Titan (London, England), D.C. Comics (New York, NY), 1996.

Death: The Time of Your Life, illustrated by Mark Buckingham and others, D.C. Comics (New York, NY), 1997.

(Author of commentary and a story) *Dustcovers: The Collected Sandman Covers, 1989-1997*, illustrated by Dave McKean, Vertigo/D.C. Comics (New York, NY), 1997, published as *The Collected Sandman Covers, 1989-1997*, Watson-Guptill (New York, NY), 1997.

Sandman: The Wake, illustrated by Michael Zulli, Charles Vess, and others, Titan (London, England), D.C. Comics (New York, NY), 1997.

(Reteller) *Sandman: The Dream Hunters*, illustrated by Yoshitaka Amano, Titan (London, England), D.C. Comics (New York, NY), 1999.

The Quotable Sandman: Memorable Lines from the Acclaimed Series, D.C. Comics (New York, NY), 2000.

The Sandman: Endless Nights, illustrated by P. Craig Russell, Milo Manara, and others, D.C. Comics (New York, NY), 2003.

FICTION

(With Terry Pratchett) *Good Omens: The Nice and Accurate Prophecies of Agnes Nutter, Witch* (novel), Gollancz (London, England), 1990, revised edition, Workman (New York, NY), 1990.

(With Mary Gentle) *Villains!* (short stories), edited by Mary Gentle and Roz Kaveney, ROC (London, England), 1992.

(With Mary Gentle and Roz Kaveney) *The Weerde: Book One* (short stories), ROC (London, England), 1992.

(With Mary Gentle and Roz Kaveney) *The Weerde: Book Two: The Book of the Ancients* (short stories), ROC (London, England), 1992.

Angels and Visitations: A Miscellany (short stories), illustrated by Steve Bissette and others, DreamHaven Books and Art (Minneapolis, MN), 1993.

Neverwhere (novel), BBC Books (London, England), 1996, Avon (New York, NY), 1997.

Smoke and Mirrors: Short Fictions and Illusions (short stories), Headline Feature (London, England), Avon (New York, NY), 1998.

American Gods (novel), Headline Feature (London, England), William Morrow (New York, NY), 2001.

(Reteller) Snow Glass Apples, illustrated by George Walker, Biting Dog Press (Duluth, GA), 2003.

EDITOR

(With Kim Newman) *Ghastly Beyond Belief*, Arrow (London, England), 1985.

(With Stephen Jones) *Now We Are Sick: A Sampler*, privately published, 1986, published as *Now We Are Sick: An Anthology of Nasty Verse*, DreamHaven (Minneapolis, MN), 1991.

(With Alex Stewart) *Temps*, ROC (London, England), 1991.

(With Alex Stewart) *Euro Temps*, ROC (London, England), 1992.

SCREENPLAYS

(With Lenny Henry) *Neverwhere*, BBC2 (London, England), 1996.

Signal to Noise, BBC Radio 3 (London, England), 1996.

Day of the Dead: An Annotated Babylon 5 Script (originally aired as the episode "Day of the Dead" for the series *Babylon 5*, Turner Broadcasting System, 1998), DreamHaven (Minneapolis, MN), 1998.

Princess Mononoke (motion picture; English translation of the Japanese screenplay by Hayao Miyazak), Miramax (New York, NY), 1999.

OTHER

Duran Duran: The First Four Years of the Fab Five (biography), Proteus (New York, NY), 1984.

Don't Panic: The Official Hitch-Hiker's Guide to the Galaxy Companion, Titan (London, England), Pocket Books (New York, NY), 1988, revised edition with additional material by David K. Dickson as *Don't Panic: Douglas Adams and the Hitchhiker's Guide to the Galaxy*, Titan (London, England), 1993.

Warning: Contains Language (readings; compact disc), music by Dave McKean and the Flash Girls, DreamHaven (Minneapolis, MN), 1995.

(Co-illustrator) *The Dreaming: Beyond the Shores of Night*, D.C. Comics (New York, NY), 1997.

(Co-illustrator) *The Dreaming: Through the Gates of Horn and Ivory*, D.C. Comics (New York, NY), 1998.

Neil Gaiman: Live at the Aladdin (videotape), Comic Book Legal Defense Fund (Northampton, MA), 2001.

(With Gene Wolfe) *A Walking Tour of the Shambles* (nonfiction), American Fantasy Press (Woodstock, IL), 2001.

Murder Mysteries (play), illustrated by George Walker, Biting Dog Press (Duluth, GA), 2001.

Adventures in the Dream Trade (nonfiction and fiction), edited by Tony Lewis and Priscilla Olson, NESFA Press (Framingham, MA), 2002.

Also author of the comic book *Outrageous Tales from the Old Testament*. Creator of characters for comic books, including Lady Justice; Wheel of Worlds; Mr. Hero, Newmatic Man; Teknophage; and Lucifer. Co-editor of *The Utterly Comic Relief Comic*, a comic book that raised money for the UK Comic Relief Charity in 1991. Contributor to *The Sandman Companion*, D.C. Comics (New York, NY), 1999, and has contributed prefaces and introductions to several books. Gaiman's works, including the short story "Troll Bridge," have been represented in numerous anthologies. Contributor to newspapers and magazines, including *Knave, Punch, Observer, Sunday Times* (London, England) and *Time Out*. Gaiman's books have been translated into other languages, including Bulgarian, Danish, Dutch, Finnish, French, German, Greek, Hungarian, Italian, Japanese,

Norwegian, Spanish, and Swedish. He has written scripts for the films *Avalon, Beowulf, The Confessions of William Henry Ireland, The Fermata, Modesty Blaise,* and others.

Adaptations

The Books of Magic was adapted into novel form by Carla Jablonski and others into several individual volumes, including *The Invitation, The Blindings,* and *The Children's Crusade,* issued by HarperCollins (New York, NY). *Neverwhere* was released on audio cassette by HighBridge (Minneapolis, MN), 1997; *American Gods* was released on cassette by Harper (New York, NY), 2001; *Coraline* was released as an audio book read by the author, Harper (New York, NY), 2002; *Two Plays for Voices* (*Snow Glass Apples* and *Murder Mysteries*) was released as an audio book and on audio CD, Harper (New York, NY), 2003. Several of Gaiman's works have been optioned for film, including *Sandman,* by Warner Bros., Inc.; *The Books of Magic,* by Warner Bros., Inc.; *Death: The High Cost of Living,* by Warner Bros., Inc.; *Good Omens,* by Renaissance Films; *Neverwhere,* by Jim Henson Productions; *Chivalry,* by Miramax; *Stardust,* by Miramax and Dimension Films; and *Coraline,* by Pandemonium Films. *Signal to Noise* was made into a stage play by NOWtheater (Chicago, IL).

Work in Progress

1602, a serialized story for Marvel Comics; *The Graveyard Book,* for HarperCollins (New York, NY); *Mirror Mask,* a film directed by Dave McKean for Jim Henson Productions and Columbia Tristar; a script for *A Short Film about John Bolton;* a television series based on *The Day I Swapped My Dad for Two Goldfish,* for Sunbow; an album of original songs for the record label Dancing Ferret Discs.

Sidelights

An English author of comic books, graphic novels (text and pictures in a comic-book format published in book form), prose novels, children's books, short fiction, nonfiction, and screenplays, Neil Gaiman is a best-selling writer who is considered perhaps the most accomplished and influential figure in modern comics as well as one of the most gifted of contemporary fantasists. Characteristically drawing from mythology, history, literature, and popular culture to create his works, Gaiman blends the everyday, the fantastic, the frightening, and the humorous to present his stories, which reveal the mysteries that lie just outside of reality as well as the insights that come from experiencing these mysteries. He refers to the plots and characters of classical literature and myth—most notably fairy tales, horror stories, science fiction, and traditional romances—while adding fresh, modern dimensions. In fact, Gaiman is credited with developing a new mythology with his works, which address themes such as what it means to be human; the importance of the relationship between humanity and art; humanity's desire for dreams and for attaining what they show; and the passage from childish ways of thinking to more mature

Book cover photograph by J.K. Potter of Smoke and Mirrors, *a collection of imaginative stories where extraordinary things happen. Written by Neil Gaiman.*

understanding. Although most of the author's works are not addressed to children, Gaiman often features child and young adult characters in his books, and young people are among Gaiman's greatest and most loyal fans. The author has become extremely popular, developing a huge cult-like following as well as a celebrity status. The author perhaps is best known as the creator of the comic-book and graphic-novel series about the Sandman. This character, which is based loosely on a crime-fighting superhero that first appeared in D.C. Comics in the 1930s and 40s, is the protagonist of an epic series of dark fantasies that spanned eight years and ran for seventy-five monthly issues. Gaiman introduces the Sandman as an immortal being who rules the Dreaming, a surreal world to which humans go when they fall asleep. As the series progresses, the Sandman discovers that he is involved with the fate of human beings on an intimate basis and that his life is tied intrinsically to this relationship. The "Sandman" series has sold millions of copies in both comic book and graphic novel formats and has inspired companion literature and a variety of related merchandise.

As a writer for children, Gaiman has been the subject of controversy for creating *Coraline,* a fantasy for middle-graders about a young girl who enters a bizarre alternate world that eerily mimics her own. Compared to Lewis Carroll's nineteenth-century fantasy *Alice's Adventures in Wonderland* for its imaginative depiction of a surreal adventure, *Coraline* has been questioned as an appropriate story for children because it may be too frightening for its intended audience. Gaiman also is the creator of two picture books for children, *The Day I Swapped My Dad for Two Goldfish,* a comic-book-style fantasy about a boy who trades his dad for two attractive goldfish, and *The Wolves in the Walls,* which features a brave girl who faces the wolves that have taken over her house. The author's adult novel *American Gods,* the tale of a young drifter who becomes involved with what appears to be a magical war, was a critical and popular success that helped to bring Gaiman to a mainstream audience. Among his many works, Gaiman has written a biography of the English pop/rock group Duran Duran; a comic book with shock-rocker Alice Cooper that the latter turned into an album; a satiric fantasy about the end of the world with English novelist Terry Pratchett; comic books about Todd MacFarlane's popular character Spawn; and screenplays for film, television, and radio, both original scripts and adaptations of his own works. Gaiman wrote the English-language script for the well-received Japanese anime film *Princess Mononoke;* the script of the episode "Day of the Dead" for the television series *Babylon 5;* and both a television script and a novel called *Neverwhere* that describes how an office worker rescues a young woman who is bleeding from a switchblade wound and is transported with her to London Below, a mysterious and dangerous world underneath the streets of England's largest city. Throughout his career, Gaiman has worked with a number of talented artists in the fields of comic books and fantasy, including John Bolton, Michael Zulli, Yoshitaka Amaro, Charles Vess, and longtime collaborator Dave McKean.

As a prose stylist, Gaiman is known for writing clearly and strongly, using memorable characters and striking images to build his dreamlike worlds. Although his books and screenplays can range from somber to creepy to horrifying, Gaiman is commended for underscoring them with optimism and sensitivity and for balancing their darkness with humor and wit. Reviewers have praised Gaiman for setting new standards for comic books as literature and for helping to bring increased popularity to both them and graphic novels. In addition, observers have claimed that several of the author's works transcend the genres in which they are written and explore deeper issues than those usually addressed in these works. Although Gaiman occasionally has been accused of being ponderous and self-indulgent, he generally is considered a phenomenon, a brilliant writer and storyteller whose works reflect his inventiveness, originality, and wisdom. Writing in *St. James Guide to Horror, Ghost, and Gothic Writers,* Peter Crowther noted that when Gaiman "is on form (which is most of the time), he is without peer. . . . [H]is blending of poetic prose, marvelous inventions, and artistic vision has assured him of his place in the vanguard of modern-day dark fantasists." Keith R. A. DeCandido of *Library*

Journal called Gaiman "arguably the most literate writer working in mainstream comics." Referring to Gaiman's graphic novels, Frank McConnell of *Commonweal* stated that the author "may just be the most gifted and important storyteller in English" and called him "our best and most bound-to-be-remembered writer of fantasy."

Born in Portchester, England, Gaiman was brought up in an upper-middle-class home. His father David acted as the director of a company, while his mother Sheila worked as a pharmacist. As a boy, Gaiman was "a completely omnivorous and cheerfully undiscerning reader," as he told Pamela Shelton. In an interview with Ray Olson of *Booklist,* Gaiman recalled that he first read *Alice in Wonderland* "when I was five, maybe, and always kept it around as default reading between the ages of five and twelve, and occasionally picked up and reread since. There are things Lewis Carroll did in *Alice* that are etched onto my circuitry." Gaiman was a voracious reader of comic books until the age of sixteen, when he felt that he outgrew the genre as it existed at the time. At his grammar school, Ardingly College, Gaiman would get "very grumpy . . . when they'd tell us that we couldn't read comics, because 'if you read comics you will not read OTHER THINGS.'" He asked himself, "Why are comics going to stop me reading?" Gaiman proved that his teachers were misguided in their theory: he read the entire children's library in Portchester in two or three years and then started on the adult library. He told Shelton, "I don't think I ever got to 'Z' but I got up to about 'L'"

When he was about fourteen, Gaiman began his secondary education at Whitgift School. When he was fifteen, Gaiman and his fellow students took a series of vocational tests that were followed by interviews with career advisors. Gaiman told Shelton that these advisors "would look at our tests and say, 'Well, maybe you'd be interested in accountancy,' or whatever. When I went for my interview, the guy said, 'What do you want to do?' and I said, 'Well, I'd really like to write American comics.' And it was obvious that this was the first time he'd ever heard that. He just sort of stared at me for a bit and then said, 'Well, how do you go about doing that, then?' I said, 'I have no idea—you're the career advisor. Advise.' And he looked like I'd slapped him in the face with a wet herring; he sort of stared at me and there was this pause and I went on for a while and then he said, 'Have you ever thought about accountancy?'" Undeterred, Gaiman kept on writing. He also was interested in music. At sixteen, Gaiman played in a punk band that was about to be signed by a record company. Gaiman brought in an attorney who, after reading the contract being offered to the band, discovered that the deal would exploit them; consequently, Gaiman refused to sign the contract. By 1977, he felt that he was ready to become a professional writer. That same year, Gaiman left Whitgift School.

After receiving some rejections for short stories that he had written, Gaiman decided to become a freelance journalist so that he could learn about the world of publishing from the inside. He wrote informational articles for British men's magazines with titles like *Knave.* Gaiman told Shelton that being a journalist "was terrific in giving me an idea of how the world worked. I was the kind of journalist who would go out and do interviews with people and then write them up for magazines. I learned economy and I learned about dialogue." In 1983, he discovered the work of English comic-strip writer Alan Moore, whose *Swamp Thing* became a special favorite. Gaiman told Shelton, "Moore's work convinced me that you really could do work in comics that had the same amount of intelligence, the same amount of passion, the same amount of quality that you could put in any other medium." In 1984, Gaiman produced his first book, *Duran Duran: The First Four Years of the Fab Five.* Once he had established his credibility as a writer, Gaiman was able to sell the short stories that he had done earlier in his career. In 1985, Gaiman married Mary Therese McGrath, with whom he has three children: Michael, Holly, and Madeleine (Maddy). At around this time, Gaiman decided that he was ready to concentrate on fiction. In addition, the comics industry was experiencing a new influx of talent, which inspired Gaiman to consider becoming a contributor to that medium.

In 1986, Gaiman met art student Dave McKean, and the two decided to collaborate. Their first work together was the comic book *Violent Cases.* Serialized initially in *Escape,* a British comic that showcased new strips, *Violent Cases* was published in book form in 1987. The story recounts the memories of an adult narrator—pictured by McKean as a dark-haired young man who bears a striking resemblance to Gaiman—who recalls his memories of hearing about notorious Chicago gangland leader Al Capone from an elderly osteopath who was the mobster's chiropractor. As a boy of four, the narrator had his arm broken accidentally by his father. In the office of the osteopath, the boy was transfixed by lurid stories about Chicago of the 1920s but, in the evenings, he had nightmares in which his own world and that of Capone's would intersect. As the story begins, the adult narrator is trying to make sense of the experience. According to Joe Sanders of *Dictionary of Literary Biography,* the narrator "discover[s] that grownups are as prone to uncertainty, emotional outbursts, and naïve rationalization as children. The boy is delighted, the grownup narrator perplexed, to see how 'facts' change to fit an interpreter's needs." Writing in the *Sunday Times* (London, England), Nicolette Jones called *Violent Cases* "inspired and ingenious," while Cindy Lynn Speer, writing in an essay on the author's Web site, dubbed it "a brilliant tale of childhood and memory."

At around the same time that *Violent Cases* was published in book form, Gaiman produced the comic book *Outrageous Tales from the Old Testament,* which is credited with giving him almost instant notoriety in the comic-book community. Gaiman teamed with McKean again to do a limited-run comic series, *Black Orchid,* the first of the author's works to be released by D.C.

Comics, the publisher of the original "Superman" and "Batman" series. A three-part comic book, "Black Orchid" features an essentially nonviolent female heroine who fights villains that she hardly can remember. Gaiman then was offered his choice of inactive D.C. characters to rework from the Golden Age of Comics (the 1930s and 1940s). He chose the Sandman. Originally, the character was millionaire Wesley Dodds who hunted criminals by night wearing a fedora, cape, and gas mask. Dodds would zap the crooks with his gas gun and leave them sleeping until the police got to them. When Gaiman began the series in 1988, he changed the whole scope of the character. The Sandman, who is also called Dream, Morpheus, Oneiros, Lord Shaper, Master of Story, and God of Sleep, became a thin, enigmatic figure with a pale face, dark eyes, and a shock of black hair. The Sandman is one of the Endless, immortals in charge of individual realms of the human psyche. The Sandman's brothers and sisters in the Endless are (in birth order) Destiny, Death, Destruction, the twins Desire and Despair, and Delirium (formerly Delight); Dream (the Sandman) falls between Death and Destruction.

In the "Sandman" book *Preludes and Nocturnes,* Gaiman introduces the title character, the ageless lord of dreams, who has just returned home after being captured by a coven of wizards and held in an asylum for the criminally insane for seventy-two years. Dream finds that his home is in ruins, that his powers are diminished, and that his three tools—a helmet, a pouch of sand, and a ruby stone—have been stolen. He finds his missing helpers and the young girl who has become addicted to the sand from his pouch; he also visits Hell to find the demon who stole his helmet and battles an evil doctor who has unleashed the power of dreams on the unsuspecting people of Earth. Dream comes to realize that his captivity has affected him: he has become humanized, and he understands that he eventually will have to die. In *The Doll's House,* Dream travels across the United States searching for the Arcana, the stray dreams and nightmares of the twentieth century that have taken on human form; the story is interwoven with a subplot about a young woman, Rose Walker, who has lost her little brother. In *Dream Country,* Gaiman features Calliope, a muse and the mother of Dream's son, Orpheus; the story also brings in a real character, actor/playwright William Shakespeare. In *Season of Mists,* Dream meets Lucifer, who has left his position as ruler of Hell and has left the choice of his successor to Dream.

A Game of You features Barbara (nicknamed Barbie), a character who had appeared in *The Doll's House.* Barbie is drawn back into the dream realm that she ruled as a child in order to save it from the evil Cuckoo, who plans to destroy it. *Fables and Reflections* is a collection of stories featuring the characters from the series and includes Gaiman's retelling of the Greek myth of Orpheus. In *Brief Lives,* Dream and Delirium embark on a quest to find their little brother Destruction, who exiled himself to Earth three hundred years before. *World's End* includes a collection of tales told by a group of travelers who are waiting out a storm in an inn. *The Kindly Ones* brings the series to its conclusion as Hippolyta (Lyta) Hall takes revenge upon Dream for the disappearance of her son. Lyta, who has been driven mad by anger and grief, asks the help of the title characters, mythological beings also known as the Furies. The Kindly Ones take out Lyta's revenge on Dream, who succumbs to their attack. The tale comes full cycle, and Dream's destiny is joined with that of humans in death. In the final chapter of the series, *The Wake*, a funeral is held for Dream; however, as Gaiman notes thematically, dreams really never die, and Dream's role in the Endless is taken on in a new incarnation. The Sandman also appears in a more peripheral role in *The Dream Hunters*, a retelling of the Japanese folktale "The Fox, the Monk, and the Mikado of All Night's Dreaming."

Next to the Sandman, Death, Dream's older sister, is the most frequently featured and popular character in the series. Death is charged with shepherding humans who are about to die through their transitions. Once a century, she must come to Earth as a sixteen-year-old girl in order to remind herself what mortality feels like. In contrast to Dream, who characteristically is isolated, brooding, and serious, Death, who is depicted as a spike-haired young woman who dresses like a punk rocker or Goth girl, has a more open and kindly nature. Death is featured in two books of her own, *Death: The High Cost of Living* and *Death: The Time of Your Life*. In the first story, she helps Sexton, a teen who is contemplating suicide, rediscover the joys in being alive as they journey through New York City and, in the second, she helps Foxglove, a newly successful musician, to reveal her true sexual orientation as her companion Hazel prepares to die. Death and the rest of the Endless are also featured in *The Sandman: Endless Nights,* in which Gaiman devotes an individual story to each of the seven siblings.

Writing in *Commonweal* about the "Sandman" series, Frank McConnell stated, "*Sandman* is not just one of the best pieces of fiction being done these days; . . . it emerges as *the* best piece of fiction being done these days." McConnell stated that what Gaiman has done with the series "is to establish the fact that a comic book can be a work of high and very serious art—a story that other storytellers, in whatever medium they work, will have to take into account as an exploration of what stories can do and what stories are for." The critic concluded, "I know of nothing quite like it, and I don't expect there will be anything like it for some time. . . . Read the damn thing; it's important." Peter Crowder of *St. James Guide to Horror, Ghost, and Gothic Writers* noted that, with the "Sandman" series of comic books, Gaiman "has truly revolutionized the power of the medium." Crowder called the various volumes of collected stories "almost uniformly excellent, and any one of them would make a good starting point

From Gaiman's fantasy graphic novel The Sandman: Ramadan. *(Illustrated by P. Craig Russell.)* "Sandman" #50 ©1993 DC Comics. All Rights Reserved. Used with Permission.

for those readers who, while well-versed in the field of Gothic prose literature, have yet to discover the rare but powerful joy inherent in a great comic book." In 1996, D.C. Comics surprised the fans of "Sandman" by announcing the cancellation of the series while it was still the company's best-seller; however, D.C. had made this arrangement with Gaiman at the beginning of the series. "Sandman" has sold more than seven million copies; individual copies of the stories also have sold in the millions or in the hundreds of thousands. "A Midsummer's Night's Dream," a story from *Dream Country,* won the World Fantasy Award for the best short story of 1991. This was the first time that a comic book had won an award that was not related to its own medium, and the event caused an uproar among some fantasy devotees. The "Sandman" stories have inspired related volumes, such as a book of quotations from the series, and merchandise such as action figures, stuffed toys, trading cards, jewelry, and watches.

In 1994, Gaiman told Ken Tucker of *Entertainment Weekly,* "Superhero comics are the most perfectly evolved art form for preadolescent male power fantasies, and I don't see that as a bad thing. I want to reach other sorts of people, too." In 1995, he told Pamela Shelton, "If you're too young for 'Sandman,' you will be bored silly by it. It's filled with long bits with people having conversations." Speaking to Nick Hasted of the *Guardian* in 1999, Gaiman said, "Right now, as things stand, Sandman is my serious work. . . . It is one giant, overarching story, and I'm proud of it. Compared to Sandman, all the prose work so far is trivia." In 2003, Gaiman wrote an introduction to *The Sandman: King of Dreams,* a collection of text and art from the series with commentary by Alisa Kwitney. He commented, "If I have a concern over *The Sandman,* the 2,000 page story I was able to tell between 1988 and 1996, it is that the things that have come after it, the toys (whether plastic and articulated or soft and cuddly), the posters, the clothes, the calendars and candles, the companion volume, and even the slim book of quotations, along with the various spin-offs and such—will try people's patience and goodwill, and that a book like this will be perceived, not unreasonably, as something that's being used to flog the greasy patch in the driveway where once, long ago, a dead horse used to lie. The ten volumes of *The Sandman* are what they are, and that's the end of it."

Throughout his career, Gaiman has included young people as main characters in his works. For example, *The Books of Magic,* a collection of four comics published in 1993, predates J. K. Rowling's "Harry Potter" series by featuring a thirteen-year-old boy, Tim Hunter, who is told that he has the capabilities to be the greatest wizard in the world. Tim, a boy from urban London who wears oversized glasses, is taken by the Trenchcoat Brigade—sorcerers with names like The Mysterious Phantom Stranger, the Incorrigible Hellblazer, and the Enigmatic Dr. Occult—on a tour of the universe to learn its magical history. Tim travels to Hell, to the land of Faerie, and to America, among other places, each of them showing him a different aspect of the world of magic. He also searches for his girlfriend Molly, who has been abducted into the fantasy realms; after he finds her, the two of them face a series of dangers as they struggle to return to their own world. At the end of the story, Tim must make a decision to embrace or reject his talents as a wizard. *The Books of Magic* also includes cameos by the Sandman and his sister Death. Writing in *Locus,* Carolyn Cushman said, "It's a fascinating look at magic, its benefits and burdens, all dramatically illustrated [by John Bolton, Scott Hampton, Charles Vess, and Paul Johnson], and with a healthy helping of humor." Speaking of the format of *The Books of Magic,* Michael Swanwick of *Book World* noted, "The graphic novel has come of age. This series is worth any number of movies."

In 1994, Gaiman produced *The Tragical Comedy, or Comical Tragedy, of Mr. Punch* (also published as *Mr. Punch*), a work that he considers one of his best. In this graphic novel, which is illustrated by Dave McKean, a young boy is sent to stay with his grandparent by the seaside while his mother gives birth to his baby sister. While on his visit, the boy encounters a mysterious puppeteer and watches a Punch and Judy show, a sometimes violent form of puppet-theater entertainment. Through a series of strange experiences, he ends up rejecting Mr. Punch's promise that everyone in the world is free to do whatever they want. Sanders of *Dictionary of Literary Biography* called *Mr. Punch* "perhaps Gaiman and McKean's most impressive collaboration," while Crowder called it "an impressive work, rich not only in freshness and originality but also in compassion, Gaiman's hallmark. . . . The collective impact is literally breathtaking." Writing in *Commonweal,* Frank McConnell noted, "This stunning comic book-graphic novel—whatever—is easily the most haunting, inescapable story I have read in years."

In 1996, Gaiman and McKean produced their first work for children, the picture book *The Day I Swapped My Dad for Two Goldfish.* In this tale, a little boy trades his father for two of his neighbor's goldfish while his little sister stares, horrified. When their mother finds out what has happened, she is furious. She makes the children go and get back their father who, unfortunately, has already been traded for an electric guitar. While on their quest to find him, the siblings decide that their father is a very good daddy after all. The children finally retrieve their father, who has been reading a newspaper all during his adventure. At home, their mother makes the children promise not to swap their dad any more. Writing in *Bloomsbury Review,* Anji Keating called *The Day I Swapped My Dad for Two Goldfish* "a fabulously funny tale" and dubbed the protagonists' journey to fetch their father "delightful." Malcolm Jones of *Newsweek* predicted that Gaiman and McKean "may shock a few grandparents . . . but in fact the most shocking thing they've done in this droll story is to take the illegible look of cutting-edge magazines like Raygun and somehow make it readable."

In 2003, Gaiman and McKean produced a second picture book, *The Wolves in the Walls.* In this work, young Lucy hears wolves living in the walls of the old house where she and her family live; of course, no one believes her. When the wolves emerge to take over the house, Lucy and her family flee. However, Lucy wants her house back, and she also wants the beloved pig-puppet that she left behind. She talks her family into going back into the house, where they move into the walls that had been vacated by the wolves. Lucy and her family frighten the usurpers, who are wearing their clothes and eating their food. The wolves scatter, and everything seems to go back to normal until Lucy hears another noise in the walls; this time, it sounds like elephants. In her *Booklist* review of *The Wolves in the Walls,* Francisca Goldsmith found the book "visually and emotionally sophisticated, accessible, and inspired by both literary and popular themes and imagery." Writing in *School Library Journal,* Marian Creamer commented that "Gaiman and McKean deftly pair text and illustration to convey a strange, vivid story," and predicted that "Children will delight in the 'scary, creepy tone.'"

Gaiman's first story for middle-graders, *Coraline,* outlines how the title character, a young girl who feels that she is being ignored by her preoccupied parents, enters a terrifying, malevolent alternate reality to save them after they are kidnapped. The story begins when Coraline and her parents move into their new house, which is divided into apartments. Left to her own devices, bored Coraline explores the house and finds a door in the empty flat next door that leads to a world that is a twisted version of her own. There, she meets two odd-looking individuals who call themselves her "other mother" and "other father." The Other Mother, a woman who looks like Coraline's except for her black-button eyes and stiletto fingernails, wants Coraline to stay with her and her husband. Tempted by good food and interesting toys, Coraline considers the offer. However, when the girl returns home, she finds that her parents have disappeared. Coraline discovers that they are trapped in the other world, and she sets out to save them. The Other Mother, who turns out to be a soul-sucking harpy, enters into a deadly game of hide-and-seek with Coraline, who discovers new qualities of bravery and resolve within herself. Before returning home, Coraline saves herself, her parents, and some ghost children who are trapped in the grotesque world.

After its publication, *Coraline* became a subject of dispute. Some adult observers saw it as a book that would give nightmares to children. However, other observers have noted that the children of their acquaintance who read the book consider it an exciting rather than overly frightening work. A reviewer in *Publishers Weekly* noted that Gaiman and illustrator McKean "spin an electrifyingly creepy tale likely to haunt young readers for many moons. . . . Gaiman twines his tale with a menacing tone and crisp prose fraught with memorable imagery . . ., yet keeps the narrative just this side of terrifying." Writing in *School Library Journal,* Bruce Anne Shook commented that "the story is odd, strange, even slightly bizarre, but kids will hang on every word. . . . This is just right for all those requests for a scary book." Stephanie Zvirin of *Booklist* added that Gaiman offers "a chilling and empowering view of children, to be sure, but young readers are likely to miss such subtleties as the clever allusions to classic horror movies and the references to the original dark tales of the Brothers Grimm." A critic in *Kirkus Reviews* found *Coraline* "not for the faint-hearted—who are mostly adults anyway—but for stouthearted kids who love a brush with the sinister, *Coraline* is spot on." *Coraline* has won several major fantasy awards and has become an international best-seller.

In his interview with Pamela Shelton, Gaiman said, "What I enjoy most is when people say to me, 'When I was sixteen I didn't know what I was going to do with my life and then I read "Sandman" and now I'm at university studying mythology' or whatever. I think it's wonderful when you've opened a door to people and showed them things that would never have *known* they would have been interested in." Gaiman finds it satisfy-

ing to introduce his readers to mythology. He told Shelton, "You gain a cultural understanding to the last 2500 to 3000 years, which, if you lack it, there's an awful lot of stuff that you will simply never quite understand." He noted that, in "Sandman," even readers unfamiliar with the Norse god Loki or the three-headed spirit of Irish mythology "sort of half-know; there's a gentle and sort of delightful familiarity with these tales. It feels right. And I think that's probably the most important thing. Giving people this stuff, pointing out that it can be interesting, but also pointing out what mythologies do know. And how they affect us." In an interview with Hasted in the *Guardian,* Gaiman stated, "What I'm fighting now is the tendency to put novelists in a box, to make them write the same book over and over again. I want to shed skins. I want to keep awake. I definitely have a feeling that if I'm not going forward, if I'm not learning something, then I'm dead."

Biographical and Critical Sources

BOOKS

Authors and Artists for Young Adults, Volume 42, Gale (Detroit, MI), 2002.
Dictionary of Literary Biography, Volume 261: *British Fantasy and Science Fiction Writers since 1960,* Gale (Detroit, MI), 2002.
Gaiman, Neil, in an interview with Pamela Shelton, *Authors and Artists for Young Adults,* Volume 19, Gale (Detroit, MI), 1996
Kwitney, Alisa, *The Sandman: King of Dreams,* introduction by Neil Gaiman, Chronicle Books (San Francisco, CA), 2003.
St. James Guide to Horror, Ghost, and Gothic Writers, St. James Press (Detroit, MI), 1998.

PERIODICALS

Bloomsbury Review, July-August, 1997, Anji Keating, review of *The Day I Swapped My Dad for Two Goldfish,* p. 21.
Booklist, August, 2002, Ray Olson, "The *Booklist* Interview: Neil Gaiman," p. 19, and Stephanie Zvirin, review of *Coraline,* p. 1948; August, 2003, Francisca Goldsmith, review of *The Wolves in the Walls,* p. 1989.
Book World, April 7, 2002, Michael Swanwick, "Reel Worlds," p. 3.
Commonweal, December 2, 1994, Frank McConnell, review of *Mister Punch,* p. 27; October 20, 1995, Frank McConnell, review of *Sandman,* p. 21; June 19, 1998, Frank McConnell, review of *Neverwhere,* p. 21
Entertainment Weekly, June 24, 1994, Ken Tucker, review of *Sandman,* pp. 228-229.
Guardian (London, England), July 14, 1999, Nick Hasted, "The Illustrated Man," p. 12.
Kirkus Reviews, June 15, 2002, review of *Coraline,* p. 88.
Library Journal, September 15, 1990, Keith R. A. DeCandido, review of *The Golden Age,* p. 104.

Locus, April, 1993, Carolyn Cushman, review of *The Books of Magic,* p. 29.

Newsweek, December 1, 1997, Malcolm Jones, review of *The Day I Swapped My Dad for Two Goldfish,* p. 77.

Publishers Weekly, June 24, 2002, review of *Coraline,* p. 57.

School Library Journal, August, 2002, Bruce Anne Shook, review of *Coraline,* p. 184; September, 2003, Marian Creamer, review of *The Wolves in the Walls,* p. 178.

Sunday Times (London, England), July 15, 1990, Nicolette Jones, review of *Violent Cases.*

ONLINE

Neil Gaiman Home Page, http://www.neilgaiman.com/ (May, 2002), Cindy Lynn Speer, "An Essay on Neil Gaiman and Comics."*

--Sketch by Gerard J. Senick

*   *   *

GARRISON, Mary 1952-

Personal

Born April 22, 1952, in Augusta, GA; daughter of H. Levy, Jr. (a South Carolina Methodist minister) and Ruth (a homemaker; maiden name, Gilstrap) Rogers; married William T. Garrison (a dentist), August 12, 1973; children: Patrick, Anne. *Ethnicity:* "Caucasian." *Education:* Attended Columbia College, 1970-1972; Emory University, B.A., 1974. *Hobbies and other interests:* Reading, hiking, traveling, family, community volunteering.

Addresses

Agent—c/o Author Mail, White Mane Publishing Company, P.O. Box 708, 63 West Burd St., Shippensburg, PA 17257. *E-mail*—mmrgarrison@mchsi.com.

Career

Freelance writer. *Times-News,* Hendersonville, NC, community columnist, 1984—; previously worked as a teacher assistant and foundation director. Volunteer in local schools.

Member

NC Press Club, National Federation of Press Women.

Awards, Honors

First place, NC Press Club Communications Contest, 2002, for columns; first place, National Federation of Press Women Communications Contest, 2003, for columns; Juvenile Book Award, NC Press Club, Juvenile Book Award, National Federation of Press Women, and

Mary Garrison

Top Forty Young Adult Books selection, Pennsylvania School Librarians Association, all 2003, all for *Slaves Who Dared: The Stories of Ten African-American Heroes.*

Writings

Slaves Who Dared: The Stories of Ten African-American Heroes, White Mane Publishing Company (Shippensburg, PA), 2002.

Sidelights

Mary Garrison was drawn to writing by her father-in-law, Webb Garrison. A prolific writer (over sixty books in his lifetime) with a particular interest in the Civil War, he involved his family in developing book ideas, research, and proofreading. In an effort to interest his family members in writing during his last year of life, he strongly encouraged them to write books for children and young adults on Civil War topics. Garrison took up the challenge, ultimately publishing *Slaves Who Dared: The Stories of Ten African-American Heroes.*

In describing her interest to *SATA,* Garrison wrote, "Why would a fifty-year-old white Southern woman want to write a book about slavery? I have a personal interest in this since I attended the first public school in South Carolina that desegregated during the 1960s. It was a tumultuous time, both personally and historically, and sparked an interest in race relations for me. I think the history of slavery is something that we often react to with anger, shame, defensiveness, or denial. . . . Why not talk about it head on, acknowledge it for what it was, and see what we can learn from it? Some people . . . especially some Southerners, will say things like, 'well, all slave owners were not bad. . . .' But stop and put yourself in that situation. Think about . . . being owned by another human being even under the best of circumstances. When your freedom, your civil liberties, and your dignity, your time, even your spouse and your children belong to someone else, what kind of life is that really?"

In *Slaves Who Dared,* Garrison recounts the remarkable stories of ten men and women who were born into but escaped from slavery. While some, like Frederick Douglass, Sojourner Truth, and Booker T. Washington are famous, others are not and their stories bear telling, remarked reviewers, not only for the exceptional courage they showed individually, but for the creativity with which they sought escape and established new lives. These stories are drawn directly from narratives that these individuals either wrote themselves or told to someone. In her review for *Booklist,* Hazel Rochman noted favorably the author's "weaving into each narrative many actual quotes, illustrations . . ., and the drama of how and where the stories were recorded." Historical photos, captions, and sidebars that explained concepts presented in the text were found useful by Linda Greengrass in her review for *School Library Journal.* A comprehensive index and bibliography, Web sites for locating original narratives, and an extensive suggested reading list complete this book.

In reaching her decision to write *Slaves Who Dared,* Garrison concluded that, "the stories of these slaves are more than worthy of preservation. Young people need heroes and they should be the right kinds of heroes. Sure, there are those in TV and comic books. And there's Nintendo, and the computer, and the Internet. But how many worthy role models are they exposed to today? What do they really know about courage in the face of adversity? How do these heroes that escaped from slavery stack up against . . . a video game? There's no comparison."

Biographical and Critical Sources

PERIODICALS

Booklist, September 1, 2002, Hazel Rochman, review of *Slaves Who Dared: The Stories of Ten African-American Heroes,* p. 73.

Civil War Book Review, winter, 2003, Carolyn P. Yoder, review of *Slaves Who Dared,* p. 19.

Savannah Morning News, August 4, 2002, Doug Wyatt, "Flights to Freedom: Remarkable stories of slaves who refused to quit dreaming," pp. 8, 15.

School Library Journal, July, 2002, Linda Greengrass, review of *Slaves Who Dared,* p. 134.

*   *   *

GLUBOK, Shirley (Astor) 1933-

Personal

Surname is pronounced "*Glue*-bach"; born June 15, 1933, in St. Louis, MO; daughter of Yale I. (a merchant) and Ann (a merchant; maiden name, Astor) Glubok; married Alfred H. Tamarin (an author and photographer), February 25, 1968 (died August 19, 1980). *Education:* Washington University, A.B.; Columbia University, M.A., 1958; graduate study in art history at New York University Institute of Fine Arts. *Religion:* Jewish.

Addresses

Home—50 East 72nd St., New York, NY 10021.

Career

Writer. Teacher in St. Louis, MO, and New York, NY, 1955-64; lecturer in art history at the Metropolitan Museum of Art in New York, NY, 1958—, in lecture series for the National Endowment for the Arts Humanities Series, 1972, at America's Society in New York, NY, 1988-90, at the Cooper Hewitt Museum in New York, NY, 1989-90, and at the Spanish Institute in New York, NY, 1991—; author-in-residence at Greenhill School, Dallas, TX, 1977; taught graduate course at Boston University, 1987. Guest lecturer in Boston public schools, 1981-2003; lecturer in museums, to various professional educators' and librarians' associations, and to university groups.

Member

Authors Guild of America, Archaeological Institute of America, Washington University Archaeological Society, College Art Association, Coffee House Club, Riverside Tennis Association, Club Taurino, Victorian Society, Temple Emanu-El.

Awards, Honors

Lewis Carroll Shelf Award, 1963, for *The Art of Ancient Egypt;* Spur Award, Western Writers of America, 1971, for *The Art of the Southwest Indians* and *The Art of the Old West; Boston Globe-Horn Book* award for best nonfiction book, 1976, for *Voyaging to Cathay;* Nonfiction Author of the Year award for body of work, Children's Book Guild of Washington, DC, 1980; Central Missouri State University award, 1987, for outstanding contribution to children's literature; MacDowell Colony Fellow, 1991; American Library Association notable book citations for *The Art of Ancient Egypt, The Art of Ancient Greece, The Art of the Eskimo, Discover-*

ing Tut-ankh-Amen's Tomb, The Art of Ancient Peru, and *Voyaging to Cathay;* American Institute of Graphic Arts awards for *The Art of Ancient Egypt, The Fall of the Aztecs,* and *Voyaging to Cathay;* Children's Book Showcase award for *The Art of the Northwest Coast Indians.*

Writings

CHILDREN'S NONFICTION; ALL WITH PHOTOGRAPHS BY ALFRED TAMARIN UNTIL 1979

The Art of Ancient Egypt, Atheneum (New York, NY), 1962.

The Art of Lands in the Bible, Atheneum (New York, NY), 1963.

The Art of Ancient Greece, Atheneum (New York, NY), 1963.

The Art of the North American Indian, Harper & Row (New York, NY), 1964.

The Art of the Eskimo, Harper & Row (New York, NY), 1964.

The Art of Ancient Rome, Harper & Row (New York, NY), 1965.

The Art of Africa, Harper & Row (New York, NY), 1965.

Art and Archaeology, Harper & Row (New York, NY), 1966.

The Art of Ancient Peru, Harper & Row (New York, NY), 1966.

The Art of the Etruscans, Harper & Row (New York, NY), 1967.

The Art of Ancient Mexico, Harper & Row (New York, NY), 1968.

Knights in Armor, Harper & Row (New York, NY), 1969.

The Art of India, Macmillan (New York, NY), 1969.

The Art of Colonial America, Macmillan (New York, NY), 1970.

The Art of Japan, Macmillan (New York, NY), 1970.

The Art of the Old West, Macmillan (New York, NY), 1971.

The Art of the Southwest Indians, Macmillan (New York, NY), 1971.

The Art of the New American Nation, Macmillan (New York, NY), 1972.

The Art of the Spanish in the United States and Puerto Rico, Macmillan (New York, NY), 1972.

The Art of America from Jackson to Lincoln, Macmillan (New York, NY), 1973.

The Art of China, Macmillan (New York, NY), 1973.

The Art of America in the Early Twentieth Century, Macmillan (New York, NY), 1974.

The Art of America in the Gilded Age, Macmillan (New York, NY), 1974.

The Art of the Northwest Coast Indians, Macmillan (New York, NY), 1975.

The Art of the Plains Indians, Macmillan (New York, NY), 1975.

Dolls, Dolls, Dolls, Follett (Chicago, IL), 1975.

(With Alfred H. Tamarin) *Ancient Indians of the Southwest,* Doubleday (New York, NY), 1975.

(With Alfred H. Tamarin) *Voyaging to Cathay: Americans in the China Trade,* Viking (New York, NY), 1976.

(With Alfred H. Tamarin) *Olympic Games in Ancient Greece,* Harper & Row (New York, NY), 1976.

The Art of America since World War II, Macmillan (New York, NY), 1976.

The Art of the Woodland Indians, Macmillan (New York, NY), 1976.

The Art of Photography, Macmillan (New York, NY), 1977.

The Art of the Vikings, Macmillan (New York, NY), 1978.

The Art of the Southeastern Indians, Macmillan (New York, NY), 1978.

(With Alfred H. Tamarin) *The Mummy of Ramose: The Life and Death of an Ancient Egyptian Nobleman,* Harper & Row (New York, NY), 1978.

The Art of the Comic Strip, Macmillan (New York, NY), 1979.

The Art of Ancient Egypt under the Pharaohs, Macmillan (New York, NY), 1980.

Dolls' Houses: Life in Miniature, Harper & Row (New York, NY), 1984.

Great Lives: Painting, Charles Scribner's Sons (New York, NY), 1994.

EDITOR

The Fall of the Aztecs, by Bernal Diaz del Castillo, St. Martin's Press (New York, NY), 1965.

The Fall of the Incas, by Garcilaso de la Vega, and Pedro Pizarro, Macmillan (New York, NY), 1967.

Discovering Tut-ankh-Amen's Tomb, by Howard Carter and A. C. Mace, Macmillan (New York, NY), 1968.

Discovering the Royal Tombs at Ur, by Leonard Woolley, Macmillan (New York, NY), 1969.

Home and Child Life in Colonial Days, by Alice Morse Earle, photographs by Tamarin, Macmillan (New York, NY), 1969.

Digging in Assyria, by Austin Henry Layard, Macmillan (New York, NY), 1970.

OTHER

Contributor to "Basic Reading Textbook" series, Holt/ Silver Burdett, including Holt Satellite book *American Sculpture;* contributor of articles to various magazines and journals, including *Connoisseur, Antiques, Teacher, Scanorama, Scholastic, Review: Latin American Arts and Literature, Columbia Magazine, New York Review of Art, Auction Forum, La Voz Hispana, Art and Auction,* and *House and Garden.*

Glubok's papers are collected at the de Grummond Archives, University of Southern Mississippi.

Work in Progress

Young Pablo Picasso, a work of children's nonfiction.

Sidelights

The author of various books for young readers, Shirley Glubok introduces children to the art of numerous cultures with a blend of photographs and simple text in her

"The Art of" series. Her award-winning books single out a particular area or time period and attempt to give a general idea of the customs and how they influenced the art that was created. Glubok has examined the art of such areas as Japan, India, and Africa, and of such people as the North American Indians and the Vikings. May Hill Arbuthnot and Zena Sutherland maintained in their *Children and Books* that Glubok's books "are impressive because of the combination of authoritative knowledge, simple presentation, dignified format, and a recurrent emphasis on the relationship between an art form and the culture in which it was created."

Glubok was born and raised in St. Louis, Missouri and enjoyed an active childhood of swimming, reading, and visiting art museums. At Washington University she majored in art and archeology, and after teaching briefly in St. Louis, she moved to New York City to attend graduate school. After earning her master's degree she taught in a private school and gave Saturday lectures for youngsters at the famed Metropolitan Museum of Art. This busy schedule notwithstanding, she decided to write a book based on her experiences blending art and archeology. *The Art of Ancient Egypt,* her first title, was published in 1962. The book sold so briskly that author and publisher decided to produce a series of art books for young readers, using text and primarily black-and-white photographs.

All of the books in the series maintain a similar format, containing large photographs with limited but clear and simple text. Such books as *The Art of Lands in the Bible, The Art of Ancient Rome, The Art of Japan,* and *The Art of the Southwest Indians* all introduce children to a variety of cultures and customs and art. "In each book [Glubok] writes she continues her marriage between children and art," asserted Lee B. Hopkins in *More Books by More People: Interviews with Sixty-five Authors of Books for Children.* Hopkins added "For each one she recruits one or more 'junior literary advisors' who read over her manuscript and help her select the works of art to be photographed. And she listens to them!" In addition to collaborating with young people on her many books, Glubok also worked with her husband, Alfred Tamarin, until his death in 1980. He photographed Hatshepsut's tomb for *The Art of Ancient Egypt* and went on to provide photographs for almost all of her books. The couple traveled all over the world to gather visual material, and they also co-wrote such books as *The Mummy of Ramose: The Life and Death of an Ancient Egyptian Nobleman* and *Olympic Games in Ancient Greece.*

Critics have often praised the clear prose style, carefully selected artwork, and remarkable photographs of Glubok's books. The only complaints seem to be that Glubok sometimes tries to cover too much, and that color photographs would be more effective for some of the artwork. A *Kirkus Reviews* contributor pointed out that Glubok's approach "gives primacy to experiencing art over studying art, which is not inappropriate for the age level, but it also has a built-in limitation: the author tells only what *she* thinks the child wants to know or should know." Hopkins, however, believed that Glubok's books "open the door to the world of art and history to readers of all ages. Leafing through [the books] is almost as good as going to the best museum, for they impart tremendous understanding and appreciation of the art world."

In *Great Lives: Painting,* Glubok introduces twenty-three European and American painters, with brief biographies and comments on their art and their personalities. Most of the entrants are well-known painters, such as Picasso and Michaelangelo, but, as Chris Sherman mentioned in *Booklist,* Glubok also includes "a few surprises," including the American painter of the Southwest, Georgia O'Keefe, and the Impressionist Mary Cassatt. In brief sketches, Glubok gives a feeling of the artist's character as well as his or her work, pulling no punches as to which are "eccentric" or "disagreeable," as Sherman remarked.

Glubok once commented on what she wishes her writing to achieve: "My aim is to introduce young readers to the great art treasures of the world and to try and understand the people who made them. By appreciating the beauty of other cultures, we can all make our own lives more beautiful and understand ourselves a little bit better."

Biographical and Critical Sources

BOOKS

Arbuthnot, May Hill, and Zena Sutherland, *Children and Books,* 4th edition, Scott, Foresman (New York, NY), 1972, pp. 598-599.
Children's Literature Review, Volume 1, Gale (Detroit, MI), 1976.
Hopkins, Lee B., *More Books by More People: Interviews with Sixty-five Authors of Books for Children,* Citation, 1974.

PERIODICALS

Booklist, September 1, 1970; July 1, 1972; January 1, 1973; July 1, 1973; July, 1994, Chris Sherman, review of *Great Lives: Painting,* p. 1939.
Bulletin of the Center for Children's Books, July-August, 1970; December, 1970; November, 1972; March, 1973; September, 1973; April, 1974; September, 1974; July-August, 1975; May, 1976; January, 1977; May, 1977; February, 1978; September, 1978; October, 1978; April, 1979; October, 1979; June, 1980; October, 1984.
Childhood Education, January, 1974.
Cricket, May, 1978.
Horn Book, February, 1970; February, 1973; August, 1973; April, 1974; April, 1976; June, 1976; August, 1976; December, 1976; December, 1977; June, 1978; August, 1979; January-February, 1985, pp. 68-69.

Kirkus Reviews, May 1, 1968, p. 514; April 1, 1970; May 1, 1972; October 1, 1972; April 15, 1973; November 1, 1973; April 1, 1974; April 15, 1975.
Library Journal, January 15, 1974.
New York Times Book Review, June 2, 1974; April 9, 1978; April 14, 1978; April 30, 1978.
Publishers Weekly, January 15, 1973; May 6, 1974; April 28, 1975; January 5, 1976; August 15, 1977.

School Library Journal, September, 1970; September, 1975; December, 1976; January, 1978; September, 1979; September, 1980; February, 1985, p. 84; May, 1989; May, 1990; July, 1994, p. 108.
Science Books, May, 1970.

Autobiography Feature

Shirley Glubok

It all seems so very long ago. Some people recall their childhood as if it were yesterday, but I could hardly remember anything about mine until I went back to St. Louis where it all began. After my family moved away I had returned to my birthplace only once, in 1969, to lecture at the library in the neighborhood where I grew up.

Then, last spring, I was invited to speak at a children's book conference at Southwest Missouri State University. Another St. Louis author, whom I met at the conference, drove me from Warrensburg to St. Louis. On the way we talked about growing up in our hometown. She writes stories that draw on her experience and could speak easily about her past, but I could think only of my present.

I had been warned that St. Louis has changed a great deal but I found that in many ways it is the same. When we zipped in from the highway onto the street where my new friend lives, I felt comforted. Even though the neighborhood I had grown up in was miles away, this was a street I knew well, and now it was just as I remembered. Appearing in a familiar area with a new friend was a welcome combination. Suddenly the trip I had dreaded for so long became a solace.

Once back at the "source" I was finally able to begin looking back on my childhood, and I realized that delving into my memory was something I had never allowed myself to enjoy, partly because I have always been too busy with the present to have a place in my mind for reliving the past. I have a tendency to block out memories, for if they are good memories I would regret their passing, and if bad, would be glad they are over. I once read a book by a famous actress that began with her admission that she never kept a diary because "once a day is gone it's gone." I more or less agree.

Now that I am finally looking backwards after all these years, it seems that everything I have become was

Shirley Glubok

predictable. Perhaps some of us determine at an early age who we are going to be and what we are going to do, then spend the rest of our lives acting it out. "Shirley was born wanting to be a writer," I overheard my mother say after I spoke at a luncheon. There was never any question in my mind. I inherited this ambition from Mother, who had a natural talent for writing but could not do much of it because she had a husband, three children, and two fashionable retail stores to look after. She expressed herself beautifully, wrote a few short stories as a young woman, and continued to send me exquisite letters all her life.

Mother had inherited the talent to write from her own mother, my maternal grandmother, who was never able to fulfill her own desire for a literary career because she had nine children to look after. Our ancestors in Europe had been scholars for centuries. Among them were scribes who wrote the Torah, so writing must be in my blood.

Some people can express themselves well in speech but I find it easier to put my feelings down on paper. When I was in the fifth grade my teacher, Miss Mitchell, had chosen a few members of my class to read stories we had written. When she came to mine she said, "Now we'll hear Shirley's; hers are always good." I felt proud, and from then on I wanted not only to write but for my writing to be read. Later in grade school I wrote stories with my friends when we came home from school. I always thought I would write a novel; but they say first novels are autobiographical and it has become obvious that I have difficulty thinking about my past.

Perhaps the earliest memory of my lifetime was of Quincy, Illinois, where I lived when I was three years old and where my younger brother, Allan, was born. I believe I remember going to a park with my father where we fed the pigeons and to the beach on Lake Michigan where I played in the sand with my favorite cousin, Maurice. I say "I believe I remember" because it is possible that I remember these events only because I grew up looking at snapshots that recorded them. In the same way, with the help of photographs, I remember my grandparents' backyard where I played with my two brothers and our cousins Maurice and Sheldon. I was the only girl.

Actually the earliest memory I have without the help of photographs is the birth of my brother Allan. He was a beautiful, chubby baby with big brown eyes and black hair. I was crazy about him and so was Hattie, our housekeeper. Hattie had been a cook for a family whose friends included Colonel Charles Lindbergh, and they entertained him on frequent occasions after his nonstop solo flight across the Atlantic Ocean. Cooking for the aviator-hero made Hattie feel proud. When she wanted to do things her own way she reminded Mother she had cooked for Colonel Lindbergh. Sometimes she would get temperamental and threaten to quit, but then she would start to cry at the prospect of leaving Allan and she would decide to stay. When she finally did leave to be near her son in New York, she addressed all postcards to Allan.

Hattie would take us for a walk after our naps, freshly bathed and powdered. I remember the odor of

Shirley, age three, "holding up a classical column"

the talcum and that of the freshly mown grass, which has always been my favorite smell. We had dinner early, before the grown-ups, and were tucked into bed soon afterwards. I remember the anguish of trying to fall asleep in the summertime when it was still light outside, and my mother coming into my bedroom to soothe me.

*

Friday night was special because it was our Sabbath. The children dined with the grown-ups on this sacred occasion. Everything was sparkling and so were we, and we had to be on our best behaviour. The tablecloth was smooth white linen, the candle sticks shiny Dutch silver, and the chinaware white with a narrow green trim and little pink roses. A crisp white napkin covered a "challah" (a twisted bread) and a knife, which my father used to slice the "challah" before he sprinkled salt on it and said a blessing in Hebrew. We also sipped red wine, ceremonially, thanking God for the "fruit of the vine." Our dinner was traditional, always starting with clear golden chicken soup. Sometimes one of the children spilled dark red wine on the snowy white table-cloth, causing our father to rebuke us.

I remember little about kindergarten, only that I kept drawing the same picture over and over again: a house with a tree and a flower. It was a country cottage, not the kind of house we lived in; we lived in a three-storey apartment house. But I thought the cottage was the kind of house I was supposed to draw. All I recall about my kindergarten teacher was her thick ankles. When I grew up I taught school with that same teacher. By then she had a different name through marriage, but I knew who she was when I looked down at her legs. Alas! She denied having been my kindergarten teacher, thinking it made her seem old.

All I remember about first grade was that a boy named Don, whose sister Jane was in my class, liked me and he hit me over the head with a book. I learned early that love can be painful. And I can also recall winning races I ran against my classmates. I have always loved outdoor exercise and the thrill of competing in sports. Mother insisted that her children get plenty of fresh air every day. She and my father liked to be outdoors whenever possible and they took long walks on Sundays and summer evenings. They made it a point to be sure we never stayed inside on a fine day, and even now I would feel guilty if I went to a movie in the afternoon.

My parents were avid readers and encouraged us to read. Mother loved poetry, especially Longfellow, and I remember her reciting "Under the spreading chestnut tree / The village smithy stands," which she had learned as a schoolgirl. We had shelves full of books all around, especially the classics. I was surprised when friends who came over would remark about them. I thought everybody must have shelves full of books in their living room.

Having a library card, and using it, was a major requirement in our home. I still recall a particular Saturday morning when I walked through freshly fallen snow in my galoshes to the public library for story hour. When I arrived the librarian gave me a dreary storybook about bears that talk. Except for the British teddy bear Winnie-the-Pooh, I never cared much for talking animals simply because they were not convincing, and I expected animals to act like animals, not people. It should not be surprising that I grew up to be a writer of nonfiction.

It seems that most of my grade-school years were uneventful. The mother of my classmate Jane sometimes invited me to dinner and admired my table manners. When she pointed this out I felt proud but slightly embarrassed. And I had a friend named Alice whose house I liked to visit after school, partly because her mother made fresh candy. Alice liked to visit my house because my mother made delicious pumpkin pie.

The two friends I played with the most were both named Betty. One lived across the street and the other next door. Both Bettys were far more sophisticated than

"My father and mother with me, Norman, and Maurice"

I because their families talked about worldly things in front of them, whereas mine tried to shelter us from any conversation they considered inappropriate for children.

The mother of Betty across the street had been divorced. When she remarried, they moved to a hotel and sent Betty to a Catholic boarding school. On weekends we sometimes had dinner in the hotel dining room. It was the most glamourous thing I could imagine, ordering anything we wanted from the menu and signing a check for our dinner. We once saw Frank Sinatra at the hotel when he came through St. Louis to sing in a nightclub. Since we loved his records we were thrilled to get a glimpse of him. (Even more thrilling was meeting the brilliant, gracious Eleanor Roosevelt when she spoke at a luncheon some years later.) My friendship with Betty ended when I loaned her my entire savings to buy her boyfriend a Christmas gift and she never paid me back.

In seventh grade I secretly liked a boy named Bill and then found out that all of the other girls liked him, too. Bill went off to boarding school two years later but came back to spend his junior year in St. Louis and he was in my physics class. I was not very good at math or science and only took those courses because I thought I was supposed to. With Bill in my physics class I did even worse than I normally would have, but I had great fun with him.

When I was eleven years old I started to swim on the "Y" team. My older brother, Norman, showed some promise as a swimmer and Rudy Brand, the coach, said as much to my mother. I was very determined and made up my mind that I, myself, would make the team—and I did.

Swimming in competition was far and away the most important activity in my youth. Rudy was a dedicated teacher and he instilled good sportsmanship and a feeling of team spirit in all of us. I wanted ever so much to be a champion athlete and put absolutely everything I had into my effort to reach that goal. I had to ask myself, "How can I win?" The first step was to have hope that it was possible, and then the only answer was to train. I knew I would have to concentrate and to work hard, consistently, and forgo activities that would distract me or tighten my muscles or do anything harmful to my body in any way. Concern with physical conditioning and the ability to "give it all I've got" to succeed in an endeavor are qualities that have continued to help me in life.

I trained to swim in freestyle races, which literally means "any stroke," but everybody swims "the crawl" in a freestyle race because it is the fastest. One summer night in an outdoor meet at the municipal pool in St. Louis, I was behind my opponents in a 100-yard sprint, and I turned over on my back and won. Moreover, I was high-point winner in this important swim meet and saw my name in headlines on the sports page of the morning paper. What a thrill!

Now I knew that the stroke that came naturally to me was the backstroke, and I changed my workout routine. My arms were stronger than my legs, so one summer Rudy instructed me to lie on my back in the water with my arms stretched over my head, tediously kicking the length of a fifty-yard pool for at least an hour every single day. It was torture but I was devoted to my coach and would have done anything he wanted me to do. It did improve my speed. For three years I reigned undefeated in the Ozark district of the Amateur Athletic Union in the 100-yard backstroke event, both indoors and outdoors, and held all of the local pool records.

The outdoor swim meets were fun because friends from other local teams were around, and swimmers came from as far away as Hawaii. The big indoor meet was on February 22, George Washington's birthday. One Valentine's Day, a week before the meet, a boy on the team named Johnny, who was three years older than I, gave me a silver necklace inscribed with the date and I wore it all the time.

When I was a senior in high school I went to the National A.A.U. indoor swim meet to enter the 100-yard backstroke. I lost but went on to win that event in

the National Intercollegiates as a freshman in college. I enjoyed swimming on the team and it certainly broadened my world, but I could not stand the intense pressure of rigourous training and the tension that would grip me before and after a meet. I was relieved to give up competitive swimming and enjoy a full social life in college. After college I started playing tennis seriously; I still play tennis and swim, purely for pleasure.

It was my mother who inspired me to swim well when I was quite young. It seems that she had a "close call" in the water when she went on an outing with some friends, so it became important to her that her children learn the sport for safety reasons. Mother believed that everything should be done to the best of one's ability, so I not only learned the sport, but made sure that I did it well.

*

I loved and admired my mother and depended on her more than anyone in the world. She, in turn, had great affection and admiration for her own mother, a tiny woman who always seemed ancient to me even though she died when she was only in her early fifties. "Grandma Astor," as we called her, was wrinkled and wore a crisp cotton scarf over her hair and her dresses nearly covered her shoes which laced over her ankles. I can recall seeing her with my grandfather sipping tea sweetened with strawberry preserves in their kitchen, which seemed ever so big, but I am certain that is because I was ever so small.

Grandma Astor was a wonderful person. Although tiny, she was very strong and extremely courageous. She came to America to join her young husband who had fled czarist Russia and settled in Newport News, Virginia where he had relatives. "Grandma" traveled by train and steamship with four tiny children. All of their luggage was stolen en route. It broke my heart to hear about those evil thieves. Altogether, my grandmother bore nine children, all of whom survived. My mother, Ann, was the eldest. Mother inherited my grandmother's courage as well as her keen intelligence and combined these qualities with a penetrating understanding of people, plus the ability to get to the heart of a problem in a flash.

Mother was a successful working woman at a time when few females were out in the world. She became a fashion model in the finest women's store in St. Louis, Missouri where her parents finally settled. She held onto her job for a time after she married, then she left her work to become a housewife and mother of three. Alas! Because of economic difficulties her retirement was short-lived. When her third child was but an infant she suddenly found herself back in business with her own store, called, after her maiden name, the Ann Astor Shop. The clothes she chose were beautiful; I can still remember a black silk dress in the shop window that I

"Grandma and Grandpa Astor in their backyard," St. Louis, 1924

wanted her to save for me until I grew up. That dress was sold to a wealthy customer, but I still wear one of Mother's very own silk beaded "flapper dresses" that all my friends admire.

My maternal grandfather was an imposing man, tall with a dark beard, and he wore a black suit and black hat with a brim. I have no memory of any conversation with him; he died when I was eight. I shall never forget the night of his death. It was the evening of the Veiled Prophet Parade, an annual event that was very exciting for St. Louis children. Prominent citizens of the city dressed in costume and masks and rode on imaginatively decorated floats. The Veiled Prophet himself, whose identity was kept secret, chose a young woman to be queen and reign over St. Louis society for a year. A friend's family took me to the parade and I never had such fun. We giggled all evening; we couldn't stop. When I got home my mother was crying because her father had died. The contrast between my own merriment and her grief devastated me.

My paternal grandfather was around to see me as a grown-up. "Grandpa Glubok" was a handsome, distinguished-looking man who seemed a fascinating

character to my friends. He traveled most of the time and always returned with a present for us, usually a five-dollar gold-piece. I remember struggling over thank-you letters to him. I always started them in the same way . . . "Dear Grandpa, How are you? I am fine." And I ended with . . . "Thank you for the five-dollar gold-piece."

Grandpa Glubok had a universal outlook and an intellectual interest in diverse philosophies. It seems that he left his wife and two baby boys in Russia and went off to Asia, where he fought in a war between Russia and Japan, and then in the Boxer Rebellion in China. After his discharge in Shanghai he made his way to St. Louis, attracted by the World's Fair of 1904 where the Olympic games were also being held. When my grandmother got word that her husband was in St. Louis she packed up and sailed for America with their two babies. Luckily she brought her silver and jewelry with her. I inherited her samovar that she had used in Russia to boil water for tea and silver Kiddush cups for reciting the blessing over wine on the Sabbath and some of her diamond jewelry.

My paternal ancestors also had been scholars and they, too, were strong. I vaguely remember hearing that my great grandfather went swimming in the river every day until he was 102 years old. The story is surely exaggerated but there must be a degree of truth behind it.

Daddy took after his own father inasmuch as he was always interested in new ideas. Also, he loved to talk to all sorts of people and would pick up on a conversation with anyone, anywhere, even on a street car, and listen to that person's problems. My father would have been an excellent social worker, or perhaps a rabbi, as he had great faith in God. My friends liked to be around him because he was attentive to them when often their own fathers were not. Perhaps he was too attentive to me, as he always seemed to be fussing with me. At the same time, he had confidence in me and told me I could do anything I set my mind to. I grew up believing this and it has stood me in good stead.

My father's mother, my paternal grandmother, was an eccentric woman. She lived in an old section of town but would not have considered moving away even when the neighborhood got run down. Her house was always cluttered, and the rooms were heated by individual coal stoves long after other people had central heating in their homes. My father dutifully went to see his mother every week to look after her. We rarely went to Grandma Glubok's house, but she often came to see us on Sunday nights. She brought us large juicy oranges and fresh walnuts, which we cracked with a silver nutcracker, using a little silver pick to dig out the stubborn bits from the shell. Sometimes she took me for a ride on the street-car. We rode all the way to the end of the line and back

I grew up near Forest Park where the World's Fair of 1904 was held and played on top of a hill by the pavilion that was constructed for the event. On hot summer evenings I had great fun rolling down the hill, cooling myself in the fresh dew on the grass. At the bottom of the hill was a fountain that shot forth tall spouts of colored water. It never occurred to me that the water itself was not colored, but that the effect was controlled by colored lights. Forest Park was wonderful. We had picnics in the summertime, and in freezing weather I skated on a lake that was amazingly quiet even though it was next to the main boulevard, just five minutes' walk from our house. I was usually the only person on the lake.

Ours was a solid neighborhood. One house we lived in for a time was just behind the home where the heroine of the musical play *Meet Me in St. Louis* supposedly lived. And the setting for Tennessee Williams's play *The Glass Menagerie* was also nearby. St. Louis is a wonderful city, originally established by fur traders and rich in history. My parents were always conscious of the cultural life all around us. We went often to the Municipal Opera, an outdoor theater for light opera in Forest Park, and to the symphony, theater, and, of course, the zoo, which is famous.

*

St. Louis is on the Mississippi River where it meets the Missouri River, so it is the "Gateway to the West." In fact, a fountain statue group designed by Carl Milles, a Swedish sculptor, stands in front of the city's railway station to commemorate the meeting of the waters. The nineteenth-century artist George Caleb Bingham, who lived in St. Louis, painted river scenes of fur traders in dugout canoes and of men who traveled the Mississippi on flat boats. It was a joy to see Bingham's paintings in the art museum. And it was fun to walk along the Mississippi and dream about the past and to have lunch in an old-fashioned German restaurant near the river. Needless to say, I did this alone, as it would not have interested many, if any, of my friends.

St. Louis is a wonderful city, but I wanted to get away. I did not like the way people gossiped and I was distressed by their unwillingness to judge others on their own merit instead of money and family background. I cared about people if they were interesting and nice, no matter what their social standing; and I felt that I was a little "different" in a society where everyone was supposed to be "alike." As far as I could see, the people I admired the most were not "alike" and most of them were far away.

The Wabash Railroad ran along tracks near our house and at night I would lie in bed listening to the railway whistle, longing to be on a train. I always knew I would move away, perhaps to the Pacific, if not the Atlantic Coast, or maybe even to Paris. I managed to get to Chicago now and then to visit my favorite aunt, Tillie, and to see friends who attended the University of Chicago. I loved to be in that city; it seemed so sophis-

ticated next to St. Louis. Chicago is built on Lake Michigan, which gives it a beautiful setting. I liked to stand alone and look at Lake Michigan, even in the wintertime when bitter winds blew off the water. One January day, while visiting Aunt Tillie, I stood gazing at the freezing waves, happy to be on the lake again; I stood there for such a long time that two policemen who came by stayed to watch me, perhaps fearing I would jump in.

Chicago is a great city. It has the Art Institute, with my favorite collection of French impressionist paintings, Michigan Avenue with its shops and restaurants, a long tradition of great jazz, and, in the summertime, international polo matches. Chicago seemed to have everything, but then I had not yet seen New York.

High school is but a blur in my memory. The school I attended was big, the classes large, and somehow I never felt part of it. The only course that inspired me was English. My teacher Miss Koch read the works of her favorite authors with such energy and enthusiasm that in my mind I can still hear her reciting Chaucer and Shakespeare. Miss Koch instilled in me a love for English literature that will be with me always. I enjoyed my French class as well, probably because it nourished my dreams of going to Paris.

The first summer after high school I landed a job as lifeguard at an exclusive country club and got a glimpse of an atmosphere I had not known before. After witnessing the life-style of the wealthy members I thought I wanted their kind of luxurious life. It took me awhile to put things in perspective. In time I began to be thankful that I was brought up in a family atmosphere where values were solid and people were not judged by the size of their purse.

Washington University, where I went to college, was only a couple of miles from my home but it was like a different world. The university campus is among the most beautiful in the country and the faculty is first rate. Freshman year I took Art and Archaeology 101 to fulfill a requirement, and my professors were so inspiring that I found myself involved in a study that I had never really been aware of. I decided to major in art and archaeology because I loved the subject, without any thought of making art history my career.

My interest in art came to me naturally. From the time I was two years old my parents had taken me to the St. Louis Art Museum in Forest Park (when I would get tired of walking my father would pick me up and carry me). Also, we had reproductions of famous paintings on our walls. Vincent van Gogh's *Starry Night,* an exciting painting of a swirling sky with yellow spots and a twisted cypress tree, hung in our hallway. A print of van Gogh's bedroom in a boardinghouse in the South of France hung in my room. His was a simple room (as was mine), with an orange bedstead, yellow chairs, and bright blue walls, on which hung a small mirror and some pictures. I often thought, "What a primitive room for such a great painter!" I did not realize that this artist, who is among the most popular painters in the world today, was not appreciated during his lifetime. Now I often admire the original *Starry Night* in the Museum of Modern Art in New York.

Gainsborough's *Blue Boy* hung in our living room in a gold frame. What a thrill for me when I later saw it first hand at the Huntington Library in Pasadena, California! I was interested to learn that the youth in the painting was an ordinary neighborhood boy who posed for the portrait dressed in an antique costume. And when a Millet exhibition was held in Boston and I saw *The Sowers* and *The Reapers* in the flesh, I remembered the reproductions we had in our home and how sorry I had felt for those poor peasants in France who worked so desperately hard and yet were so very poor.

Not only did I go to the art museum with my family and have reproductions at home, but I looked at paintings with my friends, the two Bettys. The "Y" where I swam had a little gallery, where new works of local painters were shown. Also, a group of Midwestern painters exhibited at the Artists Guild, which occupied an attractive building around the corner from my house, and I often went there with my friends when we played together in the afternoon.

The study of art history and archaeology was so appealing to me that I ended up enrolling in every course possible in college. At the same time I knew I wanted to be a writer, so I took every composition course available and wrote articles for the campus magazine. And, at my parents' urging, I took two years of public speaking. This combination of courses eventually made sense in a practical way. As it turned out I earn my living by writing and lecturing on art.

Among my friends at college was a girl from Toronto named Joan who had taken a summer job as counselor at a coeducational camp on a lake in Northern Ontario. Through Joan I managed to land a position as waterfront director. I traveled by train: first to Chicago where I made a quick visit to the Art Institute and then to Toronto to meet the camp director and his staff. For the first time I slept in a pullman berth. What fun! I awoke in the morning to look out at evergreen trees.

I loved Northern Ontario: the quiet of the woods, the clean air, and the fresh clear lake, with water pure enough to drink. I loved the starry nights and the sound of the waves lapping on the shore as I fell asleep in my cabin. At the end of the summer I proceeded to New York to meet my mother who was buying costume jewelry for her stores. The big city seemed like the most glamourous place in the world to me. I began longing to live there, to be a writer and live in an apartment near Central Park. In time my dream would come true.

*

After college I took a job writing advertising copy. I thought it was fun to work in a downtown office building and meet friends for lunch. Writing an ad was a challenge; a strong message had to be spelled out in few words. It was an experience that would later prove valuable, but I longed for work with deeper meaning. Through the inspiration of a friend who was deeply religious, I had begun teaching Sunday school at a temple and found it fulfilling. Before long I left my job in the advertising business and went to Florida with my mother for a winter vacation. Back in St. Louis I fell into a temporary job teaching physical education in a public high school. I loved the work and enjoyed the students. Although it had never occurred to me before this, I now wanted to pursue teaching as a career and enrolled in summer courses taught by Miss Jenny Wahlert at Washington University.

Miss Wahlert was a superb person who had devoted her life to teaching St. Louis children. I loved to hear her stories about the Great Depression when she fed hot oatmeal to the little ones when they came to school. Miss Wahlert continued to live in the same house where she had been born even after the neighborhood became dangerous, so that she could best serve the people who lived there. She encouraged me to pursue a career in teaching and I have been grateful to her ever since.

At the suggestion of a tennis friend, I took a position teaching a second-grade class in the suburbs of St. Louis. The first thing I did was to fill the room with interesting books and pictures; next, I arranged for a school bus to take the class to the St. Louis Art Museum. Without consciously setting out to do so, I was developing a technique of introducing works of art to schoolchildren. I prepared my students in advance by showing them a catalogue of the museum's collection. When we arrived, our lecturer was amused. I had told her we wanted to see North American Indian art because that was what *my* class was shown when I was in the second grade. But the children said, "No! We want to see a knight, a mummy, and Jesus-on-a-cross!" These were the things they liked best in the museum catalogue.

On the next visit I took the children through the museum myself and I let each of them choose a favorite painting and talk about it. The child would tell the class why he liked it and then the others would voice their opinions before we went on to the next. I thought it was important for the children to know that they did not have to like a work of art just because they thought they were supposed to; they should form their own opinions. I also thought it was important for them to learn to express their ideas in spoken words as well as in writing, and to learn to listen to each other attentively. After each museum visit we would go outside and have recess in Forest Park. Back at school the children would write stories and draw pictures about the trip.

At Miss Wahlert's urging I went for a master's degree in early childhood education. She suggested that I go to Stanford University in California or Columbia in New York. By now I had taken two trips to the West Coast and I loved California, but I chose Columbia because I had friends in New York whom I had met in Florida and on a summer trip to Europe. My classes at Columbia were huge and most of them were dreadfully dreary. The professors droned on about things I had either worked out for myself in the classroom or I had learned from Miss Wahlert. Luckily I was required to write a lot of papers. These were admired by my professors who encouraged me to do more writing.

Meanwhile, the head of the education department at the Metropolitan Museum of Art expressed interest in my original approach for teaching children about art, and he hired me to give gallery talks to young people when my course work at Columbia was finished. My job at the Met involved lecturing on Saturdays. During the week I was a classroom teacher in a private school that was more "progressive" than I had bargained for. It was a difficult situation. I brought a wide-eyed naiveté with me from the Midwest. My third-grade students mistook gentleness for weakness and took advantage of me. In addition, I did not fit in with the other teachers. One of them, the only one who was friendly to me, told me frankly that the others did not like me. I was devastated. It was an excruciatingly painful year, but my courage and strength pulled me through, whereas another teacher, in the very same position as I, left before Halloween and went back to her hometown. My sensitivity has always made it hard for me to deal with difficult people, but in the long run that same quality has been an important element in my approach to young children and in introducing them to the wonderful world of art.

In contrast to the school, the museum was a kind of haven for me. The children who came to my lectures were appreciative and well mannered, as were their parents, and the quiet galleries filled with masterpieces of art offered a refuge from the outside world. My lectures covered a wide range of topics from ancient Egyptian to contemporary American art. The children and I explored the galleries together. I urged them to look at a work and try to react to it personally before I gave them information about the materials, the artist who created it, when and how it was made, and what it stood for.

Through the museum I learned about a small furnished apartment that I could sublet for a year, only a block and a half from the Metropolitan. The apartment had real character; it was filled with eighteenth-century Dutch paintings and antique furniture. The disadvantage was that I had to walk up five flights to get there, but it was worth the effort. Everything was in one room, including the so-called kitchen, which was separated from the combination bedroom/living room/dining room by a mere screen.

I felt very much at home in the building because the tenants were either museum people or were related to the owner, who was an art dealer, so living there was

"Lecturing on knights in armor at the Metropolitan Museum of Art"

like being in a college dormitory. By good fortune, just as my year's sublet was up, the man who lived across the hall told me he was getting married and his apartment would be available. It was even smaller than the first, but it was my own. I had the walls painted peach, dyed some plain white curtains the same color, and bought a bed that doubled as a sofa. Gradually, I furnished the place with things Mother sent me or the landlord gave me or that I bought from a secondhand furniture store. It was a cozy, cheerful little home.

I even had my own "penthouse" garden, which was actually a part of the roof. To get there I climbed through a window and across a wobbly steel "balcony," and there I was in the tops of trees, with ivy from the garden below spilling over the railing. Now for the first time I took up gardening. I acquired some window boxes, and I dug up earth when I went to the country and hauled it back to New York, dragging it up five flights of stairs. I raised mostly marigolds and geraniums and now and then a cherry tomato, which I was too proud of to eat.

The neighborhood was wonderful . . . a touch of old New York as it will never be again. All the buildings along my street, which was lined with trees, were attractive town houses, one quite different from the other. Many of them had been converted into apartments but some were still privately owned, and each had its own little garden in back. At one corner there was a shop where rich ladies could have their poodles clipped and manicured. On the street at that corner, Park Avenue, there were tall apartment houses with trees growing on the terraces of the penthouses. It amused me to bend my head back to look up and see trees in the sky.

After dark a private night watchman was on duty on the block so I always felt quite safe, even though he spent much of his time hanging out in a nearby delicatessen. The "deli" was on Madison Avenue, a commercial street at the other end of the block. My favorite shop on Madison was the French dry cleaner. The owner would hang beautiful clothes he had cleaned in the window. I often looked in and thought about what glamourous lives the people who wore those clothes must lead. One night, much to my surprise, I saw my own gold blouse with rhinestone buttons in the window. I did not think of it at the time but my own life in New York had become as glamourous as the lives of some of the other people who wore the clothes that hung beside my blouse. I was so excited that I asked a friend who earned extra money by painting portraits, to paint *me* wearing that blouse.

My days were filled with work. Every morning I would walk a block and a half to Central Park and take the Fifth Avenue bus to school. In the afternoons I headed straight for the Metropolitan Museum to prepare for my Saturday lectures. In the meantime I wanted in the worst way to get a book published. The last few years I was in St. Louis I had been trying to get a publisher interested in a picture book I had written. It was about a little boy who did not like to go to school. One morning he had a series of misadventures because he didn't know how to read or count. Well, he never did get to school and the book never was published, but my persistent efforts on that story, writing and rewriting it a hundred times, eventually paid off. A literary agent read the story and liked the way I wrote. She knew that Atheneum, a new publishing company, had started a children's book department and the editor was interested in art books. Atheneum invited me to submit a proposal. Since one of the most popular subjects, both with the children at the Metropolitan Museum and with my third-grade class, was ancient Egyptian art, and since there were no children's books on the subject, I decided to write one. I chose the obvious title, *The Art of Ancient Egypt.*

*

Everything seemed to fall into place. One of the fathers who brought his children to my lectures was an art director of a magazine, and he wanted to design my book. We worked out a format together . . . a large square book with clear photographs and the text describing them always on the same page as the pictures. Three days after I delivered the layout and a sample of the text to the publisher, they offered me a contract. Usually publishers take months to react. I was so excited to be having a book published that I threw a party, inviting all my friends.

Months of hard work followed. I was determined to write a book that would be beautiful and readable as well as thoroughly understandable and useful. It would be a visual book with emphasis on masterpieces of art and, at the same time, would reflect the culture in which the works were created. I made a thorough search through the Egyptian collection at the Metropolitan, looking for works of art that would photograph well, be appealing to children, and could illustrate the kind of information I thought would be interesting. I also went to museums in Brooklyn, Boston, Cleveland, Chicago, and St. Louis to choose works from each, so that children in other cities would know that they might find Egyptian art in their own hometown. At the same time I wanted high quality photographs of the original works of art, rather than using line drawings, which would have been much cheaper to reproduce. I ordered photographs by mail from museums and private photographers in England, France, Italy, and Germany.

When I had gathered the photographs, I got together with the designer and we organized them into categories. Over the course of many, many meetings we chose those we wished to use and he made "doodles," tiny pencil sketches of page layouts on a huge sheet of paper. In that way we could view an overall plan for the entire book. Next the designer made a "dummy," a mock-up of the book in its actual size; he determined how big each picture should be and ordered a photostatic copy, to size, of each photograph. When these were pasted down he drew lines on the pages to indicate how much space I would have for the words.

In the meantime I read every book I could find on the subject of Egypt, spending day after day in the library. The research seemed never to end, but when the "dummy" was ready there was nothing left to do except begin writing . . . by far the hardest part. (I write in pencil on a lined pad, and make continuous corrections, and when I can no longer read what I have written I type, continuing to make corrections in pencil and retyping.) I must have written twenty or more drafts before the final manuscript went to the publisher to be edited. One of the most demanding aspects was cutting down the text to fit the page. I had to make every single word count. My advertising copy-writing experience came in handy.

While working on *The Art of Ancient Egypt* I met a very nice man named Alfred Tamarin at a party. He called himself "Al Tamarin" (as if it were all one word), and was very attractive, a good deal older than I, and worldly wise. For years he had been active in public relations work in theater and movies and he knew all the "stars," which I thought was glamourous. Alfred was a gifted writer and an excellent photographer as well, but took pictures only as a hobby. I was not satisfied with the Metropolitan Museum's own photograph of the pink granite sphinx of Queen Hatshepsut that stood in the main hall. Queen Hatshepsut was an ancient Egyptian queen who lived around 3500 years ago. She usurped the throne from her stepson and declared herself ruler, then had herself shown in all the poses of a male king. One of the standard poses for portraying a king was in the form of a recumbent lion with a human head to emphasize the combination of intelligence and strength. A friend tried photographing the sphinx on two different occasions, but her flash broke each time. Alfred came to the rescue and took the picture, partly with the idea of getting a date with me. Both the photography and the maneuver were successful.

The Art of Ancient Egypt was an instant success when it came out in September 1962. The *New York Times, New Yorker, Saturday Review of Literature,* and many other major magazines and newspapers throughout the country gave it rave reviews. This was the first serious art history book of its kind for young readers. Reviewers said that it was interesting and informative to grown-ups as well as children, and they pointed out that I do not talk down to children. As soon as my first book was finished I had started on the next, which covered the ancient Near East and was called *The Art of Lands in the Bible.* My agent and editor had argued that we should not have a "series," so my designer and I conceived a book in a different size and format; but when reviews on *The Art of Ancient Egypt* came out they changed their minds, and by 1980 thirty books in "The Art of" series had been published, on subjects that ranged from the ancient world to Far Eastern, American, and primitive art. These included two "mini-series," one on American art that began with colonial America and ended with contemporary American culture and another which had to do with our own native Americans. With the encouragement of the director of the Museum of the American Indian I had written *The Art of the North American Indian,* and for the first time I could see how very different the native peoples in various parts of our continent were from each other. In time I wrote six more volumes on these people, starting with the Eskimos and ending with the southwestern Indians. Perhaps the most interesting aspect of the differences in their art is the way each group adapts to its environment and uses the materials found around them to express themselves.

All the while I also wrote books in different formats, including *Art and Archaeology,* which covered important excavations throughout the world, and *Knights in Armor,* which was the most popular subject for children at the Metropolitan Museum.

*

M y work took me all over the world. I went to Greece, Peru, and India with university or museum groups. My mother accompanied me to Italy, France, and England where the great museums are filled with treasures from every corner of the world, and to Mexico, which became the subject of a book on pre-Columbian art. Sometimes I got culture shock, moving from one continent to the next, and through different

"With my beloved mother in Coronado, on our last holiday together"

time periods. I can remember trying to finish my book on ancient Mexico while on my first trip to Asia, which took me to India and Nepal. Studying various cultures gave me a broader outlook and learning about the history of other people enriched my own life. By meeting people in other countries I learned that there are different ways of living and acting from those I had always known.

In the meantime Alfred Tamarin had become my most frequent escort and best friend. He was always helpful and supportive in every kind of problem dealing with my work. Alfred was my own private photographer as well, and referred to himself as "a photographer with one client." When he traveled for his work with Inflight Motion Pictures, which put the first movies in airplanes, he would take pictures for my books. Most important of these were the ones he took in the Etruscan tombs and in Mexico, both resulting in photographs that were used as covers for books.

In 1968 Alfred and I were married in a simple ceremony in the rabbi's study with only a few friends and relatives attending. My seven-days-a-week work pace never ceased, and Alfred worked along with me. Our collaboration as a husband and wife team began the day after our wedding when we went to a friend's country house in Connecticut and spent our days sitting in front of a blazing fireplace editing Alice Morse Earle's two 1890s volumes, *Home Life in Colonial Days* and *Child Life in Colonial Days,* consolidating them into one volume. Later that winter and spring we traveled around New York State and New England to take photographs for new illustrations for the project. For our official wedding trip we went to the Yucatan Peninsula to study Maya ruins and to snorkel off Cozumel Island. In October of that year we flew to Japan and Taipei to gather material for three different books. Not only did Alfred photograph for my books, but he wrote his own and eventually we put out four books as coauthors.

Some of our most enjoyable and productive travels were in the American West. My parents moved to Colo-

"With Alfred, in a rare moment of relaxation," Estes Park, Colorado, 1974

rado in 1968, where my brother Allan taught at a university, and we started going out West to visit them several times a year. I loved the state of Colorado and we enjoyed driving down to New Mexico and Arizona where we studied the art and archaeology of the Indian people, as well as the Spanish-American culture in the area. We also collected Navajo blankets and silver and turquoise jewelry, which I love to wear. In the course of our direct contact with the Navajo and Pueblo people, Alfred grew curious about the Indians who live on the eastern seaboard of the United States and he set out to write about them. To research Alfred's book we called on the leaders of Indian tribes from Maine and Quebec all the way down to the tip of Florida. I was awed to be visiting the leaders of Indian nations. Some of these people became our friends and came to see us in New York. One Saturday night when we were having dinner the chief of the Onandaga nation showed up at our door without notice. Alfred's book *We Have Not Vanished* came as a revelation to those who thought there are no more Indians in the United States today.

The books that we coauthored required extensive travel. A trip to Greece in the spring of 1975 for *The Olympic Games in Ancient Greece* was especially memorable. I had wanted to write about the ancient games for a long time, because it combined my studies in Greek archaeology with my love for sports; so a dream was fulfilled. And then a trip to Egypt provided material for another book that had been in the back of my mind for years . . . *The Mummy of Ramose,* about ancient mummification and burial practices. We focused on an eighteenth dynasty nobleman who lived around the time of Tutankhamen. He was buried in a tomb with beautiful carvings and paintings on the walls that told about his life and his beliefs in his life after death.

Alfred fell ill in 1976 but we were able to proceed with our lives without much change until the doctor diagnosed lung cancer in the beginning of 1980. I could not believe it when our physician said he would be dead "within months." I thought this was one of those

things that only happens to somebody else. Alfred died at home on a hot night in late August. It was a difficult adjustment for me. Our lives had been so closely intertwined emotionally, socially, and professionally. Two years later my mother, to whom I was deeply devoted, also died. I knew I would have to change my life drastically and I immediately began doing as many different things as I possibly could in order to change my routine and decide which direction to take with my life. I began traveling to Boston where I lecture to schoolchildren several weeks a year, and I also taught a graduate course on museum training at Boston University. Almost every summer I go abroad to gather material for lectures and articles. I also manage to go to California to play tennis twice a year. Wherever I am, in this country or another, I wander through museums always feeling at home surrounded by treasures created through the centuries by people who probably had some of the same problems as I.

Now that I have had time to sort things out in my head and rethink my life and make new friends, I am starting a new life. As I finish this first chapter of my autobiography I am sitting in the sun between tennis games at the Racquet Club in Palm Springs, California, before returning to New York for another season of hard work. The next chapter of my life will be told in the second edition, to be read by children yet unborn.

[Shirley Glubok contributed the following update to *SATA* in 2004:]

When I sat down to write the first part of my autobiography I found it very difficult, and this update is just as hard. To review my past I must pull off layer after layer of memories, many of them painful. I have to examine everything I did, determine what was important, and lay it out for the world to see.

It took me all last summer to start writing. A quiet holiday on Nantucket, an island off the coast of Massachusetts, and then a trip to my "old haunts" in Colorado and New Mexico, did not inspire me to sit down and write.

Then one day in late summer, while sightseeing in Vienna, Austria, I stepped into a little museum just beside my hotel, where Wolfgang Amadeus Mozart, the great composer, lived more than two hundred years ago while working on his opera *The Marriage of Figaro.* Mozart was an artistic genius; he started writing beautiful music when he was still a little boy.

The following morning I awoke with the thought, "Mozart's apartment where he composed some of the world's most magnificent music is just on the other side of the wall in the room where I am sleeping. Why can't I take inspiration from him to get started *now?*" My hotel room was large and comfortable, in an old part of town on a narrow street paved with cobblestones. For further inspiration I listened to the clippity-clop of horses' hooves pulling buggies over the same cobblestone streets as in Mozart's day. And so I began this chapter.

The author with her cousin Larry in the garden at the Hotel del Coronado

My memories flashed back to the tennis courts in Palm Springs, where I had ended the first part of this autobiography. I thought of my cousin Maurice who owned the Racquet Club where I was staying. Somewhere along the line he had started calling himself by the nickname "Larry." From the time he was a little boy he was determined to become a "big-shot." Indeed, he succeeded, by becoming a political leader and an immensely rich real-estate developer in Southern California. In addition to the Racquet Club, which is a desert resort where old-time Hollywood movie stars spent winter weekends, he owned the Del Coronado, an historic resort hotel on the Pacific Ocean in San Diego. In keeping with his success Larry developed a grace and presence that caused people to turn their heads when he walked by.

Larry was kind and attentive to me and he made it possible for me to spend a block of time in California every summer and every winter for two decades. What a perfect balance to my big city life in New York! In California everything is different, not just the climate, but the people, and the things they do and what they think about.

Instead of sitting in the library working, and going to museums, as I do in New York, I played tennis and swam every day. Of course, as a writer, the first thing I would do after unpacking was to borrow a typewriter. I had my manuscripts and research materials with me; so I could set up my little office and work a few hours a day, usually very early in the morning, before tennis. It was refreshing to listen to the sound of the ocean, or to mourning doves, instead of city traffic.

In winter, in Palm Springs, I basked in the warm sunshine while gazing at the mountain peaks. In summer, at the Del Coronado, I walked the beach and swam in the Pacific when the water was warm enough and calm.

The Del Coronado is a huge wooden structure right on the beach, just off the coast of the city of San Diego. People call Coronado an island because one has to take a ferry boat or go over a bridge to get there; but it is really a peninsula. It is less than twenty miles from Mexico, so diplomatic meetings with Mexican presidents have been held at the hotel, and several American presidents have vacationed there as well. One of Hollywood's great movies, *Some Like it Hot* with Marilyn Monroe, was filmed at the Del Coronado, even though the setting is supposed to be in Florida.

I got to know everyone in the hotel and made friends with people in town who play tennis. But I always felt like an outsider. Often I played tennis with vacationers who came to the hotel for a weekend or, at most, a week, and then they would leave, while I stayed all month, waiting for new tennis players to check in. Townsfolk played with me when someone in their regular group had to drop out, but then they would go home right after our game and leave me alone to figure out what to do by myself. Worst of all were the times when members of my own family would come to the hotel. They all live in California and see each other often, and they made me feel left out. I have a different kind of life from theirs and I have very different interests. They think it is peculiar that I talk more about books than movies, and most peculiar of all is that I do not have an automobile and do not want one. When they came to the hotel waves of loneliness would come over me. Luckily my cousin Larry would rescue me when he saw that I was in distress. Larry was more important to me than he could ever have known.

Boarding an airplane in New York did not always mean that I was on my way to California. Often I was bound for Boston to give art history lectures to schoolchildren. I welcomed the chance to be back in the classroom, finding it a challenge to walk into a room filled with totally strange children and show them slides of great masterpieces, Some of the paintings and statues that I showed were in the Boston Museum of Fine Arts, not far from their schools, but they seemed worlds away. I wanted to enrich these children's lives by letting them know that these masterpieces are theirs to enjoy.

Often the teacher would slip out of the room, leaving me alone with big, tough male students who belonged to gangs and might even have been in jail. The

With actor Stacy Keach in a celebrity tennis tournament at the Hotel del Coronado

students would start to bully me, and I was often terrified, wondering if I would get out of the classroom in one piece. But then my adrenalin would start pumping as I showed them I could stand up to them.

Boston is a wonderful city, rich in history, with a tradition of education and culture. The work I do is really interesting, but nights were lonely, even though I stayed in a great hotel where I could look out at the ever-growing skyline and down on the trees in the Public Garden. I jogged in the Garden every morning, and after work I could sit at my window and gaze at the trees, particularly a weeping willow, which seemed to be the last tree in the Garden to lose its leaves in the fall and the first to bloom in the spring. And at night when I went into the hotel dining room alone I was offered a special table in the middle of the room by the elegant headwaiter, Joseph. As I sat down the pianist, John, started playing "St. Louis Blues" in honor of my home town. Nowadays I stay in a club that I joined. It was once a private home and has a friendly atmosphere.

*

Somewhere along the line I had stepped "out of the loop" in the children's book world, especially because writing a book involves sitting in one place for days on end. And I suppose I was secretly afraid that Alfred's "ghost" might enter the room and say, "Time for lunch." Again, I wanted something new. Luckily, because of the research I had done in Europe while working on my books I was able to connect with airline magazines abroad, as well as major publications in the United States, to write articles.

Some of the articles were about dollhouses, the subject of one of my books. By these I do not mean children's toys; the ones I wrote about were too important to play with. They are in museums.

Major craftsmen made miniature silverware and furniture and even paintings, as far back as the seventeenth century, especially in Holland, Germany, then England and America. Grown women who ran households would organize these miniatures into little rooms. Since they stayed intact, while actual homes that were lived in were changed through the years, the miniature rooms show us how people lived hundreds of years ago. The Dutch dollhouses were the oldest and most interesting, especially the ones for which we know the entire history of the women who owned them. And it is interesting to compare them with seventeenth-century Dutch paintings to see how authentic the dollhouses really are.

Viking art was the subject of one of the books in my "Art of" series and it stirred interest in Scandinavia as well as the United States. Vikings arrived in Newfoundland before the earliest European explorers, and archaeologists have excavated remains of their settlements in Canada, as well as Europe. My first article was about Viking dress. I like the idea that Viking chieftains who grew wealthy from foreign trade, and perhaps raids, bought beautiful jewelry for themselves, which they wore with pride. The magazine editor wanted me to tell about the women, so I wrote about the fact that they could inherit property and could take their wealth with them if they divorced their husbands. And of

In Sweden celebrating midsummer holiday

course they, too, wore wonderful gold and silver jewelry, usually acquired as gifts from their husbands after a successful trade or raid. The Vikings have a bad reputation as raiders; but many of them were peaceful farmers.

Perhaps the most interesting study I did for an article was on the archaeology of Gotland, an island off the coast of Sweden. I traveled with an archaeologist who had studied there and now works in a museum in Stockholm. We stayed in an official house for archaeological field-workers in Visby, in the medieval city in the town center. The old city was closed to automobile traffic, but we were allowed to drive because we were living there. I had a rental car in my name, courtesy of the Tourist Board, but my very bossy Swedish friend would not allow me to drive it. In fact, I was never once behind the wheel. Worst of all, she raced through the streets honking the horn at pedestrians until they jumped onto the curb for fear of being run over. I was furious with her; but I got nowhere.

Recently I have been going to Nantucket Island, in Massachusetts, in the summertime and it reminds me very much of Gotland. Instead of ancient Viking remains and a medieval settlement, Nantucket has a rich history of the whaling industry which was so important to our economy in nineteenth-century America. The sperm oil was used to make candles before people had electricity to light their homes.

There were other changes in my work. I continued giving gallery talks at the Metropolitan Museum, and since I have always felt that I must do three times as much as everyone else, I started a program to bring classes into the Spanish Institute during the school year. I give slide lectures on art that focus on Spanish history and culture, which includes Spanish settlers in America. Most of the groups are either classes in Spanish language or the students are of Spanish heritage. They should feel proud that their ancestors were in America to found colonies before the first permanent English settlements.

The Spanish Institute is in a 1930s town house on Park Avenue in New York City, designed by the famous

One of the many book jackets photographed by the author's husband Alfred

architectural firm of McKim, Mead and White. It was built for the daughter of the people who lived in the larger house next door, when she got married. These magnificent houses were about to be torn down, as had been the fate of so many other New York houses that were architectural treasures. Luckily a wealthy woman who lived across the street saw what was happening, saved them from the bulldozers, then donated them to cultural societies for educational purposes.

Houses that were torn down were replaced by ugly high-rise apartment and office buildings, gradually destroying the beauty of New York City. Thankfully a law went into effect, with the encouragement of Mrs. John F. Kennedy and other concerned citizens, establishing a Landmarks Commission to prevent changes to important buildings, preserving the beauty of this wonderful city.

To be able to lecture on Spanish art I had to go back to graduate school for further study. I was not only inspired intellectually, but I met some wonderful young friends, who have helped me in developing the fresh outlook I am always striving for.

In the meantime I got involved in a whole new social life, quite by chance. A group of bright, energetic people banded together and became great friends after the unexpected death of a young banker who was important to each of us. We began seeing each other regularly, having dinner parties and traveling together. Someone nicknamed us the "rat-pack," after Frank Sinatra's group of actor friends who went around together in Hollywood and Las Vegas. We have had fun together, renting houses in Tuscany near Florence, Italy, and San Miguel, Mexico. And we celebrate holidays and birthdays together

At home in New York entertaining friends

When I started writing books again they took a different direction. Scribner's had launched a series of reference books on lives of famous people in different categories and they asked me to do one on painters. I set out to choose two dozen artists who produced some of the great masterpieces. I wanted to find out what kinds of people they were and to connect them in a personal way with the works of art they produced. Sometimes I got quite involved with the personalities I was writing about.

At times I disliked the painter intensely and could not wait to finish writing about him. For instance, Paul Gaugin, who led a colorful life in the South Pacific, took advantage of the local people, especially the young girls. I had such a strong reaction to him that I could not wait to finish that chapter.

On the other hand, Peter Paul Rubens was a prince of a man. He was a diplomat and scholar as well as an artist. Rubens was very well-mannered and he was able to talk to royalty as easily as he could deal with the person next door. He was good at keeping secrets and he was very loyal to his friends. Kings and queens called on him to decorate their palaces and sometimes they asked him to deliver precious gifts and secret messages from one country to another.

Leonardo da Vinci was probably the greatest genius of them all. He was left-handed and could write from right to left, so that you need a mirror to read it. Some people think that his mirror writing was a secret code. Leonardo was generous and kind. to everyone. He loved wild creatures so much that he would not eat meat. When he saw a songbird in a cage in the marketplace he would buy it in order to set it free. Leonardo's portrait of the Mona Lisa is so well known that a popular song was written about it.

Michelangelo devoted himself to his work and lived like a poor man, even after he became rich. From the time he was fifteen he was earning money from his art and supporting his family, sending them all the money he had. Michelangelo was trained from childhood as a stone carver and yet he is best known for painting the ceiling of the Sistine Chapel, in the Vatican in Rome. Painting the ceiling required great physical labor. He had to work on a high scaffold with his head turned upward, paint dripping on his face.

Picasso was the last of my painters and the one I spent the most time on. Picasso was not his real name—it was his mother's family name; but it sounded special, so he decided to use it instead of his father's name, Ruiz. His father was an art teacher, so Pablo learned to draw and paint as a little boy. When he was nineteen, he moved to Paris, where he liked going around town with his bohemian friends. Max Jacob was the most interesting and amusing. He taught Picasso to love poetry. For a time they were roommates and were so poor they had to share the same small bed. Max slept while Picasso stayed up all night painting. Then Max would go to work in the morning and Picasso would sleep in the bed.

From a feature article in a Japanese magazine on the author's life in New York

Now I am working on Picasso again, writing a book on his early years, beginning with his childhood. I hope it will be an inspiration to children everywhere who want to become artists.

*

All the while I am examining my life and watching it change, as the world around me changes, and as my needs and interests change. Last summer a Japanese journalist wrote an article about me for a special New York issue of a new magazine, calling the article "Life Style of a True New Yorker." Reading what the Japanese said about my own life made me see myself in ways I never thought about before. The article talked about the "ease with which I move about in my own neighborhood" (the Upper East Side of Manhattan) and the way in which I "merge my social life with my professional life." I had never thought of expressing it this way before. I just took it for granted, because the two aspects of my life are so closely interwoven. Nor had I thought about the way in which I entertain my friends in my own home, and the fact that my friends are of all different ages. A close observer recently pointed out that I balance my professional life with my social life, and still "manage to keep in shape."

Reading about my own lifestyle in the Japanese magazine was like looking into a mirror that goes deeper than an ordinary looking-glass, and it brought out things that I would never think of, because I take them for granted. For instance, the article pointed out that my apartment is attractive and cozy and bright and very near Central Park. Once I started to realize what a privilege it is to live near this superb plot of land in the middle of this great city, I began to make sure that I took advantage of it to the fullest, with great appreciation.

Not only am I near this wonderful park, but I am around the corner from the Frick Collection, a magnificent museum that was one man's private home. People who come from all over the world make it one of their important destinations. So certainly I should go inside more frequently. And my beloved Metropolitan Museum, where I am still working, is just ten blocks away.

It amuses me that the Japanese journalist noted that I am less than a block away from the house where the Pope stayed when he came to New York. One morning during his visit I walked out of my apartment building just as he was passing by in his "Popemobile" and he blessed me as they drove by.

Another observation described in the magazine is that I make my life as compact as possible. Actually my apartment is quite small, and it doubles as a library and an office. So I must be just as compact with my space as I am with my time.

As I wind up this second chapter of my autobiography, I am meeting new challenges in my work and my life. I am unsure of my role in the children's book business as I observe the recent batch of books that have cartoony drawings when they are meant to introduce the children to great masterpieces by the world's most gifted artists. Why not show the art instead of a silly cartoon? At the same time I have more ideas than ever and I think my writing has improved enormously through years of practice. So I sign off with the only

Shirley's niece Sheryl, a budding young author

thing I know for sure . . . that there are further challenges around the corner, and I pray for the wisdom and strength to meet them.

GRIEVE, James 1934-

Personal

Born November 14, 1934, in Belfast, Northern Ireland; son of William Shanks Grieve (a telephone engineer) and Christina Storrie Mason; divorced; father of three children and two stepchildren. *Education:* Queens University, B.A. (with honors; French and Spanish); Australian National University, M.A. (with honors). *Politics:* "Left of centre." *Hobbies and other interests:* Writing, bottling wine, squash.

Addresses

Home—15 McGowan St., Dickson, Australian Capital Territory 2602, Australia. *Office*—School of Language Studies, Australian National University, Canberra, Australian Capital Territory 0200, Australia. *E-mail*—James. Grieve@anu.edu.au.

Career

Lecturer in French language and literature, author on French language, translator of French literature, book reviewer, and fiction writer for young adults. Visiting fellow, Australian National University. Also worked variously as an apprentice spy in Melbourne, Australia, and in heavy industry, also in Australia.

Member

Abortion Law Reform Association (officer), Homosexual Law Reform Association (officer), Euthanasia Law Reform Association.

Awards, Honors

Guardian Children's Fiction Award shortlist, 1988, for *A Season of Grannies.*

Writings

(Translator) Robert Lacour-Gayet, *A Concise History of Australia* (adult title), Penguin Books Australia (Ringwood, Victoria, Australia), 1975.

(Translator) Marcel Proust, *A Search for Lost Time. Swann's Way* (for adults), Australian National University (Canberra, Australian Capital Territory, Australia), 1982.

A Season of Grannies (for young adults), University of Queensland Press (St. Lucia, Queensland, Australia, and New York, NY), 1987.

Dictionary of Contemporary French Connectors (for adults), Routledge (New York, NY), 1996.

They're Only Human (for young adults), Allen & Unwin (Crows Nest, New South Wales, Australia), 2001.

(Translator) Marcel Proust, *In the Shadow of Young Girls in Flower* (for adults), Viking (New York, NY), 2004.

A Season of Grannies was also published in French as *Grands-mères à louer,* by Ecole des loisirs (Paris, France), 1990.

Work in Progress

The Future Ain't What It Used to Be, Al Jolson's a Sexagenarian, Fun Times, and a translation and stage adaptation of Voltaire's *Candide,* all for adults.

Sidelights

James Grieve, who for more than thirty-five years has been a noted French language scholar, has also authored two novels for teens, *A Season of Grannies* and *They're Only Human.* Both books confront mature, sensitive subjects such as the animal rights movement, sexual abuse, and euthanasia. Grieve has lived and worked in many parts of the world, including Ireland, Scotland, France, London, and Australia, but describes himself as having no national identity.

Published in 1987, *A Season of Grannies* was Grieve's first novel for young adults. It was shortlisted for the United Kingdom's *Guardian* Children's Fiction Award and was later translated into French.

They're Only Human, Grieve's second young-adult novel, followed in 2001. Grieve tackles tough moral issues such as animal rights and sexual abuse through the life of Susie, a fourteen-year-old girl who is easily influenced by an unusual circle of friends. Susie's French teacher, Mr. Larmour, an animal rights extremist, is also a major influence in her life; while running the school Animal Rights group, he seduces students and takes sexual advantage of Susie. Writing in *Magpies,* Sally Harding called *They're Only Human* "a cracker of a book for making you think hard about human motives, hypocrisy, and behaviour." Though finding that "the sensationalist sexual abuse tends to overwhelm the thoughtful conflict," *Booklist* critic Frances Bradburn nonetheless claimed the author's "strong craftsmanship dramatizes both sides of the animal rights debate."

Biographical and Critical Sources

PERIODICALS

American Reference Books Annual, Melissa Rae Root, review of *Dictionary of Contemporary French Connectors,* p. 390.

Booklist, May 1, 2003, Frances Bradburn, review of *They're Only Human,* p. 1589.

Economist, October 5, 2002, "Love by Osmosis; Proust in translation," review of *A Search for Lost Time. Swann's Way.*

French Review, February, 1999, Thomas T. Field, review of *Dictionary of French Connectors,* p. 610.

Magpies, September, 2001, Sally Harding, review of *They're Only Human,* p. 39.

Modern Language Journal spring, 1999, Jean-Pierre Berwald, review of *Dictionary of Contemporary French Connectors,* pp. 145-146.

Reference & Research Book News, August, 1997, review of *Dictionary of Contemporary French Connectors,* p. 142.

H

HARRIS, Joan 1946-

Personal

Born August 30, 1946, in Pueblo, CO; daughter of Walter (an engineer) and Martha (a social worker) Tooke; married Tom Harris (an army career officer), 1967; children: Roe, Olen. *Ethnicity:* "Caucasian." *Education:* University of Southern Colorado, B.A., 1968; University of Alaska—Anchorage, M.A., 1997.

Addresses

Agent—c/o Author Mail, Alaska Northwest Books, P.O. Box 10306, Portland, OR 97296-0306. *E-mail*—kjharris@gci.net.

Career

Army Education Center, Fort Richardson, AK, worked as education services specialist and counselor for sixteen years; freelance illustrator, 1967—.

Member

Guild of Scientific Illustrators, Alaska Press Women, Bird Treatment and Learning Center.

Awards, Honors

First place, Alaskan Press Women Communications Contest, and third place, National Federation of Press Women Communications Contest, both 2003, both for *One Wing's Gift.*

Writings

(And illustrator) *One Wing's Gift: Rescuing Alaska's Wild Birds,* Alaska Northwest Books (Portland, OR), 2002.

Work in Progress

Writing and illustrating a book about the rehabilitation of baby birds, publication by Alaska Northwest Books (Portland, OR) expected in 2005.

Sidelights

Joan Harris told *SATA:* "I have been an illustrator for thirty-five years. I attended college on an art scholarship and since graduating have done freelance work—mostly art work focusing on scientific illustration concerned with extreme detail and accuracy. I have worked almost exclusively in graphite and prefer that medium because of its simplicity and because of the detail it allows.

"Since 1990, I have concentrated on drawing a series of birds that were all treated at the Bird Treatment and Learning Center in Anchorage, Alaska. What started as a series of drawings eventually became *One Wing's Gift: Rescuing Alaska's Wild Birds* when I felt myself compelled to write down the stories of the birds, to explain each drawing further, but also to share the fascinating tale behind each bird. The stories were so touching and compelling—and the amount of time and care expended by the caretakers so amazing—that I wanted others to know these heartwarming tales. They are stories of hope and of human beings doing such giving and unselfish things. I believe the world needs such news—and just as important is the need for children (and adult readers also) to be aware of wildlife and to develop respect for all species that share our world.

"I am currently working on another book that will be published in 2005. It will contain stories of thirteen different birds—this time from the entire country, since thirteen different wildlife rehabilitation centers will be included. The whooping crane will represent the International Crane Foundation; the sharp-shinned hawk will represent the Cornell Ornithology Center; the snowy plover comes from the Monterey Bay Aquarium; the very endangered alala represents Hawaii—and several other species round out the book. These will be, in particular, stories of baby birds from each of these centers. I'm currently doing the illustrations. A full portrait of each baby will be included, as well as the head of the adult for each species. It will be a wonderful opportunity to highlight rehabilitation facilities nationwide and share some of the special stories of different birds they have cared for.

"I try to make my illustrations as scientifically accurate as I possibly can. The ones in *One Wing's Gift* also have color overlays that were done on sheets of Mylar 'painted' with pastel dust. It gave a tint-like quality to the illustrations, which I prefer to photo-realism color. I prefer not to use any computer art in the drawings. All are hand-done, some taking hundreds of hours to complete.

"There is educational material included in *One Wing's Gift* about each species, as there will be with the baby bird rehabilitation book. Hopefully this will be an opportunity for children to learn more about birds and become interested in nature and wildlife and its preservation."

Biographical and Critical Sources

ONLINE

Epinions.com, http://www.epinions.com/ (November 17, 2002), David Abrams, "Joan Harris' Gift: A Visit with the Author."

U.S. Fish & Wildlife Service Web Site, http://alaska.fws.gov/ (June 25, 2003), review of *One Wing's Gift: Rescuing Alaska's Wild Birds.*

*   *   *

HEARNE, Betsy Gould 1942-

Personal

Born October 6, 1942, in Wilsonville, AL; daughter of Kenneth (a doctor) and Elizabeth (Barrett) Gould; married Michael Claffey; children: Joanna Hearne, Elizabeth Claffey. *Education:* Wooster College, B.A., 1964; University of Chicago, M.A., 1968, Ph.D., 1985.

Addresses

Home—Urbana, IL. *Office*—Graduate School of Library and Information Science, 501 East Daniel, Champaign, IL 61820. *Agent*—Philippa Brophy, Sterling Lord Agency, Inc., 660 Madison Ave., New York, NY 10021. *E-mail*—hearne@alexia.lis.uiuc.edu.

Career

Wayne County Public Library, Wooster, OH, children's librarian, 1964-65; University of Chicago Laboratory Schools, Chicago, IL, children's librarian, 1967-68; *Booklist,* Chicago, reviewer, 1968-69, children's books editor, 1973-85; *Bulletin of the Center for Children's Books,* children's books editor, 1985-94, consulting edi-

tor, 1994—. University of Illinois—Chicago, instructor, 1970-71; University of Chicago, assistant professor, 1985-92; University of Illinois—Urbana-Champaign, assistant professor, 1992-94, associate professor, 1994-99, professor, 1999—. Judge, National Book Awards, 1975, American Book Awards, 1981, *Boston Globe/Horn Book* Awards, 1997. Speaker at colleges, conferences, and libraries.

Member

International Research Society for Children's Literature, International Board on Books for Young People, American Library Association (consultant, Mildred Batchelder Committee, Newbery-Caldecott Award Committee, and Notable Books Committee, 1973-78; chair, Caldecott Award Committee, 2005), Children's Reading Round Table.

Awards, Honors

Agnes Sayer Klein Award for Graduate Study, American Library Association (ALA), 1979; Children's Reading Round Table Award, 1982; Best Books for Young Adults citation, ALA, 1987, for *Love Lines: Poetry in Person;* Carl Sandburg Award, 1988, for *Eli's Ghost;* first place, Chicago Women in Publishing Competition, 1989, for *Beauty and the Beast: Visions and Revisions of an Old Tale;* Parents' Choice Award, 1990, for *Choosing Books for Children: A Commonsense Guide;* Anne Izard Award, 1993, for *Beauties and Beasts;* Choice Book citation, Cooperative Children's Book Center (CCBC), 1996, for *Eliza's Dog;* Jane Addams Children's Book Award, *Boston Globe/Horn Book* Honor Book, *New York Times* Notable Book, Children's Book of the Year, Child Study Children's Book Committee, Notable Book for Children citation, *Smithsonian* magazine, Notable Book selection, ALA, *Booklist* Editors' Choice, Notable Children's Trade Book in the Field of Social Studies, National Council for the Social Studies/Children's Book Council (NCSS/CBC), Best Book selection, *Working Mother* magazine, and Best Book selection, *New York Family* magazine, all 1998, all for *Seven Brave Women;* Centennial Scholar Award, University of Illinois—Urbana-Champaign, 1998; Notable Children's Trade Book in the Field of Social Studies, NCSS/CBC, 1999, for *Listening for Leroy;* University Scholar Award, University of Illinois—Urbana-Champaign, 2000-03; Children's Choice selection, International Reading Association/CBC, and Choice Book citation, CCBC, both 2001, both for *Who's in the Hall?: A Mystery in Four Chapters;* Parents' Choice Silver Honor Award, and "Outstanding Book" citation, *Horn Book,* both 2003, both for *The Canine Connection: Stories about Dogs and People.*

Writings

CHILDREN'S BOOKS

South Star, illustrated by Trina Schart Hyman, Atheneum (New York, NY), 1977.

Home, illustrated by Trina Schart Hyman, Atheneum (New York, NY), 1979.

Eli's Ghost, illustrated by Ronald Himler, Simon & Schuster (New York, NY), 1987.

Love Lines: Poetry in Person (poetry for young adults and adults), Simon & Schuster (New York, NY), 1987.

Polaroid and Other Poems of View (poetry for young adults and adults), photographs by Peter Kiar, Macmillan (New York, NY), 1991.

(Editor) *Beauties and Beasts,* illustrated by Joanne Caroselli, Oryx Press (New York, NY), 1993.

Eliza's Dog, illustrated by Erica Thurston, Simon & Schuster (New York, NY), 1996.

Seven Brave Women, illustrated by Bethanne Andersen, Greenwillow (New York, NY), 1997.

Listening for Leroy, Simon & Schuster (New York, NY), 1998.

Who's in the Hall?: A Mystery in Four Chapters, illustrated by Christy Hale, Greenwillow (New York, NY), 2000.

Wishes, Kisses, and Pigs, illustrated by Leslie A. Baker, Simon & Schuster (New York, NY), 2001.

The Canine Connection: Stories about Dogs and People, Simon & Schuster (New York, NY), 2003.

NONFICTION; FOR ADULTS

(Editor, with Marilyn Kaye) *Celebrating Children's Books: Essays on Children's Literature in Honor of Zena Sutherland* (reference), Lothrop, Lee & Shepard (New York, NY), 1981.

Choosing Books for Children: A Commonsense Guide (reference), Delacorte (New York, NY), 1981, 3rd edition, University of Illinois Press (Urbana, IL), 1999.

Beauty and the Beast: A Study of Aesthetic Survival (thesis), University of Chicago (Chicago, IL), 1985, published as *Beauty and the Beast: Visions and Revisions of an Old Tale,* University of Chicago Press (Chicago, IL), 1989.

(Editor, with Zena Sutherland and Roger Sutton) *The Best in Children's Books: The University of Chicago Guide to Children's Literature, 1985-1990,* University of Chicago Press (Chicago, IL), 1991.

(Editor, with Roger Sutton) *Evaluating Children's Books: A Critical Look,* University of Illinois (Urbana, IL), 1993.

(Editor) *The Zena Sutherland Lectures, 1983-1992,* Clarion (New York, NY), 1993.

(Editor, with Janice Del Negro, Christine Jenkins, and Deborah Stevenson) *Story: From Fireplace to Cyberspace,* Graduate School of Library and Information Science (Champaign, IL), 1999.

Also contributor of articles, reviews, and editorials to periodicals such as *Library Quarterly, New York Times Book Review, American Journal of Sociology,* and *Signal.* Recordings include "Evaluating Children's Books," Children's Book Council (New York, NY), 1979, and videorecording, *Sharing Books with Young Children,* American Library Association (Chicago, IL), 1986.

Sidelights

Since Betsy Gould Hearne began work as a children's librarian in the 1960s, she has made a variety of contributions to children's literature. During her career, Hearne has worked as a critic, editor, scholar, and children's book writer, and she has also earned advanced degrees and developed her talents as a poet. Hearne's commentaries on children's books can be found in *Booklist* and *Bulletin of the Center for Children's Books.* Her books for educators, librarians, and parents include *Choosing Books for Children: A Commonsense Guide* and *Evaluating Children's Books: A Critical Look* (which she edited with Roger Sutton) among others. Indeed, Humphrey Carpenter of the *New York Times Book Review* has described Hearne as "a distinguished cataloger of children's books." Many of Hearne's children's books, such as *South Star, Eli's Ghost, Seven Brave Women,* and *The Canine Connection: Stories about Dogs and People,* have been well received. Additionally, Hearne's two volumes of poetry have been recommended for mature young adults.

Hearne was born in rural Alabama, the daughter of a country doctor. On her Web site she stated: "I grew up in an Alabama pine forest with no one to play with except a dog, cat, horse, cow, alligator, raccoon, possum, owl, and garter snake. None of them talked much. They were pretty good listeners, though, and I learned from them to listen and also not to be afraid of silence." Hearne's mother taught her to read and write and also entertained her with tales of her ancestors and how they forged lives in a new land. When Hearne was older, the family moved to Tennessee in order to find better schooling, and Hearne grew into a tall, shy young woman who sought solace in literature and music. After earning a college degree, she went to work in the children's department of a public library, and it was there that she found her life's work: evaluating, creating, and relating stories to young audiences. She brought her hands-on experience with youngsters to bear on her own book reviewing and writing, while she also extended the study of children's literature from a scholarly point of view. To quote Mary M. Burns in *Horn Book,* Hearne's efforts result in "a significant contribution to understanding contemporary children's literature."

A *Publishers Weekly* critic described Hearne's first children's book, *South Star,* as "an exciting fantasy." It tells the story of Megan, a young giant girl who has escaped her family's castle, and the Screamer that has frozen the castle and her parents in ice. As Megan flees across a plain from the terrible Screamer, she is befriended and aided by a boy, Randall, who is also on his own. A bear helps the pair find the southern star to follow, and they begin a difficult journey. They finally find a valley populated by Megan's relatives and led by her sister. According to Ethel L. Heins of *Horn Book,* Hearne "successfully creates suspense and casts an atmosphere of primeval magic" in *South Star.*

In *Home,* the sequel to *South Star,* Megan is living with her sister. When Megan dreams that her sister's missing husband is calling for help, she leaves the peaceful valley to find him. While she waits at the seaside for the storms to go away and to train for a trip across the sea, she once again encounters her friend Randall. They journey across the sea to a desert land ruled by lion people, where Megan's brother-in-law is alive in prison. After battling the king of the land, the three return to the valley. "Both Brendan and Megan return home with a new appreciation for the people and places they left" and "better knowledge of themselves," explained Karen M. Klockner of *Horn Book.* Writing in *School Library Journal,* Margaret A. Dorsey commented that this book is "good stuff for growing girls."

Despite its title, according to Elizabeth S. Watson of *Horn Book, Eli's Ghost* "is definitely not scary." The action, set in the southern United States, begins when Eli runs away to a swamp to find his long-lost mother. When Eli falls into the water, his mother arrives just in time to save him. Still, Eli's ghost escapes his body and has some fun with the rescue party that arrives. Furthermore, Eli's ghost is nothing like him. "For Eli Wilson," observed a critic in *Bulletin of the Center for Children's Books,* "life will never be the same." Watson concluded in *Horn Book,* "the humor and suspense will appeal to intermediate readers."

In *Eliza's Dog,* "Hearne shapes a convincing portrait of a feisty, resourceful girl," according to a *Publishers Weekly* reviewer. Eliza, who has always wanted a dog, finds a border collie while on vacation with her parents in Ireland. Although Eliza manages to convince her parents to let her keep the dog, she worries that it will grow too large to fit in its carry-cage for the trip back home from Ireland. In addition, Eliza must learn to deal with her new pet and his many needs. "This book has appeal," wrote a *Kirkus Reviews* critic, "mainly for other dog-obsessed children." Some critics noted that the value of *Eliza's Dog* lies in its realistic depiction of pet care, a job that is sometimes tedious and unpleasant. "The story clearly sends the message that owning a dog entails hard work," pointed out Carol Schene in *School Library Journal. Horn Book* critic Maeve Visser Knoth styled *Eliza's Dog* "a pleasing, well-told story."

In 1979, Hearne went back to graduate school; by 1985, she had completed a dissertation. She published this work, in revised form, in 1989 as *Beauty and the Beast: Visions and Revisions of an Old Tale.* This work traces the beauty and the beast motif from its origins, and takes a look at how it has been revised by various authors, storytellers, and illustrators throughout time for children. "Hearne's conclusions are provocative, illuminating, and stimulating," commented Mary M. Bush in *Horn Book.* "This book is a fine example of critical analysis of a traditional tale" and "offers a wealth of material for adults to use in fostering critical thinking in children," explained Jane Anne Hannigan in *School Library Journal.* Hearne's related book for children, *Beau-*

ties and Beasts, features twenty-seven beauty and the beast folktales from different cultures and time periods. According to Judy Constantinides of *School Library Journal,* this book "will attract the attention of older primary grade children" and it will be useful to "adults teaching multiculturalism."

Hearne is also the author of two volumes of poetry. *Love Lines: Poetry in Person* includes fifty-nine poems about love, family, and friends that Hearne wrote over the course of twenty-five years. According to *Voice of Youth Advocates* contributor Becki George, the work provides "quickly readable free verse" and "includes many sexual references." However, "None of the book's three sections . . . seems to speak directly to young adult readers," observed Kathleen Whalin of *School Library Journal.* A critic for *Kirkus Reviews* asserted that the volume, "rich in ideas and imagery," "should appeal to anyone mature enough to yearn after love." *Polaroid and Other Poems of View* contains forty-three poems. Many critics enjoyed the black-and-white photos by Peter Kiar, which help introduce each section of poetry. This volume, in the words of Brooke Selby Dillon of *Voice of Youth Advocates,* "will enthrall and delight the mature poetry reader." The "rhythms . . . are capricious and compelling," and the poems are "clearly the work of an artist in control of her medium," related Nancy Vasilakis of *Horn Book.*

Hearne's conviction that the best stories are often the most personal ones led her to write *Seven Brave Women.* This award-winning book for middle readers introduces the former generations of Hearne's family and tells of their adventures, beginning with her great-great-great grandmother, who arrived in America prior to the Revolutionary War. As the book explores each succeeding generation—down to the young narrator, who is still a student—it highlights the courageous acts performed by each woman, even though none of them ever fought in a war or earned headlines in the newspaper. "Although this is about one family of women . . . children will grasp the universality in these lives," wrote Ilene Cooper in *Booklist.* Writing in *Horn Book,* Mary M. Burns liked the way the women in *Seven Brave Women* "surmount difficulties with grace, imagination, determination, and faith." The she concluded that the work provides "a splendid tribute to women and their history."

Memories of a lonely childhood inform Hearne's novel *Listening for Leroy.* Ten-year-old Alice is growing up in rural Alabama in a home ruled by her strict but principled father. Since she is schooled at home, Alice has no friends her age, but she does find a confidant in Leroy, a hired hand who works for her family. Leroy gives Alice much valuable advice, and when he is run out of town by bigots, she misses him sorely. Even after her family moves to a more populous part of the South, Alice continues to remember Leroy and to wonder what happened to him. A *Publishers Weekly* critic called *Listening to Leroy* a "gentle, reflective coming-of-age novel" that "subtly conveys Alice's revelations about herself, her family, and a prejudiced society." *Booklist*'s Shelle Rosenfeld likewise styled the work "a heartfelt look at the growing pains of an idealistic girl experiencing a less than ideal reality."

Hearne adopts a lighter tone in *Who's in the Hall?: A Mystery in Four Chapters.* In this picture story for younger readers, three sets of children, baby-sitters, and pets in an eight-story apartment building all face the same dilemma: Do they answer the door when a stranger knocks and identifies herself as the janitor? How the children band together to solve the mystery of the unidentified knocker forms the crux of the plot. In *Booklist,* Connie Fletcher concluded: "Suspense in a mundane setting, rhyming games, and tongue twisters make this fun for reading aloud." *School Library Journal* correspondent Marlene Gawron called the book "an excellent blend of good writing and fine illustration," while *Horn Book*'s Joanna Rudge Long found it "a dandy choice for newly independent readers."

Wishes, Kisses, and Pigs brings new life to the old adage, "be careful what you wish for, you just might get it." Quarreling with her brother, Louise Tolliver inadvertently calls him a pig while simultaneously wishing on a star. When her brother disappears, and a strange, white pig with blue eyes appears on the farm, Louise realizes what she has done and seeks to undo it. Complications arise as she tries to formulate a magic spell that will restore her brother before he is chosen to be a menu item at an upcoming picnic. As a reviewer in *Horn Book* put it, the plot's "fairy-tale resolution satisfyingly admits 'how nature's magic and magic's natural.'" In *School Library Journal,* Betsy Fraser deemed *Wishes, Kisses, and Pigs* "a delightful novel about the dangers of getting what you wish for."

The twelve stories collected in *The Canine Connection: Stories about Dogs and People* explore the interaction between young people and their dogs—with emphasis on the people. The stories range widely in subject matter. In one, a blind and bereft young girl begins to reconnect with the world through the howling of her recently acquired guide dog. In another, a boy and a pit bull band together to protect each other from bullies in a bad neighborhood. Willa, the heroine of "Lab," must help her mother deliver a baby while the family dog, Millie, tends to orphaned kittens. A *Kirkus Reviews* contributor wrote that each story in the collection "chimes to the rhythm . . . best suited for the unique characters involved. Best of all, Hearne writes the concerns and challenges of teens as if each word came from their hearts." In *School Library Journal,* Alison Follos observed: "These stories are well drawn, told with refinement, and enlivened with credible characters." *Booklist* contributor Ellen Mandel concluded that *The Canine Connection* is "a rewarding collection that will stay with readers."

In addition to her steady publishing schedule, Hearne continues to teach courses on children's literature and storytelling at the University of Illinois—Urbana-Champaign. On her Web site she wrote, "The heart of my work is stories, what they tell us and how they are told. Whether stories appear in the oral, print, or electronic traditions, they reflect and shape us." In *Horn Book,* Mary M. Burns commended Hearne for offering works that "lure readers into confronting issues important to intelligent reading of today's literature for children."

Biographical and Critical Sources

PERIODICALS

Booklist, April 1, 1996, Lauren Peterson, review of *Eliza's Dog,* p. 1364; June 1, 1997, Ilene Cooper, review of *Seven Brave Women,* p. 1694; November 15, 1998, Shelle Rosenfeld, review of *Listening for Leroy,* p. 587; September 15, 2000, Connie Fletcher, review of *Who's in the Hall?: A Mystery in Four Chapters,* p. 240; March 1, 2001, Michael Cart, review of *Wishes, Kisses, and Pigs,* p. 1278; April 15, 2003, Ellen Mandel, review of *The Canine Connection: Stories about Dogs and People,* p. 1471.

Bulletin of the Center for Children's Books, March, 1987, review of *Eli's Ghost,* p. 126.

Horn Book, June, 1979, Karen M. Klockner, review of *Home,* p. 301; September-October, 1987, Elizabeth S. Watson, review of *Eli's Ghost,* p. 612; May-June, 1990, Mary M. Bush, review of *Beauty and the Beast: Visions and Revisions of an Old Tale,* pp. 353-354; July-August, 1991, Nancy Vasilakis, review of *Polaroid and Other Poems of View,* p. 471; May-June, 1993, Mary M. Burns, review of *The Zena Sutherland Lectures: 1983-1992,* p. 345; July-August, 1994, Mary M. Burns, review of *Evaluating Children's Books: A Critical Look,* p. 476; September-October, 1996, Maeve Visser Knoth, review of *Eliza's Dog,* p. 596; September-October, 1997, Mary M. Burns, review of *Seven Brave Women,* p. 558; December, 1997, Ethel L. Heins, review of *South Star,* pp. 662-663; November, 2000, Joanna Rudge Long, review of *Who's in the Hall?,* p. 746; May, 2001, review of *Wishes, Kisses, and Pigs,* p. 326; May-June, 2003, Joanna Rudge Long, review of *The Canine Connection,* p. 348.

Kirkus Reviews, August 1, 1987, review of *Love Lines: Poetry in Person,* p. 1157; March 15, 1996, review of *Eliza's Dog,* p. 448; February 15, 2003, review of *The Canine Connection,* p. 307.

Libraries and Culture, summer, 2000, Jennifer Stevens, review of *Story: From Fireplace to Cyberspace,* p. 484.

New York Times Book Review, March 25, 1990, Humphrey Carpenter, review of *Beauty and the Beast,* p. 25.

Publishers Weekly, September 19, 1977, review of *South Star,* p. 146; March 18, 1996, review of *Eliza's Dog,* p. 70; May 19, 1997, review of *Seven Brave Women,* p. 75; October 26, 1998, review of *Listening for Leroy,* p. 66; July 3, 2000, review of *Who's in the Hall?,* p. 70; March 26, 2001, review of *Wishes, Kisses, and Pigs,* p. 93; February 10, 2003, review of *The Canine Connection,* p. 188.

School Library Journal, May, 1979, Margaret A. Dorsey, review of *Home,* p. 62; February, 1988, Kathleen Whalin, review of *Love Lines,* p. 88; February, 1990, Jane Anne Hannigan, review of *Beauty and the Beast,* p. 38; June, 1994, Judy Constantinides, review of *Beauties and Beasts,* p. 55; May, 1996, Carol Schene, review of *Eliza's Dog,* p. 113; August, 2000, Marlene Gawron, review of *Who's in the Hall?,* p. 156; April, 2001, Betsy Fraser, review of *Wishes, Kisses, and Pigs,* p. 140; April, 2003, Alison Follos, review of *The Canine Connection,* p. 164.

Voice of Youth Advocates, February, 1988, Becki George, review of *Love Lines,* p. 296; August, 1991, Brooke Selby Dillon, review of *Polaroid and Other Poems of View,* p. 189.

ONLINE

Betsy Hearne Home Page, http://alexia.lis.uiuc.edu/ (June 26, 2003).*

*   *   *

HEELAN, Jamee Riggio 1965-

Personal

Born May 3, 1965, in Deerfield, IL; daughter of John Albert II (a salesman) and Julia Joyce (a registered nurse; maiden name, Pope) Riggio; married Robert Charles Heelan (a broker), November 14, 1987; children: Dominic Vincent Lemieux, Grant Patrick Roy, Gianna Ashley Maree, Anthony Joseph LeClair. *Education:* University of Kansas, B.S., 1986. *Religion:* Catholic. *Hobbies and other interests:* Jogging, golfing, boating, fishing, biking, pencil drawing.

Addresses

Home—Mundelein, IL. *Office*—Rehabilitation Institute of Chicago, 345 East Superior St., Chicago, IL 60611. *E-mail*—Jheelan@rehabchicago.org.

Career

Rehabilitation Institute of Chicago, Chicago, IL, registered occupational therapist, 1987—, coordinator of the Children's Amputee Program, 1992—. Center on International Rehabilitation/Physicians Against Landmines, Chicago, IL, occupational therapist consultant, 1999-2002.

Member

Association for Children's Prosthetic and Orthotics Clinics (board of directors, 1996-1999; vice president, 2000-2002; president, 2003-2005).

Awards, Honors

Outstanding Books for Young People with Disabilities, International Board on Books for Young People, 2002, for *Can You Hear A Rainbow?: The Story of a Deaf Boy Named Chris.*

Jamee Riggio Heelen

Writings

The Making of My Special Hand: Madison's Story, Peachtree Publishing (Atlanta, GA), 1998.

Rolling Along: The Story of Taylor and His Wheelchair, Peachtree Publishing (Atlanta, GA), 2000.

Can You Hear a Rainbow?: The Story of a Deaf Boy Named Chris, Peachtree Publishing (Atlanta, GA), 2002.

Work in Progress

A Canine Companion, about the friendship between a dog and child, for Peachtree Publishing (Atlanta, GA).

Sidelights

Jamee Riggio Heelan is an occupational therapist who specializes in working with children with disabilities and physical deformities. Heelan has held a variety of jobs and high-level positions in professional organizations in the field of occupational therapy, such as being the coordinator of the Children's Amputee Program at the Rehabilitation Institute of Chicago and the president of the Association for Children's Prosthetic and Orthotics Clinics. This background gives her a unique, behind-the-scenes perspective of the daily challenges faced by children living with physical handicaps. She brings her knowledge and her compassion for these children to the public through her books.

"My greatest goal," she told *SATA,* "is to remove the fears behind a disability. By explaining through words and pictures why someone is the way they are then maybe each individual that reads my books will see a child with a disability as a child first and see their disability second."

In the three books Heelan has written, which are part of a series, she uses a first-person narrative to tell the story of a child with a disability. As a young girl, Heelan told *SATA,* she knew several children with serious disabilities. One lost both arms following an accident, another was deaf, one was blind, and one had cancer.

These experiences left her with many questions. Heelan says her parents encouraged her not to treat people differently or unfairly. This background influenced Heelan to become an occupational therapist, working with children with all kinds of physical disabilities.

"I began writing about children with disabilities in hopes to better educate the community about real children that surround us," Heelan told *SATA.* "Disabilities can bring upon many fears to the onlooker especially if it brings with it a lot of unanswered questions."

The Making of My Special Hand: Madison's Story was Heelan's first book. Born with only one hand, Madison goes through the process of acquiring a prosthetic hand. *School Library Journal* reviewer Linda Beck called the book "unique," noting that it would be "an excellent addition to collections on children with special needs." Readers join Madison and her family on their visit to the hospital and learn about "helper hands," which is the term Heelan uses for the prosthesis being made for Madison. Writing in *Booklist,* Ilene Cooper praised the book as "extrememly informative," noting that "children will have no problem understanding" the medical procedures describing the fitting of Madison's new hand.

Heelan's second book in the series, *Rolling Along: The Story of Taylor and His Wheelchair,* describes the daily life and routines of Taylor, a young boy with cerebral palsy. "While he has been trained to use a walker, he prefers a wheelchair as it enables him to go faster and not tire as quickly," noted *School Library Journal*'s Margaret C. Howell, explaining Taylor's desire for independence. *Booklist* critic Hazel Rochman described the use of Taylor's own voice as "direct and immediate," observing that what makes the book effective "is that there's a story, not just a situation."

In *Can You Hear a Rainbow?: The Story of a Deaf Boy Named Chris* Heelan narrates through ten-year-old Chris, who explains to readers how he uses sign language, hearing aids, and lipreading to communicate. Chris shows how his days aren't much different from hearing children's, and relates that some things—like a rainbow—are the same for both deaf and hearing children. While not finding the information in the book new, *School Library Journal* critic Nancy A. Gifford, nonetheless, found it "accurate and worth repeating."

"Being an author," Heelan told *SATA,* "has given me the special gift to teach those I do not have personal contact with but now have the opportunity to guide." She said, "Keep your dreams big, bright, and full of energy, and in time you can do anything your heart desires. . . . Anything is a possibility."

Biographical and Critical Sources

BOOKS

Heelan, Jamee Riggio, *The Making of My Special Hand: Madison's Story,* Peachtree Publishing (Atlanta, GA), 1998.

PERIODICALS

Booklist, April 1, 2000, Ilene Cooper, review of *The Making of My Special Hand,* p. 1462; September 1, 2000, Hazel Rochman, review of *Rolling Along: The Story of Taylor and His Wheelchair,* p. 120.
Horn Book Guide, July-December, 2000, Gail B. Hedges, review of *The Making of My Special Hand* and *Rolling Along,* p. 124.
School Library Journal, September, 2000, Linda Beck, review of *The Making of My Special Hand,* p. 217; December, 2000, Margaret C. Howell, review of *Rolling Along,* p. 133; September, 2002, Nancy A. Gifford, review of *Can You Hear a Rainbow?: The Story of a Deaf Boy Named Chris,* p. 213.
Skipping Stones, September, 2001, review of *The Making of My Special Hand,* p. 33.*

* * *

HELQUIST, Brett

Personal

Born in Gonado, AZ; married Mary Jane Callister. *Education:* Brigham Young University, B.F.A., 1993.

Addresses

Home—New York, NY. *Agent*—c/o Author Mail, HarperCollins, 10 E. 53rd St., 7th Floor, New York, NY 10022.

Career

Illustrator.

Writings

(And illustrator) *Roger, the Jolly Pirate,* HarperCollins (New York, NY), 2004.

ILLUSTRATOR

Tor Seidler, *The Revenge of Randal Reese-Rat,* Farrar, Straus & Giroux (New York, NY), 2001.

Shana Corey, *Milly and the Macy's Parade,* Scholastic (New York, NY), 2002.

Peter W. Hassinger, *The Book of Alfar: A Tale of the Hudson Highlands,* Geringer (New York, NY), 2002.

Blue Balliett, *Chasing Vermeer,* Scholastic (New York, NY), 2003.

ILLUSTRATOR; "SERIES OF UNFORTUNATE EVENTS" SERIES

Lemony Snicket, *The Bad Beginning,* HarperCollins (New York, NY), 1999.

Lemony Snicket, *The Reptile Room,* HarperCollins (New York, NY), 1999.

Lemony Snicket, *The Wide Window,* HarperCollins (New York, NY), 2000.

Lemony Snicket, *The Miserable Mill,* HarperCollins (New York, NY), 2000.

Lemony Snicket, *The Austere Academy,* HarperCollins (New York, NY), 2000.

Lemony Snicket, *The Ersatz Elevator,* HarperCollins (New York, NY), 2001.

Lemony Snicket, *The Vile Village,* HarperCollins (New York, NY), 2001.

Lemony Snicket, *The Hostile Hospital,* HarperCollins (New York, NY), 2001.

Lemony Snicket, *The Carnivorous Carnival,* HarperCollins (New York, NY), 2002.

Lemony Snicket, *The Slippery Slope,* HarperCollins (New York, NY), 2003.

ILLUSTRATOR; "TALES FROM THE HOUSE OF BUNNICULA" SERIES

James Howe, *It Came from beneath the Bed!,* Atheneum Books for Young Readers (New York, NY), 2002.

James Howe, *Howie Monroe and the Doghouse of Doom,* Atheneum Books for Young Readers (New York, NY), 2002.

James Howe, *Invasion of the Mind Swappers from Asteroid Six!,* Atheneum Books for Young Readers (New York, NY), 2002.

James Howe, *Screaming Mummies of the Pharaoh's Tomb II,* Atheneum Books for Young Readers (New York, NY), 2003.

James Howe, *Budd Barkin, Private Eye,* Atheneum Books for Young Readers (New York, NY), 2003.

James Howe, *The Amazing Odorous Adventures of Stinky Dog,* Atheneum Books for Young Readers (New York, NY), 2003.

OTHER

Contributor of illustrations to publications such as *New York Times, Time for Kids,* and *Cricket.*

Sidelights

Illustrator Brett Helquist has what some children might consider the best job in the world: he's the illustrator of Lemony Snicket's highly popular "Series of Unfortu-

Three children are sent to live with a distant relative who turns out to be evil. From Lemony Snicket's A Series of Unfortunate Events: The Bad Beginning, *illustrated by Brett Helquist.*

nate Events" books. Since graduating with a Bachelor of Fine Arts degree from Brigham Young University in 1993, Helquist has worked consistently as an illustrator. Among his more high-profile assignments has been the artwork for volumes of Snicket's books chronicling the downbeat, sometimes entirely grim adventures of the Baudelaire orphans—fourteen-year-old Violet, twelve-year-old Klaus, and baby Sonny. The children become orphans when a fire destroys their home and kills their parents in *The Bad Beginning.* The executor of their parents' estate completely ignores any of the children's wishes. Count Olaf, their new guardian, is a villainous figure intent on making the Baudelaire family fortune his own—no matter what he has to do to the rightful heirs. Peril follows upon misfortune for the Baudelaire children, and narrator Snicket takes pains to warn the readers that a happy ending will not be found in that particular book. A *Publishers Weekly* reviewer remarked on Helquist's illustrations, noting that "Exquisitely detailed drawings of Gothic gargoyles and mischievous eyes echo the contents of this elegantly designed hardcover."

More woe and danger plague Violet, Klaus, and Sonny through the volumes that follow. In *The Vile Village,*

In A Series of Unfortunate Events: The Miserable Mill, *the Baudelaire orphans are subjected to darkly amusing misadventures. Written by Snicket. (Illustrated by Helquist.)*

they are adopted by the entire village of V.F.D., because of the old saying that "it takes a village to raise a child." They continue to elude Count Olaf by relying on their own talents and resourcefulness, as the idea of being adopted by a village looks more and more like a bad one. The threats get more personal in *The Hostile Hospital,* where Count Olaf and his henchmen threaten to behead anesthetized Violet, try to crush the children with filing cabinets, and trap them in a burning building. "Perfectly capturing the atmosphere of the stories, Helquist's stylized pencil sketches are among his best yet," commented Carolyn Phelan in *Booklist.* The children disguise themselves to investigate a fortune teller in *The Carnivorous Carnival* but find that carnival life is not the constant fun it seems to be—especially when one of the performers is about to be thrown to the lions. "Children faithful to the series won't be surprised when the book does not end happily," wrote Susan Dove Lempke in *Booklist.*

For his contribution to the series, Helquist has earned high remarks from critics. "Some brilliant publishing person or cabal saw the pleasure in these tales—anarchy masked as propriety—and decided, brilliantly, to

engage Brett Helquist to do the spiky and droll line drawings," wrote Gregory Maguire in a review of *The Austere Academy* in *New York Times Book Review.* "The illustrations and the writing parody juvenile literature of an earlier time; so do the production values." Physically, the *Series of Unfortunate Events* books are "evocative of gift books of an earlier day," Maguire remarked, and "the presentation is inspired."

Helquist's illustrations can also be found in more whimsical and lighthearted books and series. James Howe's *Tales from the House of Bunnicula* series features puppy Howie Monroe, the Monroe family's wirehaired dachshund. Howie seeks literary glory with his imaginative tales and undertakes a number of creative writing projects. In *Howie Monroe and the Doghouse of Doom,* Howie writes himself into a parody of the Harry Potter books. Howie's friend Delilah finds herself being transformed into a squirrel by aliens (in another of Howie's stories, of course) in *Invasion of the Mind Swappers from Asteroid Six!* And, Howie acquires Harold, an unwanted editor, in *It Came from beneath the Bed!,* wherein Howie writes, Harold criticizes, and a typically Howie-like story takes shape about a crazed stuffed koala bear that has come to life. Wendy S. Carroll, writing in *School Library Journal,* called *Invasion of the Mind Swappers from Asteroid Six!* "lighthearted fun, . . . with humorous black-and-white drawings" of the character's experiences.

Isabel Moberly-Rat is marrying Montague Mad-Rat in *The Revenge of Randal Reese-Rat,* and Randal is broken-hearted and jealous. Isabel had earlier rejected high-rat-society Randal and instead fell in love with working-class rodent Montague, who prevented the city's rats from being poisoned and rescued their wharfside home. When a fire nearly kills the newly-married rats, Randal is the chief suspect, but while he desired revenge of some sort, there is doubt that murder was ever in his plans. Randal's life is complicated further by his increasing affection for Maggie Mad-Rat, his rival Montague's cousin. Nora Krug, writing in *New York Times Book Review,* observed that Helquist's illustrations, "though lovely, are a bit too dark for the story. The rats look too much like, well, rats." However, Helquist's detailed black-and-white illustrations "make it clear that these lithe, sociable New York rodents have busy lives and unique personalities," wrote Eva Mitnick in *School Library Journal.* A *Kirkus Reviews* commentator called the story "Loyally and lovably ratty."

Helquist's illustrations in *Milly and the Macy's Parade,* based on archival material from Macy's own historical collections, were called "charming" by Deborah Hopkinson in a *BookPage* review. Offering an imaginative tale about the origins of the annual parade, author Shana Corey's story involves Milly, a Polish immigrant who visits her father every day at his job at the famed Macy's department store. While in the store, Milly luxuriates in the atmosphere, riding the escalators and delightedly inspecting all the bright and cheerful holiday items on sale. However, during the 1924 holiday season, Milly finds her father and his friends depressed and wistful for the music, caroling, and parades they knew in their homelands. Milly bravely suggests to Mr. Macy himself that a parade would cheer up his workers and give them holiday spirit. He agrees, and a yearly holiday tradition is born. Helquist's pictures "depict scenes from the original 1924 parade, including floats, storybook characters, and animals borrowed from the Central Park Zoo," Hopkinson wrote. The "lusciously illustrated tale" contains richly colored, stylized illustrations that "convey a sense of luxury associated with Macy's," observed a *Kirkus Reviews* critic. Susan Pine, writing in *School Library Journal*, called *Milly and the Macy's Parade* "an entertaining and lively variation on holiday stories."

Biographical and Critical Sources

PERIODICALS

Booklist, October 15, 2001, Carolyn Phelan, review of *The Hostile Hospital*, p. 392; October 1, 2002, Kathleen Odean, review of *Howie Monroe and the Doghouse of Doom*, p. 326; December 15, 2002, Susan Dove Lempke, review of *The Carnivorous Carnival*, p. 761.
Childhood Education, winter, 2001, Elizabeth K. Liddicoat, review of *The Ersatz Elevator*, p. 112.
Family Life, November 1, 2001, Sara Nelson, review of *The Hostile Hospital*, p. 95.
Kirkus Reviews, August 15, 2001, review of *The Revenge of Randal Reese-Rat*, p. 1221; October 1, 2002, review of *Milly and the Macy's Parade*, p. 1464; November 15, 2002, review of *Screaming Mummies of the Pharaoh's Tomb II*, p. 1695.
New York Times Book Review, October 15, 2000, Gregory Maguire, review of *The Austere Academy*, p. 30; June 17, 2001, review of *The Vile Village*, p. 24; November 18, 2001, Nora Krug, review of *The Revenge of Randal Reese-Rat*, p. 52.
Publishers Weekly, September 6, 1999, review of *The Bad Beginning*, p. 104; July 30, 2001, review of *The Revenge of Randal Reese-Rat*, p. 85.
School Library Journal, January, 2000, Marlene Gawron, review of *The Wide Window*, p. 136; October, 2000, Ann Cook, review of *The Austere Academy*, p. 171; August, 2001, Farida S. Dowler, review of *The Vile Village*, p. 188; October, 2001, Eva Mitnick, review of *The Revenge of Randal Reese-Rat*, p. 170; November, 2001, Jean Gaffney, review of *The Hostile Hospital*, p. 164; October, 2002, Susan Pine, review of *Milly and the Macy's Parade*, pp. 99-100; November, 2002, JoAnn Jonas, review of *Howie Monroe and the Doghouse of Doom*, p. 169, Wendy S. Carroll, review of *Invasion of the Mind Swappers from Asteroid Six*, p. 169, and John Sigwald, review of *It Came from beneath the Bed!*, p. 169; August, 2003, Elaine E. Knight, review of *Bud Barkin, Private Eye*, p. 129.

ONLINE

BookPage, http://www.bookpage.com/ (May 21, 2003), Deborah Hopkinson, review of *Milly and the Macy's Parade*.
Shannon Associates Web Site, http://www.shannonassociates.com/ (June 26, 2003), "Talent: Brett Helquist."*

* * *

HEO, Yumi 1964-

Personal

Born 1964, in Korea; married; children: Auden, Sara Jane. *Education:* New York School of Visual Arts, M.F.A., c. 1991. *Hobbies and other interests:* Gardening, antique hunting.

Addresses

Home—97 Sterling Ave., White Plains, NY 10606. *E-mail*—yumiheo@earthlink.net.

Career

Author and illustrator of children's books, 1994—. Metropolitan Transit Authority, New York, NY, creator of "Q Is for Queens" glass art installation, 1997-2000.

Awards, Honors

New York Times Best Illustrated Book of the Year, 1996, for *The Lonely Lioness and the Ostrich Chicks: A Masai Tale*, written by Verna Aardema; Notable Books for Children selection, *Smithsonian* magazine, 2001, for *Henry's First-Moon Birthday*, written by Lenore Look.

Writings

SELF-ILLUSTRATED

One Afternoon, Orchard (New York, NY), 1994.
Father's Rubber Shoes, Orchard (New York, NY), 1995.
(Reteller) *The Green Frogs: A Korean Folktale*, Houghton Mifflin (Boston, MA), 1996.
One Sunday Morning, Orchard (New York, NY), 1999.

ILLUSTRATOR

Suzanne Crowder Han, reteller, *The Rabbit's Judgment*, Holt (New York, NY), 1994.
Suzanne Crowder Han, reteller, *The Rabbit's Escape*, Holt (New York, NY), 1995.
Verna Aardema, reteller, *The Lonely Lioness and the Ostrich Chicks: A Masai Tale*, Knopf (New York, NY), 1996.

Cynthia Chin-Lee, *A Is for Asia,* Orchard (New York, NY), 1997.

Melrose Cooper, *Pets!,* Holt (New York, NY), 1998.

Nancy Van Laan, *So Say the Little Monkeys,* Atheneum (New York, NY), 1998.

The Not So Itsy-Bitsy Spider: A Pop-Up Book, Piggy Toes Press (Santa Monica, CA), 1999.

Kimiko Kamikawa, *Yoshi's Feast,* DK Ink (New York, NY), 2000.

Lenore Look, *Henry's First-Moon Birthday,* Atheneum (New York, NY), 2001.

Rachel Vail, *Sometimes I'm Bombaloo,* Scholastic (New York, NY), 2001.

Marguerite W. Davol, *The Snake's Tales,* Orchard (New York, NY), 2002.

Hugh Lupton, reteller, *Pirican Pic and Pirican Mor,* Barefoot Books (Cambridge, MA), 2003.

Candace Fleming, *Smile, Lily!,* Simon & Schuster (New York, NY), 2004.

Alice Hoffman and Wolfe Martin, *Moondog,* Scholastic (New York, NY), 2004.

Lenore Look, *Uncle Peter's Amazing Chinese Wedding,* Atheneum (New York, NY), 2004.

Several books illustrated by Heo have been published in French-language editions. Contributor to *This Place I Know: Poems of Comfort,* compiled by Georgia Heard, Candlewick Press (Cambridge, MA), 2002.

Work in Progress

Lady Hahn and her Seven Friends.

Sidelights

Yumi Heo's distinctive artwork, which appears in her own picture books as well as those written by others, has garnered enthusiastic responses from critics impressed with her eccentric use of perspective, her energetic use of color, and her unique blend of primitive and sophisticated styles. The illustrator described her excitement at getting the assignment for her first book, Suzanne Crowder Han's retelling of a Korean folktale titled *The Rabbit's Judgment,* to Sally Lodge in a *Publishers Weekly* interview. "This was a tale I had known since I was a child in Korea, and I felt a real connection with it," Heo said. "I was very comfortable with it from the start," she remarked of the artistic process that culminated in the illustrations for Han's text. "I would say that this art came from inside of me."

The story of *The Rabbit's Judgment* tells of a man lured into rescuing a tiger from a pit; though the tiger promises not to attack the man, once he is freed from the pit, he changes his mind. The man looks first to a pine tree, then to an ox, and finally to a rabbit for a judgment that will rescue him; the first two are unsympathetic, but the rabbit slyly tricks the tiger back into the pit, and the man goes on his way. "The text . . . highlights amus-

ingly eloquent interchanges" between the characters, noted a *Publishers Weekly* contributor, "while arrestingly skewed illustrations in a rich, natural palette illuminate the story's childlike wisdom." Other reviewers similarly highlighted Heo's winning addition to Han's well-told story; a *Kirkus Reviews* critic characterized the artist's style as "a pleasing blend of sophisticated design, ethnic reference, and visual storytelling."

Heo paired up with Han for another adaptation of a Korean folktale in *The Rabbit's Escape,* in which a rabbit is tricked into visiting the Dragon King of the East Sea, who wants to eat the rabbit's liver in order to cure his own illness. The fast-talking rabbit assures the king that he keeps his liver in a safe place and manages to escape when given permission to return to land to retrieve it. "Heo's original, quirky illustrations, with their Klee-like seas of floating figures, contribute significantly to the book's appeal," averred Nancy Vasilakis in *Horn Book.* This judgment was echoed by other reviewers, who, as with the duo's earlier collaborative effort, commented on the happy synergy between author and artist. Lisa S. Murphy, a contributor to *School Library Journal,* concluded: "Whimsical details [in the illustrations] reveal themselves with each new look, and this folktale is engaging enough to warrant many such readings!"

Equally successful, claim reviewers, are Heo's collaborations with other writers. Her artwork for *A Is for Asia* experiments in both traditional and tradition-breaking styles, according to a *Publishers Weekly* reviewer who added: "Heo's illustrations make turning every page an adventure into contemporary and historical Asia." In Nancy van Laan's 1998 book *So Say the Little Monkeys,* Heo's "stylishly drawn illustrations" keep pace with an animated rainforest tale about a group of devil-may-care monkeys, "maintaining a sense of animated glee," in the opinion of *School Library Journal* contributor Alicia Eames. And in *Pirican Pic and Pirican Mor,* Hugh Lupton's humorous retelling of a Scots folktale, Heo complements Lupton's text with "stylized" paintings that employ what *School Library Journal* contributor Mirima Lang Budin dubbed Heo's characteristic "wildy out-of-kilter perspective," resulting in a "jaunty, humorous" picture-book offering.

Pets! features a rhyming text by Melrose Cooper that tracks a young boy searching for the perfect pet in a circus tent. Commenting on Heo's illustrations, *School Library Journal* contributor Judith Constantinides praised her colorful contributions, which "reflect the rhymes with whimsy and humor, totally disregarding normal size relationships and perspective." The illustrator whips up another dose of stylized art for *The Snake's Tales,* Marguerite W. Davol's retelling of a Seneca tale. The story of a greedy snake that trades stories for food benefits from "cheerfully cluttered pencil-and-oil compositions [that] burn with activity," according to a *Publishers Weekly* reviewer. And in the wacky *Sometimes*

Anger over missing walnuts leads one on an unexpected journey. From **Pirican Pic and Pirican Mor,** *written by* **Hugh Lipton. Illustrated by Yumi Heo.**

I'm Bombaloo, Heo brings to life the tantrum protocol of author Rachel Vail's diminutive—and highly excitable—narrator, Katie, whose temper sometimes takes control. The illustrator employs "vibrant backgrounds, blocks of color, and carefully chosen images to depict Katie's emotional tornado," explained a *Publishers Weekly* contributor, while in *Kirkus Reviews,* a critic dubbed Heo's highly textural renderings "gloriously outlandish."

Heo's self-authored picture books combine her signature illustrations with original stories. In her first effort, *One Afternoon,* "the kinetic energy of life in the big city motors this zippy picture book right along," ac-

cording to a *Publishers Weekly* critic. The story of a little boy named Minho who spends his day running errands with his mother, *One Afternoon* emphasizes the loud noises the pair encounter everywhere they go, noises which appear as words within the illustrations. In addition, the illustrator presents each destination from the child's viewpoint; "perspective, comparative size, and realistic details are forgotten" in the process, explained Nancy Seiner in *School Library Journal,* who feared that Heo's "extraordinary arrangements of details" in her pictures might captivate some children, but would confound others. In *Booklist,* Nancy Vasilakis reveled in the author-artist's "freewheeling style," and

Katie gives her temper tantrums a name in **Sometimes I'm Bombaloo,** *written by Rachel Vail. (Illustrated by Heo.)*

concluded that the "vibrant look at bustling city life . . . offers ample opportunity for creative applications in group story sessions."

Minho appears again in *One Sunday Morning,* the 1999 sequel to *One Afternoon.* On a treasured day with his father, the young boy rides the subway, is entertained by street clowns, visits the zoo, and rides the carousel. It seems like a perfect day . . . until Minho wakes up

in his bed and realizes that it has all been a dream. Author and illustrator Heo supplements her simple story with kinetic illustrations, according to a *Kirkus Reviews* critic; Minho's busy day "is depicted in exuberant paintings filled with the artist's signature shapes and forms." Several contributors praised the book's onomatopoeic text—"clickety clack" goes the zoo train and "Whoosh" signals a passing bicyclist, while the footsteps of joggers make a rhythmic "thumpa-thumpa"—which com-

bines with Heo's illustrations to create a book tha"hums with energy and offers plenty to hear and behold," according to *Booklist* contributor Shelley Townsend-Hudson.

Father's Rubber Shoes tells the story of a young boy whose family has just moved to the United States from Korea. Yungsu is understandably lonely at his new school, but his father tells the story of the poverty he endured as a child in Korea—carrying his precious rubber shoes instead of wearing them—and explains that the family came to America so that Yungsu would have an easier childhood. "Heo's innovative compositions— flat, kinetic paintings incorporating many patterns and details—reflect Yungsu's changing feelings," observed Martha V. Parravano in *Horn Book*. While some critics found "the understated story too elusive for young children," as did *Booklist* reviewer Hazel Rochman, Heo's illustrations, which John Philbrook described in his review for *School Library Journal* as "primitive and appealing in [their] simplicity," were almost universally admired.

Heo retells a Korean folktale in her third self-illustrated picture book, *The Green Frogs: A Korean Folktale,* a *pourquoi* tale that explains why green frogs sing when it rains. The story of two naughty little frogs who love to disobey their mother comes to its "gleefully fatalistic" ending, according to a *Kirkus Reviews* critic, when their dying mother tries to trick them into burying her on a sunny hill by requesting that they bury her by the side of the stream. For once the frogs obey their mother's wish and thus, every time it rains, they sit by the side of the stream and cry, afraid that the rain will wash her grave away. "This is a quirkier pourquoi tale than most," *Horn Book* critic Nancy Vasilakis observed, "but it's too mischievous to be morbid." Others reached similar opinions, some pointing to what a critic for *Kirkus Reviews* called Heo's "magnificently eccentric illustrations" as the most successful element in the book. A reviewer for *Publishers Weekly* enthusiastically enjoined, "This Korean folktale is so beguilingly retold and visualized with such individuality that it deserves a wide audience."

Taking a break from picture-book illustration in the summer of 1997, a pregnant Heo left her studio to wander the subway stations and neighborhoods of Queens, New York, searching for inspiration for a new project: a thirty-piece colored-glass art installation sponsored by the New York Metropolitan Transit Authority. Dubbed "Q Is for Queens," the work was inspired by Heo's work on *A Is for Asia;* it includes a panel for each letter of the alphabet, as well as four additional panels denoting special landmarks and events. From "A Is for Aqueduct Raceway" to "Z Is for Zoo," the brightly colored glass panels are installed in subway stops at Thirty-third Street, Fortieth Street, and Forty-sixth Street in Queens. Commenting on the completed installation to *Publishers Weekly* contributor Karen Kawaguchi, Queens's borough president Claire Shulman praised Heo's work: "It represents what Queens is all about."

Biographical and Critical Sources

BOOKS

Heo, Yumi, *One Sunday Morning,* Orchard (New York, NY), 1999.

PERIODICALS

Booklist, June 1, 1994, Deborah Abbott, review of *The Rabbit's Judgement,* p. 1825; August, 1994, Mary Harris Veeder, review of *One Afternoon,* p. 2048; September 15, 1995, Hazel Rochman, review of *Father's Rubber Shoes,* p. 175; July, 1996, Stephanie Zvirin, review of *The Green Frogs: A Korean Folktale,* p. 1827; November 15, 1996, p. 589; March 1, 1997, Hazel Rochman, review of *A Is for Asia,* p. 1165; April 1, 1999, Shelley Townsend-Hudson, review of *One Sunday Morning,* p. 1420; March 1, 2000, Gillian Engberg, review of *Yoshi's Feast,* p. 1242; April 1, 2003, John Peters, review of *Pirican Pic and Pirican Mor,* p. 1394.
Bulletin of the Center for Children's Books, February, 1997, p. 198; November, 1997, Deborah Stevenson, "Yumi Heo."
Horn Book, November, 1994, Nancy Vasilakis, review of *One Afternoon,* pp. 719-720; September, 1995, Nancy Vasilakis, review of *The Rabbit's Escape,* p. 613; November-December, 1995, Martha V. Parravano, review of *Father's Rubber Shoes,* p. 733; November, 1996, Nancy Vasilakis, review of *The Green Frogs,* pp. 748-749; March, 1999, Nancy Vasilakis, review of *One Sunday Morning,* p. 190; May, 2000, review of *Yoshi's Feast,* p. 325; July-August, 2003, Susan Dove Lempke, review of *Pirican Pic and Pirican Mor,* p. 471.
Kirkus Reviews, March 1, 1994, review of *The Rabbit's Judgment,* p. 305; June 1, 1996, review of *The Green Frogs,* p. 823; September 1, 1996, review of *The Lonely Lioness and the Ostrich Chicks,* p. 1318; March 15, 1997, p. 459; February, 1999, review of *One Sunday Morning,* p. 300; January 1, 2002, review of *Sometimes I'm Bombaloo,* p. 53; August 15, 2002, review of *The Snake's Tales,* p. 1221.
Publishers Weekly, March 7, 1994, review of *The Rabbit's Judgment,* pp. 70-71; July 4, 1994, Sally Lodge, "Flying Starts: Seven Talents New to the Children's Book Scene Talk about Their Debuts," pp. 36-41; July 11, 1994, review of *One Afternoon,* p. 77; April 3, 1995, review of *The Rabbit's Escape,* p. 62; October 2, 1995, review of *Father's Rubber Shoes,* p. 72; August 26, 1996, review of *The Green Frogs,* pp. 96-97; October

7, 1996, p. 73; February 3, 1997, review of *A Is for Asia,* p. 106; January 19, 1998, review of *Pets!,* p. 377; August 17, 1998, review of *So Say the Little Monkeys,* p. 70; February 8, 1999, review of *One Sunday Morning,* p. 212; February 28, 2000, review of *Yoshi's Feast,* p. 80; March 13, 2000, Karen Kawaguchi, "'Q Is for Queens' Lights up the Flushing Line," p. 33; April 9, 2001, review of *Henry's First-Moon Birthday,* p. 73; December 24, 2001, review of *Sometimes I'm Bombaloo,* p. 63; July 22, 2002, review of *The Snake's Tales,* p. 177; February 17, 2003, review of *Pirican Pic and Pirican Mor,* p. 75.

School Library Journal, June, 1994, p. 119; November, 1994, Nancy Seiner, review of *One Afternoon,* pp. 81-82; June, 1995, Lisa S. Murphy, review of *The Rabbit's Escape,* pp. 101-102; November, 1995, John Philbrook, review of *Father's Rubber Shoes,* p. 74;

April, 1998, Judith Constantinides, review of *Pets!,* p. 97; September, 1998, Alicia Eames, review of *So Say the Little Monkeys,* pp. 198-199; April, 1999, Carol Schene, review of *One Sunday Morning,* p. 97; June, 2001, Alice Casey Smith, review of *Henry's First-Moon Birthday,* p. 126; September, 2002, Susan Pine, review of *The Snake's Tales,* p. 183; May, 2003, Miriam Lang Budin, review of *Pirican Pic and Pirican Mor,* p. 138.

ONLINE

Cooperative Children's Book Center Web Site, http://www.soemadison.wisc.edu/ccbc/ (June 26, 2003), "Yumi Heo."

Storyopolis Art Gallery, http://www.storyopolis.com/ (September 17, 2003), artist portfolio of Yumi Heo.

I

ICHIKAWA, Satomi 1949-

Personal

Born January 15, 1949, in Gifu, Japan; moved to Paris, France, 1971; daughter of Harumi (a teacher) and Nobuko Ichikawa. *Education:* Attended college in Japan. *Hobbies and other interests:* Collecting dolls (used), piano, dance.

Addresses

Home—Paris, France. *Agent*—c/o Author Mail, Philomel Books, 375 Hudson St., New York, NY 10014.

Career

Author and illustrator of books for children, 1974—. *Exhibitions:* Gallery Printemps Ginza, Japan, 1984.

Awards, Honors

Special mention for Prix "Critici in Erba," Bologna Children's Book Fair, 1978, for *Suzette et Nicolas au marché;* Kodansha Prize (Japan), 1978, for illustrations in *Sun through Small Leaves: Poems of Spring;* Sankei Prize (Japan), 1981, for illustrations in *Keep Running, Allen!;* Notable Book selection, American Library Association, for *Dance, Tanya.*

Writings

SELF-ILLUSTRATED

A *Child's Book of Seasons* (poetry), Heinemann (London, England), 1975, Parents' Magazine Press (New York, NY), 1976.

Friends, Heinemann (London, England), 1976, Parents' Magazine Press (New York, NY), 1977.

Suzette et Nicolas dans leur jardin, Gautier-Languereau (Paris, France), 1976, translated by Denise Sheldon as *Suzanne and Nicholas in the Garden,* F. Watts (New York, NY), 1977.

Satomi Ichikawa

Suzette et Nicolas au marché, Gautier-Languereau (Paris, France), 1977, translated by Denise Sheldon as *Suzanne and Nicholas at the Market,* F. Watts (New York, NY), 1977, adaptation by Robina Beckles Wilson published as *Sophie and Nicky Go to Market,* Heinemann (London, England), 1984.

Let's Play, Philomel (New York, NY), 1981.

Children through Four Seasons, Kaisei-sha (Tokyo, Japan), 1981.

Angels Descending from the Sky, Kaisei-sha (Tokyo, Japan), 1983.

Children in Paris (two volumes), Kaisei-sha (Japan), 1984.

Furui oshiro no otomodachi, Kaisei-sha (Tokyo, Japan), 1984, translated as *Nora's Castle,* Philomel (New York, NY), 1986.

Beloved Dolls, Kaisei-sha (Tokyo, Japan), 1985.

Nora's Stars, translated from the Japanese, Philomel (New York, NY), 1989.

Nora's Duck, translated from the Japanese, Philomel (New York, NY), 1991.

Nora's Roses, translated from the Japanese, Philomel (New York, NY), 1993.

(With Patricia Lee Gauch) *Fickle Barbara,* Philomel (New York, NY), 1993.

Nora's Surprise, translated from the Japanese, Philomel (New York, NY), 1994.

Please Come to Tea!, Heinemann (London, England), 1994.

Isabela's Ribbons, Philomel (New York, NY), 1995.

La robe de Nöel, L'école des loisirs (Paris, France), 1999, translated as *What the Little Fir Tree Wore to the Christmas Party,* Philomel (New York, NY), 2001.

The First Bear in Africa!, Philomel (New York, NY), 2001.

My Pig Amarillo: A Tale from Guatemala, Philomel (New York, NY), 2003.

La-La Rose, Philomel (New York, NY), 2003.

ILLUSTRATOR

Elaine Moss, compiler, *From Morn to Midnight* (poetry), Crowell (New York, NY), 1977.

Clyde R. Bulla, *Keep Running, Allen!,* Crowell (New York, NY), 1978.

Marie-France Mangin, *Suzette et Nicolas et l'horloge des quatre saisons,* Gautier-Languereau (Paris, France), 1978, published as *Suzanne and Nicholas and the Four Seasons,* F. Watts (New York, NY), 1978, translation by Joan Chevalier published as *Suzette and Nicholas and the Seasons Clock,* Philomel (New York, NY), 1982, adaptation by Robina Beckles Wilson published as *Sophie and Nicky and the Four Seasons,* Heinemann (London, England), c. 1985.

Cynthia Mitchell, *Playtime* (poetry), Heinemann (London, England), 1978, Collins (New York, NY), 1979.

Cynthia Mitchell, compiler, *Under the Cherry Tree* (poetry), Collins (New York, NY), 1979.

Michelle Lochak and Marie-France Mangin, *Suzette et Nicolas et le cirque des enfants,* Gautier-Languereau (Paris, France), 1979, translation by Joan Chevalier published as *Suzanne and Nicholas and the Sunijudi Circus,* Philomel (New York, NY), 1980.

Marcelle Vérité, *Suzette et Nicolas aiment les animaux,* Gautier-Languereau (Paris, France), 1980.

Marcelle Vérité, *Suzette et Nicolas au Zoo,* Gautier-Languereau (Paris, France), 1980.

Robina Beckles Wilson, *Sun through Small Leaves: Poems of Spring,* Collins (New York, NY), 1980.

Marcelle Vérité, *Shiki no kodomotachi,* Kaisei-sha (Tokyo, Japan), 1981.

Martine Jaureguiberry, *La joyeuse semaine de Suzette et Nicolas,* Gautier-Languereau (Paris, France), 1981, translation by Joan Chevalier published as *The Wonderful Rainy Week: A Book of Indoor Games,* Philomel (New York, NY), 1983.

Resie Pouyanne, *Suzette et Nicolas: L'Annee en fetes,* Gautier-Languereau (Paris, France), 1982.

Robina Beckles Wilson, *Merry Christmas! Children at Christmastime around the World,* Philomel (New York, NY), 1983.

Resie Pouyanne, *Suzette et Nicolas font le tour du monde,* Gautier-Languereau (Paris, France), 1984.

Cynthia Mitchell, editor, *Here a Little Child I Stand: Poems of Prayer and Praise for Children,* Putnam (New York, NY), 1985.

Marie-France Mangin, *Sophie bout de chou,* Gautier-Languereau (Paris, France), 1987.

Elizabeth Laird, *Happy Birthday!: A Book of Birthday Celebrations,* Philomel (New York, NY), 1988.

Sylvia Clouzeau, *Butterfingers,* translated from the French by Didi Charney, Aladdin Books (New York, NY), 1988.

Marie-France Mangin, *Sophie and Simon,* Macmillan (New York, NY), 1988.

Patricia Lee Gauch, *Dance, Tanya* (also see below), Philomel (New York, NY), 1989.

Elizabeth Laird, *Rosy's Garden: A Child's Keepsake of Flowers,* Philomel (New York, NY), 1990.

Patricia Lee Gauch, *Bravo, Tanya,* Philomel (New York, NY), 1992.

Patricia Lee Gauch, *Fickle Barbara,* Philomel (New York, NY), 1993.

Patricia Lee Gauch, *Tanya and Emily in a Dance for Two* (also see below), Philomel (New York, NY), 1994.

Patricia Lee Gauch, *Tanya Steps Out,* Philomel (New York, NY), 1996.

Patricia Lee Gauch, *Tanya and the Magic Wardrobe,* Philomel (New York, NY), 1997.

Eiko Kadono, *Grandpa's Soup,* Eerdmans (Grand Rapids, MI), 1999.

Janet Taylor Lisle, *The Lost Flower Children,* Puffin (New York, NY), 1999.

Patricia Lee Gauch, *Presenting Tanya, the Ugly Duckling* (also see below), Philomel (New York, NY), 2000.

Maryann K. Cusimano, *You Are My I Love You,* Philomel (New York, NY), 2001.

Patricia Lee Gauch, *Tanya and the Red Shoes,* Philomel (New York, NY), 2002.

Patricia Lee Gauch, *The Tanya Treasury* (contains *Dance, Tanya, Tanya and Emily in a Dance for Two,* and *Presenting Tanya, the Ugly Duckling,* Philomel (New York, NY), 2002.

Sidelights

Japanese-born Satomi Ichikawa lives in Paris, France, where she creates books and illustrations for children. Ichikawa's life has not lacked adventure or daring. She taught herself to draw after being inspired by a famous French illustrator and then submitted her work to an English publisher without benefit of agent or network contacts. More than thirty years after deciding to illustrate books, she is still kept busy on her own stories and those of others, including the popular "Tanya" series about a budding young ballerina. *School Library Journal* correspondent Jacqueline Elsner called

An aspiring young dancer and mentor put on a performance—backstage. From **Tanya and the Magic Wardrobe,** *written by Patricia Lee Gauch. (Illustrated by Satomi Ichikawa.)*

Ichikawa's illustrations "masterful," adding that each figure the artist draws, "whether animal, toy, or person, is full of life, humor, and expression in every gesture."

Unlike many prominent illustrators, Ichikawa had not been drawing for years before submitting her work to publishers. She had not thought, as a child, that she would be interested in illustrating children's books. "I had no idea what I wanted to become," she once told *SATA.* "I took a general course of study for women in college. Girls in Japan were usually expected to work for a few years after college and then get married."

Although she was unsure of her career goals, Ichikawa was sure that she wanted to experience life beyond the small town in which she grew up. Some Italian friends she had met in Japan persuaded her to visit them in Italy, and from there she took a trip to France. When she explored Paris, as she recalled, "I felt at home right away. . . . Japan is beautiful, all of my family is there,

but I grew up in the countryside where people are more conservative and where traditions tend to be restrictive." In Paris, Ichikawa "discovered true freedom of spirit." She decided to live permanently in Paris, and while working as an *au pair* (a live-in governess) to support herself, she began to study French.

It was at that time that Ichikawa encountered the work of illustrator Maurice Boutet de Monvel, who died in 1913. Moved by his gentle watercolors, she began to search for his books in second-hand book shops. "I didn't know whether Boutet de Monvel was alive or dead," she told Herbert R. Lottman in *Publishers Weekly.* "But I fell in love with his work and wanted to try something of my own. In Paris you are nothing if you don't work."

Inspired by Boutet de Monvel's example, Ichikawa began to draw. "Since I had never drawn before, I started by observing real life in the gardens and in the playgrounds of Paris," she once related to *SATA*. While she viewed the reality she was drawing with the images of Boutet de Monvel in mind, Ichikawa gradually began to develop her own style. "Although I am Japanese," she explained, "my drawings are more European, because my awakening happened here. While I lived in Japan, I never paid much attention to its special beauty, so that it is difficult for me to draw Japanese children and scenes." What has transpired for the well-traveled artist is a bibliography that celebrates multiculturalism. She has written and illustrated books set in Guatemala, Africa, Japan, France, and England, and some of her work—especially that featuring animals—is quite simply universal.

As Lottman noted in *Publishers Weekly,* "Ichikawa's initial attempts to have her work published were filled with as much verve . . . as the rest of her life." During a vacation in England, Ichikawa walked into a London bookstore and copied the names and addresses of children's book editors from the books on the shelf. She then visited the editor with the closest address, Heinemann. After perusing the thirty drawings Ichikawa had brought with her, the editor decided to publish her illustrations and the ideas behind them as *A Child's Book of Seasons.* In a review for *Horn Book,* Ethel L. Heins described the illustrations as "charming, beautifully composed." Ichikawa's career as an illustrator had begun.

Since the publication of that first work, Ichikawa has seen her own books and books that she has illustrated published in various languages in England, France, the United States, and Japan. Especially notable among these books is the "Suzanne and Nicholas" series. In the first, *Suzanne and Nicholas in the Garden,* originally published as *Suzette et Nicolas dans leur jardin,* the children enjoy a summer day in the garden. When Nicholas informs Suzanne that another world exists outside the garden, Suzanne decides that the garden is big enough, "for the moment." As Gayle Celizic wrote in *School Library Journal,* the book conveys a "sense of peace and contentment."

Suzanne and Nicholas continue their adventures in *Suzanne and Nicholas at the Market,* originally published as *Suzette et Nicolas au marché,* and *Suzanne and Nicholas and the Seasons Clock,* written by Marie-France Mangin and first appearing in France as *Suzette et Nicolas et l'horloge des quatre saisons.* *Junior Bookshelf* critic Berna Clark found the illustrations in *Suzanne and Nicholas at the Market* to be "very charming." Similarly, *School Library Journal* correspondent Jane F. Cullinane commended *Suzanne and Nicholas and the Seasons Clock* for its "delightful pastel illustrations."

Also prominent in Ichikawa's work is the series of "Nora" books that she conceived and wrote herself. The inspiration for the creation of the first of these came from Ichikawa's summer stay in a friend's castle. As she once remembered in *SATA,* "There was no electric-

ity, and every night I went to my room with a candle—going up and down stairs and walking along endless hallways. I stayed there for a month and a half and had no intention of working. But I was so inspired that I wrote the story of a little girl visiting this castle and in every room she discovers a presence—a king, an old piano—reminders of another life." Ichikawa especially enjoyed the creation of *Nora's Castle,* the first book which she developed "from beginning to end—a very satisfying experience," she said, adding, "I have come to see that this is the best way to work."

The "Nora" books have been generally well received. *Nora's Stars,* in which Nora's toys come alive at night and help her gather the stars from the sky, was described as "charming" and "cozy" by Jane Yolen in the *Los Angeles Times Book Review.* Sally R. Dow, writing for *School Library Journal,* noted favorably the "whimsical mood of this quiet bedtime fantasy." In *Nora's Duck,* Nora finds a wounded duckling and takes it to Doctor John, who provides care and a home for other stricken animals on his farm. Doctor John lovingly tends to the duckling, and Nora takes it back to its pond to be reunited with its mother. Ann A. Flowers wrote in *Horn Book* that the "quiet delicacy" of Ichikawa's illustrations "mirrors the compassion and trust of the story." A reviewer for *Kirkus Reviews* commented that Ichikawa's "sweet, precise style is perfect for this idyll," and Jody McCoy related in *School Library Journal* that the book is an "excellent choice to encourage discussion of the humane treatment of animals."

In *Nora's Roses,* Nora is home with a bad cold. She passes the time by watching passersby enjoy her blooming rose bush. When a hungry cow robs the bush of all but one last bloom, Nora preserves the only rose left by drawing a picture of it. Carolyn Phelan of *Booklist* observed that Ichikawa's technique "captures . . . the beauty of a rose in bloom, and the determination of a young child." A critic for *Quill & Quire* also praised Ichikawa, proclaiming that her "illustrative technique is a delight." In her *School Library Journal* review, Lori A. Janick commented: "The story has a gentle sweetness enhanced by exquisite watercolor illustrations."

Ichikawa once told *SATA* that the books *Dance, Tanya; Bravo, Tanya;* and *Tanya and Emily in a Dance for Two,* the first three installments in the "Tanya" series, are very important in her life. "This is the first time that my love for dance and my drawing have joined," she said. "Thanks to P. L. Gauch, who wrote these stories of Tanya especially for me!" When readers first meet Tanya in *Dance, Tanya,* she is a preschooler who loves to dance and who envies her older sister, who gets to go to dancing school and be in recitals. After attending her sister's recital, Tanya beguiles her family by dancing her own version of "Swan Lake." Her reward comes soon after: her own leotard and dancing slippers, and lessons at her sister's school. Denise Wilms said of *Dance, Tanya* in *Booklist,* "Gauch's sweet story gains strength from Ichikawa's soft watercolor paintings."

Tanya's adventures continue in further books, including *Bravo, Tanya, Tanya and the Red Shoes, Tanya and Emily in a Dance for Two, Presenting Tanya, the Ugly Duckling,* and *Tanya Steps Out.* All of these stories communicate not only a love of classical ballet, but also the frustrations and challenges of learning to perform a demanding art. In *Tanya and the Red Shoes,* for instance, Tanya gets the pointe shoes she has longed for—and the blisters, calluses, and clumsiness that goes with them. *Tanya and Emily in a Dance for Two* describes the budding friendship between Tanya and Emily, the best dancer in the class. The girls find inspiration from each other when Tanya teaches Emily to dance like the animals at the zoo, and Emily helps Tanya to perfect her *cabriolet. Bravo, Tanya* was commended by a *Kirkus Reviews* contributor, who wrote that "Ichikawa captures the joy and energy of the dance in her sensitive paintings." In her *Horn Book* review of *Tanya and Emily in a Dance for Two,* Hanna B. Zeiger noted that Tanya's escapades provide "a delight for the dancer hidden in all of us."

Ichikawa has set some of her picture books in locations far removed from her home in Paris. *Isabela's Ribbons* features a Puerto-Rican youngster in her verdant tropical milieu. Isabel loves ribbons and hide-and-seek, but no other children want to play with her. However, when her fantasies begin to run away with her, she finally makes new friends. A *Publishers Weekly* critic wrote: "Gaily patterned watercolors packed with playful details make this book a joy to behold."

The animals of the African savanna work together with a young boy to help reunite a teddy bear with its owner in *The First Bear in Africa!* Meto is fascinated when a family of tourists visits his village with a teddy bear as he has never seen a bear before. When the toy gets left behind, Meto runs across the savanna after the family, pausing only to show the strange beast to the lion, hippo, giraffe, and elephant that he meets on the way. A *Publishers Weekly* reviewer deemed the book "a light, appealing caper," while *School Library Journal* contributor Alicia Eames called it "a sweet and idealized tale of universal fellowship."

Ichikawa spins another universal tale through an exotic location in *My Pig Amarillo: A Tale from Guatemala.* Pablito is delighted when he is given a pet pig, and soon pig and boy have become fast friends. When Amarillo the pig disappears without a trace, Pablito searches endlessly and weeps into his pillow when Amarillo fails to return. It falls to Pablito's grandfather to school the boy on coping with grief and loss. Claiming the work is "sure to become a classic," a *Kirkus Reviews* critic called the volume "a masterpiece of picture-book making." *Booklist*'s Ilene Cooper commented favorably on the way Ichikawa "wraps the story in universal emotions: love, longing, grief, hope."

Although Ichikawa is writing more of her own books, she still finds time to illustrate some titles by other authors. *You Are My I Love You,* written by Maryann K. Cusimano, explores the love between a mother and child teddy bear as they share a day together. A *Publishers*

Meto calls upon his jungle friends to help him return a stuffed bear to its rightful owner, in Ichikawa's self-illustrated story The First Bear in Africa.

Weekly reviewer noted that the text and illustrations work together, "instantly communicating all that the reader needs to know about the wonders of loving and being loved." In *Grandpa's Soup,* written by Eiko Kadono, a grieving widower learns to communicate with the world again by trying over and over to re-create his wife's meatball soup. The story made its debut in Japan, but according to Marta Segal in *Booklist,* its "gentle lessons on coping with grief are applicable to any culture."

Ichikawa works very hard at her craft, often turning out as many as three books a year. According to Michael Patrick Hearn in a *Horn Book* article, Boutet de Monvel's work "is kept alive" through Ichikawa's art; as her illustrations continue to delight children around the world. Several decades after her departure from Japan, she continues to live in Paris. Because, as she once commented, an "artist must feel complete freedom in order to create," her work is enriched by her life in the city. Ichikawa once asserted, "Coming to Paris was a rebirth for me." Her paintings that capture the exuberance, imagination, and joy of childhood have found fans all over the world.

Biographical and Critical Sources

BOOKS

Children's Literature Review, Volume 62, Gale (Detroit, MI), 2000.

Pablito and Amarillo are the best of friends in* My Pig Amarillo, *written and illustrated by Ichikawa.

Ichikawa, Satomi, *Suzanne and Nicholas in the Garden,* F. Watts (New York, NY), 1977.

PERIODICALS

Booklist, September 1, 1989, Denise Wilms, review of *Dance, Tanya,* pp. 70-71; March 15, 1993, Carolyn Phelan, review of *Nora's Roses,* p. 1360; December 1, 1999, Marta Segal, review of *Grandpa's Soup,* p. 712; September 1, 2001, GraceAnne A. DeCandido, review of *What the Little Fir Tree Wore to the Christmas Party,* p. 120; April 1, 2003, Ilene Cooper, review of *My Pig Amarillo: A Tale from Guatemala,* p. 1396.

Five Owls, September-October, 1994, review of *Nora's Surprise,* p. 12.

Horn Book, June, 1976, Ethel L. Heins, review of *A Child's Book of Seasons,* pp. 280-281; April, 1979, Michael Patrick Hearn, "Satomi Ichikawa," p. 180; March, 1992, Ann A. Flowers, review of *Nora's Duck,* p. 191; November-December, 1994, Hanna B. Zeiger, review of *Tanya and Emily in a Dance for Two,* p. 718; May, 1999, review of *The Lost Flower Children,* p. 333.

Junior Bookshelf, April, 1978, Berna Clark, review of *Suzanne and Nicholas at the Market,* p. 89.

Kirkus Reviews, May 1, 1989, review of *Nora's Stars,* p. 693; November 1, 1991, review of *Nora's Duck,* p. 1404; April 1, 1992, review of *Bravo, Tanya,* p. 464; May 1, 2003, review of *My Pig Amarillo,* p. 678.

Los Angeles Times Book Review, June 4, 1989, Jane Yolen, review of *Nora's Stars,* p. 11.

Publishers Weekly, June 7, 1993, Herbert R. Lottman, "In the Studio with Satomi Ichikawa," p. 19; August 21, 1995, review of *Isabela's Ribbons,* p. 65; April 12, 1999, review of *The Lost Flower Children,* p. 75; November 8, 1999, review of *Grandpa's Soup,* p. 66; March 12, 2001, review of *The First Bear in Africa!,* p. 90; April 9, 2001, review of *You Are My I Love You,* p. 73; May 12, 2003, review of *My Pig Amarillo,* p. 66.

Quill & Quire, April, 1993, Joanne Schott, review of *Nora's Roses,* p. 36.

School Library Journal, April, 1983, Jane F. Cullinane, review of *Suzette and Nicholas and the Seasons Clock,* p. 104; March, 1987, Gayle Celizic, review of *Suzette and Nicholas in the Garden,* p. 146; July, 1989, Sally R. Dow, review of *Nora's Stars,* pp. 66-67; November, 1991, Jody McCoy, review of *Nora's Duck,* p. 1404; June, 1993, Lori A. Janick, review of *Nora's Roses,* pp. 77-78; May, 1994, Jacqueline Elsner, review of *Nora's Surprise,* p. 96; September, 1994, Cheri Estes, review of *Tanya and Emily in a Dance for Two,* p. 184; June, 1999, Susan Pine, review of *Presenting Tanya, the Ugly Duckling,* pp. 95-96; June, 2001, Alicia Eames, review of *The First Bear in Africa!,* p. 118; October, 2001, review of *What the Little Fir Tree Wore to the Christmas Party,* p. 66; May, 2003, Marge Loch-Wouters, review of *My Pig Amarillo,* p. 122.*

J

JAMES, J. Alison 1962-

Personal

Born March 8, 1962, in Escondito, CA; daughter of Norman and Ednah Illsley; married Joplin James (a teacher), June 21, 1986; children: Anika, McKinley. *Education:* Vassar College, A.B., 1983; Simmons College, M.A., 1985. *Politics:* "Progressive." *Religion:* Society of Friends (Quaker).

Addresses

Agent—Robert Lescher, Lescher & Lescher, 47 East 19th St., New York, NY 10003.

Career

Author and translator, 1984—. Librarian in Everett, MA, Milton, VT, Lincoln, VT, and Lake Placid, NY, 1985-91; English as a second language teacher in Okayama, Japan, 1994-95, and Oslo, Norway, 1995-96. Director of Kindling Words, an annual conference for published authors and illustrators of children's books, 1992—.

Awards, Honors

Highest honor for fiction award, Society of School Librarians International, Best Books for Young Adults selection, American Library Association, Young Adults Choice selection, Children's Book Council/International Reading Association, and Book for the Teen Age, New York Public Library, all for *Sing for a Gentle Rain;* Notable Social Studies Trade Book, National Council for the Social Studies/Children's Book Council, 2000, for *The Drums of Noto Hanto;* Christopher Medal for translation of *The Rainbow Fish.*

Writings

Sing for a Gentle Rain, Atheneum (New York, NY), 1990.
Runa, Atheneum (New York, NY), 1993.

Eucalyptus Wings, illustrated by Demi, Atheneum (New York, NY), 1995.
The Drums of Noto Hanto, illustrated by Tsukushi, DK Ink (New York, NY), 1999.

Also contributor of entries to *The Reader's Companion to Children's Literature,* edited by Anita Silver, Houghton (Boston, MA), 1995. Contributor of "The Audition," to *What a Song Can Do,* edited by Jennifer Armstrong, Knopf (New York, NY), 2004.

FOR CHILDREN; TRANSLATOR

Tilde Michels, *Rabbit Spring,* illustrated by Käthi Bhend, Harcourt (New York, NY), 1988.
Marcus Pfister, *The Rainbow Fish,,* North-South Books (New York, NY), 1992.
Ingrid Ostheeren, *Fabian Youngpig Sails the World,* illustrated by Serena Romanelli, North-South Books (New York, NY), 1992.
Eleonore Schmid, *The Air around Us,* North-South Books (New York, NY), 1992.
Ursel Scheffler, *Rinaldo the Sly Fox,* illustrated by Iskender Gider, North-South Books (New York, NY), 1992.
Hans de Beer, *The Little Polar Bear and the Brave Little Hare,* North-South Books (New York, NY), 1992.
Gerda Marie Scheidl, *Loretta and the Little Fairy,* illustrated by Christa Unzner-Fischer, North-South Books (New York, NY), 1992.
Coby Hol, *Niki's Little Donkey,* North-South Books (New York, NY), 1993.
Pirkko Vainio, *The Snow Goose,* North-South Books (New York, NY), 1993.
Marcus Pfister, *The Christmas Star,* North-South Books (New York, NY), 1993.
Ingrid Ostheeren, *The New Dog,* illustrated by Jean-Pierre Corderoc'h, North-South Books (New York, NY), 1993.
Ursel Scheffler, *The Return of Rinaldo the Sly Fox,* illustrated by Iskender Gider, North-South Books (New York, NY), 1993.

Winfried Wolf, *Christmas with Grandfather,* pictures by Eugen Sopko, North-South Books (New York, NY), 1994.

Dominique Falda, *Night Flight,* North-South Books (New York, NY), 1994.

Ingrid Ostheeren, *Martin and the Pumpkin Ghost,* illustrated by Christa Unzner-Fischer, North-South Books (New York, NY), 1994.

Gerda Marie Scheidl, *The Moon Man,* illustrated by Jozef Wildon, North-South Books (New York, NY), 1994.

Wolfram Hänel, *Lila's Little Dinosaur,* illustrated by Alex de Wolf, North-South Books (New York, NY), 1994.

Wolfram Hänel, *The Extraordinary Adventures of an Ordinary Hat,* illustrated by Christa Unzner-Fischer, North-South Books (New York, NY), 1994.

Wolfram Hänel, *Mia the Beach Cat,* illustrated by Kirsten Höcker, North-South Books (New York, NY), 1994.

Burny Bos, *Meet the Molesons,* illustrated by Hans de Beer, North-South Books (New York, NY), 1994.

Marcus Pfister, *Dazzle the Dinosaur,* North-South Books (New York, NY), 1994.

Marcus Pfister, *Rainbow Fish to the Rescue!,* North-South Books (New York, NY), 1995.

Marianne Busser and Ron Schröder, *On the Road with Poppa Wopper,* illustrated by Hans de Beer, North-South Books (New York, NY), 1995.

Dominique Falda, *The Angel and the Child: An Incidental Incident in Twelve Scenes,* North-South Books (New York, NY), 1995.

Ursel Scheffler, *Rinaldo on the Run,* illustrated by Iskender Gider, North-South Books (New York, NY), 1995.

Jürgen Lässig, *Spiny,* illustrated by Uli Waas, North-South Books (New York, NY), 1995.

Krista Ruepp, *Midnight Rider,* illustrated by Ulrike Heyne, North-South Books (New York, NY), 1995.

Burny Bos, *More from the Molesons,* illustrated by Hans de Beer, North-South Books (New York, NY), 1995.

Hannelore Voigt, *Not Now, Sara!,* illustrated by Olivier Corthésy and Nicolas Fossati, North-South Books (New York, NY), 1995.

Antonie Schneider, *You Shall Be King,* illustrated by Christa Unzner, North-South Books (New York, NY), 1995.

Burny Bos, *Leave It to the Molesons!,* illustrated by Hans de Beer, North-South Books (New York, NY), 1995.

Antonie Schneider, *The Birthday Bear,* illustrated by Uli Waas, North-South Books (New York, NY), 1996.

Tanja Székessy, *A Princess in Boxland,* North-South Books (New York, NY), 1996.

Dorothea Lachner, *A Gift from Saint Nicholas,* North-South Books (New York, NY), 1996.

Marianne Busser and Ron Schröder, *King Bobble,* North-South Books (New York, NY), 1996.

Marcus Pfister, *Wake Up, Santa Claus!,* North-South Books (New York, NY), 1996.

Wolfram Hänel, *The Other Side of the Bridge,* illustrated by Alex de Wolf, North-South Books (New York, NY), 1996.

Ingrid Uebe, *Melinda and Nock and the Magic Spell,* illustrated by Alex de Wolf, North-South Books (New York, NY), 1996.

Wolfgang Bittner, *Wake Up, Grizzly!,* illustrated by Gustavo Rosemffet, North-South Books (New York, NY), 1996.

Dorothea Lachner, *Meredith, The Witch Who Wasn't,* illustrated by Christa Unzner, North-South Books (New York, NY), 1997.

Gerda Marie Scheidl, *Andy's Wild Animal Adventure,* illustrated by Gisela Dürr, North-South Books (New York, NY), 1997.

Krista Ruepp, *Horses in the Fog,* North-South Books (New York, NY), 1997.

Pirkko Vainio, *The Dream House,* North-South Books (New York, NY), 1997.

Gerda Wagner, *The Ghost in the Classroom,* illustrated by Uli Waas, North-South Books (New York, NY), 1997.

Wilhelm Gruber, *The Upside-Down Reader,* illustrated by Marlies Rieper-Bastian, North-South Books (New York, NY), 1998.

Marcus Pfister, *Rainbow Fish and the Big Blue Whale,* North-South Books (New York, NY), 1998.

Marcus Pfister, *How Leo Learned to Be King,* North-South Books (New York, NY), 1998.

Antonie Schneider, *Good Bye, Vivi!,* illustrated by Maja Dusíková, North-South Books (New York, NY), 1998.

Udo Weigelt, *The Strongest Mouse in the World,* illustrated by Nicolas d'Aujourd'hui, North-South Books (New York, NY), 1998.

Antonie Schneider, *Luke the Lionhearted,* illustrated by Cristina Kadmon, North-South Books (New York, NY), 1998.

Brigitte Schär, *The Blind Fairy,* illustrated by Julia Gukova, North-South Books (New York, NY), 1998.

Adele Sansone, *The Little Green Goose,* North-South Books (New York, NY), 1999.

Wolfram Hänel, *Mary and the Mystery Dog,* illustrated by Kirsten Höcker, North-South Books (New York, NY), 1999.

Anne Liersch, *A House Is Not a Home,* illustrated by Christa Unzner, North-South Books (New York, NY), 1999.

Udo Weigelt, *All Weather Friends,* illustrated by Nicolas d'Aujourd'hui, North-South Books (New York, NY), 1999.

Udo Weigelt, *Hiding Horatio,* illustrated by Alexander Reichstein, North-South Books (New York, NY), 1999.

Ulli Schubert, *Harry's Got a Girlfriend,* illustrated by Wolfgang Slawski, North-South Books (New York, NY),1999.

Antonie Schneider, *Come Back, Pigeon,* illustrated by Uli Waas, North-South Books (New York, NY), 1999.

Rolf Siegenthaler, *Never Fear, Snake My Dear,* North-South Books (New York, NY), 1999.

Gerda Marie Scheidl, *Tommy's New Sister,* illustrated by Christa Unzner, North-South Books (New York, NY), 1999.

Bruno Hächler, *The Bears' Christmas Surprise,* illustrated by Angela Kehlenbeck, North-South Books (New York, NY), 2000.

Brigitte Weninger, adapter, *Elf's Hat,* North-South Books (New York, NY), 2000.

Wolfram Hänel, *Little Elephant's Song,* illustrated by Christa Kadmon, North-South Books (New York, NY), 2000.

Ursel Scheffler, *Be Brave, Little Lion!,* illustrated by Ruth Scholte van Mast, North-South Books (New York, NY), 2000.

Udo Weigelt, *Who Stole the Gold?,* illustrated by Julia Gukova, North-South Books (New York, NY), 2000.

Dorothea Lachner, *Danny, the Angry Lion,* illustrated by Gusti, North-South Books (New York, NY), 2000.

Burny Bos, *Fun with the Molesons,* illustrated by Hans de Beer, North-South Books (New York, NY), 2000.

Dorothea Lachner, *Meredith's Mixed-Up Magic,* illustrated by Christa Unzner, North-South Books (New York, NY), 2000.

Brigitte Weninger, *Special Delivery,* illustrated by Alexander Reichstein, North-South Books (New York, NY), 2000.

Burny Bos, *Alexander the Great,* illustrated by Hans de Beer, North-South Books (New York, NY), 2000.

Marcus Pfister, *Happy Hedgehog,* North-South Books (New York, NY), 2000.

Udo Weigelt, *The Easter Bunny's Baby,* illustrated by Rolf Siegenthaler, North-South Books (New York, NY), 2000.

Kerstin Chen, *Lord of the Cranes,* illustrated by Jian Jiang Chen, North-South Books (New York, NY), 2000.

Pirkko Vainio, *Best of Friends,* North-South Books (New York, NY), 2000.

Francesca Bosca, *The Apple King,* illustrated by Giuliano Ferri, North-South Books (New York, NY), 2001.

Wolfram Hänel, *Little Elephant Runs Away,* illustrated by Christina Kadmon, North-South Books (New York, NY), 2001.

Anne Liersch, *Nell and Fluffy,* illustrated by Christa Unzner, North-South Books (New York, NY), 2001.

Gerlinde Wiencirz, *Teddy's Easter Secret,* illustrated by Giuliano Lunelli, North-South Books (New York, NY), 2001.

Susi Bohdal, *Tiger Baby,* North-South Books (New York, NY), 2001.

Miriam Monnier, *Just Right!,* North-South Books (New York, NY), 2001.

Gerlinde Wiencirz, *Teddy's Halloween Secret,* illustrated by Giuliano Lunelli, North-South Books (New York, NY), 2001.

Raoul Krischanitz, *Molto's Dream,* North-South Books (New York, NY), 2001.

Marcus Pfister, *Rainbow Fish and the Sea Monster's Cave,* North-South Books (New York, NY), 2001.

Burny Bos, *Good Times with the Molesons,* North-South Books (New York, NY), 2001.

Krista Ruepp, *The Sea Pony,* North-South Books (New York, NY), 2001.

Udo Weigelt, *It Wasn't Me!,* illustrated by Julia Gukova, North-South Books (New York, NY), 2001.

Christophe Loupi, *Hugs and Kisses,* illustrated by Eve Tharlet, North-South Books (New York, NY), 2001.

Ivan Gantschev, reteller and illustrator, *The Three Little Rabbits,* North-South Books (New York, NY), 2001.

Nannie Kuiper, *Bailey the Bear Cub,* illustrated by Jeska Verstegen, North-South Books (New York, NY), 2002.

A puppy gets a muddy kiss from a pig in Hugs and Kisses, *written by Christophe Loupy, translated by J. Alison James, with illustrations by Eve Tharlet.*

Linard Bardill, *The Great Golden Thing,* illustrated by Miriam Monnier, North-South Books (New York, NY), 2002.

Udo Weigelt, *Alex Did It!,* illustrated by Christina Kadmon, North-South Books (New York, NY), 2002.

Birte Müller, *Giant Jack,* North-South Books (New York, NY), 2002.

Karl Rühmann, *Who Will Go to School Today?,* illustrated by Miriam Monnier, North-South Books (New York, NY), 2002.

Karl Rühmann, *But I Want To!,* illustrated by John A. Rowe, North-South Books (New York, NY), 2002.

Bruno Hächler, *Pablo the Pig,* illustrated by Nina Spranger, North-South Books (New York, NY), 2002.

Ulrich Karger, *The Scary Sleepover,* illustrated by Uli Waas, North-South Books (New York, NY), 2002.

Hubert Flattinger, *Stormy Night,* illustrated by Nathalie Duroussy, North-South Books (New York, NY), 2002.

Brigitte Weninger, *Davy, Help! It's a Ghost!,* illustrated by Eve Tharlet, North-South Books (New York, NY), 2002.

Udo Weigelt, *What Lies on the Other Side?,* illustrated by Maja Dusikova, North-South Books (New York, NY), 2002.

Krista Ruepp, *Winter Pony,* illustrated by Ulrike Heyne, North-South Books (New York, NY), 2002.

Geraldine Elschner, *Moonchild, Star of the Sea,* illustrated by Lieselotte Schwarz, North-South Books (New York, NY), 2002.

Udo Weigelt, *Fair-Weather Friend,* illustrated by Nora Hilb, North-South Books (New York, NY), 2003.

Karl Rühman, *The Little Christmas Tree,* illustrated by Anne Möller, North-South Books (New York, NY), 2003.

Udo Weigelt, *The Sandman,* illustrated by Sibylle Heusser, North-South Books (New York, NY), 2003.

Udo Weigelt, *Sleepy Bear's Christmas,* illustrated by Cristina Kadmon, North-South Books (New York, NY), 2003.

Peter Horn, *The Best Father of All,* illustrated by Cristina Kadmon, North-South Books (New York, NY), 2003.

Dorothea Lachner, *Meredith and Her Magical Book of Spells,* illustrated by Christina Unzner, North-South Books (New York, NY), 2003.

Jean-Pierre Jaggi, *Pirate Pete Sets Sail,* illustrated by Alan Clarke, North-South Books (New York, NY), 2003.

Mariana Fedorova, *The Smallest Circus in the World,* illustrated by Eugen Sopko, North-South Books (New York, NY), 2003.

Christophe Loupy, *Don't Worry, Wags,* illustrated by Eve Tharlet, North-South Books (New York, NY), 2003.

Francesca Bosca, *Christmas Cakes,* illustrated by Giuliano Ferri, 2003.

Isabel Pin, *Bumblebee Blues,* North-South Books (New York, NY), 2004.

Work in Progress

Two picture books; a children's novel; two adult novels; several translations for North-South Books (New York, NY), including Udo Weigelt's *King Ironfoot,* illustrated by Angelika Nieser; Nancy E. Walker-Guye's *Merry Christmas, Mama Mouse,* illustrated by Nora Hilb; Udo Weigelt's *Finn and Max and the Gang of Cats,* illustrated by Nora Hilb; Birte Müller's *Finn Cooks;* Kristina Franke's *Kindergarten Year,* illustrated by Sigrid Leberer; Antonie Schneider's *Little Fay and the Big Black Dog,* illustrated by Quentin Grèban; Nannie Kuiper's *Beaver Danger,* illustrated by Jeska Verstegen; Udo Weigelt's *The Bad Mood,* illustrated by Amélie Jackowski; Brigitte Luciani's *The Hempels Clean Up,* illustrated by Vannessa Hié; and Eva Montanari's *Dino Bikes.*

Sidelights

An award-winning author of children's books, J. Alison James once shared with *SATA* her start as a writer. "When I was in college, I was admitted to a poetry class taught by Nancy Willard. That year, as she was encouraging us to listen to the Giver of Dreams, she was writing the Newbery/Caldecott winner, *A Visit to William Blake's Inn.* She knew long before I did that I was going to write for children. When I was almost finished at Vassar, I discovered that there was a field that covered the two things that I loved the most: children and books. I found a master's degree program in children's literature and studied the art and text of children's books with a critical eye. I had two years of luxury in that program and began my first novel with Nancy Bond, who had just received a Newbery Honor

Stormy Night *helps young readers conquer nighttime fears. (Written by Hubert Flattinger, translated by James, with illustrations by Nathalie Duroussy.)*

for her first book, *A String in the Harp.*" Studying under other notable names in children's literature, including Ethel and Paul Heins, and Betty Levin, while at Simmons College, James began her first novel *Sing for a Gentle Rain,* as a creative thesis, a book that was eventually published by Atheneum.

James got her inspiration for *Sing for a Gentle Rain* in a most unconventional way. As she once related to *SATA,* "One Sunday morning, at the end of September, I walked into the Quaker meeting house and saw a beautiful man. I sat down and for twenty minutes tried to silently get his attention. Finally, chagrined, I closed my eyes to worship. In the next forty minutes, the entire plot and characters, parallels and details, of my first book came to life, as if I was watching the story play out in a movie. By the rise of meeting, I was shaking and awed. I had my book to write. It took me three hours to meet this man, but when we at last overcame the shyness, we spent the day together, and by midnight, waltzing at a folk dance, we knew we were going to get married. It took six years to write *Sing for a Gentle Rain,* and twelve revisions, but I never lost what came that morning."

Sing for a Gentle Rain is a time-travel fantasy about a high school student named James Winter who is pulled back to the year 1280 where he meets a young Anasazi woman, Spring Rain. Her people are threatened by extinction because of an extended drought. It is Spring Rain's desperate prayers that bring James back in time. Her grandfather, Anasan, is the tribal shaman and leader. He has reluctantly taught Spring Rain their songs of power, but Anasan cannot bring himself to reveal their meaning to a girl, even though she is the last of their line. Their people cannot move forward until Spring Rain has a son who can lead them to a new land. The problem is that there are no young men in their community to father her child. James, himself half-Pueblo, finds many things that he has in common with Spring Rain. For him, a painful discovery of culture and language evolves into a rich love for Spring Rain. A critic for *Kirkus Reviews* called *Sing for a Gentle Rain* a "beautifully imagined story" and Roger Sutton, writing for the *Bulletin of the Center for Children's Books,* commented that "Both teens are convincingly of their respective times, and their cross-cultural romance is realistically awkward." In *Horn Book,* Nancy Vasilakis praised James's "unobtrusive blending of the real and fantastic. . . . The shifts in time are smooth and plausible, the author's vivid detailing of scenes giving life to both modern and ancient episodes."

Switching from the American Southwest to a limestone island off the coast of Sweden, James's second novel, *Runa,* tells about a twelve-year-old girl named Runa who travels to Sweden to visit her grandfather. While there, she learns of a curse begun a thousand years ago in which all girls in her family born on Midsummer Day must die on their thirteenth birthday. Runa turns thirteen in three days and must solve the mystery of how to avoid her fate. James told *SATA* about this book: "Runa's evolution was more organic; ideas stuck together like atoms to a molecule, each idea changing the structure and forming something new. Powerful, mythic stories clustered around a theme of sacrifice, like the story of Iphigenia, the daughter of King Agamemnon who he had to sacrifice at the start of the Trojan War; or the play *Equus.* The central catalyst for Runa, was a more personal tragedy. One month before my wedding, my beloved grandmother died. Two years later, a month before my first daughter was born, my mother was killed in a car accident. I was struggling with the unanswerable question of why I had to give up so much to gain such blessings."

The curse of Runa's family began centuries before, when one of Runa's ancestors refused to sacrifice her beloved horse and offered her thirteen-year-old daughter as a sacrifice instead. A reviewer for *The Bulletin of the Center for Children's Books* wrote, "the mythic core of the novel is fierce and dark." Ann Welton, reviewing for *Voice of Youth Advocates,* noted, "The setting, the Swedish island of Gotland is beautifully described in visual language." Wendy E. Betts, writing for *The WEB Online Review,* (now called *Notes from the Windowsill*) stated, "*Runa* is a haunting, beautifully written book,

In **Midnight Rider,** *only a girl named Charlie and a reclusive old man know the truth about a mysterious island legend. (Written by Krista Ruepp, translated by James, with illustrations by Ulrike Heyne.)*

with a mystical quality that does not stop it from being painfully real and believable."

James told *SATA* that the way she sees the world is more like the genre of magic realism than anything else. Her first original picture book, *Eucalyptus Wings,* is a story of magic and friendship. Drawing from early childhood memories of a swing that her father built high in a eucalyptus tree in their back yard, James wrote a story about two girls who find a magical cocoon that, for just one night, gives them the ability to fly. When the magic is finished, they are left with the realization that it will never happen again. Their seemingly endless joy is suddenly like the rubber pieces of a popped balloon: lifeless. But when Kiria goes back home, she discovers the swing that her father has been making for her: "a swing with ropes so long it will give you wings!" Referring to her book, James told *SATA,* "Sometimes we have an experience that is unrepeatable. *Eucalyptus Wings* is about allowing that experience to internalize, to become part of the story that makes us who we are."

Where James lives, as she revealed to *SATA,* there is a drumming group of Japanese Taiko, and she has always been riveted by their performances. One year, they played a piece that had a program note about its story. A small village in ancient Japan frightened off invading samurai warriors by wearing demon masks and pounding on their drums. It immediately struck James as a perfect story for a picture book. When their family moved to Okayama, Japan, the following year, she took a research trip to the peninsula of Noto Hanto, where the event took place. She met with the descendants of the original villagers, saw them perform their drumming, and photographed their masks. Then she wrote the story, using strongly rhythmic language for the sounds of the drums: "Don kada Don Don!" In the picture book, the peaceful villagers of Noto Hanto rely upon their drums to signal changes in the seasons and other important events. When samurai warriors threaten the town, the drummers don masks, build fires, and use their drums to intimidate their foes. In the end they triumph, and the village returns to peace. A *Publishers Weekly* reviewer found *The Drums of Noto Hanto* "dramatic" and a "splendid picture book." The critic also observed that James's "text exudes a palpable energy." Describing the book as a "simply yet powerfully told tale," *School Library Journal* contributor Grace Oliff concluded that *The Drums of Noto Hano* provides "a unique and interesting" story.

Of the many titles James has translated, none has been so popular as Marcus Pfister's "Rainbow Fish" series. Rainbow Fish is a colorful character made iridescent by the use of holographic foil. James translated the debut title, *Rainbow Fish* in 1992 and has done several sequels. *Rainbow Fish* and its sequels have become international bestsellers, with more than four million copies in print. It is widely considered one of the most successful children's book series of the 1990s.

Biographical and Critical Sources

BOOKS

James, J. Alison, *The Drums of Noto Hanto,* illustrated by Tsukushi, DK Ink (New York, NY), 1999.

PERIODICALS

Bulletin of the Center for Children's Books, December, 1990, Roger Sutton, review of *Sing for a Gentle Rain;* August 4, 1993, review of *Runa.*
Horn Book, January, 1991, Nancy Vasilakis, review of *Sing for a Gentle Rain,* p. 74.
Kirkus Reviews, October, 1990, review of *Sing for a Gentle Rain.*
Magpies, November, 1995, Anne Freier, review of *Rainbow Fish* and *Rainbow Fish to the Rescue!,* p. 12.
Publishers Weekly, July 12, 1999, review of *The Drums of Noto Hanto,* p. 94.
School Library Journal, November, 1992, Ellen Fader, review of *Rainbow Fish,* pp. 75-76; August, 1999, Grace Oliff, review of *The Drums of Noto Hanto,* p. 137.
Voice of Youth Advocates, December, 1990, Lucinda Snyder Whitehurst, review of *Sing for a Gentle Rain,* p. 298; October, 1993, Ann Welton, review of *Runa.*

A fish learns beauty is only scale-deep, from the **Rainbow Fish,** *written and illustrated by Marcus Pfister. (Translated by James.)*

ONLINE

Alison James Web site, http://www.JAlisonJames.com/ (January 10, 2004).
Notes from the Windowsill (formerly *WEB Online Review*), http://deeptht.armory.com/~web/notes.html/ (September, 1993).

*   *   *

JOHNSON, D(onald) B. 1944-

Personal

Born November 30, 1944, in Derry, NH; son of Douglas S. and Ruth Phillips Johnson; married Linda Michelin (a writer), August 28, 1971; children: three. *Ethnicity:* "Scotch/English/Norwegian." *Education:* Boston University, B.A., 1966. *Hobbies and other interests:* Hiking, backpacking.

Addresses

Home—40 Wolf Rd., #31, Lebanon, NH 03766. *E-mail*—dbjohnson@gis.net.

Career

Freelance technical illustrator, comic strip artist, cartoonist, art director, and syndicated editorial artist, 1971—; children's book author and illustrator, 2000—.

D. B. Johnson

Member

Society of Illustrators.

Awards, Honors

Boston Globe/Horn Book Picture Book Award, *New York Times* Best Illustrated Children's Books selection, *Publishers Weekly* Best Books of the Year selection, *School Library Journal* Best Books of the Year selection, and *Parenting* magazine Best Books of the Year selection, ages 4-8, all 2000, Massachusetts Book Award for Best Children's Picture Book, Ezra Jack Keats New Writer Award, and National Parenting Publications Award (NAPPA), all 2001, all for *Henry Hikes to Fitchburg; Publishers Weekly* Best Books of the Year selection, 2002, for *Henry Builds a Cabin.*

Writings

Henry Hikes to Fitchburg, Houghton Mifflin (Boston, MA), 2000.
Henry Builds a Cabin, Houghton Mifflin (Boston, MA), 2002.
Henry Climbs a Mountain, Houghton Mifflin (Boston, MA), 2003.
Henry Works, Houghton Mifflin (Boston, MA), 2004.

Adaptations

Henry Hikes to Fitchburg was adapted for videocassette (closed captioned), narrated by James Naughton with background music by Jon Carroll, Weston Woods (Weston, CT), 2001.

Sidelights

With the publication of his first illustrated children's book, *Henry Hikes to Fitchburg,* in 2000, D. B. Johnson quickly made his mark in the world of children's literature. For more than twenty-five years, Johnson has been a nationally recognized freelance illustrator for such publications as the *New York Times Book Review, Newsday,* and the *Washington Post.* His editorial art was widely distributed through the *Los Angeles Times* syndicate.

Henry the bear, Johnson's main character, is now the hero in a series of picture books. The character and stories are based on nineteenth century writer-philosopher Henry David Thoreau, who recommended a simple way of life, unencumbered by material possessions. *Henry Hikes to Fitchburg* is the story of Henry and one of his bear friends who plot two different itineraries as they travel from Concord to Fitchburg, MA, seeing who will arrive first. Underscoring different paths to life, Henry takes the slower, scenic route with his carved walking stick, all the while enjoying the natural surroundings of his journey. His friend prefers to work at different odd jobs to earn enough money to take the train to their eventual meeting point. Along the way, readers get the practice of counting the miles and adding up the wages. Writing in *School Library Journal,* Nina Lindsay noted that "Johnson makes this philosophical musing accessible to children, who will recognize a structural parallel to 'The Tortoise and the Hare.'" A reviewer for *Horn Book* called *Henry Hikes to Fitchburg* "an auspicious picture book debut." *Concord* magazine contributor Deborah Bier noted that in its first year, the book was "already in its fourth printing with 60,000 copies in print."

"This splendid book works on several levels," noted Tim Arnold, a *Booklist* reviewer. "Johnson's adaptation of a paragraph taken from Thoreau's *Walden* . . . illuminates the contrast between materialistic and naturalistic views of life without ranting or preaching." In a *Publishers Weekly* interview with Shannon Maughan, Johnson stated, "We don't know if this actually happened [to Thoreau]," referring to the Fitchburg challenge. "But I wondered what would happen if it really took place, and I wanted to write it in a way that children could understand. *Walden* inspired the story, but it's not necessary that readers be familiar with Thoreau to 'get it.'" *Henry Hikes to Fitchburg* went on to win the 2000 *Boston Globe/Horn Book* Award for Best Picture Book, as well as the Ezra Jack Keats New Writer Award, and was a New York Times Bestseller, among other honors.

Johnson was first attracted to the powerful teachings of Thoreau after reading his book *Walden* in high school. He read it again in college. But Johnson revealed to

SATA that his lifelong attraction to the beauty of nature and the principles of living a simple life began as a young child when his father moved the family to a home he built himself on a country road in New Hampshire. Johnson's childhood memories suggest the playful influence he brings to his storytelling and his devotion to the natural world. "That first winter we kids, all five of us, scrunched up around the fireplace at night before racing through the walls to our cold bedrooms. There inside the covers at the foot of our beds, my mother had placed warm bricks wrapped in newspaper. . . . It was a great polar adventure," Johnson told SATA. Johnson and his wife returned to the rural town to raise their own family.

Called a "worthy sequel" by a Publishers Weekly reviewer, Henry Builds a Cabin was published in 2002. As spring approaches, Henry decides to construct a dwelling for himself, a small, one-room building sufficient enough to service his simple needs. His bear friends Emerson, Alcott, and Miss Lydia, however, wonder if Henry's new house will even be large enough to fit the bear. But Henry proves that he only wants a roof over his head to shelter him from inclement weather, as a bean patch serves as his dining area and his other natural surroundings happily satisfy all of Henry's needs. A Kirkus Reviews critic wrote, "In an effective retelling of . . . Thoreau's cabin-building project, Johnson relates with lighthearted humor how Henry builds a cabin barely big enough for himself." According to Horn Book contributor Mary M. Burns, "That Johnson is able to translate Thoreau's philosophy into a picture-book format . . . is an example of ingenuity at work."

The frugal bear's story continues in Henry Climbs a Mountain, an imaginative story featuring Henry meeting a runaway bear-slave. Accepting his punishment for refusing to pay taxes to a state that allows slavery, Henry daydreams about hiking while serving his sentence in a jail cell. Using the wall as a canvas, the bear depicts an imaginary outdoor scene where he meets a fellow bear, obviously an escaped slave. After helping the stranger on his journey north, Henry returns to his small cell and finds himself freed in the morning by someone who has paid his tax bill. However, keen readers will observe that the bear has been free, if only in his mind, during the entire experience. "Despite dealing with complex themes," wrote School Library Journal critic Eve Ortega, "Johnson's text does a fine job of explaining the essential conflicts without oversimplifying them." While admitting that younger children probably will not grasp the themes of taxes and slavery, a Kirkus Reviews critic nonetheless predicted that fans of the series "would welcome another story about a familiar and unique character whose deep moral convictions are expressed in simple, daily deeds."

Johnson told SATA that he was inspired by the childhood summer visits of an uncle who brought boxes of left-over printing paper and another uncle, an architect,

who "drew wild characters he dreamed up on the spot. Once he gave us a Walter Foster drawing book. That year I used hundred of sheets of paper copying his crazy faces and adding others from the drawing book. Every summer after that, I dived into that big box of paper and drew some more. All that drawing got me a lot of friends." Johnson continued, "In school I became the 'class artist,' but I didn't take art very seriously." It was during his college studies re-reading Thoreau that made the lasting impact. As he told SATA, "This time I understood, not just [Thoreau's] ideas about nature, but also his ideas about how to live. If people weren't working so hard to buy stuff, he said, they could spend more time doing what they love. That was an important idea. I decided to spend my life doing art."

Biographical and Critical Sources

PERIODICALS

Book, January, 2001, Kathleen Odean, review of Henry Hikes to Fitchburg, p. 83.
Booklist, April 15, 2000, Tim Arnold, review of Henry Hikes to Fitchburg, p. 1548; October 1, 2003, Carolyn Phelan, review of Henry Climbs a Mountain, p. 324.
Bulletin of the Center for Children's Books, May, 2002, Janice M. DelNegro, review of Henry Builds a Cabin, p. 328.
Horn Book, May, 2000, review of Henry Hikes to Fitchburg, p. 296; July-August, 2002, Mary M. Burns, review of Henry Builds a Cabin, p 448.
Kirkus Reviews, February 15, 2002, review of Henry Builds a Cabin,, p. 259; September 1, 2003, review of Henry Climbs a Mountain, p. 1125.
Language Arts, March, 2002, review of Henry Hikes to Fitchburg, p. 355.
New York Times Book Review, October 15, 2000, Simon Rodberg, review of Henry Hikes to Fitchburg, p. 31; May 19, 2002, Maud Lavin, review of Henry Builds a Cabin, p. 18.
Publishers Weekly, April 10, 2000, review of Henry Hikes to Fitchburg, p. 98; June 26, 2000, Shannon Maughan, "Flying Starts," p. 30; February 4, 2002, review of Henry Builds a Cabin, p. 76; September 1, 2003, review of Henry Climbs a Mountain, p. 91.
Reading Today, June, 2001, "Ezra Jack Keats Awards Presented," p. 9.
School Library Journal, June, 2000, Nina Lindsay, review of Henry Hikes to Fitchburg, p. 116; December, 2000, review of Henry Hikes to Fitchburg, p. 54; March, 2002, review of Henry Builds a Cabin, p. 190; September, 2003, Eve Ortega, review of Henry Climbs a Mountain, p. 181.

ONLINE

Concord Magazine, http://www.concordma.com/magazine/ (July-August, 2000), Deborah Bier, "Henry Hikes to a Surprise Success," review of Henry Hikes to Fitchburg.

D. B. Johnson Home Page, www.henrybuilds.com/ (December 26, 2003).

* * *

JOHNSTON, Tim(othy Patrick) 1962-

Personal

Born July 16, 1962, in Iowa City, IA. *Education:* University of Iowa, B.A., 1985; University of Massachusetts—Amherst, M.F.A., 1989.

Addresses

Home—Los Angeles, CA. *Agent*—Marianne Merola, Brandt & Hochman Literary Agents Inc., 1501 Broadway, New York, NY 10036. *E-mail*—jstoneink@earthlink.net.

Career

Writer. Also works as a carpenter.

Member

Authors Guild, Authors League of America.

Awards, Honors

Notable Children's Book citation, International Reading Association, 2003, for *Never So Green;* O. Henry Prize, 2003, for the short story "Irish Girl."

Writings

Never So Green (young adult novel), Farrar, Straus & Giroux (New York, NY), 2002.

Contributor of "Irish Girl" to *O. Henry Prize Stories, 2003.* Contributor of short stories to periodicals, including *New England Review, Missouri Review, Confrontation, DoubleTake, Sycamore Review, Crescent Review, Puerto del Sol,* and *Iowa Review.*

Work in Progress

Jewel of Nebraska, a novel about "a young man who abruptly leaves his Massachusetts home in search of the key to his unknown origins."

Sidelights

Tim Johnston told *SATA:* "As a writer who still makes his living as a carpenter, I get up very early or I don't get any writing done. It took nine months to write the first draft of *Never So Green,* and it took another five years (and countless revisions) for the book to find the right agent, and another year after that for my agent to find the right publisher, and another two years (and more revisions) for the book to hit the bookshelves.

"I always believed in the book, tried to have patience, worked hard, mostly enjoyed the process, felt great joy and gratitude to hold it, at last, in my hands.

"The film rights for *Never So Green* have been optioned, which is one nice thing that's come out of my living in Los Angeles."

Biographical and Critical Sources

PERIODICALS

Booklist, September 1, 2002, John Peters, review of *Never So Green,* p. 127.
Los Angeles Times, February 5, 2003, Renee Tawa, "Building a Reputation, One Nail at a Time."
Publishers Weekly, October 14, 2002, review of *Never So Green,* p. 85; December 23, 2002, Shannon Maughan, "Flying Starts," p. 32.
School Library Journal, October, 2002, Linda Binder, review of *Never So Green,* p. 167.

ONLINE

Never So Green: A Novel, http://www.neversogreen.com/ (June 27, 2003) "About the Author."

K

KJELLE, Marylou Morano 1954-

Personal

Born August 7, 1954, in Plainfield, NJ. *Education:* Cook College, B.S., 1976; Rutgers University, M.S., 1978.

Addresses

Office—P.O. Box 4202, Metuchen, NJ 08840. *E-mail*—mmoranokjelle@aol.com.

Career

Writer. *Westfield Leader/Times of Scotch Plains Fanwood,* Westfield, NJ, reporter/correspondent; Institute of Children's Literature, instructor; tutor of reading and writing. Publisher of *Gabriel's Message,* a free e-zine for Christian single mothers. Middlesex County Commission on Status of Women, vice chair, 1998, chair, 1999.

Member

Society of Children's Book Writers and Illustrators.

Writings

The Waco Siege, Chelsea House (Philadelphia, PA), 2002.
Helping Hands: A City and a Nation Lend Their Support at Ground Zero, Chelsea House (Philadelphia, PA), 2003.
Raymond Damadian and the Story of the Open MRI, Mitchell Lane (Bear, DE), 2003.
Hitler's Henchmen, Lucent (San Diego, CA), 2003.
Arkansas: A MyReportLinks.com Book, Enslow (Berkeley Heights, NJ), 2003.
Alabama: A MyReportLinks.com Book, Enslow (Berkeley Heights, NJ), 2003.
Henry Louis Gates, Jr., Chelsea House (Philadelphia, PA), 2003.

Katherine Paterson, Mitchell Lane (Hockessin, DE), 2004.

Contributor of "Children's Book Nook" column to the *Westfield Leader/Times of Scotch Plains Fanwood.*

Sidelights

Marylou Morano Kjelle's books cover a wide range of recent history, from the 1993 siege of the Branch Davidian compound in Waco, Texas, to the rescue and recovery efforts that followed the terrorist attacks on the World Trade Center in 2001. In *The Waco Siege,* Kjelle examines the events leading up to the federal government's lethal raid, which left seventy-three Branch Davidians dead. The book is part of the "Great Disasters: Reforms and Ramifications" series, whose purpose is to "examine disasters and look at the changes made so that they would not be repeated," as Betsy Fraser explained in *School Library Journal.* In another book, *Hitler's Henchmen,* Kjelle profiles top Nazi officials, including Hermann Göring, commander-in-chief of the Luftwaffe (Air Force) and Hitler's designated successor; Joseph Goebbels, who was in charge of Nazi propaganda; Heinrich Himmler, head of the Gestapo (Germany's secret police) and organizer of the concentration camps; Rudolph Hess, third in command in the Nazi hierarchy; and Baldur von Schirach, the head of the Hitler Youth. The book "use[s] primary-source documents extensively," Paula J. LaRue noted in *School Library Journal.*

Kjelle told *SATA:* "After nineteen years in a completely unrelated field, I took a leap of faith and became a full-time writer. In addition to writing nonfiction books for middle grade students and young adults, I also am a reporter for a local newspaper, an instructor for the Institute of Children's Literature, and a tutor of reading and writing for the Department of English at a local community college. I recently was awarded a county grant to teach journaling to middle school students at risk for anti-social behavior.

"One of the loves of my life is food, and currently I am studying for a certificate in culinary arts. My hope is to one day write with authenticity about food and its preparation.

Volunteers from AT&T pitch in to make sandwiches for rescue workers. From Helping Hands: A City and a Nation Lend Their Support at Ground Zero, *written by Marylou Morano Kjelle.*

"I am passionate about nonfiction because I believe we—society as a whole and each of us individually—can learn from people, places, and events, especially those that came before our time. I especially love writing (and reading) biographies. There is so much to learn from those who have already made their mark in the world. By writing about influential people, I hope to create a bridge, through my books, that connects what came before us with what is to come. To me, what is to come is the hopes, dreams, and potential stored in the hearts and minds of those who read my books and learn from the past how to create a better future."

Biographical and Critical Sources

PERIODICALS

School Library Journal, December, 2002, John Peters, review of *Helping Hands: A City and a Nation Lend Their Support at Ground Zero,* p. 163; January, 2003,

Linda Wadleigh, review of *Raymond Damadian and the Story of the Open MRI;* April, 2003, Betsy Fraser, review of *The Waco Siege,* p. 184; July, 2003, Paula J. LaRue, review of *Hitler's Henchmen,* p. 140.

ONLINE

Marylou Morano Kjelle Home Page, http://ourcreativespace.com/maryloukjelle/ (December 11, 2003).

*   *   *

KOTZWINKLE, William 1938-

Personal

Born November 22, 1938, in Scranton, PA; son of William John (a printer) and Madolyn (a housewife; maiden name, Murphy) Kotzwinkle; married Elizabeth Gundy (a writer), 1970. *Education:* Attended Rider College and Pennsylvania State University. *Hobbies and other interests:* Folk guitar.

Addresses

Agent—c/o Author Mail, Frog, 1435-A Fourth St., Berkeley, CA 94710.

Career

Writer. Worked as a short-order cook and an editor in the mid-1960s.

Awards, Honors

National Magazine Awards for fiction, 1972, 1975; O'Henry Prize, 1975; World Fantasy Award for best novel, 1977, for *Doctor Rat;* North Dakota Children's Choice Award, 1983, and Buckeye Award, 1984, both for *E.T., the Extra-Terrestrial: A Novel;* Breadloaf Writer's Conference Scholarship.

Writings

FOR CHILDREN

The Fireman, illustrated by Joe Servello, Pantheon (New York, NY), 1969.
The Ship That Came Down the Gutter, illustrated by Joe Servello, Pantheon, 1970.
Elephant Boy: A Story of the Stone Age, illustrated by Joe Servello, Farrar, Straus & Giroux (New York, NY), 1970.
The Day the Gang Got Rich, illustrated by Joe Servello, Viking (New York, NY), 1970.

William Kotzwinkle

The Oldest Man and Other Timeless Stories, illustrated by Joe Servello, Pantheon (New York, NY), 1971.

The Return of Crazy Horse, illustrated by Joe Servello, Farrar, Straus & Giroux (New York, NY), 1971.

The Supreme, Superb, Exalted, and Delightful, One and Only Magic Building, illustrated by Joe Servello, Farrar, Straus & Giroux (New York, NY), 1973.

Up the Alley with Jack and Joe, illustrated by Joe Servello, Macmillan (New York, NY), 1974.

The Leopard's Tooth, illustrated by Joe Servello, Houghton (Boston, MA), 1976.

The Ants Who Took Away Time, illustrated by Joe Servello, Doubleday (Garden City, NY), 1978.

Dream of Dark Harbor, illustrated by Joe Servello, Doubleday (Garden City, NY), 1979.

The Nap Master, illustrated by Joe Servello, Harcourt (New York, NY), 1979.

E.T., the Extra-Terrestrial: A Novel (novelization of screenplay by Melissa Mathison), Putnam (New York, NY), 1982.

Superman III (novelization of screenplay by David and Leslie Newman), Warner (New York, NY), 1983.

Great World Circus, illustrated by Joe Servello, Putnam (New York, NY), 1983.

Trouble in Bugland: A Collection of Inspector Mantis Mysteries, illustrated by Joe Servello, David R. Godine (Boston, MA), 1983.

E.T., the Book of the Green Planet: A New Novel (based on a story by Steven Spielberg), Putnam (New York, NY), 1985.

The World Is Big and I'm So Small, illustrated by Joe Servello, Crown (New York, NY), 1986.

Hearts of Wood and Other Timeless Tales, David R. Godine (Boston, MA), 1986.

The Million Dollar Bear, illustrated by David Catrow, Knopf (New York, NY), 1995.

Tales from the Empty Notebook, illustrated by Joe Servello, Marlowe (New York, NY), 1996.

(With Glenn Murray) *Walter, the Farting Dog,* illustrated by Audrey Colman, Frog (Berkeley, CA), 2001.

(With Glenn Murray) *Walter, the Farting Dog: Trouble at the Yard Sale,* illustrated by Audrey Colman, Frog (Berkeley, CA), 2004.

FOR ADULTS

Elephant Bangs Train (short stories), Pantheon (New York, NY), 1971.

Hermes 3000, Pantheon (New York, NY), 1972.

The Fan Man, Avon (New York, NY), 1974.

Night-Book, Avon (New York, NY), 1974.

Swimmer in the Secret Sea, Avon (New York, NY), 1975, reprinted, Chronicle Books (San Francisco, CA), 1994.

Doctor Rat, Knopf (New York, NY), 1976.

Fata Morgana, Knopf (New York, NY), 1977.

Herr Nightingale and the Satin Woman, illustrated by Joe Servello, Knopf (New York, NY), 1978.

Jack in the Box, Putnam (New York, NY), 1980, published as *Book of Love,* Houghton (Boston, MA), 1982.

Christmas at Fontaine's, illustrated by Joe Servello, Putnam (New York, NY), 1982.

Queen of Swords, illustrated by Joe Servello, Putnam (New York, NY), 1983.

Seduction in Berlin (poetry), illustrated by Joe Servello, Putnam (New York, NY), 1985.

Jewel of the Moon (short stories), Putnam (New York, NY), 1985.

The Exile, Dutton (New York, NY), 1987.

The Midnight Examiner, Houghton (Boston, MA), 1989.

Hot Jazz Trio, illustrated by Joe Servello, Houghton (Boston, MA), 1989.

The Game of Thirty, Houghton (Boston, MA), 1994.

The Bear Went Over the Mountain, Doubleday (New York, NY), 1996.

Also author of screenplays, including *Nightmare on Elm Street Four: The Dream Master* and *Dreaming of Babylon.* Author of screen adaptations of *Book of Love, The Exile,* and *Christmas at Fontaine's.* Contributor of short stories to books and periodicals, including *Great Esquire Fiction, Redbook's Famous Fiction,* and *O. Henry Prize Stories,* 1975. Contributor to magazines and newspapers, including *New York Times* and *Mademoiselle.*

A troll causes a wooden carousel to come to life in Hearts of Wood and Other Timeless Tales, *written by William Kotzwinkle and illustrated by Joe Servello.*

Adaptations

Jack in the Box was filmed as *Book of Love* in 1992; Jim Henson Productions has optioned *The Bear Went Over the Mountain.*

Work in Progress

More "Walter, the Farting Dog" titles with Glenn Murray and Audrey Colman.

Sidelights

William Kotzwinkle is a versatile writer who has penned books for all sorts of reading tastes. His fertile imagination has produced science fiction, children's stories, mysteries, and satire. Perhaps the easiest way to characterize his work is to say that it does not fit into any particular category. Even in the realm of writing novelizations of popular movies, Kotzwinkle has excelled. His *E.T., the Extra-Terrestrial: A Novel,* based on the film by the same name, offers a completely different point of view and a great deal more detail than

the film contains. Though better known for his adult novels, Kotzwinkle has written numerous books for children and young adults and has done so throughout his career. In an interview with *Publishers Weekly* correspondent Walter Gelles, the author said: "I always think I'll never do another [children's book], but something in me keeps bubbling up, the inner child who wants us to reexperience the world in a spontaneous way."

Kotzwinkle was born in 1938 in Scranton, Pennsylvania, a mid-sized city near the New York border. He was the only child and enjoyed a warm relationship with his father, a printer, and his stay-at-home mother. A *Dictionary of Literary Biography* contributor observed: "In describing the beginnings of his awareness of himself as a writer, Kotzwinkle recalls his father on a hike pointing to the Lackawanna Valley as if presenting the richness of the world to him and his mother taking him to a wading pool where a tadpole in his hand seemed, he said, like an 'exquisite jewel.'" Certainly the young Kotzwinkle was taken by the beauty of nature, but he did not gravitate to serious writing until he became a student at Pennsylvania State University. There he began writing poetry and honing his narrative skills in drama and playwrighting seminars.

In 1957, Kotzwinkle dropped out of Penn State and went to live in New York City, where he embraced the bohemian lifestyle so popular then among younger writers. He supported himself by working as a short-order cook, a department store Santa Claus, a promotions writer for Prentice-Hall, and a reporter for a tabloid, among other odd jobs. An old school friend, Joe Servello, helped Kotzwinkle to sell his first book in 1969. That book, *The Fireman,* is based on one of Kotzwinkle's fondest childhood memories—the day his grandfather, a fireman, allowed him to sit behind the wheel of the fire truck. "After such excitement, no ordinary profession could hold me," Kotzwinkle is quoted as saying in *Dictionary of Literary Biography.* Kotzwinkle added that he thought the book was successful because it was the first piece of work in which he was able to reconnect with one of the peak moments of his childhood.

Kotzwinkle established himself in the 1970s as a prolific author who never seemed to repeat himself. Some of his best known adult books were published during this time, including *The Fan Man,* a lyrical meditation on the Greenwich Village art scene of the 1960s. His 1976 book *Doctor Rat* was one of the first to denounce scientific experimentation on animals. An eco-fable, *Doctor Rat* introduces readers to the title character, an educated rat who undertakes experiments on other animals. A movement of free animals of all species makes attempts to break into the lab and uncage the imprisoned animals. In his *Harper's* review of the book,

Robert Stone called Kotzwinkle an author who is "not afraid to take the kind of risks that are necessary for the production of a serious novel."

It was also during the early part of his career that Kotzwinkle wrote *Jack in the Box,* perhaps his most autobiographical work. Set in a coal mining region of Pennsylvania, *Jack in the Box* explores the slow maturation process of one Jack Twiller, who is bewildered by much of what he sees around him and is just as uncomfortable within his own mind. "The novel is an audacious attempt to join the ends of the spectrum of YA literature, the fading wonder of the child's world with the bleakness of a looming adult life stretching onward through decades of boredom," observed a contributor to the *St. James Guide to Young Adult Writers.* "Kotzwinkle's narration of Twiller's maturation, full of screw-ups and failed schemes, is an illuminating account of how small gains in self-awareness and a deepening understanding of the world can lead to a construction of the self that can withstand the inevitable further screw-ups and failures of existence."

Film director Steven Spielberg became acquainted with Kotzwinkle's work by reading *The Fan Man.* While preparing the movie *E.T.,* Spielberg invited Kotzwinkle to Hollywood and asked him to write the film's novelization. Novels based on movies are generally done quickly and without much attention to style or substance, but Kotzwinkle was quite taken by the character of the empathetic extra-terrestrial. His adaptation of Melissa Mathison's screenplay was written from E.T.'s point of view, stressing the evolution of love and humanity on the character's home planet. Kotzwinkle is quoted in *Dictionary of Literary Biography* as saying that E.T. "is definitely not human. . . . [He has] a quality of humanity *that is yet to come,* and it has to do with love."

E.T., the Extra-Terrestrial made the bestseller lists and has sold more than three million copies. The contributor to *Dictionary of Literary Biography* observed: "The public accepted it as a separate work of art. In a sense, it is the culmination of Kotzwinkle's previous writing for younger readers; he presents E.T. as a manifestation of humanity's undeveloped cosmic consciousness that finds its expression in imagination and fantasy but which can be objectified because it is so much a part of common human desire." The critic added: "Kotzwinkle uses E.T. to present the positive side of his environmental concerns through a figure whose strength and appeal comes from his symbiotic bond with every sentient organism in the universe. . . . Kotzwinkle is emphasizing his belief that environment is life and that proper care and concern for the planet is essential for the survival of every form of life, as well as a source of nourishment for the soul."

In his *Publishers Weekly* interview with Gelles, Kotzwinkle said that his book version of E.T. communicates, to adults as well as children, "a powerful archetype that is dawning for humanity, the little helper from the stars. UFO visitations represent the alien within us. The alien is a missing link for us, a missing piece of our awareness."

Together, Spielberg and Kotzwinkle plotted another E.T. story that was published as *E.T., the Book of the Green Planet: A New Novel.* In this book, E.T. has returned to his home planet but longs to go back to Earth—"the green planet"—to visit Elliott and help him through adolescence. According to Jill Grossman, who assessed the book in the *New York Times Book Review,* Kotzwinkle's "strong suit here is his imagination and playfulness with language." The *Dictionary of Literary Biography* essayist wrote of the novel: "Even more than *Doctor Rat,* it is a revealing allegory relating human nature to aspects of biodiversity."

It is no coincidence that Kotzwinkle feels so strongly about environmental concerns. Since the early 1970s, he has avoided big cities, preferring to live in rural seaside Maine with his writer wife. He rarely does book tours, does not keep a Web site, and does not court celebrity the way some authors do. In a rare *People* magazine interview, he told Brenda Eady: "I want children to think the guy who wrote *E.T.* is weird."

Kotzwinkle has a low opinion of much of children's literature, as he explained to Gelles: "When Robert Louis Stevenson wrote *Treasure Island* there was no such thing as 'children's books.' But once they became a separate category, it unleashed a river of trash. So much of this writing is condescending, permeated with an austere sense of looking down at the child." Critics rarely note these tendencies in Kostwinkle's work. Some of his adult novels could easily be understood by younger readers, and some of his children's books provide diversion for adults. *Trouble in Bugland: A Collection of Inspector Mantis Mysteries,* for instance, borrows from Sherlock Holmes for a series of stories featuring a praying mantis detective who solves crimes in the insect world. While the insects in the stories speak and act somewhat like people, each different species behaves according to its characteristics in the natural world. It is no surprise, then, that Inspector Mantis is calm and calculating, able to detect other insects's weaknesses.

"Initially, Mantis and Hopper resemble the anthropomorphic equivalents of animated cartoons, cute creatures with human attributes," observed an essayist in *St. James Guide to Young Adult Writers.* "As the tales progress, the characters, especially Mantis, assume an allegorical ambiguity closer to the complexity of human nature than the single-trait dominance required by children's books. The struggle to overcome evil and seek justice has an essential appeal to any reader not consumed by cynicism, while the satisfaction inherent

***Billy and Betty must find a way to convince their father to let them keep their beloved dog. From* Walter the Farting Dog,
*written by Kotzwinkle and Glenn Murray. (Illustrated by Audrey Colman.)***

in seeing a riddle revealed is an important element of a story for young adults discovering the increasingly ambiguous nature of almost everything." In her *New York Times Book Review* assessment of *Trouble in Bugland*, Ann Cameron concluded that readers of all ages would "appreciate the book's sly mock seriousness and flights of rhetoric and imagination."

The author is also at home with more conventional picture books for the youngest readers. In *The Million Dollar Bear*, a valuable teddy bear—the first ever made, in fact—is languishing in the locked safe of a stingy business tycoon. Eventually the bear escapes and finds its way into a home with children—and a grandfather who proclaims it worthless and allows them to play with it as freely as they wish. Writing in the *Washington Post Book World*, Michael Dirda concluded: "All in

all, this is a very good picture book. . . . If you find the moral a tad sappy, well, you'll just have to grin and bear it."

Walter the dog has quite another problem in *Walter, the Farting Dog*. His gas attacks have landed him in the pound, and the family that has just adopted him discovers that they, too, cannot stand the stink. Just in time to save himself, however, Walter foils a burglary at his new home with his secret weapon: flatulence. A *Publishers Weekly* reviewer declared that Walter's antics "should have children rolling in the aisles during read-aloud." *Booklist*'s Ilene Cooper likewise felt that children would find the book "hysterical."

The success of *Walter, the Farting Dog* has only verified what Kotzwinkle wants his audience to think: that he is weird, unpredictable, and very much in touch with what makes children laugh—and think. Though he is uncertain of what books may lie in his future, Kotzwinkle told *People* interviewer Eady, "I know I'll end up a little old guy telling stories on a mountain somewhere."

Biographical and Critical Sources

BOOKS

Beacham's Popular Fiction Update, Beacham Publishing (Washington, DC), 1991, pp. 693-704.
Children's Literature Review, Volume 6, Gale (Detroit, MI), 1994, pp. 180-185.
Contemporary Literary Criticism, Gale (Detroit, MI), Volume 5, 1976, Volume 14, 1980, Volume 35, 1985.
Contemporary Novelists, 7th edition, St. James (Detroit, MI), 2001.
Dictionary of Literary Biography, Volume 173: *American Novelists since World War II, Fifth Series,* Gale (Detroit, MI), 1996, pp. 98-107.
St. James Guide to Fantasy Writers, St. James (Detroit, MI), 1996.
St. James Guide to Young Adult Writers, 2nd edition, St. James (Detroit, MI), 1999.
Twentieth-Century Science-Fiction Writers, 3rd edition, St. James (Detroit, MI), 1991.

PERIODICALS

Atlantic, May, 1974; June, 1976; July, 1977.
Booklist, February 15, 2002, Ilene Cooper, review of *Walter, the Farting Dog,* p. 1020.
Chicago Tribune, May 5, 1989.
College Literature, spring, 2000, Robert E. Kohn, "The Ambivalence in Kotzwinkle's Beat and Bardo Ties," p. 103.
Harper's, June, 1976, Robert Stone, review of *Doctor Rat.*
Listener, July 22, 1976.
Los Angeles Times Book Review, January 22, 1984, p. 8; June 14, 1987, p. 10; April 30, 1989; November 19, 1989, p. 8; September 11, 1994, Susan Salter Reynolds, review of *Swimmer in the Secret Sea,* p. 6.
Nation, November 4, 1996, Dan Wakefield, review of *The Bear Went Over the Mountain,* p. 31.
New Republic, March 2, 1974.
Newsweek, May 31, 1982, p. 63.
New Yorker, March 25, 1974; July 25, 1977.
New York Times, April 9, 1971, Thomas Lask, "Of Elephants and Air Strikes," p. 29.
New York Times Book Review, January 10, 1974; November 2, 1975; May 30, 1976, Richard P. Brickner, review of *Doctor Rat,* p. 8; May 1, 1977; November 9, 1980; July 11, 1982, pp. 31-32; January 1, 1984, Ann Cameron, review of *Trouble in Bugland: A Collection*

of Inspector Mantis Mysteries,* p. 23; May 5, 1985, Jill Grossman, review of *E.T., the Book of the Green Planet: A New Novel,* p. 24; January 4, 1987, p. 33; May 10, 1987, pp. 1, 38; May 14, 1989, p. 27; February 25, 1990, p. 13.
Observer, January 8, 1978.
People, April 22, 1985, Ralph Novak, review of *E.T., the Book of the Green Planet,* p. 26; May 27, 1985, Brenda Eady, "From Any Angle, E.T.'s Biographer William Kotzwinkle Is Not an Alien to Success."
Publishers Weekly, November 10, 1989, Walter Gelles, "William Kotzwinkle," pp. 46-47; October 16, 1995, review of *The Million-Dollar Bear,* p. 60; October 8, 2001, review of *Walter, the Farting Dog,* p. 63.
San Francisco Review of Books, spring, 1985, R. E. Nowicki, "An Interview with William Kotzwinkle," pp. 7-8.
Saturday Review, May 29, 1976; April 30, 1977.
School Library Journal, February, 1984, p. 74; January, 1996, Patricia Pearl Dole, review of *The Million-Dollar Bear,* p. 86.
Times Literary Supplement, January 7, 1983, p. 13.
Village Voice, September 15, 1975; June 28, 1976, Anne Larsen, "Did Doctor Rat Sell Out?," p. 45; August 24, 1982, Ariel Dorfman, "Norteamericanos, Call Home," pp. 39-40; August 8, 1989, p. 49.
Washington Post Book World, October 1, 1995, Michael Dirda, review of *The Million-Dollar Bear,* p. 6.
Writer's Digest, July, 1992, Michael Schumacher, "The Inner Worlds of William Kotzwinkle," p. 34.*

*   *   *

KOUTSKY, Jan Dale 1955-

Personal

Born March 24, 1955, in Seattle, WA; daughter of Eugene and Mary (Kinzel) Dale; married James Koutsky, February 18, 1983; children: Tessa, Dylan. *Education:* Central Washington University, B.A., 1976.

Addresses

Home—Seattle, WA. *Agent*—Barbara S. Kouts, P.O. Box 560, Bellport, NY 11713. *E-mail*—jankoutsky@attbi.com.

Career

College art instructor in Seattle, WA, 1978—. Artist, creating mixed-media collages to be sold through galleries; work also represented in exhibitions and private collections.

Member

Society of Children's Book Writers and Illustrators, Arts West Artists Association.

Awards, Honors

Teachers' Choice selection, International Reading Association, 2003, for *My Grandma, My Pen Pal.*

Writings

(And illustrator) *My Grandma, My Pen Pal,* Boyds Mills Press (Honesdale, PA), 2002.

Work in Progress

Another children's picture book.

Sidelights

Jan Dale Koutsky told *SATA:* "We live in an age of the global community. Many families are spread all over the world. As the world becomes smaller, I fear we will lose our unique cultural identities. I believe in the old saying that 'variety is the spice of life.' It is my hope that families will keep their cultural traditions alive.

"My book *My Grandma, My Pen Pal* is the story of a grandmother and grandchild who are a part of each other's lives through letters and occasional visits. The book encourages the generations to talk with each other and get to know each other's lives, but there is also a hope that family traditions will be passed from one generation to the next. Our elders carry rich history and tradition that needs to be shared and understood by the next generation. Our world will become a boring place if we all are too much alike. I hope that the book will encourage children and grandparents to write to each other and get to know each other. We have valuable resources in each other.

"I am working on my next children's picture book. It is based on a true drama that we witnessed in our backyard. Our dog hated crows because they would eat her dog food. One day a baby crow landed in our yard before it could fly. Our dog protected it until it could take off on its own. As I saw the transformation in the dog's behavior, I couldn't help but wish that we humans could be just as understanding and compassionate. My book tries to encourage children to rethink the situations when someone makes them angry. If a dog can learn to get along, maybe we humans can, too."

Biographical and Critical Sources

PERIODICALS

Booklist, May 15, 2002, Kathy Broderick, review of *My Grandma, My Pen Pal,* p. 1596.
School Library Journal, June, 2002, Be Astengo, review of *My Grandma, My Pen Pal,* p. 98.

L

LANDSTRÖM, Lena 1943-

Personal
Born July 12, 1943, in Stockholm, Sweden; daughter of Bertil Löfquist (a doctor of engineering) and Ingrid Bern (a homemaker); married Olof Landström (an author and illustrator), June 11, 1971; children: Albin, Karl, Viktor. *Ethnicity:* "Swedish." *Education:* Attended Beckman's School of Design, 1966-69.

Addresses
Home—Sweden. *Agent*—Rabén & Sjögren, Box 2052, 10312 Stockholm, Sweden.

Career
Children's book author, illustrator, and filmmaker. Freelance author and filmmaker creating projects for Swedish television, 1970—.

Member
Föreningen Svenska Tecknare (Swedish Association of Illustrators and Graphic Designers), Sveriges Författarförbund (Swedish Writers' Union).

Awards, Honors
Parents Choice award for picture book, 1992, for *Will's New Cap;* several international awards.

Lena Landström

Writings

"WILL" SERIES; WITH HUSBAND, OLOF LANDSTRÖM

Nisses my mössa, Rabén & Sjögren (Stockholm, Sweden), 1990, translated by Richard E. Fisher as *Will's New Cap,* R & S Books (New York, NY), 1992.

Nisse hos frisören, Rabén & Sjögren (Stockholm, Sweden), 1991, translated by Elisabeth Dyssegaard as *Will Gets a Haircut,* R & S Books (New York, NY), 1993.

Nisse på stranden, Rabén & Sjögren (Stockholm, Sweden), 1992, translated by Carla Wiberg as *Will Goes to the Beach,* R & S Books (New York, NY), 1995.

Nisse gå till posten, Rabén & Sjögren (Stockholm, Sweden), 1993, translated by Elisabeth Dyssegaard as *Will Goes to the Post Office,* R & S Books (New York, NY), 1994.

"BOO AND BAA" SERIES; WITH HUSBAND, OLOF LANDSTRÖM

Bu och Bä på kalashumör, Rabén & Sjögren (Stockholm,

Sweden), 1995, translated by Joan Sandin as *Boo and Baa in a Party Mood*, R & S Books (New York, NY), 1996.

Bu och Bä i blåsväder, Rabén & Sjögren (Stockholm, Sweden), 1995, translated by Joan Sandin as *Boo and Baa in Windy Weather*, R & S Books (New York, NY), 1996.

Bu och Bä i städtagen, Rabén & Sjögren (Stockholm, Sweden), 1996, translated by Joan Sandin as *Boo and Baa on a Cleaning Spree*, R & S Books (New York, NY), 1997.

Bu och Bä på sjö, Rabén & Sjögren (Stockholm, Sweden), 1996, translated by Joan Sandin as *Boo and Baa at Sea*, R & S Books (New York, NY), 1997.

Bu och Bä i skogen, Rabén & Sjögren (Stockholm, Sweden), 1999, translated by Joan Sandin as *Boo and Baa in the Woods*, R & S Books (Stockholm, Sweden), 2000.

Bu och Bä blir blöta, Rabén & Sjögren (Stockholm, Sweden), 1999, translated by Joan Sandin as *Boo and Baa Get Wet*, R & S Books (London, England), 2000.

OTHER

En flodhästsaga, Rabén & Sjögren (Stockholm, Sweden), 1993.

(Self-illustrated) *Småflodhästarnas äventyr*, Rabén & Sjögren (Stockholm, Sweden), 2000, translated by Joan Sandin as *The Little Hippos' Adventure*, R & S Books (New York, NY), 2002.

(Self-illustrated) *De nya flodhästarna*, Rabén & Sjögren (Stockholm, Sweden), 2002, translated by Joan Sandin as *The New Hippos*, R & S Books (New York, NY), 2003.

Landström's books have been translated into over a dozen languages, including French and Persian.

Work in Progress

Four Hens and a Rooster, illustrated by husband, Olof Landström.

Sidelights

Together with her husband Olof Landström, author and illustrator Lena Landström has created several picture-book series that have captivated young readers both in Sweden and in the United States. Translated into over a dozen languages and published worldwide, the Landströms's engaging books include four volumes about a young boy named Will as well as the "Boo and Baa" series, which follow a pair of wide-eyed lambs through a series of humorous mishaps. *Will's New Cap* was the first Landström book to appear in English; since then the couple has produced three other "Will" books as well as six books in the humorous "Boo and Baa" series. In praise of 1994's *Will Gets a Haircut, School Library Journal* reviewer Anna DeWind commented: "this Swedish import has a wonderfully kooky visual style and a positive, self-affirming, heartwarming message."

Diving off of a tall cliff seems like a fun idea. From **The Little Hippos' Adventure.** *(Written and illustrated by Lena Landström. Translated by Joan Sandin.)*

The Landströms's "Will" books feature the day-to-day activities of a young boy, all drawn in a cartoon style where characters are "brightly colored to stand out against the prevalent beiges and grays," explained a *Publishers Weekly* contributor. In *Will's New Cap*, the boy rushes out to show his friends his new baseball cap, but panics when a sudden cloudburst wilts the brim and, unable to see, he tumbles onto the sidewalk. With Mom to the rescue, all is made well in a book that *Five Owls* reviewer Barbara Knutson praised for its ability to focus on childhood concerns with "a satisfying simplicity." *Horn Book* critic Martha V. Parravano also offered warm words for the book, finding *Will's New Cap* "fresh and wonderfully child centered." *Will Gets a Haircut* finds Will nervously awaiting the barber's shears, until he realizes that he can make his hair cut unique and one-of-a-kind, while a huge box sent by an uncle holds tantalizing mysteries for the young boy in *Will Goes to the Post Office*. Praising the latter book for its "brief text" and evocative yet simple illustrations, *Horn Book* contributor Parravano dubbed *Will Goes to the Post Office* a "slightly offbeat, very funny book," while in her *School Library Journal* review, Pamela K. Bomboy called it "a charmer." In *Will Goes to the Beach*, a rainy day at the seashore becomes an opportunity for Will to practice his swimming without distractions. Olof Landström's watercolor-and-ink drawings "deftly express nuances of action and feeling," according to Carolyn Phelan in a *Booklist* review.

From Boo and Baa Get Wet, *written and illustrated by Olof and Lena Landström.* (*Translated by Joan Sandin.*)

In the Landström's "Boo and Baa" series, a pair of round-eyed sheep go about typical sheep business: practicing for dancing lessons, going to birthday parties, and playing croquet. Praised by many critics for their cheerful texts, these stories of two sheep who make out okay despite a host of small-scale setbacks encourage young readers to take things in stride. Praising the creators of these "guileless sheep" in *Booklist,* Ilene Cooper commended the Landströms for creating stories with "a good balance of action and homey detail."

The "Boo and Baa" books have allowed Landström and her husband to indulge in their "talent for imbuing their bare-bones stories with funny narrative" asides, according to a *Publishers Weekly* reviewer who commented on the continual mishaps confounding the two sheep's efforts to get ready for a friend's birthday party in *Boo and Baa in a Party Mood.* Noting the "satisfying" nature of *Boo and Baa Get Wet*—where a sudden shower puts a damper on the sheep's croquet plans—and *Boo and Baa in the Woods*—where a berry-picking trip find the pair hunted by ants—in her *School Library Journal*

review of the two titles, Denise Reitsma noted that the illustrators' attention to Boo and Baa's facial expressions "add charm to the simple, pleasing stories."

In addition to her many collaborations with her husband, Landström has also branched out on her own with several books featuring a hippo family and her own illustrations. In *The Little Hippos' Adventure,* she introduces the hippo characters featured throughout the series. *The Little Hippos' Adventure* finds the trio of small hippos dissatisfied with the amenities at their family watering hole and wishing there was a higher diving board available. After repeated naggings by the young hippos, their fatigued parents relent and give their permission for the excited youngsters to clamber through the jungle to a new jumping-off spot high up on Tall Cliffs. Once granted, however, their wish brings worry, as the hippos realize that the dark, mysterious jungle and its hidden creatures is not such a fun place after all. Praising Landström's text and illustrations, a *Publishers Weekly* contributor cited in particular the "endearing images of the diminutive threesome . . . as they timidly make their way through the jungle." Reviewer Be Astengo echoed this praise in *School Library Journal,* noting that Landström's "cartoonlike" drawings create "a lovely, jungly effect" in a picture book that is "charming" over all.

Landström told *SATA:* "My husband Olof and I have been working together with animated films for Swedish television and on picture books for children. We both write and illustrate."

Biographical and Critical Sources

PERIODICALS

Booklist, November 1, 1993, Carolyn Phelan, review of *Will Gets a Haircut,* p. 530; November 1, 1994, Carolyn Phelan, review of *Will Goes to the Post Office,* p. 507; September 1, 1995, Carolyn Phelan, review of *Will Goes to the Beach,* p. 87; November 1, 1996, Carolyn Phelan, review of *Boo and Baa in Windy Weather* and *Boo and Baa in a Party Mood,* p. 507; July, 1997, Ilene Cooper, review of *Boo and Baa at Sea* and *Boo and Baa on a Cleaning Spree,* p. 1822; November 15, 2000, Ilene Cooper, review of *Boo and Baa Get Wet* and *Boo and Baa in the Woods,* p. 648; April 15, 2003, Carolyn Phelan, review of *The New Hippos,* p. 1478.

Five Owls, November-December, 1992, Barbara Knutson, review of *Will's New Cap,* p. 32.

Horn Book, March-April, 1993, Martha V. Parravano, review of *Will's New Cap,* p. 199; March-April, 1994, Martha V. Parravano, review of *Will Gets a Haircut,* p. 224; March, 1995, Martha V. Parravano, review of *Will Goes to the Post Office,* p. 184.

Kirkus Reviews, July 1, 1995, review of *Will Goes to the Beach,* p. 948.

Publishers Weekly, October 26, 1992, review of *Will's New Cap,* p. 69; August 5, 1996, review of *Boo and Baa in Windy Weather* and *Boo and Baa in a Party Mood,* p. 440; April 7, 1997, review of *Boo and Baa on a Cleaning Spree,* p. 93; September 11, 2000, review of *Boo and Baa Get Wet,* p. 92; April 8, 2002, review of *The Little Hippos' Adventure,* p. 225.

School Library Journal, February, 1994, Anna DeWind, review of *Will Gets a Haircut,* p. 88; December, 1994, Pamela K. Bomboy, review of *Will Goes to the Post Office,* p. 78; November, 1995, Ann Cook, review of *Will Goes to the Beach,* p. 74; November, 1996, Sharon R. Pearce, review of *Boo and Baa in Windy Weather* and *Boo and Baa in a Party Mood,* pp. 87-88; July, 1997, Darla Remple, review of *Boo and Baa on a Cleaning Spree* and *Boo and Baa at Sea,* p. 70; September, 2000, Denise Reitsma, review of *Boo and Baa in the Woods* and *Boo and Baa Get Wet,* p. 203; April, 2002, Be Astengo, review of *The Little Hippos' Adventure,* p. 114; April, 2003, Bina Williams, review of *The New Hippos,* p. 130.

Tribune Books (Chicago, IL), October 10, 1993, Mary Harris Veeder, review of *Will Gets a Haircut,* p. 6.*

LANDSTRÖM, Olof 1943-

Personal

Born April 9, 1943, in Åbo, Finland; married Lena Löfquist (a children's book author, illustrator, and filmmaker), June 11, 1971; children: Albin, Karl, Viktor. *Ethnicity:* "Swedish." *Education:* Konstfackskolan University College of Arts, 1959-63.

Addresses

Home—Sweden. *Agent*—Rabén & Sjögren, Box 2052, 10312 Stockholm, Sweden.

Career

Illustrator, animator, and author; filmmaker for Swedish television.

Member

Föreningen Svenska Tecknare (Swedish Association of Illustrators and Graphic Designers), Sveriges Författarförbund (Swedish Writers' Union).

Awards, Honors

First prize, Prix Jeunesse (Germany), 1976, for *Charlie's Climbing Tree;* second prize, Los Angeles Film Festival and Biennial of Illustration Bratislava, both 1985, both for *Teacher Haze;* first prize, Prix Jeunesse (Germany), 1988, for *Mr. Bohm and the Herring* (animated film); *New York Times* Best Illustrated Book Award, 1989, for *Olson's Meat Pies;* Parents Choice Award for picture book, 1992, for *Will's New Cap;* Children's Book of Distinction, *Riverbank Review,* 2000, for *Benny's Had Enough!;* recipient of several international awards.

Writings

"WILL" SERIES; WITH WIFE, LENA LANDSTRÖM

Nisses my mössa, Rabén & Sjögren (Stockholm, Sweden), 1990, translated by Richard E. Fisher as *Will's New Cap,* R & S Books (New York, NY), 1992.

Nisse hos frisören, Rabén & Sjögren (Stockholm, Sweden), 1991, translated by Elisabeth Dyssegaard as *Will Gets a Haircut,* R & S Books (New York, NY), 1993.

Nisse på stranden, Rabén & Sjögren (Stockholm, Sweden), 1992, translated by Carla Wiberg as *Will Goes to the Beach,* R & S Books (New York, NY), 1995.

Nisse gå till posten, Rabén & Sjögren (Stockholm, Sweden), 1993, translated by Elisabeth Dyssegaard as *Will Goes to the Post Office,* R & S Books (New York, NY), 1994.

"BOO AND BAA" SERIES; WITH WIFE, LENA LANDSTRÖM

Bu och Bä på kalashumör, Rabén & Sjögren (Stockholm, Sweden), 1995, translated by Joan Sandin as *Boo and Baa in a Party Mood,* R & S Books (New York, NY), 1996.

Bu och Bä i blåsväder, Rabén & Sjögren (Stockholm, Sweden), 1995, translated by Joan Sandin as *Boo and Baa in Windy Weather,* R & S Books (New York, NY), 1996.

Bu och Bä i städtagen, Rabén & Sjögren (Stockholm, Sweden), 1996, translated by Joan Sandin as *Boo and Baa on a Cleaning Spree,* R & S Books (New York, NY), 1997.

Bu och Bä på sjö, Rabén & Sjögren (Stockholm, Sweden), 1996, translated by Joan Sandin as *Boo and Baa at Sea,* R & S Books (New York, NY), 1997.

Bu och Bä i skogen, Rabén & Sjögren (Stockholm, Sweden), 1999, translated by Joan Sandin as *Boo and Baa in the Woods,* R & S Books (Stockholm, Sweden), 2000.

Bu och Bä blir blöta, Rabén & Sjögren (Stockholm, Sweden), 1999, translated by Joan Sandin as *Boo and Baa Get Wet,* R & S Books (London, England), 2000.

ILLUSTRATOR

Peter Cohen, *Olssons pastejer,* Rabén & Sjögren (Stockholm, Sweden), 1988, translated by Richard E. Fisher as *Olson's Meat Pies,* R & S Books (New York, NY), 1989.

Barbro Lindgren, *Sunkan flyger,* Rabén & Sjögren (Stockholm, Sweden), 1989, translated from the Swedish by Richard E. Fisher as *Shorty Takes Off,* R & S Books (New York, NY), 1990.

Peter Cohen, *Herr Bohm och sillen,* Rabén & Sjögren (Stockholm, Sweden), 1991, translated by Richard E. Fisher as *Mr. Bohm and the Herring,* R & S Books (New York, NY), 1992.

Viveca Lärn Sundvall, *Ruben,* Rabén & Sjögren (Stockholm, Sweden), 1994, translated by Kjersti Board as *Santa's Winter Vacation,* R & S Books (New York, NY), 1995.

Barbro Lindgren, *Nämen Benny,* Rabén & Sjögren (Stockholm, Sweden), 1998, translated by Elisabeth Kallick Dyssegaard as *Benny's Had Enough,* R & S Books (New York, NY), 1999.

Barbro Lindgren, *Jamen Benny,* Rabén & Sjögren (Stockholm, Sweden), 2001, translated by Elizabeth Kallick Dyssegaard as *Benny and the Binky,* R & S Books (New York, NY), 2002.

Peter Cohen, *Boris glasögon,* Rabén & Sjögren (Stockholm, Sweden), 2002, translated by Joan Sandin as *Boris's Glasses,* R & S Books (New York, NY), 2003.

Barbara Bottner and Gerald Kruglik, *Wallace's Lists,* Katherine Tegen Books (New York, NY), 2004.

OTHER

Also animator of *Charlie's Climbing Tree,* 1975, *Teacher Haze,* 1984, and *Mr. Bohm and the Herring,* 1987. Landström's books have been translated into over a dozen languages, including French and Persian.

Work in Progress

Illustrating *Four Hens and a Rooster,* written by wife, Lena Landström.

When Boris gets new glasses, not only does the picture on his TV get clearer, but so does his outlook on life. From **Boris's Glasses,** *written by Peter Cohen, translated by Joan Sandin. (Illustrated by Olof Landström.)*

Sidelights

Together with his wife, Lena Landström, Swedish author and illustrator Olof Landström is the cocreator of two popular Swedish imports: the "Will" and "Boo and Baa" picture books, which began arriving in North American libraries in 1992. A professional illustrator, Olof Landström has also created artwork for several other Swedish authors whose books have traveled across the ocean to reach U.S. readers. His cartoon art for Peter Cohen's picture book *Olson's Meat Pies,* originally published as *Olssons pastejer,* received special attention from *School Library Journal* contributor Jane Saliers, who wrote that Landström's use of "softly outlined, subdued colors" and "simple lines humorously depict the eccentric cartoon characters," while the illustrator's off-kilter perspective reinforces his art's humorous impact. According to a *Publishers Weekly* critic, Landström's "remarkably wry illustrations" for *Benny's Had Enough,* first appearing in Swedish as *Nämen Benny,* "inject charm into a familiar tale" about a young pig who thinks his life will be vastly improved once he finds a new home. In Barbro Lindgren's picture book *Benny and the Binky,* originally published as *Jamen Benny,* which finds the porcine toddler jealous of his new sibling's rubber pacifier, Landström's drawings enhance "the slightly absurd tone of the text and expand the narrative with great expression, movement, and detail," according to *Horn Book*'s Lauren Adams.

Landström told *SATA:* "Mostly, I take full responsibility for the entire design of the books I illustrate. Besides acting as the director and scenographer of the story, I also do the typographical design because it is such an integral part of an illustrated book. When planning and illustrating a picture book, my experience in filmmaking is of great advantage."

For more information, see entry on wife Lena Landström.

Biographical and Critical Sources

PERIODICALS

Booklist, November 1, 1993, Carolyn Phelan, review of *Will Gets a Haircut,* p. 530; November 1, 1994, Carolyn Phelan, review of *Will Goes to the Post Office,* p. 507; September 1, 1995, Carolyn Phelan, review of *Will Goes to the Beach,* p. 87; November 1, 1996, Carolyn Phelan, review of *Boo and Baa in Windy Weather* and *Boo and Baa in a Party Mood,* p. 507; July, 1997, Ilene Cooper, review of *Boo and Baa at Sea* and *Boo and Baa on a Cleaning Spree,* p. 1822; November 15, 2000, Ilene Cooper, review of *Boo and Baa Get Wet* and *Boo and Baa in the Woods,* p. 648.

Five Owls, November-December, 1992, Barbara Knutson, review of *Will's New Cap,* p. 32.

Horn Book, March-April, 1993, Martha V. Parravano, review of *Will's New Cap,* p. 199; March-April, 1994, Martha V. Parravano, review of *Will Gets a Haircut,* p. 224; March, 1995, Martha V. Parravano, review of *Will Goes to the Post Office,* p. 184; January-February, 1996, Maeve Visser Knoth, review of *Santa's Winter Vacation,* p. 69; May-June, 2002, Lauren Adams, review of *Benny and the Binky,* p. 317.

Kirkus Reviews, July 1, 1995, review of *Will Goes to the Beach,* p. 948.

Publishers Weekly, October 26, 1992, review of *Will's New Cap,* p. 69; August 5, 1996, review of *Boo and Baa in Windy Weather* and *Boo and Baa in a Party Mood,* p. 440; April 7, 1997, review of *Boo and Baa on a Cleaning Spree,* p. 93; November 15, 1999, review of *Benny's Had Enough,* p. 64; September 11, 2000, review of *Boo and Baa Get Wet,* p. 92; September 8, 2003, review of *Boris's Glasses,* p. 76.

School Library Journal, April, 1990, Jane Saliers, review of *Olson's Meat Pies,* p. 88; April, 1993, Nancy A. Gifford, review of *Mr. Bohm and the Herring,* p. 94; February, 1994, Anna De Wind, review of *Will Gets a Haircut,* p. 88; December, 1994, Pamela K. Bomboy, review of *Will Goes to the Post Office,* p. 78; November, 1995, Ann Cook, review of *Will Goes to the Beach,* p. 74; November, 1996, Sharon R. Pearce, review of *Boo and Baa in Windy Weather* and *Boo and Baa in a Party Mood,* pp. 87-88; July, 1997, Darla Remple, review of *Boo and Baa on a Cleaning Spree* and *Boo and Baa at Sea,* p. 70; December, 1999, Nancy Menaldi-Scanlan, review of *Benny's Had Enough,* pp. 102-103; September, 2000, Denise Reitsma, review of *Boo and Baa in the Woods* and *Boo and Baa Get Wet,* p. 203; April, 2002, Martha Topol, review of *Benny and the Binky,* p. 116; September, 2003, Edith Ching, review of *Boris's Glasses,* p. 176.

Tribune Books (Chicago, IL), October 10, 1993, Mary Harris Veeder, review of *Will Gets a Haircut,* p. 6.*

*   *   *

LEE, Dom 1959-

Personal

Born May 4, 1959, in Seoul, Korea; immigrated to United States, 1990; son of Myung-eui (a painter and art teacher) and Young-sook (a homemaker and sculptor; maiden name, Park) Lee; married Keunhee (a painter), November 15, 1982; children: Brian, Eun. *Ethnicity:* "Korean." *Education:* Seoul National University, B.F.A., 1985; School of Visual Arts, M.F.A., 1992. *Hobbies and other interests:* Woodworking.

Addresses

Home and office—8 Insley St., Demarest, NJ 07627. *Agent*—Kirchoff/Wohlberg, Inc., 866 United Nations Plaza, New York, NY 10017. *E-mail*—domandkay@ hotmail.com.

Career

Hyang-Lin Institute, Seoul, Korea, drawing instructor, 1985-89; painter and illustrator of children's books, 1990—. *Exhibitions:* Exhibitor at one-man shows, including *Generations,* School of Visual Arts Gallery, New York, NY, 1991; *Urbanscapes: Images of New York City* (with wife, Keunhee Lee), Bread and Roses Cultural Project, Gallery 1199, New York, NY, 1993; *Works with Wax,* Indeco Gallery, Seoul, Korea, 1995, and *Works on Wax by Dom Lee,* Works Gallery, New York, NY, 2000. Exhibitor in group shows, including *Best Children's Book Illustration in 1993,* Society of Illustrators, Museum of American Illustration, New York, NY, 1993; *A Selection of Works from the Editorial and Book Categories of the Thirty-sixth Annual Exhibition,* Society of Illustrators, Museum of American Illustration, New York, NY, 1994; *Exposition découvirir la corée livres et illustrations pour enfants,* Centre Georges Pompidou, Paris, France, 1995; *Exhibition of Children's Book Illustrators,* Bologna, Italy, 1996; *The Art of Dom and Keunhee Lee,* Morning Calm Gallery, New York, NY, 1998, and Pangborn Gallery, Detroit, MI, 1999; *The Art of Dom and K. Lee,* Works Gallery, New York, NY, 2002; and *The Magazine Rack,* School of Visual Arts Gallery, New York, NY, 2003.

Awards, Honors

Parents' Choice Award, Cuffies Award for the Best Multicultural Title, *Publishers Weekly,* Pick of the Lists selection, American Booksellers Association, Best Bets of 1993, *San Francisco Chronicle,* all 1993, and Washington Governor's Writers Award, 1994, all for *Baseball Saved Us;* Teachers' Choice Award, Notable Children's Book citation, *Smithsonian* magazine, "Editors' Choice"

Dom Lee

award, *San Francisco Chronicle,* and Notable Children's Trade Book in the Field of Social Studies citation, National Council for the Social Studies/Children's Book Council, all 1996, all for *Heroes;* Notable Book selection, American Library Association, Reading Magic Award, *Parenting* magazine, Best Books selection, Society of School Librarians International, Notable Books for a Global Society selection, International Reading Association, and Picture Book Honor, Jane Addams Children's Book Award, 1998, all for *Passage to Freedom: The Sugihara Story.*

ILLUSTRATOR:

Ken Mochizuki, *Baseball Saved Us,* Lee & Low Books (New York, NY), 1993.

Ken Mochizuki, *Heroes,* Lee & Low Books (New York, NY), 1995.

(With wife, Keunhee Lee) *Fireworks,* Gilbut Children's Publishing Company (Seoul, South Korea), 1996.

Ken Mochizuki, *Passage to Freedom: The Sugihara Story,* Lee & Low (New York, NY), 1997.

(With Keunhee Lee) Lawrence McKay, *Journey Home,* Lee & Low Books (New York, NY), 1998.

Kirk Douglas, *Young Heroes of the Bible,* Simon & Schuster (New York, NY), 1999.

Also illustrator, with Keunhee Lee, of elementary school reading books, including *A Railroad on Gold Mountain,* by Fay Chiang; *Flat as a Pancake,* by Sheila Black;

Grandmother and I, by Anne Miranda, and *Quinto's Volcano,* by Aileen Friedman, all for Macmillan (New York, NY). Contributor of an illustration to *On the Wings of Peace,* edited by Sheila Hamanaka, Clarion (New York, NY), 1995. Illustrator of book jackets, *After the War* and *The Garden,* both by Ruth Mendenberg, for Simon & Schuster (New York, NY).

Work in Progress

More picture books and a series of urban and suburban landscapes of Seoul.

Sidelights

Korean-born Dom Lee has won awards and gained international recognition for his children's book illustrations. As an art student, Lee developed a new technique for illustrations, an encaustic method in which images are literally scratched out of and painted on beeswax applied to paper. This style projects a three-dimensional effect on two dimensions and fits particularly well the historic subject matter of such Lee-illustrated books as *Baseball Saved Us, Heroes,* and *Passage to Freedom: The Sugihara Story,* all written by Ken Mochizuki. In tandem with his work as an illustrator, Lee has also continued to produce fine art, in many cases using the same method. In a review of *Passage to Freedom,* a *Publishers Weekly* reviewer called Lee's work "precise, haunting art" that "unites carefully balanced compositions and emotional intensity."

In an essay for *Something about the Author Autobiography Series,* Lee described himself as a youngster who immersed himself in art from an early age. Lee grew up in a painting milieu. His father is an abstract painter, and his mother is an avid art lover. Though a housewife while Lee was growing up, she has since become a sculptor, working in terra-cotta. Lee's older sister also was involved in the art world, working in traditional oriental brush technique. Thus, there was never any doubt that Lee would follow in his family's footsteps and become an artist; the only question was in which medium. "When I was a kid," Lee told *SATA* in an interview, "I always liked to draw and everybody told me I was good. But I never drew kid's pictures. No stick figures or big suns in the sky. My drawings were always adult pictures."

Lee's father founded the Hyang-Lin Institute, the first of its kind in Korea, which trained young artists for either a professional career or entrance to the College of Fine Arts at Seoul National University. "Competition for entry to the university is very stiff," Lee told *SATA,* "and my father's institute helped prepare many artists." Art was second nature to Lee growing up, but during high school he wondered about it as a career. "I thought for a time of being maybe a guitar player or a tennis player, but finally I went back to art. Sculpture was very important to me then; also, I loved the works of Rodin and working in three dimensions. In the end, though, I settled on painting."

Lee earned his B.F.A. at Seoul's College of Fine Arts in 1985, but artistically speaking this was not an easy time for him. He explained to *SATA:* "I love painting and drawing, especially narrative and realistic forms. I like to tell stories about people in my paintings, but in Korea there was a big push for abstract and conceptual painting. I felt very lonely in Korea because I was developing a very realistic style. I took as my models such painters as the Europeans Vermeer, Rembrandt, Delacroix, and Daumier, and the Americans George Bellows, Andrew Wyeth, and Edward Hopper." Isolated or not, Lee continued to work in Korea after graduation, teaching drawing at his father's art institute as well as helping to manage it; the institute had grown to some two hundred to three hundred students. At the same time, he was beginning to see that illustration, the most basic narrative use of art, might hold possibilities for him. "But I knew that in order to learn illustration, I would have to leave Korea. The history of book illustration is very short there. There was not even a department for it in the college. The center for illustration is New York. My older sister was living in New York at the time, managing a framing shop and art gallery, and she encouraged me to come."

Picking up and moving to a new country with no security in the future was not an easy decision to make, especially since Lee was married and the father of two children. He had met his wife in high school, and she had attended the Hyang-Lin Institute as well as the College of Fine Arts at Seoul National University with Lee. In 1990, however, Lee was finally ready. "I had seen the works of Marshall Arisman, the American illustrator, at an exhibition in Korea," Lee told *SATA,* "and wanted to study under him." Both Lee and his wife attended the School of Visual Arts in New York; Lee received his M.F.A. in 1992 in illustration. New York was a revelation for Lee. "The art supply stores here were unlike anything I had seen at home," he recalled. "There was everything any artist could want and more. This allowed me to begin experimenting with technique."

Out of these experiments, Lee developed an encaustic wax technique, his own unique invention. The encaustic method is a way of painting on statues or providing architectural detail with colored wax which is later fused with hot irons. But Lee, a sculptor himself, brought the technique to two-dimensional art. "Basically, I melt beeswax onto paper and then scratch out the images like an etching," Lee said in his *SATA* interview. "I'm always looking for the best tools to do this scratching out. Kmart, for example, has a surprising number of useful articles like pins and needles. Once I have the images scratched out of the wax, I apply the oil paint. What results is a kind of relief sculpture on the paper, and working like this is a kind of sculpturing. For me it's a bridge between painting and sculpture, both of which I love." By scraping away the wax, Lee leaves a surface to his paintings that duplicates the effects of nature—of wind and rain and temperature eroding the surfaces of buildings or the landscape. The monochromatic, almost sepia, quality enhances this time-worn look.

It is a technique that exactly fit his first major exhibit, one that he and his wife shared, *Urbanscapes: Images of New York City.* Imbued with the sense of the urban landscape both in Seoul where he grew up and in New York, Lee captured the feel of the city with his encaustic beeswax technique in pictures somewhat reminiscent of Edward Hopper. "Lee deftly creates his dolorous moods with subdued colors of pigmented wax on paper," Charles Keller noted in a review of the exhibition in *People's Weekly World.* But if his painting career was moving along with group and one-man shows, Lee's attempts at finding illustration work were proving more difficult. "I would bring my portfolio to all sorts of magazine offices," Lee explained to *SATA,* "and they liked my work, but I just had no luck in landing a job. There was the language problem, partly, but also the fact that I had no real professional experience, only exhibitions and degrees." Finally, however, it was the exhibitions that provided a break for Lee. A chance cancellation at a showing allowed Lee to hang his paintings, and an editor from Putnam saw his work and liked it. "I showed him my portfolio and he introduced me to Philip Lee of Lee & Low Books, who was looking for illustrators. That's how I got the contract to do the illustrations for *Baseball Saved Us.*"

If the encaustic technique fit the urban landscape, it was also one well suited to the desert landscape where much of *Baseball Saved Us* takes place. The book tells the story of a young Japanese-American boy, Shorty, who is relocated along with his family to an internment camp during the Second World War. It is a bleak and barren desert where the camp is located. Ken Mochizuki, whose parents were sent to the Minidoka internment camp in Idaho, wrote a solemn and understated evocation of that experience, told from a young child's point of view. It was a degrading experience, one of the darker moments in U.S. history, and the family structure of these Japanese Americans began to break down at the camp.

Baseball Saved Us tells the story of how one group of internees fought against such a breakdown. "One day," Shorty relates in the book, "my dad looked out at the endless desert and decided then and there to build a baseball field. He said people needed something to do in camp." From that simple vision grew a team effort to construct a diamond out of sagebrush wasteland, to find gloves, balls, and bats, and to fashion baseball uniforms out of mattress coverings. The story is not only about the perseverance of a people, however; it is also the story of Shorty, last chosen and never very good at baseball, who learns to "do something" on his own. With his team down in the bottom of the ninth inning of the final game, Shorty is at bat and, inspired by the anger he feels at the ever-watchful eye of one of the guards on a tower, he manages to get a hit and win the game. Once the war is over, however, Shorty's trials have not ended. Back home, he is called the "Jap" by kids at school, and once again it is baseball that saves him when he hits a home run to win the big game. "In a sense," noted Ira Berkow in the *New York Times Book Review,* "it is a despairing commentary that so many boys' and men's self-respect has too often been dependent on such athletic, or physical, moments." But Shorty does manage to prove himself by this deed; he has made a physical as well as spiritual journey throughout the course of the book.

"When I read the text of the story," Lee told *SATA,* "I knew I wanted to make the feeling of a movie with the book. Recently movies have become increasingly realistic and much more visually powerful. If we look at an old James Bond movie, for example, it seems so dated and not really suspenseful at all. Movies are much more *now,* much more in the moment. And it is this hyperrealism that I tried for in my illustrations." In order to achieve that realism, Lee immersed himself in physical artifacts of the time. He gathered pictures—many by the photographer Ansel Adams—of internment camps. Additionally, he collected baseball paraphernalia and placed it around his work space and his living environment. "I try to get into the mind of the main characters of the story I'm illustrating. I even kept a baseball on my bedside table when I was doing *Baseball Saved Us.* I try to live in that stuff. Clothes, hats, old photos, videos—all this stuff helps me to understand the story and the characters. But it makes for a pretty crazy working space." Most difficult of all for Lee was coming up with an appropriate model for Shorty. Lee tried using his son Brian, but soon the boy came up with the very valid complaint, "I'm not a Japanese boy, I'm a Korean boy," Lee recalled for *SATA.* Luck again played a part in Lee's career in the form of a neighbor child, a Japanese American, whom Lee saw playing baseball one day. Lee had his model for Shorty.

It took Lee several months to gather his references for *Baseball Saved Us,* but the actual painting on paper took only one month, with Lee finishing up to one plate per day once he had the story and characters firmly in mind. His own illustrations served as further references as he would tack them up on the walls, creating a moving picture of the action. These he would further condense or elaborate on to achieve his realistic movie approach. From the cover of the book on, Lee creates the mood of the story. The boy Shorty is wielding a bat on the book's cover, teammates seated excitedly behind him. And behind them is a high-wire fence surmounted by rolls of barbed wire, providing a stark contrast to the youthful elation of the kids playing baseball. With a mixture of full-page and multi-panel illustrations, Lee sets the rhythm and pace of the book, taking Shorty and his family from the dreary scene of a house in chaos as they are being moved, to a full-page illustration of their arrival at the camp. Here the color is so monochromatic as to recall an old black and white photo, and the resemblance to photos of Europe's concentration camps is

at once startling and evocative. Once the father has decreed that the camp should build a baseball diamond, the action sequences move briskly, with three panels showing the men and boys digging up the sagebrush and building stands and the women sewing the uniforms. Tight close-ups alternate with longer shots as perspective changes from Shorty to a more general point of view. Lee follows cinematic precepts closely in this regard. All is not bleakness, though, for the pages of jubilation at Shorty's victory hits—both at the camp and back home—are full of exuberance and lighter colors. Kids leap and fly about, looking as if they are about to come out of the page—an added advantage to the dimensionality that Lee's encaustic technique lends the illustrations.

"Dom is a diligent worker, spending long hours on his research to insure the project's authenticity," Philip Lee, his publisher, said in an interview with Alex Jay in *Asian New Yorker.* "He also possesses a wonderful creative vision, presenting his work in a unique and appealing way." Most reviewers of *Baseball Saved Us* offered similar opinions as the publisher. Ellen Fader, writing in *Horn Book,* noted that "Lee's pictures . . . are highly accomplished." Fader also pointed out how the monochromatic views of the camp contrast sharply with the brighter blue skies at the end of the book as Shorty is cheered by his team. Many reviewers commented on how Lee's style fit the theme of the book. Hazel Rochman, writing in *Booklist,* commented particularly on Lee's illustrations, inspired by Ansel Adams' photographs of the Manzanar camp in 1943. "Lee's images evoke the bleak desert isolation," Rochman noted. Berkow, in his *New York Times Book Review* critique, concluded that Lee's illustrations "add a proper serious mood to this fine book." Awards followed critical acclaim, and *Baseball Saved Us* garnered not only a Parents' Choice Award, but also a Cuffies Award as the Best Multicultural Title of 1993. Such a reception was a blessing not only for Lee but for his publishers, a new and small press committed to multicultural themes.

For his second book, Lee once again teamed with Mochizuki on a book with a multicultural theme. The story of a Japanese-American boy, Donnie, growing up in the 1960s, *Heroes* asks hard questions about what really makes a hero and about fitting in. Donnie is tired of being the "bad guy" when he and his friends play war, but his friends insist that he looks like the enemy, as it is the era of the Vietnam War. When he tells his friends that his dad and uncle served in the U.S. Army, they only laugh at him, and when he asks his father and uncle to give him the proof he needs, they advise him to play something else besides war. "Real heroes don't brag. They just do what they are supposed to do," his Uncle Yosh tells him. A selection of the Children's Book-of-the-Month Club, *Heroes* tells a story not likely to be found in traditional children's books.

"With this book I did not have to go so far for references," Lee said in his interview with *SATA.* "The father and uncle run a gas station, and I was lucky enough to find a mock-up of one in a museum in Indiana where I was attending a workshop. So I took a photo of it and that helped a lot. For the country setting and playground, I could use just about anything, but the gas station from the 1960s was one thing I badly needed."

The work on *Heroes* took less time than *Baseball Saved Us*. "Searching for references only took a month and then the actual drawing and painting was another month. You get to know the process, the ins and outs of publishing, and that helps. And I have more confidence now," Lee said. With *Heroes*, Lee was also able to choose which illustrations and how many he wanted, a process that liberates him, he says. Lee again employed his encaustic technique with a somewhat monochromatic sepia tone, especially effective in panels in which the young boy Donnie is in the attic picking through old photos and memorabilia of his father's military life. In her *Horn Book* review of *Heroes*, Ellen Fader wrote: "Lee has done a superb job of creating realistic, individualized faces for each of the characters." A *Publishers Weekly* critic concluded that Lee's "burnished paintings exude the patina of age and the glint of hard-won experience."

While both *Baseball Saved Us* and *Heroes* were for ages four and up, a later assignment has taken Lee to material for the fourth-to sixth-grade level. *On the Wings of Peace* is a compilation of short stories edited by Sheila Hamanaka. "I found that doing illustrations for this level was a little bit better for me because my style in general suits an older audience," Lee explained to *SATA*. "It is a little heavy for younger readers, but doing illustrations for older kids you find the stories are longer and have more weight and can carry the heavier painting style I have. I like to paint and draw the real things in life. The everyday. I find my strengths are in structure and line. I am not a strong colorist. For that I often consult my wife."

Lee again teamed with Mochizuki on the picture book *Passage to Freedom: The Sugihara Story*, the true story of a Japanese consul in Lithuania who helped Jewish refugees escape during World War II. *Passage to Freedom* is told from the point of view of Hiroki Sugihara, the consul's son, who despite his youth, understands how his father's decisions put the whole family in peril. In her *Booklist* review of the work, Hazel Rochman found Lee's mixed-media illustrations "stirring . . . humane and beautiful." Writing in *School Library Journal*, Shirley Wilton found Lee's illustrations "dramatic," remarking favorably on how the artist focused his efforts on capturing the faces of the men, women, and children during this difficult period in history.

An Asian theme also animates Lawrence McKay's *Journey Home*, on which Lee worked with his wife. In this story, a young girl named Mai returns to Vietnam to search for her birth parents, her only clue being a kite that they gave her as an infant. The illustrations in *Jour-*

ney Home demonstrate a collaborative effort between the Lees that resulted, as critics noted, in more colorful and varied panels. According to a *Publishers Weekly* reviewer, the duo's "realistic art, by turns brightly lighted and almost oppressively dark, seamlessly matches the changing moods of the text." *Booklist*'s Hazel Rochman similarly found the Lee's efforts "a powerful part of the narrative."

When not illustrating, Lee is still busy painting on canvas. "I like to do both illustration and painting," Lee said in his interview. "Making a picture book that works is great fun. . . . When I work, I concentrate on it with a feeling of love, wanting to share that kind of feeling with the kids who will be looking at it between covers. And when I walk around the city and see even tragic scenes like a homeless person, I still feel a kind of love. It comes with both types of painting for me. That's why I want to continue doing both illustration and fine art painting, and in many ways I believe there is no difference between the two."

Biographical and Critical Sources

BOOKS

Ken Mochizuki, *Baseball Saved Us,* illustrated by Dom Lee, Lee & Low Books (New York, NY), 1993.

Ken Mochizuki, *Heroes,* illustrated by Dom Lee, Lee & Low Books (New York, NY), 1995.

Something about the Author Autobiography Series, Volume 26, Gale (Detroit, MI), 1999.

PERIODICALS

Asian New Yorker, August, 1993, Alex Jay, "Seoul Artist Captures the Soul of America," p. 7.

Booklist, April 15, 1993, Hazel Rochman, review of *Baseball Saved Us,* pp. 1523-1524; May 15, 1997, Hazel Rochman, review of *Passage to Freedom: The Sugihara Story,* p. 1574; May 1, 1998, Hazel Rochman, review of *Journey Home,* p. 1518.

Bulletin of the Center for Children's Books, May, 1993, p. 290.

Horn Book, July-August, 1993, Ellen Fader, review of *Baseball Saved Us,* pp. 453-454; May-June, 1995, Ellen Fader, review of *Heroes,* p. 327.

Kirkus Reviews, March 1, 1993, p. 303.

New York Times Book Review, April 4, 1993, Ira Berkow, review of *Baseball Saved Us,* p. 26.

People's Weekly World, May 15, 1993, Charles Keller, "Two Koreans Look at New York," p. 21.

Publishers Weekly, March 29, 1993, p. 55; March 6, 1995, review of *Heroes,* p. 69; April 21, 1997, review of *Passage to Freedom,* p. 71; May 25, 1998, review of *Journey Home,* p. 90; September 27, 1999, review of *Young Heroes of the Bible,* p. 98.

Baseball Saved Us *tells the story of how forming a baseball field gave Japanese Americans a reason to live while forced to reside in internment camps during World War II, illustrated by Dom Lee*

School Library Journal, June, 1993, p. 84; July, 1997, Shirley Wilton, review of *Passage to Freedom,* p. 86; June, 1998, Diane S. Marton, review of *Journey Home,* p. 114; January, 2000, Elizabeth Maggio, review of *Young Heroes of the Bible,* p. 119.

ONLINE

Dom Lee Home Page, http://www.domandk.com/ (December 26, 2003).

Houghton Mifflin Reading, http://www.eduplace.com/kids/hmr/mtai/dlee.htm/ (May 29, 2003), "Meet the Illustrator: Dom Lee."

Lee & Low Books, http://www.leeandlow.com/booktalk/ (May 29, 2003), "Booktalk with Dom and Keunhee Lee."

OTHER

Lee, Dom, telephone interview with J. Sydney Jones for *Something about the Author,* February 22, 1995.

In Journey Home, *Mai travels to Vietnam, her mother's birthplace. (Written by Lawrence McKay, Jr. Illustrated by Dom and Keunhee Lee.)*

*   *   *

LEUCK, Laura 1962-

Personal

Surname is pronounced "luke"; born July 9, 1962, in Toms River, NJ; daughter of John L. (a health care consultant) and Gwen (a homemaker; maiden name, Youngworth) Yoder; married Arthur R. Leuck (a facilities manager), September 15, 1984; children: Matthew, Shane. *Education:* Monmouth College, B.A. *Hobbies and other interests:* Traveling, hiking, films, theatre.

Addresses

Home and office—19 Benjamin Rush Ln., Princeton, NJ 08540. *E-mail*—lauraleuck@patmedia.net.

Career

Poet and author of children's books. Worked for *Asbury Park Press,* Neptune, NJ.

Member

Authors Guild, Authors League of America, Society of Children's Book Writers and Illustrators, Electronic Writer's Association.

Awards, Honors

Ben-Yitzhak Award, 1996, for *Sun Is Falling, Night Is Calling;* Children's Choice Award, 1999, for *My Monster Mama Loves Me So.*

Writings

Sun Is Falling, Night Is Calling, illustrated by Ora Eitan, Simon & Schuster (New York, NY), 1994.

My Brother Has Ten Tiny Toes, illustrated by Clara Vulliamy, A. Whitman (Morton Grove, IL), 1997.

Teeny, Tiny Mouse: A Book about Colors, illustrated by Pat Schories, BridgeWater Books (Mahwah, NJ), 1998.

My Monster Mama Loves Me So, illustrated by Mark Buehner, HarperCollins (New York, NY), 1999.

Goodnight, Baby Monster, illustrated by Nigel McMullen, HarperCollins (New York, NY), 2002.

Jeepers Creeper: A Monstrous ABC, illustrated by David Parkins, Chronicle Books (San Francisco, CA), 2003.

One Witch, illustrated by S. D. Schindler, Walker (New York, NY), 2003.

Twenty-six monsters use their names to teach each other the alphabet, in Jeepers Creepers: A Monstrous ABC. *(Written by Laura Leuck, with illustrations by David Parkins.)*

My Beastly Brother, illustrated by Scott Nash, HarperCollins (New York, NY), 2003.

My Creature Teacher, illustrated by Scott Nash, HarperCollins (New York, NY), 2004.

Contributor of poetry and stories to periodicals, including *Hopscotch* and *Turtle.* Leuck's books have been translated into French.

Work in Progress

Santa Claws, for Chronicle Books (San Francisco, CA).

Sidelights

Through the use of verse, Laura Leuck creates picture books for young readers that teach children about the joy of language and illustrate several basic concepts. In *Teeny, Tiny Mouse: A Book about Colors,* for example, Leuck employs a simple, repetitive text in describing a young mouse touring his home—actually a lavishly furnished doll's house—with his mother in tow. *Children's Book Review Service* contributor Arlene Wartenberg dubbed the book "clever" in its interactive concept, as the pair travel from room to room, each time posing readers a color-related question. Noting that the "book invites sharing and further color exploration," *Christian Science Monitor* contributor Karen Carden commended *Teeny, Tiny Mouse* for its "clear concepts and reassuring repetition."

Leuck relates the rituals associated with night and getting ready for bed in *Sun Is Falling, Night Is Calling.* Such things as the moon in the sky, a bedtime story, a song, a teddy bear, and sweet dreams are described as a mother rabbit guides her young one towards sleep. "In spare, gently cadenced verse, newcomer Leuck beckons readers into the soothing rituals of nighttime," commented a *Publishers Weekly* reviewer, while *School Librarian* contributor David Lewis wrote that Leuck's rhythmic text, which describes "the gradual winding down of the toddler's day," is "genuinely charming."

In 1999's *My Monster Mama Loves Me So,* Leuck spins a tender tale of a green, round-eyed, sharp-toothed monster that only a monster mother could love. A reviewer for *Early Childhood Educational Journal* found the story "captivating" and maintained that the humorously illustrated book "hits the spot," while in *School Library Journal,* Amy Lilien-Harper praised Leuck for providing story-time aficionados with "a reassuring message" packaged in "a funny, mildly scary story." A *Publishers Weekly* contributor had special praise for the author-illustrator collaboration, calling Mark Buehner's soft-edged illustrations "vibrant" and "cuddly," and predicting that Leuck's text with its "tender tone" will make the book a sure-fire "bedtime favorite for drowsy toddlers."

Monsters also figure in *Goodnight, Baby Monster* and *Jeepers Creepers: A Monstrous ABC,* the latter illustrated by David Parkins. In *Goodnight, Baby Monster,* which *School Library Journal* reviewer Rosalyn Pierini described as "a gentle, rhyming story chock-full of nighttime creatures both real and imaginary," Leuck uses poetic prose to offset imaginary terrors of the night and render them harmless, as a host of scary nocturnal creatures are revealed to be stuffed animals sharing the bed with a mother and child reading a good-night tale. Twenty-six monstrous children, arranged alphabetically according to type, march across the pages of *Jeepers Creepers.* The group gathers together for a fun-filled first day of school in this picture book that a *Kirkus Reviews* critic called a "cheerful offering" from Leuck.

Other picture books penned by Leuck include *My Beastly Brother* and *My Creature Teacher,* both featuring quirky illustrations by artist Scott Nash and "a steady beat of humorous, monster-inspired verse," in the opinion of a *Publishers Weekly* critic, reviewing *My Beastly Brother.* Idiosyncratic illustrations by S. D. Schindler grace the pages of *One Witch,* a counting book with a difference. Readers learn the recipe for a distasteful witches' brew, containing everything from straw-stuffed scarecrows to fish tails and bird claws, through Leuck's rhyming text that a *Kirkus Reviews* contributor described as "jaunty" and *School Library Journal* reviewer James K. Irwin praised as "romping" and spiced with "plenty of alliteration." Writing in

From **Goodnight, Baby Monster,** *written by Leuck. (Illustrated by Nigel McMullen.)*

Booklist, Gillian Engberg found *One Witch* "a great choice for October preschool read-alouds."

Biographical and Critical Sources

PERIODICALS

Booklist, June 1, 1994, Carolyn Phelan, review of *Sun Is Falling, Night Is Calling,* p. 1841; April 15, 1997, Julie Corsaro, review of *My Baby Brother Has Ten Tiny Toes,* p. 1436; September 1, 2003, Gillian Engberg, review of *One Witch,* p. 136.

Children's Book Review Service, spring, 1998, Arlene Wartenberg, review of *Teeny, Tiny Mouse: A Book about Colors,* p. 136.

Christian Science Monitor, September 24, 1998, Karen Carden, "Bright Books Teach Smart Concepts," p. B9.

Early Childhood Educational Journal, winter, 1999, review of *My Monster Mama Loves Me So,* p. 106.

Horn Book Guide, fall, 1997, Martha V. Parravano, review of *My Baby Brother Has Ten Tiny Toes,* p. 253.

Kirkus Reviews, July 1, 2003, review of *One Witch,* p. 912; August 1, 2003, review of *Jeepers Creepers: A Monstrous ABC,* p. 1019.

Publishers Weekly, April 11, 1994, review of *Sun Is Falling, Night Is Calling,* p. 63; March 15, 1999, review of *Teeny, Tiny Mouse,* p. 61; September 27, 1999, review of *My Monster Mama Loves Me So,* p. 103; August 4, 2003, reviews of *One Witch,* p. 77, and *My Beastly Brother,* p. 79.

School Librarian, November, 1996, David Lewis, review of *Sun Is Falling, Night Is Calling,* p. 147.

School Library Journal, March, 1997, Patricia Pearl Doyle, review of *My Brother Has Ten Tiny Toes,* pp. 160-161; May, 1998, Jody McCoy, review of *Teeny, Tiny Mouse,* p. 120; January, 2000, Amy Lilien-Harper, review of *My Monster Mama Loves Me So,* pp. 106-107; September, 2002, Rosalyn Pierini, review of *Goodnight, Baby Monster,* p. 198; August, 2003, James K. Irwin, review of *One Witch,* p. 136.

Times Educational Supplement, September 27, 1996, Ann Treneman, review of *Sun Is Falling, Night Is Calling,* p. 2.

ONLINE

Laura Leuck Home Page, http://www.patmedia.net/aleuck/ (December 17, 2003).*

*   *   *

LEVINE, I(srael) E. 1923-2003

OBITUARY NOTICE—See index for *SATA* sketch: Born August 30, 1923, in New York, NY; died of complications following vascular surgery May 10, 2003, in Queens, NY. Publicist and author. Levine was a former director of public affairs at City College of the City University of New York, and he also wrote books for young readers. After serving in the U.S. Army Air Forces during World War II and being decorated with an Air Medal, he graduated from City College in 1946 with a B.S.S. He then joined the staff at his alma mater as a publicity assistant, moving up to director of public relations from 1954 to 1977 and assistant to the president from 1964 to 1966. He left city college to edit *Health Care Week* for two years, followed by two more years as an editor for William H. White Publications. From 1981 to 1987 Levine was the director of communications for the American Jewish Congress. He then became chief operating officer for Richard Cohen Associates, where he remained until 1999. The next year he formed his own company, I. E. Levine Public Relations. Besides his work in public relations, Levine authored over a dozen nonfiction books for young readers, many of which are biographies, including *Conqueror of Smallpox: Dr. Edward Jenner* (1960), *Inventive Wizard: George Westinghouse* (1962), *Young Man in the White House: John Fitzgerald Kennedy* (1964), and *The Many Faces of Slavery* (1975).

OBITUARIES AND OTHER SOURCES:

BOOKS

Writers Directory, 18th edition, St. James Press (Detroit, MI), 2003.

PERIODICALS

New York Times, May 18, 2003, p. A33.

M

MARSDEN, John 1950-

Personal

Born September 27, 1950, in Melbourne, Victoria, Australia; son of Eustace Cullen Hudson (a banker) and Jeanne Lawler (a homemaker; maiden name, Ray) Marsden. *Ethnicity:* "Anglo-Australian." *Education:* Mitchell College, diploma in teaching, 1978; University of New England, B.A., 1981. *Hobbies and other interests:* Conservation.

Addresses

Home—RMB 1250, Romsey, Victoria 3434, Australia. *Agent*—Jill Grinberg, Anderson Grinberg Literary Management, 266 West 23rd St., New York, NY 10011.

Career

Geelong Grammar School, Geelong, Victoria, Australia, English teacher, 1982-90; writer, 1991—; primary school teacher, c. 1995. Worked at various jobs, including truck driver, hospital worker, and delivery person, c. 1968-77.

Awards, Honors

Children's Book of the Year Award, Children's Book Council of Australia (CBCA), 1988, Premier's Award (Victoria, Australia), 1988, Young Adult Book Award (New South Wales, Australia), 1988, Alan Marshall Award, 1988, Christopher Award, 1989, KOALA (Kids Own Australian Literature Awards), 1989, Notable Book, American Library Association, 1989, and COOL Award (Canberra's Own Outstanding List), 1995, all for *So Much to Tell You . . .;* Writers' Fellowship, Australia Council, 1993; Australian Multicultural Children's Book Award, 1994, YABBA (Young Australians Best Book Award), 1995, WAYRBA (West Australian Young Readers' Books Award), 1995, KOALA Award, 1995, COOL Award, 1996 and 2001, BILBY Award (Books I Love Best Yearly), 1998, CYBER Award (Children's

John Marsden

Yearly Best Ever Reads), 2000, and New South Wales Talking Book Award, all for *Tomorrow, When the War Began;* Grand Jury Prize for Austria's favorite young person's novel, 1996, for *Letters from the Inside;* New South Wales Talking Book Award, and CYBER Award, both for *The Dead of Night;* Book of the Year Award, Australian Booksellers Association, 1998, and WAYRBA Award, 1999, both for *Burning for Revenge;* WAYRBA Award, 1998, COOL Award, 1999, and Buxtehude Bulle (Germany), 2000, all for *The Third Day, the Frost;* KOALA Award, 1999, for *Cool School: You Make It Happen;* Children's Book of the Year Award,

179

CBCA, 1999, for *The Rabbits;* COOL Award, and WAYRBA Award, both 2000, both for *The Night Is for Hunting.*

Writings

So Much to Tell You . . ., Walter McVitty (Glebe, Australia), 1988, Little, Brown (Boston, MA), 1989.

The Journey, Pan (Sydney, Australia), 1988.

The Great Gatenby, Pan (Sydney, Australia), 1989.

Staying Alive in Year Five, Piper (Sydney, Australia), 1989.

Out of Time, Pan (Sydney, Australia), 1990.

Letters from the Inside, Pan Macmillan (Sydney, Australia), 1991, Houghton Mifflin (Boston, MA), 1994.

Take My Word for It: Lisa's Journal, Pan Macmillan (Sydney, Australia), 1992.

Looking for Trouble, Pan Macmillan (Sydney, Australia), 1993.

Cool School: You Make It Happen, Pan Macmillan (Sydney, Australia), 1995.

Checkers, Pan Macmillan (Sydney, Australia), 1996, Houghton Mifflin (Boston, MA), 1998.

Creep Street: You Make It Happen, Macmillan (Sydney, Australia), 1996.

Dear Miffy, Pan Macmillan (Sydney, Australia), 1997.

Winter, Pan Macmillan (Sydney, Australia), 2000, Scholastic (New York, NY), 2002.

Millie, Pan Macmillan (Sydney, Australia), 2002.

"TOMORROW, WHEN THE WAR BEGAN" SERIES

Tomorrow, When the War Began, Pan Macmillan (Sydney, Australia), 1993, Houghton Mifflin (Boston, MA), 1995.

The Dead of Night, Pan Macmillan (Sydney, Australia), 1994, Houghton Mifflin (Boston, MA), 1997.

The Third Day, the Frost, Pan Macmillan (Sydney, Australia), 1995, published as *A Killing Frost,* Houghton Mifflin (Boston, MA), 1998.

Darkness, Be My Friend, Pan Macmillan (Sydney, Australia), 1996, Houghton Mifflin (Boston, MA), 1999.

Burning for Revenge, Pan Macmillan (Sydney, Australia), 1997, Houghton Mifflin (Boston, MA), 2000.

The Night Is for Hunting, Pan Macmillan (Sydney, Australia), 1998, Houghton Mifflin (Boston, MA), 2001.

The Other Side of Dawn, Pan Macmillan (Sydney, Australia), 1999, Houghton Mifflin (Boston, MA), 2002.

While I Live: The Ellie Linton Chronicles, Pan Macmillan (Sydney, Australia), 2003.

OTHER

Everything I Know about Writing (nonfiction), Macmillan (Sydney, Australia), 1993.

So Much to Tell You: The Play, Walter McVitty (Montville, Australia), 1994.

(Editor) *This I Believe: Over 100 Eminent Australians Explore Life's Big Questions* (essays), Random House (Milsons Point, Australia), 1996.

(Editor) *For Weddings and a Funeral* (poetry), Pan Macmillan (Sydney, Australia), 1996.

Prayer for the Twenty-first Century (picture book), Lothian (Port Melbourne, Australia), 1997, Star Bright Books (New York, NY), 1998, also published as *Message for the Twenty-first Century,* Ticktock (Tonbridge, England), 1999.

Secret Men's Business: Manhood: The Big Gig (nonfiction), Pan Macmillan (Sydney, Australia), 1998.

Norton's Hut (picture book), illustrated by Peter Gouldthorpe, Lothian Books (Port Melbourne, Australia), 1998, Star Bright Books (New York, NY), 1999.

The Rabbits (picture book), illustrated by Shaun Tan, Lothian Books (Port Melbourne, Australia), 1998.

Marsden on Marsden: The Stories behind John Marsden's Bestselling Books, Pan Macmillan (Sydney, Australia), 2000.

The Head Book, Pan Macmillan (Sydney, Australia), 2001.

The Boy You Brought Home: A Single Mother's Guide to Raising Sons, Pan Macmillan (Sydney, Australia), 2002.

A Day in the Life of Me, Lothian Books (Port Melbourne, Australia), 2002.

Contributor to *Goodnight & Thanks for the Teeth: A Fairies' Tale,* Pan Macmillan (Sydney, Australia), 1999.

Adaptations

The Journey was adapted into an opera of the same name and published by the Australian Music Centre (Grosvenor Place, Australia), 1999.

Sidelights

John Marsden is one of the most popular writers for teens in Australia and the author of the critically acclaimed "Tomorrow, When the War Began" series. The reasons for Marsden's international fame are twofold, claim critics. First, he is known for not talking down to his audience, fully aware that for many teenagers, life is bleak, challenging, and dangerous. Second, he is applauded for his ability to craft exciting adventure stories in which the young protagonists are called to adult action—with all its moral and ethical implications. This is particularly the case in the "Tomorrow, When the War Began" series, in which a group of teens engage in a guerilla war against a vastly superior force that has occupied Australia. Noting that Marsden's titles "have consistently met with overwhelming critical and commercial success," *Horn Book* reviewer Karen Jameyson concluded: "Marsden has always touted the importance of writing honestly, of not shielding the young from topics that some might see as too depressing or shocking. And this frankness and honesty have clearly struck a chord with young adults."

Marsden debunked some of the myths of his native Australia in an essay he wrote for the *Something about the Author Autobiography Series* (*SAAS*). "Growing up in Australia wasn't a matter of kangaroos, surfboards, and the wild outback," he said. "Not for me, anyway.

Book jacket illustration by Vivienne Goodman from The Night Is for Hunting, *written by John Marsden.*

My childhood was spent in the quiet country towns in the green southern states of Victoria and Tasmania. It was peaceful, secure, and often very boring." Marsden's father managed a bank, a responsibility he held for forty-eight years. This had a marked yet contrary effect on the young Marsden. He related: "Perhaps one of the things I've done in my adult life is to react against that kind of commitment. At the latest count, I've had thirty-two different jobs."

Growing up in small Australian towns during the 1950s gave Marsden experiences that were quite different from children in urban America during the same era. In Marsden's village, ice was still delivered to people for their iceboxes, cooking was mainly done on stoves powered by fuel, and no one he knew owned a television set. "I first saw television when I was ten years old. In our small Tasmanian town, an electrical shop brought in a TV and put it in their window for the wedding of Princess Margaret. On the great day, the whole town gathered in front of the shop and the set was switched on. All we saw was 'snow'—grey and white static, with a few figures vaguely visible through the murk," Marsden wrote in *SAAS*.

Marsden was too infatuated with literature to care if his family had a television. "I read and read and read," he commented. "When I ran out of books for boys I read the girls' books. . . . Some days, I'd borrow three titles (the maximum allowed) from the town library, read them, and get them back to the library by five o'clock, in time to exchange them for three more before the library shut. I'd become a speed reader without really trying!" Marsden also found another pastime that was to help him with his later writing. "My favourite game was to draw a town layout on the driveway with chalk and use little model cars to bring the town to life. Perhaps that's how I first became used to creating and living in imaginary worlds," he recalled in *SAAS*.

Marsden became such a lover of books that by the time he was in grade three, he had memorized *The Children of Cherry Tree Farm.* His teacher would use him when she wanted to take a break. "She'd have me stand up in front of the class and recite the next chapter to the other kids . . . from memory. She'd go off to the staff room and leave me there. I loved it! Maybe that's where I got my first taste of the power of storytelling."

That school year was also a difficult one for Marsden. His teacher would fly into rages and yell at the children. She believed in corporal punishment and would cane the children for the slightest disobedience. Each Friday, the teacher would give the class a ten-question quiz; if a student failed to answer at least seven questions correctly, he was beaten. "Recently, I met up with a girl who'd been in that class with me," Marsden related. "As she talked about those Friday tests, she started to tremble with the memories. At the age of forty-four, she was still haunted by her grade three days." When Marsden was promoted to the next grade, he was rewarded in two ways. His teacher was much more nurturing, and she saw in him the seeds of a writer, letting him edit the school paper. "This was my first taste of publication," he told *SAAS*. "It was a heady experience. Seeing my name in print, having people—even adults—reacting to and commenting on what I'd written was powerful stuff."

At the age of ten, Marsden moved with his family to Sydney. Having mainly grown up in country towns, he was fascinated by the switch from rural to urban life. "I thought Sydney was huge and exotic, and wildly exciting," Marsden commented. "I spent my first week collecting bus tickets, to the amusement of the staff in the hotel where we stayed. Riding on the escalators was as good as Disneyland."

Marsden's parents enrolled him at King's School, a prestigious private school that was run like a military establishment. There was very little Marsden liked about the place, from the stuffy uniforms to the military drills they were required to perform. He also felt out of touch with happenings in the world. "The rest of the Western world was embarking on a decade of drugs, free love, and the Beatles, but at King's, boys continued to salute their teachers, drill with rifles for hours every week, and stand to attention when speaking to prefects." Marsden spent his time in somewhat subversive activities. He wrote short books with plots that were stolen from famous mystery novels, distributed his underground newspaper about new rock bands, and read books under his desk during class.

At the time, Marsden found that there was very little literature written for adolescents. He read adult literature but was quite taken aback by his first experience with J. D. Salinger's *Catcher in the Rye,* a classic coming-of-age story that was—and still is—controversial. The book "had me gasping for breath," Marsden commented in *SAAS.* "I'd never dreamt you were allowed to write like that. . . . For the first time I was reading a genuine, contemporary teenage voice. If I've had any success at capturing teenage voices on paper, it's because of what I learnt at the age of fifteen from J. D. Salinger."

School had very little settling influence on Marsden. He continued being a rebel despite the conservative atmosphere. "I began to question everything: religion, education, law, parenting. All the institutions and customs that I'd been taught to accept unquestioningly," he related to *SAAS.* It is of little surprise that when Marsden graduated from King's he had not received any military awards or promotions. He did, however, win some academic prizes, including one for a 40,000-word essay on poets of World War I.

After graduating, Marsden enrolled at the University of Sydney but soon lost interest in his studies and dropped out. He then tried his hand at many exotic jobs. He told *SAAS* that some of his employment included "collecting blood, looking after a mortuary at nights, working in a side-show, being a night clerk in the casualty department of Sydney Hospital, and guarding Australia's oldest house from vandals." Marsden's interest in these occupations, however, generally waned rather quickly. "Once I mastered a job, I got bored with it and started restlessly looking for the next challenge. Maybe that was a reaction to the boredom of my early life and the tedium of most of my years in schools."

Marsden continued to write and submitted a novel to a publisher that was rejected. He drifted from job to job, yet somehow succeeded in finishing the first year of a law school course. However, he slipped into a deep depression and ended up in a psychiatric institution, where he met a fourteen-year-old girl who would not speak to anyone. Marsden wondered about this, and on the girl's last day at the institution, he got to talk to her. The girl's plight became the inspiration for Marsden's novel *So Much to Tell You . . .*

At the age of twenty-seven, bored with his latest promotion to a desk job at a delivery company, Marsden saw a newspaper advertisement about teaching classes and decided to apply. "I'd always had a vague idea that

Ellie and her friends contemplate returning to their families in Australia after being airlifted to New Zealand and safety during the war, in Darkness, Be My Friend. *(Written by Marsden. Book jacket illustration by Goodman.)*

I might enjoy teaching, but then I'd had the same vague ideas about other jobs and they hadn't worked out. . . . From the very first day, however, I knew I'd found my vocation." Marsden soon had a position teaching at Geelong Grammar School, a very famous Australian school. After several years of teaching, he was encouraged to resume writing.

Marsden told *SAAS* that during a school holiday "I sat down and started to write. I made two decisions that turned out to be critical. One was to use the diary format, the other was to aim it at teenage readers. These two decisions seemed to free me to write more fluently than before. I worked in an intensity of emotion, a state that I often slip into when writing." On the very last day of his vacation, Marsden finished the book. He sent it off to a variety of publishers but received only negative responses. Luckily, a chance meeting with a bookseller helped Marsden get the manuscript into the right hands.

So Much to Tell You . . . focuses on a mute girl who is sent to a special boarding school rather than a psychiatric hospital. The girl has been physically scarred in an accident. Readers get to know her through her diary entries, where her secrets are gradually revealed: her father scarred her with acid that was meant to injure her mother. One of the girl's teachers is able to break into her silent world, and at the end of the novel, there is the hope that she will begin coming out of her isolation. The book caught on quickly and soon became an Australian bestseller. "A good proportion of the first print run was bought by my students, who were smart enough to know how to improve their grades in English," Marsden joked.

Many reviewers offered favorable comments about *So Much to Tell You . . .* Jo Goodman, writing in *Magpies,* declared that the book was "a riveting first novel which grips the reader from the start," adding: "I found the observation and the characters authentic, the suspense gripping, and the slow and subtle revelation of the truth both painful and illuminating." *School Library Journal* contributor Libby K. White asserted: "Marsden is a master storyteller." I. V. Hansen, commenting in *Children's Literature in Education,* claimed that the novel offers "a moving story, tragic, simple, generous, tender. It is the kind of novel that seems to come from nowhere, yet we know it has been with us all the time."

In *The Journey,* Marsden built a fable around adolescent coming-of-age rituals. In this tale, a society sends its adolescents on a journey of self-discovery; the youths return with seven stories of experience and enlightenment. The local council then judges whether the stories are sufficient to allow the youths to pass into adulthood. Margot Nelmes commented in *Reading Time* that "this is a rare book, fortifying to the spirit, gripping, and worthy of reading more than once."

Marsden turned to lighter works with the publication of *The Great Gatenby* and *Staying Alive in Year Five. The Great Gatenby* is about the popular but reckless Erle Gatenby, who causes trouble wherever he goes. *Staying Alive in Year Five* offers one boy's perspective on his class's experience with an unusual teacher named Mr. Merlin. *Reading Time* reviewer Halina Nowicka termed *Staying Alive* "a really good, humorous story."

Marsden's *Letters from the Inside* and *Dear Miffy* have evoked controversy. *Letters from the Inside* centers around two girls, Mandy and Tracy, who have become pen pals. After a few exchanges of letters, Tracy reveals that she is actually serving time in a maximum security prison. Mandy admits that her brother is quite violent, and the end of the novel alludes to the fact that Mandy might have been attacked by him. In *Reading Time,* Ashley Freeman called *Letters from the Inside* a "compelling story, which totally involves the reader." Other critics were alarmed by the manner in which Marsden presented the subject of domestic violence. Elizabeth Gleick contended in the *New York Times Book Review* that the book "might be faulted for one reason and one reason alone: it offers not the palest glimmer of hope."

Dear Miffy, which features a jacket notice warning that its contents "may offend some readers," has engendered a similar reaction. In this novel, institutionalized teenager Tony, who comes from a broken home and a working-class environment, writes to his girlfriend Miffy, a beautiful girl from a wealthy and very troubled family. Tony's letters, which are never mailed, recount their relationship from its turbulent beginnings through its tragic conclusion. *Dear Miffy* is filled with violence, sex, and profanity set against a backdrop of corruption, injustice, and dysfunctional families. Discussing the controversy surrounding the work in *Horn Book,* Jameyson wrote: "In inevitable parallel with the U.S. discussion about *The Chocolate War,* [critics] point out that the shades of gray in this book are so dark as to be unrealistic. Surely no life can be so dismal; surely no group of characters can be so totally lacking in redeeming features; surely no slice of life can be so void of . . . hope." Other commentators have rallied to Marsden's support, however, commending his forthright treatment of difficult subjects and his capacity to endow his protagonists with an authentic teenage voice.

Marsden's best known work, the "Tomorrow, When the War Began" series, has made him an international writer of renown. The multi-volume series begins with a simple premise. A small group of Australian teens returns from a camping trip in the bush to discover that, in their absence, Australia has been invaded and occupied by an enemy country. The politics behind the war is kept deliberately vague as the teens themselves decide to do what they can to help push the invaders from Australian soil. The plot thickens quickly because this is not fantasy or science-fiction; it is a plausible, realistic adventure saga in which the young heroes face life-threatening situations and respond to them in very human ways. Marsden told *SAAS* that the series was born from one of his own childhood fantasies, "of a world without adults, a world in which the adults had magically disappeared and the kids were left to run the place."

The first book in the series, *Tomorrow, When the War Began,* introduces the narrator, Ellie Linton, and the mixed-gender group of friends who will join her to fight the war. Returning from a camping trip in a canyon they have nicknamed "Hell," Ellie and her friends discover that everyone in their town has been captured, and they must fend for themselves. Quickly, the group organizes to resist the invaders, blowing up a lawn mower to kill one soldier. Theirs is not the mindless violence of a video game, however. Each character reacts to the trauma of war and displacement differently, and Ellie is only one of the teens who struggles with the ethics of killing on one hand and the grip of mortal fear on the other. *Horn Book* contributor Maeve Visser Knoth described *Tomorrow, When the War Began* as "a riveting adventure through which Marsden explores the capacity for evil and the necessity of working together to oppose it."

In Marsden's novel Tomorrow, When the War Began, *Australian teens must find ways to survive the military force taking over their town. (Jacket art by Will Hillenbrand.)*

Subsequent volumes in the series have generated a high level of excitement among the author's fans. Marsden has said that he wanted all of his "Tomorrow, When the War Began" books to have the same level of style and execution that the first one had. Judging by the reaction of some reviewers, he has succeeded in that goal. *The Dead of Night* and *The Third Day, the Frost* further the story of the teenagers as the war in their country continues. Reviewing *The Dead of Night* for *Voice of Youth Advocates,* Alice F. Stern commented: "If you hope for a plot with any closure, you will not find it here. What you will find is a strong adventure story, a little romance, and an excellent psychological study." *Horn Book* reviewer Jennifer M. Brabander praised *The Dead of Night* as "riveting," citing favorably the depth of Marsden's characters and adding: "Thoughtful explorations of the nature of fear, bravery, and violence—natural conversations during wartime—add depth and balance to the edge-of-the-seat action and intense first-person narration."

By the time *Burning for Revenge* appeared, Marsden was a celebrity with a shelf full of Australian awards,

most of them voted upon by his teenaged readers. *Burning for Revenge* lifted him into another category altogether. This novel, in which Ellie, Fi, Kevin, Homer, and Lee launch an attack on an airfield and try to civilize a gang of feral children, won the prestigious Book of the Year Award from the Australian Booksellers Association. What made this award particularly special was that Marsden's work was judged not against other young adult novels, but against adult fiction—and he won. He is the first children' author ever to win that particular citation. In her *School Library Journal* review of *Burning for Revenge,* Susie Paige noted that the characters "are so believable that readers forget that the story is fiction." Calling Marsden "a master at creating tension and excitement," *Booklist* critic Frances Bradburn declared *Burning for Revenge* "riveting."

"Tomorrow, When the War Began" found its conclusion in the seventh novel, *The Other Side of Dawn,* in which Ellie and her surviving friends finally find reunion with their loved ones after a final, climactic battle. A *Kirkus Reviews* critic predicted that the many fans of the series worldwide "will be sorry to reach their final chapter in such an outstanding story of friendship, courage, and survival." Fortunately, those legions of readers need not part with Ellie entirely—Marsden has commenced a new, post-war series also featuring the courageous narrator.

Marsden has written numerous other titles in tandem with his series. *The Rabbits* and *Norton's Hut* are picture books, but their intended audience is not necessarily children. *Norton's Hut* is a ghost story about a group of hikers caught out by a blizzard and the strange, silent fellow who shares his home with them during the storm. *The Rabbits* is an allegory of the European conquest of Australia, using the metaphor of the destructive rabbit population that has been such a plague to the continent. "This book is a title to jolt readers," Jameyson said in her *Horn Book* review of *The Rabbits.* "There is no doubt as to the writer's intentions: to sober, sadden, and provoke."

Marsden's novels *Checkers* and *Winter* each feature female protagonists at odds with the adults around them. The heroine of *Checkers* tells her tale from a mental hospital to which she has been sent after a nervous breakdown. Bit by bit, the character reveals the events that led to a family crisis, brought on by her father's unethical business practices. *Booklist* critic Shelle Rosenfeld called *Checkers* a "fascinating, intricately woven novel" notable for its "strong psychological exploration." In *Voice of Youth Advocates,* Gloria Grover also characterized *Checkers* as "an emotionally compelling story."

The protagonist in *Winter* is strong and determined—and she needs to be. Sixteen-year-old Winter returns alone to her estate, Warriewood, to find it neglected and ransacked by those who were paid to care for it. She sets about restoring the home, in the process becoming a detective to discover the real truth behind her parents' deaths when she was four. Winter is hardly a pushover. She takes charge of her life and does not let an adult conspiracy keep her from finding out what she needs to know. In *School Library Journal,* Miranda Doyle concluded that youthful readers would "especially enjoy the ferocity with which Winter stands up to the adults who try to take advantage of her." A *Kirkus Reviews* critic found Winter to be "an appealingly gutsy narrator who keeps the story moving."

"I imagine I'll always be writing, all my life, because there is something within me that needs to tell stories," Marsden related to *SAAS.* "The other passion of my life is the preservation of life. The older I get, the more disturbed I get by the wanton destruction of other creatures by humans. . . . I hope I continue to improve in my treatment of my fellow creatures, be they animal or vegetable."

Marsden makes no apologies for the sensitive issues he covers in his fiction, or the fact that his stories are not always happily resolved. He told *Horn Book* contributor Jameyson, "I keep reminding myself I'm not writing for babies. These are people who in any other culture or any other time would be treated as full adults."

Biographical and Critical Sources

BOOKS

Authors and Artists for Young Adults, Volume 20, Gale (Detroit, MI), 1997.

Children's Literature Review, Volume 34, Gale (Detroit, MI), 1995.

St. James Guide to Young Adult Writers, 2nd edition, St. James Press (Detroit, MI), 1999.

Something about the Author Autobiography Series, Volume 22, Gale (Detroit, MI), 1996, pp. 169-185.

Twentieth-Century Young Adult Writers, St. James Press (Detroit, MI), 1994.

PERIODICALS

Booklist, May 15, 1998, Frances Bradburn, review of *A Killing Frost,* p. 1617; October 15, 1998; Shelle Rosenfeld, review of *Checkers,* p. 412; June 1, 1999, Roger Leslie, review of *Darkness, Be My Friend,* p. 1814; October 1, 2000, Frances Bradburn, review of *Burning for Revenge,* p. 332.

Children's Literature in Education, September, 1989, I. V. Hansen, "In Context: Some Recent Australian Writing for Adolescents," pp. 151-163.

Horn Book, July-August, 1995, Maeve Visser Knoth, review of *Tomorrow, When the War Began,* p. 467; September-October, 1997, Karen Jameyson, "Contents May Offend Some Readers," pp. 549-552, and Jennifer M. Brabander, review of *The Dead of Night,* pp.

575-576; May, 1999, Karen Jameyson, "Brush Strokes with History," p. 364; November-December, 2002, Jennifer M. Brabander, review of *The Other Side of Dawn,* p. 762.

Kirkus Reviews, August 15, 2001, review of *The Night Is for Hunting,* p. 1216; July 1, 2002, review of *Winter,* p. 958; August 15, 2002, review of *The Other Side of Dawn,* p. 1229.

Magpies, March, 1988, Jo Goodman, review of *So Much to Tell You . . .,* p. 30.

New York Times Book Review, November 13, 1994, Elizabeth Gleick, review of *Letters from the Inside,* p. 29.

Publishers Weekly, May 25, 1998, review of *Prayer for the Twenty-first Century,* p. 88; September 7, 1998, review of *Checkers,* p. 96; August 26, 2002, Elizabeth Devereaux, "Bestseller Down Under," p. 70.

Reading Time, Volume 33, number 2, Margot Nelmes, review of *The Journey,* p. 28; Volume 33, number 4, Halina Nowicka, review of *Staying Alive in Year Five,* p. 24; Volume 35, number 4, 1991, Ashley Freeman, review of *Letters from the Inside,* p. 32.

School Library Journal, May, 1989, Libby K. White, review of *So Much to Tell You . . .,* p. 127; October, 2000, Susie Paige, review of *Burning for Revenge,* p. 166; August, 2002, Miranda Doyle, review of *Winter,* p. 194.

Voice of Youth Advocates, February, 1998, Alice F. Stern, review of *The Dead of Night,* p. 387; December, 1998, Gloria Grover, review of *Checkers,* p. 356.

ONLINE

John Marsden Home Page, http://www.johnmarsden.com/ (December 20, 2003).

*   *   *

MAYFIELD, Sue 1963-

Personal

Born March 15, 1963, in North Shields, England; daughter of Alexander William (a merchant naval captain) and Brenda Patricia (a teacher; maiden name, Mobberly) Kinghorn; married Timothy Mayfield (a Anglican clergyman), 1985; children: Frank Alexander, Jonah William, one other son. *Education:* Lincoln College, Oxford, B.A. (with honors), 1985; received teaching certificate from University of Bristol, 1986. *Politics:* "Left-wing." *Religion:* Christian. *Hobbies and other interests:* Photography, films, walking with her dog.

Addresses

Agent—c/o Author Mail, Hodder & Stoughton, 338 Euston Rd., London NW1 3BH, England.

Career

Novelist. Teacher of English and drama in secondary school in Bath, England, 1986-87. Involved in church activities.

Awards, Honors

North East Book Award, 2002, for *Blue.*

Writings

Timeline: Women and Power (nonfiction), Dryad (London, England), 1988.

I Carried You on Eagle's Wings (young adult novel), Deutsch (London, England), 1990, Lothrop (New York, NY), 1991.

Hands in Contrary Motion (young adult novel), Scholastic (London, England), 1993.

A Time to Be Born (young adult novel; sequel to *I Carried You on Eagle's Wings*), Scholastic (London, England), 1995.

Shoot!, illustrated by Ken Cox, Mammoth (London, England), 2000, Crabtree Publishing (New York, NY), 2001.

Blue, Hodder & Stoughton (London, England), 2001, published as *Drowning Anna,* Hyperion (New York, NY), 2002.

Reckless (young adult novel), Hodder & Stoughton (London, England), 2002.

Voices (young adult novel), Hodder & Stoughton (London, England), 2003.

The Four Franks, illustrated by Gary Parsons, Egmont Books (London, England), 2003.

Poison (young adult novel), Hodder & Stoughton (London, England), 2004.

(With Anne Butler) *Molly's Muddle Cake,* illustrated by Moira Munro, Keppel Publishing (New Galloway, Scotland), in press.

Contributor to *Youth Emmaus,* Church House Publishing (London, England), 2003.

Sidelights

British author Sue Mayfield has built a loyal following of fans since she began her career as a young adult novelist in the early 1990s. With books such as *I Carried You on Eagle's Wings* and *Blue,* published in the United States as *Drowning Anna,* she introduces likeable, intelligent, and introspective teen protagonists who attempt to understand and overcome significant emotional issues in their lives, including issues of faith and purpose. Other teen novels by Mayfield include *Reckless* and *Poison,* in addition to which she has authored the picture book *Shoot!* about a longstanding soccer rivalry.

Born in England in 1963, Mayfield did not think of herself as the bookish type as a child. As she once told *SATA:* "Writing fiction is something I have come to gradually and almost accidentally. As a child I was a keen reader and from an early age I loved stories—especially the ones my father made up. I never saw reading as a hobby, though, preferring more active outdoor pursuits such as riding horses and walking." After

graduating from Lincoln College, Oxford, in 1985, she decided to train as a secondary-school teacher. While teaching she began to seriously explore writing for the first time. "I found that in teaching my students how to improve their writing, I inadvertently taught myself a great deal," she once explained. "Teaching also led me to think a lot about teenage life and its pressures, and to be aware of the issues which faced the young people I was teaching."

Although she has gone on to make a name for herself as the author of teen fiction, Mayfield's first published book, *Timeline: Women and Power,* is a work of nonfiction. A book that explores the contributions of women to British history, *Timeline* was an eye-opening project for its twenty-something author. After the book's 1988 publication, Mayfield "expected to do further journalistic work on women's issues and it was only when a project I was working on fell through the following spring that I turned my hand . . . to writing fiction," as she once recalled to *SATA.*

I Carried You on Eagle's Wings, Mayfield's first novel for young readers, focuses on Tony Sharpe, a teen whose wheelchair-confined mother suffers from multiple sclerosis (MS). Inspired by a friend of Mayfield's who was then dying from MS, the book combines the teen's efforts to come to terms with his mother's imminent death with his own spiritual awakening.

A sequel to *I Carried You on Eagle's Wings,* Mayfield's *A Time to Be Born,* was published in 1995. Continuing Tony's story, the novel finds the young man still mourning his mother's loss and taking small consolation in his Christian faith. When a group of young evangelical Christians called the Beach Club arrive in town, the new relationships he makes forces Tony to confront questions about sexuality as well as view his relationship with God in a new light. Calling the book a challenging read for teens, *School Librarian* reviewer Susan Hamlyn praised *A Time to Be Born* as "a sensitive portrayal of a thoughtful boy" dealing with widely shared teen problems, while a *Junior Bookshelf* contributor maintained that the "challenge" Mayfield confronts her teen protagonist with is "refreshing."

Also a coming-of-age story, 1993's *Hands in Contrary Motion* takes place in Yorkshire, England, and introduces sixteen-year-old Michelle Murgatroyd, who is trying to cope with a weight problem and her parents' divorce. Additionally, the youngster also attempts to break away from the influences of friends, teachers, an unstable romantic attachment, and family to become her own person. Fortunately, Michelle finds a means of self-expression in playing the piano—the novel's title refers to a pianist's keyboard technique—a talent which sees her through some rocky times. Praised as "witty" by *School Librarian* reviewer Maggie Bignell, *Hands in Contrary Motion* offers a teen protagonist possessing "optimism and resilience," two characteristics sure to inspire the novel's young teen readers. *Hands in Con-*

The second in a series, Sue Mayfield's **A Time to Be Born** *finds Tony dealing with the death of his mother.(-Cover illustration by Syd Brak.)*

trary Motion "is great fun in spite of the traumas of adolescence" it portrays, a *Junior Bookshelf* contributor added, praising the author's use of inspiring and responsible adult characters to create a balanced portrayal of cross-generational interaction.

Smart but shy, thirteen-year-old Anna Goldsmith, the young protagonist of *Drowning Anna,* wants to be accepted in her new school, and at first, she seems to make a close friend in Hayley Parkin. When things change and Haley starts to disparage Anna behind her back, Anna is confused, and her strong exterior begins to crumble, resulting in a suicide attempt two years later. Anna's slow descent into ultimate despair is depicted through three narratives: her own diary, the reflections of her friend Melanie, and the reflections of her mother, who searches for signs of her daughter's suicidal tendencies in hindsight. Depicting character types that most readers can relate to, *Drowning Anna* was characterized by a *Kirkus Reviews* contributor as "a bleakly compelling cautionary tale for teens and their adults," while in *School Library Journal* Cindy Darling

Codell dubbed the novel "a compelling story that will strike a chord with many young teens," and praised in particular Mayfield's portrayal of the manipulative Hayley.

"I keep a journal and a book of 'scribblings' in which I constantly record thoughts and insights as well as observations of places and events," Mayfield once revealed. "I find that the process of creating characters and describing their inner lives is akin to role playing and that communicating moods and emotions through words is very similar to acting. I enjoy making people laugh and cry and I consider possession of the power to move another human being to be a great privilege."

Biographical and Critical Sources

PERIODICALS

Booklist, October 15, 2002, Debbie Carton, review of *Drowning Anna,* p. 401.
Books for Keeps, July, 1993, Adrian Jackson, review of *Hands in Contrary Motion,* p. 28.
Junior Bookshelf, June, 1993, review of *Hands in Contrary Motion,* pp. 109-110; June, 1995, review of *A Time to Be Born,* p. 109.
Kirkus Reviews, September 1, 2002, review of *Drowning Anna,* p. 1314.
Publishers Weekly, October 7, 2002, review of *Drowning Anna,* p. 73.
School Librarian, August, 1993, Maggie Bignell, review of *Hands in Contrary Motion,* p. 123; August, 1995, Susan Hamlyn, review of *A Time to Be Born,* p. 118.
School Library Journal, September, 1991, Marjorie Lewis, review of *I Carried You on Eagle's Wings,* p. 283; December, 2002, Cindy Darling Codell, review of *Drowning Anna,* p. 145.
Times Educational Supplement, March 8, 1996, Jan Mark, review of *A Time to Be Born.*

ONLINE

Calderdale Libraries Web Site, http://www.calderdale.gov.uk/libraries/readers/chatterbooks/ (June 7, 2002) interview with Sue Mayfield.*

*   *   *

McCLINTOCK, Barbara 1955-

Personal

Born May 6, 1955, in Flemington, NJ; daughter of Earl Irving (a photographer) and JoAnn (a teacher and shop owner; maiden name, Herigstad) McClintock; married Lawrence DiFiori (an illustrator), April 14, 1982 (marriage ended); children: Larson Alan. *Education:* Attended Jamestown College, 1973-75, and Art Student's League, 1985.

Barbara McClintock

Addresses

Home—Connecticut. *Agent*—c/o Author Mail, Farrar, Straus, & Giroux, 19 Union Square W., New York, NY 10003.

Career

Illustrator, 1975—. *Exhibitions:* Master Eagle Gallery, 1976; Jamestown Art Center (solo show), Jamestown, ND, 1980; Garrison Art Center, Garrison, NY, 1987.

Awards, Honors

Selected as one of *Ms.* magazine's three favorite illustrators, 1983; International Children's Reader Award, 1986, for *The Revolt of the Teddy Bears: A May Gray Mystery;* Best Illustrated Book, *New York Times,* 1989, for *The Heartaches of a French Cat;* Books of Distinction Award, *Riverbank Review,* 2003, for *Dahlia.*

Writings

SELF-ILLUSTRATED

(Reteller) *The Little Red Hen,* Random House (New York, NY), 1979.
Down at Fraggle Rock (coloring book), Holt (New York, NY), 1984.
The Heartaches of a French Cat, David R. Godine (Boston, MA), 1988.
(Adapter) *Animal Fables from Aesop,* David R. Godine (Boston, MA), 1991.
The Battle of Luke and Longnose, Houghton Mifflin (Boston, MA), 1994.

The Fantastic Drawings of Danielle, Houghton Mifflin (Boston, MA), 1996.
(Adapter) *Frances Hodgson Burnett's A Little Princess,* HarperCollins (New York, NY), 2000.
Molly and the Magic Wishbone (based on a story by Charles Dickens), Farrar, Straus & Giroux (New York, NY), 2001.
Dahlia, Farrar, Straus & Giroux (New York, NY), 2002.
Adele and Simon, Farrar, Straus & Giroux (New York, NY), 2004.
(Reteller) *Cinderella,* Scholastic (New York, NY), in press.

ILLUSTRATOR

Elizabeth Winthrop, *Potbellied Possums,* Holiday House (New York, NY), 1977.
David Young, *Marooned in Fraggle Rock,* Holt (New York, NY), 1984.
Louise Gikow, *What's a Fraggle?,* Holt (New York, NY), 1984.
Louise Gikow, *The Legend of the Doozer Who Didn't,* Holt (New York, NY), 1984.
James Duffy, *The Revolt of the Teddy Bears: A May Gray Mystery,* Crown (New York, NY), 1985.
H. B. Gilmour, *Why Wembley Fraggle Couldn't Sleep,* Holt (New York, NY), 1985.
Stephanie Calmenson, *Waggleby of Fraggle Rock,* Holt (New York, NY), 1985.
James Duffy, *The Christmas Gang: A May Gray Mystery,* Scribner (New York, NY), 1989.
Jim Aylesworth, reteller, *The Gingerbread Man,* Scholastic (New York, NY), 1998.
Eric A. Kimmel, *When Mindy Saved Hanukkah,* Scholastic (New York, NY), 1998.
Jim Aylesworth, reteller, *Aunt Pitty Patty's Piggy,* Scholastic (New York, NY), 1999.
Beatrix Potter, *A Tale of Two Bad Mice,* Simon & Schuster (New York, NY), 1999.
C. Drew Lamm, *The Prog Frince: A Mixed-Up-Tale,* Orchard Books (New York, NY), 1999.
Eric Metaxas and Madame d'Aulnoy, *The White Cat,* Simon & Schuster (New York, NY), 2000.
Jim Aylesworth, reteller, *The Tale of Tricky Fox: A New England Trickster Tale,* Scholastic (New York, NY), 2001.
Jim Aylesworth, reteller, *Goldilocks and the Three Bears,* Scholastic (New York, NY), 2003.
Robert Louis Stevenson, *A Child's Garden of Verses,* HarperCollins (New York, NY), 2003.
Kate Douglas Wiggin, *Rebecca of Sunnybrook Farm,* Houghton (Boston, MA), 2003.

Contributor to *Little Lit: Strange Stories for Strange Kids,* edited by Art Spiegelman and Françoise Mouly, HarperCollins (New York, NY), 2001.

Adaptations

The Minneapolis Children's Theatre adapted *Animal Tales from Aesop* as an opera/ballet.

Sidelights

Barbara McClintock's lushly detailed pen and ink and watercolor artwork often features the expressive animals she loved to draw as a child. Frequently, these animals are dressed in nineteenth-century costume and set in famous European locales, also depicted in minute period detail. McClintock counts Victorian-era artists including Grandville, Delacroix, Dore, Leech, and Caldecott as important influences on her work. In her books, which often draw comparisons to Randolph Caldecott in particular, McClintock sometimes sets her characters upon the pages as if they were actors upon a stage. The author-illustrator once explained to *SATA* that her success is the result of labor and love: "Making pictures is hard work, but the most pleasurable and rewarding work I can think of!"

The daughter of parents who ran a photography shop, McClintock began to develop her talent when she was very young. Tirelessly, she drew animals in action and cartoon figures. As she once told *SATA,* "By the time I was in second grade, I had . . . a callous on the index finger of my drawing hand from holding pencils and crayons!" McClintock was just seven years old when her sister suggested she become a children's book illustrator. McClintock agreed, "and so began my career!"

As a young adult, McClintock studied the work of her favorite artists. She also spent a great deal of time sketching people and animals she saw outside. She sketched on the subway, in the market, and in restaurants. She made copies of the drawings of others that she especially liked. McClintock studied art in college, but she was not quite sure how to go about beginning the career she desired. She decided to ask a successful children's book illustrator, and telephoned the renowned artist Maurice Sendak. "Mr. Sendak was so helpful, kind and supportive. He told me how to put together a dummy book and suggested I move to New York," McClintock once recalled for *SATA*. She followed Sendak's advice, moving to Manhattan and supporting herself while continuing her art studies. It did not take her long to find an agent, "and in several months I had my first book. I was extremely lucky. It was very, very hard for the first several years."

Especially during the first years of her career, McClintock illustrated books written by other authors. *Potbellied Possums,* by Elizabeth Winthrop, features a garbage-eating possum named Gertrude. McClintock conducted research in Paris for her illustrations for James Duffy's *Revolt of the Teddy Bears: A May Gray Mystery,* which won an International Children's Reader Award in 1986. *The Christmas Gang,* another "May Gray Mystery" book that McClintock illustrated, is also set in Paris. In this work, May Gray (a poodle) reminisces about a mystery she solved when she was a young police officer. McClintock has also illustrated several "Fraggle Rock" books.

During the late 1980s and into the 1990s, McClintock created books that showcased her skill as an illustrator and author. McClintock once explained to *SATA* that a "wordless book that I have loosely based on stories by P. J. Stahl and Honore de Balzac," *The Heartaches of a French Cat,* was another result of the research she conducted in Paris. The action in this book occurs as if on stage; the characters, a young female cat, her mother, and a villain, tell the story with their poses and expressions. At the end of the story, Minette the cat writes a memoir, which succeeds. "If there is any justice, so will this comic biography," wrote Stefan Kanfer in *Time* magazine.

Animal Fables from Aesop, with McClintock's revisions of nine of Aesop's tales, begins with the introduction of the book's characters on a stage. The animal characters, including a crane and a fox dressed in Victorian clothing, present the fables "The Town Mouse and the Country Mouse" and "The Wolf and the Dog," among others. When they finish presenting the fables, the actors reveal that they are really children in costume. The illustrations are "finely detailed line drawings, with . . . leafy, verdant settings," Nancy Vasilakis related in *Horn Book.* With its "gracefully phrased" text and illustrations providing "drama, comedy, and exquisite detail," the book, according to a *Kirkus Reviews* critic, is a "delight."

The Battle of Luke and Longnose presents a familiar story with McClintock's fanciful illustrations on what Luann Toth described in *School Library Journal* as "dramatic double-page spreads." While playing with his miniature theater, Luke falls asleep. Miraculously, the theater, along with Luke's toy soldiers, grows to become life-sized. Luke wakes up, and with his cat, he leads the soldiers in battle against the ruffian Longnose. When they finally defeat Longnose, Luke and his cat go back to bed. "A superb and inventive book by a truly talented illustrator," concluded a *Kirkus Reviews* critic.

McClintock sends a message to young artists in *The Fantastic Drawings of Danielle,* which features a young woman artist living in nineteenth-century Paris who paints surreal scenes. Her father, a photographer, cannot understand Danielle's style and tells her to paint more realistically. Danielle tries to follow his suggestions, but she cannot. Finally, she finds a woman painter who has turned her own vision into a successful career. The illustrations in this book, wrote Shirley Wilton in *School Library Journal,* "are delightfully antique." In the words of a *Publishers Weekly* reviewer, the book is a "delicious celebration of creativity" and "an inspiration to young artists."

Beginning in 1998, McClintock paired with author Jim Aylesworth to publish a series of picture books offering fresh retellings of favorite trickster tales. In *The Gingerbread Man,* the title character jumps from the oven and escapes from his creators, determined not to be eaten by them or by any of the hungry animals he finds outside. A *Publishers Weekly* reviewer felt that most of

Barbara McClintock's lively illustrations bring to life the tale of **The Gingerbread Man,** *who dares the butcher to catch him if he can. (Story retold by Jim Aylesworth.)*

the book's "readers will be utterly disarmed—and may well wish to come back again and again." *Aunt Pitty Patty's Piggy* is another silly story that builds upon itself—and then reverses for a happy ending. A *Publishers Weekly* critic concluded of that title: "Narrative and art pull equal weight in this cheerful reworking." A contributor to *Horn Book* especially liked "McClintock's humorously expressive, delicately characterized cast." *The Tale of Tricky Fox* is a lesser-known folktale about a conniving fox who gets his own tricks turned against him by a potential victim who is smarter than he is. In her *School Library Journal* review of the book, Barbara Buckley wrote: "The expressions on Tricky and his unsuspecting victims are priceless." A *Horn Book* correspondent also praised the animals' "energetic poses of deception and delight."

As its title implies, *The Prog Frince: A Mixed-Up-Tale* builds upon the premise that a hapless prince and his true love have gotten confused about everything from kissing to their true identities. When a talking frog steals Jane's dime, she reluctantly agrees to hear his story—only to discover that the same spell that turned him from a frog to a prince turned her from a happy, imaginative girl to a diehard skeptic. Writing in *Horn*

Book, Joanna Rudge Long found McClintock's illustrations for this title "elegantly limned" and "full of fun."

Molly and the Magic Wishbone is based on a Charles Dickens' tale, but McClintock recasts it with animal characters in Victorian costumes and settings. Sent out to shop while her mother is sick, Molly meets a Fairy Godmother who gives her a magic wishbone—in this case a fishbone. Molly's younger siblings are full of advice about what she should wish for, but in the end she saves her wish for a sensible, and life-saving, event. In her *School Library Journal* review of *Molly and the Magic Wishbone,* Kathleen Kelly MacMillan declared the book "a charmer" and maintained that "the expressions of the characters are endearing." A contributor to *Kirkus Reviews* also commended the "wonderful cast of animals and fine, handsome drawings," while Ilene Cooper concluded in *Booklist:* "Oh, the charm of the pictures. The Dickensian world is fully realized. . . . Practically purr-fect."

Dahlia is McClintock's story of a tomboy and her doll. Edwardian-era heroine Charlotte likes playing in the mud with her teddy bear Bruno, so she is less than thrilled when her Aunt Edme sends her a doll that is swathed in satin and lace. Charlotte informs her doll that there will be no tea parties or other ladylike play, and the doll—named Dahlia—soon comes to enjoy the rough-and-tumble sports of her owner. All is well in the end when prim Aunt Edme sees the worse-for-wear Dahlia and pronounces her well-loved. "*Dahlia* will be loved by young girls who are forging their first friendships," observed Susan Marie Pitard in *School Library Journal.* A *Publishers Weekly* reviewer deemed the book "a doll story that will win over even confirmed tomboys." In *Kirkus Reviews,* a critic commended *Dahlia* as "elegantly subversive and utterly charming," and *Booklist* contributor Julie Cummins likewise concluded that *Dahlia* "simply blooms with charm."

McClintock has also enjoyed success illustrating and adapting several classic children's novels. *Frances Hodgson Burnett's A Little Princess* tells the poignant story of Sara Crewe, left at an exclusive boarding school while her father goes to war. When news of her father's death and financial ruin reaches the school, Sara is reduced to servitude and a grim life in a garret. In the *New York Times Book Review,* Jane Fritsch declared that McClintock's adaptation of the novel "brings it to life with . . . richly detailed illustrations intended to engage the imaginations of the youngest girls." *Rebecca of Sunnybrook Farm* is another turn-of-the-twentieth-century novel about an orphaned youngster who goes to live with her aunts on a Maine farm. In 2003, McClintock was selected to provide the illustrations to Houghton Mifflin's 100th anniversary edition of the book.

In an interview published on *HarperChildren's.com,* McClintock said that the kind of illustrating she does takes a great deal of time and that she has to work hard to meet her deadlines. "I often get up at 2:00 a.m. to work, go back to bed around 4:30, get up again at 6:00 to get my son off to school, work 'til he gets home, make dinner, work in the evening, sometimes work after my son is in bed," she said. "I am exhausted by the end of a book!" She added that she has enough plans to fill her working hours for quite some time to come. "I'd love to do more picture book adaptations of Victorian-era stories," she concluded. "Expect to see more McClintock retellings in the future!"

Biographical and Critical Sources

PERIODICALS

Booklist, September 15, 1999, Hazel Rochman, review of *Aunt Pitty Patty's Piggy,* p. 258; February 1, 2001, Gillian Engberg, review of *The Tale of Tricky Fox: A New England Trickster Tale,* p. 1055; September 1, 2001, Ilene Cooper, review of *Molly and the Magic Wishbone,* p. 110; September 1, 2002, Julie Cummins, review of *Dahlia,* p. 121.

Horn Book, January-February, 1992, Nancy Vasilakis, review of *Animal Fables from Aesop,* p. 83; March, 1999, Joanna Rudge Long, review of *The Prog Frince: A Mixed-Up Tale,* p. 194; September, 1999, review of *Aunt Pitty Patty's Piggy,* p. 618; March, 2001, review of *The Tale of Tricky Fox,* p. 217; January-February, 2002, Joanna Rudge Long, review of *Molly and the Magic Wishbone,* p. 70; September-October, 2002, Susan Bloom, review of *Dahlia,* p. 555.

Kirkus Reviews, November 15, 1991, review of *Animal Fables from Aesop,* p. 1472; September 15, 1994, review of *The Battle of Luke and Longnose,* p. 1276; September 15, 2001, review of *Molly and the Magic Wishbone,* p. 1362; June 1, 2002, review of *Dahlia,* p. 807.

New York Times Book Review, November 19, 2000, Jane Fritsch, review of *Frances Hodgson Burnett's A Little Princess,* p. 45.

Publishers Weekly, August 19, 1996, review of *The Fantastic Drawings of Danielle,* p. 65; January 26, 1998, review of *The Gingerbread Man,* p. 90; August 2, 1999, review of *Aunt Pitty Patty's Piggy,* p. 83; March 12, 2001, review of *The Tale of Tricky Fox,* p. 88; November 5, 2001, review of *Molly and the Magic Wishbone,* p. 66; June 24, 2002, review of *Dahlia,* p. 55; August 18, 2003, review of *Goldilocks and the Three Bears,* p. 77.

School Library Journal, March, 1995, Luann Toth, review of *The Battle of Luke and Longnose,* p. 183; September, 1996, Shirley Wilton, review of *The Fantastic Drawings of Danielle,* p. 184; March, 2001, Barbara Buckley, review of *The Tale of Tricky Fox,* p. 192; October, 2001, Kathleen Kelly MacMillan, review of *Molly and the Magic Wishbone,* p. 124; November, 2002, Susan Marie Pitard, review of *Dahlia,* p. 130.

Time, December 11, 1989, Stefan Kanfer, "Of Cats, Myths and Pizza," review of *The Heartaches of a French Cat,* pp. 100, 102.

ONLINE

HarperChildren's.com, http://www.harperchildrens.com/ (July 2, 2003), "Barbara McClintock Talks about *A Little Princess.*"

Visiting Authors, http://www.visitingauthors.com/authors/ (July 2, 2003), "Barbara McClintock's Biography."*

* * *

McCLOSKEY, (John) Robert 1914-2003

OBITUARY NOTICE—See index for *SATA* sketch: Born September 15, 1914, in Hamilton, OH; died June 30, 2003, in Deer Isle, ME. Artist, illustrator, and author. McCloskey was a Caldecott Award-winning children's book author and illustrator best known for his 1941 picture book *Make Way for Ducklings.* As a child, he was initially interested in music and learned to play the piano, oboe, harmonica, and percussions; he was also a great tinkerer, and his parents thought he might become an inventor, if not a musician. However, he surprised them by turning to art after an engraving and printmaking class he took in high school sparked his interest. He won a scholarship to Vesper George Art School in Boston, completing courses there in 1936, and then moved on to the National Academy of Design, from which he graduated in 1938. Although he won the Prix de Rome in 1939, his early work as an artist afforded him little financial security until he started illustrating children's books. His first book, *Lentil,* was published in 1940, and *Make Way for Ducklings* was released the following year, earning him his first of two Caldecotts. *Homer Price* came out in 1943, but McCloskey's career was by then interrupted by the start of World War II; the artist enlisted in the U.S. Army, becoming a technical sergeant. When the war ended, he continued his art studies in Italy, as well as continuing his illustration work. McCloskey completed five more self-illustrated children's books, including *Blueberries for Sal* (1948), *One Morning in Maine,* and his second Caldecott winner, *Time of Wonder* (1957). He also illustrated books by other children's writers, including Claire Huchet Bishop, Tom Robinson, and Ruth Sawyer. Despite the attention he got for the books he wrote, McCloskey always considered himself an artist first and an author second. He stopped writing after *Burt Dow, Deep-Water Man: A Tale of the Sea in the Classic Tradition* (1963), and focused on his art work for the rest of his life. Nevertheless, McCloskey will likely always be remembered as a classic children's author whose books will continue to be treasured by children, teachers, and parents for years to come.

OBITUARIES AND OTHER SOURCES:

BOOKS

St. James Guide to Children's Writers, fifth edition, St. James Press (Detroit, MI), 1999.

PERIODICALS

Los Angeles Times, July 6, 2003, p. B16.
New York Times, July 1, 2003, p. C17.
Washington Post, July 2, 2003, p. B7.

McDANIEL, Lurlene 1944-

Personal

Born Lurlene Nora Gallagher, April 5, 1944, in Philadelphia, PA; daughter of James (a chief petty officer in the U.S. Navy) and Bebe (a homemaker; maiden name, Donaldson) Gallagher; married Joe McDaniel, March 12, 1966 (divorced, 1987); children: Sean Clifford, Erik James. *Education:* University of South Florida, B.A., 1965. *Politics:* Republican. *Religion:* Conservative Presbyterian.

Addresses

Agent—Meg Ruley/Jane Rotrosen, 318 East 51st St., New York, NY 10022.

Career

Novelist and freelance writer; author of works, including radio and television scripts, and promotional and advertising copy. Fiction editor for the children's magazine *Guideposts for Kids.* Frequent speaker and lecturer at writers' conferences.

Member

Romance Writers of America, East Tennessee Romance Writers of America.

Awards, Honors

Six Months to Live was placed in a literary time capsule in the Library of Congress, November, 1990; RITA Award, 1991, for *Now I Lay Me Down to Sleep;* Children's Choice Books, International Reading Association, for *Somewhere between Life and Death, Too Young to Die,* and *Goodbye Doesn't Mean Forever.*

Writings

YOUNG ADULT NOVELS

What's It Like to Be a Star?, Willowisp Press (Worthington, OH), 1982.

I'm a Cover Girl Now, Willowisp Press (Worthington, OH), 1982.

Will I Ever Dance Again?, Willowisp Press (Worthington, OH), 1982.

Head over Heels, Willowisp Press (Worthington, OH), 1983.

If I Should Die before I Wake, Willowisp Press (Worthington, OH), 1983.

Sometimes Love Just Isn't Enough, Willowisp Press (Worthington, OH), 1984.

Three's a Crowd, Willowisp Press (Worthington, OH), 1984.

The Secret Life of Steffie Martin, Willowisp Press (Worthington, OH), 1985.

Lurlene McDaniel

Eternal Flame (Serenade/Serenata, No. 13), Zondervan (Grand Rapids, MI), 1985.

Hold Fast the Dream (Serenade/Serenata, No. 20), Zondervan (Grand Rapids, MI), 1985.

Love's Full Circle (Serenade/Serenata, No. 33), Zondervan (Grand Rapids, MI), 1986.

Why Did She Have to Die?, Willowisp Press (Worthington, OH), 1986.

More Than Just a Smart Girl, Willowisp Press (Worthington, OH), 1987.

Mother, Please Don't Die, Willowisp Press (Worthington, OH), 1988.

My Secret Boyfriend, Willowisp Press (Worthington, OH), 1988.

When Dreams Shatter, Willowisp Press (Worthington, OH), 1988.

Too Young to Die, Bantam (New York, NY), 1989.

Goodbye Doesn't Mean Forever, Bantam (New York, NY), 1989.

Somewhere between Life and Death, Bantam (New York, NY), 1991.

Time to Let Go, Bantam (New York, NY), 1991.

Now I Lay Me Down to Sleep, Bantam (New York, NY), 1991.

When Happily Ever After Ends, Bantam (New York, NY), 1992.

Baby Alicia Is Dying, Bantam (New York, NY), 1993.

Don't Die, My Love, Bantam (New York, NY), 1995.

Angels Watching over Me, Bantam (New York, NY), 1996.

Saving Jessica, Bantam (New York, NY), 1996.

I'll Be Seeing You, Bantam (New York, NY), 1996.

Lifted Up by Angels, Bantam (New York, NY), 1997.
Till Death Do Us Part (also see below), Bantam (New York, NY), 1997.
For Better, for Worse, Forever (also see below), Bantam (New York, NY), 1997.
Starry, Starry Night, Bantam (New York, NY), 1998.
Until Angels Close My Eyes, Bantam (New York, NY), 1998.
Angel of Mercy, Bantam (New York, NY), 1999.
The Girl Death Left Behind, Bantam (New York, NY), 1999.
Angel of Hope, Bantam (New York, NY), 2000.
How Do I Love Thee?: Three Stories, Bantam (New York, NY), 2001.
Telling Christina Goodbye, Bantam (New York, NY), 2002.
A Rose for Melinda, Bantam (New York, NY), 2002.
Garden of Angels, Bantam (New York, NY), 2003.
The Time Capsule, Delacorte (New York, NY), 2003.
As Long As We Both Shall Live (contains *Till Death Do Us Part* and *For Better, for Worse, Forever*), Bantam (New York, NY), 2003.
Always and Forever, Bantam (New York, NY), 2004.

"DAWN ROCHELLE" YOUNG ADULT SERIES

Six Months to Live (also see below), Willowisp Press (Worthington, OH), 1985.
I Want to Live (also see below), Willowisp Press (Worthington, OH), 1987.
So Much to Live For (also see below), Willowisp Press (Worthington, OH), 1991.
No Time to Cry (also see below), Willowisp Press (Worthington, OH), 1993.
Dawn Rochelle: Four Novels (contains *Six Months to Live, I Want to Live, So Much to Live For,* and *No Time to Cry*), Bantam (New York, NY), 2000.
To Live Again, Bantam (New York, NY), 2001.

"ONE LAST WISH" YOUNG ADULT SERIES

A Time to Die, Bantam (New York, NY), 1992.
Mourning Song, Bantam (New York, NY), 1992.
Mother, Help Me Live, Bantam (New York, NY), 1992.
Someone Dies, Someone Lives, Bantam (New York, NY), 1992.
Sixteen and Dying, Bantam (New York, NY), 1992.
Let Him Live, Bantam (New York, NY), 1992.
The Legacy: Making Wishes Come True, Bantam (New York, NY), 1993.
Please Don't Die, Bantam (New York, NY), 1993.
She Died Too Young, Bantam (New York, NY), 1994.
All the Days of Her Life, Bantam (New York, NY), 1994.
A Season for Goodbye, Bantam (New York, NY), 1995.
Reach for Tomorrow, Bantam (New York, NY), 1999.

CHILDREN'S NOVELS

A Horse for Mandy, Willowisp Press (Worthington, OH), 1981.
The Pony Nobody Wanted, Willowisp Press (Worthington, OH), 1982.
The Battle of Zorn, Willowisp Press (Worthington, OH), 1983.
Peanut Butter for Supper Again, Willowisp Press (Worthington, OH), 1985.

OTHER

McDaniel's books have been translated into German, Norwegian, and Dutch.

Adaptations

Sound recordings of McDaniel's books include *Don't Die, My Love, Lifted Up by Angels, Angels Watching over Me,* and *Until Angels Close My Eyes; Don't Die, My Love* was adapted for television by NBC-TV and broadcast as a prime time television movie titled *A Champion's Fight,* 1999.

Work in Progress

Six more novels for Delacorte (New York, NY).

Sidelights

More often than not, some form of the word "death" finds its way onto the covers of Lurlene McDaniel's young adult novels, as it does in *A Time to Die, Sixteen and Dying,* and *She Died Too Young.* As the titles suggest, McDaniel's specialty is dealing with some of life's most difficult events. In *Somewhere between Life and Death,* Erin's younger sister is severely injured in a car accident. When the doctors declare her brain dead, Erin and her family must decide if they should turn off life-support systems and donate her organs for transplant. In *Please Don't Die,* heart transplant recipient Katie O'Roark spends the summer at "Jenny House," a retreat for critically ill adolescents. She befriends three girls: Chelsea, a candidate for a heart transplant; Amanda, a victim of leukemia; and Lacey, a diabetic. Not everyone makes it through the summer. Desi, the protagonist of *Baby Alicia Is Dying,* is a teenage volunteer at a home for babies with AIDS. She becomes very attached to a baby who seems healthy but then suddenly succumbs to the disease.

Such books are not exactly the stuff of young adult romances, or even the horror novels that fill the shelves in teen sections of bookstores. Nevertheless, McDaniel has carved out a niche in the publishing world—one that some people never dreamed existed. "Adults are often prejudiced against my books," McDaniel said in her interview with Sarah Verney. "They don't understand why kids would want to read them." The problem, McDaniel speculates, may be that the adults have not read the books themselves. "They look at the titles and erroneously assume that the books are morbid. They aren't," McDaniel claimed.

Illness, death, and dying may be at the core of McDaniel's novels, but the stories themselves are really about life and getting beyond the grieving process.

While some people have referred to her books as "ten-hankie novels," McDaniel prefers to think of them as "bibliotherapy"—a means of working out one's grief in a book. To do that, her readers need to get a glimpse of the big picture—"the totality of life, not just the individual moments," as McDaniel told Verney.

According to McDaniel, it is important that her readers also feel hope. "I end all my stories on a note of hope," she explained to Verney. Hope is the one thing McDaniel most wants to give her readers, whether they are kids like her characters, facing extraordinary challenges, or ordinary teens with basic problems. McDaniel recognizes that many teens face difficulties that those of her own generation never even imagined. "We worried about someone cutting in line," she related. "They worry about getting shot." When terrible things do happen in their lives, teens may have nowhere to turn.

"No one is talking to teenagers about the grieving process," asserted McDaniel in an interview with Mark Curnutte for the *News & Observer* (Raleigh, NC). So McDaniel fills this void by offering kids a look into the lives of characters who have been through the process and emerged on the other side. As she attests, positive messages abound in her books, as they do in the following passage from *Somewhere between Life and Death:* "The flowers, the butterflies, the greening of the grass, told her that life was cyclic, season after season. It came, it went. It came again. . . . Erin gazed at Amy's coffin . . . and knew with certainty that Amy wasn't in it. Maybe her body would be buried, but the person of Amy, her spirit, would not. For Amy was with Erin still and would live in her heart for all the days of her life." And a similar theme of hope and peace is found in the following excerpt from *All the Days of Her Life:* "As she turned to go inside, she saw a shooting star arc through the darkness. . . . Was it an answer sent to her from a world beyond the rainbows? Lacey found renewed hope within her heart. She'd been given a second chance for all the days of her life. Beginning now, she'd make the most of it."

The hope reaching out to young adults in McDaniel's novels springs from the author's own personal well, which is fed by her faith. A devout Christian, McDaniel offers books which reflect the inspiration she receives from her religion. But while McDaniel strives to maintain "a biblical perspective" and "a sense of eternal purpose" in her novels, she makes a point of not being dogmatic. "I don't push a Christian agenda on my readers," McDaniel told Verney, pointing out that they come from a variety of religious backgrounds. "I don't preach to them—if someone wants a sermon, they can go to church."

One obvious way McDaniel's Christian perspective comes through is in her treatment of death. "I never send a character to the grave without the hope of eternal life," she explained to Verney. And although her doomed characters suffer plenty, in the end they generally make their peace with God. As Melissa, a high school junior dying of leukemia writes to her best friend in *Goodbye Doesn't Mean Forever:* "I'm not mad at God anymore. . . . I've had some heart-to-heart talks with Him and I've come to believe that He loves me enough to want me with Him in heaven. And that once I'm in heaven, I'll never have to die again." In coming to terms with her own death, Melissa also seems confident that she is going on to an afterlife. She finishes her letter with, "I'll be watching you. And when you least expect it, you'll hear me call you in the wind. I promise."

McDaniel's faith, in addition to inspiring her young protagonists, helps her through the tough times in her own life. The most difficult of these resulted from her older son's diabetes. Sean, who is now an athletic, healthy (though still diabetic) adult, was only three when diagnosed with the disease. At the time, he was losing weight and was constantly fatigued—all classic signs of diabetes; McDaniel consulted a doctor, but he failed to recognize Sean's illness. "I was getting him undressed that night," McDaniel remembered, "and I could count every rib on his little body. It was as if there was a voice in my head—I just knew he wasn't going to make it through the night," she told Verney. McDaniel, who was then in the early stages of her second pregnancy, took her son to an emergency room, and the doctors there immediately recognized his condition. Still, it took a tremendous medical effort to stabilize Sean, and he came perilously close to dying in McDaniel's arms.

When Sean's crisis was over, McDaniel turned to the business of learning everything she could about diabetes management, a process that includes monitoring blood sugar levels and being extremely careful about diet and exercise. She quickly saw how chronic illness takes over one's life, and how it affects the dynamics of a family. Nevertheless, she feels her own experiences with Sean's illness support two of the hopeful messages she tries to convey in her novels: "Good can come from bad" and "life works out if you give it a chance." "What possible good could come of my beautiful little red-haired boy having diabetes?," she asked in her interview with Verney, then answered her own question: "If it weren't for Sean's illness, I don't know that I would ever have written my first novel. Would I go back and give up writing if it meant Sean wouldn't have diabetes? Absolutely. But you don't get to pick what happens to you. You do get to pick how you respond to it, however."

One way McDaniel responded to Sean's illness was to choose to work at home as a freelance writer, so that she would be available to care for him. She had previously worked as a promotion copywriter for television stations in Florida and Michigan, and so was able to write advertising and promotional copy at home for a number of different sources. Among the things McDaniel wrote were commercials for local companies, public service announcements, and promotional materials for real estate agencies. The beginning of McDaniel's career as a novelist can be traced back to when Sean was ten or eleven and was asked to model in a poster for the Diabetes Research Institute. As McDaniel waited for Sean, she happened to strike up a conversation with a woman there whose father had founded a company, School Book Fairs, that sold remainders of already published books to schools. The company was just starting to branch out into publishing its own titles, and the woman suggested that McDaniel write one. "I think they were just looking for someone who could meet a deadline, and I was used to that," McDaniel related to Verney.

McDaniel wrote several children's books for School Book Fairs, including picture books, before publication of her *Will I Ever Dance Again?* This book, which is the story of how diabetes changes the life of a teenage ballet student, did very well for Willowisp, School Book Fairs' imprint. Asked to do more titles that featured teenage characters overcoming physical adversity, McDaniel followed up with *If I Should Die before I Wake,* and later, *Six Months to Live,* which eventually sold more than 500,000 copies and was placed in a literary capsule at the Library of Congress.

McDaniel had found her voice and her subject matter, but it was not until she ended her relationship with Willowisp that she hit her stride as a writer. She and her husband of twenty-one years divorced in 1987, and McDaniel suddenly needed to earn more money. She felt she had stayed at home too long to go back out into the work force, so she concentrated on making her career as a novelist more lucrative. She found a literary agent and within weeks had a contract with Bantam Books. In addition to increasing her financial security, the move to Bantam gave McDaniel an opportunity to work with an editor in a way she had not previously experienced. Her books for Willowisp were edited and then sent to press without McDaniel participating in the process. Looking back, she realizes that, due to lack of constructive feedback, she wrote "a lot of bad books" before signing on with Bantam. She now works more closely with her editor and feels that the editorial give-and-take has helped her to grow artistically. Nevertheless, McDaniel is grateful to her two editors at Willowisp for their instrumental role in establishing her as an author, and they remain friends to this day.

In spite of her feeling that some of her earlier books were not as well-crafted as they might have been, McDaniel commented to Verney that she "did have an ability to tap into the reader's emotions," and credits that skill with much of her success. "Fiction is about feelings," she said, "and empathy is the name of the game." Without that empathy, McDaniel might never be able to get her message of hope across to readers. Such empathy comes easily to McDaniel, even though she has not experienced the diseases that her characters endure. She has, however, had serious illness touch her life. In addition to Sean's diabetes, her father-in-law had multiple sclerosis, a progressive nerve disease, and her mother-in-law died of liver cancer while still relatively young. "I felt like I was always standing at a hospital bedside," McDaniel remembered for Verney.

From this vantage point, she had the opportunity to observe both the emotional effects of illness and the high-tech world of medicine. "I was always fascinated by things medical," McDaniel explained to Verney. "Maybe I'm really a frustrated doctor." This interest led to another hallmark of McDaniel's novels, perhaps the flip side to her inspirational themes: realistically stark portrayals of illness and medical procedures. This is another aspect of her books that parents sometimes fail to understand, but judging by the comments in her fan mail, McDaniel's readers are as interested in the details as she is. (One girl, a pre-med student, wrote that she had become so intrigued with medicine while reading McDaniel's novels that she intended to become a pediatric oncologist.)

In order to keep the medical information as up-to-date and accurate as possible, McDaniel sometimes employs the services of a librarian, who faxes her information from medical journals, and she interviews scores of medical experts. She also works with cancer societies, hospice organizations, the Tennessee Organ Donor Services, and an AIDS agency in Atlanta. All of this research, coupled with McDaniel's graphic descriptions, leads to passages that should put to rest anyone's fears that McDaniel somehow romanticizes illness or dying. "I have a responsibility to my readers to be accurate," McDaniel related in her interview with Curnutte. "If somebody vomits, they vomit." Her dedication to realism results in passages like the following, which appears in *She Died Too Young:* "Jillian was on the bed, lead wires from monitors snaking to her chest. Two tubes protruded from her groin area, from the femoral arteries, and led to the ECMO machine. One tube carried her oxygen-poor blood into the machine, where it was oxygenated by a special membrane, and the other tube carried the blood into her body to her oxygen-starved system. The machine was eerily quiet."

In a two-book series, McDaniel follows teenage missionary Heather Barlow as she faces mortality and poverty. In *Angel of Mercy,* Heather journeys to Africa, "filled with idealism," according to Shelley Townsend-Hudson in *Booklist.* But the reality is much different: Uganda is rife with disease and famine. But Heather's spirits are lifted by her growing attraction to Ian McCollum, a fellow missionary from Scotland. When Ian undertakes a mission to save a dying baby, "readers will know there's tear-jerking tragedy in store," as Townsend-Hudson put it. A sequel, *Angel of Hope,* finds Heather back in the United States mourning Ian, who was killed by rebels. Though she falls ill, Heather convinces her self-centered younger sister, Amber, to go in her place back to Uganda to continue her mission of

An Amish family give Leah a new outlook on life in Angels Watching Over Me, *written by Lurlene McDaniel. (Book cover illustration by Kamil Vojnar.)*

mercy. In another *Booklist* piece, Townsend-Hudson found that while this plot "verges on melodrama, the love between the sisters is realistically portrayed."

Two more books with "Angels" in their titles made a bow. *Angels Watching over Me* tells of Leah, who at age sixteen is handed a devastating diagnosis: bone cancer. Forced to take treatment alone in hospital over the Christmas holidays, Leah finds strength and inspiration in little Rebekah, an Amish child "possessing strong religious beliefs and a very supportive family," noted *School Library Journal* contributor Cynthia Schulz. Leah also finds a budding romance in Rebekah's brother, Ethan. "With a little angelic assistance, Leah's prognosis improves," Schulz recounted. The teenager heals enough to take a summer job in *Lifted Up by Angels.* Leah works at an inn near Ethan's family and finds herself with a question of faith: can she adapt to traditional Amish ways, or will Ethan forsake his upbringing to be with her?

In 2001, McDaniel produced *How Do I Love Thee?: Three Stories,* all of which center on young adults facing critical illness. Elizabeth Maggio of *School Library Journal* found "a level of realism" in McDaniel's writing, set off by "a strong dose of drama."

Unfortunately McDaniel also knows what it feels like to be on the receiving end of all the medical care she describes in her novels. In August, 1993, the author was diagnosed with breast cancer. Although the diagnosis was frightening, McDaniel considers herself lucky: the disease was caught early enough that she was able to have a lumpectomy (removal of just the cancerous lump, not the entire breast) plus radiation treatment, and she is considered to have made a full recovery. Still, the act itself of facing the cancer gave her a slightly different outlook. And McDaniel believes this comes through in one of her 1995 novels, *Don't Die, My Love,* in which a high school football star fights Hodgkin's disease, a form of cancer that affects the lymphatic system.

It is this realistic portrayal of teen crisis that is praised by some critics. In a review of *Now I Lay Me Down to Sleep,* a *Booklist* contributor asserted that "McDaniel deals honestly and directly with the emotional and physical challenges of her characters." *Voice of Youth Advocates* critic Barbara Flottmeier pointed out in a review of *Somewhere between Life and Death* and *Time to Let Go:* "The issues of healing after a loved one dies, sustaining or ending life support systems, and organ donation are handled with care and thoughtfulness."

On the other hand, those who disparage McDaniel's work describe her novels as being too contrived and predictable. "The plot is trite and overly sentimental, with obvious twists and a predictable ending," said Tina Smith Entwistle in a review of *Mourning Song* for *School Library Journal. Somewhere between Life and Death* and its sequel, *Time to Let Go,* are similarly criticized by a *Publishers Weekly* contributor: "These forgettable, lightweight novels have no place among the many wonderful books that offer young readers an authentic vision of what it means to love and lose."

McDaniel takes an upbeat view of negative reviews. "I'm a mass market writer, a commercial writer," she explained to Verney. "I'll never win a Newbery Award." The author remarked on her Web site that her goal is always "to write a good book and a fresh interesting story. But I have reader expectations to fulfill. It's not always in the front of my mind. At this point, I think it's more instinctive. But my readers expect an intriguing story, a challenge to overcome, a romantic element, and a certain morality."

Biographical and Critical Sources

BOOKS

McDaniel, Lurlene, *Goodbye Doesn't Mean Forever,* Bantam (New York, NY), 1989.

Erin suffers painful headaches for a year following the death of her sister, in McDaniel's novel Time to Let Go. *(Book cover illustration by Phil Hefferman.)*

McDaniel, Lurlene, *Somewhere between Life and Death,* Bantam (New York, NY), 1991.

McDaniel, Lurlene, *All the Days of Her Life,* Bantam (New York, NY), 1994.

McDaniel, Lurlene, *She Died Too Young,* Bantam (New York, NY), 1994.

McDaniel, Lurlene, in an interview with Sarah Verney, *Authors and Artists for Young Adults,* Volume 15, Gale (Detroit, MI), 1995.

PERIODICALS

Booklist, March 15, 1991, review of *Time to Let Go* and *Somewhere between Life and Death,* p. 1506; June 15, 1991, review of *Now I Lay Me Down to Sleep,* p. 1977; October 1, 1993, review of *Baby Alicia Is Dying,* p. 331; September 15, 1995, review of *Don't Die, My Love,* p. 153; March 15, 1996, review of *A Season for Goodbye,* p. 1294; July, 1996, Laura Tillotson, review of *I'll Be Seeing You,* p. 1819; September 15,

1998, review of *Don't Die, My Love,* p. 220; March 15, 1999, review of *Till Death Do Us Part,* p. 1316; January 1, 2000, Shelley Townsend-Hudson, review of *Angel of Mercy,* p. 906; May 1, 2000, Shelley Townsend-Hudson, review of *Angel of Hope,* p. 1659; March 1, 2001, Shelley Townsend-Hudson, review of *To Live Again,* p. 1272; September 15, 2001, Anne O'Malley, review of *How Do I Love Thee?: Three Stories,* p. 217; December 15, 2001, review of *To Live Again,* p. 729; September 15, 2002, Patricia Austin, review of *Angel of Mercy,* p. 252.

Bulletin of the Center for Children's Books, May, 1993, review of *Baby Alicia Is Dying,* p. 287.

Journal of Adolescent and Adult Literacy, November, 1995, review of *Saving Jessica,* p. 27.

Journal of Reading, November, 1990, review of *Too Young to Die* and *Goodbye Doesn't Mean Forever,* p. 231; November, 1993, review of *Now I Lay Me Down to Sleep,* p. 225.

Los Angeles Times Book Review, June 10, 2001, review of *Dawn Rochelle: Four Novels,* p. 16.

News & Observer (Raleigh, NC), April 10, 1992, Mark Curnutte, interview with Lurlene McDaniel, pp. 1D, 6D.

Publishers Weekly, June 9, 1989, review of *Too Young to Die* and *Goodbye Doesn't Mean Forever,* pp. 70-71; November 23, 1990, Tina Smith Entwhistle, review of *Time to Let Go* and *Somewhere between Life and Death,* p. 66; April 6, 1992, pp. 23-24; June 7, 1993, review of *Baby Alicia Is Dying,* p. 71; September 28, 1998, review of *Starry, Starry Night,* p. 64.

Reading Teacher, October, 1990, review of *Too Young to Die* and *Goodbye Doesn't Mean Forever,* p. 141.

School Library Journal, August, 1989, review of *Too Young to Die* and *Goodbye Doesn't Mean Forever,* pp. 152-154; March, 1991, review of *Time to Let Go* and *Somewhere between Life and Death,* p. 215; June, 1993, Tina Smith Entwistle, review of *Mourning Song,* pp. 130, 132; July, 1993, review of *Baby Alicia Is Dying,* pp. 101-102; June, 1995, review of *A Season for Goodbye,* p. 130; October, 1995, review of *Don't Die, My Love,* p. 156; December, 1996, review of *I'll Be Seeing You,* p. 139; March, 1997, review of *Angels Watching over Me,* p. 188; October, 1998, review of *Starry, Starry Night,* p. 138; March, 1999, review of *The Girl Death Left Behind,* p. 211; December, 1999, review of *Search for Tomorrow,* p. 137; April, 2000, Cynthia Schulz, review of *Angels Watching over Me,* p. 78; July, 2000, Lynda Short, review of *Don't Die, My Love,* p. 56; November, 2001, Elizabeth Maggio, review of *How Do I Love Thee?: Three Stories,* p. 161; July, 2002, Rebecca Hogue Wojahn, review of *Telling Christina Goodbye,* p. 122.

Voice of Youth Advocates, December, 1989, review of *Too Young to Die* and *Goodbye Doesn't Mean Forever,* p. 279; April, 1991, Barbara Flottmeier, review of *Time to Let Go* and *Somewhere between Life and Death,* pp. 32-33; June, 1991, review of *Now I Lay Me Down to Sleep,* p. 98; February, 1992, review of *So Much to Live For,* p. 373; August, 1992, p. 169; December, 1992, review of *A Time to Die, Mourning Song,* and *Mother, Help Me Live,* pp. 283-284; June, 1993, review of *Baby Alicia Is Dying,* p. 154; August, 1993, p. 154; October, 1994, review of *She Died Too Young,* p. 210; June, 1995, review of *A Season for Goodbye,* p. 96; October, 1995, review of *Baby Alicia Is Dying,* p. 210; December, 1995, review of *Don't Die, My Love,* p. 306; April, 1996, review of *Saving Jessica,* p. 27; August, 1998, review of *Angels Watching over Me, Until Angels Close My Eyes,* and *Lifted up by Angels,* p. 193; December, 1998, review of *Starry, Starry Night,* p. 356; February, 1999, review of *One Last Wish,* p. 423; April, 1999, review of *The Girl Death Left Behind,* p. 28; December, 2001, review of *How Do I Love Thee?: Three Stories,* p. 361.

ONLINE

Bookpage, http://www.bookpage.com/ (July, 2000), Jamie Whitfield, "Missions of Mercy Inspire Lurlene McDaniel's Angelic Series," interview with Lurlene McDaniel.

Lurlene McDaniel Home Page, http://www.eclectics.com/ (July 17, 2002).*

*   *   *

McDONNELL, Flora (Mary) 1963-

Personal

Born July 11, 1963, in London, England; daughter of Alexander, Earl of Antrim (a picture restorer) and Sarah (an artist; maiden name, Harmsworth) Gates. *Education:* Attended Exeter College, Oxford, 1982-84; City and Guilds of London Art School, diploma (illustrative arts; with distinction), 1989. *Politics:* "Left of Centre." *Religion:* "Lapsed Roman Catholic."

Addresses

Home—The Mill House, Glenarm, County Antrim BT440BQ, Northern Ireland.

Career

Painter and illustrator, 1989—. Creator of commissioned work for clients, including Savoy Hotel, 1989, and Ulster Television, 1992. *Exhibitions:* Work has been exhibited at galleries, including Kerlin Gallery, Belfast, Northern Ireland, 1991; St. Martin's Gallery, London, England, 1991; Cadogan Gallery, London, 1992; No. 1 Oxford St., Belfast, 1993; and Cadogan Contemporary Gallery, London, 1995.

Awards, Honors

Mother Goose Award for most exciting newcomer to British children's book illustration, 1995, for *I Love Animals; Parenting* Best Book of the Year designation, 1997, for *Flora McDonnell's ABC,* and 1999, for *Splash!*

Writings

SELF-ILLUSTRATED

I Love Animals, Walker (London, England), Candlewick Press (New York, NY), 1994.
I Love Boats, Walker (London, England), Candlewick Press (New York, NY), 1995.
Flora McDonnell's ABC, Walker (London, England), Candlewick Press (New York, NY), 1997.
Splash!, Walker (London, England), Candlewick Press (New York, NY), 1999.
Giddy-Up! Let's Ride!, Walker (London, England), Candlewick Press (New York, NY), 2002.
Sparky, Walker (London, England), Candlewick Press (Cambridge, MA), 2004.

McDonnell's works have been translated into other languages, including Danish, Urdu, Spanish, and Japanese.

ILLUSTRATOR

Ted Hughes, *The Mermaid's Purse,* Faber and Faber (London, England), 1999, Random House (New York, NY), 2000.
Ted Hughes, *The Cat and the Cuckoo,* Faber and Faber (London, England), 2002, Roaring Brook Press (Brookfield, CT), 2003.

Sidelights

Artist and author Flora McDonnell, winner of 1995's Mother Goose Award for most exciting newcomer to British children's book illustration, has produced a number of titles popular with the picture-book set. Focusing primarily on depictions of animals in a variety of natural settings, McDonnell draws on her training as a fine-art painter in her work for such self-penned books as *I Love Animals, Splash!,* and *Giddy-Up! Let's Ride!* Reviewing *Giddy-Up! Let's Ride!* for *School Library Journal,* Patricia Pearl Dole remarked favorably upon McDonnell's "well-arranged" acrylic-and-gouache paintings, overflowing with "fun and action," and noted that the author/illustrator's onomatopoetic text makes the 2002 volume "a perfect read-aloud."

Born in London, England, in 1963, McDonnell now makes her home in Northern Ireland, where she has roots that go back many generations on her father's side. She once admitted to *SATA* that when she was a teen, she lost an argument with her parents about "whether to study chemistry or art." As a result, she postponed serious art study until she was a university student, eventually earning her diploma in illustrative arts at a London art school. Although she originally intended to devote her life to painting, McDonnell was wooed into working as an illustrator by an editor from Walker Books who saw examples of the recent graduate's art work and knew that McDonnell would be perfect for the world of children's picture books.

McDonnell's first book was 1994's *I Love Animals,* which features large, full-spread illustrations of her favorite animals (and frequently their young). According to a critic for *Kirkus Reviews,* it is McDonnell's art work that truly shines, creating a "visual exuberance." A *Publishers Weekly* critic described McDonnell's renderings in acrylics and gouache as similar in style to "primitive folk-art," while Charlotte Voake wrote in *Books for Keeps* that she found the illustrations "lovely, bold, and thrilling."

I Love Boats, in the words of a *Publishers Weekly* critic, is "awash with color," an "exuberant paean to all things afloat." The work showcases a variety of boats within large acrylic and gouache paintings. Houseboats, racing boats, fishing boats, and sailboats are all depicted. At the end of the book, readers find that all the boats are toys, floating in a happy little girl's bathtub. *Horn Book* critic Nancy Vasilakis concluded of *I Love Boats,* "boat lovers young and old will want to share it with friends."

The award-winning *Flora McDonnell's ABC,* which a London *Observer* reviewer described as a "grand way to learn letters," firmly cemented the author/illustrator's position as a top talent. "Whimsy rules" in what *Bulletin of the Center for Children's Books* contributor Elizabeth Bush dubbed "a back-to-basics alphabet book" in which brightly colored images of cats in cars are followed by jelly-bean jugglers, tigers with teapots, and yo-yoing yaks. In a review for *Christian Science Monitor,* Karen Williams praised McDonnell's illustrations for their "clarity, color, and pure sense of fun," going on to claim that the pictures are sure to appeal to small children.

A story book rather than a concept book, *Splash!* allows McDonnell to indulge in her love of animal illustration through the tale of three animals languishing in the heat of an Indian summer. A tiger, an elephant family, and a rhinoceros listlessly endure the midday heat at the edge of a local watering hole until the playful elephant child decides this is the perfect time for a cooling water fight. A *Kirkus Reviews* critic praised the book's bold, painted illustrations for their "mythopoetic radiance," while in *Publishers Weekly,* a contributor maintained that *Splash!* "showcases McDonnell's keen sensitivity to the visual and verbal needs of the very young."

Acting as illustrator, McDonnell provided artwork for poet Ted Hughes's *The Mermaid's Purse* and *The Cat and the Cuckoo.* Containing twenty-eight short poems penned by the late British poet laureate about the ocean and its inhabitants, *The Mermaid's Purse* features paintings that "capture the wildness of the sea and the poet's dark humor with sensitivity and panache," according to a *Horn Book* reviewer. *The Cat and the Cuckoo* also features McDonnell's impressionistic illustrations, this time focusing on creatures of farm and field. The two-toned graphic artwork in this small-scale book, described as "whimsical and folksy" by a *Kirkus Reviews*

In **Flora McDonnell's ABC,** *T is for Teapot and Tiger, in McDonnell's self-illustrated picture book.*

contributor, provides a "comforting feel to these poems that sometimes veer wonderfully into dark animal thoughts."

A fan of children's literature greats such as Maurice Sendak, Helen Oxenbury, and Ludwig Bemelmans, McDonnell advises aspiring illustrators "to express what you enjoy and make small compromises but keep the essence of what you want to say." Indeed, McDonnell's own compromise—from painter to illustrator—was painless. "Luckily for me," she once commented to *SATA,* "what I want to express about what I see falls quite naturally into children's book illustration."

Biographical and Critical Sources

PERIODICALS

Booklist, October 15, 1994, Ellen Mandel, review of *I Love Animals,* p. 438; August, 1995, Hazel Rochman, review of *I Love Boats,* p. 1956; April 15, 1997, Shelley Townsend-Hudson, review of *Flora McDonnell's ABC,* p. 1432; July, 1999, Ilene Cooper, review of *Splash!,* p. 1952; May 1, 2002, GraceAnne A. DeCandido, review of *Giddy-Up! Let's Ride!,* p. 1534; April 1, 2003, Hazel Rochman, review of *The Cat and the Cuckoo,* p. 1406.

Books for Keeps, July, 1995, Charlotte Voake, review of *I Love Animals,* p. 8.

It is a hot day and baby elephant knows just how to help others cool off. From Splash, *written and illustrated by McDonnell.*

Bulletin of the Center for Children's Books, July, 1997, Elizabeth Bush, review of *Flora McDonnell's ABC,* p. 402; September, 1999, Elizabeth Bush, review of *Splash!,* p. 22.

Christian Science Monitor, September 25, 1997, Karen Williams, review of *Flora McDonnell's ABC,* p. B1.

Horn Book, July-August, 1995, Nancy Vasilakis, review of *I Love Boats,* p. 452; September, 2000, review of *The Mermaid's Purse,* p. 59; July-August, 2003, Joanna Rudge Long, review of *The Cat and the Cuckoo,* p. 473.

Kirkus Reviews, July 15, 1994, review of *I Love Animals,* p. 989; May 15, 1999, review of *Splash!,* p. 803; May 15, 2002, review of *Giddy-Up! Let's Ride!,* p. 736; February 15, 2003, review of *The Cat and the Cuckoo,* p. 308.

Observer (London, England), March 30, 1997, review of *Flora McDonnell's ABC,* p. 17.

Publishers Weekly, August 1, 1994, review of *I Love Animals,* p. 77; May 22, 1995, review of *I Love Boats,* p. 58; June 7, 1999, review of *Splash!,* p. 81; May 6, 2002, review of *Giddy-Up! Let's Ride!,* p. 56.

School Library Journal, October, 1994, Sally R. Dow, review of *I Love Animals,* p. 94; August, 1995, Steven Engelfried, review of *I Love Boats,* p. 126; October, 2000, Kathleen Whalin, review of *The Mermaid's Purse,* p. 186; July, 2002, Patricia Pearl Dole, review of *Giddy-Up! Let's Ride!,* p. 95; May, 2003, Kathleen Whalin, review of *The Cat and the Cuckoo,* p. 136.

ONLINE

BookPage, http://www.bookpage.com/ (July 2, 2003), Alice Cary, review of *Giddy-Up! Let's Ride!**

*   *   *

MEAD, Alice 1952-

Personal

Born January 11, 1952, in Portchester, NY; daughter of Richard and Jeanne Weber; children: Jeffrey O'Hara, Michael O'Hara. *Education:* Bryn Mawr College, B.A., 1973; Southern Connecticut State University, M.Ed., 1975; University of Southern Maine, B.A. (art education), 1985. *Politics:* Democrat. *Hobbies and other interests:* Flute, gardening, painting, photography, clay.

Addresses

Home—Cape Elizabeth, ME. *Agent*—c/o Author Mail, Farrar, Straus, & Giroux, 19 Union Square W., New York, NY 10003. *E-mail*—amead@maine.rr.com.

Career

Has worked as an art teacher in Connecticut and Maine, 1974-92, and as a preschool teacher in Maine, 1980-83. Board member for Project Co-Step for developmentally delayed preschoolers; active in efforts to aid children in Kosovo, Serbia.

Member

Society of Children's Book Writers and Illustrators, New England Children's Book Writers and Illustrators, Kosova Action Network, Maine Writers and Publishers Alliance.

Writings

Crossing the Starlight Bridge, Bradbury (New York, NY), 1994.

Walking the Edge, A. Whitman (Morton Grove, IL), 1995.

Junebug, Farrar, Straus & Giroux (New York, NY), 1995.

Journey to Kosovo, Loose Cannon Press (Cumberland Center, ME), 1995.

(Editor, with Arnold Neptune) *Giants of the Dawnland: Ancient Wabanaki Tales,* Loose Cannon Press (Cumberland Center, ME), 1996.

Adem's Cross, Farrar, Straus & Giroux (New York, NY), 1996.

Junebug and the Reverend, Farrar, Straus & Giroux (New York, NY), 1997.

Soldier Mom, Farrar, Straus & Giroux (New York, NY), 1999.

Billy and Emma, illustrated by Christy Hale, Farrar, Straus & Giroux (New York, NY), 2000.

Girl of Kosovo, Farrar, Straus & Giroux (New York, NY), 2001.

Junebug in Trouble, Farrar, Straus & Giroux (New York, NY), 2002.

Year of No Rain, Farrar, Straus & Giroux (New York, NY), 2003.

Madame Squidley and Beanie, Farrar, Straus & Giroux (New York, NY), 2004.

Work in Progress

Isabella's Above-Ground Pool and *Lindi Meholli: Origin Unknown,* both for Farrar, Straus & Giroux (New York, NY).

Sidelights

Alice Mead's novels for young adults and middle graders often feature young people coping with dire circumstances, who with ingenuity, determination, and the aid of helpful adults make positive, if small, changes in their own lives and the lives of those around them. Mead does not shrink from difficult subjects. She has written about the war in Kosovo, famine and civil war in the Sudan, and the perils of reaching manhood in an inner-city housing project. Mead once told *SATA:* "I have always been interested in writing about children who—for some reason—live on the edge of the mainstream society. I feel that authors and artists should travel to these edges, to widen the circle of inclusion through empathy and art."

What Mead's heroes and heroines share is a resiliency of spirit and an ability to find humanity in themselves and others. Junebug, an African-American boy growing up in New Haven, Connecticut, stands up to bullies when they threaten smaller children and nurtures a dream of owning his own boat. Zana Dugolli in *Girl of Kosovo* saves the lives of her Serbian neighbors during an ethnic-inspired riot. *Adem's Cross* features a young teen who comes to understand the meaninglessness of war after being attacked and disfigured. As Susan Dove Lempke observed in *Booklist,* Mead "offers children a glimpse into realistically difficult lives faced with courage, optimism, and conviction."

Mead was born in Portchester, New York, in 1952. On her Web site, she maintains that she began to entertain flights of imagination during a two-year stay in an industrial city in the north of England. The majority of her childhood was spent in America, where she developed an interest in the countries behind the Iron Curtain in Eastern Europe. One summer, when she was twenty, she worked at a camp for inner-city children. Observing their delight in the art supplies she provided helped her to decide to be a teacher. "For many years I was an art teacher working with low-income children," Mead once explained. "In America, wealth abounds yet a large proportion of American children are poor. Everyone tells poor kids to have hopes, to dream—but how do you go about it? We have a society that sees children in very negative ways. I like to celebrate the intensity and steadfastness of kids, their creativity and fresh energy."

When an illness made it impossible for Mead to teach anymore, she stayed home and began writing. Her books reflect her experience with youngsters here and abroad, as well as her beliefs in peaceful cooperation and nonviolence. An early inspiration to write about her adopted state of Maine led to the creation of her first novel, *Crossing the Starlight Bridge.*

Rayanne, the central character in *Crossing the Starlight Bridge,* is a member of the Penobscot tribe of Native Americans. She and her parents have always lived on their island reservation, but now her father, who is unable to find work there, decides to leave. "Mead deftly establishes a child's point of view with simple and unpretentious language," observed Deborah Stevenson in the *Bulletin of the Center for Children's Books,* noting that Rayanne's misery over her father's absence is deepened when she realizes that she and her mother must leave the island, and her pet rabbit, behind. References to traditional Penobscot lore arise in the character of the grandmother, with whom Rayanne and her mother go to live, "a strong, contemporary, optimistic woman whose warmth and encouragement are restorative," Susan Scheps asserted in *School Library Journal.* A *Kirkus Reviews* critic called *Crossing the Starlight Bridge* "a believable and compelling portrayal of a Native-American family coexisting with white society while retaining its own traditions."

Like Rayanne, Scott, the main character in *Walking the Edge,* looks to something positive outside of himself to give him strength to endure the poverty and unhappiness of his life. Set in Maine and based on real events, *Walking the Edge* describes Scott's involvement in a science project that aims to restock the local bay with clams. The title of the book refers to Scott's penchant for perching on a high cliff overlooking the harbor, even though the footing there is precarious. *School Library Journal* contributor Connie Tyrrell Burns, commenting favorably on Mead's realistic depiction of the turbulent emotions of her adolescent hero, concluded that Scott's "amazement at the delicate and relentless process of life will be shared by readers."

Reeve McClain, known as Junebug, reluctantly approaches his tenth birthday in Mead's novel *Junebug,* knowing that he will then be recruited to join one of the gangs that terrorize his housing project. Junebug develops an idea he hopes will help him realize his dream of learning to sail and captaining his own boat. He collects and cleans fifty glass bottles and seals in each a piece of paper describing his dream, then sets the bottles free on a boat trip around the harbor in New Haven, Connecticut. "The novel is a hopeful one," Maeve Visser Knoth commented in *Horn Book,* "in spite of the vivid portrait of the housing project's grim realities." Elizabeth Bush, on the other hand, writing in *Bulletin of the Center for Children's Books,* called *Junebug's* happy ending "soothing but decidedly too easy," though her conclusion echoed that of a critic in *Kirkus Reviews,* who wrote that "readers will be rooting for

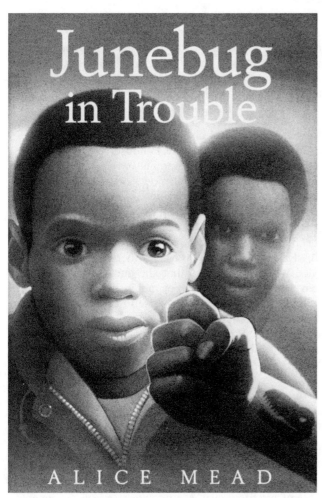

Junebug in Trouble

ALICE MEAD

A ten-year-old boy worries that his friend Robert will join a gang, in Junebug in Trouble, *written by Alice Mead. (Book jacket illustration by Michael Hays.)*

Junebug and his dreams all the way." Mead once commented to *SATA:* "I grew up near the water and have always loved boats. I wanted to be either a sea captain or a lighthouse keeper and live on an island. Writing a book is a lot like putting a message in a bottle and tossing it overboard—you never know who will read it! Or where!"

Junebug proved such a popular character that Mead has built a series around him. In *Junebug and the Reverend,* he moves away from the projects and begins sailing lessons, but still struggles with bullies and with his new duties as an assistant to an elderly emphysema patient. *Junebug in Trouble* finds the hero trying to maintain his friendship with a buddy from the projects while also developing a mature, realistic view of his incarcerated father. In a *Horn Book* review of *Junebug and the Reverend,* Maeve Visser Knoth felt that the themes addressed by Junebug "speak to the life of a young boy faced with many changes." A *Kirkus Reviews* critic called *Junebug in Trouble* "a realistic and touching" tale, concluding that the novel offers "a hopeful, yet hard look at youth growing up in the inner city." In her *Booklist* review of the same novel, Susan Dove Lempke

called the novel's hero "a touching character with sensitivity and a loving heart." *School Library Journal* contributor B. Allison Gray concluded that *Junebug in Trouble* "will ring true to many young readers and expose others to the challenges faced by children today."

Mead has set two stories in the war-torn state of Kosovo: *Adem's Cross* and *Girl of Kosovo.* Both novels take a candid approach to describing the lives of children in a war zone—something the author observed first-hand during visits to the former Yugoslavia. In *Adem's Cross,* Kosovo has been taken over by Serbian soldiers bent on "cleansing" the population of Albanians, descendants of the land's ancient conquerors. Twelve-year-old Adem and his family have been waiting for the Serb troops to leave their hometown for four years when Adem's older sister takes the bold stance of participating in a peaceful demonstration against the invaders. She is subsequently killed by Serb soldiers, and Adem, enraged at his family's passivity, rebels by going out alone one night. He is caught by three soldiers who break his hand and carve a Serbian symbol, a Cyrillic cross, into his chest with a knife. He decides to leave Kosovo and is aided in his flight by a Serb and a gypsy, both of whom teach him lessons in practical politics. "Mead preps readers with a quick, efficient sketch of Yugoslavia's recent history before jumping into this disturbing society," observed Marilyn Payne Phillips in *School Library Journal.* Critics noted that Mead does not take sides in the real-life deadly conflict. Instead, she "writes powerfully and eloquently about Adem's attempt to understand why people mistreat each other," Susan Dove Lempke remarked in *Booklist.*

Mead herself once told *SATA:* "For the past [several] years, I have been traveling to Eastern Europe. When I was little, I was told that these countries lay behind the Iron Curtain, a place Americans didn't go. Since the collapse of communism, I have traveled there . . . to document the conditions of children's lives. My novel, *Adem's Cross,* is about the cleansing of Albanian children in southern Serbia. I have brought nine teenagers to the United States to study in high schools in Maine. In addition, a group of schools got together and sent a truckload of toys to Kosovo, Serbia."

Girl of Kosovo presents the civil war in Kosovo from the point of view of Zana Dugolli, an Albanian girl who also suffers at the hands of the Kurds. Zana witnesses the murders of her father and brothers and is herself injured in the same attack. As she recuperates slowly, she struggles to remember her father's advice: "Don't let them fill your heart with hate." It is this advice that ultimately guides Zana as she returns to her village and her friendship with a Serbian girl her age. In *Booklist,* Hazel Rochman described *Girl of Kosovo* as a "moving novel," adding: "The power in the story is the personal drama." Describing the story as "powerful and hard-hitting," a *Publishers Weekly* critic remarked that Mead's book "places a human face on the Kosovo crisis."

Billy was a blue-gold macaw. Emma was a lovely green. They were best friends, and they lived in a bird cage at the Willowby Zoo.

Macaws, **Billy and Emma,** *are friends who live in the zoo until someone steals Emma. (Written by Mead. Jacket illustration by Christy Hale.)*

Continuing to deal with the theme of war, but from a different perspective, Mead's novel *Soldier Mom* deals with a problem inherent when countries go to war: how families continue with their daily lives as their soldier relatives are sent abroad to fight. Eleven-year-old Jasmyn Williams finds her life turned upside down when her mother, an Army Reservist, is called to active duty in the Persian Gulf War. Suddenly Jasmyn faces an onslaught of adult responsibilities—cooking, cleaning, caring for her baby half-brother—while all she wants to do is play basketball for her school team. Jasmyn's mother's boyfriend, Jake, proves inept as a substitute parent, leaving Jasmyn frustrated and overwhelmed. A *Horn Book* reviewer found Jasmyn to be "a realistically prickly heroine" and the book "an entirely convincing and involving picture." A *Publishers Weekly* critic praised Mead's "sharply focused" writing, noting that the "emotions of the heroine are consistently authentic." In *Reading Today,* Lynne T. Burke concluded that *Soldier Mom* "provides insight and confidence that families can survive."

Year of No Rain visits another brutal civil war, this time in Sudan. In a region laid waste by drought, Stephen Kajok becomes the sole survivor of his family after his father goes away to fight, his two brothers die of disease, and his mother and his sister are kidnapped by rebels. In order to avoid the violence, Stephen and his friend Wol strike out on their own to find a refugee camp. *School Library Journal* contributor Sue Giffard maintained that Mead "gives voice to a vulnerable, often forgotten group of people," while a *Kirkus Reviews* critic called *Year of No Rain* "an artfully told story" in which "Mead puts civil war in human terms through the eyes of one young boy."

Mead lives in a house that overlooks Casco Bay off the coast of Maine. On her Web site the author said, "When I'm stuck writing a story, I can go sit on the rocks and watch the water for a while, something I have enjoyed doing throughout my life."

Biographical and Critical Sources

PERIODICALS

Booklist, November 15, 1996, Susan Dove Lempke, review of *Adem's Cross,* pp. 579, 581; September 1, 1998, Susan Dove Lempke, review of *Junebug and the Reverend,* p. 120; September 1, 1999, Chris Sherman, review of *Soldier Mom,* p. 127; March 15, 2001, Hazel Rochman, review of *Girl of Kosovo,* p. 1401; April 15, 2002, Susan Dove Lempke, review of *Junebug in Trouble,* p. 1402; August, 2003, Hazel Rochman, review of *Year of No Rain,* p. 1983.

Bulletin of the Center for Children's Books, June, 1994, Deborah Stevenson, review of *Crossing the Starlight Bridge,* p. 329; December, 1995, Elizabeth Bush, review of *Junebug,* pp. 133-134; December, 1999, Deborah Stevenson, review of *Soldier Mom,* p. 142.

Horn Book, March, 1996, Maeve Visser Knoth, review of *Junebug,* p. 198; September-October, 1998, Maeve Visser Knoth, review of *Junebug and the Reverend,* p. 612; September, 1999, review of *Soldier Mom,* p. 614; May-June, 2002, Roger Sutton, review of *Junebug in Trouble,* p. 334.

Kirkus Reviews, May 1, 1994, review of *Crossing the Starlight Bridge,* p. 634; September 1, 1995, review of *Junebug,* p. 1284; February 1, 2002, review of *Junebug in Trouble,* p. 184; May 1, 2003, review of *Year of No Rain,* p. 680.

New York Times Book Review, January 14, 1996, pp. 23, 66.

Publishers Weekly, December 6, 1999, review of *Soldier Mom,* p. 77; March 19, 2001, review of *Girl of Kosovo,* p. 100; May 19, 2003, review of *Year of No Rain,* p. 74.

Reading Today, February-March, 2002, Lynne T. Burke, review of *Soldier Mom,* p. 32.

School Library Journal, June, 1994, Susan Scheps, review of *Crossing the Starlight Bridge,* pp. 132-133; December, 1995, Connie Burns Tyrrell, review of *Walking the Edge,* p. 106; November, 1996, Marilyn Payne Phillips, review of *Adem's Cross,* p. 109; May, 2000, Susan Hepler, review of *Billy and Emma,* p. 150; March, 2001, Kathleen Isaacs, review of *Girl of Kosovo,* p. 254; March, 2002, B. Allison Gray, review of *Junebug in Trouble,* p. 235; May, 2003, Sue Giffard, review of *Year of No Rain,* p. 157.

ONLINE

Alice Mead Home Page, http://www.alicemead.com/ (July 2, 2003).

* * *

MENENDEZ, Shirley (C.) 1937-

Personal

Born February 5, 1937, in Richmond, VA; daughter of Daniel and Madeline (Euting) Corbin; married Albert John Menendez (an author and editor), June 15, 1974. *Ethnicity:* "White." *Education:* Mary Baldwin College, B.A., 1961; Drexel University, M.L.S., 1965.

Addresses

Home—12625 Timonium Terrace, Gaithersburg, MD 20878-3428. *Office*—Georgetown University, 37th and O Streets NW, Washington, DC 20057. *E-mail*—menendez@georgetown.edu.

Career

Federal Reserve Bank, Philadelphia, PA, cataloger and reference librarian, 1963-65; Prince George's County Memorial Library System, Prince George's County,

Shirley Menendez

MD, adult services librarian, 1965-69, branch librarian at the College Park Library, 1969-71, assistant to the assistant director for public services, 1971-78; Westchester Library System, Westchester County, NY, assistant director, 1979-81; Georgetown University, Washington, DC, coordinator of administrative services for the Kennedy Institute of Ethics, 1981, coordinator of administrative services for the office of the president, 1982-86, director of housing services, 1987—.

Awards, Honors

Vicennial Medal, Georgetown University, 2003.

Writings

Allie, the Christmas Spider (picture book), illustrated by Maggie Kneen, Dutton (New York, NY), 2002.

WITH HUSBAND, ALBERT J. MENENDEZ

Maryland Trivia, Rutledge Hill Press (Nashville, TN), 1992.

New Jersey Trivia, Rutledge Hill Press (Nashville, TN), 1993.

South Carolina Trivia, Rutledge Hill Press (Nashville, TN), 1996.

(As Shirley C. Menendez) *Christmas Songs Made in America: Favorite Holiday Melodies and the Stories of Their Origins,* Cumberland House (Nashville, TN), 1999.

Joy to the World: Sacred Christmas Songs through the Ages, Cumberland House (Nashville, TN), 2001.

B Is for Blue Crab: A Maryland Alphabet, illustrated by Laura Stutzman, Sleeping Bear Press (Chelsea, MI), 2004.

Sidelights

Shirley Menendez's first children's book, *Allie, the Christmas Spider,* is a "gentle story . . . true to the holiday spirit," as Hazel Rochman wrote in *Booklist.* Allie the spider has taken up residence in the house of a poor rabbit family. The rabbit-parents have told their daughter, Beth, that their Christmas will be very simple this year, with homemade decorations and presents, because the rabbits cannot afford anything else. But after Beth spares Allie's life on Christmas Eve, Allie spends the entire night covering the family's Christmas tree in a beautiful, sparkling garland of spider webs. "The rabbit family is duly impressed with their Christmas surprise," a critic explained in *Kirkus Reviews,* and Allie ends the book considering what kind of art she should try next.

Menendez told *SATA:* "My husband and I are Christmas buffs and have collected over 1,000 books about the customs and traditions of Christmas, as well as novels, mysteries, and stories with Christmas settings. We especially enjoy the music of the Christmas season, which inspired us to research the stories behind our familiar Christmas songs and carols. This resulted in the publication of two books, *Christmas Songs Made in America* and *Joy to the World.* And, of course, my first children's book is about a little spider who gives a special gift to the rabbit family at Christmas."

Biographical and Critical Sources

PERIODICALS

Booklist, September 15, 2002, Hazel Rochman, review of *Allie, the Christmas Spider,* p. 246.

Kirkus Reviews, November 1, 2002, review of *Allie, the Christmas Spider,* pp. 1622-1623.

Publishers Weekly, September 24, 2001, review of *Joy to the World: Sacred Christmas Songs through the Ages,* p. 61.

School Library Journal, October, 2002, Eva Mitnick, review of *Allie, the Christmas Spider,* p. 61.

*   *   *

MOCHIZUKI, Ken 1954-

Personal

Surname pronounced "Moh-chee-*zoo*-kee"; born May 18, 1954, in Seattle, WA; son of Eugene (a social worker) and Miyeko (a clerical worker; maiden name, Nakano) Mochizuki. *Ethnicity:* "Third-generation American of Japanese descent." *Education:* University of Washington—Seattle, B.A., 1976.

Addresses

Home—25426 213th Ave., S.E., #51, Maple Valley, WA 98038. *Agent*—Stimola Literary Studio, 308 Chase Ct., Edgewater, NJ 07020. *E-mail*—kenmoch@aol.com.

Career

Journalist and children's book author. Actor in Los Angeles, CA, 1976-81; *International Examiner* (newspaper), Seattle, WA, staff writer, 1985-89; *Northwest Nikkei* (newspaper), Seattle, assistant editor, 1990-97. Gives presentations to schools and other groups.

Member

Society of Children's Book Writers and Illustrators.

Awards, Honors

Parents' Choice Award, Washington State Governor's Writers Award, *Publishers Weekly* Editor's Choice, and American Bookseller Pick of the List, all 1993, all for *Baseball Saved Us;* Notable Children's Trade Book in the Field of Social Studies, National Council for the Social Studies/Children's Book Council (NCSS/CBC), Notable Book for Children, *Smithsonian* magazine, both 1995, and Teachers' Choices selection, International Reading Association (IRA), 1996, all for *Heroes; Parenting* Best Book of the Year designation, Notable Book for Children, *Smithsonian* magazine, both 1997, Notable Children's Trade Book in the Field of Social Studies, NCSS/CBC, Notable Books for a Global Society, IRA, Notable Children's Book in the Language Arts, National Council of Teachers of English, all 1998, and Utah Beehive Award, 1999, all for *Passage to Freedom: The Sugihara Story.*

Writings

Baseball Saved Us, illustrated by Dom Lee, Lee & Low (New York, NY), 1993.

Heroes (picture book), illustrated by Dom Lee, Lee & Low (New York, NY), 1995.

Passage to Freedom: The Sugihara Story (nonfiction), illustrated by Dom Lee, Lee & Low (New York, NY), 1997.

Beacon Hill Boys, Scholastic (New York, NY), 2002.

Contributor to *A Different Battle: Stories of Asian Pacific American Veterans,* edited by Carina A. del Rosario, University of Washington Press (Seattle, WA), 1999. Some of Mochizuki's works have been translated into Spanish.

Adaptations

Passage to Freedom: The Sugihara Story was adapted as an audiocassette by Live Oak Media (Pine Plains, NY), 2000; *Baseball Saved Us* was adapted into a stage musical by the Fifth Avenue Theatre and produced in Seattle, WA, 2003.

Because of Donnie's Japanese heritage, his friends make him play the "bad guy" in their games of war, in Heroes. *(Written by Ken Mochizuki and illustrated by Dom Lee.)*

Sidelights

Through his award-winning 1993 picture book *Baseball Saved Us,* journalist and children's book author Ken Mochizuki was credited by a *Publishers Weekly* contributor with introducing young readers "to a significant and often-neglected . . . chapter in U.S. history," the imprisonment of Americans of Japanese descent in internment camps during the early 1940s. Mochizuki, whose parents were sent from their home on the West Coast to Idaho's Minidoka camp during World War II, explains the history surrounding his story and attempts to illustrate for children the difficulties caused by living with racism. Ira Berkow wrote in the *New York Times Book Review* that in *Baseball Saved Us,* Mochizuki "captures the confusion, wonder, and terror of a small child in such stunning circumstances with convincing understatement."

Shorty, the book's young Japanese-American narrator, begins the story by remembering how he was ostracized, how other children called him "Jap," and how voices on the radio talked on and on about Pearl Harbor

before his family was sent to live in the crowded, dusty camp. Life in the camp was stressful as well as boring, causing tension within families. Shorty's father decides to do something: "One day, my dad looked out at the endless desert and decided then and there to build a baseball field." Everyone's efforts and talents are marshaled and scarce resources are cleverly used: water is channeled to pack down earth for a field, uniforms are sewn from mattress covers, bleachers are constructed, and friends from home are asked to send bats, balls, and gloves. Baseball begins to occupy the minds and time of the camp's captives. For Shorty, baseball becomes a way to excel and battle the racism that follows him even after leaving camp and returning home.

Reviewers recognized the importance of the message in *Baseball Saved Us,* although several voiced concerns regarding the story's presentation. *Horn Book* contributor Ellen Fader maintained that Mochizuki "effectively conveys the narrator's sense of isolation, his confusion about being a target of prejudice, and the importance of baseball in his life." *Bulletin of the Center for Children's*

Mochizuki's **Passage to Freedom: The Sugihara Story** *tells how one Japanese family helped thousands of Jews during World War II. (Illustrated by Dom Lee.)*

Books writer Roger Sutton, however, thought that while the "political consciousness" reflected in Mochizuki's book rings true, the "children's book vehicle it rides in is dated and sentimental." Hazel Rochman of *Booklist* concluded, nonetheless, that "the baseball action will grab kids—and so will the personal experience of bigotry."

In the 1995 picture book *Heroes,* Mochizuki once again mines his roots as a Japanese American growing up in mid-twentieth century America by telling the story of Donnie Okada, a young boy who always gets stuck playing the part of the evil enemy when he and his friends play battleground games. The reason? he looks like "them": the Koreans and Japanese that the men of the boys' father's generation fought against in World War II and the Korean War. Although Donnie tries to explain that his father and uncles served on the American side in the same wars, his friends do not believe him. It is only after his uncles arrive at his school in full uniform that Donnie's friends begin to understand. Noting that Mochizuki intended *Heroes* as a tribute to the Japanese-American 442nd Regimental Combat Team, a *Kirkus Reviews* contributor praised the book

for illustrating "how subtly prejudice was passed on to . . . children" in the postwar years. Comparing the book to *Baseball Saved Us,* a *Publishers Weekly* contributor praised both Mochizuki and illustrator Dom Lee for "adroitly" causing young readers to think about an important social issue by working it into the life of a child, "neither trivializing the issues nor condescending to their audience."

Mochizuki's nonfiction work *Passage to Freedom: The Sugihara Story* was inspired by news articles that circulated in 1994 that focused on a Japanese diplomat stationed in Lithuania during World War II. In 1940, so the news stories explained, Chiune Sugihara issued handwritten visas to hundreds of Polish Jews, allowing them to escape through the USSR into Japan and thus be spared shipment by the Nazis to concentration camps. In his book, Mochizuki adopts the point of view of Sugihara's son, five-year-old Hiroki, and tells the story of the diplomat's courage through youthful eyes. Drawing on his journalist's training, the author met with Hiroki Sugihara in 1995, and was able to obtain a great deal of background information—Sugihara and his family were subsequently interred for over a year in

In Beacon Hill Boys, *four Asian American teens come of age in 1970s Seattle. Written by Mochizuki. (Book jacket photograph by Marc Tauss.)*

a Soviet detention camp and the diplomat released of his rank—and personal reflections on the man's childhood experiences during World War II. Scenes of desperate Jewish refugee families huddled at the door of the Japanese embassy and a boy's attempts to understand his parent's fear and agitation are brought to life in a "narrative [that] will grab kids' interest and make them think" according to *Booklist* contributor Hazel Rochman.

Discussing the inspiration for his picture books in an essay posted on the *Lee & Low* Web site, Mochizuki commented: "The basic theme of . . . *Baseball Saved Us* was the power of positive thinking and believing in oneself. One of the themes implicit in . . . *Heroes* was the definition of a hero as one who knows that actions speak louder than words. . . . *Passage to Freedom* is about the moral choice: Does one do what is considered 'correct' at the time? Or does one do what is 'right' for all time?" Issues of similar import, which *Booklist* contributor Gillian Engberg listed as "racial and cultural identity, prejudice, and family," are woven into the author's first young-adult novel, *Beacon Hill Boys*. Tak-

ing place in a Seattle neighborhood during the early 1970s, the novel focuses on a group of teens who are frustrated that the social and political changes sweeping the country in the wake of the civil rights movement are passing Asian Americans by, leaving them to bear the legacy of their traditionalist parents to conform and excel within the "system." Mochizuki's depiction of teenage life in the seventies earned praise from reviewers, with a *Publishers Weekly* critic remarking that "the author's understanding of teen conflicts and the need to forge an individual identity should resonate" with many readers.

"My grandparents were from Japan," Mochizuki once told *SATA,* "but my parents, brothers and I grew up and have lived in the U.S.A. all our lives. I have never been to Japan, nor do I speak any Japanese. Yet, I am still sometimes asked, 'Do you speak English?' or . . . 'Where are you from?' I am from Seattle, Washington, and learned my English in an American school like anyone else. When I am asked those kind of questions, I am being judged solely on what I look like. And that is a big reason why I write: to show that people of Asian and Pacific Islander descent in this country are Americans who are a part of everyday American life, and that they have been Americans for a long time.

"I hope to convey to young readers that they should actually get to 'know' others, rather than to 'assume' things about them—that really, all people are basically the same, and that there are only two types of people in this world: good and bad. I also try to communicate to young people a sense of positive thinking and self-esteem—that they should believe in themselves and what they can do, rather than listen to others who tell them what they cannot."

Biographical and Critical Sources

BOOKS

Mochizuki, Ken, *Baseball Saved Us,* Lee & Low (New York, NY), 1993.
Something about the Author Autobiography Series, Volume 22, Gale (Detroit, MI), 1996.

PERIODICALS

Booklist, April 15, 1993, Hazel Rochman, review of *Baseball Saved Us,* pp. 1523-1524; May 15, 1997, Hazel Rochman, review of *Passage to Freedom: The Sugihara Story,* p. 86; November 15, 2002, Gillian Engberg, review of *Beacon Hill Boys,* p. 595.
Bulletin of the Center for Children's Books, May, 1993, Roger Sutton, review of *Baseball Saved Us,* p. 290.
Horn Book, July-August, 1993, Ellen Fader, review of *Baseball Saved Us,* pp. 453-454; May-June, 1995, Ellen Fader, review of *Heroes,* p. 327.

Kirkus Reviews, March 1, 1993, p. 303; March 15, 1995, review of *Heroes,* p. 389; November 15, 2002, review of *Beacon Hill Boys,* p. 1689.

New York Times Book Review, April 4, 1993, Ira Berkow, review of *Baseball Saved Us,* p. 26.

Publishers Weekly, March 29, 1993, review of *Baseball Saved Us,* p. 55; March 6, 1995, review of *Heroes,* p. 69; April 21, 1997, review of *Passage to Freedom,* p. 71; November 11, 2002, review of *Beacon Hill Boys,* p. 65.

Reading Teacher, September, 1998, review of *Passage to Freedom,* p. 58.

School Library Journal, June, 1993, Tom S. Hurburt, review of *Baseball Saved Us,* pp. 84-85; July, 1995, John Philbrook, review of *Heroes,* p. 79; June, 2000, Patricia Mahoney Brown, review of *Passage to Freedom,* p. 89; January, 2003, Alison Follos, review of *Beacon Hill Boys,* p. 140.

ONLINE

Children's Literature: Meet Authors and Illustrators, http://www.childrenslit.com/ (December 30, 2003), "Ken Mochizuki."

Lee & Low, http://www.leeandlow.com/ (July 2, 2003), "Book Talk with Ken Mochizuki."

Scholastic, http://www.scholastic.com/ (July 2, 2003), "Ken Mochizuki."

* * *

MONTGOMERY, Hugh (Edward) 1962-

Personal

Born October 20, 1962, in Plymouth, England; son of Nelson (a doctor) and Bridget (a nurse) Montgomery; married; wife's name, Mary; children: Oscar Nelson. *Education:* University College London, B.Sc. (circulatory/respiratory physiology and neuropharmacology; first class honors), 1984; University of London, Bachelor of Medicine and Surgery, 1987, M.D., 1997. *Hobbies and other interests:* Skydiving, scuba diving, mountaineering.

Addresses

Agent—Caroline Sheldon, Thorley Manor Farm, Thorley, Yarmouth P04 1055, England. *E-mail*—h.montgomery@ucl.ac.uk.

Career

Doctor; consultant in intensive care. Division of Cardiovascular Genetics, Department of Medicine, British Heart Foundation, University College London, senior lecturer. Practiced medicine in Africa for a year.

Member

Royal College of Physicians; London Hypertension Society, British Hypertension Research Group, Intensive Care Society, European Society of Intensive Care Medicine, British Society for Cardiovascular Research, International Society for Heart Research (European Section), British Society of Echocardiography, European Society for Clinical Investigation, Royal Geographic Society (fellow).

Awards, Honors

Young Investigators Award, British Cardiac Society, 1996; Martii Karvonen Young Investigator Award, Pujko Symposium (Finland), 1998; Medal for Basic Science, European Society of Cardiology, 2001; Award for Excellence in Clinical Investigation, European Society for Clinical Investigation, 2002; Gillian Hanson Award, Intensive Care Society, 2002; self-published poetry book of the year and self-published book of the year awards, Independent Publishing Awards, 2002, for *The Voyage of the Arctic Tern.*

Writings

The Voyage of the Arctic Tern, illustrated by Nick Poullis, Synapse GB (Hants, England), 2000, Walker Books (London, England), Candlewick Press (Cambridge, MA), 2002.

(Editor, with D. Holdright) *100 Questions in Cardiology,* BMJ Publishing (London, England), 2001.

My First MRCP Book, ReMedica (London, England), 2002.

Contributor to radio and television programs and to over 200 print publications, including *Scientific American, New Scientist, Science, Newsweek, Focus, Men's Health,* and *Hola.*

Work in Progress

Morchilla and Ptarmagon, for Walker Books (London, England) and Candlewick Press (Cambridge, MA); *Cloudsailors,* for Candlewick Press (Cambridge, MA); *Consciousness,* a television drama; and *Reputation,* an adult film thriller.

Sidelights

British writer Hugh Montgomery's first book, *The Voyage of the Arctic Tern,* is a sea yarn, "an epic poem that delivers a spine-tingling tale of treachery and redemption, pirates and ghost ships," a reviewer wrote in *Publishers Weekly.* Bruno is the captain of a fishing boat, the *Arctic Tern.* Long ago, he committed a horrendous crime against his country, and as a result, he has been cursed. To lift the curse, he must save a life, rescue someone who has been betrayed, and give treasure back to the people, a process that ends up taking hundreds of years. He rescues the King of Spain from being poisoned by an aide when Queen Elizabeth sends Bruno to Spain with a message, taking care of two components of the curse. He has found the treasure that he wants to

Hugh Montgomery's novel The Voyage of the Arctic Tern *spins a tale in verse about Bruno, the skipper, and the adventures of his crew. (Illustrated by Nick Poullis.)*

return, too. When the aide's plot is foiled, he steals a chest of gold and sails away with it. However, the ship sinks, taking the aide and the gold down with it. The *Arctic Tern* sails for centuries, trying to find this gold, until the age of scuba gear allows Bruno and his crew to bring the treasure up from the sea floor and give it to the poor.

The fact that *The Voyage of the Arctic Tern* is composed entirely in rhyming verse sets it apart from most adventure novels for middle graders. Writing in verse "is a rollicking, rolling, driving form of storytelling," claimed *School Librarian* contributor Chris Brown, making the book "attractively different and . . . well worth seeking out."

Montgomery told *SATA:* "I was raised in Plymouth, Devon, in England, from whence the Pilgrim fathers set sail. Being raised by the sea was a powerful influence, and I spent a great deal of my youth either on or under it. By fifteen, I was a diver working on the salvage of King Henry VIII's flagship 'The Mary Rose,' and I went on to salvage other wrecks around the world. Perhaps the oldest was that of an Etruscan vessel, which sank off Italy in 621 B.C.

"I inherited some nautical genes—my grandfather was a ship's captain. My other grandfather had also written a novel. My father was a children's doctor, and my mother a children's nurse, so I suppose that I was always destined to write fiction for families, and with this upbringing and inheritance, the first book was always likely to be about the sea.

"I qualified as a doctor in 1987, and found myself alone in Edinburgh doing research in 1993. Having failed to buy my godchildren a present, I set out to write them a short story. To my amusement, it started writing itself in verse . . . and two years later I finished it! Not surprisingly, twenty-eight publishers rejected the book, but I persisted; I knew that what I had written was worthy. I self-published in 2000 to prove that the book *would* sell . . . and was right. Two thousand hardback copies went in two months. Candlewick (Walker in the UK) bought the rights . . . and the rest is history!

"I continue to work in medicine, as a specialist in intensive care. I also run a research group (finding the first 'gene for human fitness'). However, my writing career has moved on: I am working on four films (having sold the options to two), and have finished two more books.

The next book is *Morchilla and Ptarmagon,* a myth (and love story) set high in the mountains.

"I hate to hear of books being compartmentalized. If it is a good read, then who cares what age group reads it? I suspect, therefore, that my books are as much read by adults as children. This is certainly true for *The Voyage of the Arctic Tern.* I thus like to think of my books as 'family books,' not just 'books for children.'

"As to the future? Well, that depends on sales. Ultimately, I see myself as a writer."

Biographical and Critical Sources

PERIODICALS

Bookseller, April 19, 2002, Caroline Horn, profile of Hugh Montgomery, p. 35.

Kirkus Reviews, July 15, 2002, review of *The Voyage of the Arctic Tern,* p. 1038.

Publishers Weekly, October 7, 2002, review of *The Voyage of the Arctic Tern,* p. 73.

School Librarian, summer, 2001, Chris Brown, review of *The Voyage of the Arctic Tern,* p. 90.

School Library Journal, August, 2002, John Peters, review of *The Voyage of the Arctic Tern,* p. 195.

ONLINE

Voyage of the Arctic Tern Web Site, http://www.arctictern. com/ (August 25, 2003).

N

NEWMAN, Marjorie

Personal

Born in England. *Education:* Attended Southlands Teacher Training College (Wimbledon, England). *Religion:* Christian. *Hobbies and other interests:* Reading, drawing, painting, music, collecting second-hand books, playing guitar, violin, piano, and recorder.

Addresses

Agent—Eunice McMullen, Low Ibbotsholme Cottage, Troutbeck, Windermere, Cumbria LA23 1HU, England.

Career

Teacher and writer. Worked variously in offices, retail shops, and snack bars.

Member

Society of Children's Book Writers and Illustrators.

Awards, Honors

Christopher Award, 2003, for *Mole and the Baby Bird.*

Writings

Wilkins the Armchair Cat, illustrated by Clare Beaton, A. & C. Black (London, England), 1978.

Wilkins Gets a Job, illustrated by Clare Beaton, A. & C. Black (London, England), 1980.

The Amazing Pet, illustrated by Janet Duchesne, Hamish Hamilton (London, England), 1982.

Concert at School, Help the Aged Education Department (London, England), 1982.

Mr Green Can't Sleep, Help the Aged Education Department (London, England), 1982.

Letters, Help the Aged Education Department (London, England), 1982.

Skipping Surprise, Help the Aged Education Department (London, England), 1982.

Knocked Out, illustrated by Nicole Goodwin, Hamish Hamilton (London, England), 1983.

Wilkins Gets a Blanket, illustrated by Clare Beaton, A. & C. Black (London, England), 1984.

Dan and the Football and *Dan and the Special Badge,* Pickering (Basingstoke, England), 1984.

Dan and the Breakdown and *Dan and the Night Visitor,* Pickering (Basingstoke, England), 1984.

Burnt Sausages and Custard, illustrated by Catherine Bradbury, Hamish Hamilton (London, England), 1985.

Andrew and the Special Sunday, Pickering (Basingstoke, England), 1986.

Andrew and the Thank You Cat, Pickering (Basingstoke, England), 1986.

A Room for Neil, illustrated by Catherine Bradbury, Hamish Hamilton (London, England), 1986.

The School Concert, illustrated by Nicole Goodwin, Hamish Hamilton (London, England), 1986.

Police Horse, illustrated by David Saunders, A & C Black (London, England), 1986, published as *Lloyd, the Police Horse,* Scholastic (London, England), 1988.

Storytime One, illustrated by Eileen Madison, Scripture Union (London, England), 1986.

Family Saturday, illustrated by Pamela Southgate, Hamish Hamilton (London, England), 1987.

The Scary Mouse, illustrated by Pamela Southgate, Hamish Hamilton (London, England), 1987.

Party Day and Other Stories, Scripture Union (London, England), 1988.

Michael and the Jumble-Sale Cat, illustrated by Pamela Southgate, Hamish Hamilton (London, England), 1988.

Look at Me Now, illustrated by Kathy James, Macdonald (London, England), 1988.

Green Monster Magic, illustrated by Pamela Southgate, Hodder and Stoughton (London, England), 1988.

The Pirates and the Cats, illustrated by Graham Round, Hodder and Stoughton (London, England), 1988.

(Reteller) *The First Christmas,* illustrated by Edgar Hodges, World International (Manchester, England), 1988.

(Reteller) *Joseph and His Coat of Many Colours,* illustrated by Edgar Hodges, World International (Manchester, England), 1988.

(Reteller) *Noah Builds an Ark,* illustrated by Edgar Hodges, World International (Manchester, England), 1988.

(Reteller) *The Good Samaritan,* illustrated by Edgar Hodges, World International (Manchester, England), 1988.

(Reteller) *Children's Illustrated Bible,* illustrated by Michael Codd, World International (Manchester, England), 1989.

My Book of Prayers, illustrated by Linda Pasifull, World International (Manchester, England), 1989, published as *My Book of Favorite Prayers,* Augsburg (Minneapolis, MN), 1990.

The Pirates and the Spring Cleaning, illustrated by Graham Round, Hodder and Stoughton (London, England), 1989.

Songs for Jesus, illustrated by Dianne Stuchbury, World International (Manchester, England), 1990.

The Children at Willow Green, illustrated by Joanna Williams, Scripture Union (London, England), 1990.

(Reteller) *The Lord's Prayer,* illustrated by Dianne Stuchbury, World International (Manchester, England), 1990.

(Reteller) *The Christmas Story,* illustrated by Robin Lawrie, World International (Manchester, England), 1990.

(Reteller) *The Easter Story,* illustrated by Robin Lawrie, World International (Manchester, England), 1990.

(Reteller) *The Boy Jesus,* illustrated by Edgar Hodges, World International (Manchester, England), 1990.

(Reteller) *The Boy with Loaves and Fishes,* illustrated by Edgar Hodges, World International (Manchester, England), 1990.

(Reteller) *Daniel and the Lion's Den,* illustrated by Edgar Hodges, World International (Manchester, England), 1990.

(Reteller) *David and Goliath,* illustrated by Edgar Hodges, World International (Manchester, England), 1990.

Robert and the Giant, illustrated by Sally Gardner, Hamish Hamilton (London, England), 1990.

Horace, illustrated by Kay Widdowson, Hodder and Stoughton (London, England), 1990.

The Christmas Puzzle Book, illustrated by Peter Kent, Scholastic (London, England), 1990.

(Reteller) *Bible People,* World International (Manchester, England), 1990.

The Pirates and Captain Bullseye, illustrated by Graham Round, Hodder and Stoughton (London, England), 1991.

Bible Questions and Answers, illustrated by Michael Codd, World International (Manchester, England), 1991.

A Child's First Book of Prayers, illustrated by Elvira Dadd, Hunt and Thorpe (Alresford, England), Revell (Tarrytown, NY), 1991.

Skipper at School, Hamish Hamilton (London, England), 1992.

(Reteller) *A Boy Helps Jesus,* illustrated by Edgar Hodges, Tyndale House (Wheaton, IL), 1994.

(Reteller) *The Good Neighbor,* illustrated by Edgar Hodges, Tyndale House (Wheaton, IL), 1994.

(Reteller) *Noah Builds a Boat,* illustrated by Edgar Hodges, Tyndale House (Wheaton, IL), 1994.

Tiger, Tiger, illustrated by Isabel Rayner, Collins (London, England), 1995.

(With others) *Footprint Detective,* Ginn (Aylesbury, England), 1995.

Steve: A Story about Death, Franklin Watts (New York, NY), 1995, Franklin Watts (New York, NY), 1998.

Yo Ho Ho!, Corgi (London, England), 1996.

Science Magic, illustrated by Margaret Clark-Jones, Collins (London, England), 1996.

Sir Garibald and Hot Nose, illustrated by Christopher Masters, Macdonald (Hove, England), 1996.

Time for a Party, Heinemann Educational Secondary Division (London, England), 1997.

Hornpipe's Hunt for Pirate Gold, illustrated by Ben Cort, Walker (London, England), Candlewick Press (Cambridge, MA), 1998.

The Wonderful Journey of Cameron Cat, illustrated by Charlotte Hard, Walker (London, England), Candlewick Press (Cambridge, MA), 1998.

Is That What Friends Do?, Hutchinson Children's Books (London, England), 1998.

Sir Garibald and the Damsel in Distress, illustrated by Christopher Masters, Macdonald (Hove, England), 1998.

Ned the Fighting Donkey, Oxford University Press (Oxford, England), 1999.

Gordon the Clever Goat, Oxford University Press (Oxford, England), 1999.

Rabbit's Trick, Oxford University Press (Oxford, England), 1999.

The King and the Cuddly, Hutchinson Children's Books (London, England), 1999.

Dogs, Oxford University Press (Oxford, England), 2000.

Mole and the Baby Bird, illustrated by Patrick Benson, Bloomsbury Children's Books (London, England, and New York, NY), 2002.

Boswell the Kitchen Cat, Little Tiger Press (London, England), 2002.

Captain Pike Looks after the Baby, Macmillan Children's Books (London, England), 2004.

Author of other books for children, as well as scripts for radio, television, and audio cassette.

Work in Progress

Just Like You Did, a picture book for Bloomsbury Children's Books (London, England).

Sidelights

Children's author Marjorie Newman has been writing and publishing for more than twenty-five years. Her first children's book, *Wilkins the Armchair Cat,* was published in 1978. Since then, Newman has written more than ninety books for young people from publishers such as Ginn, Hodder, Scholastic, Hamish Hamilton, Scripture Union, and more.

Born in England, Newman has worked at a variety of jobs, including office work and retail sales. Newman began writing when she was about seven years old, as

A monkey and elephant learn about friendship in **Is That What Friends Do?,** *written by Marjorie Newman, with illustrations by Peter Bowman.*

she said on the *Word Pool* Web site. She attended Southlands Teacher Training College and worked for many years as a "full-time infant teacher," as she remembered in a *Bloomsbury Web Site* author profile. Newman gradually moved to teaching part-time and writing part-time, then became a full-time writer.

Some of Newman's books have been written in as little as two days, as she noted in her *Word Pool* author profile. Other books have taken up to a year, or more. She gets her ideas from a variety of sources, including television, or other books she has read, or from things she sees children do. Offering advice on the *Word Pool* Web site, Newman urges people who want to write children's books to work hard at thinking like a child, to read kids' books, to talk to children, and to watch television aimed at young people.

Although she is an avid artist who draws and paints, so far others have illustrated her books. The "editors won't let me do the illustrations although it's still one of my ambitions to manage this one day," Newman quipped on *Word Pool* Web site.

Puzzles and games add an interactive element to some of Newman's books. In *The Wonderful Journey of Cameron Cat,* curious feline Cameron's sense of adventure and exploration gets him stuck in the back of a furniture van. Readers solve puzzles throughout the story as they read about Cameron's attempts to get back to his owner, Ann.

A number of Newman's works revolve around Biblical teachings and stories from the Bible. In *A Child's First Book of Prayers,* Newman provides a selection of prayers for children newly introduced to religion. The *Children's Illustrated Bible* presents the Bible in a format accessible to younger readers. Newman offers stories of Biblical characters, themes, and events in titles such as *Noah Builds a Boat, A Boy Helps Jesus,* and *The Good Neighbor.*

Many of Newman's works are populated by gentle and understanding animals, some of whom have the same reactions to the world that the children often have. Other animals in the stories represent different personalities— some difficult—that children may encounter. In *Is That What Friends Do?,* Elephant believes he has found his first and best friend in Monkey. But Monkey is sometimes thoughtless and selfish, often bossy, and frequently unpleasant to Elephant. Though he tries hard to be Monkey's friend, Elephant wonders about their relationship. Monkey's poor treatment of Elephant makes him ask the question that forms the title of the book: is this what friends do? "Being kind and sharing is the answer in this very traditional type English nursery story," wrote Barbara James in *Magpies.*

Cuthbert the lion, the hero of *The King and the Cuddly,* must continually uphold his reputation for ferocity and fearlessness. To do so, he has to keep his comforting toy, Cuddles, a secret. If the other animals in the jungle found out about Cuddles, they might think Cuthbert is not really as brave and bold as he claims to be. But when Cuddles comes up missing, Cuthbert worries little about his reputation and instead becomes determined to find his absent friend, no matter what others may think. In the process, he learns that others may have little secret friends of their own. Deepa Earnshaw, writing in *School Librarian,* called *The King and the Cuddly* a "charming story" with "a nice, but perhaps obvious, conclusion" that should nonetheless appeal to preschoolers and young children.

In the award-winning *Mole and the Baby Bird,* young Mole adopts a baby bird that has fallen out of its nest. Although Mole takes good care of the little bird, his parents tell him it may die and repeatedly warn him that it is a wild creature, not a pet. The bird gains strength and grows quickly with Mole's care, but when it shows signs of wanting to fly, Mold builds a cage to make sure it cannot leave. Captivity, however, does not suit the bird; its condition worsens even though Mole continues to give it plenty of attention and loving care. Mole continues to ignore his parents' gentle cautions that the bird is not intended to be a pet and should be free.

When Grandpa Mole visits and sees the situation, he takes Mole for a walk up a high hillside. There, Mole sees birds in their natural setting and realizes that his pet should be allowed to fly free, no matter how much he might want to keep the bird for his own. While Grandpa demonstrates to his young grandson "what is right and what is natural, . . . it is Mole who makes the decision to set the bird free," wrote Kathy Broderick in *Booklist.* Newman "conveys to youngest readers the importance of allowing others to be free to be themselves," wrote a reviewer in *Publishers Weekly,* while Marlene Gawron, writing in *School Library Journal,* observed that "the message of making others happy through a selfless act and the true meaning of love comes across gently" in the pages of *Mole and the Baby Bird.* A writer in *Kirkus Reviews* called the book a "sweet story," going on to predict that young readers "will eagerly read between the lines" and reach their own conclusions about how and why Mole decides to release the bird.

Newman's works also strive to explain the sometimes bewildering, sometimes painful events in a child's world. *Steve: A Story about Death,* a specially commissioned work concerning the death of a parent, is intended for children in the seven to nine year age range. More mildly, *The Scary Mouse* tells the story of how Paul conquers his fear of touching mice when he is asked to take care of his friend Annette's mouse while she is in the hospital. "How Paul overcomes his distaste is well told," wrote a reviewer in *Books for Keeps.*

Cuthbert has a secret, in **The King and the Cuddly,** *written by Newman and illustrated by Bowman.*

Biographical and Critical Sources

PERIODICALS

Booklist, October 15, 2002, Kathy Broderick, review of *Mole and the Baby Bird,* p. 413.

Books for Keeps, July, 1990, review of *The Scary Mouse,* p. 9.

Kirkus Reviews, August 5, 2002, review of *Mole and the Baby Bird,* p. 1231.

Magpies, March, 1999, Barbara James, review of *Is That What Friends Do?,* p. 26.

Publishers Weekly, June 29, 1998, review of *The Wonderful Journey of Cameron Cat,* p. 61, and review of *Hornpipe's Hunt for Pirate Gold,* p. 61; July 15, 2002, review of *Mole and the Baby Bird,* pp. 72-73.

School Librarian, spring, 2001, Deepa Earnshaw, review of *The King and the Cuddly,* p. 20.

School Library Journal, December, 2002, Marlene Gawron, review of *Mole and the Baby Bird,* p. 104.

Times Educational Supplement, February 14, 1992, Carol Fox, "Sharing the Story," review of *Skipper at School,* p. 31.

ONLINE

Bloomsbury Web Site, http://www.bloomsbury.com/ (July 7, 2003), profile of Marjorie Newman. Word Pool, http://www.wordpool.co.uk/ (July 7, 2003), profile of

NIXON, Joan Lowery 1927-2003

OBITUARY NOTICE—See index for *SATA* sketch: Born February 3, 1927, in Los Angeles, CA; died of complications from pancreatic cancer June 28, 2003, in Houston, TX. Author. Nixon was a prolific author of young adult literature who was best known for her Edgar Award-winning mystery novels. She was a graduate of the University of Southern California, where she earned a B.A. in 1947, and California State College, where she received her certification in elementary education in 1949. Nixon began her career teaching elementary school in Los Angeles in the late 1940s, but after marriage she focused on raising her children for several years. She began writing—something she could do while at home—in the 1950s and had her first book, *The Mystery of Hurricane Castle,* published in 1964. Nixon enjoyed writing mysteries because she found them comforting—the bad guy always gets caught in her stories, which she felt was reassuring. In addition to many other honors, she won Edgar Allan Poe Awards for best juvenilenovel for *The Kidnapping of Christina Lattimore* (1979), *The Seance* (1980), *The Other Side of Dark* (1986), and*The Name of the Game Was Murder* (1993). Although Nixon wrote mainly mysteries, she also penned a number of historical novels and nonfiction books. During the 1970s she taught creative writing at Midland College and at the University of Houston, and she also authored a book offering advice to aspiring writers titled *If You Were a Writer* (1988). Some of her more recent books include *The Haunting* (1998), *Nancy's Story* (2000), *Caesar's Story* (2000), and *Gus and Gertie and the Missing Pearl* (2000).

*   *   *

OBITUARIES AND OTHER SOURCES:

BOOKS

St. James Guide to Young Adult Writers, second edition, St. James Press (Detroit, MI), 1999.
Writers Directory, 18th edition, St. James Press (Detroit, MI), 2003.

PERIODICALS

Houston Chronicle, July 1, 2003, p. 1.
Los Angeles Times, July 13, 2003, p. B19.
New York Times, July 7, 2003, p. A14.

*   *   *

NOONAN, Diana 1960-

Personal

Born January 7, 1960, in Dunedin, New Zealand; daughter of Valerie Popham; married Keith Olsen (an artist), 1984; children: one son. *Ethnicity:* "European."
Education: Attended Auckland Secondary Teachers College; Otago University, B.A., 1980. *Religion:* Christian. *Hobbies and other interests:* Swimming.

Addresses

Home—Catlins, New Zealand. *Agent*—Richards Literary Agency, P.O. Box 31240, Milford, Auckland, New Zealand.

Career

Writer and educator. Worked as a secondary school teacher prior to 1986. Full-time writer, 1986—; editor, *New Zealand School Journal,* 1996—. Writer-in-residence, Dunedin College of Education, 1993. Received two writing bursaries from Creative New Zealand.

Awards, Honors

Queen Elizabeth II Arts Council Children's Writer Bursary, 1991; White Raven Award, International Library of Munich, 1992, for *Leaving the Snow Country* and 1993, for *A Sonnet for the City;* AIM Children's Book Award for junior fiction, 1994, for *A Dolphin in the Bay;* AIM Children's Book Award for picture books, 1995, for *The Best-Loved Bear;* New Zealand Library and Information Association Book Award for nonfiction, 1997, for *I Spy Wildlife* and *The Field;* New Zealand Post Children's Book Award for nonfiction, 1998, for *The Know, Sow, and Grow Kids' Book of Plants.*

Writings

The Silent People, John McIndoe (Dunedin, New Zealand), 1990.
Leaving the Snow Country, John McIndoe (Dunedin, New Zealand), 1991.
A Sonnet for the City, John McIndoe (Dunedin, New Zealand), 1992.
The Bump, illustrated by Lyn Kreigler, Murdoch Books (North Sydney, Australia), 1992.
Oswald Bear's Night by the Sea, illustrated by Bryan Pollard, Murdoch Books (Sydney, Australia), 1992.
Right Now, illustrated by Trevor Pye, Murdoch Books (North Sydney, Australia), 1992.
The Dragon's Egg, illustrated by Gabriela Klepatski, Murdoch Books (North Sydney, Australia), 1992.
Trees Belong to Everyone, illustrated by Liz Dodson, Shortland Publications (Auckland, New Zealand), 1992.
Listening in Bed, illustrated by Warren Crossett, Nelson Price Milburn (Petone, NZ), Wright Group (Bothell, WA), 1992.
The Super-Duper Sunflower Seeds, illustrated by Annie Quinn, Nelson Price Milburn (Petone, New Zealand), Wright Group (Bothell, WA), 1992.

A Storm on the Beach, illustrated by Betty Greenhatch, Nelson Price Milburn (Petone, NZ), Wright Group (Bothell, WA), 1992.

Out after Dark, illustrated by Mark Sofilas, Nelson Price Milburn (Petone, NZ), Wright Group (Bothell, WA), 1992.

Gladys and Max Love Bob, illustrated by Philip Webb, Nelson Price Milburn (Petone, NZ), Wright Group (Bothell, WA), 1992.

The Adventures of Greanwald: The Fish Are Jumping, illustrated by Tony Hadlow, Little Mammoth (Auckland, New Zealand), 1992.

What Would You Do?, illustrated by Mitch Vane, Lands End (Lower Hutt, New Zealand), Wright Group (Bothell, WA), 1992.

The Last Steam Train, illustrated by Brent Putze, Ashton Scholastic (Auckland, New Zealand), 1992.

A Dolphin in the Bay, Omnibus (Norwood, South Australia), 1993.

Goodbye Toss, illustrated by Keith Olsen, HarperCollins (Auckland, New Zealand), 1993.

The Birthday Bicycle, illustrated by Sandra Cammell, Murdoch Books (North Sydney, Australia), 1993.

Who's Maxwell?, illustrated by Kevin Hawley, Murdoch Books (North Sydney, Australia), 1993.

A Crocodile to Tea, illustrated by Clive Taylor, Murdoch Books (North Sydney, Australia), 1993.

Baby and Me, illustrated by Trevor Pye, Murdoch Books (North Sydney, Australia), 1993.

Old Teeth, New Teeth (also see below), illustrated by Clare Bowes, Lands End (Wellington, New Zealand), 1993.

The Teddy Snatcher, illustrated by Gabriela Klepatski, Murdoch Books (North Sydney, Australia), 1993.

Where Is My Caterpillar? (also see below), illustrated by Isobel Lowe, Lands End (Lower Hutt, New Zealand), 1993.

Porridge, illustrated by Trevor Pye, Lands End (Wellington, New Zealand), 1993.

If You Like Strawberries, Don't Read This Book, photographs by Michelle Moir, Shortland Publications (Auckland, New Zealand), 1993.

Everybody Eats Bread, photographs by Peter Garland, Shortland Publications (Auckland, New Zealand), 1993.

Skin, Skin (also see below), Lands End (Lower Hutt, New Zealand), 1993.

Fly Away Home (also see below), illustrated by Audrie Leslie, Lands End (Lower Hutt, New Zealand), 1993.

Food Trappers (also see below), illustrated by John Parsons, Lands End (Lower Hutt, New Zealand), 1993.

The Big Roundup (also see below), illustrated by Mark Coote, Lands End (Lower Hutt, New Zealand), 1993.

Bird Beaks (also see below), illustrated by Veronica Alkema, Lands End (Lower Hutt, New Zealand), 1993.

Hide & Seek (also see below), illustrated by Audrie Leslie, Lands End (Lower Hutt, New Zealand), 1993.

Hay Making (also see below), illustrated by Mark Coote, Lands End (Lower Hutt, New Zealand), 1993.

Milking (also see below), illustrated by Julie McCormack, Lands End (Lower Hutt, New Zealand), 1993.

My Friend Jess (also see below), illustrated by Clare Bowes, Lands End (Lower Hutt, New Zealand), 1993.

I Spy (also see below), illustrated by Astrid Matijasevic, Applecross (Auckland, New Zealand), 1993.

The Old Green Machine, illustrated by Carlos Freire, Applecross (Auckland, New Zealand), Wright Group (Bothell, WA), 1993.

The Whaler's Garden, John McIndoe (Dunedin, New Zealand), 1994.

Room Four at Cattle Creek, HarperCollins (Auckland, New Zealand), 1994.

The Deer, Ashton Scholastic (Auckland, New Zealand), 1994.

The Best-Loved Bear, illustrated by Elizabeth Fuller, Ashton Scholastic (Auckland, New Zealand), 1994.

Kangaroo Bill and the Forest Behind the Bay, Reed (Auckland, New Zealand), 1994.

Fat Cat Tompkin, illustrated by Craig Smith, SRA School Group (Santa Rosa, CA), 1994.

Shooting It Straight, photographs by Audrie Leslie, SRA School Group (Santa Rosa, CA), 1994.

Donkeys, illustrated by Don Black, SRA School Group (Santa Rosa, CA), 1994.

Houses That Move, illustrated by Don Black, SRA School Group (Santa Rosa, CA), 1994.

I Spy a Fly (also see below), illustrated by Nic Bishop, Lands End (Lower Hutt, New Zealand), 1994.

On the Move (also see below), illustrated by Nic Bishop, Lands End (Lower Hutt, New Zealand), 1994.

(With Keith Olsen) *Let's Look after Our World,* Applecross (Auckland, NZ), Wright Group (Bothell, WA), 1994.

From Camel Cart to Canoe: Transportation in India and Nepal, photographs by Chloe Dear, Applecross (Auckland, New Zealand), Wright Group (Bothell, WA), 1994.

A Touch of Jungle Fever, HarperCollins (Auckland, New Zealand), 1995.

Sleeping, Dreaming (also see below), illustrated by Caroline Campbell, Lands End (Lower Hutt, New Zealand), 1995.

Dazzling Miss Dynamo Dials for Help, illustrated by Philip Webb, Telecom New Zealand (Wellington, New Zealand), 1995.

The Lunchbox, illustrated by Philip Webb, Learning Media (Wellington, New Zealand), 1995.

A Cupboard Full of Summer, illustrated by Christine Ross, Learning Media (Wellington, New Zealand), 1995.

Olivia Agnew's Wild Imagination (also see below), illustrated by Sarah Farman, Lands End (Lower Hutt, New Zealand), 1995.

Storm! (also see below), illustrated by Julie McCormack, Lands End (Lower Hutt, New Zealand), 1995.

Our Solar System (also see below), illustrated by Christine Tate, Lands End (Lower Hutt, New Zealand), 1995.

The Burglar's Ball (also see below), illustrated by Lyn Kriegler, Lands End (Lower Hutt, New Zealand), 1995.

Danny to the Rescue, HarperCollins (Auckland, New Zealand), 1995.

Packing (also see below), illustrated by Caroline Campbell, Lands End (Lower Hutt, New Zealand), 1995.

Feed Me!, illustrated by John Bennett, Murdoch Books (North Sydney, Australia), 1995.

Birds' Nests (also see below), illustrated by Paul Gay, Lands End (Lower Hutt, New Zealand), 1995.

The Picnic (also see below), illustrated by Rick Youmans, Lands End (Lower Hutt, New Zealand), 1995.

Potatoes, Potatoes (also see below), illustrated by Donna McKenna, Lands End (Lower Hutt, New Zealand), 1995.

Stop!, illustrated by Nicola Belsham, Lands End (Lower Hutt, New Zealand), Wright Group (Bothell, WA), 1995.

A Writer's Work, Lands End (Lower Hutt, New Zealand), Wright Group (Bothell, WA), 1995.

My Story, illustrated by Andrea Jaretzki, Lands End (Lower Hutt, New Zealand), Wright Group (Bothell, WA), 1995.

Don't Throw It Away, illustrated by Donna McKenna, Lands End (Lower Hutt, New Zealand), Wright Group (Bothell, WA), 1995.

Amazing Maps, Lands End (Lower Hutt, New Zealand), Wright Group (Bothell, WA), 1995.

Bird-Watcher, illustrated by Jan van der Voo, Lands End (Lower Hutt, New Zealand), Wright Group (Bothell, WA), 1995.

Bludger, illustrated by Brent Putze, Lands End (Lower Hutt, New Zealand), 1995.

Traffic Light Sandwich, illustrated by Marjory Gardner, Lands End (Lower Hutt, New Zealand), 1995, Wright Group (Bothell, WA), 1996.

Dear Tom, illustrated by Fifi Colston, Lands End (Lower Hutt, New Zealand), 1995, Wright Group (Bothell, WA), 1996.

Donkey Work, Lands End (Lower Hutt, New Zealand), 1995, Wright Group (Bothell, WA), 1996.

Rockets, illustrated by Peter Campbell, Lands End (Lower Hutt, New Zealand), Wright Group (Bothell, WA), 1995.

All about Bicycles, Wendy Pye Group (Auckland, New Zealand), 1995, Wright Group (Bothell, WA), 1996.

The Giant's Stew, illustrated by Johanna Voss, Wendy Pye Group (Auckland, New Zealand), Wright Group (Bothell, WA), 1995.

I Know That Tune! (also see below), illustrated by Fraser Williamson, Lands End (Lower Hutt, New Zealand), 1996.

I Spy Wildlife, Heinemann Education (Auckland, New Zealand), 1996.

Hercules, Omnibus (Norwood, South Australia), 1996.

The Farmer's Journey: A Greek Fable, illustrated by Vivi Escriva, Celebration Press (Glenview, IL), 1996.

Whizz! Click!, illustrated by Philip Webb, Learning Media (Wellington, New Zealand), 1996.

The Biggest Bear in the Woods, illustrated by Dorothy Donahue, Celebration Press (Glenview, IL), 1996.

Hello, Dad!, illustrated by Annabel Craighead, Learning Media (Wellington, New Zealand), 1996.

A House with Character,, illustrated by Keith Olsen, Rigby Heinemann (Port Melbourne, Victoria, Australia), 1996.

What If—?, illustrated by Jan van der Voo, Murdoch Books (North Sydney, Australia), 1996.

Why Cry?, illustrated by Jacqui Thomas, Wendy Pye Group (Auckland, New Zealand), Wright Group (Bothell, WA), 1996.

Animal Inventions, Wendy Pye Group (Auckland, New Zealand), Wright Group (Bothell, WA), 1996.

A Name Garden, illustrated by Toni Goffe, Wendy Pye Group (Auckland, New Zealand), Wright Group (Bothell, WA), 1996.

Lift Off!, illustrated by Scott Kennedy, Learning Media (Wellington, New Zealand), 1996.

What's Up?, Learning Media (Wellington, New Zealand), 1996.

The Great Bean Race, illustrated by Christine Ross, Learning Media (Wellington, New Zealand), 1996.

Too Little, illustrated by Christine Ross, Learning Media (Wellington, New Zealand), 1996.

The Tricky, Sticky Problem, illustrated by Christine Ross, Learning Media (Wellington, New Zealand), 1996.

Up Went Edmond, illustrated by Jennifer Lautusi, Learning Media (Wellington, New Zealand), 1996.

Wild Cats (also see below), illustrated by Julie McCormack, Lands End (Lower Hutt, New Zealand), 1996.

A Silent World, illustrated by Bryan Pollard, Shortland Publications (Auckland, New Zealand), 1996.

Open It!, photography by Michael Overend, Learning Media (Wellington, New Zealand), 1996.

Our Car, illustrated by Nick Price, Wendy Pye Group (Auckland, New Zealand), Wright Group (Bothell, WA), 1996.

A Fire at the Zoo, illustrated by Terry Burton, Wendy Pye Group (Auckland, New Zealand), Wright Group (Bothell, WA), 1996.

An Elephant for the Holidays, illustrated by Paolo Bellini, Wendy Pye Group (Auckland, New Zealand), Wright Group (Bothell, WA), 1996.

After the Dinosaurs, illustrated by Geoffrey Cox, Lands End (Lower Hutt, New Zealand), Wright Group (Bothell, WA), 1996.

We All Play Sports, Learning Media (Wellington, New Zealand), 1996.

Time for a Change, Learning Media (Wellington, New Zealand), 1996.

Mrs. Barnett's Birthday, illustrated by Celia Canning, Wendy Pye Group (Auckland, New Zealand), Wright Group (Bothell, WA), 1996.

Making Friends, illustrated by Helen Casey, Lands End (Lower Hutt, New Zealand), 1996, Wright Group (Bothell, WA), 1997.

The Picnic in the Sky, illustrated by Clive Taylor, Lands End (Lower Hutt, New Zealand), 1996, Wright Group (Bothell, WA), 1997.

The Birthday Sleep-Over, photographs by Dean Zillwood, Learning Media (Wellington, New Zealand), 1997.

The Know, Sow, and Grow Kids' Book of Plants, Bridge Hill Publishing (Alexandra, New Zealand), 1997.

What about Bennie?, illustrated by Ralph Whirly, Shortland (Auckland, New Zealand), Rigby (Barrington, IL), 1997.

It's My Bread, Learning Media (Wellington, New Zealand), 1997.

Stop That Noise!, Learning Media (Wellington, New Zealand), 1997.

Snakes, Wendy Pye Group (Auckland, New Zealand), 1997, Wright Group (Bothell, WA), 1998.

Busking, illustrated by Kiki Ketcham-Neumann, Wendy Pye Group (Auckland, New Zealand), 1997.

Flora: A Friend for the Animals, Wendy Pye Group (Auckland, New Zealand), 1997, Wright Group (Bothell, WA), 2000.

Off We Go!, Learning Media (Wellington, New Zealand), 1997.

Hedgehog Fun, photographs by Dean Zillwood, Learning Media (Wellington, New Zealand), 1997.

My Chair, Learning Media (Wellington, New Zealand), 1997.

Pedal Power, Learning Media (Wellington, New Zealand), 1997.

Simple Solution!, illustrated by Bryan Pollard, Rigby (Barrington, IL), 1997.

My Nest, illustrated by Wendy Smith-Griswold, Celebration Press (White Plains, NY), 1997.

The Desert Machine (also see below), Wendy Pye Group (Auckland, New Zealand), 1997.

Under the City (also see below), Wendy Pye Group (Auckland, New Zealand), 1997.

Oh, No!, illustrated by Clare Bowes, Learning Media (Wellington, New Zealand), 1998.

The Pyjama Hunt, illustrated by Christine Ross, Learning Media (Wellington, New Zealand), 1998.

Rabbits in Space, illustrated by Andrew Geeson, Dominie Press (Carlsbad, CA), 1998.

The New Forest, illustrated by David House, Dominie Press (Carlsbad, CA), 1998.

The Grass Circles Mystery, illustrated by E. Silas Smith, Dominie Press (Carlsbad, CA), 1998.

King Glitter and the Stars, illustrated by David P. Smith, Dominie Press (Carlsbad, CA), 1998.

Not Enough Cupcakes, illustrated by Denise Elliott, Dominie Press (Carlsbad, CA), 1998.

Three, Two, One, Blast-Off!, illustrated by Deidre Grant, Dominie Press (Carlsbad, CA), 1998.

Two of Everything, illustrated by Denise Elliott, Dominie Press (Carlsbad, CA), 1998.

Who's Afraid of Shadows?, illustrated by Carol Daniel, Dominie Press (Carlsbad, CA), 1998.

The Best Birthday Gift Ever, illustrated by Elizabeth Sawyer, Dominie Press (Carlsbad, CA), 1998.

Beating the Drought, ("Skyrider Yellow" series), Learning Media (Wellington, New Zealand), 1999.

Hang in There, Oscar Martin!, ("Skyrider Blue" series), Learning Media (Wellington, New Zealand), 1999.

Lake Critter Journal, photographs by Nic Bishop, Longman (South Melbourne, Australia), 1999.

Double Switch, ("Skyrider Blue" series), Learning Media (Wellington, New Zealand), 1999.

McGinty's Friend, Rigby (Barrington, IL), 1999.

Mr. Merton's Vacation, illustrated by Paul Konye, Rigby (Barrington, IL), 1999.

Colour It My Way, photographs by Mary Foley, Shortland Publications (Auckland, New Zealand), published as *Color It My Way,* Rigby (Barrington, IL), 2000.

A Whistle from the Blunder, Longacre Press (Dunedin, New Zealand), 2000.

Dangerous Work, Heinemann Library (Port Melbourne, Victoria, Australia), 2001.

Edmond Went Splash, Learning Media (Wellington, New Zealand), 2001.

(With Keith Olsen) *What Is Recycling?,* Wendy Pye Group (Auckland, New Zealand), 2001.

How Do You Say "Hello"?, Learning Media (Wellington, New Zealand), 2001.

Auntie Rosie & the Rabbit, illustrated by Christina Ross, Scholastic New Zealand (Auckland, New Zealand), 2002.

The Best-Dressed Bear, (sequel to *The Best-Loved Bear*), Scholastic New Zealand (Auckland, New Zealand), 2002.

Don't Shout, illustrated by Karen Odiam, Learning Media (Wellington, New Zealand), 2003.

Also author of *Deadbeat, Street Musician,* and *Oatmeal.* Other titles by Noonan have been published in the United States by the Wright Group (Bothell, WA), including *The Big Roundup, Bird Beaks, Birds' Nests, The Burglar's Ball, The Desert Machine, Fly Away Home, Food Trappers, Hay Making, Hide and Seek, I Know That Tune!, I Spy, I Spy a Fly, Milking, Storm!, Under the City, Where Is My Caterpillar, Wild Cats, My Friend Jess, Old Teeth, New Teeth, Olivia Agnew's Wild Imagination, On the Move, Our Solar System, Packing, The Picnic, Potatoes, Potatoes, Skin, Skin,* and *Sleeping, Dreaming.* Contributor of short story to *Personal Best,* edited by Tessa Duder Tessa and P. McFarlane, Reed (Auckland, New Zealand), 1997.

"LIFE CYCLES" SERIES

The Green Turtle, Chelsea Clubhouse Books (Philadelphia, PA), 2003.

The Frog, Chelsea Clubhouse Books (Philadelphia, PA), 2003.

The Butterfly, Chelsea Clubhouse Books (Philadelphia, PA), 2003.

The Emperor Penguin, Chelsea Clubhouse Books (Philadelphia, PA), 2003.

The Kangaroo, Chelsea Clubhouse Books (Philadelphia, PA), 2003.

The Crocodile, Chelsea Clubhouse Books (Philadelphia, PA), 2003.

"I SPY WILDLIFE" SERIES; WITH NIC BISHOP

The Field, Heinemann Education (Auckland, New Zealand), 1995.

The Rocky Shore, Heinemann Education (Auckland, New Zealand), 1996.

The Pond, Heinemann Education (Auckland, New Zealand), 1996.

The Garden, Heinemann Education (Auckland, New Zealand), 1996.

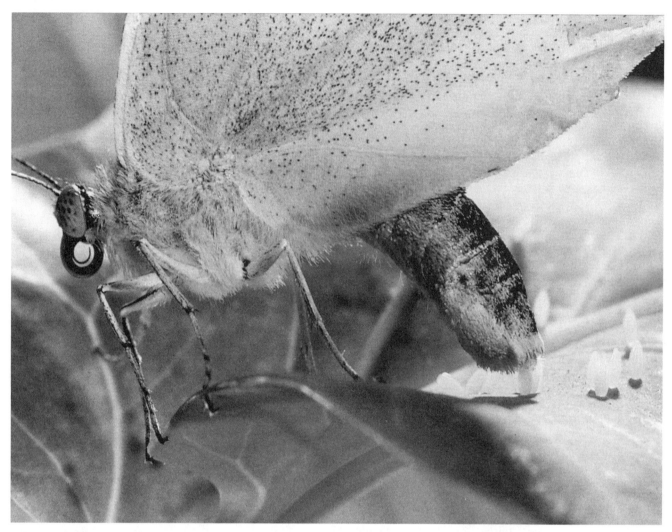

The Butterfly *traces this insect's life cycle from egg to caterpillar and finally butterfly.* (*Written by Diana Noonan. Book photograph by Pascal Goetgheluck.*)

Sidelights

New Zealand-born writer Diana Noonan is a prolific and award-winning author of books for children and young readers with more than 100 volumes to her credit. Her works include young adult novels, picture books for beginning readers, and books for elementary school-age children.

Born in 1960, Noonan graduated from the Otago University in 1980 with a degree in English and was awarded her teaching diploma in 1981. She taught secondary school for four years before becoming a full-time writer. Noonan originally wanted to be a painter; when she could not do it to her satisfaction, she turned to writing and "painted with words instead," she said in an interview on the *Christchurch City Libraries* Web site.

Noonan's "Life Cycles" series of books gives younger readers an introduction to a variety of wild animals, including frogs, butterflies, emperor penguins, green turtles, kangaroos, and crocodiles. Each book in the se-

ries includes a physical description of the animal and its habitat, types of food eaten, breeding cycle, and types of natural predators. The books also include information on human predators and threats to the animals and their environment. Hazel Rochman, writing in *Booklist,* called the "Life Cycles" series "an attractive series for group sharing as well as for first science reports."

Noonan demonstrates her skills at writing fiction in *Hercules,* the story of nine-year-old Sam who is facing the addition of a sibling to his family and the loss of his only-child status. When out exploring, Sam and his elderly neighbor Mabel find a pair of oyster catcher birds tending a nest containing two fragile eggs. Sam and Mabel become protectors of the birds and their eggs while anticipating the arrival of Sam's new sibling. The book addresses themes of human family relationships, wildlife conservation, and positive relationships with elders, observed Joan Zahnleiter in *Magpies.* "This is an elegantly crafted and designed book with something worthwhile to say on three levels," Zahnleiter commented.

In Noonan's The Emperor Penguin, *young readers learn about the behavior and life of these Antarctica birds. (Book jacket photograph by Colin Blobel.)*

In *The Best-Loved Bear,* Noonan's award-winning picture book effort, Tim's teacher, Mr. McDonald, organizes a Best-Loved Bear competition for the students in his class. He appoints Mrs. Hall, the headmistress, to be the judge, and the children begin their plans to enter their newest, most beautiful bears in the contest. Tim would very much like to see his bear, Toby, win, but the bear has seen better days. Toby is torn and ragged from all the attention Tim has given him. Tim does his best to clean and repair Toby, sewing up his ear, bandaging his nose, cleaning and fluffing his fur. But Tim's efforts can only accomplish so much for a toy worn almost to threads, and he ends up taking Toby to the competition hidden in a paper bag. The perceptive Mrs. Hall, however, can clearly see how well Toby has been loved and declares the worn but cherished toy the winner. "This endearing, gentle tale for pre-school and even older children who still cherish their battered old teds has a charm of its own," wrote Cynthia Anthony in *Magpies.* A *Books for Keeps* reviewer called it "a de-lightful story," while Julia Marriage, writing in *School Librarian,* called *The Best-Loved Bear* a "gentle story" and "a well-told tale" that will appeal to children with its heartfelt message that a toy worn out by love and attention can be "as precious as newer, smarter types."

Biographical and Critical Sources

BOOKS

St. James Guide to Children's Writers, 5th Edition, St. James Press (Detroit, MI), 1999.

PERIODICALS

Australian Book Review, December, 1993, Stephen Matthews, "From the Word Go," review of *A Dolphin in the Bay,* pp. 69-70.

Booklist, January 1, 2003, Hazel Rochman, review of *The Crocodile* and *The Kangaroo,* p. 900.

Books for Keeps, September, 1995, review of *The Best-Loved Bear,* p. 9.

Junior Bookshelf, August, 1995, review of *The Best-Loved Bear,* p. 129.

Magpies, March, 1995, Cynthia Anthony, review of *The Best-Loved Bear,* p. 22; May, 1996, Joan Zahnleiter, review of *Hercules,* p. 39; March, 1997, review of *I Spy Wildlife: The Garden,* p. 2; March, 1997, review of *I Spy Wildlife: The Rocky Shore,* p. 2.

School Librarian, August, 1995, Julia Marriage, review of *The Best-Loved Bear,* p. 104.

ONLINE

Christchurch City Libraries Web Site, http://library. christchurch.org.nz/ (April 18, 2003), interview with Diana Noonan.

New Zealand Book Council Web Site, http://www. bookcouncil.org.nz/ (July 7, 2003), profile of Diana Noonan.

P

PEARCE, Jacqueline 1962-

Personal

Born January 27, 1962, in Vancouver, British Columbia, Canada; daughter of John (a log scaler) and Rochelle (a nurse; maiden name, Arnot) Pearce; married Craig Naherniak (a humane educator), 1991; children: Danielle. *Ethnicity:* "English/French/Italian." *Education:* University of Victoria, B.A., 1985; York University, M.E.S., 1990. *Hobbies and other interests:* Art, photography.

Addresses

Home—7757 Royal Oak Ave., Burnaby, British Columbia V5J 4K2, Canada. *E-mail*—jacquiep@island.net.

Career

Canadian Children's Book Centre, Toronto, Ontario, Canada, information officer, 1990; Vancity Credit Union, Vancouver, British Columbia, Canada, environmental specialist, 1990-94; freelance writer, 1994—. Georgia Strait Alliance (environmental group), board member, 2001-03.

Member

Children's Writers and Illustrators of British Columbia.

Awards, Honors

Grant from Canada Council.

Writings

The Reunion (junior novel), Orca Book Publishers (Victoria, British Columbia, Canada), 2002.
Weeds and Other Stories (young adult novel), Thistledown Press (Saskatoon, Saskatchewan, Canada), 2003.

Jacqueline Pearce

Author of poetry for adults.

Work in Progress

Discovering Emily, a junior novel, publication by Orca Book Publishers (Victoria, British Columbia, Canada) expected in 2004; *River Stones,* a young adult novel; *Emily's Dream,* a sequel to *Discovering Emily,* about the childhood of artist Emily Carr, publication by Orca Book Publishers (Victoria, British Columbia, Canada) expected in 2005.

Sidelights

Jacqueline Pearce told *SATA:* "I've always liked books, but I became particularly excited by them when I was about twelve years old and discovered the novels of C. S. Lewis, Lloyd Alexander, Lucy Maud Montgomery, and others. From that time on, I wanted to write books like theirs. Even as an adult with a degree in English literature, I still love to read a good book for children, and I still want to write the same type of book. In a way, with each book I read or story I write, I return to that time in my life of excitement and discovery when so many things seemed possible. In fact, writing for children helps me continue to see magic in the world around me.

"Although I've wanted to write novels since I was twelve, it took many years before I finished my first one. *The Reunion* actually started as a picture book story, which the publisher asked me to try expanding into a junior novel. My second junior novel also started out this way. Both stories take place in the past, so I had to do a lot of research for both. Interviewing people who grew up in a small multi-cultural sawmill town during World War II was especially interesting.

"In contrast, *Weeds and Other Stories,* my collection for young adults, takes place in the present and is influenced by my interest in people's relationships to nature and to animals. The short stories take place in a large city where the presence of wild nature may not be obvious at first, but it ends up touching the lives of many of the characters.

"I love writing but am forced to take breaks, and when I do, I like to explore intriguing areas of the city around me or work on art projects. One day I may illustrate some of my own writing."

Biographical and Critical Sources

PERIODICALS

Resource Links, December, 2002, Victoria Pennell, review of *The Reunion,* p. 28.

*   *   *

PETERSON, Shelley 1952-

Personal

Born March 17, 1952, in London, Ontario, Canada; daughter of Donald (an engineer and developer) and Joyce (a schoolteacher) Matthews; married David Rob-

Shelley Peterson

ert Peterson (a lawyer and former premier of Ontario, Canada), January 12, 1974; children: Ben, Chloë, Adam. *Ethnicity:* "WASP: English, Scottish, French." *Education:* Attended Dalhousie University, Banff School of Fine Arts, and University of Western Ontario. *Politics:* Liberal. *Hobbies and other interests:* Horse riding, training, and breeding.

Addresses

Home—8 Gibson Ave., Toronto, Ontario M5R 1T5, Canada. *E-mail*—shelleypeterson@earthlink.net.

Career

Actress and author. Actress in numerous stage performances, including (debut) *Pinocchio,* London, Ontario, Canada, 1962; *The Donnellys, A Midsummer Night's Dream, Anne of Green Gables, Run for Your Wife;* and *Steel Magnolias.* Actress for film, including *The Housekeeper,* RawiFilm, and *Einstein: Light to the Power of Two,* HBO/Family Channel. Actress in television, including the series *Not My Department,* Canadian Broadcasting Corporation, and *Doghouse,* YTV/USA Network; telefilms *Kiss and Kill* and *An Equal Right to Die;* and specials.

Member

Actor's Equity; Alliance of Canadian Cinema, Television, and Radio Artists; Writer's Union of Canada; Canada Sport Horse Association; Canadian Equine Federation.

Writings

"CALEDON" TRILOGY

Dancer, Porcupine's Quill (Erin, Ontario, Canada), 1996.
Abby Malone, illustrated by Marybeth Drake, Porcupine's
    Quill (Erin, Ontario, Canada), 1999.
Stagestruck, Key Porter (Toronto, Ontario, Canada), 2002.

Work in Progress
Son of Dancer; Confessions.

Sidelights
Canadian stage and television actress and horse trainer
Shelley Peterson has somehow managed to find enough
hours in her busy schedule to write three young adult
novels that feature young women building their skills as
equestrians while also practicing their detective ability.
Peterson's "Caledon" trilogy, which takes place in the
author's Ontario hometown, features teen protagonists
who lead lives almost as busy as that of their author,
but still find time to tackle a mystery or two along the
way to winning a ribbon or trophy at the next horse
show.

In *Dancer,* readers meet Hilary James, otherwise known
as "Mousie," a sixteen-year-old equestrian whose temperamental mount, Daring Dancer, has caught the eye
of a horse thief. After a winning performance at the
Toronto Royal Winter Fair jumping competition, an invitation is offered to Mousie to put Dancer through her
paces before the Queen of England, bringing both horse
and rider to Great Britain. There, in between fox hunting with the royals, the teen soon discovers signs that a
premonition about the theft of her horse may in fact
come to pass, while ghostly apparitions and the rekin-
dling of a fairytale romance separate the novel from
typical "horse-meets-girl" fiction, claim reviewers. Noting that Peterson's story line "seems a bit farfetched,"
Quill & Quire reviewer Anne Louise Mahoney nonetheless praised the high-adventure novel as a "fun read"
that "is sure to please horse fans."

In *Abby Malone,* readers meet a young teen who inherited a love of horses from her father, a former horse
racer. Fortunately, she did not inherit his suspected tendency to break the law, but dealing with a father who
claims innocence while in prison is not easy. Abby's alcoholic mother is unable to care for either the girl or
herself, and Abby feels many of the responsibilities and
stresses of adulthood falling on her shoulders at an
early age. When the opportunity comes to ride her favorite horse, Moonlight Sonata, in a local steeplechase
event, Abby finds that the task of training the horse—
and uncovering a sequence of mysteries involving her
father, her pet coyote Cody, and various friends—allows her to break away from her unpleasant family
circumstances. While noting the old-fashioned quality
of the novel, Deborah Dowson praised *Abby Malone* in

Shelley Peterson's novel Dancer, *about a sixteen-year-
old girl and her beloved horse, was inspired by a dream.
(Cover photograph by Karl Leck/USESA.)*

her review for *Canadian Book Review Annual,* noting
that Peterson "skillfully" combines "mystery, suspense,
romance, and family drama to create an exciting read."
Writing in the *Free Press* (London, Ontario, Canada),
Nancy Schiefer had special praise for the novel's protagonist, noting that Abby "combines an adventurous
spirit with sensitivity, common sense, and a good degree of feisty courage."

Dancer's story continues in the final installment of
Peterson's "Caledon" trilogy. In *Stagestruck,* Mousie
James is off at college, leaving her beloved mount in
the hands of Abby Malone, now age sixteen. Things are
looking up in Abby's life: her mother is attempting to
seek treatment for her drinking problem, her father is
out of jail, and she has a horse to care for full time.
While busy training Dancer to compete in the Grand In-
vitational Horse Show, Abby discovers that the horse is
still being sought after by thieves; other echoes of
Peterson's first novel also enter the plot. Though considering some of the information provided in the book a
hindrance to plot development, Joan Marshall acknowl-

A young woman copes with family dysfunctions in **Abby Malone,** *written by Peterson. (Book jacket photograph by Christina Handley.)*

edged that the novel contains "some genuinely gripping and dramatic moments," as she remarked in her *Resource Links* review of *Stagestruck.*

Peterson told *SATA:* "I grew up as the second eldest of six children, surrounded by activity and animals. Dogs, cats, hamsters, turtles, fish, and best of all, horses. Every birthday and Christmas I had one request only, 'PLEASE can I have riding lessons?' Finally, at age eleven, my wish came true. Our family moved to the country shortly after, and the barn was always full. To this day, I raise and train horses, now understanding how little I knew way back then, and how forgiving my beloved horses were.

"I became enthralled at a very young age with the stories I found in books. Saturday morning would find me standing in front of the library, arms full of read books,

waiting for the librarian to unlock the door to allow me to restock for the upcoming week. Mystery, adventure, fairy tales, and legends; they silently waited for young fingers to lift open their covers and enter their worlds.

"My love of stories led quite naturally to theater, where characters, plot, interaction, motives, and emotions lift off the page and come to life. The world of theater captivated me, and I started acting lessons at age ten and turned professional at the age of twenty. Since then, I've performed in well over one hundred plays and have starred in two television series, as well as dozens of roles in film and television.

"Along the way, I fell in love and married David, and we were lucky enough to give birth to three enchanting children: Ben, Chloë, and Adam. As they were growing, I reveled in their expanding minds and sense of fun, which is quite likely why I write for young adults. It is an extremely impressionable time in a person's life. Certainly it was for me.

"In the 'Caledon' trilogy, my writing combines all my loves: stories, young people, excitement, horses, theater, intrigue. They're written for ages nine to fourteen, but my hope is that all ages might enjoy reading them, and perhaps even rediscover something of their youth." With her children grown, Peterson and her husband spend much of their time at Fox Ridge Farm, a sixty-five-acre farm where Peterson raises and trains horses.

Biographical and Critical Sources

PERIODICALS

Books in Canada, October, 1997, Alex Browne, review of *Dancer,* pp. 35-36.
Canadian Book Review Annual, 1996, Dave Jenkinson, review of *Dancer,* p. 489; 1999, Deborah Dowson, review of *Abby Malone,* pp. 513-514.
Chatelaine, August, 1986, Robert Collision, "David and Shelley: The Politics of Style," pp. 60-61.
Free Press (London, Ontario, Canada), April, 1997, Barbara Novak, review of *Dancer;* August 14, 1999, Nancy Schiefer, review of *Abby Malone.*
Quill & Quire, December, 1996, Anne Louise Mahoney, review of *Dancer,* p. 40.
Resource Links, February, 2003, Joan Marshall, review of *Stagestruck,* p. 43.

ONLINE

Porcupine's Quill Web Site, http://www.sentex.net/~pql/ (January 19, 2002).

R

READ, Nicholas 1956-

Personal

Born December 19, 1956, in Vancouver, British Columbia, Canada; son of Anthony Mark (a doctor) and Nina (a teacher; maiden name, Kusnetzov) Read. *Education:* University of British Columbia, B.S.; Langara College, journalism degree. *Politics:* Green. *Religion:* Russian Orthodox. *Hobbies and other interests:* Reading, hiking, art, music, boxing.

Addresses

Home—122-2255 West 8th Ave., Vancouver, British Columbia V6K 2A6, Canada. *Office*—Vancouver Sun, Suite 1, 200 Granville St., Vancouver, British Columbia V66 3N3, Canada. *E-mail*—nicholasr@axion.net.

Career

Vancouver Sun, Vancouver, British Columbia, Canada, journalist and editor.

Awards, Honors

International Media Award, Royal Society for the Prevention of Cruelty to Animals; Genesis Award.

Writings

One in a Million, Polestar (Vancouver, British Columbia, Canada), 1996.
Saving Emily, illustrated by Ellen Klem, Prometheus Books (Amherst, NY), 2001.

Work in Progress

A third novel for young adults.

Sidelights

Nicholas Read's books for young adults, including *One in a Million* and *Saving Emily,* are intended to teach children about cruelty towards animals in a way that

Nicholas Read

makes the reader empathize with the animal—a dog in *One in a Million* and a cow in *Saving Emily.* Joey, the German shepherd puppy at the center of *One in a Million,* is part of an unwanted litter that is brought to an animal shelter. Joey's friends, fellow dogs Mick, Blackie, and Dumpster and human shelter worker Marjorie, teach him about the hardships that unwanted dogs face in life and that the most important thing is to find a family to love him. Deborah Dowson, writing in *Canadian Book Review Annual,* praised the book for its "excellent descriptive prose" and "deep understanding of animal behavior."

Saving Emily is told from two perspectives, that of Emily, a beef cow with a human personality, and Chris, a boy whose newly remarried mother has moved him from his native city to a small ranching town where he does not feel like he fits in. "Chris's role as newcomer gives Reid the opportunity to teach readers about ranching realities like tagging, branding, castration, rodeos, feedlots, auction, and transport operations," Cora Lee explained in *Canadian Materials.* As Chris discovers these things and becomes friends with his school's free spirit, Gina, he joins her and others in trying to save Emily from the slaughterhouse. The book "contains a clear vegetarian message," Debra Probert wrote on the *Vancouver Humane Society* Web site, but "no one, regardless of his or her opinion on the ethics of eating meat, could ever question its validity as a straightforward children's story."

Read told *SATA:* "I write books with animal themes. I've always had a passion for animals and this is my way of expressing it. I enjoy the feedback I get from young readers who are touched by what I've written and want to share their animal stories with me. I'm also pleased by the number of adults who read my books.

"I believe it's the storyteller's first duty to tell a good story. I try to do that. But I also believe there should be something behind the story, something to give it resonance and substance. I hope I achieve that."

Biographical and Critical Sources

PERIODICALS

Canadian Book Review Annual, 1996, Deborah Dowson, review of *One in a Million,* p. 490.
Canadian Materials, November 30, 2001, Cora Lee, review of *Saving Emily.*
Globe and Mail (Toronto, Ontario, Canada), April 7, 2001, review of *One in a Million,* p. D23.

ONLINE

Vancouver Humane Society Web Site, http://www. vancouverhumanesociety.bc.ca/ (July 7, 2003), Debra Probert, review of *Saving Emily.**

*   *   *

RODDA, Emily 1948-
(Jennifer Rowe; Mary-Anne Dickinson)

Personal

Real name Jennifer Rowe; born 1948, in New South Wales, Australia; married; children: one girl, three boys. *Education:* University of Sydney, M.A., 1973. *Hobbies and other interests:* Reading.

Addresses

Home—Sydney, Australia. *Agent*—c/o Author Mail, Omnibus Books, 52 Fullarton Rd., Norwood, South Australia 5067, Australia.

Career

Full-time writer, 1994—. Former editor, Angus & Robertson publishers; former editor, *Australian Women's Weekly.*

Awards, Honors

Children's Book of the Year, Children's Book Council of Australia (CBCA), 1985, for *Something Special,* 1987, for *Pigs Might Fly,* 1989, for *The Best-Kept Secret,* 1991, for *Finders Keepers,* and 1994, for *Rowan of Rin;* Bilby Award, Ipswich Festival of Children's Literature, 1995, for *Rowan of Rin;* Dromkeen Medal, Courtney Oldmeadow Children's Literature Foundation, 1995, for contributions to Australian children's literature; Children's Honour Book of the Year, CBCA, 1997, for *Rowan and the Keeper of the Crystal.*

Writings

FOR CHILDREN

Something Special, illustrated by Noela Young, Angus & Robertson (Sydney, Australia), 1984, Holt (New York, NY), 1989.
Pigs Might Fly, illustrated by Noela Young, Angus & Robertson (Sydney, Australia), 1986, published as *The Pigs Are Flying!,* Greenwillow (New York, NY), 1988.
The Best-Kept Secret, illustrated by Noela Young, Angus & Robertson (North Ryde, Australia), 1988, Holt (New York, NY), 1990.
Finders Keepers, illustrated by Noela Young, Omnibus Books (Norwood, Australia), 1990, Greenwillow (New York, NY), 1991.
Crumbs!, illustrated by Kerry Argent, Omnibus Books (Norwood, Australia), 1990.
The Timekeeper, illustrated by Noela Young, Omnibus Books (Norwood, Australia), 1992, Greenwillow (New York, NY), 1993.
Power and Glory, illustrated by Geoff Kelly, Allen & Unwin (St. Leonards, Australia), 1994, Greenwillow (New York, NY), 1996.
Yay!, illustrated by Craig Smith, Omnibus Books (Norwood, Australia), 1996, Greenwillow (New York, NY), 1997.
Game Plan, illustrated by Craig Smith, Omnibus Books (Norwood, Australia), 1998.
Green Fingers, illustrated by Craig Smith, Omnibus Books (Norwood, Australia), 1998.
Where Do You Hide Two Elephants?, illustrated by Andrew McLean, Omnibus Books (Norwood, Australia), 1998, Gareth Stevens (Milwaukee, WI), 2001.
Fuzz, the Famous Fly, illustrated by Tom Jellett, Omnibus Books (Norwood, Australia), 1999.

The Julia Tapes, Puffin (Ringwood, Australia), 1999.

Bob the Builder and the Elves, illustrated by Craig Smith, ABC Books (Sydney, Australia), 2000, published in Britain as *Bob and the House Elves,* illustrated by Tim Archbold, Bloomsbury (London, England), 2001.

Gobbleguts, ABC Books (Sydney, Australia), 2000.

Dog Tales, Omnibus Books (Norwood, Australia), 2001.

Squeak Street, illustrated by Andrew McLean, Working Title Press (Kingswood, Australia), 2002.

The Long Way Home, illustrated by Danny Snell, Working Title Press (Kingswood, Australia), 2002.

Editor of anthology *She's Apples: A Collection of Winning Stories for Young Australians.*

"ROWAN OF RIN" SERIES

Rowan of Rin, Omnibus Books (Norwood, Australia), 1993, Greenwillow (New York, NY), 2001.

Rowan and the Travellers, Omnibus Books (Norwood, Australia), 1994, published as *Rowan and the Travelers,* Greenwillow (New York, NY), 2001.

Rowan and the Keeper of the Crystal, Omnibus Books (Norwood, Australia), 1996, Greenwillow (New York, NY), 2002.

Rowan and the Zebak, Omnibus Books (Norwood, Australia), 1999, Greenwillow (New York, NY), 2002.

Rowan of the Buckshah, Omnibus Books (Norwood, Australia), 2003, published as *Rowan and the Ice Creepers,* Greenwillow (New York, NY), 2004.

"DELTORA QUEST" SERIES

The Forests of Silence, Scholastic Australia (Sydney, Australia), Scholastic (New York, NY), 2000.

The Lake of Tears, Scholastic Australia (Sydney, Australia), 2000, Scholastic (New York, NY), 2001.

City of the Rats, Scholastic Australia (Sydney, Australia), 2000, Scholastic (New York, NY), 2001.

The Shifting Sands, Scholastic Australia (Sydney, Australia), 2000, Scholastic (New York, NY), 2001.

Dread Mountain, Scholastic Australia (Sydney, Australia), 2000, Scholastic (New York, NY), 2001.

The Maze of the Beast, Scholastic Australia (Sydney, Australia), 2000, Scholastic (New York, NY), 2001.

The Valley of the Lost, Scholastic Australia (Sydney, Australia), 2000, Scholastic (New York, NY), 2001.

Return to Del, Scholastic Australia (Sydney, Australia), 2000, Scholastic (New York, NY), 2001.

The Deltora Book of Monsters: By Josef, Palace Librarian in the Reign of King Alton, illustrated by Marc McBride, Scholastic Australia (Sydney, Australia), 2001.

Cavern of the Fear, Scholastic Australia (Sydney, Australia), Scholastic (New York, NY), 2002.

The Isle of Illusion, Scholastic Australia (Sydney, Australia), 2002.

The Shadowlands, Scholastic Australia (Sydney, Australia), 2002.

ORIGINALLY PUBLISHED UNDER NAME MARY-ANNE DICKINSON IN "STORYTELLING CHARMS" SERIES; REPRINTED UNDER NAME EMILY RODDA IN "FAIRY REALM" SERIES

The Charm Bracelet (also see below), Bantam Books (Sydney, Australia), 1994, HarperCollins (New York, NY), 2003.

The Flower Fairies (also see below), Bantam Books (Sydney, Australia), 1994, HarperCollins (New York, NY), 2003.

The Third Wish (also see below), Bantam Books (Sydney, Australia), 1995, HarperCollins (New York, NY), 2003.

The Last Fairy-Apple Tree (also see below), Bantam Books (Sydney, Australia), 1995, HarperCollins (New York, NY), 2003.

The Magic Key (also see below), Bantam Books (Sydney, Australia), 1995, HarperCollins (New York, NY), 2004.

The Unicorn (also see below), Bantam Books (Sydney, Australia), 1996, HarperCollins (New York, NY), 2004.

The Fairy Realm (contains *The Flower Fairies, The Charm Bracelet, The Third Wish, The Last Fairy-Apple Tree, The Magic Key,* and *The Unicorn*), ABC Books (Sydney, Australia), 2002.

"TEEN POWER INC." SERIES

The Secret of Banyan Bay, Ashton Scholastic (Sydney, Australia), 1994.

The Sorcerer's Apprentice, Ashton Scholastic (Sydney, Australia), 1994.

The Bad Dog Mystery, Ashton Scholastic (Sydney, Australia), 1994.

Beware the Gingerbread House, Ashton Scholastic (Sydney, Australia), 1994.

Cry of the Cat, Ashton Scholastic (Sydney, Australia), 1994.

The Disappearing TV Star, Ashton Scholastic (Sydney, Australia), 1994.

The Ghost of Raven Hill, Ashton Scholastic (Sydney, Australia), 1994.

Green for Danger, Ashton Scholastic (Sydney, Australia), 1994.

Poison Pen, Ashton Scholastic (Sydney, Australia), 1994.

Breaking Point, Ashton Scholastic (Sydney, Australia), 1994.

Nowhere to Run, Ashton Scholastic (Sydney, Australia), 1995.

Crime in the Picture, Ashton Scholastic (Sydney, Australia), 1995.

The Case of Crazy Claude, Ashton Scholastic (Sydney, Australia), 1995.

Fear in Fashion, Ashton Scholastic (Sydney, Australia), 1995.

Dangerous Game, Ashton Scholastic (Sydney, Australia), 1995.

Danger in Rhyme, Ashton Scholastic (Sydney, Australia), 1995.

The Missing Millionaire, Ashton Scholastic (Sydney, Australia), 1995.

Haunted House, Ashton Scholastic (Sydney, Australia), 1995.

Cry Wolf, Ashton Scholastic (Sydney, Australia), 1996.

Photo Finish, Ashton Scholastic (Sydney, Australia), 1996.

Stage Fright, Ashton Scholastic (Sydney, Australia), 1996.

St. Elmo's Fire, Ashton Scholastic (Sydney, Australia), 1996.

Bad Apples, Ashton Scholastic (Sydney, Australia), 1996.

Dirty Tricks, Ashton Scholastic (Sydney, Australia), 1996.

The War of the Work Demons, Ashton Scholastic (Sydney, Australia), 1997.

Hit or Miss, Ashton Scholastic (Sydney, Australia), 1998.

Hot Pursuit, Ashton Scholastic (Sydney, Australia), 1998.

Deep Freeze, Ashton Scholastic (Sydney, Australia), 1999.

The Secret Enemy, Ashton Scholastic (Sydney, Australia), 1999.

Dead End, Ashton Scholastic (Sydney, Australia), 1999.

AS JENNIFER ROWE

The Commonsense International Cookery Book, Angus & Robertson (Sydney, Australia), 1978.

(Editor) *More Poems to Read to Young Australians,* Royal New South Wales Institute for Deaf and Blind Children (North Rocks, Australia), 1980.

Eating Well in Later Life, Angus & Robertson (Sydney, Australia), 1982.

Grim Pickings, Allen & Unwin (Sydney, Australia), 1988.

Murder by the Book, Allen & Unwin (Sydney, Australia), 1989.

Death in Store, Allen & Unwin (Sydney, Australia), 1991, Doubleday (Garden City, NY), 1993.

The Makeover Murders, Allen & Unwin (St. Leonards, Australia), 1992, Doubleday (Garden City, NY), 1993.

Stranglehold, Allen & Unwin (St. Leonards, Australia), 1993, Bantam (New York, NY), 1995.

(Editor) *Love Lies Bleeding: A Crimes for a Summer Christmas Anthology,* Allen & Unwin (St. Leonards, Australia), 1994.

Lamb to the Slaughter, Allen & Unwin (St. Leonards, Australia), 1996, Bantam (New York, NY), 1996.

Deadline, Allen & Unwin (St. Leonards, Australia), 1997, published as *Suspect,* Ballantine (New York, NY), 1999.

Something Wicked, Allen & Unwin (St. Leonards, Australia), Ballantine (New York, NY), 1999.

Angela's Mandrake and Other Feisty Fables, Allen & Unwin (St. Leonards, Australia), 2000, published as *Fairy Tales for Grown-Ups,* Allen & Unwin (St. Leonards, Australia), 2001.

Sidelights

When she finished her first children's book, Emily Rodda submitted it to a publisher under her grandmother's maiden name rather than use her own birth name of Jennifer Rowe. Little did she know at the time that "Emily Rodda" would become one of Australia's favorite children's authors and a five-time winner of the Children's Book Council of Australia's

Children's Book of the Year Award. Rodda has written numerous picture books as well as several series for older readers, most notably the "Rowan of Rin" and "Deltora Quest" books. Her fantasy novels are said to introduce carefully-drawn imaginary realms where quests are complicated by riddles, magic, and mixed motives. Rodda also helped launch an adventure/mystery series for young readers for Scholastic Australia, "Teen Power Inc.," to which she has contributed more than two dozen titles. Writing under her real name, Jennifer Rowe, she has produced adult mysteries as well as cookbooks. This prolific output is particularly remarkable because Rodda did not become a full-time writer until 1994. Before that she held a job as a magazine editor, while raising four small children. "I feel very lucky to have a job I love so much," she said on her Web site.

Born in New South Wales, Rodda worked as an editor at both an Australian publishing house and at a woman's magazine before turning her hand to juvenile fiction. She chose her grandmother's maiden name as a pseudonym because at the time of her first publication, her publisher, Angus & Robertson, was also her employer. Rodda's first novel, *Something Special,* was an attempt to document her daughter's growth, and with four children, Rodda had a lot of material at hand for subsequent titles. Aimed at primary graders, *Something Special* tells the story of a little girl, Samantha, who becomes involved in her mother's rummage sale. Set in contemporary times and with a realistic setting, the book nonetheless contains an element of fantasy: Samantha and her friend, Lizzie, become involved with the spirits of the former owners of the clothing donated for the sale.

At the sale, Sam's friend Lizzie leaves the stall for a while. Sam takes a short nap and is surprised by a quartet of spirits who are admiring their donated clothes. Upon Lizzie's return, these visitors have gone and she suspects they were just a dream of Sam's, but the next day one of them actually returns in the flesh to reclaim a favorite "second skin," a tartan dressing gown he had for years. Ron Morton, writing in *Books for Your Children,* noted: "This is a well written book. . . . Its strength is perhaps its warm, embracing dialogue." Morton concluded that though the "essence" of the story was fantasy, "there is still something quite believable about what happened." A *Books for Keeps* critic called *Something Special* a "thought-provoking and eerie tale" which "catches quite brilliantly the dash, excitement, and movement of the preparations" for the sale. Writing about the U.S. edition, a *Kirkus Reviews* critic commented that the book offers an "unusual story, beautifully structured and simply but gracefully told," while *School Library Journal* contributor Elisabeth LeBris noted that the book "is told in a light tone with lots of dialogue."

With this first book, Rodda won the Australian Children's Book of the Year Award, one of the most prestigious prizes in Australia, which not only helped sales of the initial title, but also had reviewers and readers alike awaiting a second book. Rodda commented in an interview in *Magpies:* "I was astounded and surprised because I hadn't held out the faintest hope of actually winning. . . . As a child I had always wanted to be a writer; now maybe I really was one." Rodda also noted in the interview, however, that "second books are much harder to pull off than first ones."

Rodda's second book, *Pigs Might Fly,* is a lighthearted fantasy that employs mystery and magical travel to another world. Rachel, about age seven, is in bed with a cold and longs for some excitement to break up her boring days. A picture drawn by a sign-painting friend of her father's is meant to cheer Rachel up but leads to much more radical results. The picture shows Rachel riding a unicorn in her pajamas while pigs fly overhead. Soon Rachel finds herself on the unicorn while actual pigs are playing in the sky. Left at the door of a peasant couple who insist on calling her Grace, Rachel soon discovers that what is transpiring is known locally as a flying pig storm. The peasants think that Rachel has come from "Outside," a rare event that has also initiated the pig storm. Rachel stays in this fabulous land a day and a half, filled with anxiety about how she will get back home, but she eventually does return through the aid of a rhyme discovered at the library. Many reviewers have noted the parallels in the book to *Alice's Adventures in Wonderland* as well as to *The Wizard of Oz,* though Rodda's tale is much shorter and far less complex than either of those two. Howard George, writing in *Reading Time,* commented that Rodda's second novel was "bound to be a great success with young readers" because "only people with a sense of the ridiculous can appreciate unlikely events." George concluded that "this is a finely crafted book" and that "the humour used is never slapstick nor banal." Reviewing the U.S. edition, published as *The Pigs Are Flying!,* Karen P. Smith commented in *School Library Journal* that this is "an engaging fantasy for beginning fans of the genre," while Karen Jameyson called the story a "comfortable swirl of suspense, adventure, and amusing characters" in *Horn Book.* A *Books for Keeps* contributor concluded by stating that *Pigs Might Fly* is a "beautifully unfolded tale from an illuminating, fresh-voiced writer." Award committees reached similar conclusions as reviewers, for this second book also earned a Children's Book of the Year Award from the Children's Book Council of Australia (CBCA).

Rodda stuck with fantasy for her third title, *The Best-Kept Secret,* which features a magical carousel ride. When this carousel comes to town, the residents all find reasons why they should take a ride on it into the future, including young Joanna, who rescues a boy lost in the future. None of the characters who take the magic ride realize that they are at crossroads in their lives; Joanna has just learned she is to become a big sister. Rescuing the young boy in the future, then, is an unconscious acceptance of this new role. Gerald Haigh,

reviewing the book in the *Times Educational Supplement,* noted that Rodda's story "is subtle and layered, and pricks at the emotions in all sorts of ways." A *Kirkus Reviews* critic dubbed it a "deceptively simple tale" and a "charmingly original, neatly structured story," while *School Library Journal* contributor Joanne Aswell concluded that *The Best-Kept Secret* is an "amusing, optimistic chapter book fantasy to read alone or aloud."

Rodda's first male protagonist appears in her fourth book, *Finders Keepers,* a longer and more sophisticated juvenile novel. Rodda herself has characterized the book as being special not only for the use of a boy as the central character, but also for the fact that she used "family relationships as a background to the fantasy," as she explained in *Reading Time.* When Patrick takes part in a novel interactive quiz game on his television, he has no idea he will pass through the "Barrier" separating his reality from the "Other Side," but that in fact is exactly what happens. Patrick becomes a Finder of all those things people misplace day to day. His prize is a computer he has been longing for. As Laurie Copping commented in *Reading Time,* the story moves at "a rapid pace, fantasy and reality interchanging so rapidly that sometimes the reader may wonder whether or not they are experiencing the real or the unreal." A *Publishers Weekly* reviewer also noted the "lightning speed" at which Rodda keeps her story going and concluded that the book was "an uncommonly satisfying read."

Patrick reappears in *The Timekeeper,* a sequel to *Finders Keepers,* in which he is once again summoned through the Barrier, this time to prevent the destruction of worlds on both sides. Obstacles make his mission all the harder, and Rodda blends elements of computer technology to create "an action-filled fantasy with warm, believable depictions of family relationships," according to Anne Connor in *School Library Journal.* A *Kirkus Reviews* commentator called *The Timekeeper* an "engaging light fantasy."

Rodda has also used the contemporary world of high tech in other books for young readers, including *Crumbs!* and the picture book *Power and Glory.* The successive competency levels of a video game form the core of the latter title, which Carolyn Phelan dubbed an "unexpected pleasure" in a starred *Booklist* review. John Sigwald, writing in *School Library Journal,* called *Power and Glory* a "big, bold, colorful and cartoony quest for control over electronic nemeses," while a *Kirkus Reviews* contributor noted the "clever analogies" Rodda makes between the witch, goblin, and ogre of the video game and family members of the boy who is playing the game. "Rodda builds up a throbbing rhythm that approximates the intensity of the play," observed a *Publishers Weekly* reviewer of this "rousing" picture book.

Far afield from the techno world of the 1990s are Rodda's series of novels about the adventures of Rowan, two of which have been honored by the CBCA. The first title in the series, *Rowan of Rin,* tells the magical story of the village of Rin, where the locals awake one morning to discover that their source of water, a nearby river, has slowed to a mere trickle. As the days pass, matters get worse and the stream almost totally dries up. The villagers depend on this stream to water their animals, the "bukshah," and these can no longer get enough water. Something must be done. The villagers agree that someone must travel up the Mountain, an eerie and frightening place, to find out what the problem is. The Wise Woman provides the villagers with a map along with a guiding chant, but it is only the boy who tends the bukshah, Rowan, who can figure out the meaning of the map. Rowan sets out on his quest with six others, braving obstacles, including a dragon, until he reaches the top of the Mountain and is able to restore the stream to life. In the process, Rowan also saves the life of his protector, Strong John.

Horn Book correspondent Karen Jameyson called *Rowan of Rin* a "quest adventure of the highest order" and a "riveting fantasy." Jameyson also noted that Rodda's characters "step off the page as individuals." *Magpies* contributor Joan Zahnleiter commented that the "text is very visual, sparkling with vivid imagery. It would lend itself to an exciting TV production." The "Rowan of Rin" series has become popular worldwide, with Internet chat rooms dedicated to its plots. Throughout the series, Rowan has evolved from a sickly and timid youngster to a careful but courageous lad to whom others look for leadership. In a discussion of *Rowan and the Travelers,* published in Australia as *Rowan and the Travellers,* a *Kirkus Reviews* critic commended Rodda for her novels that "prove . . . that a weak body can hide a hero's heart."

In *Rowan and the Travelers,* it falls to Rowan to save his fellow villagers from a strange curse that causes them to fall asleep where they stand. "Once again Rodda's fantasy world, a folkloric Anytime, becomes a vivid reality for readers," commented Kay Weisman in *Booklist.* In *School Library Journal,* Trish Anderson observed that *Rowan and the Travelers* "proves heroism comes in many sizes." *Rowan and the Keeper of the Crystal,* the third book in the series, finds Rowan in a desperate quest to put together an antidote after his mother is poisoned at the critical moment in which she must choose a new leader for the village. *Horn Book* correspondent Anne St. John felt that the novel "offers an ideal mix of suspenseful plot, unusual characters, and an engaging hero."

The Zebak are the historic enemies of Rowan's people, and in *Rowan and the Zebak,* the young hero must journey to their land to rescue his kidnapped sister. As with the previous titles in the series, Rowan's success depends upon his courage and upon his ability to understand magic and the enigmatic riddles posed to him by the wise woman Sheba. In her *Booklist* review of the title, Weisman declared that "Rowan's adventures are riveting, with plot twists sufficient to keep the outcome

in doubt." Writing in *School Library Journal,* Mara Alpert noted that Rowan "is not the flashiest of heroes, but in each story he grows a little more confident."

While the "Rowan of Rin" series is perhaps better known internationally, Rodda is also building an audience for her "Deltora Quest" fantasies, which number a dozen titles. In this series, three friends—Leif, Jasmine, and Barda—face perils both ordinary and fantastic to retrieve a set of seven precious stones that their people have used to ward off enemies in the past. When the stones are restored to the Belt of Deltora, the land will be freed of the Shadow Lord, a force with evil intentions. In the Australian editions of each "Deltora" novel, the belt appears on the spine of the book, with the stones that have been rescued in each previous volume. In his *Magpies* review of books five to eight in the "Deltora Quest" series, Russ Merrin wrote: "The full series is quite simply, a huge achievement. It is vividly written, rich in detail and highly imaginative in its execution. It melds together well, flows cohesively, and reads easily."

Rodda's "Fairy Realm" series, originally published as the "Storytelling Charms" series under the name Mary-Anne Dickinson, is aimed at middle-grade readers having their first taste of fantasy. Jessie, the heroine of these volumes, is an ordinary girl who discovers that her destiny lies equally in the everyday world and in an alternative universe peopled by fairies, elves, trolls, ogres, and other fabulous creatures. In the series debut, *The Charm Bracelet,* Jessie discovers that her grandmother is actually queen of the fairies, and that the two of them must go into the fairy realm to renew its magic and ensure its safety. *Booklist* critic Ellen Mandel suggested that "intergenerational teamwork and a girl's levelheaded thinking combine" in the novel to produce an "exciting fantasy." A *Publishers Weekly* reviewer called *The Charm Bracelet* a "taut, engaging fantasy tale" with "an intriguing plot and appealing characters." According to a *Kirkus Reviews* contributor, "Rodda tells a suspenseful, well-knit tale, enlivened by humor and heroism."

Through the first decade of her writing life, Rodda worked late at night after her children had gone to bed. Now she devotes her days to her craft and enjoys it so much that she says her favorite hobbies are "reading and writing," as she related on her Web site. She has written for nearly every age reader from preschool to retirement, having also penned almost a dozen crime novels for adults under her real name. Rodda said on her Web site: "I am married with four children, and live in the Blue Mountains, west of Sydney. We have a dog called Sunny. And because we live next to the bush, the garden is always full of frogs, lizards, magpies, cockatoos, and kookaburras." In a *Magpies* interview, she described the kind of book she likes to write. "I love things that all tie up and in fact I find things that don't very irritating if they're that type of book," she said. "The kind of book that I regard as an adventure or a fantasy or whatever, I think that deserves a good, neat ending. . . . There' no little clue that doesn't have a meaning. . . . Maybe it's a response to the general messiness of life, but I find it very satisfying."

Biographical and Critical Sources

BOOKS

Children's Literature Review, Volume 23, Gale (Detroit, MI), 1994, pp. 207-213.

Helbig, Alethea K. and Agnes Regan Perkins, editors, *Dictionary of Children's Fiction from Australia, Canada, India, New Zealand, and Selected African Countries,* Greenwood Press (Westport, CT), 1992.

Rodda, Emily, *Something Special,* illustrated by Noela Young, Angus & Robertson (Sydney, Australia), 1984, Holt (New York, NY), 1989.

PERIODICALS

Booklist, September 1, 1990, p. 52; April 15, 1996, Carolyn Phelan, review of *Power and Glory,* p. 1441; January, 1997, p. 768; November 15, 2001, Kay Weisman, review of *Rowan and the Travelers,* p. 574; January 1, 2002, Kay Weisman, review of *Rowan and the Keeper of the Crystal,* p. 859; March 1, 2002, Kay Weisman, review of *Rowan and the Zebak,* p. 1133; January 1, 2003, Ellen Mandel, review of *The Charm Bracelet,* p. 892.

Books for Keeps, September, 1986, review of *Something Special,* p. 23; March, 1989, review of *Pigs Might Fly,* p. 18; January, 1996, p. 10; May, 2001, Annabel Gibb, review of *Bob and the House Elves,* p. 21.

Books for Your Children, spring, 1985, Ron Morton, review of *Something Special,* p. 11.

Horn Book, November-December, 1988, Karen Jameyson, review of *The Pigs Are Flying!,* p. 784; November-December, 1993, Karen Jameyson, "News from Down Under," review of *Rowan of Rin,* pp. 778-780; September, 2001, Anne St. John, review of *Rowan and the Travelers,* pp. 593-594; March-April, 2002, Anne St. John, review of *Rowan and the Keeper of the Crystal,* pp. 217-218.

Kirkus Reviews, November 1, 1989, review of *Something Special,* p. 1597; May 15, 1990, review of *The Best-Kept Secret,* p. 802; October 1, 1993, review of *The Timekeeper,* p. 1278; February 15, 1996, review of *Power and Glory,* p. 299; October 1, 2001, review of *Rowan and the Travelers,* p. 1432; January 1, 2002, review of *Rowan and the Keeper of the Crystal,* p. 50; May 1, 2002, review of *Rowan and the Zebak,* p. 666; January 1, 2003, review of *The Charm Bracelet,* p. 65.

Magpies, July, 1990, "Emily Rodda," pp. 19-21; November, 1993, Joan Zahnleiter, review of *Rowan of Rin,* p. 31; September, 1998, Rayma Turton, review of *Bob the Builder and the Elves,* p. 35; March, 2001, Russ Merrin, "Two Series for Independent Readers," review of *Dread Mountain, The Maze of the Beast, The Valley of the Lost,* and *Return to Del,* p. 35.

Publishers Weekly, October 18, 1991, review of *Finders Keepers,* p. 25; May 6, 1996, review of *Power and Glory,* p. 81; June 9, 1997, p. 46; February 10, 2003, review of *The Charm Bracelet,* p. 188.

Reading Time, Number 3, 1987, Howard George, review of *Pigs Might Fly,* p. 66; Number 4, 1990, Laurie Copping, review of *Finders Keepers,* p. 25; Number 4, 1991, Emily Rodda, "CBCA Acceptance Speech," p. 5.

School Library Journal, September, 1988, Karen P. Smith, review of *The Pigs Are Flying!,* pp. 185-186; January, 1990, Elisabeth LeBris, review of *Something Special,* pp. 106, 108; January, 1991, Joanne Aswell, review of *The Best-Kept Secret,* pp. 79-80; October, 1993, Anne Connor, review of *The Timekeeper,* p. 128; May, 1996, John Sigwald, review of *Power and Glory,* p. 97; January, 2002, Trish Anderson, review of *Rowan and the Travelers,* p. 140; May, 2002, Janet Gillen, review of *Rowan and the Keeper of the Crystal,* p. 160; July, 2002, Mara Alpert, review of *Rowan and the Zebak,* p. 124; August, 2003, Debbie Whitbeck, review of *The Charm Bracelet,* p. 140.

Times Educational Supplement, February 17, 1989, Gerald Haigh, "Daredevils," review of *The Best-Kept Secret,* p. B28.

ONLINE

Emily Rodda Home Page, http://www.emilyrodda.com/ (February 20, 2003).

Scholastic Australia, http://www.scholastic.com.au/ (February 20, 2003), "Profile: Emily Rodda."*

*   *   *

ROWE, Jennifer
See RODDA, Emily

*   *   *

ROWE, John A. 1949-

Personal

Born 1949, in Kingston-upon-Thames, Surrey, England; son of Alfred and Joan Elaine (Hazell) Rowe; married Lisbeth Zwerger (divorced, 1990); married Michelle Kuipers (a manager), March 8, 1992. *Ethnicity:* "White British." *Education:* Attended Richmond School of Art, 1968, Twickenham College of Technology, 1970, and Hochschule für Angewandte Kunst, 1974; Epsom School of Art & Design, fine arts diploma, c. 1974. *Hobbies and other interests:* Mountain biking, walking, reading, music, history, playing flute and recorder.

Addresses

Home and office—The Cottage, Higher Putham, Cutcombe, Minehead, Somerset TA24 7AS, England. *E-mail*—jonnyarowe@aol.com.

John A. Rowe

Career

Writer and illustrator. Worked variously as a grave digger, bicycle mechanic, plumber, cinema cleaner, and TV set maker. *Exhibitions:* Royal Academy Summer Show, London, England, 1973; Royal Academy, London, England, 1974, 1977, 1979, 1982; Galerie Wittman, Vienna, Austria, 1975; Surrey Artists Exhibition, Surrey, England, 1976; United Nations, Vienna, Austria, 1978, 1980; Freie Kunst Exhibition, Künstlerhaus, Vienna, Austria, 1981; Galerie im Kelterhaus, Hochheim, Germany, 1998; Every Picture Tells a Story, Los Angeles, CA, 2000.

Awards, Honors

Golden Apple, Biennial of Illustrations Bratislava (BIB), 1991; UNICEF Honorary Diploma, Bologna Book Fair, 1992; Rattenfänger Literaturepreis, 1992; Österreichischer Kinder-und Jugendbuchpreis, 1993, 1995; UNICEF Recognition Award, 1995; Storytelling World Award, 1995; Grand Prix, BIB, 1995; Fällt aus dem Rahmen, 1996; Federhasenpreis Design (Austria), 1997; Austrian Honors List, 2000; Deutscher Jugendliteratur Preis nomination, 2000; UNICEF Books of Tolerance nomination, 2002.

Writings

SELF-ILLUSTRATED

Rabbit Moon, Picture Book Studios (Saxonville, MA), 1992.

How Many Monkeys?: A Counting Book in English, French, German, Hutchinson (London, England), 1993.

Jack the Dog, Picture Book Studios (Saxonville, MA), 1993.

Baby Crow (also see below; originally published in Switzerland as *Raben-Baby*), North-South Books (New York, NY), 1994.

Can You Spot the Spotty Dog?, Red Fox (London, England), 1996, published as *Can You Spot the Spotted Dog?,* Doubleday Books for Young Readers (New York, NY), 1996.

Peter Piglet (also see below; originally published in Switzerland as *Ferkel Ferdinand*), North-South Books (New York, NY), 1996.

Smudge (also see below; originally published in Switzerland as *Schmutzfink*), North-South Books (New York, NY), 1997.

Monkey Trouble (originally published in Switzerland as *Affenzoff*), North-South Books (New York, NY), 1999.

Favorite Stories by John A. Rowe: Three Complete Tales (contains *Baby Crow, Peter Piglet,* and *Smudge*), Smithmark (New York, NY), 1999.

Jasper the Terror (originally published in Switzerland as *Theodor Terror*), North-South Books (New York, NY), 2001.

Tommy DoLittle (originally published in Switzerland under the same title), North-South Books (New York, NY), 2002.

Amazing Animal Hide and Seek, Hutchinson Children's (London, England), Barron's (Hauppauge, NY), 2003.

ILLUSTRATOR

Rudyard Kipling, *The Sing-Song of Old Man Kangaroo,* Picture Book Studios (Saxonville, MA), 1990.

The Gingerbread Man: An Old English Folktale, Picture Book Studios (London, England), 1993, North-South Books (New York, NY), 1996.

Rudyard Kipling, *The Beginning of the Armadillos,* North-South Books (New York, NY), 1995.

Rudyard Kipling, *The Elephant's Child,* North-South Books (New York, NY), 1995.

Brigitte Weninger, reteller, *Zwergen Mütze,* translated by J. Alison James as *The Elf's Hat,* North-South Books (New York, NY), 2000.

Karl Rühmann, *Aber Ich Will,* translated by J. Alison James as *But I Want To!,* North-South Books (New York, NY), 2002.

Work in Progress

Hamster Hamlet.

Sidelights

British-born author and illustrator John A. Rowe's numerous books have garnered consistent high praise for the quality of the artwork. In *Jack the Dog,* one of his early works, Rowe takes readers on a trip to unfamiliar places in the canine's dreams. Jack wanders onto a ship and sails to Japan, where he has to overcome cultural barriers and follow unusual procedures to get a cup of tea. Before he can sample the beverage, however, he wakes up in his own home, safe and far from Japan. A *Publishers Weekly* reviewer called *Jack the Dog* a "sophisticated flight of fancy, a story whose illustrations might be more at home on a gallery wall."

In *Baby Crow,* originally published in Switzerland as *Raben-Baby,* a little bird discovers that he cannot caw or call or sing like his well-mannered family, but instead is only able to make a beeping noise. But Grandpa Crow, a former opera singer, is a wise old bird, and he helps the baby find his real voice. *Baby Crow's* "haunting pictures are rich in color and tone and have a dreamlike reality," wrote Raymond Briggs in *Times Educational Supplement,* while a *Books for Keeps* reviewer commented that *Baby Crow* is "unusual and visually striking."

Originally published under the title *Ferkel Ferdinand,* in *Peter Piglet,* Peter finds a pair of beautiful golden shoes. The shoes become his prized possession, and he learns to walk, dance, swim, and do other amazing things while wearing them. The next morning, however, the shoes are gone, and Peter sets out to find the scoundrel he thinks took his shoes. What he finds is something entirely different than what he expected. One shoe is being used by an old tortoise who lost his home in a storm. The other serves as a nest for a blackbird family with new babies. Realizing that the shoes were a frivolous plaything to him, Peter finds that the new owners can get far better and more practical use from them. He also discovers that the happiness of others leads to happiness of his own. "This touching message is delivered in a gentle manner," complemented by "Rowe's accomplished artwork," observed Julie Corsaro in a *Booklist* review of *Peter Piglet.* "Rowe's prose is image-rich throughout," wrote Lee Bock in *School Library Journal,* concluding that *Peter Piglet* "is an exquisitely designed book that children will love."

Smudge, the lead character of Rowe's book of the same name, is an old rat, a grandfatherly storyteller with a vivid imagination and a clear recollection of the adventures he had in his youth. In *Smudge,* first published as *Schmutzfink,* the rodent tells how, as a child, he was abducted by a bird. Smudge tries to fit in with the bird family, but eventually the birds fly off and leave him behind. Through a series of surrogate families—dogs, rabbits, fish, squirrels, and more—Smudge tries again and again to fit in but is eventually abandoned by everyone. He cannot hop like rabbits, swim like fish, or run like dogs. One day, Smudge encounters a brown rat with a familiar smile: his mother has found him and brings him back into the rat family where he belongs.

Anji Keating, writing in *Bloomsbury Review,* commented that *Smudge* "is not only humorous but enchanting," while *School Librarian* critic Hazel Townson found the book to be "clever and amusing." A *Kirkus Reviews* contributor called Smudge a "delightfully eccentric character," declaring the author's own illustrations to be "dauntingly emotional," with varying depictions of the titular rat reflecting the feelings or situation Smudge has found himself in. In a *Booklist* review, Michael Cart commented favorably on "Rowe's striking pictures" and called *Smudge* "an eccentric but engaging book."

Little Monkey finds himself in difficult situations in *Monkey Trouble,* a work first published as *Affenzoff.* But the fault is no one's but his own, as he does not listen to the advice of his elders. Because "Little Monkey never listened," and instead "made faces and never did what he was told," the wind takes the startled primate on a teaching journey. Far from home, Little Monkey is mistaken for an elephant couple's new baby and is clad in a pink dress, though he is not a little girl (and tells every animal he meets this fact). When he finally arrives home, Little Monkey is given a special present to discourage him from repeating his adventure. "The author's whimsical artistic interpretation adds a sense of character to each animal and humor to each situation," wrote Tina Hudak in *School Library Journal.* A *Publishers Weekly* reviewer noted that "the artwork is the real draw" of the book.

Originally appearing as *Theodor Terror, Jasper the Terror* is an earnest but accident prone young dragon whose allergy-induced sneezing causes fires, sets his friends' pants ablaze, and leads to his banishment—purely for the sake of everyone else's safety. Eventually, Professor Owl discovers that Jasper has tickleyitis from the tall grass that constantly tickles his nose and offers a solution that pleases everyone. *Jasper the Terror's* "bold cartoon illustrations are strong crowd pleasers," claimed Eunice Weech in *School Library Journal.* Christine Sarazin, writing in *Horn Book Guide,* observed that "Jasper is an appealing character," but found the solution to the problem "too silly." On the other hand, Stephanie Merrit, reviewing *Jasper the Terror* in London, England's *Observer,* remarked positively on the story's "ingenious solution."

"I was born in Kingston-upon-Thames, Surrey, England, in 1949," Rowe told *SATA.* "My parents separated when I was three to four years old, so, along with my three sisters and one brother, I was raised by my mother. I started drawing more and more around this time.

"After the usual soul-destroying school years, I worked, amongst other things, as a bicycle mechanic, grave digger, cinema cleaner, plumber, and TV set maker, before attending life drawing classes at Richmond School of Art in 1968," Rowe continued. "This led on to a Foundation Year at Twickenham College of Technology, and then a three-year fine art (painting) course at Epsom School of Art & Design.

"In 1974, I moved to Vienna, Austria, after a two-week holiday there, during which time I fell in love with Lisbeth Zwerger. I studied two semesters at the Hochschule für Angewandte Kunst. I also worked in a design studio, did some set painting at a theatre, but mainly painted and exhibited. Lisbeth and I married, and I stayed in Vienna for sixteen years, until our divorce.

"After a trip to Australia, I started a series of small paintings based on Kipling's 'The Sing-Song of Old Man Kangaroo' from his *Just-So Stories,*" Rowe told *SATA.* "These pictures were not intended to be illustrations, but they were seen by the Austrian Publisher Michael Neugebauer, and I was offered the chance to turn them into a book. This was a major turning point for me and the point where my life as an illustrator, and author, of children's books began."

Biographical and Critical Sources

BOOKS

Rowe, John A., *Monkey Trouble* (originally published in Switzerland as *Affenzoff*), North-South Books (New York, NY), 1999.

PERIODICALS

Bloomsbury Review, November-December, 1997, Anji Keating, review of *Smudge,* p. 33; September-October, 1999, review of *Monkey Trouble,* p. 22.

Bookbird, summer, 1995, review of *Baby Crow,* p. 56.

Booklist, November 1, 1996, Ellen Mandel, review of *Can You Spot the Spotted Dog?,* p. 510; December 1, 1996, Julie Corsaro, review of *Peter Piglet,* p. 669; December 1, 1997, Michael Cart, review of *Smudge,* pp. 643-644.

Books for Keeps, July, 1996, review of *Raben-Baby,* p. 7; November, 1996, review of *Jack the Dog,* p. 7.

Horn Book Guide, spring, 1997, Carolyn Shutt, review of *Peter Piglet,* p. 45; spring, 2002, Christine Sarazin, review of *Jasper the Terror,* p. 57.

Kirkus Reviews, April 15, 1996, review of *The Gingerbread Man,* p. 606; September 1, 1996, review of *Peter Piglet,* p. 1327; October 1, 1997, review of *Smudge,* p. 1536.

Observer (London, England), October 28, 2001, Stephanie Merrit, review of *Jasper the Terror,* p. 16.

Publishers Weekly, November 23, 1992, review of *Rabbit Moon,* p. 61; April 26, 1993, review of *Jack the Dog,* p. 77; April 15, 1996, review of *Baby Crow,* p. 70; December 2, 1996, review of *Jack the Dog,* p. 62; May 12, 1997, review of *Rabbit Moon,* p. 77; September 17, 2001, review of *Monkey Trouble,* p. 82.

School Librarian, spring, 1998, Hazel Townson, review of *Smudge,* p. 22.

School Library Journal, June, 1993, Anna Biagioni Hart, review of *Rabbit Moon,* p. 88; August, 1993, Steven Engelfried, review of *Jack the Dog,* p. 151; November, 1994, Christine A. Moesch, review of *Baby Crow,* p. 90; January, 1996, Patricia Lothrop Green, review of *The Beginning of the Armadillos,* p. 86; August, 1996, Pam Gousner, review of *The Gingerbread Man,,* p. 136; November, 1996, Lee Bock, review of *Peter Piglet,* pp. 91-92; December, 1996, Martha Topol, review of *Can You Spot the Spotted Dog?,* p. 104; February, 1998, Alicia Eames, review of *Smudge,* p. 90; October, 1999, Tina Hudak, review of *Monkey Trouble,* p. 125; March, 2002, Eunice Weech, review of *Jasper the Terror,* p. 200; July, 2002, Bina Williams, review of *But I Want To!,* pp. 97-98; November, 2003, Rachel G. Payne, review of *Amazing Animal Hide and Seek,* p. 114.

Times Educational Supplement, December 2, 1994, Raymond Briggs, review of *Baby Crow,* p. 14; May 19, 2000, Ted Dewan, review of *The Elf's Hat,* p. 23.

S

SCHROEDER, Russell (K.) 1943-

Personal

Born May 2, 1943, in Cambria Heights, Long Island, NY; son of Henry and Helen (Voigt) Schroeder. *Education:* St. Petersburg Junior College, A.A., 1963; Eckerd College, B.A., 1965.

Addresses

Home—16 Algonquin Dr., Queensbury, NY 12804.

Career

Walt Disney World, Lake Buena Vista, FL, artist, 1971-89 and 1990-91; Walt Disney Company, Burbank, CA, artist, 1989-90, art director, 1991-99.

Writings

The Road Runner and the Very Scary Lesson, illustrated by Bob Toten and Phil DeLara, Golden Press (New York, NY), 1973.

(Illustrator, with Don Williams) Michael Teitelbaum, *Walt Disney's Winnie the Pooh and the Missing Bullhorn,* Golden Press (New York, NY), 1990.

(Illustrator, with Don Williams) Joan Phillips, *Walt Disney's Winnie the Pooh and the Toy Airplane,* Golden Press (New York, NY), 1990.

(Illustrator, with Don Williams) Fran Manushkin, adapter, *Walt Disney Presents The Prince and the Pauper,* Golden Press (New York, NY), 1990.

(Illustrator, with Don Williams) Bruce Isen, *Huey, Dewey, and Louie's Campfire Surprise: A Book about Time,* Golden Press (New York, NY), 1990.

(Editor and author of introduction) Jim Fanning, *Disney's Sing-Along Song Book,* Hyperion (New York, NY), 1995.

(Editor) *Walt Disney: His Life in Pictures,* introduction by Diane Disney Miller, Disney Press (New York, NY), 1996.

Mickey Mouse: My Life in Pictures, Disney Press (New York, NY), 1997.

(With Kathleen W. Zoehfeld) *Disney's Mulan,* Disney Press (New York, NY), 1998.

(With Victoria Saxon) *Disney's Tarzan,* Disney Press (New York, NY), 1999.

Disney: The Ultimate Visual Guide, Dorling Kindersley (New York, NY), 2002.

Work in Progress

A book about the creation of song scores for Disney films.

Sidelights

Russell Schroeder, a now-retired artist for the Walt Disney Company, has written several books about Disney characters and films and even about company founder Walt Disney himself. *Walt Disney: His Life in Pictures* features 178 photographs of Disney, some of which are captioned with quotations from Disney. Other photos feature comments from his friends and family or "engaging trivia," such as the fact that "Disney kept two fawns on the studio lot for *Bambi* animators to study," as a reviewer commented in *Publishers Weekly.*

Like *Walt Disney, Mickey Mouse: My Life in Pictures* is built around images taken from the Disney archives. Told from the animated rodent's point of view, *Mickey Mouse* begins with Mickey recalling how he met Walt Disney on a train and then chronicles his animated career decade by decade. In addition to stills of Mickey himself, the book also includes photographs of the animators who drew him and the Disney lots on which they worked. Although the most obvious attraction of the book is visual, "much of the material, especially that surrounding the war years, is of genuine historical interest," Tim Wadham noted in *School Library Journal.*

Schroeder told *SATA:* "Even during my pre-school years I liked to draw, and along with wielding my crayons in the creation of barnyard and other animals, I copied

Disney characters from my storybooks. In addition to the inspiration found in the colorful Disney illustrations in books around the house, I was fascinated by the enchanting magical worlds of *Pinocchio, Snow White,* and other animated classics presented on the large movie screen at our local theater. By the time I was ten, I knew I wanted to be an artist for Walt Disney some day.

"I kept up my art studies throughout school, but added to that an appreciation for literature, and its power to speak to people and give relevance to their lives throughout history. Whether relating legendary sagas, such as the stories of the Trojan War or the Arthurian tales, or the novels of Charles Dickens (a personal favorite), the written word has been a source of enjoyment and enrichment.

"Having had the goal of working for Disney from a very early age, I feel very fortunate that that dream did come true for me. Although I was principally an artist for my twenty-nine years with the Walt Disney Company, I enjoyed the benefit of working in many different areas—at the Walt Disney World theme parks in Florida, the motion picture studio in Burbank, California, and even, briefly, at Disneyland in Anaheim, California. I created illustrations for posters, advertising, publications and brochures, and souvenir items, and I designed ceramic figurines, which other artists turned into dimensional sculptures. Along with other artists, architects, and engineers, I worked on the full-size interactive area of the Magic Kingdom that opened in 1988 as Mickey's Birthdayland. (This area has since been redesigned and renamed Mickey's Toontown Fair.) In addition to the wide variety of applications for my illustration projects, another benefit has been the opportunity to meet and interact with inspiring creative personnel throughout the Disney company, both in the U.S. and from around the world.

"When you are interested in something, it is very easy to learn all about it. I always read any books or magazine articles I can find about the process of making the Disney animated movies and of Walt Disney as a person. That knowledge, acquired over the years, in addition to the firsthand experience of my job, has given me the opportunity to write about the Walt Disney Company and its activities on several occasions. And even though I have been retired for several years, it was one of the reasons I was recommended to the publisher Dorling Kindersley when they first proposed their book *Disney: The Ultimate Visual Guide.*"

Biographical and Critical Sources

PERIODICALS

Booklist, March 15, 1998, review of *Mickey Mouse: My Life in Pictures,* p. 1225.

Horn Book Guide, spring, 1998, Peter D. Sieruta, review of *Mickey Mouse,* p. 146.

Publishers Weekly, July 29, 1996, review of *Walt Disney: His Life in Pictures,* p. 88.

Reading Teacher, December, 1997, review of *Walt Disney,* p. 328.

School Library Journal, October, 1996, Pamela K. Bomboy, review of *Walt Disney,* p. 140; February, 1998, Tim Wadham, review of *Mickey Mouse,* p. 126.

Voice of Youth Advocates, April, 1998, review of *Mickey Mouse,* p. 40.

*   *   *

SEINFELD, Jerry 1954-

Personal

Born April 29, 1954, in Brooklyn, NY; son of Kalman (in business) and Betty Seinfeld; married Jessica Sklar (a publicist), 1999; children: Sascha, Julian. *Education:* Queens College, graduated with degree in communications and theater, 1976. *Religion:* Jewish. *Hobbies and other interests:* Baseball, sports cars.

Addresses

Home—Los Angeles, CA; and New York, NY. *Office*—147 El Camino Dr., #215, Beverly Hills, CA 90212. *Agent*—c/o Author Mail, Little, Brown, 1271 Avenue of the Americas, New York, NY 10020.

Career

Stand-up comedian, actor, and screenwriter. Worked variously as a light bulb salesman, a waiter, and a jewelry street vendor. Creator, with Larry David, and producer and star of *Seinfeld,* National Broadcasting Company, Inc. (NBC-TV), 1990-98. Tours frequently as a stand-up comic. Made regular appearances on *The Tonight Show* and *Late Night with David Letterman.* Appeared briefly as the governor's joke writer, *Benson,* American Broadcasting Companies, Inc. (ABC-TV), 1980. Appeared in numerous television specials, including *The Tonight Show Starring Johnny Carson Nineteenth Anniversary Special,* NBC-TV, 1981; "Rodney Dangerfield—It's Not Easy Bein' Me," *On Location,* Home Box Office (HBO), 1986; "Jerry Seinfeld—Stand-Up Confidential," *On Location,* HBO, 1987; *Late Night with David Letterman Seventh Anniversary Show,* NBC-TV, 1989; *Today at Forty,* NBC-TV, 1992; *Twenty Years of Comedy on HBO,* HBO, 1995; *Comedy Club Superstars,* ABC-TV, 1996; *Jerry Seinfeld: I'm Telling You for the Last Time,* HBO, 1998; *Seinfeld: The Chronicle,* NBC-TV, 1998; *Saturday Night Live: Twenty-fifth Anniversary,* NBC-TV, 1999; and *Larry David: Curb Your Enthusiasm,* HBO, 1999. Produced and appeared in documentary *Comedian,* Miramax, 2002.

Jerry Seinfeld

Awards, Honors

American Comedy Award, funniest male comedy club stand-up, 1988; Clio Award, best announcer in a radio commercial, 1988; American Comedy Award, funniest actor in a television series, 1992 and 1993, Emmy Award for outstanding comedy series, 1993, and Golden Globe Awards for best television series and best actor in a television comedy, 1994, all for *Seinfeld;* honorary doctorate, Queens College of the City University of New York, 1994.

Writings

(With others) *Seinfeld* (television series), NBC-TV (New York, NY), 1990-98.
SeinLanguage, Bantam Books (New York, NY), 1993.
(With others) *The Seinfeld Scripts: The First and Second Seasons,* HarperTrade (New York, NY), 1998.
Sein Off: The Final Days of Seinfeld, HarperEntertainment (New York, NY), 1998.
Halloween (picture book), illustrated by James Bennett, Little, Brown, (Boston, MA), 2002.

Also author of stand-up routines. Author of introduction, *Letters from a Nut* and *More Letters from a Nut,* by Ted L. Nancy, and *The Moron Stories of Ed Broth,* St. Martin's Press (New York, NY), 2003.

Work in Progress

Writing, producing, and starring in *Bee Movie,* a computer-animated feature, for DreamWorks Pictures.

Sidelights

Jerry Seinfeld is best known as one of the most successful comedians of the 1990s, the star of *Seinfeld* and a stand-up comic with specials on Home Box Office and network television. Seinfeld has used his own life as grist for his comedy, from his childhood on Long Island to his daily rounds of Manhattan with his friends. In all of his work, Seinfeld is just himself—an ordinary guy who finds humor in the Laundromat and the deli, the frantic search for the perfect piece of Halloween candy, and the perfect one-liner with which to end a routine. In an interview with *New York* magazine, he said: "Superman is my role model. I have this very romantic image of the stand-up comic, the solitary challenge of being out there on your own, using whatever you have on you. Every man thinks of himself as a low-level superhero. And it came true for me. I got to do what I wanted to do in life. To me, that's being Superman."

Growing up in Massapequa, Long Island, Seinfeld learned comic traits early—from his father. "My dad was very funny," Seinfeld recalled in an interview with *People* magazine. "He turned me on that it's fun to be funny. That's really why I do it." Seinfeld himself was a self-described television junkie who spent hours and hours of his childhood watching situation comedies and dramas. At thirteen, he started making comic audio tapes of his own, including interviews he conducted with his pet parakeet. "When you retreat from contact with other kids, your only playground left is your own mind," he explained in *GQ* magazine. "You start exploring your own ability to entertain yourself."

Seinfeld was still a teenager when he decided to pursue stand-up comedy as a career. After graduating from Queens College of the City University of New York in 1976 with a dual major in theater and communication arts, he began haunting comedy clubs in Manhattan, working on his material in front of audiences and earning a mere thirty to forty dollars per gig. In order to make ends meet, he also held a series of daytime jobs, including selling jewelry from a cart outside Bloomingdale and trying to sell light bulbs over the telephone. After putting in four years on the New York circuit, he had twenty-five minutes of solid material and decided to make the big move to Los Angeles.

What followed was not overnight success, but rather another decade of steadily-improving venues for Seinfeld. He made his debut on the *Tonight Show* in 1981 and thereafter made semi-regular appearances on talk shows and comedy specials, rounding out his schedule with tours of universities and larger clubs in the bigger cities. By 1989, he was making almost 300 appearances per year. It was at that moment that he was approached about doing a television show.

Jerry Seinfeld covers the topic of Halloween in hilarious fashion, in **Halloween,** *illustrated by James Bennett.*

What the National Broadcasting Corporation (NBC) proposed was a special, on the topic of Seinfeld's choice. He and a friend, Larry David, sat down and discussed what the show would be about—and decided that it would be about how comedians come up with their material. This idea evolved into the hugely successful *Seinfeld,* a show that features Jerry Seinfeld interacting with his friends and using his and their insights to create stand-up routines that appear at the beginning and end of each show. In an interview with *TV Guide,* Seinfeld called his show "micro-concept

TV." He added: "It's long bank lines, subway muggings, missing rent-a-car reservations, rude waiters. Sneezing is good. No cute kids, no morals tacked onto the end." Conceived as a show about conversation, *Seinfeld* became so popular that its catch-phrases, such as "yada yada yada," became part of the national slang.

From its debut in 1990 through its final episode in 1998, *Seinfeld* regularly topped the ratings. Seinfeld and his co-stars became international celebrities, with all the scrutiny that stardom brings. Most observers were surprised in 1998 when Seinfeld decided not to renew the show for another year, but the entertainer himself was ready to return to his first love, stand-up comedy. The 2002 film *Comedian* chronicles his return to small stages and the not-so-simple craft of making audiences laugh.

Seinfeld has spent some of his time writing books as well. His 2002 work *Halloween* is a picture book that includes Seinfeld's recollection of the Halloweens of his youth. Culled from a stand-up routine he once performed, *Halloween* chronicles Seinfeld's devotion to amassing huge amounts of candy, his humiliation at having to wear a winter coat over his Superman costume, and his frustration at items as varied as the flimsy rubber bands on the back of masks and orange marshmallow circus peanuts. *Booklist* contributor Ilene Cooper wrote of *Halloween:* "The premise is funny, and the art is fantastic," while a *Publishers Weekly* reviewer called the work a "sugar-fueled nostalgia trip." However, not all reviewers found children as the intended audience. In *Kirkus Reviews,* a critic noted: "What do you get when you cross one of America's most successful comedians with one of childhood's most sacred days? A very funny picture book . . . for adults." *Horn Book* contributor Peter D. Sieruta conversely concluded, however, that children would "relate to the subject matter." Sieruta observed: "The book's holiday theme and humorous voice will draw readers of all ages."

In an interview on *Bookreporter.com,* Seinfeld quipped that he found childhood so memorable because "the colors were so strong and bright. I'm sure if I grew up in Eastern Europe, with its more muted gray-brown palette, I wouldn't remember a thing."

Biographical and Critical Sources

BOOKS

Authors and Artists for Young Adults, Volume 11, Gale (Detroit, MI), 1993.
Contemporary Theatre, Film and Television, Volume 29, Gale (Detroit, MI), 2000.
Oppenheimer, Jerry, *Seinfeld: The Making of an American Icon,* HarperCollins (New York, NY), 2002.

PERIODICALS

Booklist, September 1, 2002, Ilene Cooper, review of *Halloween,* p. 140.
Detroit Free Press, November 20, 1992, Section F, p. 4; December 22, 1992, Section B, p. 6; February 11, 1993, Section D, p. 6.
Entertainment Weekly, March 1, 1991, pp. 29-30; September 11, 1992, p. 35.
GQ, May, 1992, pp. 136-141, 202, 204-205.
Horn Book, September-October, 2002, Peter D. Sieruta, review of *Halloween,* p. 560.

Kirkus Reviews, July 15, 2002, review of *Halloween,* p. 1043.
Mirabella, October, 1991, pp. 48, 50.
New York, February 3, 1992, pp. 32-37.
New York Times, September 29, 1991, Section H, pp. 33-34; September 16, 1992, Section C, p. 20.
People, June 4, 1990, p. 14; December 2, 1991, pp. 87-88.
Publishers Weekly, June 24, 2002, review of *Halloween,* p. 54.
School Library Journal, September, 2002, John Sigwald, review of *Halloween,* p. 205.
Time, August 24, 1992, p. 63.
TV Guide, May 23, 1992, pp. 11-15.
Us, April 4, 1991, pp. 16-19.
USA Today, October 2, 1991, Section D, p. 1.

ONLINE

Books & Authors, http://www.booksandauthors.net/ (July 7, 2003), interview with Seinfeld.
Bookreporter.com, http://www.bookreporter.com/ (July 7, 2003), interview with Seinfeld.*

*   *   *

SHAW, Janet 1937-
(Janet Beeler, Janet Beeler Shaw)

Personal

Born September 30, 1937, in Springfield, IL; daughter of Russel Henry (a teacher) and Nadina (a homemaker; maiden name, Boardman) Fowler; married Thomas Beeler, August 22, 1959 (divorced); married Robert C. Shaw (a counselor), September 12, 1978; children: (first marriage) Kristin, Mark, Laura. *Education:* Stephens College, A.A., 1957; Goucher College, B.A., 1959; Cleveland State University, M.A., 1975. *Hobbies and other interests:* Teaching children and adults, reading, gardening, biking, hiking.

Addresses

Home—46 Newcross N., Asheville, NC 28805-9213. *Agent*—Ned Leavitt, William Morris Agency, 1350 Avenue of the America, New York, NY 10019.

Career

Novelist. Freelance writer, 1959-80, 1986—. University of Wisconsin—Madison, lecturer, beginning 1980; Edgewood College, Madison, WI, lecturer, 1985. Writer-in-residence, Associated Colleges of the Twin Cities, 1983; visiting writer, Florida State University, 1986. Administrator for South Dakota Arts Board, 1981, Wisconsin Arts Board, 1981-83, Illinois Arts Board, 1985, and National Endowment for the Arts, 1987-88. Member, Dane County Cultural Affairs Commission, 1983-86.

Member

Phi Beta Kappa.

Awards, Honors

Mademoiselle award, 1958, for "A Day for Fishing;" Devins Foundation Award for Poetry, 1978, for *Dowry;* Wisconsin Arts Board fellow, 1981-82; *Seventeen* magazine Poetry Contest award, 1985; Outstanding Literary Achievement citation, Wisconsin Library Association, 1987, for *Taking Leave.*

Writings

"KIRSTEN" SERIES

Meet Kirsten: An American Girl, 1854 (also see below), illustrated by René Graef, Pleasant Company (Madison, WI), 1986.

Kirsten Learns a Lesson: A School Story, 1854 (also see below), illustrated by René Graef, Pleasant Company (Madison, WI), 1986.

Kirsten's Surprise: A Christmas Story, 1854 (also see below), illustrated by René Graef, Pleasant Company (Madison, WI), 1986.

Happy Birthday, Kirsten! A Springtime Story, 1854 (also see below), illustrated by René Graef, Pleasant Company (Madison, WI), 1986.

Changes for Kirsten: A Winter Story, 1854 (also see below), illustrated by René Graef, Pleasant Company (Madison, WI), 1988.

Kirsten Saves the Day: A Summer Story, 1854 (also see below), illustrated by René Graef, Pleasant Company (Madison, WI), 1988.

Kirsten on the Trail, illustrated by René Graef, Pleasant Company (Middleton, WI), 1999.

Kirsten and the New Girl, illustrated by René Graef, Pleasant Company (Middleton, WI), 2000.

Kirsten's Story Collection (contains *Meet Kirsten, Kirsten Learns a Lesson, Kirsten's Surprise, Happy Birthday, Kirsten!, Changes for Kirsten,* and *Kirsten Saves the Day*), illustrated by René Graef, Pleasant Company (Middleton, WI), 2001.

Kirsten Snowbound! illustrated by René Graef, Pleasant Company (Middleton, WI), 2001.

Kirsten and the Chippewa, illustrated by René Graef, Pleasant Company (Middleton, WI), 2002.

Kirsten's Promise, illustrated by René Graef, Pleasant Company (Middleton, WI), 2003.

"KAYA" SERIES

Meet Kaya: An American Girl: 1764 (also see below), illustrated by Bill Farnsworth, Pleasant Company (Middleton, WI), 2002.

Kaya's Escape!: A Survival Story: 1764 (also see below), illustrated by Bill Farnsworth, Pleasant Company (Middleton, WI), 2002.

Mountain fires make rescuing her horse difficult in **Changes for Kaya: A Story of Courage: 1764,** *written by Janet Shaw and illustrated by Bill Farnsworth.*

Kaya's Hero: A Story of Giving: 1764 (also see below), illustrated by Bill Farnsworth, Pleasant Company (Middleton, WI), 2002.

Kaya and Lone Dog: A Friendship Story: 1764 (also see below), illustrated by Bill Farnsworth, Pleasant Company (Middleton, WI), 2002.

Kaya Shows the Way: A Sister Story: 1764 (also see below), illustrated by Bill Farnsworth, Pleasant Company (Middleton, WI), 2002.

Changes for Kaya: A Story of Courage: 1764 (also see below), illustrated by Bill Farnsworth, Pleasant Company (Middleton, WI), 2002.

Kaya and the River Girl: 1764, illustrated by Bill Farnsworth, Pleasant Company (Middleton, WI), 2003.

Kaya's Story Collection (contains *Meet Kaya, Kaya's Escape, Kaya's Hero, Kaya and Lone Dog, Kaya Shows the Way,* and *Changes for Kaya*), illustrated by Bill Farnsworth, Pleasant Company (Middleton, WI), 2003.

OTHER

(Under name Janet Beeler) *How to Walk on Water* (poems), Cleveland State University Poetry Forum (Cleveland, OH), 1973.

(Under name Janet Beeler) *Dowry* (poem), University of Missouri Press (Columbia, MO), 1978.

In Shaw's novel **Kaya's Escape: A Survival Story: 1764,** *Kaya and her sister must find their way back home after being kidnapped. (Illustrated by Farnsworth.)*

(Under name Janet Beeler Shaw) *Some of the Things I Did Not Do* (short stories), University of Illinois Press (Urbana, IL), 1984.

Taking Leave, Viking (New York, NY), 1987.

Also author of "A Day for Fishing." Short stories represented in anthologies, including *Prize Stories of 1960: The O. Henry Awards,* 1960; *Mademoiselle Prize Stories,* 1975; *The Editors' Choice: New American Stories,* Bantam (New York, NY), 1985; *Family: Stories from the Interior,* Grey Wolf Press (Minneapolis, MN), 1987; *The Norton Anthology of Short Fiction,* Norton (New York, NY), 1988; *Stiller's Pond,* New Rivers Press (St. Paul, MN), 1988; and *Prime Number,* University of Illinois Press (Champaign, IL), 1988. Poetry represented in anthologies, including *Bear Crossings: An Anthology of North American Poets,* 1978; *Poems Out of Wisconsin V,* 1980; and *In the Middle: Ten Midwestern Women Poets,* 1985.

Contributor of stories to periodicals, including *Atlantic, Denver Quarterly, Family Circle, Fiction Journal, Indiana Review, Mademoiselle, McCall's, Milwaukee Journal, Missouri Review, Redbook, Sewanee Review, Shenandoah, Southwest Review,* and *TriQuarterly*

Review. Contributor of poetry to *American Poetry Review, Antaeus, Esquire, New Catholic World, New Orleans Review, Open Places, Perspective, Poet Lore,* and *Primavera.*

Adaptations

Many of Shaw's books in the "Kirsten" series have been adapted for videocassette by Pleasant Company (Middleton, WI).

Sidelights

In addition to writing many works of short fiction and verse for adult readers, Janet Shaw has established a prolific career penning historical novels focusing on young girls that tie in to the collectible dolls designed and marketed by the Wisconsin-based Pleasant Company. In both the "Kirsten" and "Kaya" books, which contain less that eighty pages and are geared for elementary-grade readers, Shaw introduces plucky and resourceful heroines who deal with the hardship of life in an earlier era and encounter a series of adventures on the way.

As she once explained in *SATA,* in the "Kirsten" series of "American Girl" novels, Swedish-born Kirsten and her family experience the loss of their homeland and all that is familiar to them when they immigrate to the United States in 1854. In their new home on the frontier in Minnesota, they create a new life as Americans. The family's strong bonds of love stretch to include their community's new teacher in *Kirsten Learns a Lesson,* a Sioux Indian friend in *Kirsten on the Trail,* and the children and adults they meet in the harsh world they have made home. Taking a great deal of time to research the world of her protagonist, Shaw also works to keep the "Kirsten" books free of sentimentality, preferring to portray the world of the mid-nineteenth-century settlers in a realistic light.

"Kirsten is a resourceful girl with heart," Shaw once commented. "She shows real courage when she saves her father in the blizzard and also makes real mistakes when she thinks she can outsmart the bears. She faces her fears and forms deep bonds of love and friendship—qualities I'd certainly wish for all of us."

Shaw delves even further into America's past in her "Kaya" series, which features a nine-year-old girl of the Nez Perce tribe. The time is 1764, and in the region now divided into the states of Washington, Idaho, and Oregon, Kaya is living among a close family and building her understanding of both her tribe and the natural world around her. In *Meet Kaya: An American Girl: 1764,* the girl and her horse try to win a bareback race, in the process forgetting to care for her younger twin brothers. In *Kaya's Hero: A Story of Giving: 1764,* the girl seeks to win the respect of a highly-regarded member of her community. In writing the "Kaya" novels, Shaw benefited from the help of the Nez Perce Tribal

Kaya is a young Nez Perce Indian from 1764, who wishes to gain the respect and friendship of a strong woman in her tribe. From Kaya's Hero: A Story of Giving: 1764, *written by Shaw and illustrated by Farnsworth.*

Executive Committee, which assisted the author in getting the details of life in the Northwest Territories correct. Reviewing several books in the "Kaya" series for *School Library Journal,* Carolyn Janssen described Shaw's protagonist as "well developed through her actions and words," while in *Booklist,* Karen Hutt commended the books for being "historically accurate and culturally sensitive . . . a noteworthy result of a unique collaboration."

In an interview for *Kidsreads.com,* Shaw described her hopes for the "Kaya" books: "I hope that by looking at the world through Kaya's eyes, . . . readers will learn to understand, appreciate, and respect a rich and intriguing way of life very different from their own. Kaya and her people were strengthened by their powerful sense of community and their relationship with the world around them. They prized justice, independence, bravery, generosity, and spirituality—enduring values we badly need in our lives today."

Shaw, whose short fiction and poetry has been widely anthologized and who published the 1987 adult novel *Taking Leave* as well as several poetry collections, once explained in *SATA* that "the skills in writing for chil-

dren are as much the same as in writing for adults: the story has to have drive and a dramatic question to be resolved; the characters must be believable and empathetic and the source for the conflict within the story; dialogue must be natural. Of course, you must write in shorter sentences, but my husband pointed out to me that I write in short sentences anyway! My pleasure in writing the children's books has been to create stories I'd like my own daughters to read."

Biographical and Critical Sources

PERIODICALS

Booklist, January 1, 2003, Karen Hutt, review of *Meet Kaya: An American Girl: 1764* and *Kaya's Escape! A Survival Story: 1764,* p. 893.
Library Journal, April 15, 1987, Maurice Taylor, review of *Taking Leave,* p. 101.
Publishers Weekly, October 31, 1986, review of "Kirsten" series, p. 68; February 13, 1987, review of *Taking Leave,* p. 82; June 24, 2002, review of "Kaya" series, p. 59.
School Library Journal, November, 1986, Elaine Fort Weischedel, review of *Meet Kirsten: An American Girl: 1854,* p. 85; May, 1988, Sylvia S. Marantz, review of *Happy Birthday, Kirsten! A Springtime Story: 1854,* p. 88; October, 1988, Ruth K. MacDonald, review of *Kirsten Saves the Day: A Summer Story: 1854,* p. 148; December, 2002, Carolyn Janssen, review of *Kaya's Escape!* and *Kaya's Hero: A Story of Giving: 1764,* p. 108.

ONLINE

Kidsreads.com, http://aol.kidsreads.com/ (June 3, 2003), interview with Shaw.

OTHER

Meet Janet Shaw: An American Girls Author (short film), Pleasant Company, 1991.*

*   *   *

SHAW, Janet Beeler
See SHAW, Janet

*   *   *

SHULMAN, Dee 1957-

Personal

Born July 8, 1957, in South Africa; married Chris Barton (a writer, teacher, and theatre director), August 19, 1983; children: Esther, Max. *Education:* University of York, B.A. *Religion:* Jewish.

Addresses

Agent—Kathryn Ross, Fraser Ross Associates, 6 Wellington Pl., Edinburgh EH6 7EQ, Scotland. *E-mail*—dee.shulman@blueyonder.co.uk.

Career

Writer and illustrator. Middlesex University, lecturer in creative writing.

Member

Society of Authors, Association of Illustrators.

Awards, Honors

Children's Book Award shortlist, Federation of Children's Book Groups.

Writings

SELF-ILLUSTRATED

One Day, Janie!, Puffin (London, England), 1990.
Jessie's Special Day, Puffin (London, England), 1990.
Roaring Billy, Bodley Head (London, England), 1991.
The Visit, Bodley Head (London, England), 1991.
Grandad and Me, Red Fox (London, England), 1991.
Dora's New Brother, Bodley Head (London, England), 1993.
My Mum, A & C Black (London, England), 1996.
Katie's Special Tooth, Oxford University Press (Oxford, England), 1997.
Aunt Bella's Cat, Barrington Stoke (Edinburgh, Scotland), 2001.
Hetty the Yeti, A & C Black (London, England), 2003.

SELF-ILLUSTRATED; "MAGENTA" SERIES

Magenta and the Ghost Babies, A & C Black (London, England), 2002.
Magenta and the Ghost Bride, A & C Black (London, England), 2002.
Magenta and the Ghost School, A & C Black (London, England), 2002.
Magenta and the Scary Ghosts, A & C Black (London, England), 2002.

"CUDDLY BOARD BOOKS" SERIES

A Perfect Cuddle, illustrated by Sue Porter, Scholastic (New York, NY), 2000.
Birthday Bunny, illustrated by Sue Porter, Scholastic (New York, NY), 2000.
Fluffy Kitten, illustrated by Sue Porter, Scholastic (New York, NY), 2000.
Our New Baby, illustrated by Sue Porter, Scholastic (New York, NY), 2000.

ILLUSTRATOR

Paul and Emma Rogers, *Amazing Babies,* Dent (London, England), 1990.

Paul and Emma Rogers, *Billy Buzoni and Friends,* Dent (London, England), 1991.
Chris Barton, *Cream Cake,* Bodley Head (London, England), 1992.
Michaela Morgan, *Pickles Sniffs It Out,* A & C Black (London, England), 1994.
Hiawyn Oran, *Wilf, the Black Hole, and the Poisonous Marigold,* A & C Black, 1994, published as *Wilf and the Black Hole,* Puffin (London, England), 1996.
Philip Wooderson, *The Baked Bean Cure,* A & C Black (London, England), 1995.
Michaela Morgan, *Cool Clive* (also see below), Oxford University Press (Oxford, England), 1995.
Philip Wooderson, *The Mincing Machine,* A & C Black (London, England), 1996.
Michaela Morgan, *Clive Keeps His Cool* (also see below), Oxford University Press (Oxford, England), 1996.
Michaela Morgan, *Invasion of the Dinner Ladies,* A & C Black (London, England), 1997.
Philip Wooderson, *Dad's Dodgy Lodger,* A & C Black (London, England), 1997.
Kaye Umansky, Stephen Chadwick, and Kate Buchanan, *Three Rapping Rats,* A & C Black (London, England), 1998.
Michaela Morgan, *Shelley Holmes, Ace Detective,* Oxford University Press (Oxford, England), 1998.
Michaela Morgan, *The True Diary of Carly Ann Potter,* Oxford University Press (Oxford, England), 1999.
Michaela Morgan, *Yum! Yuck!,* Rigby (Port Melbourne, Australia), 2000.
Michaela Morgan, *Shelley Holmes, Animal Trainer,* Oxford University Press (Oxford, England), 2000.
Michaela Morgan, *Pompom,* Barrington Stoke (Edinburgh, Scotland), 2000.
Michaela Morgan, *Cool Clive and the Little Pest,* Oxford University Press (Oxford, England), 2001.
Michaela Morgan, *Cool Clive, the Coolest Kid Alive* (contains *Cool Clive* and *Clive Keeps His Cool*), Oxford University Press (Oxford, England), 2001.
Bobbie Gargrave and others, *Let's Go Zudie-O: Creative Activities for Dance and Music,* A & C Black (London, England), 2001.
Kes Gray and Linda Jennings, *Toffee and Marmalade: Two Pet Stories,* Oxford University Press (Oxford, England), 2002.
Ivan Jones, *The Lazy Giant,* Oxford University Press (Oxford, England), 2003.

Contributor of illustrations to a variety of magazines and periodicals.

ILLUSTRATOR; "SILLY SAUSAGE" SERIES

Michaela Morgan, *School for Sausage,* A & C Black (London, England), 2001.
Michaela Morgan, *Sausage and the Spooks,* A & C Black (London, England), 2001.
Michaela Morgan, *Sausage and the Little Visitor,* A & C Black (London, England), 2001.
Michaela Morgan, *Sausage in Trouble,* A & C Black (London, England), 2001.

Preschoolers will warm up to Sue Porter's cuddly illustrations in the board book **Birthday Bunny,** *by Dee Shulman.*

Work in Progress

The Marsh Monster, Howling Moon, and a sequel to *Hetty the Yeti.*

Sidelights

Many of writer and illustrator Dee Shulman's books are intended for the very youngest book lovers. Four of Shulman's books for beginning readers are from the "Cuddly Board Books" series—*Birthday Bunny, Fluffy Kitten, A Perfect Cuddle,* and *Our New Baby.* Illustrated by Sue Porter, the books have physical features designed to appeal to youngsters, including lift-up flaps, cut-outs that add an interactive element to the stories, and swatches of fur and other materials to appeal to the

sense of touch. A *Publishers Weekly* reviewer remarked that the books "are sure to stimulate any toddler's tactile senses."

In *One Day, Janie!,* three-year-old Janie tries to do the things her older sister can do, with unintentionally destructive results. A reviewer in *Books for Keeps* called *One Day, Janie!* "great fun" and a "perfect" book for readers in Janie's age range.

The Visit follows young Dora as she stays with her grandparents for a day. Though she tries to be good, Dora does eventually annoy her grandfather, and she worries what kind of report she will get when her parents come to pick her up. The story "demonstrates the warmth and security that a good relationship with grand-parents can bring," observed Cathy Sutton in *School Librarian.*

Roaring Billy presents a small mystery—why has smil-ing and happy Billy suddenly been turned into a cranky and crying child who cannot be pleased no matter what his family tries? Attempts to soothe him only make him cry and roar louder. But the next morning, Billy smiles again and reveals the culprit behind his problems—his first tooth. Reviewer J. Haydn Jones, writing in *Books for Your Children,* called *Roaring Billy* a "visually bright book." Jones also claimed that the author "cap-tures so accurately" all the emotions, turmoil, and con-cern of a family and child experiencing teething. A re-viewer in *Books for Keeps* remarked on how well Shulman's "zany [art] style" reflected the growing dis-tress and eventual relief of Billy and his family.

Shulman has also written stories for older children. In *Aunt Bella's Cat,* Kate accompanies her Aunt Bella, a Hollywood star, to a cat show where Bella exhibits Bashir, a superb Abyssinian cat. *Times Educational Supplement* critic Michael Thorn remarked that the "pet appeal" and "crime climax" would appeal to children in the three to four-year-old age range.

"When my children were small, I abandoned the fast and furious world of magazine illustration and cartoon strips, and began to write and illustrate books for chil-dren," Shulman told SATA. "Many titles later, my chil-dren and their world continue to be my inspiration.

"As writer/illustrator, I have been published by Bodley Head, Red Fox, Puffin, A & C Black; HarperCollins, Dent, Barrington Stoke, Scholastic, and Oxford Univer-sity Press, with co-editions in the United States, Japan, China, the Netherlands, Italy, Finland, and South Africa.

"My books have been highly recommended in numer-ous publications, and on Radio 4's *Treasure Islands,* and I was recently shortlisted for the Federation of Children's Book Groups Children's Book Award."

Biographical and Critical Sources

PERIODICALS

Books for Keeps, January, 1991, review of *One Day, Janie!,* p. 6; November, 1992, review of *Roaring Billy,* p. 15.
Books for Your Children, spring, 1993, J. Haydn Jones, re-view of *Roaring Billy,* p. 8.
Publishers Weekly, May 1, 2000, "Getting Touchy-Feely," review of *Fluffy Kitten, Birthday Bunny, A Perfect Cuddle,* and *Our New Baby,* p. 73.

From **Our New Baby,** *written by Shulman and illus-trated by Porter.*

School Librarian, May, 1992, Cathy Sutton, review of *The Visit,* p. 58.
Times Educational Supplement, November 16, 2001, Michael Thorn, review of *Aunt Bella's Cat,* p. 20.

*   *   *

SIEVERT, Terri
See DOUGHERTY, Terri (L.)

*   *   *

SMALLS, Irene
See SMALLS-HECTOR, Irene

*   *   *

SMALLS-HECTOR, Irene 1950-
(Irene Smalls)

Personal

Born February 11, 1950, in Harlem, NY; daughter of Charles Smith and Mary Smalls; married Derek C. Hec-tor, May 13, 1989; children: Jonathan, Kevin Logan, Dawn. *Education:* Cornell University, B.A., 1971; New York University, M.B.A., 1974. *Hobbies and other in-terests:* Reading, shopping, traveling.

Addresses

Home—Boston, MA. *Agent*—c/o Author Mail, Little, Brown, 34 Beacon St., Boston, MA 02108. *E-mail*—Ismalls107@aol.com.

Career

Children's book author and storyteller. Smalls-Dawn Associates (marketing consultants), affiliate, 1978-80; voice-over actress, beginning 1988. Presenter at workshops and school assemblies.

Member

Screen Actors Guild, American Federation of Television and Radio Artists, Society of Children's Book Writers and Illustrators, Cornell Black Alumni Association.

Awards, Honors

Miss Black New York State, 1967-68; Global Cultural Awareness Award, International Reading Association, 1996; Children's Book Author of the Year, Chicago Black History Association, 1999.

Writings

Irene and the Big, Fine Nickel, illustrated by Tyrone Geter, Little Brown (Boston, MA), 1991, published under name Irene Smalls, 2003.

Jonathan and His Mommy, illustrated by Michael Hays, Little, Brown (Boston, MA), 1992.

Dawn's Friends, illustrated by Tyrone Geter, D. C. Heath (Lexington, MA), 1993.

AS IRENE SMALLS

Dawn and the Round To-It, illustrated by Tyrone Geter, Simon & Schuster (New York, NY), 1994.

The Alphabet Witch, illustrated by Kevin McGovern, Longmeadow Press (Stamford, CT), 1994.

Father's Day Blues: What Do You Do about Father's Day When All You Have Are Mothers? Longmeadow Press (Stanford, CT), 1995.

Ebony Sea, illustrated by Jon Enyé Lockard, Longmeadow Press (Stanford, CT), 1995.

Irene Jennie and the Christmas Masquerade: The Johnkankus, illustrated by Melodye Rosales, Little, Brown (Boston, MA), 1996.

Jenny Reen and the Jack Muh Lantern, illustrated by Keinyo White, Atheneum (New York, NY), 1996.

Louise's Gift; or, What Did She Give Me That For?, illustrated by Colin Bootman, Little, Brown (Boston, MA), 1996.

Beginning School, illustrated by Toni Goffe, Silver Burdett Press (Parsippany, NJ), 1996.

Because You're Lucky, illustrated by Michael Hays, Little, Brown (Boston, MA), 1997.

A Strawbeater's Thanksgiving, illustrated by Melodye Benson Rosales, Little, Brown (Boston, MA), 1998.

Kevin and His Dad, illustrated by Michael Hays, Little, Brown (Boston, MA), 1999.

I Can't Take a Bath!, illustrated by Aaron Boyd, Scholastic (New York, NY), 2003.

Don't Say Ain't, illustrated by Colin Bootman, Charlesbridge Publishing (Watertown, MA), 2003.

My Nana and Me, illustrated by Cathy Ann Johnson, Little, Brown (Boston, MA), 2004.

Sidelights

Irene Smalls-Hector keeps to the time-honored traditions of the African-American storyteller, allowing the events of her life and ideas gained through dreams to inspire her simple yet universal tales. In addition to molding her stories into picture-book texts, Smalls-Hector also enjoys spending time talking to children and telling her stories aloud. As she once told *SATA:* "My approach to writing children's books is that I write about what I know, what I see, and what I feel. I write very simple stories. . . . I try to write musically, because it was the sounds of . . . words that moved me as a child. My stories almost always have songs or children's rhymes in them."

Born in New York in 1950, Smalls-Hector shares with readers her memories of a childhood spent in Harlem during the mid-1950s in *Irene and the Big, Fine Nickel.* An enclave of Southern-born blacks and not yet affected by drugs and drug-related violence, Harlem reflected a Southern culture and attitude, both of which are brought to life in Smalls-Hector's depiction of a typical Saturday for seven-year-old Irene. After visiting neighbors, planting a window-box garden, climbing some rocks, and spotting a nickel, Irene finds herself sharing a bakery-store raisin bun with best friends Lulabelle and Lulamae. Smalls-Hector's "nostalgic text" and "richly textured language" bring to life a time and place that today's urban children can only dream about, according to a *Publishers Weekly* reviewer.

Of her 1992 picture book *Jonathan and His Mommy,* Smalls-Hector once explained: "It's the story of my son Jonathan and I, and the walks we used to take when he was ages four-and-a-half to five. This book is for every adult who has ever loved a child and for every child who knows or remembers quiet talks, long walks, and smiles." Praising Smalls-Hector's depiction of an "imaginative mother" who energetically dances along the sidewalk with her laughing son astride her back as "an inspiration to us all," Betsy Hearne added in her *Bulletin of the Center for Children's Books* review that *Jonathan and His Mommy* may focus on a black family, but "the scenario is the envy of every child."

The parent-child bond is celebrated in several other books by Smalls-Hector, among them *Kevin and His Dad* and *Father's Day Blues: What Do You Do about*

An everyday adventure unfolds for a young girl and her friends in 1950s Harlem. From **Irene and the Big Fine Nickel,** *written by Irene Smalls-Hector. (Illustrated by Tyrone Geter.)*

Father's Day When All You Have Are Mothers? Published in 1999, *Kevin and His Dad* celebrates the special relationship between a boy and his father on a day when Mom has been called away from home. Cleaning the house is usually a chore, but done with Dad it becomes fun to young Kevin, especially when it is followed by a quick game of baseball. Folding laundry, dusting, and washing windows? No problem, because any time spent alone with Dad is fun. Reviewing the book, critics observed that Smalls-Hector brings every moment to life with her simple, rhythmic, repetitious text. While creating a gentle story line, Smalls-Hector also manages to interject "a bit of lighthearted silliness" which, according to *School Library Journal* contributor

Marian Drabkin, "transforms ordinary chores into something special."

Kevin's special day is something Cheryl, the protagonist of *Father's Day Blues,* cannot relate to. The young girl has difficulty imagining spending an entire day with her dad, and a school assignment to write an essay titled "My Dad" causes the young girl to question her lack of a father. Fortunately, the women in her life— including her teacher—are understanding and help Cheryl realize that her father's absence is not her fault. *Father's Day Blues* is a story that a *Publishers Weekly* reviewer claimed reinforces "the importance of familial love whatever its source." Reviewing the book for *Booklist,* Hazel Rochman had special praise for the

In Smalls-Hector's story **Kevin and His Dad,** *a boy spends the whole day with his father, first cleaning the house then going out to a movie. (Illustrated by Michael Hays.)*

author's success in creating "strongly individualized" characters and a picture-book text that provides young readers—many of whom may share Cheryl's concerns—an "honest, sensitive treatment" of a situation that is not uncommon.

While the day-to-day events of life with her three children sparked several of her early works, Smalls-Hector has also written about African-American history. In the mid-1990s, she embarked on an ambitious project: to create twelve books, one for each month of the calendar year, with each book focusing on a unique aspect of a child's life during the days of slavery. Among these books are *Ebony Sea, A Strawbeater's Thanksgiving,* and *Irene Jennie and the Christmas Masquerade: The Johnkankus,* the last which focuses on a Christmas tradition that dates back several centuries to Africa. *Ebony Sea* also has its roots in fact. It is based on an actual incident that took place along the South Carolina coastline during the first half of the nineteenth century. A young boy wins the right to be the musical center of attention in *A Strawbeater's Thanksgiving,* a book offering a look at how some slaves celebrated the ending of the growing season. Reviewing *A Strawbeater's Thanksgiving* for *School Library Journal,* Beth Tegart noted that the 1998 picture book "helps to fill out the life stories of slaves and presents an interesting glimpse of a harvest celebration" as it occurred before the U.S. Civil War. Hazel Rochman heaped praise on Smalls-Hector's Halloween installment, *Jenny Reen and the Jack Muh*

Lantern, about a foul creature that roams the countryside in search of children on All-Hallows Eve. *Jenny Reen and the Jack Muh Lantern* "is told with rhythm and shivery immediacy," noted Rochman, going on to praise Smalls-Hector for her "poetic, colloquial voice."

Biographical and Critical Sources

PERIODICALS

American Visions, December, 1991, review of *Irene and the Big, Fine Nickel,* p. 36; December-January, 1997, Yolanda Robinson Coles, review of *Because You're Lucky,* p. 33.

Booklist, October 1, 1992, Deborah Abbott, review of *Jonathan and His Mommy,* p. 338; July, 1995, Hazel Rochman, review of *Father's Day Blues: What Do You Do about Father's Day When All You Have Are Mothers?,* p. 1884; September 15, 1996, Hazel Rochman, review of *Jenny Reen and the Jack Muh Lantern,* p. 137; September 1, 1997, Hazel Rochman, review of *Because You're Lucky,* p. 135; February 15, 1999, Ilene Cooper, review of *Kevin and His Dad,* p. 1076; February 13, 2003, Hazel Rochman, review of *Don't Say Ain't,* p. 1090.

Bulletin of the Center for Children's Books, January, 1993, Betsy Hearne, review of *Jonathan and His Mommy,* p. 157; November, 1997, Pat Matthews, review of *Because You're Lucky,* p. 102.

Horn Book, July-August, 1991, Lois F. Anderson, review of *Irene and the Big, Fine Nickel,* p. 452; November-December, 1992, Maeve Visser Knoth, review of *Jonathan and His Mommy,* p. 719.

Publishers Weekly, April 12, 1991, review of *Irene and the Big, Fine Nickel,* p. 57; November 9, 1992, review of *Jonathan and His Mommy,* p. 83; June 19, 1995, review of *Father's Day Blues,* p. 59; September 30, 1996, *Jenny Reen and the Jack Muh Lantern,* p. 85; December 9, 2002, review of *Don't Say Ain't,* p. 84.

Reading Teacher, November, 1997, review of *Irene Jennie and the Christmas Masquerade,* p. 256.

School Library Journal, December, 1991, Ruth Semrau, review of *Irene and the Big, Fine Nickel,* p. 102; November, 1992, Marie Orlando, review of *Jonathan and His Mommy,* p. 78; July, 1996, Carol Jones Collins, review of *Ebony Sea,* p. 86; July, 1996, Karen James, review of *Louise's Gift,* p. 73; August, 1996, Virginia Opocensky, review of *Beginning School,* p. 130; October, 1996, Mane Marino, review of *Irene Jennie and the Christmas Masquerade,* p. 85; October, 1997, Dawn Amsberry, review of *Because You're So Lucky,* p. 111; October, 1998, Beth Tegart, review of *A Strawbeater's Thanksgiving,* p. 113; May, 1999, Marian Drabkin, review of *Kevin and His Dad,* p. 97; March, 2003, Alicia Eames, review of *Don't Say Ain't,* p. 207.

ONLINE

National School Network, http://nsn.bbn.com/community/ (June 30, 2003), "Chat with Irene Smalls."*

T-U

TORRES, Laura 1967-

Personal

Born March 21, 1967, in Yakima, WA; daughter of James R. (a data technician) and Shirley (a loan officer; maiden name, Gray) Hofmann; married John C. Torres (an assistant professor of sociology), December 19, 1987; children: Brennyn, John Andrew. *Education:* Brigham Young University, A.A., 1987. *Religion:* Church of Jesus Christ of Latter-day Saints (Mormon).

Addresses

Home—1643 North 1100 W., Mapleton, UT 84664.

Career

Freelance writer, 1990—; creative consultant, 1995—; workshop presenter. Former editor, *American Girl* magazine; Klutz Press, Palo Alto, CA, senior editor.

Member

International Society of Altered Book Artists.

Awards, Honors

National Parenting Publications Award (NAPPA) and Cuffie Award, both 1994, both for *The Incredible Clay Book: How to Make and Bake a Million-and-One Clay Creations;* NAPPA Award, 1999, for *Create Anything with Clay* (with Sherri Haab), and 2001, for *Paper Punch Art.*

Writings

NONFICTION

Beads, Glorious Beads, Klutz Press (Palo Alto, CA), 1994.
(With Sherri Haab) *The Incredible Clay Book: How to Make and Bake a Million-and-One Clay Creations,* Klutz Press (Palo Alto, CA), 1994.

Laura Torres

Beads: A Book of Ideas and Instructions, Klutz Press (Palo Alto, CA), 1996.
Friendship Bracelets, Klutz Press (Palo Alto, CA), 1996.
The Sticker Book, Klutz Press (Palo Alto, CA), 1996.
Pipe Cleaners Gone Crazy: A Complete Guide to Bending Fuzzy Sticks, Klutz Press (Palo Alto, CA), 1997.
The Fantastic Foam Book, Klutz Press (Palo Alto, CA), 1998.
Clay Modeling with Pooh, illustrated by Francese Rigoli, Mouse Works (New York, NY), 1999.
(With Sherri Haab) *Create Anything with Clay,* Klutz Press (Palo Alto, CA), 1999.
Pompoms Gone Crazy: How to Make Any Pompom Project in Three Easy Steps, Klutz Press (Palo Alto, CA), 1999.
Disney's Ten-Minute Crafts for Preschoolers, Disney Press (New York, NY), 2000.

(With Sherri Haab) *Wire-o-Mania,* Klutz Press (Palo Alto, CA), 2000.

Don't Eat Pete, Klutz Press (Palo Alto, CA), 2000.

Salt Dough!, illustrated by Wendy Wallin Malinow, Pleasant Company (Middleton, WI), 2001.

Paper Punch Art, Pleasant Company (Middleton, WI), 2001.

Disney Princess Crafts, photographs by Sherri Haab, Disney Press (New York, NY), 2001.

OTHER

November Ever After (young adult fiction), Holiday House (New York, NY), 1999.

Crossing Montana (young adult fiction), Holiday House (New York, NY), 2002.

Contributor to periodicals, including *Children's Digest* and *Jack and Jill.*

Work in Progress

A third novel; a line of books for girls.

Sidelights

Laura Torres has taken a talent for making all manner of things and transformed that talent into a career as a children's how-to-book author. A senior editor at the California-based publisher Klutz Press, Torres is the brainchild behind such works as *Pompoms Gone Crazy: How to Make Any Pompom Project in Three Easy Steps, Wire-o-Mania, The Fantastic Foam Book,* and *Salt Dough!,* the last a 2001 book that helps students concoct the stiff, dyeable bread dough that has been a classic for creating topographical maps for school geography projects for years. In the late 1990s, Torres expanded her own craft as a writer and has garnered praise for several works of young adult fiction.

Torres had aspirations to be a writer even as a child; quiet and shy, she came into her own writing stories others could enjoy. While working in a publishing company for several years, she submitted stories to children's periodicals and sold several. However, it was not until she persuaded the publisher she worked for—Klutz Press—to let her develop a book on polymer clay projects for kids that she began writing nonfiction. Talented at explaining techniques in simple terms that children can understand, Torres has since gone on to produce over a dozen books that celebrate the virtues of crafts from the mid-twentieth century, many of which use materials such as pipe cleaners, Styrofoam, and pompoms. In a *Threads* review of Torres' craft manual *The Incredible Clay Book: How to Make and Bake a Million-and-One Clay Creations,* David Page Coffin praised Torres and frequent collaborator Sherri Haab for doing "a witty, imaginative, and attractive job of presenting clay projects," and noted that the book—geared toward younger readers—makes "the whole idea of clay molding seem fun and approachable."

Secrets test the bonds of friendship between Amy and Sara, in Laura Torres's novel November Ever After.

In 1999, Torres made the break into young adult fiction with her first novel, *November Ever After.* The book introduces sixteen-year-old Amy, whose pastor father is too busy dealing with his parishioners to help Amy cope with the grief over her mother's recent death in a car accident. Turning not only from her father but from her faith as well, Amy clings to her friend Sara for support. More confusion comes when Sara is found in a secret homosexual relationship with another young woman, leaving Amy with feelings of abandonment that a young man named Peter ultimately helps her deal with. A *Kirkus Reviews* critic noted that in response to the questions she raises regarding organized religion's views on homosexuality, Torres "timidly suggest[s] that . . ., in real life, personal bonds may be more powerful than belief systems." Praising the novel's protagonist as "a refreshingly wholesome yet completely realistic teen," *Booklist* contributor Debbie Carton added that the many "lighthearted" turns the plot takes help balance the book's serious focus. In *Publishers Weekly,* a reviewer concluded of *November Ever After* that Torres's "promising prose and credible characterizations make this writer one to watch."

Another young teen figures in Torres's second novel, *Crossing Montana,* which appeared in 2002. At age fif-

Callie Gray sets out to find her grandfather, in **Crossing Montana,** *written by Torres. (Book jacket illustration by Lisa Cinelli.)*

teen, coping with the death of her father and now living with her grandfather and a mother who cannot cope with life, Callie had proved herself a survivor. When her grandfather disappears, Callie decides to go in search of him herself, stealing the family car and a credit card and heading out on the highway. Grandpa, an alcoholic, is ultimately found fishing and brought home, but his condition and her self-reflection while driving cause Callie to realize that her family harbors demons of alcoholism and depression. A fighter, she vows to find a way to make her life better in a novel *Booklist* contributor Hazel Rochman called "stark and beautiful," adding that "Callie's brave, desperate . . . narrative tells the truth and doesn't let you go."

Biographical and Critical Sources

PERIODICALS

Booklist, December 1, 1999, Debbie Carton, review of *November Ever After,* p. 697; August, 2002, Hazel Rochman, review of *Crossing Montana,* p. 1963.

Kirkus Reviews, November 15, 1999, review of *November Ever After,* p. 1816.

Lambda Book Report, April, 2000, Nancy Garden, review of *November Ever After,* p. 27.

Publishers Weekly, October 7, 1996, review of *Friendship Bracelets,* p. 78; April 7, 1997, review of *Pipe Cleaners Gone Crazy: A Complete Guide to Bending Fuzzy Sticks,* p. 94; June 15, 1998, review of *The Fantastic Foam Book,* p. 61; January 3, 2000, review of *November Ever After,* p. 77.

School Library Journal, January, 2000, Connie Tyrell Burns, review of *November Ever After,* p. 136; July, 2002, Diane P. Tuccillo, review of *Crossing Montana,* p. 126.

Threads, June-July, 1996, David Page Coffin, review of *The Incredible Clay Book: How to Make and Bake a Million-and-One Clay Creations,* p. 82.*

*   *   *

URIS, Leon (Marcus) 1924-2003

OBITUARY NOTICE—See index for *SATA* sketch: Born August 3, 1924, in Baltimore, MD; died of renal failure June 21, 2003, in Shelter Island, NY. Novelist. Uris was a bestselling author who is best known for his 1957 novel *Exodus.* Determined to become a writer from a young age, despite getting bad grades in English, he quit high school in his senior year after the Japanese attack on Pearl Harbor and joined the U.S. Marines. Uris, who served as a radio operator, saw action at Guadalcanal and Tarawa. After the war he was hired as a newspaper delivery manager for the San Francisco *Call-Bulletin* and began writing articles for magazines. His first novel, *Battle Cry* (1953), was based on his war experiences and sold so well that he was asked to write a screenplay for the book. The movie was released the next year and was followed in 1955 with Uris's second novel, *The Angry Hills.* Although not known for his writing style, Uris focused more on story than characterization and was fanatical about research. He read hundreds of books, interviewed over a thousand people, and traveled for miles through Israel to write his blockbuster *Exodus,* which is about the founding of the state of Israel. *Exodus* was also adapted to film, although disagreements with producer Otto Preminger prevented Uris from writing the screenplay. Uris's *Gunfight at the O.K. Corral* (1957), however, was a widely praised film. The author gave up writing for Hollywood after this project and focused on historical novels, including *Mila 18* (1960), *Topaz* (1967), *Trinity* (1976), *Redemption* (1995), and *A God in Ruins* (1999). His final novel, *O'Hara's Choice,* was released posthumously. Uris also wrote a book about the places he describes in *Exodus* called *Exodus Revisited* (1959) and authored a play based on the novel titled *Ari* (1971). His 1970 novel *QB VII,* which was later adapted to television, is based on a libel suit filed against Uris by a Polish doctor who complained that in *Exodus* Uris identifies him as committing crimes against humanity. In what became the longest libel case in history at the time, Uris lost the case, but the plaintiff was awarded only a halfpenny and ordered to pay all legal costs.

OBITUARIES AND OTHER SOURCES:

BOOKS

Writers Directory, 18th edition, St. James Press (Detroit, MI), 2003.

PERIODICALS

Los Angeles Times, June 25, 2003, p. B13.
New York Times, June 25, 2003, p. A25.
Times (London, England), June 25, 2003.
Washington Post, June 25, 2003, p. B7.

WARD, Jennifer 1963-

Personal

Born December 4, 1963; daughter of Paul (an economics professor) and Charlene Sultan; married; children: Kelly. *Education:* University of Arizona, B.A.

Addresses

Home—745 West Landoran Ln., Oro Valley, AZ 85737. *E-mail*—jenward@comcast.net.

Career

Teacher in the Tucson, AZ, elementary schools for eleven years.

Member

Society of Children's Book Writers and Illustrators, Society of Southwestern Authors.

Awards, Honors

Parents' Choice Award for a picture book, Parents' Choice Foundation, for *Somewhere in the Ocean.*

Writings

(With T. J. Marsh) *Way Out in the Desert,* illustrated by Kenneth J. Spengler, Northland Publishing (Flagstaff, AZ), 1998.

(With T. J. Marsh) *Somewhere in the Ocean,* illustrated by Kenneth J. Spengler, Northland Publishing (Flagstaff, AZ), 2000.

Over in the Garden, illustrated by Kenneth J. Spengler, Northland Publishing (Flagstaff, AZ), 2002.

The Seed and the Giant Saguaro, Northland Publishing (Flagstaff, AZ), 2003.

Sidelights

Jennifer Ward's first three books for children, *Way Out in the Desert, Somewhere in the Ocean,* and *Over in the Garden,* are musical counting books, all set to the tune of the old song "Over in the Meadow." In each book, Ward chooses ten animals native to the area about which she is writing and then fits them into the verse pattern from "Over in the Meadow." *Way Out in the Desert,* Ward's first book and the one set closest to her home, has horned toads, hummingbirds, rattlesnakes, Gila monsters, jackrabbits, and road runners. *Somewhere in the Ocean* stars clown fish, hermit crabs, tiger sharks, jellyfish, manatees, sea turtles, and sea horses, while *Over in the Garden* features ladybugs, bees, butterflies, pill bugs, and other insects. Besides teaching counting, the books also include other activities for children: Kenneth J. Spengler's double-page spreads each contain a picture of the numeral for that page hidden in the illustration, and all of the books conclude with an appendix of "Fun Facts" about the animals mentioned in that volume. The finished product, as *School Library Journal* critic Mollie Bynum wrote of *Way Out in the Desert,* is "absolutely delightful."

Ward told *SATA:* "I am fairly new to the field of writing for children, but like many in the field, I began my career writing for children with a simple but passionate love of children's literature combined with a desire to write.

"My career as a writer literally fell into my lap. My first manuscript submitted for publication, *Way Out in the Desert,* was accepted by the first publisher it was sent to. It was critically acclaimed and picked up by the Scholastic market and later released in a board book format. As many know, the road to publication is usually not that simple or quick. Call it beginner's luck!

"I do not have an agent. My manuscript was 'pulled from the slush'—meaning it made its way into an editor's hand via regular mail.

"My first picture books are patterned after the old song, 'Over in the Meadow,' which was written by Olive Wadsworth in the 1800s. For my books, I patterned the existing melody to various habitats, such as a desert, an

In Over in the Garden, *families of insects go about their day and night. (Written by Jennifer Ward and illustrated by Kenneth J. Spengler.)*

ocean, and a garden. I make it sound so simple, but many hours and many revisions go into selecting the exact words used.

"I believe writers must write about what they know and what they love. I love nature and animals and thus, find them easy subjects to write about. I write every day and am disciplined about it, even if it's just a few words.

"If I could offer advice to aspiring writers or illustrators, it would be to read a lot of children's books. Consistently. Also, the professional organization SCBWI (Society of Children's Book Writers and Illustrators) offers tremendous resources for writers and illustrators of all levels, from aspiring, yet unpublished, to advanced and well known. If you're serious about wanting to write for children, follow your dream!"

Biographical and Critical Sources

PERIODICALS

Booklist, April 1, 2000, Carolyn Phelan, review of *Somewhere in the Ocean,* p. 1472.
Childhood Education, fall, 2002, Elizabeth Bacon and Patricia A. Crawford, review of *Over in the Garden,* p. 53.

Publishers Weekly, March 20, 2000, review of *Somewhere in the Ocean,* p. 94; March 4, 2002, review of *Over in the Garden,* p. 78.
School Library Journal, June, 1998, Mollie Bynum, review of *Way Out in the Desert,* p. 115; July, 2000, Lisa Gangemi Krapp, review of *Somewhere in the Ocean,* p. 90; August, 2002, Susan Scheps, review of *Over in the Garden,* p. 172.

ONLINE

Jennifer Ward Home Page, http://www.jenniferwardbooks. com/ (July 1, 2003).

*   *   *

WATTS, Leander 1956-
(A pseudonym)

Personal

Born September 2, 1956, in Rochester, NY; married Eileen Lavelle Metzger, September 22, 1979. *Ethnicity:* "White." *Education:* State University of New York—College at Geneseo, B.A., M.L.S., 1979. *Religion:* Mennonite. *Hobbies and other interests:* Shape-note singing, jazz, collecting books, nineteenth-century technology.

Addresses

Office—Department of English, State University of New York—College at Brockport, Brockport, NY 14420. *Agent*—Christopher Schelling, Ralph Vicinanza Ltd., 303 West 18th St., New York, NY 10011.

Career

State University of New York—College at Brockport, Brockport, NY, lecturer in English, 1995—; *City* (newspaper), Rochester, NY, feature writer, 1999—.

Writings

YOUNG ADULT NOVELS

Stonecutter, Houghton Mifflin (Boston, MA), 2002.
Wild Ride to Heaven, Houghton Mifflin (Boston, MA), 2003.
Ten Thousand Charms, Houghton Mifflin (Boston, MA), in press.

Sidelights

Young adult novelist Leander Watts, who writes under a pseudonym, is the author of gothic stories that have been considered by critics to have the same tone as works written by Edgar Allan Poe. His first novel,

Stonecutter, set in 1835 in New York, is told through the diary of Albion Straight, a young apprentice stonecutter whose work on memorials and tomb stones has caught the attention of John Good. Good hires Albion to design a memorial for his late wife, using his daughter Michal, who is the image of her dead mother, as the model. Albion feels that Good's mansion-in-progress is like a prison, and when he discovers that Michal also feels trapped by her father, the two flee the Good mansion, trying to escape from Good's influence. Though some reviewers criticized that the plot was not as strong as the atmosphere and historical setting, others found the work to be a strong first novel for young adults. Mary M. Burns of *Horn Book* called *Stonecutter* "a haunting story to discuss and to savor." Todd Morning, writing for *School Library Journal* praised, "all the elements are here for a classic gothic novel, and the story delivers the goods." Commenting on the novel's archaic style, *Kliatt* reviewer Claire Rosser noted, "The language sets this tale apart from other YA fiction." Paul Di Filippo of *Asimov's Science Fiction* called *Stonecutter* "a period thriller for all ages," while a reviewer for *Publishers Weekly* noted, "the ominous, claustrophobic tone that Watts sustains marks this writer as one to watch."

Wild Ride to Heaven is also set in nineteenth-century New York. The story is told by Hannah Renner, a girl who is an outcast due to her eyes; one of her eyes is a deep green, the other is milky-white. Her father is a treasure hunter, deeply in debt; in order to free himself of his debts, he "sells" Hannah to the Barrow brothers, two oafs who treat her as a slave. The only escape Hannah has from her drudge work is her relationship with the Barrow brothers' youngest brother, an albino who lives apart from them to avoid the sun and calls himself Brother Boy. When Hannah finds out that the elder Barrow intends to marry her, she enlists Brother Boy to help her escape, and the pair flee into the wilderness, stumbling onto a treasure that may satisfy Hanna's father. But the Barrow brothers hunt for them, and it is only through Hannah's father's help that she manages to escape a violent conclusion. A reviewer for *Publishers Weekly* called *Wild Ride to Heaven* "as grippingly oppressive as Watts's debut novel," and a critic for *Kirkus Reviews* noted, "Hannah's voice is both lyrical and straightforward." Though commenting that the book's ending happens too easily, *Booklist* critic Rebecca Platzner still found Hannah "a strong female character" and thought that the conclusion serves "to highlight the vulnerability of youth."

Watts told *SATA:* "I spend a lot of my time in another century. Through reading, traveling, exploring, singing, and thinking, I try to get myself back to an earlier day. In the nineteenth century, before television and radio, before cars and computers and airplanes to everywhere, people were more connected to each other. I value community, and it seems to me that we've lost that in our present age of speed and convenience. So the books I've written are of another time, when family and religion, home-made music, and passed-on stories were more important.

"Still, I'm a born-and-bred New Yorker. When you read those words, you probably think of skyscrapers and bustling crowds. But there's another New York, hundreds of miles from Manhattan. Indeed, my home is closer to Wheeling, West Virginia, than it is to the Brooklyn Bridge. This place was once called the Burnt-Over District, for all the ordinary folks whose spirits were set on fire by various preachers and prophets. Still, farmers plow and reap here. Still, the beautiful landscape of lakes and rivers and green hills is an inspiration.

"The books I've written go back to a better time, to a place I can still glimpse here and there on my wanderings. My novels allow me to travel back to a world where work had dignity, faith had power, and human voices joined each other in real communion. My hope is that I can take my readers there, too."

Biographical and Critical Sources

PERIODICALS

Asimov's Science Fiction, June, 2003, Paul Di Filippo, review of *Stonecutter.*
Booklist, September 15, 2002, Hazel Rochman, review of *Stonecutter,* p. 224; November 1, 2003, Rebecca Platzner, review of *Wild Ride to Heaven,* p. 491.
Horn Book, November-December, 2002, Mary M. Burns, review of *Stonecutter,* p. 765.
Kirkus Reviews, August 15, 2002, review of *Stonecutter,* p. 1239; September 1, 2003, review of *Wild Ride to Heaven,* p. 1132.
Kliatt, September, 2002, Claire Rosser, review of *Stonecutter,* p. 14; September, 2003, Claire Rosser, review of *Wild Ride to Heaven,* p. 14.
Publishers Weekly, July 29, 2002, review of *Stonecutter,* p. 72; October 27, 2003, review of *Wild Ride to Heaven,* p. 70.
School Library Journal, December, 2002, Todd Morning, review of *Stonecutter,* p. 150; November, 2003, Kimberly Monaghan, review of *Wild Ride to Heaven,* p. 150.

ONLINE

Houghton Mifflin Web Site, http://www.houghtonmifflinbooks.com/ (July 1, 2003), publisher's description of *Stonecutter.*

*   *   *

WREDE, Patricia C(ollins) 1953-

Personal

Surname is pronounced "Reedy"; born March 27, 1953, in Chicago, IL; daughter of David Merrill (a mechani-

Patricia C. Wrede

cal engineer) and Monica Marie (an executive; maiden name, Buerglar) Collins; married James M. Wrede (a financial consultant), July 24, 1976 (divorced, 1992). *Education:* Carleton College, A.B., 1974; University of Minnesota, M.B.A., 1977. *Politics:* Independent. *Religion:* Roman Catholic. *Hobbies and other interests:* Sewing, embroidery, gardening, reading.

Addresses

Home—Edina, MN. *Agent*—Valerie Smith, Route 44-55, R.R. Box 160, Modena, NY 12548. *E-mail*—Pwrede6492@aol.com.

Career

Novelist. Minnesota Hospital Association, Minneapolis, rate review analyst, 1977-78; B. Dalton Bookseller, Minneapolis, financial analyst, 1978-80; Dayton-Hudson Corporation, Minneapolis, financial analyst, 1980-81, senior financial analyst, 1981-83, senior accountant, 1983-85; full-time writer, 1985—. Laubach reading tutor.

Member

Science Fiction Writers of America, Novelists, Inc.

Awards, Honors

Books for Young Adults Recommended Reading List citation, 1984, for *Daughter of Witches,* and 1985, for *The Seven Towers;* Minnesota Book Award for Fantasy and Science Fiction, 1991, and Best Books for Young Adults citation, American Library Association (ALA), both for *Dealing with Dragons;* ALA Notable Book designation, and Best Books for Young Adults designation, both for *Searching for Dragons.*

Writings

The Seven Towers, Ace Books (New York, NY), 1984.
(With Caroline Stevermer) *Sorcery and Cecelia,* Ace Books (New York, NY), 1988, published as *Sorcery and Cecelia; or, The Enchanted Chocolate Pot: Being the Correspondence of Two Young Ladies of Quality Regarding Various Magical Scandals in London and the Country,* Harcourt (Orlando, FL), 2003.
Snow White and Rose Red, Tor Books (New York, NY), 1989.
Mairelon the Magician, Tor Books (New York, NY), 1991.
Book of Enchantments (short stories), Harcourt (San Diego, CA), 1996.
The Magician's Ward (sequel to *Mairelon the Magician*), Tor Books (New York, NY), 1997.
Star Wars: Episode I: The Phantom Menace (novelization; based on the screenplay and story by George Lucas), Scholastic (New York, NY), 1999.
Star Wars: Episode II: Attack of the Clones (novelization; based on the screenplay and story by George Lucas), Scholastic (New York, NY), 2002.

Contributor of short stories to anthologies, including *Liavek,* Ace Books (New York, NY), 1985; *Liavek: The Players of Luck,* Ace Books (New York, NY), 1986; *Spaceships and Spells,* Harper (New York, NY), 1987; *The Unicorn Treasury,* Doubleday (New York, NY), 1988; *Liavek: Spells of Binding,* Ace Books (New York, NY), 1988; *Liavek: Festival Week,* Ace Books (New York, NY), 1990; *Tales of the Witch World Three,* Tor Books (New York, NY), 1990; *A Wizard's Dozen,* Harcourt (San Diego, CA), 1993; and *Blackthorn, White Rose,* Morrow (New York, NY), 1994.

"LYRA" FANTASY SERIES

Shadow Magic (see also below), Ace Books (New York, NY), 1982.
Daughter of Witches (see also below), Ace Books (New York, NY), 1983.
The Harp of Imach Thyssel (see also below), Ace Books (New York, NY), 1985.
Caught in Crystal, Ace Books (New York, NY), 1987.
The Raven Ring, Tor Books (New York, NY), 1994.
Shadows over Lyra (includes *Shadow Magic, Daughter of Witches,* and *The Harp of Imach Thyssel*), Tor Books (New York, NY), 1997.

"CHRONICLES OF THE ENCHANTED FOREST" FANTASY SERIES

Talking to Dragons (Volume 4), Tempo/MagicQuest Books (New York, NY), 1985.

Dealing with Dragons (Volume 1), Harcourt (San Diego, CA), 1990, published as *Dragons Bane,* Scholastic (New York, NY), 1993.

Searching for Dragons (Volume 2), Harcourt (San Diego, CA), 1991, published as *Dragon Search,* Scholastic (New York, NY), 1994.

Calling on Dragons (Volume 3), Harcourt (San Diego, CA), 1993.

Enchanted Forest Chronicles (contains *Dealing with Dragons, Searching for Dragons, Calling on Dragons,* and *Talking to Dragons*), Harcourt (San Diego, CA), 2003.

Adaptations

Books in Wrede's "Chronicles of the Enchanted Forest" series have been adapted as audiobooks by Listening Library (New York, NY), 1997-2002.

Sidelights

The author of almost a score of novels and as many short stories, Patricia C. Wrede is a popular writer of fantasy. Her novels and stories, ranging from modern versions of traditional fairy tales to comic fantasy, break new ground in the genre. According to an essayist in *St. James Guide to Young Adult Writers,* the "two trademarks" of her work "are humor and light romance, two elements sure to appeal to the young adult audience." While much fantasy uses a pseudo-medieval, vaguely Celtic setting, Wrede expands these boundaries to include Renaissance and Regency-era England in *Snow White and Rose Red, Sorcery and Cecelia, Mairelon the Magician,* and *The Magician's Ward.* She has also helped to establish the strong-minded female protagonist as a mainstay in the modern fantasy genre. Among her other novels are the "Lyra" tales, which take place in Wrede's own created world, and the "Enchanted Forest" books, which present comic variations on fairy-tale motifs.

"I was an omnivorous reader as a child," Wrede once commented to *Authors and Artists for Young Adults* (*AAYA*). "I don't think I ever read anything only once. I read the Oz books, and I still treasure a set of those that I collected over the years. *Mrs. Piggle Wiggle* and *The Borrowers,* the Walter Farley horse books, Robert Lawson animal stories, the Narnia Chronicles—practically everything I could get my hands on. They knew me very well down at the library. I also told stories to my younger siblings (I am the eldest of five) and to any of my friends who would listen."

Wrede started writing, in the seventh grade, a "wildly improbable" novel. As she recalled, "I worked on it during class when I was supposed to be studying and brought it home every day. My mother aided and abetted me by typing out the pages and my father read them and told me they were great (he still thinks I should try to publish the book)."

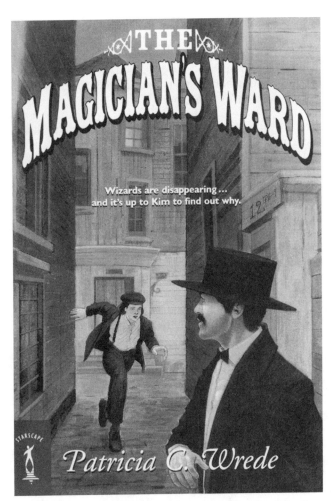

From the novel **The Magician's Ward** *by Patricia C. Wrede. (Cover illustration by Jim Madsen.)*

After graduating from high school, Wrede attended Carleton College, where she majored in biology and graduated in 1974. "Of the sciences, I liked biology the best because it dealt on a personal level with living things, as opposed to physics and chemistry, which deal with things in abstract—little molecules you can't even see. With biology you can pick up a plant and look at the roots and know what you've got."

After working as a secretary for several months, Wrede returned to school and obtained her M.B.A. in 1977. After graduating, she started work on her first novel, *Shadow Magic,* which would take five years to complete. Published by Ace Books in 1982, the novel tells the story of Alethia, daughter of a noble house of the nation of Alkyra. Alethia is of mixed blood—her mother is one of the magic-using Shee, and magic runs in her blood. She is kidnapped from her home in the city of Brenn by the Lithmern, agents of a rival nation. To carry out their plan, the Lithmern have unbound the evil Shadowborn, spirits who inhabit men's bodies and slowly destroy their minds. Alethia escapes the Lithmern with the aid of the Wyrds, a forest-dwelling, cat-like race of people, and meets her mother's folk, who train her in the use of magic. Alethia unites the four races of Alkyra—the Wyrds, the Shee, the sea-living Neira, and the humans—against the threat of the aroused Shadowborn. Finally, she discovers the lost magic treasures of the kings of Alkyra, uses them to defeat the Shadowborn, and is proclaimed queen of the land by the four reunited races.

Shadow Magic introduces the world of Lyra, an alternate earth that many of Wrede's novels share. Lyra is a land literally shaped by magic and by the threat of the Shadowborn. Its history dates from the end of the Wars of Binding, the conflict in which the Shadowborn were finally restrained by the power of the gifts of Alkyra. The land itself was broken, however, and many of its original inhabitants left homeless, forced to wander across the oceans in ships or over the lands in caravans. The ultimate result is a kaleidoscope of different cultures, from the warrior Cilhar nation to the older and more cultured society of Kith Alunel. The Kulseth sailors were left homeless when their island sank in the Wars of Binding; Varna, the island of wizards, was destroyed in a later conflict, and survivors from both places mingled with other peoples, adding to the variety and occasionally causing friction. The events of *Shadow Magic* take place more than three thousand years after the Wars of Binding, and other "Lyra" novels examine other eras in the world's history.

"For me the process of turning the story into a novel is a process of asking questions," Wrede explained to *AAYA.* "The two most useful tend to be: 'All right, what are the characters doing now?' and 'Why on earth are they doing *that?*' 'What are they doing now' applies not so much to the people who are 'onstage' as to the people who are 'offstage.' For instance, if I've written a scene in which the characters are all sitting around playing cards, I ask myself, 'What are the bad guys doing? That guy who was running away from the Indians—what's he doing? Did he get away, and if so, how did he do it? Where did he go? Did he have any help? Has he run into anybody interesting? Is he going to show up any minute? If so, why did he decide to break up this particular card game?' It's a whole process of asking questions—starting with the basic idea and asking, 'What does this mean?'"

In 1980, Wrede joined a writing group that later became known as the Scribblies. The group's members, which included Pamela Dean, Emma Bull, Will Shetterly, Steven Brust, and Nate Bucklin, all benefited from the experience because all seven sold at least one piece of writing after the group began and four went on to become professional writers.

In part because of the encouragement of her fellow Scribblies, Wrede followed *Shadow Magic* in 1983 with *Daughter of Witches,* another "Lyra" book, which tells of the sentencing of bond-servant Ranira to death on suspicion of sorcery and her escape from the prison city of Drinn. *The Seven Towers,* published in 1984, while not part of the "Lyra" cycle, nevertheless introduces

several of Wrede's most memorable characters. One of these is Amberglas, a powerful sorceress who speaks in a sort of stream-of-consciousness pattern. Another is Carachel, the wizard-king of Tar-Alem, whose struggle against the magic-devouring Matholych has led him to practice black magic. The 1985 addition to the "Lyra" cycle, *The Harp of Imach Thyssel,* is "one of the darker stories in the series," according to a reviewer for *St. James Guide to Fantasy Writers.* It is also one of the rare Wrede novels with a male protagonist and tells a tale somewhat similar to *The Seven Towers,* about a magical harp and the man destined to play it. Wrede brought out the fourth volume of the "Lyra" series in 1987 with *Caught in Crystal,* a tale of "witches who have renounced their powers, only to be called back to right a wrong committed long ago," according to the *St. James Guide to Fantasy Writers* essayist.

After a seven-year hiatus, Wrede returned readers to Lyra with *The Raven Ring,* published in 1994. Her twenty-year-old heroine, Eleret Salven, has journeyed to the city of Ciaron to claim the property of her late mother, who has been killed in battle. Eleret's efforts are interrupted, however, by villains intent on stealing those personal effects—especially the raven ring, which has great power against the Shadowborn. According to *Booklist* contributor Roland Green, Eleret is "dragged more forcibly than not into a classic tale of mayhem and magic" that he found to be up to Wrede's "usual standard." A *Publishers Weekly* reviewer characterized Eleret as "a lively, spunky heroine" who, in this "refreshingly charming story," is allowed "to find less obvious solutions to the rather typical dilemmas presented."

Talking to Dragons, Wrede's fourth book, although published in 1985, eventually became the fourth and final volume in her "Chronicles of the Enchanted Forest" series. Mixing elements of traditional fairy tales with modern wit, it tells the story of Daystar, a young man of sixteen who has lived the whole of his life on the outskirts of the Enchanted Forest with his mother, Cimorene. One day a wizard appears at his home, and the consequences of that wizard's arrival send Daystar into the Enchanted Forest, alone and armed only with a magic sword, with no idea what he is supposed to be doing. In the forest, he meets several memorable characters, including Shiara, a young fire witch who cannot quite control her magic; Morwen, a witch who lives with her umpteen cats in a cottage that is bigger on the inside than it is on the outside; and Kazul, the female King of the Dragons. The story reaches its climax as Daystar and Shiara confront the Society of Wizards at the castle of the rulers of the Enchanted Forest. Reviewing the audiobook version of that novel, *Booklist* contributor Anna Rich called it a "complex and fantastic story."

"The Enchanted Forest books did not start off as a series," Wrede once explained to *AAYA.* "Just after I finished *Daughter of Witches,* we were having trouble with the title: the publisher didn't like the title I had originally come up with. . . . My friend said to me, 'What are some of the good titles with no books?' I listed out a few for him, and the last one I mentioned was *Talking to Dragons.* He said, 'That sounds good. *Talking to Dragons* sounds like a good book; you should write that book some day.' I said, 'That's the whole problem. I've got the title; I don't have any book.'"

The book that begins the "Enchanted Forest" series chronologically is *Dealing with Dragons,* which tells how Cimorene, having been refused the right to pursue her own interests—fencing, Latin lessons, and the like—and forced into a marriage not to her liking, flees to the lair of the dragon Kazul and becomes Kazul's princess. Eventually Cimorene becomes instrumental in securing Kazul's succession as King of the Dragons and helps defeat the Society of Wizards. In *Searching for Dragons,* the second volume of the "Chronicles of the Enchanted Forest," Mendanbar and his queen go in search of Kazul after problems develop in the kingdom. In *School Librarian,* Maureen Porter noted that this "entertaining and charming novel" falls within the tradition of J. R. R. Tolkien's classic trilogy *The Lord of the Rings* while still "making the reader think of this kingdom in a different way." Kristi Beavin, writing in *Horn Book,* likewise praised the "magical landscape" Wrede creates, while *School Library Journal*'s Celeste Steward called the audiobook version a "lighthearted tale of dragon-napping and magic gone awry," and a "charming tale."

Volume three of the series, *Calling on Dragons,* is told from Morwen's perspective. Two of Morwen's highly opinionated cats accompany Queen Cimorene, Morwen, Telemain the magician, Kazul, and Killer, a sort of rabbit-like, blue donkey, on a very important quest: the evil wizards have stolen the Enchanted Sword that protects the Forest and a royal family member must retrieve it. Like the two preceding "Enchanted Forest" books, *Calling on Dragons* is a "madcap romp" with the same "bright, witty dialogue [and] clever, fairy-tale spoofs; in short, a treat from start to finish," in the opinion of Bonnie Kunzel in *Voice of Youth Advocates.* "The focus is on the comical repartee and the magic itself," noted a *Kirkus Reviews* critic, adding that several episodes are "laugh-aloud funny." Reviewing the audiobook version of the same title for *School Library Journal,* Brian E. Wilson called the tale a "lighthearted look at a group of misfits," and further commented that this "fluffy romp goes down easy, pleasing fans of the fractured fairytale genre." In fact, "humor predominates" in the entire "Chronicles of the Enchanted Forest" series, according to the critic for *St. James Guide to Young Adult Writers.* This same contributor further noted, "Wrede plays with fairy-tale convention, turning the familiar motifs upside down and inside out."

Wrede embarked on a very different type of fantasy writing with *Sorcery and Cecelia,* her seventh book. Written with friend Caroline Stevermer, *Sorcery and*

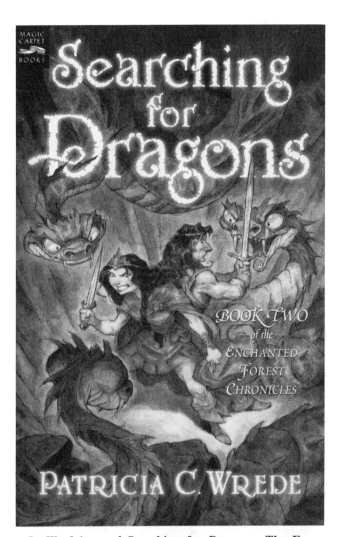

In Wrede's novel **Searching for Dragons: The Enchanted Forest Chronicles** *wizards endanger the kingdom by taking control of the Enchanted Forest.*

Cecelia is set in an alternate early-nineteenth-century England wherein magic is systematized and taught in the public schools following the Napoleonic Wars. The book consists of a series of letters written between two cousins, one of whom has gone down to London to be introduced to the social life there. The two become entangled in a power struggle between wizards but overcome their adversaries and, in true Regency fashion, marry their respective beaus. Reprinted by Harcourt in 2003 as *Sorcery and Cecelia; or, The Enchanted Chocolate Pot: Being the Correspondence of Two Young Ladies of Quality Regarding Various Magical Scandals in London and the Country,* the novel was welcomed back by a critic for *Kirkus Reviews* as a "cult epistolary fantasy." The same reviewer went on to note that this "clever romp will appeal to fans of Regency romance and light fantasy."

Wrede's *Snow White and Rose Red* is also set in an alternate England, in this case during Tudor times. It is a retelling of an ancient Grimms' fairy tale but mixes in historical characters such as Dr. John Dee, mathematician and astrologer to the court of Queen Elizabeth.

Blanche and Rosamund, the title characters, are daughters of the widow Arden. They live on the edges of a forest near the river Thames that marks the boundary of the magical realm of Faerie. Because of their isolation and occasional odd behavior, the widow and her daughters are suspected of using magic, a serious crime in Elizabethan England that is punishable by death. Through the machinations of the villagers, the Faerie Queen's court, and the magical experiments of Dr. Dee, the girls become involved with the half-human sons of the queen of Faerie.

"*Mairelon the Magician* is more like *Sorcery and Cecelia* or *Snow White and Rose Red,* which are set in an alternate England," Wrede explained of her 1991 novel. "*Mairelon the Magician* is set in this England in about 1816-17, shortly after the Napoleonic Wars ended. The main character, Kim, a street waif who has grown up in the slums, is hired to burgle the wagon of a performing magician. He turns out to be a real magician, however, and she gets caught. Since he is a rather eccentric magician, instead of turning her over to the constable, he decides to take her under his wing. He had, it turns out, five years before been framed for theft and has come back trying to find all of the various things that were stolen so he can clear his name. It turns into very much a lunatic romp. You've got a lot of character types that people who read Regency romances will recognize, although it's not a romance." Sybil Steinberg, writing in *Publishers Weekly,* was sufficiently cast under Wrede's spell to call the book "delightful," and further comment that the author's "confection will charm readers of both Regency romances and fantasies."

In 1997's *The Magician's Ward,* Wrede creates a sequel to *Mairelon the Magician* and leads readers once again into her alternate Regency universe. In this novel, Kim falls in love with her magician/mentor Richard Merrill, although Kim's aunt pushes the young woman to work on honing her feminine wiles in polite society. In *Publishers Weekly,* a reviewer praised *The Magician's Ward* as featuring Wrede's characteristic "charm, humor and intelligence," and maintained that the novel will "enthrall Regency fans and fantasy buffs looking for a new twist." According to *Booklist* reviewer Roland Green in his appraisal of *The Magician's Ward,* "The pacing, the wit, the world-building skill, and the general intelligence" found in the author's other novels are all present here.

Wrede has also written a number of short stories, published both in anthologies as well as in her own 1996 collection, *Book of Enchantments.* Mostly the tales in this collection are high fantasy, although some do have a modern setting. Based on fairy tales, ballads, biblical tales, and even humorous send-ups of fantasy traditions, the collected stories offer a "surprisingly varied" and "well-crafted" selection, according to *Booklist* reviewer Carolyn Phelan. Additionally, Wrede has turned her hand to novelizations with two "Star Wars" adaptations: 1999's *Star Wars: Episode I: The Phantom Menace* and

Star Wars: Episode II: Attack of the Clones. Based on the movies of the same titles, the books closely follow the plot lines of the popular films. *School Library Journal* contributor Wilson praised Wrede's "faithful novelization" of *Attack of the Clones,* noting that the author "does an excellent job" of "conveying [the] confusion and frustration" of Padme and Anakin when they fall in love. For Wilson, in fact, such scenes "work better in the novelization than they do onscreen because Wrede embraces the opportunity to explain what goes on in their heads."

"When you're writing fantasy you're writing about magic," Wrede explained of the genre that has occupied much of her writing life, "and magic is not something that exists in the real world, like rocks. Essentially magic is a metaphor for something else. . . . It varies from writer to writer and frequently from book to book." For Wrede, magic is a metaphor for power: "the essence of the ability to make things happen, to get things done. When you're the CEO of a corporation you can say, 'I want this to happen,' and people will go out and make it happen. You have the power to make it happen. And in my books the fundamental question is, if you can do anything, what do you do? If you've got the power to make stuff happen, good stuff or bad stuff, what do you do with it?"

Biographical and Critical Sources

BOOKS

Authors and Artists for Young Adults, Volume 8, Gale (Detroit, MI), 1992.
St. James Guide to Fantasy Writers, St. James Press (Detroit, MI), 1996.
St. James Guide to Young Adult Writers, St. James Press (Detroit, MI), 1999.

PERIODICALS

Booklist, May 1, 1993, Sally Estes, review of *Calling on Dragons,* p. 1582; August, 1993, Sally Estes, review of *Talking to Dragons,* p. 2051; October 15, 1994, Roland Green, review of *The Raven Ring,* p. 405; May 15, 1996, Carolyn Phelan, review of *Book of Enchantments,* p. 1588; November 1, 1997, Roland Green, review of *The Magician's Ward,* p. 457; April 15, 2002, Sally Estes, review of *The Magician's Ward,* pp. 357-358; June 1, 2002, p. 1753; November 1, 2002, Anna Rich, review of *Talking to Dragons* (audiobook), p. 518.
Bulletin of the Center for Children's Books, May, 1996, p. 319.
English Journal, December, 1981, review of *Daughter of Witches,* p. 67.
Horn Book, January-February, 1992, Ann A. Flowers, review of *Searching for Dragons,* p. 76; November-

December, 1993, Ann A. Flowers, review of *Talking to Dragons,* p. 760; May-June, 2002, Kristi Beavin, review of *Searching for Dragons* (audiobook), pp. 357-358.

Kirkus Reviews, March 15, 1993, review of *Calling on Dragons,* p. 382; April 15, 1996, p. 609; April 15, 2003, review of *Sorcery and Cecelia; or, The Enchanted Chocolate Pot: Being the Correspondence of Two Young Ladies of Quality Regarding Various Magical Scandals in London and the Country,* pp. 613-614.

Library Journal, November 15, 1994, Jackie Cassada, review of *The Raven Ring,* p. 90.

Publishers Weekly, April 19, 1991, Sybil Steinberg, review of *Mairelon the Magician,* p. 60; October 10, 1994, review of *The Raven Ring,* p. 66; November 24, 1997, review of *The Magician's Ward,* p. 57.

School Librarian, November, 1994, Maureen Porter, review of *Dragon Search,* p. 168.

School Library Journal, February, 1992, Cathy Chauvette, review of *Mairelon the Magician,* p. 122; June, 1993, Lisa Dennis, review of *Calling on Dragons,* p. 112; June, 1996, p. 130; June, 2002, Celeste Steward, review of *Searching for Dragons* (audiobook), p. 72; August, 2002, Brian E. Wilson, review of *Calling on Dragons* and *Star Wars: Episode II: Attack of the Clones* (audiobook), pp. 76, 77-78.

Voice of Youth Advocates, August, 1993, Bonnie Kunzel, review of *Calling on Dragons,* pp. 171-172.

ONLINE

Enchanted Chocolate Pot, http://www.tc.umn.edu/ (May 8, 2003), "Caroline Stevermer and Patricia C. Wrede Page."

Patrica C. Wrede Info Page, http://www.dendarii.co.uk/ (May 8, 2003).

SFWA, http://www.sfwa.org/ (May 8, 2003), Patricia C. Wrede, "Fantasy Worldbuilding Questions."*

Z

ZELDIS, Malcah 1931-

Personal

Born September 22, 1931, in New York, NY; daughter of Morris and Tania (Guttman) Brightman; married Chayym Zeldis, 1950 (divorced, 1974); children: David, Yona Zeldis McDonough. *Religion:* Jewish. *Hobbies and other interests:* Opera, ballet.

Addresses

Home—80 North Moore St., Apt. 30-L, New York, NY 10013.

Career

Artist. *Exhibitions:* Exhibitor in numerous group exhibits, including "Muffled Voices: Folk Artists in Contemporary America," Museum of American Folk Art, New York, NY, and a solo exhibition, "Malcah Zeldis: American Self-Taught Artist," Museum of American Folk Art, 1988; paintings held in museum collections, including the permanent collections of the Museum of American Folk Art, New York, NY, the Smithsonian Institution, Washington, DC, and the American Museum, Bath, England, and various private collections.

Member

Museum of American Folk Art.

Awards, Honors

Award from Memorial Foundation for Jewish Culture, 1981.

ILLUSTRATOR:

Mary Ann Hoberman, *A Fine Fat Pig, and Other Animal Poems,* HarperCollins (New York, NY), 1991.

Edith Kunhardt, *Honest Abe,* Greenwillow (New York, NY), 1993.

Yona Zeldis McDonough, *Eve and Her Sisters: Women of the Old Testament,* Greenwillow (New York, NY), 1994.

Rosemary L. Bray, *Martin Luther King,* Greenwillow (New York, NY), 1995.

George Shannon, *Spring: A Haiku Story,* Greenwillow (New York, NY), 1996.

Yona Zeldis McDonough, *Moments in Jewish Life: The Folk Art of Malcah Zeldis,* Michael Friedman Publishing Group (New York, NY), 1996.

Yona Zeldis McDonough, *God Sent a Rainbow: And Other Bible Stories,* Jewish Publication Society (Philadelphia, PA), 1997.

Yona Zeldis McDonough, *Anne Frank,* Holt (New York, NY), 1997.

Rosemary Bray, *Nelson Mandela,* Greenwillow (New York, NY), 1998.

Yona Zeldis McDonough, *Sisters in Strength: American Women Who Made a Difference,* Holt (New York, NY), 2000.

Yona Zeldis McDonough, *Peaceful Protest: The Life of Nelson Mandela,* Walker (New York, NY), 2002.

Work in Progress

Paintings of Biblical subjects.

Sidelights

The paintings of Malcah Zeldis, which grace such picture books as *Honest Abe* by Edith Kunhardt and Rosemary L. Bray's *Martin Luther King,* have been celebrated by folk art experts for their vivid colors, primitive representation, careful composition, and busy, detailed backgrounds. Some children may be surprised to learn that this internationally renowned artist did not develop her unique style under the influence of formal training or study. Instead, Zeldis taught herself how to paint the people, memories, ideas, and events that were important to her.

Like her evocative paintings held in private collections and museums such as the Smithsonian Museum of Art in New York City, Zeldis's paintings for children present the profound with a seemingly "naive" or childlike portrayal of historical and literary figures and personalities.

Rosemary L. Bray's visual interpretation of the life of a civil rights leader is vividly portrayed in Malcah Zeldis's folk-style art, in **Martin Luther King.**

While some critics have wondered if children will appreciate Zeldis's primitive works, which are often unrealistic in color and shape, many have asserted that her paintings allow children insight into difficult, sensitive, or heretofore neglected topics and issues. "Think explosive colors and people, people, people," N. F. Karlins wrote for the *Artnet* web site. Karlins concluded that Zeldis is a "distinctive American talent."

Zeldis was born in New York City and raised in Detroit, Michigan. There her father, a blue-collar worker, painted whenever he found the time. Zeldis left the United States for Israel when she was just eighteen years old. She explored her Jewish heritage, lived on a kibbutz, and began her own family, which later relocated to New York. It was not until the mid-1970s, after Zeldis and her husband divorced, that she began to paint seriously and zealously. Just over a decade later, her works received recognition by folk art critics. One of these critics, Henry Niemann, curated a show for the Museum of American Folk Art in New York in 1988 to introduce the general public to Zeldis's particular talent. According to a press release from the museum, the sixty paintings in this exhibit provide a sample of the range of subjects explored by Zeldis.

Zeldis made her first contribution to children's literature by illustrating Mary Ann Hoberman's book of fourteen

animal poems, *A Fine Fat Pig, and Other Animal Poems,* in 1991. The art for each poem, according to Barbara Chatton in *School Library Journal,* "reflects the content and humor" of the poetry while emphasizing the "unique features" of the animals. This whimsical work opened up a new venue for Zeldis's talents, offering her an opportunity to illustrate more than a dozen books.

Edith Kunhardt's *Honest Abe* demonstrates Zeldis's affinity for painting historical figures with bold colors against vivid patterns while providing children with a memorable history lesson. Abraham Lincoln appears on each page of this picture book in paintings that, in the words of a *Publishers Weekly* critic, seem "unpolished but genuinely American, much like the man they commemorate." In the opinion of *Booklist* writer Carolyn Phelan, *Honest Abe* is suitable for reading aloud: "this is the one teachers will be asking for come February."

In 1994, Zeldis began collaborating with her daughter, Yona Zeldis McDonough. This partnership has proven particularly fruitful for both women. Their books include biographies, a memoir, and Biblical tales. Their debut collaboration, *Eve and Her Sisters: Women of the Old Testament,* recalls the women's Jewish heritage while emphasizing the role of women in the Old Testament of the Bible. *Eve and Her Sisters* features the stories of fourteen women including Eve, Sarah, Rachel, Ruth, Deborah, Hagar, Esther, and the Queen of Sheba. While critics lauded McDonough's text, *School Library Journal* critic Patricia Dooley concluded that the style of Zeldis's full-page paintings of the women "might appeal more to sophisticated viewers." Noting that the women in the paintings "look alike," Ilene Cooper commented in *Booklist* that Zeldis's "bright, bubble gum colors" result in illustrations that are "full of energy."

A *Publishers Weekly* critic claimed that Zeldis's rendering of the renowned African-American leader in Rosemary L. Bray's *Martin Luther King* "may persuade those already familiar with his story to see it in a new light." Zeldis's "eye-catching, full-page gouache paintings," as *School Library Journal* critic Martha Rosen described them, complement Bray's detailed presentation of Dr. King's childhood, adult struggles, death, and legacy. Rosen appreciated a painting of an enlarged King in jail, "guarded by small scale policemen."

In *Spring: A Haiku Story,* Zeldis illustrated fourteen translations of haiku poetry selected by George Shannon from Japanese sources, each of which contributes to a tale of a springtime walk through the countryside. In his *New York Times Book Review* critique of the title, Bruno Navasky noted that Zeldis's "pictures help bind the sequence together, and offer up a tempting range of color and detail to stir the imagination." Navasky concluded that *Spring* "is a fine introduction to haiku, and perhaps a reminder to take notice of the world around us."

Since 1996, Zeldis has worked predominantly with her daughter, publishing another Biblical title, *God Sent a Rainbow: And Other Bible Stories,* and a memoir in paintings, *Moments in Jewish Life: The Folk Art of Malcah Zeldis.* They are better known, however, for their biographies of Nelson Mandela and Anne Frank, written for early readers. Both Mandela and Frank present challenges to children's book authors as their lives were steeped in tragedy. Zeldis and McDonough have won warm reviews for the way their text and illustrations explain difficult topics to the youngest students.

Anne Frank introduces not only the young Jewish diarist hiding from the Nazis, it also explains the Holocaust through Zeldis's signature folk art pictures. In one case, Zeldis recreates a concentration camp, with shaven-headed prisoners in close up. A *Publishers Weekly* reviewer commended Zeldis and McDonough for "address[ing] a complex subject without shying away from the gravity of the events." *Booklist*'s Hazel Rochman felt that *Anne Frank* "is a good place to start, for talking about the Holocaust and about prejudice, then and now."

Prejudice is also the central issue of *Peaceful Protest: The Life of Nelson Mandela.* Zeldis and McDonough offer young readers a portrait of the South African leader who spent more than a quarter century in jail before emerging to lead his country's government. A *Publishers Weekly* correspondent described *Peaceful Protest* as a "respectful and admiring book." Writing in *School Library Journal,* Alicia Eames particularly liked Zeldis's portrayal of Mandela's suffering in prison. The critic concluded: "Zeldis's brightly-colored folk-art illustrations reflect her subject's life and struggle with candid simplicity."

On the Web site *Walker Young Readers,* Zeldis said that she delayed becoming a painter for years because she thought she had no talent. It was only when she found idle time on her hands that she began to experiment. She said that during the painting process, the forms she creates "take on a life of their own." She added: "After a work is completed, I always look at it in amazement, since I am not exactly sure how it came to be." Zeldis lives and works in New York City.

Biographical and Critical Sources

PERIODICALS

Booklist, December 1, 1992, Carolyn Phelan, review of *Honest Abe,* p. 666; May 15, 1994, Ilene Cooper, re-

Nelson Mandela is known for his lifelong devotion to leading the fight for freedom in South Africa. From **Peaceful Protest: The Life of Nelson Mandela,** *written by Yona Zeldis McDonough. Illustrated by Zeldis.*

view of *Eve and Her Sisters: Women of the Old Testament;* February 15, 1995, Carolyn Phelan, review of *Martin Luther King,* p. 1085; October 1, 1997, Hazel Rochman, review of *Anne Frank,* p. 335; November 15, 2002, Hazel Rochman, review of *Peaceful Protest: The Life of Nelson Mandela,* p. 599.

Horn Book, May-June, 1995, Mary M. Burns, review of *Martin Luther King,* p. 340.

New York Times Book Review, July 14, 1996, Bruno Navasky, review of *Spring: A Haiku Story,* p. 19.

Publishers Weekly, December 28, 1992, review of *Honest Abe,* p. 72; April 18, 1994, review of *Eve and Her Sisters,* p. 62; November 28, 1994, review of *Martin Luther King;* July 28, 1997, review of *Anne Frank,* p. 73; October 14, 2002, review of *Peaceful Protest,* p. 84.

School Arts, October, 2000, Alice S. W. Keppley, "Malcah Zeldis: Self-Taught Artist," p. 44.

School Library Journal, April, 1991, Barbara Chatton, review of *A Fine Fat Pig;* May, 1994, Patricia Dooley, review of *Eve and Her Sisters;* February, 1995, Martha Rosen, review of *Martin Luther King;* October, 1997, Marcia W. Posner, review of *Anne Frank,* p. 120; October, 2002, Alicia Eames, review of *Peaceful Protest,* p. 148.

ONLINE

Artnet, http://www.artnet.com/ (July 1, 2003), N. F. Karlins, "Wild Folk."

Walker Young Readers, http://www.walkeryoungreaders. com/ (July 1, 2003), "Malcah Zeldis."

OTHER

Museum of American Folk Art Presents "Malcah Zeldis: American Self-Taught Artist" (press release), Museum of American Folk Art, 1988.*

DATE DUE

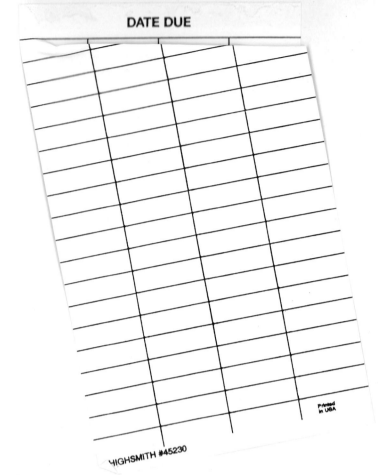

HIGHSMITH #45230

Printed
in USA